P9-DOB-147

The Decline
and Resurgence
of Congress

JK
1061
.S93

JAMES L. SUNDQUIST

The Decline and Resurgence of Congress

THE BROOKINGS INSTITUTION
Washington, D.C.

322916 Tennessee Tech. Library
Cookeville, Tenn.

Copyright © 1981 by
THE BROOKINGS INSTITUTION
1775 Massachusetts Avenue, N.W., Washington, D.C. 20036

Library of Congress Cataloging in Publication data:

Sundquist, James L.
  The decline and resurgence of Congress.

  Includes index.
  1. United States. Congresses. 2. United States—Politics and government—20th
century. I. Title.
JK1061.S93   328.73   81-66191
ISBN 0-8157-8224-1   AACR2
ISBN 0-8157-8223-3 (pbk.)

9 8 7 6 5 4 3 2 1

Board of Trustees
Robert V. Roosa
Chairman
Andrew Heiskell
Vice Chairman;
Chairman, Executive Committee
Louis W. Cabot
Vice Chairman
Vincent M. Barnett, Jr.
Barton M. Biggs
Frank T. Cary
A. W. Clausen
William T. Coleman, Jr.
Lloyd N. Cutler
Bruce B. Dayton
George M. Elsey
Hanna H. Gray
Huntington Harris
Roger W. Heyns
Carla A. Hills
Lane Kirkland
Bruce K. MacLaury
Robert S. McNamara
Arjay Miller
Herbert P. Patterson
Donald S. Perkins
J. Woodward Redmond
Charles W. Robinson
James D. Robinson III
Henry B. Schacht
Warren M. Shapleigh
Phyllis A. Wallace

Honorary Trustees

Eugene R. Black
Robert D. Calkins
Edward W. Carter
Douglas Dillon
John E. Lockwood
William McC. Martin, Jr.
H. Chapman Rose
Robert Brookings Smith
Sydney Stein, Jr.

THE BROOKINGS INSTITUTION is an independent organization devoted to nonpartisan research, education, and publication in economics, government, foreign policy, and the social sciences generally. Its principal purposes are to aid in the development of sound public policies and to promote public understanding of issues of national importance.

The Institution was founded on December 8, 1927, to merge the activities of the Institute for Government Research, founded in 1916, the Institute of Economics, founded in 1922, and the Robert Brookings Graduate School of Economics and Government, founded in 1924.

The Board of Trustees is responsible for the general administration of the Institution, while the immediate direction of the policies, program, and staff is vested in the President, assisted by an advisory committee of the officers and staff. The by-laws of the Institution state: "It is the function of the Trustees to make possible the conduct of scientific research, and publication, under the most favorable conditions, and to safeguard the independence of the research staff in the pursuit of their studies and in the publication of the results of such studies. It is not a part of their function to determine, control, or influence the conduct of particular investigations or the conclusions reached."

The President bears final responsibility for the decision to publish a manuscript as a Brookings book. In reaching his judgment on the competence, accuracy, and objectivity of each study, the President is advised by the director of the appropriate research program and weighs the views of a panel of expert outside readers who report to him in confidence on the quality of the work. Publication of a work signifies that it is deemed a competent treatment worthy of public consideration but does not imply endorsement of conclusions or recommendations.

The Institution maintains its position of neutrality on issues of public policy in order to safeguard the intellectual freedom of the staff. Hence interpretations or conclusions in Brookings publications should be understood to be solely those of the authors and should not be attributed to the Institution, to its trustees, officers, or other staff members, or to the organizations that support its research.

Foreword

THE BALANCE of power between the executive and the legislative branches of government—a recurrent issue in the U.S. political system—reached the proportions of a constitutional crisis in the early 1970s, when an aggressive president, Richard M. Nixon, confronted an equally combative Congress controlled by the opposition party. That historic conflict crystallized a determination on the part of the Congress to recapture what is considered its rightful "coequal" place in the governmental structure. And out of that determination emerged a series of events that transformed relations between the two branches.

The Congress established a new budget process, giving it a stronger and more effective voice in setting the country's fiscal policy. It stripped the president of his claimed power to impound appropriated funds. It enacted, over his veto, the War Powers Resolution in a determined effort to prevent unilateral executive action that would involve the country in hostilities. It asserted itself vigorously in foreign policy decisions. It intensified its oversight of administration. It extended the device of the legislative veto to many additional categories of administrative actions. At the same time, it speeded the pace of internal change within the Congress and vastly expanded its own staff.

James L. Sundquist undertakes in this book two tasks of historical and political analysis. First, he sets out to determine the nature, scope, and causes of the long decline of the Congress in relation to the president during this century. He investigates the extent to which the decline was an inevitable consequence of inherent weaknesses in the legislative branch, examining the relation between congressional power and performance, on the one hand, and internal organization and working habits and attitudes, on the other. Second, he recounts the resurgence of the legislative body since its historic confrontation with President Nixon in 1972–73, detailing the changes in the balance of power between the branches and the limitations of the Congress that persist, and appraises the consequences of the new balance of power for

vii

the effectiveness of government. He finds the "unending conflict" between presidents and Congresses to be an intractable problem in the American governmental system, even though he believes that the recent era of turbulence has given way to a period of relative stability.

In carrying out the study, Sundquist was assisted by Andrew Linehan, who prepared case studies on executive-legislative conflicts discussed in chapter 10; by Joy Silver, who assembled the initial bibliography of books and articles; and by Gloria Jimenez, Jo Ann Pinero, and Diane Hodges, who typed the manuscript and verified facts and figures. Alice M. Carroll edited the manuscript, and Florence Robinson prepared the index.

The Brookings Institution and the author also acknowledge the generosity of the Government Division of the Congressional Research Service, Library of Congress, in providing office space and access to its collections during the historical research phase of the project. James W. Fesler, Louis Fisher, Ralph K. Huitt, and James Sterling Young read the entire manuscript and offered extensive and detailed criticism. Valuable comments on particular chapters were received from John Barriere, Roger H. Davidson, I. M. Destler, Thomas E. Mann, and Glenn R. Parker, as well as from Martha Derthick, director of the Brookings Governmental Studies program, and from Joel D. Aberbach, Paul J. Quirk, and A. James Reichley of the Governmental Studies staff.

As in all Brookings publications, the interpretations, conclusions, and recommendations presented here are those of the author and should not be ascribed to the trustees, officers, or other staff members of the Institution.

BRUCE K. MAC LAURY
President

June 1981
Washington, D.C.

Contents

CHAPTER I

Congress at Nadir

THE Ninety-third Congress convened, in January 1973, in an angry mood. The speaker of the Democratic-controlled House of Representatives, Carl Albert of Oklahoma, sounded a keynote: The Congress must check, and reverse, the "accelerating usurpation of power by the Executive branch . . . these wholesale executive invasions of legislative powers and responsibilities." President Nixon, he charged, "is creating a crisis that goes to the very heart of our Constitutional system."[1] In the Senate the Democratic majority leader, Mike Mansfield of Montana, called similarly for "a reinforcement of the Constitution's system of checks and balances." "The people," said Mansfield, "have not chosen to be governed by one branch of government alone."[2] Many other members expressed like views.

Speaker Albert enumerated four issues that divided the Congress and President Richard M. Nixon—impoundment of appropriated funds, conduct of the war in Vietnam, executive privilege, and government reorganization. The president had impounded at least $8.7 billion that the Congress had appropriated, thus unilaterally repealing laws that the Congress, with the president's approval, had enacted.[3] While the legislature was in recess, Nixon without consultation with its leaders had intensified the bombing of North Vietnam and mined the port of Haiphong. Under the doctrine of executive privilege, the president was asserting unlimited power to withhold any information from the Congress, solely at his own discretion.[4] And, by ex-

1. Speech to fiftieth anniversary of Time, Inc., inserted in *Congressional Record*, February 5, 1973, p. 3239.
2. Address to the Senate Democratic Conference, inserted in *Congressional Record*, January 4, 1973, p. 324.
3. The $8.7 billion was the administration's figure; *Congressional Quarterly Weekly Report*, vol. 31 (February 10, 1973), pp. 270–74. Louis Fisher, *Presidential Spending Power* (Princeton University Press, 1975), pp. 171–74, applying a broader definition, arrived at a total of $17.7 billion.
4. "Statement About Executive Privilege, March 12, 1973," *Public Papers of the Presidents: Richard*

1

ecutive order, the president had put into effect the basic features of a plan for reorganizing the executive departments that the Congress had explicitly rejected.[5]

"In this second term," recalls Nixon in his memoirs, "I had thrown down a gauntlet to Congress, the bureaucracy, the media, and the Washington establishment and challenged them to epic battle. We had already skirmished over the limitations of prerogative and power represented in confirmation of appointments, the impoundment of funds, and the battle of the budget."[6] After his landslide reelection, Nixon was claiming powers for the executive beyond what preceding presidents had asserted, and was pushing those powers to the limit, in defiance of the sentiment of his political enemies who controlled the Democratic Congress. In doing so, he finally "aroused a snoozing Congress and made it mad"[7] and spurred it to organize and fight back against the presidency in order—as senators and representatives were wont to put it—to restore the Congress to "its constitutional position as a coequal branch of the government."

To Albert, impoundment was the "central and overwhelming issue." As he and others saw it, the president had assumed the power of item veto— a power some earlier presidents had sought but the Congress had never seen fit to grant—and through a process that denied to the Congress its right in ordinary circumstances to override presidential vetoes. "It is obvious," said Albert, "that what Congress has refused him, the President has undertaken to seize. What Congress had decreed, the President has circumvented."[8]

The impoundment issue of 1973 was actually an extension of "the battle of the budget" of the campaign season of the previous autumn, to which Nixon referred in his memoirs. The president had touched off that conflict in July with an "urgent appeal" to the Congress to set a firm ceiling on expenditures for the fiscal year then beginning of $250 billion, which would be several billion dollars below the spending level that then appeared in

---

Nixon, 1973 (U.S. Government Printing Office, 1975), pp. 184–86; and testimony of Attorney General Richard G. Kleindienst on April 10, 1973, in *Executive Privilege, Secrecy in Government, Freedom of Information,* Hearings before subcommittees of the Senate Government Operations and Judiciary Committees, 93 Cong. 1 sess. (GPO, 1973), vol. 1, pp. 18–52, especially 45–46, 51.

5. The president had proposed consolidating seven cabinet departments concerned with domestic matters into four; after the Congress failed to act, he appointed four cabinet members as assistants or counselors to the president to coordinate the seven.

6. *RN: The Memoirs of Richard Nixon* (Grosset and Dunlap, 1978), p. 850. The statement, made in the context of his handling of the Watergate affair, describes his posture on the whole range of issues on which he was confronting the Congress.

7. Arlen J. Large, *Wall Street Journal,* April 13, 1973.

8. Speech to fiftieth anniversary of Time, Inc., inserted in *Congressional Record,* February 5, 1973, p. 3239.

prospect.[9] Threatening to veto appropriation bills that would put spending beyond that limit, he promised to act on his own, "with or without the cooperation of the Congress," to achieve the objective. During the next few weeks, he made congressional spending a major campaign issue, and by October—when expenditures appeared likely to exceed $256 billion—the Congress was forced to confront the question. If the legislators would give him the authority, Nixon informed them, he would "face the harsh and difficult decisions" as to which governmental programs would be cut.[10] The administration continued to claim the power to make the cuts without any new delegation of authority but asked for the delegation in order to have a "clear signal" rather than "a series of confrontations."[11]

The House of Representatives proved willing to give the president the authority he sought, despite impassioned pleas from its own Democratic leaders not to yield that most cherished of congressional prerogatives, the "power of the purse." To do so would be to "knowingly and willingly abdicate not only our powers—but our responsibilities," Speaker Albert told the House. "Congress would be reduced to a debating society . . . to political impotency," declared Majority Leader Hale Boggs, Democrat of Louisiana. Majority Whip Thomas P. O'Neill, Jr., Democrat of Massachusetts, called the proposal a "domestic Gulf of Tonkin resolution"; a vote for it was a vote "for a further erosion of congressional responsibility."[12] Yet sixty Democrats, more than one-fourth of those voting, spurned their leaders' advice and provided the necessary votes to pass it.

The Senate Finance Committee recommended acceptance of the House policy, but when the measure reached the Senate floor, it encountered an aroused sensitivity, among Republicans as well as Democrats this time, to the Congress's constitutional prerogatives. If the House proposal were adopted, Majority Leader Mansfield argued, "you might just as well abolish Congress,"[13] and his sentiment was echoed on both sides of the aisle. So, by a substantial bipartisan majority of 46 to 28, the Senate voted to overrule the Finance Committee and accept the president's objective but make the cuts itself. This it did by exempting certain programs from any reduction and then directing the president to apply to the rest of the budget whatever flat

9. "Special Message to the Congress on Federal Government Spending, July 26, 1972," *Public Papers: Nixon, 1972* (GPO, 1974), pp. 741–44.

10. Testimony of Caspar W. Weinberger, director of the Office of Management and Budget, October 11, 1972, in *$465 Billion Debt Limit*, Hearings before the Senate Finance Committee, 92 Cong. 2 sess. (GPO, 1972), p. 26.

11. Ibid., p. 34.

12. *Congressional Record*, October 10, 1972, pp. 34612, 34591, 34603.

13. *New York Times*, October 13, 1972.

percentage cut would yield the necessary reduction. In the conference committee, however, the Senate members concluded that that would be unworkable, and they accepted a compromise that gave the president a delegation of authority, more restricted than in the original House version but nonetheless a delegation. But on October 17 the Senate rejected that compromise, 39 to 27.

Next day the Congress adjourned, a spectacle of futility. Both houses had separately reached the conclusion, in effect, that the fiscal policy they had written for the nation had turned out to be unsound. Both had agreed that corrective action should be taken. But they had proposed different solutions, and in the end the Congress proved impotent to pull itself together even to rectify the errors it acknowledged. Conceding that the president was right in the direction he was proposing to lead, the Congress could not even organize itself to follow. Then Nixon went ahead anyway, simply proceeding to exercise the impoundment authority that he had sought. October 17, 1972, the day the legislature lost the battle of the budget to Richard Nixon, marks the low point in the modern history of congressional power vis-à-vis the president.

The Congress Looks Inward

The imbalance between the president and the Congress was "the dominant theme" in Washington in those early days of 1973, said Representative Lee H. Hamilton, an Indiana Democrat just elected to his fifth term. "A mood of anxiety about the expansion of presidential power at the expense of the Congress dominates the speeches and the conversations of the lawmakers. The mood of Congress today is more assertive and aggressive than at any time since I have been in Washington." In regard to foreign affairs, "the question is not whether but what the Congress should do to retain its traditional role."[14]

The "mood of anxiety" on Capitol Hill that winter reflected the pervasive feeling that the problem lay far deeper than just Richard Nixon and his aggressive "usurpation" of power. If the Congress looked down Pennsylvania Avenue and condemned the president, it also looked inward and asked probing questions of itself. Why had the legislative branch allowed itself to sink to such a low estate? And did the Congress have the will, and the capacity, to take steps necessary to regain its rightful place? Member after

14. *Congressional Record*, February 20, 1973, pp. 4517–18.

member rose to ask questions such as these, in a remarkable period of congressional introspection—surely the most intense such period, perhaps the only one, in the history of that institution. Members observed that the Congress had been declining for a long time—indeed, that legislatures the world over had been declining in favor of the executive—and they wondered openly whether in their own case abdication to the president had become a habit too deeply ingrained to shake. Nixon's defiance of the Congress was a timely prod, but in its absence would the Congress have been able to bestir itself? And could it succeed in doing so even now, given its organization and its habits?

"We have seen congressional powers eroded and weakened over the years," said Representative Joe L. Evins, a Tennessee Democrat. For at least forty years, said Senator George McGovern, Democrat of South Dakota, there had been a "steady deterioration" of the power of Congress. Few described the imbalance as something new, that had begun with Richard Nixon. "Growing," "accelerating," "continuing" were the adjectives used, and "erosion"— a slow and long-term process—was the noun. "The fault lies not in the Executive Branch but in ourselves, in the Congress," said Mansfield, referring to the "failure" of budget control. "The Congress must regain the will to govern," said Barbara Jordan, the new Democratic congresswoman from Texas.[15] And outside opinion did not spare the Congress. It had lost its powers by "default," by "failure," by "abdication," by "irresponsibility," in the prevailing view of editorial writers and columnists during the long debate.[16] "Congress already has enormous power, if it only had the guts to use it," was the view of one observer with experience in both branches, Theodore C. Sorensen, the former special counsel to President John F. Kennedy.[17]

The Congress knew that it stood low in the public esteem as well as in its own. From a positive rating of 64 percent in the Harris poll in 1965—an uncommon high, to be sure—it had slipped to 38 percent in 1973.[18] And when it declined to 21 percent in February 1974, it was actually 8 points lower

15. Ibid., February 6, 1973, p. 3653; January 16, 1973, p. 1136; January 4, 1973, p. 324; April 18, 1973, p. 13170. A poll of members early in 1969, when relations with Nixon were still cordial, had shown only 15 percent believing firmly that legislative initiative had not shifted too much to the executive branch. *Nation's Business*, June 1969, p. 57.

16. See, for instance, *Chicago Tribune*, November 12, 1972; *Time*, January 15, 1973, p. 12; Roscoe Drummond, *Christian Science Monitor*, December 14, 1972; *Wall Street Journal*, November 30, 1972; *New Orleans Times Picayune*, December 19, 1972.

17. "The Case for a Strong Presidency," in Charles Roberts, ed., *Has the President Too Much Power?* (Harper's Magazine Press, 1974), p. 27.

18. The 1965 high point came when the Congress was passing a wide range of long-deferred measures—civil rights, aid to education, medicare, employment and antipoverty programs, environmental measures, and so on. See James L. Sundquist, *Politics and Policy: The Eisenhower, Kennedy, and Johnson Years* (Brookings Institution, 1968), pp. 1–2.

in that poll than even so unpopular a president as Nixon—and after the Watergate scandal had broken. Two other national surveys at that time showed the Congress getting somewhat higher approval than the president— Gallup showed 30 percent as against 25 percent[19]—but whatever the relative rating, the Congress clearly did not command a full measure of popular respect.

Members of the Congress could even tie the two phenomena together. The "crisis of confidence" in the Congress, suggested Representative John B. Anderson, Republican of Illinois, had its roots in "the emergence of a strong presidency and congressional acquiescence in that development over the past 40 years."[20] The polls seemed to give at least some support to that position; certainly the public in these years wanted a more assertive Congress. "People would . . . like to see a redistribution of power," the University of Michigan's Survey Research Center found late in 1973. Among other things, they wanted "more power invested in Congress" and "some reduction in the influence of . . . the President."[21] One congressman who polled his constituents on the question in 1974—Gus Yatron, Democrat of Pennsylvania—found that 87 percent of those responding agreed that the balance between the three branches of government had been upset, 56 percent of the respondents feeling it was the executive branch that had gained excessive power, as against only 10 percent naming the legislative branch and 21 percent the judicial.[22]

Out of anger, and anxiety, and public pressure and contempt, arose a new assertiveness. On one day, a bipartisan group of thirty-five congressmen, most of them defenders of the president, took the floor to demand that the Congress find a way to impose its own effective ceiling on the budget.[23] A few weeks later, seventeen freshman Democrats kept the House in session through a long evening to make the same plea and to confront the president as well. Said Gillis Long, of Louisiana: "Our protest is that the President has overstepped the authority of his office in the actions he has taken. Our warning is that the Congress will not stand by idly as the President reaches for more and more power. . . . Our message to the President is that he is

19. Cited by Representative John B. Anderson, *Congressional Record*, June 19, 1974, p. 19854. The Survey Research Center of the University of Michigan showed the Congress with a rating of 4.59 as against 3.30 for the president and his administration, on a scale of 0 (very poor) to 8 (very good). *Institution for Social Research Newsletter*, Winter 1974, p. 8.

20. *Congressional Record*, June 19, 1974, p. 19854.

21. *Institution for Social Research Newsletter*, Winter 1974, p. 8.

22. *Congressional Record*, September 24, 1974, p. 32510. Over 30,000 responded to the questionnaire.

23. Ibid., March 7, 1973, pp. 6730–46. The term *congressmen*, as used in this book, includes senators as well as representatives, and both male and female members.

risking retaliation from the Congress for his power grabs, that support for the counter-offensive is found in the whole range of congressional membership—old Members and new, liberal and conservative, Democratic and Republican."[24]

Earlier, a freshman senator, James Abourezk, South Dakota Democrat, had suggested in his maiden speech the form "a possible confrontation with the President" might take: "If the President persists in carrying on this illegitimate war [in Vietnam] or in defying the will of Congress by impounding billions of dollars in appropriated money, then this body should impound money for the White House staff, impound money for high executive branch officials, and refuse to approve any Presidential appointees." A veteran representative offered a like suggestion on how to beard the president. Said William Moorhead, Pennsylvania Democrat: "We know there are programs coming up that he wants, and wants badly. And the only way that we will get back the programs is to hold them ransom for the programs we need."[25]

Thus the Congress achieved in the early weeks of 1973 something close to a collective resolve—a firmness and unity of purpose extraordinarily difficult to attain in a body as diffuse as the Congress—to restore the balance between the executive and legislative branches that, in its view, had prevailed in some earlier age. The long era of congressional decline had ended. A period of resurgence had begun.

Some Persistent Questions

Once the Congress made up its mind to reassert itself, only the general direction was settled. There remained all the perplexing subsidiary questions: How? In what respects? What would be the implications for the organization of the Congress, its leadership structure, its staff facilities, its working methods? And what of the behavior patterns that its members had settled into? If the fault lay "in ourselves," as Senator Mansfield said, were the defects inherent in the very nature of the Congress, and of the political system of which it was a part? Did senators and representatives behave the way they did because of the necessities of political survival? And if they had learned, over the years, that the successful congressmen were those who tended to the local problems of their constituencies and left the big national decisions to the president, then would an attempt to reassert their leadership at the

24. Ibid., April 18, 1973, p. 13190; see pp. 13166–93.
25. Ibid., January 16, 1973, pp. 1135–36; February 21, 1973, p. 5003.

president's expense do anything more than jeopardize their futures? Would the public, which at that moment might want a particular president—Nixon— cut down to size, see things the same way once that job had been accomplished? Or would it turn on the legislative branch and exact its retribution once a more popular president came to occupy the White House?

And, from a more detached point of view, the questions could be asked: Would a resurgence of the Congress actually contribute to a better governmental product? Until Lyndon Johnson's Vietnam and Richard Nixon's Watergate, it is doubtful that most detached observers would have answered yes. Surely only a minority of political scientists would have. For at least two generations, many of the leading scholars within that discipline had thrown their prestige behind the aggrandizement of the presidency. Only under strong presidents working with compliant Congresses, this school of thought held, could progress normally be made. The American system of separated powers worked as well as it did, in other words, only because the Congress had abdicated as freely as it had. A full reassertion of those powers could well lead back to stalemate.

With Vietnam and Watergate, revisionism became the order of the day both inside and outside the Congress. But the revisionists had yet no satisfactory theory. If the balance between the president and the Congress were to be shifted, what would be the right balance? How much should the president be cut down? Where should the process stop? And how would deadlock be overcome and progress be made? If the president were evicted from the driver's seat, how could 535 members of the Congress possibly manage to sit there? Would additional restraint on the president steady the course of the nation, or would it simply lessen the chances of taking a clear course at all?

The only objective that everybody could agree on was one that begged the question: the president should have all the power he needed to do wise and proper things but be subject to restraint from doing improper and unwise things. But that goal is unattainable—and not just because people disagree on what things are wise and proper. A presidency strong enough to achieve great ends will inevitably have also the strength to produce abominations. And a presidency hamstrung by checks and balances to prevent abuse of power will be handicapped in exercising constructive leadership. In the end, it is a choice of risks. The optimist will say, "Give the president the power; most of the time it will be wisely used." And the pessimist will answer: "Oh, no! Look at Vietnam and Watergate. Better keep the presidency under wraps. Better safe than sorry."

Throughout the debate over the power of the presidency, the image of the particular president was never absent. Before the revisionism of the 1960s, three models dominated. One was Theodore Roosevelt, creator of the modern presidency—zestful fighter against monopoly and privilege, founder of the conservation movement. One was Woodrow Wilson—idealist and visionary whose dream of peace was shattered by a "band of willful men" in the Congress. The third was Franklin Roosevelt—warrior against domestic poverty and foreign totalitarianism, hampered as often as he was helped by the Congress. It was with Theodore Roosevelt and Wilson that the modern concept of the strong presidency was born, and during the New Deal and in its afterglow that the doctrine was crystallized. And now, with the images of more recent presidents to reflect on, its wisdom was in question.

If all presidents were the same, the problem of institutional design would be vastly simplified. But how can a set of presidential-congressional relations be devised that will be suitable for every circumstance? They cannot, obviously, be redesigned for every president, depending on his competence and character. Yet if the cloth is cut for a Franklin Roosevelt saving the country from depression and the world from Hitler, the garment designed for greatness will be worn also by the smaller men who come after. And it is not even that simple. Not every one agrees that Roosevelt always used the great powers of his presidency for benign, heroic ends. And Lyndon Johnson, in only five years of office, was two presidents, many would say—the farseeing crusader of the civil rights and Great Society triumphs, and the shortsighted, stubborn commander in chief who mired the nation in a lost, divisive war.

Yet institutions still have to be designed. And students of government have to try to conceive of what is best over the long run in the infinite variety of circumstances that history teaches can occur. They must think in terms of what works best for the typical or normal or average president—recognizing that presidents are perhaps of all people the most individualized, the least typical, and that no scholar, however conscientious, can ever put Franklin Roosevelt and John Kennedy and Richard Nixon wholly out of mind and think only of an abstract, nameless figure. But can a dispassionate student, assuming he can dismiss from his consciousness the individual who occupied the White House in 1973, accept, uncritically, the goal of congressional resurgence that seemed so reasonable then? Conversely, if the public mood changes when some highly popular president occupies the White House, will the student remember the reasons that a new presidential-legislative balance seemed in the Nixon era to be so urgently required? As for the Congress itself, if under Democratic control it adopted aggressive patterns of behavior in the 1970s in order to combat Republican presidents, would it institutionalize itself into a position of inevitable conflict—beyond what might be considered normal, healthy, and desirable—when the president and the congressional majorities were of the same party?

Even if, despite these problems, the answer to the question of whether Congress should reassert its power seems generally affirmative, the initial queries remain. How? In what respects? Surely, in reviewing the powers that have slipped away during the decades, the Congress would have to be selective in what it set out to recapture. If the criterion were the quality of the governmental product—assuming a definition of quality could be agreed on—that could well call for the Congress to withdraw further in some fields while asserting itself in others. Certainly, relations with the president could not be identical in every substantive field in which the Congress acts. Traditionally, a distinction had been made between matters of foreign and domestic policy, with the president conceded more independent authority in the former. Should this distinction be maintained, or abrogated, or even reversed?

As the Congress turned to the question of which powers to retrieve, the immediate priorities were clear enough. The losses of congressional authority peculiar to the Nixon period had precipitated the crisis, and these would have to be dealt with first and most emphatically. At the head of the list was the budget. When the Ninety-second Congress was floundering with the issue of budget cuts, it was plain that the budget process on Capitol Hill must inescapably be dealt with, and the Congress established a committee to begin the consideration of proposals for improving the mechanisms and procedures for relating expenditure to revenue. As an aspect of fiscal reform, the problem of impoundment would have to be confronted. And then came measures to curtail the discretion of the president to wage undeclared war on his own authority—in Southeast Asia or anywhere else. Beyond those were many other questions. If, as so many members of the Congress believed, the decline of the legislative branch had begun in New Deal days, or even earlier, then a whole range of relations beyond those dramatized in the Nixon period was in need of fresh review.

This book is an attempt to treat both the narrow and the broader issues. It first scans history, particularly recent history, to shed light on these questions, among others: In what areas of governmental responsibility has the authority, or participation, of the Congress in fact declined? In each case, when and why? Was the shift of responsibility to the executive avoidable, or was it inevitable in the nature of the modern world? Has it made for better or worse government—or, assuming that the answer in most cases is likely to be some of each, what has been the balance? Part one concludes with a chapter identifying the weaknesses the Congress explicitly or implicitly acknowledged when it acted to create and nourish the modern presidency that, by 1973, had come to tower over the legislative branch.

Part two examines what has happened since the Ninety-third Congress resolved to reverse the flow of power to the executive, including changes in congressional organization and procedure that have a bearing on that objective. Finally, part three appraises the new balance between the branches that was established by the end of the 1970s; considers whether the weaknesses of the Congress that led to its decline have been, or even can be, remedied; and examines the prospects for ameliorating the unending conflict between the branches that has marked the whole of American history.

A Semantic Digression

The decline of Congress bemoaned by members of that body in the Nixon years was described, usually, as a loss of power to the executive, and the objective the legislators set for themselves in their period of resurgence was to recapture power. But the word as used then, and as used in this book, has more than one meaning.

Power is divided among the institutions of government in the first instance by the Constitution, and the distribution is fixed, in the absence of constitutional amendment or judicial reinterpretation of the Constitution's clauses. In constitutional terms, the decline of Congress did not occur at all, because the document was neither amended nor reinterpreted to lessen the legislature's role.

But power is also distributed by custom and usage—by the unwritten constitution that amplifies, or may sometimes even contradict, the written one—as well as by statutes enacted by the Congress. There is a difference, in short, between power latent or potential under the Constitution and power exercised. In the latter sense, the Congress could decline and did.

By employing different meanings of the word in the same sentence, the Congress can be said to delegate power to the president or an executive agency while at the same time retaining the very power that has been delegated. When it authorizes an Interstate Commerce Commission to set railroad rates, for example, it loses none of its authority to set the rates directly. The same is true of every other delegation of power—whether to set tariff policy, or to make war in one or another area of the globe, or to impose price and wage controls. When the delegation is not a power to act but only responsibility to recommend—the executive budget, for instance—the Congress explicitly retains not only its full authority but also its responsibility to act.

My basic purpose is to analyze the decline and resurgence in the congressional share of governmental power and the causes and consequences, in terms of power exercised (and using the terms power, authority, and responsibility somewhat interchangeably, in accordance with common usage). In these terms, any delegation to the executive of authority to act on matters on which the Congress has customarily acted is a shift of power from the legislative to the executive branch. Even if the Congress delegates to the president no more than the responsibility to recommend, to the extent that the recommendations are not seriously reviewed and therefore become controlling, the exercise of governmental power has moved between the branches. Like the members of Congress, further, I have been concerned with the division between the two branches of the totality of governmental decision-making at any given time, disregarding the growth in the range and volume of activity over the period being covered that, as is often correctly pointed out, has resulted in a vast increase in responsibility for both branches.

Another semantic difficulty surrounds the concept of the legislative and executive branches themselves. Neither is monolithic, and many of the incidents that are presented in these pages as conflicts between branches involve only particular committees or subcommittees or individual members, on the one side, and single agencies or individuals on the other—and these contestants, moreover, may on occasion be little more than the respective agents of groups outside the government that are defining the terms of conflict. But one cannot deny that a constitutional struggle has been taking place between the branches as such, and all of the conflicts between individuals and small groups and outside interests that spread across the executive-legislative boundary have necessarily been a part of the broader competition.

PART I

Decline

CHAPTER II

Two Centuries of Ups and Downs

FOREBODINGS on Capitol Hill about the decline of Congress are nothing new. The Congress has been at low ebb many times. If it was rebelling against domination by Richard Nixon in 1973, it was no less restive under the aggression of "King Andrew" Jackson more than a century before. Or when Andrew Johnson was the chief executive—"the experience of the past quarter of a century demonstrates the fact that the whole power of the national Government is gradually but surely passing under the complete control of our Presidents," said a congressman, not in 1973 but in 1869.[1] If the Democrats were denouncing "executive usurpation" in the Nixon period, that phrase appeared also in the Democratic platform when Theodore Roosevelt was in the White House. "The Republican administration . . . made war, which is the sole power of Congress, without its authority"—words that might have been written in the Democratic platform of 1972—appeared in the 1904 platform. And sixteen years later, when a Democrat was in the White House, the Republican platform had occasion to pledge to "end executive autocracy and restore to the people their constitutional government." Yet the first century and a half of U.S. history saw, on balance, more years of congressional than of executive ascendancy.[2]

1. J. M. Ashley of Ohio, *Congressional Globe*, February 3, 1869, appendix.
2. The broadest analytical treatment of legislative-executive relations in that period is W. E. Binkley, *The Powers of the President: Problems of American Democracy* (Doubleday, Doran, 1937). Arthur M. Schlesinger, Jr., *The Imperial Presidency* (Houghton Mifflin, 1973), reviews relations in the field of foreign policy. Leonard D. White's four volumes subtitled *A Study of Administrative History* cover executive-congressional relations: *The Federalists* (Macmillan, 1948); *The Jeffersonians* (Macmillan, 1951); *The Jacksonians* (Macmillan, 1954); and *The Republican Era: 1869–1901* (Macmillan, 1958).

The Constitutional Ambiguities

The Constitution, in effect, put two combatants in the ring and sounded the bell that sent them into endless battle. The "separation of powers," of which the Founding Fathers so often spoke, turned out not to be that at all. The branches of the government were separated but the powers of government were not; they were shared.[3] While the Congress was the legislative branch, the president had a role in legislation. And while the president was head of the executive branch, the Congress had a role in administration. On essential matters that would define the boundary between the branches, and the relations between them, the Constitution was silent, or ambiguous. The opponents would have to settle those, through combat. To remove the ambiguities would require writing detailed prescriptions into the Constitution through the amendment process—and that process, requiring extraordinary majorities both of federal legislators and of state legislatures, calls for a degree of consensus that on controversial questions pertaining to the allocation of governmental power is unlikely ever to be obtained. So the fight continues. The president may appear as the heftier contestant, but he cannot win every round; the balance will continue to shift back and forth. Five main areas of ambiguity on which the executive-legislative conflict has centered can be identified.

Legislative Initiation and Leadership. The Constitution assigns legislative power to the two houses of Congress but imposes on the president the duty "to recommend to their Consideration such Measures as he shall judge necessary and expedient." This leaves open the question of the extent of the participation by the president and his subordinates once the measures have been proposed. In the Continental Congress, legislators had come to rely on the heads of executive departments not only to recommend measures but also to draft bills and even manage them through the legislature; but was that the appropriate relationship in the new republic? Should the president or his cabinet members join the legislative deliberations? Should they set the agenda for the Congress? The Constitution does not say. Consequently, presidents have varied across the spectrum in the extent to which they have tried to lead and guide the legislative process, as Congresses have in their acceptance or rejection of executive leadership.

3. Richard E. Neustadt redefined the separation of powers as "separated institutions sharing powers"; *Presidential Power* (Wiley, 1960), p. 33.

The Veto. The Constitution places no restrictions on the use of the veto power it assigns the president. But should the power be exercised freely or with restraint? Does an unrestrained use of the veto power, or even its threatened use for purposes of legislative bargaining, violate the spirit of the clause that says that "all legislative Powers herein granted . . . shall be vested in a Congress"? Some presidents have thought so and have expressly abdicated their veto power in whole or in part. Others have used the power to the full to gain sway over the legislative branch.

The Scope of Executive Power. The Constitution assigns to the president the "executive Power" but nowhere makes clear just what that power is. Does it consist only of the powers enumerated in the remainder of Article II, or does it include other powers traditionally assumed by monarchs? Does the executive power, for instance, give to the president the right to proclaim a foreign policy for the United States, or is the definition of foreign policy a legislative matter? If both branches have a say, which has the last word in cases of disagreement? In conducting foreign policy, can the president issue ultimatums, and back them up with force if they are rejected? And what is the extent of the president's authority over his cabinet officers and the departments under their control? When the Congress places authority in a department or agency head, may the president direct how that power shall be exercised and remove executive officials who resist his direction? Presidents and Congresses have quarreled over the answers to these questions throughout the country's history.

Congressional Control of Administration. The Constitution assigns to the president responsibility to "take care that the laws be faithfully executed," but the Congress by statute, including appropriations acts, can prescribe the details of administrative organization and procedure and severely limit the president's discretion in performing his duties. If it so chooses, the Senate can turn its power to confirm or reject presidential nominees into a virtual power of appointment. By using its powers as bargaining levers, the Congress can intervene in almost any matter of administration and can influence and even control the exercise by the executive branch of any of its constitutional responsibilities. As the converse of the question of limits on the president's veto power, should the Congress utilize its powers over administration freely, or with restraint? How much discretion should the executive be granted in each of the myriad administrative functions and substantive fields of governmental action? In the exercise of self-restraint, Congresses—like presidents—have ranged across the spectrum from much to virtually none at all.

The Congressional Right to Information. Nowhere in the Constitution is Congress granted the specific power to investigate the conduct of the executive branch, but investigation was recognized at the outset as an implied power, necessary to support the legislative and appropriations functions. Nevertheless, whether the executive branch was justified in withholding information sought by the investigators—thus impeding and crippling their investigations—was still unresolved in the 1970s, as the Watergate case made dramatically clear. Presidents have taken differing views as to what kinds of matters are covered by "executive privilege"—and as to what lengths it is prudent and appropriate to go in insisting on the privilege.

In constitutional crises involving a struggle between the branches, the question is always asked, "What was the intent of the drafters of the Constitution?" At the outset the Founders could be asked directly, because most of them were in the government in one branch or another. But when the Founders separately interpreted the charter they had together written, they often disagreed. James Madison and Alexander Hamilton had both been at Philadelphia, and they had collaborated on *The Federalist*, yet they had profoundly different conceptions as to how the new government should evolve. The convention had had all it could do in one summer to reach the great compromises that enabled it to create a basic structure for the government, and many details had to be left unconsidered. The delegates were satisfied that enough checks and balances had been created to safeguard against either legislative or executive despotism; the exact balance of power would have to be worked out by reasonable men striving together to make the structure that was given them succeed.

When a chief executive and a Congress have collided, the one bent on making the presidency a great office, the other determined to protect and expand its own prerogatives and restrain the executive's ambitions, the courts have rarely been a recourse. Most of the issues have not been justiciable, in some instances because of the judicial doctrine of avoiding "political questions," in others—executive privilege, for instance—because both presidents and Congresses have preferred to make timely compromises rather than push matters to a final determination. Except for a few limitations placed on the executive by the Supreme Court,[4] then, the balance of power between the branches has been left to the political process. The public, ultimately, has

4. As, for instance, the Supreme Court decision of 1952 countermanding President Truman's seizure of most of the country's steel mills. *Youngstown Sheet & Tube Co., et al.* v. *Sawyer*, 343 U.S. 579 (1952). The three-judge dissenting opinion reviews a long series of cases in which presidential use of executive power in the absence of express statutory authorization was upheld. The president's power to remove executive officials was also established in 1935 in *Humphrey's Executor* v. *U.S.*, 295 U.S. 602 (1935).

been the arbiter. In the continuing power struggle, politicians have been restrained by public opinion, or by the fear of it. Eventually, the voters pass judgment on the conduct of the combatants in this as in other matters, and they impose retribution for any unseemly power-grabbing.

Strong and Weak Presidents

The balance between executive and legislative power at any particular time seems to have depended more on the attributes of the president than on the character of the Congress, if only because the nature of the presidency has changed so often and so abruptly and varied across so wide a range. As the makeup of the Congress is altered only gradually, so is its temper and its capacity; the Revolution of 1910 in the House (discussed in chapter 7) appears as the one example of sudden change in the past one hundred years. So the legislative branch is almost a constant in the executive-legislative balance, with shifts attributable to the differing attitudes and objectives, and skill and determination, of the occupants of the presidential office.

In every age those presidents who are seen in retrospect as "strong" have been able to outshine the Congresses that have competed with them. Indeed, they earned their accolade by virtue of their ability to dominate their times and hold sway over the whole of government, including the legislative branch. Such presidents are by no means a twentieth century creation. On almost any list of strong presidents would be found Washington, Jefferson, Jackson, Lincoln, and probably Polk from the last century, along with the two Roosevelts and Wilson from this one.[5] Towering presidential figures have appeared somewhat at random in the course of history—the product of a selection process that itself has always had a random quality.

5. In a poll of historians he took in 1968, Gary M. Maranell found the "strongest" were these eight plus Harry Truman, Lyndon Johnson, and John Kennedy. (Maranell received 571 usable responses to questionnaires mailed to a random sample of 1,095 members of the Organization of American Historians.) Presidents were rated on a scale from strong to weak, using as the criterion "the strength of the role the President played in directing the government and shaping the events of the day." On a second criterion, "the approach taken by each President toward his administration, an active approach or a passive approach," these presidents were again the eleven rated "most active." Ten of them (excluding Johnson) were at the top on a scale of "general prestige," and ten (excluding Kennedy) ranked highest in "accomplishments of their administrations." "The Evaluation of Presidents: An Extension of the Schlesinger Polls," *Journal of American History*, vol. 57 (June 1970), pp. 104–13. The Schlesinger polls, taken by Arthur M. Schlesinger, Sr., in 1948 and 1962, used a single scale from "great" to "failure" and the respondents were a much smaller number of historians and political scientists. Ibid. The nine "greatest" presidents on the 1962 Schlesinger list are also the nine "strongest" and the nine "most active" in the Maranell rankings (excluding Kennedy and Johnson, who did not appear in the 1962 rankings).

But strength in a president is a compound of two factors. One has to do with his conception of his office, the other with his ability to realize that conception. Some presidents who have entered their terms with determination to lead the country and set its course have failed to make history's list of strong presidents because of personal inadequacy or exceptionally difficult political obstacles, or both. The country's presidents fall, for the most part, into three categories: those who believed in a strong presidency and succeeded in achieving it, those who believed in a strong presidency but failed to achieve it, and those who did not believe in a strong presidency at all.

What distinguishes the twentieth century from the nineteenth—and has brought about what appears as a permanent shift of some measure of authority from the legislature to the executive—is the disappearance of the type of president who believes as a matter of conviction that the presidency should be weak. In this century, only William Howard Taft, Warren G. Harding, and Calvin Coolidge openly professed the old Whig view that the Congress should set the policies of the country and let the president administer them. Even these three departed more than once from the principles they claimed, and no president since then has even espoused the Whig view; not for half a century has the country had a president who chose deliberately to be weak in his relations with Congress. Nor will the system of institutions that has been built up around the president, and the expectations of the media, the political world, and the country at large, let him be. Dwight Eisenhower's public statements on occasion convey the frustration of a man caught up in the rough and tumble of legislative politics who would have preferred to be— and, had he lived in the nineteenth century, would have been—a Whig, but circumstances would not let him.[6]

So the era of the strong president—strong in aspiration if not always achievement—has unquestionably arrived to stay, carried on the force of trends as irreversible as anything can be. And that fact limits severely the degree to which even a determined Congress can recapture lost authority. Congressional government, as Woodrow Wilson called the American system in 1885, was possible then because presidents chose to leave a leadership

6. The Maranell poll ranks Eisenhower as both weak and passive—twenty-second among thirty-three presidents in strength and twenty-third in activeness (as well as twentieth in accomplishments). The characterization of weakness would appear to reflect not Eisenhower's conception of the presidency—he laid out a program for the Congress and used the veto freely—but the relatively passive character of the program itself and perhaps what Fred I. Greenstein calls "the 'low profile' nature of [Eisenhower's] leadership style," or "hidden hand leadership." "Eisenhower as an Activist President," *Political Science Quarterly*, vol. 94 (Winter 1979–80), pp. 575–99. The other four of the five presidents between 1933 and 1968 are all rated among the top ten in both strength and activeness. Six of the top seven in activeness are twentieth century presidents; Kennedy and Johnson, of course, were being judged in even less historical perspective than Eisenhower.

vacuum that the legislature was free to fill, but no such vacuums are now conceivable. A reassertive Congress in these days will always face a president who is equally assertive. The legislature can rebound from its low point of the Nixon era—and has—but it will stop far short of the hegemony of its golden age. The major variable affecting the legislative-executive balance is the nature of the presidency, not the objectives and capacity of the Congress; with a permanent shift in the character of the presidency has come a shift in the executive-legislative balance of equal permanence.

Competition in the Early Decades

At the outset of the republic the executive branch was the focal point of government and the center of leadership. President Washington himself appears as something of a figurehead executive, or "chairman of a board,"[7] at least on domestic matters, but his secretary of the treasury, Alexander Hamilton, was the dominant figure in the earliest years of the new government. Hamilton saw himself as a kind of prime minister, and the Congress evidently saw him that way too. He served, on at least some occasions, as a channel of communication to the Congress from departments other than his own. Hamilton presented measures to raise revenue, reorganize the debt, stabilize the currency, and establish a banking system and, with the president's complete support, maintained continuous communication with the legislative managers until the bills were enacted—stopping short only of appearing on the floors of the House and Senate.[8] And there is no record that any of the eighteen members of the Constitutional Convention sitting in the First Congress suggested that such reliance on the executive branch for legislative leadership violated the constitutional intent.[9]

But so intimate an arrangement was not to last, for Hamilton's financial measures provoked fierce controversy. The outlines of the two-party system began to take form, and resolutions condemning Hamilton were introduced—

7. Joseph Charles, *The Origins of the American Party System* (Williamsburg: Institute of Early American History and Culture, 1956), p. 41. According to Charles, Washington took votes of his four-man cabinet on each issue, always accepted the majority vote, and himself voted only in case of a tie.

8. Hamilton offered to appear before the House to present a report that body had asked him to prepare, but the House, "evidently fearful of the precedents involved," asked him to submit it in writing instead. Carl Brent Swisher, *American Constitutional Development*, 2d ed. (Houghton Mifflin, 1954), p. 54.

9. W. E. Binkley, *The Man in the White House: His Powers and Duties* (Johns Hopkins Press, 1958), p. 148; Joseph Cooper, "The Origins of the Standing Committees and the Development of the Modern House," *Rice University Studies*, vol. 56 (Summer 1970), p. 5.

but not passed—and investigations were conducted. Hamilton finally re-signed—"driven" from office is the usual interpretation—but out of the conflict had grown a determination on the part of the Congress to free itself from dependence on executive leadership. In organizational terms, this meant establishing a committee system to make possible the development of leg-islative measures within the Congress. House committees on Ways and Means and on Commerce and Manufactures, hardly necessary during the Hamilton period, appeared in 1795 and other committees followed, one by one, until by 1825 they covered the full range of business in both houses.[10] In the new pattern of relations, a member of the Congress had to avoid even the appearance of being subservient to executive influence; "to be involved in a collusive relationship with the White House in any circumstances was to run a continuous risk of social stigmatization for sycophancy."[11]

Until the administration of Andrew Jackson, the balance between the branches did not again become a major issue. John Adams's relations with the Congress were unhappy but he held his own; Jefferson appears as a strong president—leader of the Congress and dominant figure of his time— but he exercised his leadership subtly, within the limits of the congressional norms. In his first message he promised to carry "into faithful execution" the "legislative judgment,"[12] and he did not use the veto. But more than anyone else, he had introduced the political party upon the American scene, and it was in his role of leader of the newly victorious Republicans that he exercised his sway over the majorities on Capitol Hill. The president and the Congress worked as a team, with the president serving as manager;[13] bills were drafted in the executive branch, much as in Hamilton's time, and relations between leaders of the two branches were not strained by major policy disputes.

In the two decades after Jefferson, presidents did not seek to exercise forceful leadership or were unable to do so, and the balance of authority swung back. A high point of congressional initiative came with the War of 1812—popularly called Henry Clay's War, after the speaker of the House who headed the War Hawks of the time. It is indicative of where the leadership lay during that period that even after a reluctant President Madison was led— or forced—into accepting the war, he stopped short of recommending it; he

10. Joseph Cooper, "Jeffersonian Attitudes toward Executive Leadership and Committee De-velopment in the House of Representatives, 1789–1829," *Western Political Quarterly*, vol. 18 (March 1965), pp. 45–63; Cooper, "Origins of the Standing Committees," note 7 on p. 135.

11. James Sterling Young, *The Washington Community 1800–1828* (Columbia University Press, 1966), p. 165.

12. James D. Richardson, comp., *A Compilation of the Messages and Papers of the Presidents* (New York: Bureau of National Literature, 1897), vol. 1, pp. 319–20. (Hereafter *Messages and Papers*.)

13. Alexander B. Lacy, Jr., "Jefferson and Congress: Congressional Method and Politics, 1801–1809" (Ph.D. dissertation, University of Virginia, 1964), p. 310.

transmitted a review of American grievances against Great Britain to the Congress with a recommendation that the legislature make them the subject of "early deliberation."[14] President James Monroe was equally passive. He expressed no view on the Missouri Compromise until after it was passed, then signed it with an expression of personal opposition. He took no part in tariff deliberations. And he insisted that the Congress make the initial policy decision on recognition of the new republics created in the Latin American wars of independence. The Monroe Doctrine, however, can be credited to executive initiative.

With the inauguration of Andrew Jackson, the executive-legislative balance changed abruptly. Energetic, opinionated, combative, and intolerant, Jackson was also the first president to win his office through a direct appeal to the electorate.[15] He came to office with both a program and a popular mandate, and as he set out to execute them he aroused both passionate devotion and fierce enmity. In the fight over the Second Bank of the United States, congressional-executive tension reached heights not experienced before—and not to be known again until Andrew Johnson held the presidency. The Senate at one point adopted a resolution censuring Jackson for his unilateral action in reversing national policy by withdrawing government deposits—but it could do nothing directly to save the bank. The funds remained withdrawn, and the bank a few years later closed its doors.

But this brand of leadership split the country. Those opposed to the policies and the high-handed tactics of "King Andrew" coalesced into a new party, which called itself the Whigs. Making political issue of the style as well as the substance of Jacksonian Democracy, the Whigs became institutionally committed to the doctrine of a weak presidency. It is difficult to see how Henry Clay, the most notable of the Whig leaders and its presidential candidate in 1844, would have fit into this mold; but his campaign failed, and the presidents the party did elect—William Henry Harrison and Zachary Taylor—espoused, verbally at least, the Whig conception of the presidency. Harrison devoted most of history's longest inaugural address to that issue, attacking concentration of power in the executive, and forswearing any "executive interference" in the legislative process, including the use of the veto "to assist or control Congress." He even advocated taking the Treasury out of the executive branch.[16] President Zachary Taylor in his inaugural

---

14. "Special Message to the Congress, June 1, 1812," in Richardson, *Messages and Papers*, vol. 2, pp. 484–90.
15. In 1828, most presidential electors were chosen by direct election. Previously, they had been chosen by state legislatures.
16. Richardson, *Messages and Papers*, vol. 5, pp. 1860–76.

address in 1849 described the veto power as "an extreme measure, to be resorted to only in extraordinary cases,"[17] and promised not to try to control congressional decisions. And even Abraham Lincoln, when a congressman, wrote: "Were I President, I should desire the legislation of the country to rest with Congress, uninfluenced by the executive in its origin or progress, and undisturbed by the veto unless in very special and clear cases."[18] The Whig record in office, however, was not quite so passive. While the Compromise of 1850—the Whigs' outstanding achievement—was initiated in the Senate by Clay and worked out in detail by a Senate committee, both Whig Presidents Taylor and Millard Fillmore took strong stands on the proposal. Taylor's opposition slowed the progress of Clay's scheme at the outset, and Fillmore's support smoothed the way to its eventual passage.

The Democrats, having the record of Jackson to defend, accepted the strong presidency as a matter of party philosophy. Tyler (who, although elected vice president on the Whig ticket, had been a Democrat and on acceding to the presidency was more Democrat than Whig) not only exercised the veto on policy grounds but secretly negotiated the treaty for Texas's annexation and successfully maneuvered it through the Congress. James K. Polk laid out a program at the outset of his term and through strong party leadership got all of it enacted. He defended the use of the veto on matters of policy disagreement—to yield that right "would be a violation of the spirit of the Constitution, palpable and flagrant"[19]—and he used it that way. Indeed, he worried that presidents would be reluctant "to come in collision with Congress" and hence would not use the veto enough.[20] The war with Mexico, to put it in its most favorable light, was the result of Polk's strong and belligerent foreign policy; at one point the House called it "unnecessarily and unconstitutionally begun by the President."[21] That the last two pre-Civil War Democratic presidents—Franklin Pierce and James Buchanan—appear weak

17. Ibid., vol. 6, p. 2561.
18. John G. Nicolay and John Hay, *Abraham Lincoln: Complete Works* (Century, 1920), vol. 1, p. 134. In *The Federalist*, no. 73, Alexander Hamilton rested his explanation of the veto on the president's need to defend the executive branch against encroachment by the legislature, which otherwise could strip the president of his authority. A secondary purpose would be to protect the community "against the passing of bad laws, through haste, inadvertence, or design." Before Jackson, however, presidents employed the veto sparingly, usually for constitutional reasons and only rarely because of a policy disagreement with the Congress. Washington and Jefferson both explicitly denied that it could properly be used in such cases and John Adams, like Jefferson, never exercised the veto power. The early vetoes are reviewed by Louis Fisher, *The Constitution between Friends: Congress, the President, and the Law* (St. Martin's, 1978), pp. 85–87.
19. "Fourth Annual Message, December 5, 1848," in Richardson, *Messages and Papers*, vol. 6, pp. 2512–13.
20. Ibid., pp. 2519–20.
21. Schlesinger, *Imperial Presidency*, pp. 42–43.

was a matter of capacity and temperament rather than philosophy. Both used the veto when they thought it appropriate, on constitutional or policy grounds, but legislative initiative passed to the Congress. The Kansas-Nebraska bill, which finally reopened the fierce sectional quarrel over slavery that the two great compromises had quieted, was the work of Senator Stephen A. Douglas, who led a complaisant President Pierce along.

But, as W. E. Binkley observed, a succession of four determined men who had brought the presidency into the slavery controversy—Tyler, Polk, Taylor, and Fillmore—had so identified that issue with the office that the irresolution of Pierce and Buchanan could not dispel its importance. So, with the election of another potentially strong president, Abraham Lincoln, by a new party committed to oppose the extension of slavery, the South seceded—without even waiting to see what the president's policies might be or whether the Congress might be able to hold him in check.[22]

The Golden Age of Congressional Ascendancy

Congressmen who dream of a return to the supremacy of the legislative branch can look back to a golden age of ascendancy that lasted virtually without interruption for a third of a century—from the time that the Congress imposed its legislative will on Andrew Johnson until the accession of Theodore Roosevelt. It was not a period distinguished for achievement, of course. If the presidents did not have a program for the country, neither did the legislators; bold legislative proposals were mainly the property of a series of third parties. But insofar as Republicans and Democrats responded to pressures for legislation, it was the Congress that devised the measures. Presidents sometimes identified the problems they thought deserving of congressional attention, but not often. The Whig philosophy, in short, carried over to the postwar era as the doctrine of Republican presidents from Ulysses S. Grant to William McKinley. The one Democratic president of that era, Grover Cleveland, entered office with a Whiggish view as well, though he distinguished himself by exercising the veto more than any other president in history—mostly on private pension bills.

Lincoln himself was a transitional figure on the way to congressional ascendancy. Confronted with disunion and war, he cast aside the Whig mantle he had worn as a congressman and from the onset of hostilities took executive measures that defied the constitutional power of the Congress.

22. Binkley, *Powers of the President*, pp. 110–13.

"No President before or since," wrote Binkley in 1937, "has pushed the boundaries of executive power so far over into the legislative sphere."[23] But the Congress had been transformed too. Secession had made it virtually a one-party body and, relieved of any troublesome minority, it achieved an extraordinary degree of unity and under able leaders battled a strong president on something like equal terms. Indeed, the leading historian of executive-legislative relations during the Civil War has concluded that by the time Lincoln was assassinated, Congress had won the struggle; the congressional radicals "had gutted his policies almost completely."[24]

However, the crucial struggle over reconstruction policy had only begun when Lincoln died, and the showdown was reserved for his successor. President Andrew Johnson adopted Lincoln's reconstruction program in its entirety and swore not to surrender. "Your President is now the Tribune of the people, and, thank God, I am, and intend to assert the power which the people have placed in me," he said.[25] Instead of calling Congress into special session in 1865, he chose to use the months before its regular meeting in December to "steal a march on his legislature and to confront them with a fait accompli"[26] by announcing and putting into effect his pardon and amnesty policies and his program for readmitting the seceded states. This very boldness "produced a reaction against him" in the Congress, and when it met in December it was determined to be the country's policymaking body. Its means to that end was the Joint Committee of Fifteen on Reconstruction, a body that came closer than any other group in the history of the Congress to performing the legislative functions of a British cabinet. [27] It produced the Congress's alternative program for reconstruction, which was enacted over a series of presidential vetoes, as well as the seizure of executive power epitomized in the Tenure of Office Act. The Congress then delivered the final humiliation to the president by impeaching him and coming within one vote in the Senate of convicting him and removing him from office.

These years represent the zenith of congressional power and initiative—the only period when the Congress has been able to enact a comprehensive program to deal with the major issues of the day over the active opposition of a determined president. Indeed, in no other period has the Congress as a whole been able even to develop, much less enact, anything approaching

23. Ibid., p. 133.
24. T. Harry Williams, *Lincoln and the Radicals* (University of Wisconsin Press, 1941), p. 18.
25. Quoted by H. K. Beale, *The Critical Years* (Ungar, 1958), p. 214.
26. J. G. Randall, *The Civil War and Reconstruction* (D.C. Heath, 1937), p. 711.
27. The committee's story is told in ibid. and in W. R. Brock, *An American Crisis: Congress and Reconstruction 1865–67* (St. Martin's, 1963). The committee followed the precedent of the Joint Committee on the Conduct of War, which had harassed Lincoln.

a comprehensive program. But when the Joint Committee of Fifteen had finished its work, after just two years, it was disbanded and the Congress returned to its accustomed ways of decentralized committee deliberations and piecemeal legislative action.

President Grant was happy to leave reconstruction policy to the Congress, described himself as a "purely administrative officer"[28]—although he did assert himself on one occasion to veto a currency bill—and yielded to the claims of the Senate for control of patronage, even including cabinet appointments. But from the pitiable state to which the presidency sank under Johnson and Grant it could only rise, and it began to do so as soon as their successors in the White House were ready to assert a greater degree of authority. Presidents Hayes, Garfield, and Cleveland all battled the Senate to a series of showdowns over patronage, and Hayes fought with his veto the House's attempt to control policy and administration through riders on appropriations bills. The presidents won these contests and succeeded in checking the erosion of their office, when it became clear to the legislators that public opinion overwhelmingly supported the executive. Even the Tenure of Office Act was finally repealed.

But the rejuvenation of the presidency did not extend to legislative leadership. The years from Grant to the end of the century saw in the White House an unbroken line of staunch conservatives—the Democrat Grover Cleveland as well as the half dozen Republicans who held the office—and their messages are singularly barren of major program proposals. The two issues of currency and tariff dominated the election campaigns of the period, and presidents felt obliged to recommend the enactment of measures to carry out their party platforms. But once they had made the recommendations, they left the Congress to work out the legislation. Cleveland stands out as a partial exception. In his first term, he initially forswore "meddling" with pending legislation and then learned, when he tried to intervene on the tariff, that he had thrown his influence away.[29] In his second term he tried to be more forceful. He pressed for, and obtained, the Silver Purchase Repeal Act of 1893 and he used his patronage to assist the House Democratic leaders to pass a tariff reduction bill in 1894 in line with the party platform. But when this bill was gutted in the Senate, his intervention was fitful and inept. In any case, the bill came out in the form desired by the bipartisan Senate coalition, and Cleveland abandoned the fight and signed it.

28. White, *The Republican Era*, p. 23.
29. Horace Samuel Merrill, *Bourbon Leader: Grover Cleveland and the Democratic Party* (Little, Brown, 1957), pp. 113–15.

Any sensitivity to domestic issues, beyond the currency and the tariff, was mainly in the Congress and initiative was taken there. The Interstate Commerce Act was the product of the legislative branch; President Cleveland had only identified the subject as one "worthy of consideration."[30] The original antitrust act is credited to Senator John Sherman, Ohio Republican, but President Benjamin Harrison had urged action. In the leading study of legislative initiation during this period, the president is viewed as the dominant influence in the enactment of only one of thirteen major legislative measures between 1873 and 1897 (the Silver Purchase Repeal Act), pressure groups in two (tariff acts in 1890 and 1897), and Congress in the other ten.[31] "The most eminent Senators," wrote Senator George F. Hoar, Republican of Massachusetts, "would have received as a personal affront a private message from the White House expressing a desire that they should adopt any course in the discharge of their legislative duties that they did not approve. If they visited the White House, it was to give, not to receive advice."[32] This was the time when the young Woodrow Wilson saw the Congress as,

> unquestionably, the predominant and controlling force, the centre and source of all motive and of all regulative power. . . . The legislature is the aggressive spirit. . . . [It] has entered more and more into the details of administration, until it has virtually taken into its own hands all the substantial powers of government. . . . the degree in which the one of these great branches of government is balanced against the other is a very insignificant degree indeed. . . . I know not how better to describe our form of government in a single phrase than by calling it a government by the chairmen of the Standing Committees of Congress.[33]

And a few years later, at the end of Cleveland's first term, Lord Bryce made similar observations:

> The President himself, although he has been voted into office by his party, is not necessarily its leader, nor even one among its most prominent leaders. . . . The expression of his wishes conveyed in a message has not necessarily any more effect on Congress than an article in a prominent party newspaper. No duty lies on Congress to take up a subject to which he has called attention as needing legislation;

30. Richardson, *Messages and Papers*, vol. 12, p. 5111.

31. Lawrence H. Chamberlain, *The President, Congress and Legislation* (Columbia University Press, 1946), pp. 450–52. Besides the Interstate Commerce Act and the Sherman Antitrust Act, he credits to the Congress the currency acts of 1873, 1878, and 1890, Chinese exclusion acts of 1882 and 1892, the General Immigration Act of 1882, the Reclamation Act of 1894, and the Tariff Act of 1894. In the 1890s two major foreign relations decisions not discussed by Chamberlain—the annexation of Hawaii and the Spanish-American War—would have to be credited also to congressional initiative. President McKinley resisted the war fever and accepted the congressional verdict with great reluctance.

32. *Autobiography of Seventy Years* (Scribner's, 1903), vol. 2, p. 46.

33. Woodrow Wilson, *Congressional Government: A Study in American Politics* (1885; World, 1956), pp. 31, 44, 49, 53, 82.

and, in fact, the suggestions which he makes, year after year, are usually neglected, even when his party has a majority in both Houses. . . .

Congress has been the branch of government with the largest facilities for usurping the powers of the other branches, and probably with the most disposition to do so. . . . Congress has succeeded in occupying nearly all of the area which the Constitution left vacant and unallotted between the several authorities it established.[34]

Yet, observed Bryce, the Congress "has not become any more distinctly than in earlier days the dominant power in the State." That was because of the weakness of the Congress itself—its division into two houses, its decentralization into independent committees, its lack of unifying leadership, its irresponsibility in legislating because of the absence of responsibility for successful administration, and for all these reasons its lack of a program. "The weakness of Congress is the strength of the President," he observed, and he presciently remarked that "a vigorous personality" in the presidency could "attract the multitude," represent and influence public opinion better than could the Congress, and hence realize the "undeveloped possibilities of greatness" that lay in that office. But, on balance, he predicted congressional ascendancy in the long run, because "a weak magistrate comes after a strong magistrate, and yields what his predecessor had fought for; but an assembly holds all it has ever won."[35]

During the next couple of decades, the Congress overcame for a time the kinds of weakness of which Bryce spoke, reaching its historic high point in the degree of internal discipline it achieved behind strong leaders. Within the House, power had been gradually accruing to the speaker, and as early as 1891 the historian Albert Bushnell Hart observed that the reformers (perhaps with Bryce in mind) had overlooked the rise in the American system of "an officer who possesses and exercises the most important powers entrusted to the head of the administration in England." The party now acted legislatively through the speaker, he said, and that officer, he predicted, "is likely to become, and perhaps is already, more powerful, both for good and evil, than the President of the United States."[36]

But, as Bryce foresaw, the personality of the president was more crucial than the structure and leadership of the Congress. Not long after the first of the modern strong presidents—Theodore Roosevelt—collided with a legislative branch as strongly organized and led as at any time in its history, the balance of authority swung decisively toward the president.

34. James Bryce, *The American Commonwealth*, 2d ed. (Macmillan, 1889), vol. 1, p. 206; vol. 2, pp. 711–12.

35. Ibid., vol. 1, pp. 223, 294–95; vol. 2, pp. 712–13; vol. 3, p. 656.

36. "The Speaker as Premier," *Atlantic Monthly*, vol. 67 (1891), pp. 380–86.

The Modern Era of the Strong President

Whereas in the nineteenth century the president who believed the office should be strong was the exception, in this century he is the norm.[37] The two Roosevelts and Wilson set a pattern that almost every president since has sought to emulate, though not always with success.

One reason, clearly, is that a "vigorous personality" does indeed "attract the multitude." It is the presidents who exerted forceful leadership who have won the most fervent popular support. When Americans look to the past, it is the strong presidents who are in the pantheon of heroes, who are commemorated by the great monuments in the nation's capital, and who are remembered at political party dinners more than a century after their administrations, while weaker presidents are forgotten. In every crisis the people look for leadership not to a Congress made up of two houses, more than five hundred individuals, and a plural set of contentious spokesmen, but to the White House. There power is concentrated in a single person, elected by all the people, highly visible and known to everyone, who is not merely head of the executive branch of the government but also chief of state—invested, as has often been observed, with many of the trappings of royalty.

The twentieth century was newly born when the potential appeal of a strong president was established. Theodore Roosevelt, he of the "strenuous life," the "big stick," and the "bully pulpit," so caught the public imagination that in his reelection campaign of 1904 he smashed his Democratic opponent by a three-to-two popular majority and swept every state but two outside the Solid South. Because the strong president had to contend with a Congress dominated by entrenched conservatives and also strong in leadership and organization, his legislative requests were modest. He did not directly challenge the ideologically hostile Republican leadership of the Congress until near the end of his second term, at which point executive-legislative relations disintegrated; before that time, he relied on negotiation and entreaty and the results were meager. Indeed, wrote Arthur S. Link, "his chief contribution to the reform cause was the publicity he gave to it."[38] But in the executive sphere, where he could proceed without congressional consent, he made a

37. Three of the five strongest presidents in Maranell's ranking—Theodore Roosevelt (fourth), Woodrow Wilson (fifth), and Franklin Roosevelt (first)—held office during the first half of the twentieth century. Moreover, three of the four later presidents who were included in the study were in the top ten—Harry Truman (seventh), Lyndon Johnson (eighth), and John F. Kennedy (tenth). "Evaluation of Presidents," p. 108. Lincoln ranked second, Jackson third, Jefferson sixth, and Washington ninth.

38. *Woodrow Wilson and the Progressive Era 1910–17* (Harper, 1954), p. 2.

more impressive record: the creation of national forests from the public lands, initiation of antitrust prosecutions, settlement of a coal strike through a threat to seize the mines. This boldness so aroused the Congress that during his first term it adopted a resolution requesting him to file copies of his executive orders and cite the legal authority on which they were based, and it provided for a commission of lawyers to pass on their legality. But he ignored this resolution.

If there were doubt as to whether congressional consent for an action was needed, he resolved it in his own favor. Identifying himself with the "Jackson-Lincoln theory of the presidency," he

> declined to adopt the view that what was imperatively necessary for the nation could not be done by the President unless he could find some specific authorization to do it. My belief was that it was not only his right but his duty to do anything that the needs of the Nation demanded unless such action was forbidden by the Constitution or by the laws. . . . I did not usurp power, but I did greatly broaden the use of executive power.[39]

Roosevelt so transformed the public conception of the presidency that when his successor, the luckless William Howard Taft, took a more restrained approach, he was decisively repudiated. Taft's view was that

> the President can exercise no power which cannot be fairly and reasonably traced to some specific grant of power or justly implied and included within such express grant as proper and necessary to its exercise. Such specific grant must be either in the Federal Constitution or in an act of Congress passed in pursuance thereof. There is no undefined residuum of power which he can exercise because it seems to him to be in the public interest. . . .
>
> My judgment is that the view of . . . Mr. Roosevelt . . . is an unsafe doctrine and that it might lead under emergencies to results of an arbitrary character, doing irremediable injustice to private right. The mainspring of such a view is that the Executive . . . is to play the part of a Universal Providence and set all things right.[40]

In the three-way contest of 1912, Roosevelt as a third-party candidate outpolled the Republican nominee Taft, despite the latter's advantage as incumbent president, and threw the election to the Democrat, Woodrow Wilson. Taft carried but two states. A Taft supporter, writing in 1910, attributed Taft's decline in public popularity to his relative inactivity as legislative leader—specifically, during the tariff debate that began early in his term—and offered a vivid commentary on the new popular view of the presidency:

> It was a shock to the public that a President, after merely submitting in calm and dispassionate tones his recommendations to Congress, should leave that body free

---

39. Theodore Roosevelt, *An Autobiography* (1913; Scribner's, 1925), p. 357.

40. *Our Chief Magistrate and His Powers* (Columbia University Press, 1967), pp. 139–40, 144. Louis Fisher, *President and Congress: Power and Policy* (Free Press, 1972), pp. 33–37, points out that Taft's actions in office and statements elsewhere in his autobiography take a less restrictive view of the president's powers.

to deliberate and frame a bill according to its best judgment. That he forbore to importune Congress, to threaten it . . . that he did not bear down upon that body with all the force and power of his high office, appeared as an unpardonable failure to perform his plain duties. . . . there has arisen the assumption that the President is not merely the administrative head of the nation, but also, and preeminently, the extraordinary representative of the people at large. . . . He is the chief, the overshadowing figure in the Government. No matter how drastic the means employed, the public will applaud the man wielding the power if their demands are satisfied. . . . They applaud the exercise of the veto power; they shriek with glee when the "big stick" is wielded on the heads of those whom they regard as their misrepresentatives.[41]

One editor, looking back on the Taft regime, put it simply: "The public expects the President to manage Congress. If he does not do this he is not considered a successful President. A failure to dominate Congress was Mr. Taft's chief shortcoming in the public mind. He was elected to get laws of a certain character passed and they were not passed." No matter that the failure could be laid to the Congress: "We merely demand that the President see that it gets results along with his other duties."[42] Taft did, in fact, make numerous legislative recommendations, and his departments even drafted bills, but that minimum fulfillment of the role of legislative leader was not enough in a country conditioned by seven and a half years of Theodore Roosevelt.

Woodrow Wilson had no qualms about dominating Congress. He had written much of the need for leadership in the American system, and he sought the presidency explicitly for purposes of leading. And he believed in party government. So his model was Thomas Jefferson, first president to exercise sway over the legislative branch in his role as the head of his party. Wilson was more fortunate than Roosevelt: the party majority elected with him consisted mostly of progressives who had nominated and supported him and looked naturally to him as their leader, while the minority of conservative Democrats went along at the outset in the interest of making a party record after their long period out of power.[43] Cohesion and discipline broke down later, but Wilson remained dominant over his party in the Congress until his incapacitation late in 1919. As Wilson's time in office approached its end, observers were writing once again that the institutional balance had been

41. Samuel J. Kornhauser, "President Taft and the Extra-Constitutional Function of the Presidency," *North American Review*, vol. 192 (1910), pp. 580–81, 586. Kornhauser may have underestimated Taft's legislative efforts and he disregards the question of the effectiveness of Theodore Roosevelt's "big stick," but his emphasis on the contrasting public reaction to the styles of the two presidents is significant. Taft is generally credited with more vigorous antitrust action than Roosevelt, but lacking the latter's flamboyant style he received less public credit.

42. "The Reason for Executive Aggression," *World's Work*, vol. 27 (1913–14), pp. 10–11.

43. Link, *Woodrow Wilson*, p. 35. The internal processes of the Congress during this period are discussed in chap. 7, below.

upset. Henry Campbell Black, editor of the *Constitutional Review*, expressed the concern of a constitutional lawyer:

> The President of the United States has grown into a position of overmastering influence over the legislative department of the government. . . . Congress is subservient to his will; its independence is in eclipse.
>
> The President of the United States occupies today a position of leadership and command over the government of the country so different from that which was intended by the framers of the Constitution that, if it were not the outcome of a natural process of evolution working through a long period of years, it would bear the stigmata of revolution, and if it had been achieved in a single presidential term, it would have been denounced as a *coup d'état*.[44]

When Wilson left the White House, the public mood was ready for a less assertive presidency, and the course of evolution was halted for a decade. But even so, the three Republican presidents of the 1920s did not go all the way back to nineteenth century Whiggery. In fact, they appear ambivalent, consciously trying to steer a middle course between the extreme activism of Wilson and the passivity that had destroyed Taft. Warren Harding began his term by denouncing "executive dictatorship" and promising not to interfere, as had Wilson, in the legislative process, yet he later went so far as to intervene directly in the legislative process on the floor of Congress, when he appeared before the Senate during consideration of a soldiers' bonus bill. On balance, however, his "occasional half-hearted intervention" was not "successful in leading Congress."[45] Calvin Coolidge wrote after his retirement that he "never felt it was my duty to attempt to coerce Senators or Representatives or to take reprisals,"[46] but he did submit a legislative program and he freely used the veto. Hoover, similarly, presented measures but declined to exert leadership in getting them enacted. He wanted limited tariff revision, but "when the high-tariff wolves took charge of the bill," according to Allan Nevins, he showed "paralysis."[47] By the end of his term, the Democrats had captured the lower house of the Congress and national policy was, on the whole, deadlocked—although when Hoover proposed a Reconstruction Fi-

44. *The Relation of the Executive Power to Legislation* (Princeton University Press, 1919), pp. v, 1. James Miller Leake, in "Four Years of Congress," *American Political Science Review*, vol. 11 (May 1917), p. 253, wrote that "at no time" in his first term had Wilson "failed to lead his party, to shape its program, to dominate its policies. . . . on one point all are agreed, friend and foe alike,— President Wilson's leadership in his party has been paramount." Leake emphasized the importance of Wilson's personal appearances on Capitol Hill to read his messages—the first president since John Adams to do so—and his conferences with legislators in the president's room at the Capitol to push legislation.

45. Lindsay Rogers, "The First (Special) Session of the Sixty-Seventh Congress," *American Political Science Review*, vol. 16 (February 1922), p. 46, and "The Second, Third, and Fourth Sessions of the Sixty-Seventh Congress," ibid., vol. 18 (February 1924), p. 91.

46. "The President Lives under a Multitude of Eyes," *American Magazine*, vol. 108 (1929), p. 147.

47. "President Hoover's Record," *Current History*, vol. 36 (1932), pp. 388–89.

nance Corporation as his central antidepression measure, the Congress passed it.

Franklin Roosevelt did not live to write his memoirs and define his philosophy of the presidency, but he expressed it through a dozen years of unremittant activism. Rewarded with three decisive reelection victories, he became still another exemplar of presidential leadership, one that every later Democratic president emulated and that had its influence as well on his Republican successors. Truman presaged Nixon in his aggressive use of presidential power—as in his unilateral action plunging the country into the Korean War, his impoundment of funds for weapons programs, and his seizure of the steel mills (declared unconstitutional by the Supreme Court[48]). On the Republican side, President Eisenhower, whatever may have been his temperamental inclinations, continued the practice of his predecessors in presenting a comprehensive legislative program, and he fully exercised the presidential veto power.

In contradiction, then, to Lord Bryce's prediction that weak presidents would give up what their predecessors had fought for, no president forswore any of the powers accumulated in his office, and by the time of Richard Nixon's inauguration the concept of strong presidential leadership was solidly implanted in the American political culture. It was accepted by the public, by the media, and by the politicians, legislators and executives alike. And a generation of students had been inculcated with the doctrine, their textbooks full of reaffirming phrases. Thomas E. Cronin has assembled some excerpts from the textbooks: the presidency is "the great engine of democracy," "the American people's one authentic trumpet," "the central instrument of democracy," "the chief formulator of public policy" and "chief architect of . . . foreign policy." "Presidential government is a superb planning institution." "He symbolizes the people." "He is . . . a kind of magnificent lion who can roam widely and do great deeds." "Few nations have solved so simply and yet grandly the problem of finding and maintaining an office of state that embodies their majesty and reflects their character."[49]

And what of the danger that a president might roam widely but do bad deeds? "Not one has been recreant to his high trust," insisted Louis Brownlow, one of the architects of the aggrandized presidency.[50] Paul Appleby saw no danger in the presidency: "Through Congress, and through elections, it

48. *Youngstown Sheet & Tube Co., et al.* v. *Sawyer*, 343 U.S. 579 (1952).

49. Excerpts quoted in Thomas E. Cronin, *The State of the Presidency*, 2d ed. (Little, Brown, 1980), pp. 78–81.

50. *The President and the Presidency* (Chicago: Public Administration Service, 1949), p. 51.

is a power popularly controlled."[51] And Richard E. Neustadt, whose *Presidential Power* became the bible of the "cult of the presidency," had no worries. A president seeking to "maximize his power" energizes the government; what is good for the president, he concluded, is therefore good for the country.[52]

There are many institutional factors, moreover, that would deter a president from surrendering power, even should he choose to do so. As each new brick was added to the structure of the strong presidency, usually during the tenure of one of the aggressive occupants of that office, it was fixed in place by the mortar of institutionalization—statutes, organizational units, reporting requirements, executive orders, written and unwritten understandings governing behavior in both branches and the relations between them.

The modern presidency is symbolized by, and embodied in, the Executive Office of the President, an apparatus of a dozen or so component offices erected as a composite policymaking, coordinating, and directing structure for the executive branch—and in many respects, in normal circumstances, for the government as a whole. As power has gravitated from the Congress to the president, it has come to reside in the Executive Office of the President, where the elaborate institutional trappings make the president perforce the leader. A president today cannot be without comprehensive policies and programs, as his nineteenth century and even early twentieth century predecessors often were. As the obverse of Woodrow Wilson's proposition, Neustadt has noted, a president now "cannot be as small as he might choose."[53]

Congressional Acquiescence in Decline

The modern aggrandizement of the presidency was the product of considered legislative decisions, neither acts of impulse by the Congress nor presidential coups d'etat. The Congress had to consent, because it had to pass the laws. But more than that, much of the transfer of power was initiated by the legislative branch itself. Legislatures in other countries have similarly declined; the growth of executive power has been a worldwide phenomenon. However, when the U.S. Congress relinquishes authority to the executive, it does not assign it to a committee of its own members under its ultimate

51. *Big Democracy* (Knopf, 1945), p. 124.
52. Pages 181–85.
53. "The Presidency at Mid-Century," *Law and Contemporary Problems*, vol. 21 (Autumn 1956), p. 610.

control—as in a parliamentary country—but to an independent branch of government. It tosses power over a barrier, so to speak, into alien territory— out of direct control, out of easy reach, even out of sight. It does so when its relations with a particular president are relatively harmonious and trustful; but when harmony turns to discord—as it always must when the two branches are controlled by opposing parties, and often does even when they are not— the powers remain with the president. That is when the urge arises in Congress to take back its power—an impulse that was never stronger than in late 1972 and early 1973 when the Congress began to reassert itself.

Presumably there were good reasons that the Congress voluntarily undertook to construct the modern presidency in the first place. If the legislative branch were to restore itself to the "co-equal status" that was the slogan of 1973, it would have to reassess those reasons.

The next four chapters, which examine the reasons for the decline of Congress in relation to the presidency, treat the growth and institutionalization of the modern presidency from the viewpoint of the institution that lost power—the legislature. The shifts in power from the Capitol to the White House coincided with the establishment or expansion of four great presidential roles in the twentieth century—the roles of general manager of the executive branch, chief stabilizer of the economy, foreign policy leader, and de facto leader of the legislative branch itself. The weaknesses in the Congress that it acknowledged, explicitly or implicitly, in relinquishing power are analyzed in chapter 7. An understanding of the reasons for the acquiescence of the Congress in its own decline is crucial to any appraisal of the possibility, or the desirability, of the Congress's regaining significant elements of its lost authority.

CHAPTER III

The President
as General Manager

WHEN the Constitution assigned the legislative power to the Congress and the executive power to the president, it offered no abstract definition of either and demarked no precise boundary between them. Authorizing the government to do things is clearly legislative; *doing* them is plainly executive. But in between is a vast borderland: *how* the executive shall go about accomplishing the objectives of the law. The Constitution allocated only a couple of regions of that borderland; it specified that the power to appoint administrative officials is in the executive branch (subject to confirmation by the Senate of the top officials), and the power to appropriate money is in the legislative. Beyond those, the terrain was left to be struggled over.

It was inevitable that the Congress should stake its claim to the maximum authority, taking the position that it has the right to prescribe the manner of program execution in whatever degree of detail it elects. At the outset, the First Congress made one concession—acknowledging the right of the president to remove cabinet members without specific statutory authority. But otherwise it established the precedent of tight control. It created by statute each organizational element of the executive branch, and after the first couple of years settled on the practice of itemizing each office and fixing the salary of every employee. All concerned, including President Washington, appear to have accepted that as the appropriate exercise of the congressional prerogative.

Throughout the nineteenth century, the tight controls established by the earliest Congresses were maintained. If anything, they were tightened. In the never-ending struggle over patronage the legislators often used the power

37

of the purse and the right of senatorial confirmation to force presidents to yield to them, as a matter of practice though not of law, the right of actual selection of the individuals whom the president would use his constitutional power to appoint. When the Congress revolted against the excesses of the patronage system, it created by law a civil service system that restricted in new ways the freedom of the president and his subordinates in their use of the appointive powers.

The Supreme Court has not found occasion to impose any constitutional limits on the extent to which the Congress may prescribe by law the organization and methods of operation of the executive branch—except for a series of somewhat inconclusive cases concerning the right of the Congress to limit the power of the president and his subordinates to remove officials and employees.[1] The legislature is checked, then, only by its own self-restraint and by the president's right to veto bills that he may feel invade his prerogatives as chief executive (and even his vetoes can, of course, be overridden). So such managerial discretion as the executive branch possesses comes to it not as a matter of constitutional right but by explicit or implicit delegation from the Congress.

The responsibility of the Congress to authorize, finance, and supervise the activities of the executive branch has been called its "board of directors" function, as distinct from its strictly legislative duties.[2] As the government grew, the sheer magnitude of its operations compelled its board of directors— like any board in a comparable situation—to delegate more and more authority to its general manager. Unlike other boards of directors, however, and unlike legislatures in parliamentary countries, the United States government's board neither selects its general manager nor has the power to remove him under ordinary circumstances; and on occasion it may be in political opposition to him. Nevertheless, much delegation perforce has occurred, and the president has been steadily strengthened as the general manager of the government's vast establishment. What had been the president as an individual, aided only by a couple of secretaries and a tiny clerical staff housed in the president's own home—the White House—in the past half century has become the

---

1. These cases are discussed in Edward S. Corwin, *The President: Office and Powers, 1787–1957,* 4th rev. ed. (New York University Press, 1957), pp. 85–110; and Louis Fisher, *The Constitution between Friends: Congress, the President, and the Law* (St. Martin's, 1978), chap. 3. In one case, *Myers* v. *United States,* 272 U.S. 52 (1926), the Court held that the Congress could not restrict the president's removal power by establishing a four-year term for postmasters, but other restrictions, including the extensive procedural safeguards that protect civil servants against arbitrary dismissal, have been upheld.

2. W. F. Willoughby, *Principles of Legislative Organization and Administration* (Brookings Institution, 1934), pp. 24–25.

presidency, an assortment of managerial and directing agencies so large that they overflow even two large buildings that look down on and dwarf the White House.

The Congress did not assign managerial responsibility to the president without strong reason. It recognized the inherent potential strength of the single-headed presidency, and the manifest weaknesses of the plural legislature, as the point of control over the operations of the executive branch. But the Congress did not relinquish any of its ultimate power to ratify or overturn executive decisions, or to intervene as it might choose in administrative matters. The proportion of decisions made on Capitol Hill was reduced, and in that sense the assignment of managerial responsibility to the president has been an important element in the decline of the Congress.

A New Executive Responsibility: Fiscal Leadership

The first major shift of managerial authority came in the fiscal field. Before 1921, a president did not have to have a program for the whole of the government, and none did; after that date, he was compelled by the Budget and Accounting Act to present a program for every department and every bureau, and to do it annually. Before 1921, a president did not have to propose a fiscal policy for the government, and many did not; after 1921, every chief executive had to have a fiscal policy, every year. That act made the president a leader, a policy and program initiator, and a manager, whether he wished to be or not. The modern presidency, judged in terms of institutional responsibilities, began on June 10, 1921, the day that President Harding signed the Budget and Accounting Act.

Before the passage of that landmark legislation, the department heads prepared annual requests for funds and submitted them directly to the Congress. For the convenience of the Congress, the secretary of the treasury assembled them into a single "book of estimates" but that was a ministerial act; he did not review or approve them nor, normally, did the president. Once arrived in the Congress, they were dispersed among various committees that had responsibilities for appropriations, and they were approved piecemeal.[3] No one at any time, in either branch of government, examined the

---

3. In 1909 eight different committees of the House produced the fourteen annual appropriation bills. In the Senate, the Appropriations Committee had jurisdiction over all but the rivers and harbors bill. Henry Jones Ford, *The Cost of the National Government: A Study in Political Pathology* (Columbia University Press, 1910), pp. 15, 20. But by 1920 appropriation measures were divided among eight Senate committees also. W. F. Willoughby, *The National Budget System with Suggestions for Its Improvement* (Washington: Institute for Government Research, 1927), pp. 16–17.

fiscal policy and position of the government as a whole. But this had not been an urgent matter; between the Civil War and the Spanish-American War, government revenues exceeded expenditures most of the time, and legislators—especially advocates of high tariffs, which provided the surpluses—had to devise "pork barrel" programs to rid themselves of embarrassing excess receipts. But early in the twentieth century, deficits began to appear, and when President Taft took office he made budget reform a matter of major concern. Among other steps, he appointed a Commission on Economy and Efficiency; it recommended that the executive branch be required to prepare a single budget, and Taft in his last week in office did just that, submitting his own consolidated budget for the executive branch as an alternative to the book of estimates.[4] But the Congress ignored it, and President Wilson did not follow Taft's precedent.

As the deficits continued and as the size and the costs of government increased, however, public agitation for a comprehensive budget system grew. By 1916 a pledge to introduce a "simple businesslike budget system" had found its way into the Republican platform (the Democrats only promised to consolidate appropriations responsibility in a single committee in each house of the Congress). Then came the explosive growth of government in World War I, and the lack of management became intolerable. Between 1916 and 1919, expenditures increased from less than $800 million to $18.5 billion, and the deficit in 1919 alone was $13.4 billion.[5] "The Government has been running wild, the ship has been rudderless, the captain has been off watch, and there has been no head who might be held responsible," declared Representative Martin B. Madden, Republican of Illinois, who served on the House Select Committee on the Budget.[6]

At this point the Congress had two options. It could organize itself to seize the tiller and steer the ship, retaining the exclusive responsibility for producing the comprehensive and unified budget, establishing a consolidated process, and equipping its committees with appropriate staff resources. Or it could assign the responsibility for preparing the national budget to the executive, reserving for itself a review capacity.

Public opinion was wholly on the latter side. Fiscal responsibility, after all, had belonged to the Congress, and that body had failed. It bore the blame

4. Taft also personally reviewed the departmental estimates; he claimed to have made reductions of $43 million in the 1911 budget. President Wilson also evidently reviewed budget estimates in cabinet meetings. Louis Fisher, *Presidential Spending Power* (Princeton University Press, 1975), pp. 29–32.

5. Louis Fisher, *President and Congress: Power and Policy* (Free Press, 1972), p. 102.

6. *Congressional Record*, October 17, 1919, p. 7093.

for pork barrel appropriations, for sitting "besottedly by its dirty political hearth, sucking at its smelly pipe of patronage."[7] In the credo of the Progressive Era, corruption centered in the legislatures at every level of government. There the secret deals were made that distributed patronage and boodle, all at the dictates of hidden party bosses. But the situation was not beyond hope: legislatures and bosses and party machines could be circumvented. Bring leadership out into the open where it could be seen and held accountable, by giving the chief executives the clear responsibility for governmental management. Elect reform candidates as mayors, as governors, and as presidents. Give them the means to achieve efficiency and economy in government.

Reinforcing this line of political reasoning in support of the strong managerial executive was the new and developing doctrine of "scientific management," borrowed from the business world. In a country enamored of its burgeoning corporate power, the ideal government was, above everything else, "businesslike." Its goals were "economy and efficiency." To achieve those ends, reformers contended, the public executive must prepare a comprehensive budget, using "scientific" measurements of work loads and resource requirements for every program. After legislative approval of the budget, the executive should control the expenditures, to prevent waste. For these purposes, he should have a professionally trained budget staff reporting directly to him. The executive budget systems introduced in states and cities that had been liberated by the Progressives from rule by entrenched political machines became the models—along with budget systems in other countries, notably Britain—for planning a national budget system for the United States. Such a system had been urged by the leaders of the fledgling public administration profession who made up President Taft's Commission on Economy and Efficiency. In 1911 the House Appropriations Committee was not yet ready to share its control over spending with the president, but in the next decade the idea gained strength inside and outside the government.

Many reformers advocated an executive budget that shifted much more responsibility from the Congress to the president than the Budget and Accounting Act eventually did. Some wanted to deny the Congress the right to increase the presidential estimates; others proposed a requirement for a two-thirds or three-fourths majority. Some defended the right of the president to impound appropriated funds that turned out to be unneeded, others

7. Herbert Quick, *Saturday Evening Post*, September 27, 1919, quoted by Chairman James W. Good, Republican of Iowa, in *National Budget System*, Hearings before the House Select Committee on the Budget, 66 Cong. 1 sess. (U.S. Government Printing Office, 1919), pp. 398–99.

proposed he be empowered to veto individual items in appropriation bills. "Many who are urging the adoption of a budget in the United States are really in favor of a very revolutionary change in our whole system of government," complained a former chairman of the House Appropriations Committee, John J. Fitzgerald, Democrat of New York, at the hearings of the special House budget committee in 1919. "What they favor is practically the elimination of Congress from very much of the work which it now does."[8] None of the public witnesses who testified at the hearings went so far as to propose that the Congress be cut out of the budget process altogether. But W. F. Willoughby, who was a consultant to the House committee and the leading academic witness at its hearings (and who had been a member of Taft's commission), had argued in his writings a year earlier:

> Foreign as is the idea to the American public . . . , there are cogent grounds for holding that the legislature should be largely, if not wholly, excluded from the direct determination of the appropriation of funds. . . .
> . . . It is of the essence of that system that the total revenue and expenditure needs of a government shall be considered and determined upon at one and the same time and that the two sides of the account shall be considered in their relations to each other. . . . The difficulties involved in securing well considered action of this kind through the customary processes of legislation are manifold.
> . . . Extravagance, waste, and misapplication of public funds have invariably resulted where the legislative branch has been given the determining voice in the enactment of budgetary proposals.[9]

The Budget and Accounting Act of 1921 went all the way with the reform movement in putting the executive into the budget process, but not in cutting the Congress out. Its congressional sponsors emphasized that the powers of the Congress would remain intact, not weakened in any way. Indeed, they argued, the legislative branch would benefit in three ways. First, it would be provided better estimates to serve as the basis of its appropriations judgments. Second, the president would be forced to accept a share of the political blame for extravagance that had hitherto been fastened disproportionately—and unfairly—on the legislators. Finally, a comptroller general would be established to act as the legislature's agent independent of the executive, with responsibility for auditing and for the final settlement of accounts.

In order for the Congress to do a better job in its appropriations function, reasoned the House committee, someone had to subject the estimates of the various departments to "scrutiny, revision, and correlation." The president was the only officer superior to the departments, the only one with a view of the whole government, while yet elected and hence politically responsible.

8. *National Budget System*, Hearings, p. 317.
9. *The Problem of a National Budget* (Appleton, 1918), pp. 39–40. President Wilson's successive secretaries of the treasury also endorsed limitations on the congressional power to increase the president's estimates. Fisher, *Constitution between Friends*, p. 177.

The bill would "definitely locate upon him responsibility for the formulation and recommendation of a financial and work program for the year to ensue."[10] In the debates the insistence on presidential "responsibility" was a constant theme. The committee's ranking Democrat, Representative Joseph W. Byrns of Tennessee, contended that the chief advantage of the bill lay "in the fact that it fixes in the most direct and positive way upon the President the responsibility for all the estimates submitted. . . . If he wishes to exercise economy, then he is given the means. . . . And if . . . Congress should prove extravagant and increase them, then the issue is made and the people will know how to judge between them. You can neither have or expect good government . . . unless there is some one at the head upon whom rests the weight of responsibility." Representative William R. Green, Republican of Iowa, concurred: The bill "will prevent the Chief Executive from dodging responsibility. . . . If waste and extravagance are proposed in these estimates, he will be responsible." And Byrns explained that the committee had omitted a requirement for senatorial confirmation of the budget director and his assistant for the very reason that they were "trying to put this responsibility directly upon the President and make him responsible and to leave no loophole whereby anyone can escape that responsibility." In the Senate Walter E. Edge, Republican of New Jersey, told his colleagues: "I believe absolutely . . . in centering responsibility. I would like to see the President . . . the actual head of the great big business of the United States" and as head of that big business to present annually a "complete scheme" embracing "the policy for the coming year."[11]

Few championed the alternative of fixing responsibility in the Congress rather than in the president. In the House hearings, John N. Garner, Texas Democrat, raised the question of whether the new budget bureau ought to be responsible to the Congress rather than the president, but the suggestion was dropped and the committee was unanimous in assigning the responsibility to the president.[12] In the floor debate a few members expressed misgivings; Representative Green "would have much preferred that this budget should have been framed by Congress in the first instance and not by any budget bureau."[13] In the Senate only James A. Reed, Missouri Democrat, seemed aroused by the prospect that the ultimate authority of the Congress

10. *Establishment of a National Budget System*, H. Rept. 362, 66 Cong. 1 sess. (GPO, 1919), pp. 5–7.

11. *Congressional Record*, October 17, 1919, pp. 7087–88; May 29, 1920, p. 7955; October 17, 1919, p. 7089; April 30, 1920, p. 6350.

12. *National Budget System*, Hearings, p. 324. The bureau was, however, required to provide information to congressional committees on request.

13. *Congressional Record*, October 21, 1919, p. 7284. Green had been the sponsor of a bill to create a legislative budget system.

would be diminished. The purpose of the bill, he grumbled, was "to enable Congress once more to abdicate its powers and transfer them to the Executive. . . . if that work can be better done by the Executive and Congress can no longer be trusted, Congress had better go out of business: we should once and for all vote our incompetency and shift the responsibility of government to the executive. . . . It is just as likely that a President, through subordinates . . . whose word he must take . . . will make mistakes as that the Representatives of the people elected by the people will make mistakes."[14] Former Speaker Joseph G. Cannon, Republican of Illinois, who had written in a magazine article that "when Congress consents to the Executive making the budget it will have surrendered the most important part of a representative government,"[15] subsequently accepted the committee's unanimous judgment. Indeed, only nine members voted against the bill on final passage in the House, and in the Senate the roll was not even called.[16]

The major enlargement of presidential responsibility represented in the Budget and Accounting Act was in no sense an executive seizure of what had been a function of the legislature. While President Taft had advocated, and in his final year actually presented, an executive budget, Wilson had not demanded the authority. He took no personal part in the drive for a budget system except for a cursory cable from the Paris Peace Conference early in 1919 and a general endorsement of the idea in his annual message in December—after the House had acted and Senate approval was assured. His secretaries of the treasury testified favorably, but the impetus came from within the Congress and from the Progressive reform movement outside.

In companion measures the Congress tidied up its own procedures. Jurisdiction over all appropriation measures was assigned to a single House committee in 1920 and to a corresponding Senate committee in 1922. But budgetary decisionmaking had effectively been passed to the executive branch. In the early years the appropriations committees accepted the president's estimates as ceilings and their cuts amounted to less than one-half of one percent.[17] The committees later showed somewhat less constraint, but

14. Ibid., June 5, 1920, pp. 8626–27.
15. "The National Budget," *Harper's Magazine,* October 1919.
16. The act was delayed until 1921 because President Wilson vetoed the measure passed in 1920, contending that its provision that the comptroller general could be removed only by concurrent resolution of the two houses of the Congress was an unconstitutional limitation on the president's power to remove officers appointed by him. The Congress simply held the bill over until the next session, and repassed it with some modifications, including the concession that removal was to require a joint resolution of the Congress approved by the president rather than a concurrent resolution of the two houses alone; President Harding signed the bill without objection.
17. Willoughby, *National Budget System,* p. 145; Joseph P. Harris, *Congressional Control of Administration* (Brookings Institution, 1964), p. 63.

the executive budget remained the starting point for congressional consideration of fiscal policy and of appropriations, and the overwhelming proportion of reductions that the Budget Bureau, acting for the president, made in agency requests for funds was sustained.[18] The Congress, relieved of the exclusive responsibility for reviewing and analyzing the agency estimates, could accept the president's judgment on the preponderance of them and concentrate its activity on items that involved policy questions or, for other reasons, were of special interest to the legislators.

The General Manager Role Develops

The first director of the budget, General Charles G. Dawes, set out explicitly to make the president the general manager of "the great big business of the United States" that Senator Edge and other reformers wanted him to become. The "great waste and extravagance" of the government in its "routine business administration," contended Dawes, were traceable to the fact that the "president of the corporation gave practically no attention to its ordinary routine business."[19] That had now changed. Dawes arranged for President Harding to inaugurate semiannual meetings of the president and budget director with what was named the Business Organization of the Government—an assembly of officials from department and agency heads to unit chiefs and chief clerks that soon numbered two thousand—and he obtained the president's signature on executive orders to establish coordinators and interdepartmental boards to improve governmental efficiency in such governmentwide business problems as purchasing, real estate management, motor transport utilization, and hospital management.

But while Dawes's reiteration of words like "routine" and "ordinary" may have helped to reconcile the hitherto autonomous departments to the new realities of control from the presidential level, it was obvious that the budget process brought the presidency into systematic policy control as well. In the 1919 House hearings, when a witness had argued that budgeting should be taken out of politics, Representative Garner had challenged him "to tell me

18. Richard F. Fenno, Jr., *The Power of the Purse: Appropriations Politics in Congress* (Little, Brown, 1965), pp. 353–54, 574–79, found that in reviewing the budget requests for 36 bureaus in the period 1947–62, the House Appropriations Committee accepted the executive estimate in about 20 percent of the cases and in a large majority of cases altered the estimate—usually downward—by less than 5 percent; and the Senate Appropriations Committee, acting as an appeals body, normally restored some of the cuts made by the House.

19. "Report of the Director of the Bureau of the Budget to the President of the United States, December 5, 1921," in Charles G. Dawes, *The First Year of the Budget of the United States* (Harper and Bros., 1923), pp. 145, 121.

of a single appropriation that does not involve a question of public policy."[20] Policy questions, in theory, would be decided by the president; as the government grew, the Budget Bureau's role in policy advice would be bound to expand along with its role in the routines of work measurement and cost standardization—but in any case the policy decisions would be made at the presidential level. One of Dawes's early directives to departments and agencies required that proposed new legislation involving new expenditure commitments be submitted to the bureau for presidential approval. The bureau thereby gained access to much of the flow of legislative recommendations from the executive branch to the Congress, though not to the entire flow for another decade.[21]

The bureau also established procedures for setting aside unneeded funds as "reserves," a practice that was confirmed by statute in 1950. Initially, presidential control over spending was undertaken, with congressional encouragement, as a strictly managerial task; yet the reserve procedures that are meant to prevent waste can also be used to curtail or eliminate expenditures that the Congress may have fully intended be made.[22] Once the president began to exercise control over agency spending, the Congress started consolidating "line items" in appropriations into fewer and fewer categories, thus granting more discretion to the executive branch.[23] It also granted limited permission to transfer funds from one project or purpose to another, sometimes subject to committee review and approval.[24] On spending decisions, however, the Congress retained the last word; in a very real sense, then, the

20. *National Budget System*, Hearings, p. 109. The witness was John T. Pratt, president of the National Budget Committee, who had presented the committee's scheme for a five-member budget commission appointed for four-year overlapping terms as the means to "take it out of politics." The Congressmen saw no merit in the proposal.

21. This directive grew out of a suggestion by Representative Madden, who in 1921 became chairman of the House Appropriations Committee. Richard E. Neustadt, "The Presidency and Legislation: The Growth of Central Clearance," *American Political Science Review*, vol. 48 (September 1954), pp. 643–44. The order, says Neustadt, aroused such opposition from cabinet members that it was not enforced until the Coolidge administration.

22. The 1950 act authorizes impoundments "whenever savings are made possible by or through changes in requirements, greater efficiency of operations, or other developments subsequent to the date on which such appropriation was made available." The "other developments" clause, in particular, gave a president great latitude, and it was deleted in 1974. Presidential use, and abuse, of this impoundment power is discussed later in this chapter and in chapters 4 and 8, and the reforms of 1974 in chapter 8. The original antideficiency act, passed in 1905 and amended in 1906, required department heads to apportion their annual appropriations by months or quarters to prevent excessive expenditures early in the fiscal year leading to requests for deficiency appropriations later.

23. By 1976 a $375 billion budget had substantially fewer "lines" than the budget of $265 million a century before. Allen Schick, "Congress and the 'Details' of Administration," *Public Administration Review*, vol. 36 (September/October 1976), p. 517.

24. The varying arrangements and understandings, along with instances of violation of them by the executive branch, are detailed in Fisher, *Presidential Spending Power*, chaps. 4, 5.

argument that establishment of an executive budget would not reduce congressional power but only enable the Congress to exercise its power more intelligently was borne out. By making fewer decisions, presumably it was making better ones.

In 1923 came another delegation of administrative authority, this time in the field of personnel management. The Congress finally concluded that it could no longer consider in the appropriation process, and establish by law, the exact number of civil servants who might be employed at every level in every agency and the compensation of each. For the Congress to pretend to evaluate each job each year, in a growing government, had become absurd; and to even approach equity in the results—"equal pay for equal work"— was impossible. The Classification Act of 1923 assigns to the executive branch the responsibility of allocating jobs among a limited number of pay grades, with only positions at the very highest levels excepted.

Ten years later, the allocation of office space among executive agencies in the District of Columbia was transferred to the executive branch from a Public Buildings Commission which had been created in 1919 as an agency of the Congress. That body, in which the president had had "absolutely no voice," consisted of seven persons, four of whom were members of Congress and a fifth an employee of the legislative branch.[25] Gradually, such government-wide service functions as building management, purchase of supplies and equipment, and records management were brought under closer control by the Bureau of the Budget, acting for the president, and eventually, in 1949, consolidated in the General Services Administration.

The General Manager as Constitutional Intent

As the presidency expanded in the 1920s and 1930s, so did the reformers' aspirations for that office. The first textbooks in public administration were standardizing the conception of chief executives—presidents, governors, mayors, and city managers—as general managers. Leonard D. White's first edition of what became the most influential volume in the training of the first generation of professional public administrators stated that the new discipline was based on "the theory that honest, efficient, and responsible government will best be secured by concentrating substantial authority in the office of the chief executive, and by establishing administrative machinery subject to his

25. Willoughby, *National Budget System*, pp. 233–35.

supervision which can make this authority effective."[26] And the prolific Willoughby in his *Principles of Public Administration* avowed that, "It can be stated without any hesitation that a prime requisite of any proper administrative system is . . . that, in a word, the chief executive shall be given all the duties and powers of a general manager and be made in fact, as well as in theory, the head of the administration."[27]

The two disagreed on terminology, however, in a dispute that reflected conceptual differences about executive-legislative relations. White defined public *administration* as synonymous with *execution* and with *management* and so wrote the legislature out of administration altogether; only in chapters on "The External Relationships of Public Administration" and "Control of Administration" are legislatures discussed. "The unfortunate use of the words 'execution' and 'administration' as almost interchangeable terms," Willoughby protested, had led to a general, but erroneous, public view that the chief executives are the custodians of administrative authority. The legislature, he reminded the public, presumably including White, is "the source of all administrative authority." "Direction, supervision, and control of the administrative activities of the government" reside with the legislature. Accordingly, his text includes a chapter on "The Legislature as a Board of Directors."[28] But it is mainly a plea for a maximum delegation by the board of directors to "the chief executive as general manager." So Willoughby joined White in a common conception of how the executive branch should be organized and run—whether the executive's authority to run it were by sufferance and delegation or by right. In their concept, agencies are grouped neatly into integrated departments. The heads of those departments are appointed by, and removable by, the chief executive. The executive—in the national government, the president—is the general manager of the whole establishment, in every sense, and he is provided with staff agencies to assist him in exercising direction and control.

By 1933, White could write, with pardonable exaggeration, that the president "is now in effective control of administrative policy and operation because he has an adequate staff agency in the Bureau of the Budget. The departments have lost their independent and uncoordinated position and

---

26. *Introduction to the Study of Public Administration* (Macmillan, 1926), p. 131.

27. W. F. Willoughby, *Principles of Public Administration* (Johns Hopkins Press, 1927), p. 36.

28. Ibid., pp. 10–11. Since the Constitution places executive authority in the president (and state constitutions in the governors), Willoughby had to distinguish between the terms, and he did so by defining the executive function as that of "representing the government as a whole and seeing that all of its laws are properly complied with by its several parts," and administration as "actually administering the law."

have been coordinated into a single national administrative machine."[29] When he revised his textbook in 1939, he included a chapter on "The Chief Executive as General Manager," and he reduced his reference to the legislature's role in administration to a few grudging paragraphs. After he acknowledged that a legislature does have "legitimate functions to perform with regard to administration," White proceeded to limit them severely:

> It may properly undertake to fix the main lines of policy and to see that administrative policy is in harmony with legislative policy; to ensure the legality and propriety of expenditures; to be satisfied that internal administrative controls are operating to secure economy and efficiency; and to inform itself of the conditions of administration in view of remedial legislation. Farther than this it does not need, and is not qualified, to go.[30]

Luther Gulick, in his theory of organization, went all the way. Coordination, he wrote in 1937, is "mandatory." It is achieved by "a structure of authority" through which orders are transmitted from "superiors to subordinates, reaching from the top to the bottom of the entire enterprise"; and by "the development of intelligent singleness of purpose" among the workers. In the structure of authority, "a single directing executive authority" at the top of a hierarchy of communication and control is essential.[31]

All of this developing theory was brought to its practical application to the federal government in the 1937 report of the President's Committee on Administrative Management, chaired by Louis Brownlow, with Gulick and Charles E. Merriam as the other members. The committee's plan, which President Roosevelt sent to the Congress with his endorsement, was clearly designed to make the president the "single directing executive authority" over a hierarchical executive branch. The independent regulatory agencies, in all but their "judicial" functions, would be brought within the hierarchical structure. Two new departments would be created, for social welfare and public works. Government corporations would be placed in the departments, under supervisory agencies, though some of them might be semiautonomous. To aid the president in his diverse and expanded functions of management, the forty-five-person Bureau of the Budget would be enlarged, and it would be augmented by a personnel agency (to be created by transfer of the Civil Service Commission), a planning agency (to be created from the temporary National Resources Board set up by executive order), and six executive

29. Leonard D. White, *Trends in Public Administration*, prepared for the President's Research Committee on Social Trends (McGraw-Hill, 1933), p. 174.

30. Leonard D. White, *Introduction to the Study of Public Administration*, rev. ed. (Macmillan, 1939), p. 567.

31. "Notes on the Theory of Organization," in Luther Gulick and L. Urwick, eds., *Papers on the Science of Administration* (Institute of Public Administration, Columbia University, 1937), pp. 6–7.

assistants in the White House—all brought together in an Executive Office of the President. The president would be "required to accept" a continuing authority to reorganize the executive branch; otherwise, he could not be held "truly responsible for administration and its efficiency."[32] (Such power had been granted previously only for temporary periods during emergencies—to President Wilson during World War I, and to Presidents Hoover and Roosevelt from June 1932 to March 1935 during the depression). The Budget Bureau's function of clearing proposed legislation with fiscal implications would be extended to all legislation recommended by executive branch agencies, and to reports on pending legislation.[33] "The President needs help," said the committee. Its answer was to complete the conversion of an individual into an echelon of government, of the president into the presidency.[34]

To support this aggrandizement of the presidential office, the committee offered a rereading of the Constitution. Gone was the Willoughby concept that administrative responsibility lay in the legislature, to be granted to the executive only by delegation. Accepted in full was White's "unfortunate"— as Willoughby had termed it—interchangeable use of *executive* and *administrative*. And since the Constitution grants the executive power to the president, he became the chief administrator not by sufferance but by constitutional right. The "effectiveness of the Chief Executive is limited and restricted, in spite of the clear intent of the Constitution to the contrary," said the committee, without attempting to prove any such intent.[35] Specifically, it argued, the Constitution was being violated in the assignment to the comptroller general (an officer of the legislative branch) of responsibility for settlement of accounts and supervision of administrative accounting systems. In a message written by Gulick transmitting the report to the Congress, President Roosevelt gladly accepted this constitutional interpretation. "The plain fact is," said the president, "that the present organization and equipment of the executive branch of the Government defeats the constitutional intent that there be a single responsible Chief Executive to coordinate and manage the

32. President's Committee on Administrative Management, *Report of the Committee with Studies of Administrative Management in the Federal Government* (GPO, 1937), p. 36.

33. The bureau had in fact been clearing all proposed legislation and legislative reports since December 1935, but without statutory authority. The National Emergency Council had first been assigned the responsibility for nonfiscal legislation, in December 1934. Neustadt, "The Presidency and Legislation," pp. 649–50.

34. William Y. Elliott and Schuyler Wallace, members of the committee's eminent staff of political scientists and specialists in administrative law, dissented from the principle of consolidating administrative power in the president and his personal staff, as did such scholars as Edward S. Corwin and Lindsay Rogers. One alternative urged was that the collective role of the cabinet be enlarged. Barry Dean Karl, *Executive Reorganization and Reform in the New Deal* (Harvard University Press, 1963), pp. 238–41.

35. President's Committee on Administrative Management, *Report*, p. 3.

departments and agencies in accordance with the laws enacted by the Congress."[36]

The plainer fact, however, was that no matter what the Constitution intended, the president could only coordinate and manage "in accordance with the laws enacted by the Congress." The Congress could define the president's constitutional rights in almost any way it chose and had always done so. Even if the Brownlow Committee's interpretation of the intent of the Constitutional Convention were correct—a highly dubious proposition, given that the Founders themselves had participated in establishing practices to the contrary—a century and a half of governmental experience had effectively overturned the intent. And any president who sought to resist the legislature's tendency to write the details of government organization and management practices into law would find few weapons, other than persuasion, at his disposal. Occasionally, a right could be asserted through the courts, as in 1926 when the congressional restriction on the presidential right of removal of postmasters was struck down. Occasionally, the president could protect or assert a claimed authority by the use of the veto power. But beyond that, no matter what he might contend his constitutional rights to be, his administrative authority came in fact not from the Constitution but from the Congress through voluntary (or bargained) delegation.

Proof of that proposition lay in the fact that the Brownlow Committee's plan itself had to be transmitted only as the president's recommendations to the Congress. Only those proposals that the Congress approved would take effect. Any new powers the president gained might not be seen by the president and his committee as "delegations" of legislative power, but they would amount to that. The organizational theories and constitutional interpretations of White, the Brownlow Committee, and Roosevelt may have won the allegiance of most of the trend-setting thinkers in the political science and public administration disciplines. But Willoughby's theory of the legislators' board-of-directors responsibility had the preponderance of support on Capitol Hill, even among fervent Roosevelt supporters, and the Hill held the power of decision.

Reorganization: "Congress Cannot Do It"

The overwhelmingly Democratic Congress carried into office by the Roosevelt landslide of 1936 almost passed a bill embodying the central features of

36. Ibid., p. iv.

the Brownlow Committee plan—and it surely would have, except for a coincidence of timing. The president's bill to "pack" the Supreme Court rent the country in 1937; it gave his opposition the issue of "dictatorship" and enabled it to inflict on him his first major legislative defeat. Three weeks after that bill was killed, two reorganization bills did get through the House by lopsided margins, but in the months before the Senate could take them up a "heated and organized furor" arose.[37] Republican leaders like Senator Arthur H. Vandenberg of Michigan again accused the president of envisioning a "potential dictatorship,"[38] and anti-New Deal newspapers took up the cry. Nevertheless, when the issue reached the Senate floor, this time in a single bill, the president's lieutenants were able to stave off a series of weakening amendments by narrow votes and then pass the measure by a margin of 49 to 42. The proponents argued that while the power to reorganize the government lay in the Congress, decades of experience had shown that the Congress could not exercise that power. "We can make Fourth of July speeches about the matter," said Senator James F. Byrnes, South Carolina Democrat, "but the history of Congress shows that Congress just cannot make these changes."[39] But when the Senate bill came before the House, that body's mood had changed. It killed the measure by 8 votes, 204 to 196, after what Representative Lindsay Warren, Democrat of North Carolina, called the bitterest House fight in fifty years.[40]

The administration and its congressional leaders tried another tack in the next Congress, offering in modified form just one of the key elements of the 1938 bill—the one delegating reorganization powers to the president, subject to a veto by a concurrent resolution of both houses.[41] The most controversial proposals—such as those pertaining to the independent regulatory commissions and those creating new departments—could be sent to the Congress subsequently, to be considered one by one. The bill introduced early in 1939, granting reorganization power only for the remainder of Roosevelt's second term, exempted a score of especially politically sensitive agencies, including

37. Karl, *Executive Reorganization*, p. 248. One bill, passed by a vote of 260 to 88, would have authorized the six presidential assistants recommended by the Brownlow Committee. The second, passed by 283 to 76, would have created a department of welfare and given the president authority to regroup agencies. Richard Polenberg, *Reorganizing Roosevelt's Government: The Controversy over Executive Reorganization, 1936–39* (Harvard University Press, 1966), pp. 49–50.

38. *Congressional Record*, March 28, 1938, p. 4191.

39. Ibid., March 8, 1938, pp. 3034–38.

40. Polenberg, *Reorganizing Roosevelt's Government*, p. 162. Polenberg notes that the Senate bill could have gone directly to a conference committee, but it went to the House floor instead through a parliamentary quirk.

41. Unlike a joint resolution, a concurrent resolution does not require presidential signature. This important limitation on the proposed reorganization powers of the president was a modification accepted by the administration during the 1938 struggle in order to gain crucial support.

the Veterans Administration, the Civil Service Commission, the Army Corps of Engineers, and the independent regulatory commissions. No new departments could be created. Several noncontroversial features of the 1938 measure, including authorization for the six administrative assistants to the president that the Brownlow group had urged, were retained in the 1939 version.

Debate turned on the simple issue of whether the Congress had the capacity to fulfill what it had always claimed to be its constitutional responsibility—rather than the president's—to keep the organization of the government up to date. The Democratic sponsors of the bill said no. Opening discussion in the House, John J. Cochran of Missouri argued that "it has long since been determined that the Congress itself will not pass the necessary specific legislation to bring about general reorganization." Said Representative Warren of North Carolina: "We now know from long and bitter experience that Congress does not want to do it. We know that Congress is not going to do it, and, furthermore, we know that Congress cannot do it." E. Eugene Cox of Georgia contended that Congress must use the president as its "agent" to get the desired results. And John W. McCormack of Massachusetts said that the "practical" members of Congress knew that "bureaucratic influence" exercised on the legislators could kill any reorganization measure submitted by any president. In the Senate, Guy M. Gillette of Iowa asked whether there were "any more logical agency . . . than the executive department to act for us in taking the preliminary steps." Majority Leader Alben W. Barkley of Kentucky reasoned that it would be "physically impossible" for the Congress to go through all the departments "with a fine-tooth comb" and determine how they should be reorganized. "That is the reason why . . . Congress . . . never will do it."[42]

The Republican opposition protested that the Congress was not incompetent but had only to assert itself. "If the Congress of the United States is willing to concede and admit that it is incapable of protecting the interests of the people as against the whims of the bureaus and bureaucrats in this Government, we had better fold our tents and go home and let them run the whole Government," declaimed Representative Frank B. Keefe of Wisconsin.[43] Passage of the bill was a foregone conclusion; the crucial vote was on an amendment offered in the Senate by Burton K. Wheeler, Montana Democrat, to require affirmative action by the Congress before a reorganization plan

42. *Congressional Record*, March 6, 1939, pp. 2305, 2310; March 7, 1939, pp. 2375, 2414; March 20, 1939, pp. 3034, 3036.
43. Ibid., March 6, 1939, p. 2319.

could take effect—in other words, to require the equivalent of a statute and thus reduce the president's reorganization plans to nothing more than ordinary recommendations. It lost by the narrowest of margins, 46 to 44.

Armed with his new reorganization powers, President Roosevelt later that year sent to the Congress five reorganization plans embodying recommendations of the Brownlow report—but excluding those that his legislative lieutenants advised him would arouse too much controversy. None of the plans was disapproved.[44] Among them was one that brought into being the Executive Office of the President, to consist of five divisions: the White House Office, with its six new administrative assistants; the Bureau of the Budget, transferred from its nominal location in the Treasury Department; the National Security Resources Board, created from the National Resources Committee; the Office of Government Reports; and the Liaison Office for Personnel Management. The last of these was what remained of the Brownlow Committee's recommendations relating to personnel management; because the Reorganization Act of 1939 had included the Civil Service Commission in the list of exempt agencies, the president could not transfer its functions, but he designated one of his new administrative assistants to advise him, and deal with the commission for him, on personnel matters.

With the act of 1939, reorganization of the executive branch came to be accepted as the president's responsibility. It was a responsibility to be exercised under specific congressional controls, however, and it was in no sense an exclusive delegation; the Congress would continue also to effect reorganization through the usual legislative process. The 1939 act was allowed to expire in January 1941, but after Pearl Harbor the First War Powers Act gave President Roosevelt broad powers to effect temporary reorganizations without congressional review. After the war President Truman was given temporary reorganization authority, with the prewar provision for legislative veto, and that authority was subsequently renewed—with occasional lapses, none of which lasted more than two years—until April 1, 1973. When the last extension ran out during the intense conflict between President Nixon and the Democratic Congress, any grant of power to the president, of any kind, was scarcely conceivable; but in 1977, with a Democrat in the White House, the procedure was reinstated. Between 1939 and 1973, a total of 105 reorganizations plans were sent to the Congress by six presidents, many of the individual plans embodying multiple proposals, and 83 of the plans were accepted.

44. The House rejected one, to put the Civil Aeronautics Administration in the Commerce Department, but the plan was sustained by the Senate.

In its repeated extensions of the Reorganization Act the Congress has modified the president's power in various ways—by reducing the number of exempted agencies; by prohibiting the use of reorganization plans to create, abolish, or consolidate departments; and by providing that a presidential plan could be vetoed by action of either house alone. But the disputes that have occurred in the Congress have been over restrictions such as these, not over the principle. Democratic Senator Harry F. Byrd of Virginia, a leading opponent of the 1939 act, expressed the conversion of reluctant members six years later: "The only way to reorganize the Government is to give the power of reorganization to the President and then depend on him to accomplish it, and hold him to strict accountability."[45] In 1971, when a Democratic Congress granted reorganization authority to a Republican president, only twenty members voted against the bill in the House and it was not even debated in the Senate.

The Unification of Military Management

A reorganization of particular significance in enhancing the president's role as general manager was the unification of the armed services in 1947. During World War II, devices for coordinating the separate War and Navy departments had been improvised both in Washington and in the theaters of operation, but coordination was far from satisfactory. When the war ended the navy had its ground forces in the marines, the army had some small seagoing vessels, and both had large air forces competing vigorously for primacy in preparing for the strategic air warfare of the future. As the War and Navy departments scrambled for their respective shares of the diminishing military budgets, it was clear that somebody had to serve as an authoritative arbiter of the roles and missions of the various elements of the armed services and the allocator of scarce resources. Neither the Congress nor the president could do that job.

President Truman offered his solution in 1945, and two years later a Republican Congress accepted it: the unification of the War and Navy departments in a single Department of Defense. In the National Security Act of 1947, the Congress declared its intent to provide for the "authoritative coordination and unified direction under civilian control" of the army, navy, and air forces. The coordinator and director would be the secretary of defense,

45. *Congressional Record*, November 9, 1945, p. 10572.

under the president as commander in chief.[46] Both houses of Congress also consolidated their military and naval affairs committees.

In adopting the plan, the Congress saw no diminution of its own responsibilities. The president, as commander in chief, would allocate roles and missions among the services, as he had done during the war, explained Republican Chan Gurney of South Dakota, chairman of the Senate Military Affairs Committee, in presenting the bill. The secretary of defense would "supervise and control as a coordinated whole the budgeted expenditures" of all of the armed services. But "what kind and how many military forces we have" would continue to be the responsibility of the Congress, as it had always been.[47]

The line between determining roles and missions and deciding what kind of military forces to maintain could not be a sharp one, however, and events shortly after the act was passed suggested that the power of decision had indeed been shifted somewhat from the legislative to the executive branch.

Repeatedly presidents have exercised the power to override the Congress in determining "what kind and how many military forces" the country would have, despite Senator Gurney's assurances, and members of the Congress have found themselves helpless to object. In April 1949, President Truman and Secretary of Defense Louis Johnson unilaterally reversed a decision of the Congress, written into statute, when they halted construction of a navy "supercarrier." Cries of "dictatorship" and charges of unconstitutionality arose in the Congress and elsewhere.[48] But the chairman of the House Armed Services Committee, Democrat Carl Vinson of Georgia, who with his Senate counterpart had given concurrence beforehand, defended the action as "simply a matter of the proper allocation of war missions between the Navy and Air Force," which was now the responsibility of the new secretary of defense.[49]

In that same year, President Truman impounded funds appropriated to increase the number of air force groups, but in this case he did have some legislative history to back him up. The Congress had deadlocked on the issue, with the House in favor and the Senate opposed. Under pressure of adjournment the Senate yielded and approved the funds, but the bill's floor manager had stated: "I do not think the money should be used. I think it should be

46. After World War I, President Harding submitted to a Joint Committee on Reorganization—consisting of six members of Congress with a presidential appointee as chairman—a proposal that the two departments be consolidated. But the committee bowed to the fierce opposition of both departments, and it required another world war to drive home the necessity of the merger.

47. *Congressional Record, I*, July 7, 1947, pp. 8297–98.

48. See remarks of Representative Edith Nourse Rogers, Republican of Massachusetts, ibid., April 27, 1949, p. 5204.

49. Ibid., April 26, 1949, p. 5053; Louis Fisher, "The Politics of Impounded Funds," *Administrative Sciences Quarterly*, vol. 15 (September 1970), pp. 367–68.

impounded, and I leave the impression that if the money is appropriated it may not be used."[50] The president did impound the money, claiming both constitutional powers as chief executive and as commander in chief and statutory powers under the Budget and Accounting Act and the Anti-Deficiency Act.[51] The House subcommittee on defense appropriations blasted the president for exceeding his powers—"there is no warrant or justification for the thwarting of a major policy of Congress by the impounding of funds"— but the president's action stuck.[52]

In 1961, Secretary of Defense Robert S. McNamara refused to spend funds appropriated for the B-70 bomber. The next year, the House Armed Services Committee approved the strongest language it could devise to force the expenditure—the secretary of defense "is directed, ordered, mandated, and required" to use the money—but President Kennedy invited Chairman Vinson to the White House and persuaded him to return to the normal word *authorize*. The settlement appeared to embody a constitutional concession on each side—one by the Congress that the president did indeed possess discretion in the absence of mandatory language, and one by the president that the mandatory language would have been, if not constitutionally binding, at least extremely difficult to ignore.[53] In a similar instance during the Johnson administration, it was the president who yielded; under attack by the House Armed Services Committee for threatening to "thwart the exercise of the constitutional powers of the Congress to provide and maintain a Navy," Johnson finally overruled Secretary McNamara and ordered construction of two nuclear frigates the Congress had authorized and funded.[54]

Command and Control

After 1939 the central organizational apparatus for the president as general manager was fixed firmly in place. The Executive Office had been established. It had been endowed with presidential staff agencies for budgeting, plan-

50. Statement of Senator Elmer Thomas, Democrat of Oklahoma, during consideration of conference committee report; *Congressional Record*, October 12, 1949, p. 14355.

51. Fisher, *President and Congress*, p. 125; Mary Louise Ramsey, "Impoundment by the Executive Department of Funds Which Congress Has Authorized It To Spend Or Obligate," Legislative Reference Service, Library of Congress, May 10, 1968, in *Executive Impoundment of Appropriated Funds*, Hearings before a subcommittee of the Senate Judiciary Committee, 92 Cong. 1 sess. (GPO, 1971), p. 299.

52. Ramsey, "Impoundment," p. 300.

53. James P. Pfiffner, *The President, the Budget, and Congress: Impoundment and the 1974 Budget Act* (Westview, 1979), pp. 37–39; Fisher, *President and Congress*, pp. 124–25.

54. Pfiffner, *The President, the Budget*, pp. 39–40, quoting *Authorizing Defense Procurement and Research and Development*, H. Rept. 221, 90 Cong. 1 sess. (GPO, 1967), p. 8.

ning,[55] personnel,[56] reorganization studies, and legislative clearance. The Brownlow-Gulick faith in developing the presidency as a powerful "directing executive authority" was clearly triumphant, within the legislative as well as the executive branch and among opinion makers outside the government as well.

The conservative and Republican opposition to this view that lingered from the anti-Roosevelt struggle of the 1930s was swept away in 1949 by the report of the first Hoover Commission on government organization.[57] Herbert Hoover a decade earlier had joined in the Republican denunciation of Franklin Roosevelt's "dictator bill,"[58] but no one could have endorsed that bill's principles more firmly than did Hoover in a commission report that he wrote, for the most part, himself. "The President," said the report in words reminiscent of Gulick, "must be held responsible and accountable . . . for the conduct of the executive branch." Responsibility and accountability "are impossible without authority—the power to direct." And that requires "a clear line of command from the top to the bottom . . . and [a] line of responsibility from each employee of the executive branch up to the President . . . a clear line of control from the President . . . cutting through the barriers which have in many cases made bureaus and agencies partially independent of the Chief Executive."[59] Staff agencies of the Executive Office should be further strengthened, said the commission.

55. The planning agency, the National Resources Planning Board, was abolished by the Congress in 1943, but other Executive Office agencies added subsequently had a planning role—though not necessarily in fields where the NRPB had been active.

56. The personnel staff, which carried various names and performed somewhat different functions in different administrations, never consisted of more than a few people, but it maintained liaison with the Civil Service Commission, which though an independent agency performed many of the activities that in other organizations are considered to be an aspect of general management. In some administrations the chairman of the commission also had status as a presidential assistant in the Executive Office.

57. This was a bipartisan body of twelve members, including two senators and two representatives, created by statute. It is known as the first Hoover Commission because the former president a few years later headed another, similar body.

58. Compared to the comments of other Republicans—and compared to his own condemnation of Roosevelt's "court-packing" plan—Hoover's criticism of the reorganization bill was mild. But he attacked several features of it. Comments at Boston and at Syracuse, in *Addresses upon the American Road, 1933–1938* (Scribner's, 1938), pp. 271, 283.

59. Commission on Organization of the Executive Branch of the Government, *General Management of the Executive Branch* (GPO, 1949), pp. 1, 3, 7. According to Herbert Emmerich, Hoover "constituted himself the task force" for preparation of this report. *Essays on Federal Reorganization* (University of Alabama Press, 1950), pp. 97, 98. For an account of the work and significance of the commission and of Hoover's personal role, see Peir E. Arnold, "The First Hoover Commission and the Managerial Presidency," *Journal of Politics*, vol. 38 (February 1976), pp. 46–70. And for a contemporary warning that a president given such power could not be held accountable by the legislature, see G. Homer Durham, "An Appraisal of the Hoover Commission Approach to Administrative Reorganization in the National Government," *Western Political Quarterly*, vol. 2 (December 1949), pp. 615–23.

Reorganization plans presented to, and accepted by, the Congress immediately after the Hoover Commission report, and in later years, were all consistent with these objectives. Many of them contributed to organizing the executive branch into a hierarchy controllable from the top. Powers lodged by statute in inferior officers were transferred to department heads, who were thereupon free to reorganize bureaus and reassign functions within their departments. In the multiheaded independent regulatory commissions, administrative authority was centered in the chairmen, and some independent administrative agencies were brought into departments. The staff agencies in the Executive Office were gradually strengthened—most notably in the Nixon reorganization plan of 1970, which created the Domestic Council.

Most important of all, after 1939, was the fact that the public administration specialists reared on the reformist doctrine of the strong presidency were able to staff the Executive Office itself—particularly the Budget Bureau—where they could devote themselves, day in and day out, to protecting and, as occasion arose, aggrandizing the presidency. The Budget Bureau steadily developed its capacity as a presidential-level coordinating agent, imposing presidential discipline on the traditionally semiautonomous departments and agencies and calling the president's attention to matters on which he needed to exert his own authority. The reorganization plans were a means to enhance the presidency; the Budget Bureau saw to it that they strengthened "the ability of the President to see that the laws are faithfully executed."[60] In the legislative clearance process, the Budget Bureau could intercept any executive agency's proposal that would chip away at presidential powers. And it could advise the president when he needed to use his veto power to block congressional encroachment on what the bureau considered—accepting the Brownlow-Roosevelt interpretation of the Constitution—the president's constitutional right to manage.

In their single-minded determination to make the presidency the directing center of the government, the men and women who made up the Budget Bureau and the other elements of the growing Executive Office were loyal to the doctrines of public administration preached by reformers for a generation before the Executive Office was created, and since, and they were faithful in serving the presidents for whom they worked. They were able to build on the public and political support that the strong presidents of the twentieth century had won for the presidential office, and they were guided by a common doctrine. The object of a presidential staff, as William D. Carey,

60. Emmerich, *Essays*, p. 8.

an assistant director of the Budget Bureau, put it, was to help the president attain "command and control."[61]

Yet the crucial factor in their success was surely the lack of resistance to the buildup of the presidency, even on Capitol Hill. Backed by the immense prestige of the Hoover Commission—and its supporting citizens' committee— most of the reorganization plans of the 1950s were approved. Those that were defeated lost because of the opposition of clientele groups defending the independence of individual bureaus, not on principle. Even as late as 1970, President Nixon could win support from an opposition-controlled Congress for a significant expansion of the Executive Office apparatus, with creation of the Domestic Council and conversion of the Bureau of the Budget into the Office of Management and Budget. There was significant opposition to some features of the plan in the House, where approval was won by a margin of only 193 to 164, but little in the Senate, where Senator Abraham A. Ribicoff, Connecticut Democrat, expressed the still-prevailing view: "I would like to give the President as much responsibility as he could possibly use to coordinate this great bureaucracy of ours. . . . It must be done, and . . . we can call the President to answer to the Nation."[62] No philosophy of government organization contradicting this concept—dominant already for half a century—had been developed and articulated. Not until the popular revulsion against the presidency in the period surrounding the Nixon resignation did serious people even begin to search for one.

61. "Presidential Staffing in the Sixties and Seventies," *Public Administration Review*, vol. 29 (September/October 1969), pp. 455–56.

62. May 8, 1970, in *Reorganization Plan No. 2 of 1970*, Hearing before the Subcommittee on Executive Reorganization and Government Research of the Senate Government Operations Committee, 91 Cong. 2 sess (GPO, 1970), p. 30.

CHAPTER IV

The President
as Economic Stabilizer

HERBERT HOOVER in his memoirs observed ruefully that, until his time, depressions "had always been left to blow themselves out" without governmental intervention. Except for "a few helpful gestures," he said, Presidents Van Buren, Grant, Cleveland, and Theodore Roosevelt "had all remained aloof."[1]

In the Panic of 1837, Van Buren found no constitutional authority for the government to "interfere" with "the ordinary operations of foreign or domestic commerce." "All communities are apt to look to government for too much . . . especially at periods of sudden embarrassment and distress," he told the Congress; "this ought not to be."[2] In the Panic of 1873 Grant proposed no emergency measures, and when the Congress passed a currency inflation bill, he vetoed it. Cleveland's program during the Panic of 1893 was limited to currency contraction to restore "confidence," and when that failed he had no other measures. Even the activist Theodore Roosevelt could simply ignore the Panic of 1907. To these four who presided aloofly over economic hardship Hoover might have added the man to whom he owed his first cabinet appointment, President Warren Harding, who said during the 1921 slump: "There has been vast unemployment before and there will be again. . . . I would have little enthusiasm for any proposed remedy which seeks either palliation or tonic from the Public Treasury."[3]

1. *The Memoirs of Herbert Hoover*, vol. 3: *The Great Depression, 1929–1941* (Macmillan, 1952), p. 29.

2. "Special Session Message, September 4, 1837," in James D. Richardson, comp., *A Compilation of the Messages and Papers of the Presidents* (New York: Bureau of National Literature, 1897), vol. 4, pp. 1561–62.

3. Address to Conference on Unemployment, September 26, 1921, quoted by Stephen K. Bailey, *Congress Makes a Law: The Story behind the Employment Act of 1946* (Columbia University Press, 1950), p. 6.

The people were always less complacent than their presidents, however, and less inclined to worry about the public treasury. So while the depressions did blow themselves out, the voters still visited retribution on the party that happened to be in power. Van Buren's Democratic party lost the White House at the next election; Grant, Cleveland, and Harding all saw heavy losses by their party at the mid-term congressional poll, and Cleveland's posture not only resulted in loss of the White House but contributed to a party split and a realignment of the party system. Herbert Hoover, who rightly claimed to have been more responsive to hard times than any of his predecessors, suffered more severely than any of them (even Cleveland, who was more vindicated than punished when his Democratic party lost, after repudiating his policies, in 1896). Hoover was overwhelmed in his bid for reelection, his partisans in the Congress were decimated, and the Republican party lost the majority status in the country it had held for four decades. Franklin Roosevelt cemented the Democratic majority when he set his party on a course of massive governmental intervention in the economy—to relieve suffering, to speed recovery, and to so reform the economic system that similar debacles would not occur again.

Roosevelt's economic recovery program did not end the depression; only the vast spending for World War II did that. But if the New Deal's success as economics can be questioned, its success as politics cannot. The political rewards of activism in coping with depression, and the penalties of aloofness, proved so great that never again could a government leave an economic disaster to simply run its course. Once this became apparent, it was a short but inevitable step from intervening after the fact of depression to intervening before the fact. So in the midst of the artificial prosperity of war, Roosevelt and his New Deal Democratic party worried about preventing a postwar return to the hard times of the prewar decade. The economist John Maynard Keynes had provided the necessary doctrine, with his theory of compensatory spending by government to make up for deficiencies in private investment, spending, and purchasing power. By 1944 Roosevelt was proclaiming a "second Bill of Rights" that would assure economic security and prosperity for all and was calling on the Congress to enact implementing legislation. Listed first was "the right to a useful and remunerative job in the industries or shops or farms or mines of the Nation."[4]

4. "Message to the Congress on the State of the Union, January 11, 1944," *The Public Papers and Addresses of Franklin D. Roosevelt, 1944–45* (Harper and Bros., 1950), p. 41. The "economic Bill of Rights" was first suggested in a report of the National Resources Planning Board. Bailey, *Congress Makes a Law*, pp. 26–27.

Congress responded with the Employment Act of 1946, which committed the government to a continuous policy of economic activism, primarily through fiscal policy, to assure "maximum employment, production, and purchasing power." In writing the act, the Congress faced the same questions about how to divide responsibility between the branches that it had confronted in drafting the Budget and Accounting Act a generation earlier. Again it assigned to the president the role of initiator and leader and created institutional facilities to enable him to serve in that capacity. In doing so, it magnified the stature and importance of the presidency and the public dependence on presidential leadership. But it yielded no ultimate power of decision. The president would have to have at all times an economic policy and program for the country, but the Congress would confirm, modify, or reject the executive's proposals.

During the next quarter century the two branches of government were in almost continuous conflict, with the Congress repeatedly thwarting the fiscal policies of the president yet failing to develop the capacity to formulate and substitute a considered policy of its own. The incessant quarreling culminated in the 1972 clash between the branches and the subsequent attempt by the legislative branch (discussed in chapter 8) to regain control of fiscal policy.

The Employment Act of 1946: The President Shall Propose

Conditioned by more than a decade of Rooseveltian leadership, the legislators might have been expected to take for granted that when the government assumed responsibility for economic prosperity and stabilization, it would be the president who would initiate—as the Employment Act of 1946 ultimately provided. However, the earliest version of the legislation—the so-called Patton amendment circulated in 1944 by Senator James E. Murray, Democrat of Montana—proposed to place the center of initiation in the Congress itself.[5] Each year the Joint Committee on Internal Revenue Taxation, using data from the executive branch, would estimate the prospective shortfall from the $40 billion investment calculated as necessary annually to sustain

5. *Congressional Record*, August 8, 1944, p. 6757. The idea, developed by Russell Smith, legislative representative of the National Farmers Union, in consultation with government economists, was presented by the union's president, James G. Patton, to Murray, who had the amendment printed and circulated for comment but did not offer it for action. Bailey, *Congress Makes a Law*, pp. 23–24, 37–38.

full employment. To the extent that the Reconstruction Finance Corporation's investment loans would not make up the shortfall, the Congress would authorize public works expenditures.

After the 1944 election confirmed Democratic control of both the legislative and executive branches,[6] an informal group of economists and legislative strategists set out to develop this germ of an idea. Its chairman was Bertram M. Gross, a staff aide to Senator Murray, but most of the participants were from the executive agencies, and the group quickly developed a unanimous view that initiative for the full employment program should be the responsibility not of the Congress but of the president. Public works and investment measures were, after all, elements of the budget that the president had been preparing for a quarter century. Indeed, the new act would only require that the administration's proposed fiscal policy be stated more specifically. Moreover, the planners reasoned that if full employment planning were incorporated in the accepted budget process, the innovation would appear more conservative and its prospects would thus be enhanced.[7] Their proposal was even couched in budget language, prescribing that the economic data, analyses, and proposals be presented in the form of a "national production and employment budget." The Patton amendment's $40 billion investment goal was eliminated as too specific.

The full employment bill introduced in January 1945 by Senator Murray called, accordingly, on the president to present annually his analysis and his recommendations to bring about full employment.[8] These recommendations would be reviewed by a congressional joint committee on the national budget, which would make its own recommendations to "serve as a guide" to the regular committees of the two houses. Along the way to passage, the bill's policy statement was modified: the aim would not be "full" but "maximum" employment, and reference to employment as a "right" was stricken;[9] the goal of "maximum employment, production, and purchasing power" would

6. President Roosevelt never specifically endorsed the legislation that became the Employment Act of 1946, although the legislative planners had no reason to doubt his commitment to the objective. The 1944 Democratic platform declared that one of the party's objectives was to "guarantee full employment." Republican candidate Thomas E. Dewey had been forthright in endorsing the concept of compensatory governmental spending to assure full employment. Bailey, *Congress Makes a Law*, pp. 45–47.

7. Ibid., p. 51.

8. *Congressional Record*, January 22, 1945, pp. 377–78.

9. The new language pledged the government to a "continuing policy and responsibility . . . to use all practicable means consistent with its needs and obligations and the essential considerations of national policy . . . to coordinate and utilize all its plans, functions, and resources for the purpose of creating and maintaining . . . conditions under which there will be afforded useful employment, for those able, willing, and seeking to work." Senator Murray, among others, contended that this language meant "full employment" even though that phrase had been dropped.

be balanced against the government's other "needs and obligations and other considerations of national policy." The president's presentation would be known as the Economic Report, and he was given a Council of Economic Advisers to assist him in preparing it. Congressional review would be performed by a Joint Committee on the Economic Report (subsequently broadened and simplified to the Joint Economic Committee).

Also removed before the bill was passed was a provision authorizing the president to vary the rates of expenditure of appropriated funds. Intended primarily to permit acceleration of public works expenditures in the event of an economic downturn, this provision would also, however, have conferred on the president a blanket permission to impound moneys. Thus the Congress would have surrendered voluntarily—to a Democratic president—the power whose seizure by a Republican president three decades later plunged the executive and legislative branches into their historic conflict.

Members of the Congress saw the new assignment of duties to the president, much as they had seen the earlier grant of authority in the Budget and Accounting Act, as enhancing the ability of the legislature to fulfill its responsibilities. The Congress had always had the job of framing economic legislation; now it would have a solid base of information and concrete recommendations from which to work. Both Congresses and presidents in the past, supporters of the bill had contended in the floor debates, had failed in part for lack of information. The bill's manager in the Senate, Robert F. Wagner, Democrat of New York, argued that a "defect" in congressional organization would be remedied by the establishment of a joint committee "to study the over-all problems of employment and production and to develop a full employment program adjusted to changing needs and changing conditions." The bill would "restore the functions of Congress," said Senator Joseph C. O'Mahoney, Wyoming Democrat, "instead of continually delegating the power to the executive branch." Far from shifting power from the legislative to the executive branch, it would simply set a congressional policy to govern the exercise by the president of his existing power. Conservatives, in fact, used that as an argument against the measure. Representative Ralph E. Church of Illinois, leading the Republican opposition, contended the economic report "adds nothing to what can now be done." The president already had the constitutional duty to advise and recommend, and that surely covered economic conditions. The proposed new council would simply add to the "innumerable" experts already at the president's command and lead to "duplication of work." Representative Carter Manasco, Alabama Democrat, agreed that nothing was added but the policy statement and the new agencies, for the president "can submit a budget any day he wants to, he can transmit a message to the Congress any day he wants to under our Constitution."[10]

But, as Senator Robert A. Taft, Ohio Republican, had pointed out, there was a difference between "the President *may* submit" and "the President *shall* submit" a program.[11] The latter provision made the president the government's chief economic analyst, program developer, and program initiator whether he wished to be or not. To make the assignment of responsibility unmistakable, the Congress rejected a proposal to set up the Council of Economic Advisers as an independent agency—"a group of economic and financial experts, sort of elder statesmen, who would be able to stand aloof from the general political struggle," as Representative Walter H. Judd, a Minnesota Republican who was an advocate of that scheme, put it.[12] An amendment to make the members of the council subject to Senate confirmation was twice rejected, in the House committee and on the House floor, with the argument that the president should not be hampered; the provision was contained, however, in the final version. But to prevent any ambiguity in the council's relation to the president, language in the House bill that would have required the council to submit its studies to the joint committee as well as to the president was dropped.[13] The outcome, said Senator Murray, was that the council would be "entirely subordinate to the President," with neither independent nor autonomous authority, and removable by the President at any time for any reason.[14]

Perhaps the best measure of the relative importance Congress attached to the respective functions of the two branches is found in the authorization for salaries in the new agencies. The Council of Economic Advisers was authorized $300,000 for its staff (in addition to $45,000 for salaries of council members), the new joint committee of Congress only $50,000.

But the Congress Shall Dispose

In a procedural sense the Employment Act of 1946 profoundly transformed economic policymaking in the United States. It compels the president to maintain a continuous surveillance of the nation's economy, to report on the

10. *Congressional Record*, September 25, 1945, p. 8954; September 27, 1945, p. 9055; December 13, 1945, pp. 11977, 11974.
11. Ibid., September 25, 1945, p. 8959. Emphasis added.
12. Ibid., December 14, 1945, p. 12074.
13. Bailey, *Congress Makes a Law*, pp. 170–71, 226–27.
14. *Congressional Record*, February 8, 1946, p. 1142. Lester G. Seligman argues, however, that the act as passed expressed a dual purpose of confirming presidential leadership yet limiting and

state of its health at least annually, and if there are signs of pathology—inflation, recession, stagnation—to recommend corrective action.

Economic analysts have been installed in the Executive Office of the President, reporting directly to the chief executive. The Economic Report has taken its place as one of the trilogy of presidential communications—with the State of the Union Message and the Budget—submitted at the opening of each session of Congress to lay the agenda for the year's deliberations. The collection and presentation of economic data have been improved. The Joint Economic Committee has regularly reviewed the president's recommendations, and in its own report has usually indicated its approval or disapproval. The formerly haphazard processes of analysis and communication have become orderly, competent, regular. Surely, Senator Taft was right in his prediction that the simple requirement that the president present a program would make a difference, and those who promised that the act would result in far better information for the Congress were wholly vindicated.

But in a substantive sense the consequences were probably less profound; as the sponsors had pointed out during the debates, none of the prerogatives of the Congress, or of any of its standing committees, was impaired. The Congress through the Employment Act set up a system to produce advice, but the way it acted on that advice was unaffected. The standing committees could proceed as usual, ignoring or contradicting both the president and the Joint Committee if they chose. Even the ringing commitment to full employment in the original bill had been rendered innocuous by the requirement that the employment goal be balanced with other national needs and objectives.

So, while the authors of the Employment Act assumed a Keynesian approach to economic policy, a pre-Keynesian president would not have to adopt that approach, and the pre-Keynesians who dominated many of the congressional committees were likewise in no way bound. For them, nothing at all had changed—except for what educational effects might accrue from a required annual exercise in Keynesian analysis.

The repeated clashes between the president and the Congress during the first couple of decades after 1946, at least, reflected a conflict between Keynesians and pre-Keynesians, between those who looked on the budget as an economic instrument and those who saw it as an embodiment of moral

---

containing it, and that the latter objective was served by provisions defining the qualifications of members of the Council of Economic Advisers, requiring Senate confirmation, and providing that the council be responsible to the Congress as well as to the president. "Presidential Leadership: The Inner Circle and Institutionalization," *Journal of Politics*, vol. 18 (August 1956), pp. 418–20.

principle. To the former a budgetary deficit might appear not as an evil but as a positive good in times of less-than-full employment, and a big deficit might be better than a small one. But to the latter, deficits were always bad: "a country like a family cannot expect to live beyond its means." It was the violation of this tenet that exposed the New Deal Democratic party most openly to political attack, and its opponents never ceased to exploit its vulnerability with charges of "profligacy," and "spendthrift," and "national bankruptcy." For their part, the practitioners of what was called the "new economics" derided the "Puritan ethic."[15]

The Congress, numbering among its elders in both parties many not wholly converted to the economic arguments for deficit spending, tended throughout the postwar decades to be less activist in fiscal policy than Democratic presidents. Yet, since it also included those who wrote the Employment Act and many who were their political and intellectual heirs, it tended to be more interventionist than Republican presidents, particularly President Eisenhower, who was an ambivalent mixture of old morals and the new economics of the time. The Congress appears, then, sometimes as a foot-dragger, stalling the president's recommendations and hindering his fiscal policy, and sometimes as an initiator and a prod, trying to bring about more vigorous action than the president desired.

But the essential fact is that most of the time the president and the Congress were out of step. If the government is to attempt a policy of countercyclical action, the crucial element is timing. Governmental policy must be able to shift as abruptly as economic trends alter or reverse themselves. "The first principle," wrote Arthur F. Burns, the former chairman of President Eisenhower's CEA and future Federal Reserve Board chairman, in 1957, "is that when the economy shows signs of faltering, prompt countermoves are required. Even mild measures on the part of government can be effective in the early stages of an economic decline. On the other hand, if action is withheld until a recession has gathered momentum, strong and costly measures may prove insufficient."[16] Promptness is just as important, presumably, if inflation is the problem. Whether or not "fine tuning" by the government's economic manipulators is possible, the Employment Act compels a president to have a policy (beyond the effects of the automatic stabilizers, like unemployment compensation), which will perforce be either expansionary, restrictive, or neutral. And every post–Employment Act president, once he had

15. The phrase was used by Walter W. Heller, chairman of the Council of Economic Advisers during the Kennedy administration.
16. *Prosperity without Inflation* (Fordham University Press, 1957), pp. 30–31.

decided what policy the economic circumstances called for, invariably asked the Congress to enact the necessary measures without delay.

The Congress, however, is a deliberative body, and its procedures were not conducive to rapid action—in fiscal policy or any other field. The Employment Act of 1946 did nothing to change the habits of the standing committees that handle legislation that cumulatively determines fiscal policy. A committee might resist a presidential initiative because of a disagreement on fundamental policy, or it might simply go through the normal slow process of hearings and debate, but in either case the president's policy could be vitiated. Yet congressional committees were not so organized that they could substitute an alternative policy. When they attempted to take the initiative, they were likely to do so in piecemeal fashion without reference to any carefully calculated, consistent fiscal policy. The dispersion of authority within the Congress, as well as between the president and the Congress, made the execution of the principles of compensatory governmental action as set out in the Employment Act excruciatingly difficult at best, and at worst impossible. The question in the case of economic stabilization is whether the Congress could properly exercise the power it retained and whether it should delegate more authority to the president.

President Truman and Congressional Dominance

Within months of enacting the Employment Act of 1946, the Congress proceeded flagrantly to ignore it. Without even waiting for President Truman's first Economic Report, the leaders of the Congress committed themselves to a fiscal policy of their own—a substantial reduction in individual income taxes. When President Truman opposed their course and proposed a different set of policies, they ignored his recommendations and eventually enacted their tax cut over his veto.

The circumstances were, of course, unusual. The Republicans had won control of the Congress for the first time since before the New Deal era. When the legislators assembled, the Republican majority had no intention of taking its leadership from Harry Truman, whom the party had humbled in the 1946 midterm election and confidently expected to send into retirement in 1948. Nor was it guided by any conceptions of compensatory fiscal policy. A pledge to cut taxes had been introduced in the 1946 campaign, in statements by prominent Republicans distributed by the party's national committee, and those promising the reduction did not make it "conditional on the economic situation being such as to make it safe, or even conditional on a substantial reduction in expenditure."[17] So the tax reduction bill, amounting to $3.8 billion annually, was introduced on the session's opening day—before the president's economic report had appeared—and given the number H.R. 1 as. a symbol of the importance the Republican leadership attached to it. Its sponsor, Harold Knutson of Minnesota, chairman of the House Ways and Means Committee, justified it as a matter of party principle rather than of countercyclical economics—as a bill that "puts the ax to punitive taxes designed by alien minds and whizzed through subservient Congresses" during the New Deal era.[18] So the Republican tax bill, too, "whizzed" through Congress, passed and ready for President Truman's signature in June. Truman, however, had meanwhile interpreted the needs of the country altogether differently. In his first economic report, prepared by his new Council of Economic Advisers and submitted at the opening of the Congress, he had declared that in a time of high employment a budget surplus should be the goal and, therefore, "it would be unsound fiscal policy to reduce taxes."[19] In June, he found that the situation had not changed; unemployment was still at a peacetime minimum, and inflationary pressures were continuing. Accordingly, he vetoed the bill.[20]

Failing to override the veto, the Republicans tried again with the same bill with a later effective date—January 1, 1948. An even greater issue than the substantive question of tax policy, said Speaker Joseph W. Martin, Jr., of Massachusetts, was "the fundamental question of whether or not the Congress shall retain its right to perform its constitutional function of determining what taxes shall be levied on the people." Only one president before Truman, Martin said, had "ever attempted to invade the tax-making power of the Congress. That effort was turned back. Shall the Members of the Eightieth Congress be less vigilant to preserve the rights of the people's representatives?"[21] But he was speaking only for his party, not for the Congress as an institution. Democrats responded that the president had not only the right but the duty to veto a measure that he believed embodied unwise policy.

In a second veto message, the president laid stress on the relation of tax

17. A. E. Holmans, *United States Fiscal Policy 1945–1959: Its Contribution to Economic Stability* (Oxford University Press, 1961), p. 59.

18. *Congressional Record*, March 26, 1947, p. 2641.

19. "Special Message to the Congress: The President's First Economic Report, January 8, 1947," *Public Papers of the Presidents: Harry S. Truman, 1947* (U.S. Government Printing Office, 1963), p. 30.

20. "Veto of Bill to Reduce Income Taxes, June 16, 1947," ibid., pp. 279–81. Consumer prices had risen 18 percent and wholesale prices 31 percent between June 1946, when wartime controls were removed, and June 1947.

21. *Congressional Record*, July 8, 1947, p. 8460. The reference was to President Franklin D. Roosevelt, whose veto of a tax reduction bill was overridden.

policy to foreign policy—presumably because the fiscal implications of the Truman Doctrine calling for aid to Greece and Turkey, which had been announced March 12, were becoming clearer. By autumn the Marshall Plan had taken form, calling for nearly $7 billion in United States aid to European countries by mid-1949, and inflation was continuing as, in the president's words, "an ominous threat to prosperity . . . already alarming . . . and . . . getting worse."[22] In a special session of the Congress, called to consider the related subjects of European assistance and inflation control, he asked authority to impose a wide range of direct controls on the economy, including price, wage, rent, and credit ceilings, consumer rationing, and allocation of scarce materials.

But on economic policy the Republican Congress was just as intent on going in the opposite direction. The president was seeking legislation that would "enable him to regiment the American people," said Representative Knutson. "Imposing government controls is a policy which I think has failed in every foreign country in which it has been tried in time of peace," averred Senator Taft.[23] Except for several of the least important, relatively noncontroversial items, the president's package of control authorities died quietly in the Republican-controlled committees. An effort to revive them on the Senate floor was defeated by nearly a straight party-line vote.

Meanwhile, the Congress made one more try to enact a tax reduction bill, this time in the amount of $5 billion. Once more it met a presidential veto, expressed in even stronger terms: the bill, said Truman, exhibited a "reckless disregard for the soundness of our economy," would greatly increase the danger of further inflation, and would weaken the United States in a world situation that was "one of uncertainty and, indeed, of danger."[24] But this time Democratic support for the president's position had weakened, and the bill was enacted over the veto.

Ironically, the congressional move proved to be right from the standpoint of compensatory fiscal policy. The inflation that so alarmed the president came to a halt in the summer of 1948, and both wholesale and consumer price indexes began actually to recede. Unemployment rose, production fell, and the long-feared postwar recession had appeared. So the tax cut that the Republican Congress forced on President Truman turned out to be almost ideally timed to help limit the recession—which continued through most of

22. "Special Message to the Congress on the First Day of the Special Session, November 17, 1947," *Public Papers: Truman, 1947,* p. 494.

23. *Congressional Record,* November 18, 1947, p. 10646; December 17, 1947, p. 11504.

24. "Veto of the Income Tax Reduction Bill, April 12, 1948," *Public Papers: Truman, 1948* (GPO, 1964), p. 200.

1949 but turned out to be brief and mild. "If there was ever a case of broadly sound economic measures being taken in very good time through good luck rather than good judgment, this was it," wrote A. E. Holmans.[25] "Correct action taken for incorrect reasons," wrote E. Cary Brown.[26]

Even more ironic was the Republicans' reward in the 1948 election. Truman, who vetoed three tax-reduction bills, was reelected. The Republicans, who finally gave the people a tax cut over the third of those vetoes, lost control of the Congress. And among the Republicans defeated for reelection was Harold Knutson.

But change in party control of the Congress did not produce the kind of "subservience" that Knutson had accused previous Democratic Congresses of displaying toward Democratic presidents. Indeed, the policy positions of the two branches, and the relations between them, were not markedly different from those of the preceding Congress. While the economy had reversed directions, President Truman did not make a similar turn. In his 1949 messages to the Congress, he welcomed the halt in the upward climb of prices but observed that there had been similar pauses in the last two years and, accordingly, he still identified inflation as the prime economic danger and asked for a $4 billion tax increase as the best means of combating it. He also renewed his request for the standby control powers denied him by the Eightieth Congress. It became clear later that had his tax proposal been promptly adopted, it could only have deepened the recession that turned out to be already under way. Undoubtedly a contributing—perhaps the principal—reason for President Truman's persistence in seeking a budgetary surplus was underlying fiscal orthodoxy; he too was in much of his thinking a pre-Keynesian.[27]

In any case, the Congress, having just reduced taxes, was in no hurry to consider raising them. Chairman Robert L. Doughton (Democrat of North

25. *United States Fiscal Policy*, p. 100.

26. In Ralph E. Freeman, ed., *Postwar Economic Trends in the United States* (Harper, 1960), p. 155. Herbert Stein, *The Fiscal Revolution in America* (University of Chicago Press, 1969), p. 217, observes that the standard view of economists during the tax cut debate and for months afterward was that the cut was a mistake, and that when the recession developed "the tax-cutters were lucky—luckier than they deserved." Stein points out that some of the pro-cut witnesses in 1947 did use the arguments that the tax cut would be desirable to counter a recession that might be in the offing, and that Senator Eugene D. Millikin, Republican of Colorado, made the same point in the Senate debate in March 1948. Ibid., pp. 214–17. However, this argument was not part of the rationale presented by the bill's sponsors during the 1946 campaign or the floor debates of 1947 or even during the House debate in 1948. Indeed, the *unlikelihood* of a recession appears in 1947 as an argument for making the tax cut. *Congressional Record*, May 21, 1947, p. 5593.

27. Wilfred Lewis, Jr., *Federal Fiscal Policy in the Postwar Recessions* (Brookings Institution, 1962), pp. 124–25. Holmans, *United States Fiscal Policy*, p. 71. Stein, *Fiscal Revolution in America*, p. 207.

Carolina) of the Ways and Means Committee saw no chance to put the matter on his committee's calendar until late in the session, by which time the downward trend of the economy was quite clear, and the president's proposals could be rejected on their economic as well as their political merits.[28] In July the president withdrew the tax increase proposal.[29] Once again, congressional inertia had produced a better policy, from the standpoint of compensatory economics, than a quick legislative response to bold presidential initiative would have brought about.

Economic policy during President Truman's last years in office was dominated by the problem of controlling the inflationary pressures created by the fighting in Korea that began in June 1950 and by the accompanying rearmament program. Within a month after President Truman ordered American troops to help throw back the North Korean invasion of South Korea, he asked for the entire battery of control powers that had previously been denied him, and a quick "interim" tax increase of $3 billion to cover the immediate rise in military spending. Under the spur of national emergency, the Congress responded with unaccustomed speed; it gave him the control authority in barely six weeks, and the tax increase in just two months.[30] Fortuitously, a tax bill reducing World War II excise taxes and accomplishing various other reforms and revisions had passed the House when the president's new recommendations arrived, so the changes were made in the Senate and taken directly to a House-Senate conference, short-circuiting one stage in the normal legislative process.

But no such dispatch was possible when the next phase of the president's "pay as we go" tax program was sent to the Congress on February 2, 1951. In response to the president's plea for $10 billion in new taxes "as rapidly as possible" to aid the fight against inflation (with further recommendations to come later in the year), the House Ways and Means Committee began

28. Holmans, *United States Fiscal Policy,* pp. 109–10.

29. Once the recession was acknowledged, the president proposed no major countercyclical legislative measures but relied on administrative action to ease credit and on the stimulating effects of already planned expenditure increases for defense and foreign aid, of a dividend to National Service Life Insurance holders that came at a fortuitous time, and of the 1948 tax cut. Ibid., pp. 128–31.

30. While Truman asked for power to impose controls, he protested when the Congress directed him to cut authorized spending for nondefense purposes by at least $500 million. Truman called it an "unwise and dangerous departure from proper budgetary practices" and "a failure by the Congress to exercise its proper responsibility." "Statement by the President Upon Signing the General Appropriation Act, September 6, 1950," *Public Papers: Truman, 1950* (GPO, 1965), p. 616. He subsequently did impound $573 million, mostly in funds for postponable construction projects. Robert Ash Wallace, *Congressional Control of Federal Spending* (Wayne State University Press, 1960), pp. 75–76.

hearings on February 5. But it bogged down at once in deep controversy over how the increased tax burden should be distributed. Nine days later—on the very day that Economic Stabilization Administrator Eric Johnston was testifying that a delay of several months would "do considerable damage" to the stabilization effort and "if taxes are not increased over a protracted period of time, you make the job of stabilization impossible"[31]—the committee voted for delay until the president's complete package of tax recommendations was received, meanwhile proceeding with six weeks of hearings. On April 1 the administration announced no further tax increase beyond the $10 billion under consideration would be necessary, but the committee still did not complete action until June 15. When the bill passed the House a week later, the Senate Finance Committee opened another set of hearings that lasted even longer—from June 27 through August 16. The bill passed the Senate September 28, but the House-Senate conference had to labor for three weeks more, and the bill could not be signed until October 20—almost nine months after the original request. By that time the $10 billion had been watered down to $5.4 billion, which the president denounced as inadequate.

What had been proposed by the President as an emergency anti-inflation measure had been handled on Capitol Hill on almost routine schedule. True, normal procedures had been expedited, but once the responsible committees had decided to hear witnesses representing every affected interest, and to consider all the inequities in the existing tax laws that ought to be corrected in any major revenue measure, the major part of a year had to be committed. If the president's countercyclical tax policy was sound—and at no time did the critics of his specific proposals question the economic need for higher taxes—then the long delay could not be other than costly. As it turned out, the administration had once again failed to perceive a shift in the economic outlook. Wages and prices were frozen in January 1951, the tax increase of 1950 had its effect, the feverish buying that marked the last half of 1950 leveled off, and by spring the inflationary pressures slackened. But the Congress's own economic authority, its Joint Committee on the Economic Report, did not perceive the shift either, and it endorsed the president's tax increase objective in its report of April 2. The economic policy record of 1951 is one of governmental tardiness in achieving a goal on which the executive and the legislative branches were fundamentally agreed. Once more, no damage was done—the fortuitous result, perhaps, of the primitive state of the art of economic forecasting.

31. On February 14, 1951, in *Revenue Revision of 1951*, Hearings before the House Ways and Means Committee, 82 Cong. 1 sess. (GPO, 1951), p. 351.

President Eisenhower and Executive Dominance

In the eight years of President Eisenhower's administration, relations between the branches were reversed; the president rather than the Congress dominated economic policy. His policies were more conservative than the legislators at times believed appropriate, but only rarely were they able to impose their more liberal views on him. The legislative branch forced him to accept an unsought tax reduction—but a small one—in 1954. And it thrust on him a few measures to raise expenditures in the recession of 1957–58. But otherwise it was the president's appraisal of the economic outlook and his resulting policy positions that set the course the country followed.

The Eisenhower era began with a rare display of presidential-congressional solidarity. As in 1946, the Republicans in 1952 had campaigned against the Democratic record of spending, deficits, and inflation and had promised balanced and lower budgets and reduced taxes. Accordingly, in 1953, as in 1947, H. R. 1 in the new Republican-controlled Congress was a tax cut bill introduced by the chairman of the Ways and Means Committee, this time seventy-seven-year-old Daniel A. Reed, who had represented an upstate New York district for thirty-five years. It proposed a cut of $3 billion annually in individual income taxes effective on July 1.

Unlike the situation in 1947, the Republican Congress faced a Republican president—and while Dwight Eisenhower had promised a tax cut, he had not specified exactly when. Before the president could make up his mind, the Ways and Means Committee reported Reed's bill by a lopsided bipartisan majority. At the behest of the White House, however, the Republican leadership arranged to bottle up the Reed bill in the House Rules Committee until the president's program could be received. When the president reported to the Congress, in May, he repudiated Reed and his committee by proposing an effective date of December 31 for the income tax reduction and asking that the excess profits levy, that was yielding $2 billion a year and was scheduled to expire June 30, be continued another six months. "Party pressure or party discipline" was applied, according to a Reed ally on the committee, and the committee reversed itself and over the chairman's negative vote reported a bill yielding to the president. "Involved here is the question of whether this Congress is going to retain its independence or abdicate to executive dictate," Reed pleaded on the House floor.[32] But the executive prevailed, by easy majorities in both the House and the Senate.

32. *Congressional Record*, July 10, 1953, p. 8491.

Yet, like Truman, Eisenhower was still fighting inflation after times had changed. During the midsummer debate, Reed had warned that "danger signals" of recession were already in the air, but like his other arguments that one went unheeded. Even as he spoke, the economy was sliding into a recession that would continue until mid-1954—a recession that should not have caught the government by surprise, since it was brought on largely, if not entirely, by the government's own decision to sharply reduce military expenditures in the spring of 1953 as the fighting in Korea ended.[33] While the tax cut that went into effect at the beginning of 1954 was well timed to check the economic decline, it would have been better timed if it had been allowed to take effect six months earlier, as Reed had proposed.[34] Yet the indicators of a recession were not clear, and the majorities in the Congress—the first Republican majorities with an opportunity to support a Republican president in more than two decades—fell into line behind the party's leader, while the Democratic minority found no ground on which to mount a challenge.

In 1954, however, the Republican-controlled Congress asserted a degree of independence. President Eisenhower, arguing that the earlier tax cuts plus those contained in a comprehensive tax reform measure he had proposed were all the reductions the budget could afford, again asked the Congress to extend excise taxes, this time $2 billion scheduled to expire on March 31. The Congress, responding to intense pressure from affected industries, would grant him only half that amount, and the president had to take what he could get.

During the next three years of economic expansion and general prosperity, President Eisenhower pursued a conservative economic course and the Congress, even though the Democrats resumed control in 1955, supported him. Each year, he propose to maintain existing tax rates in order to produce a budgetary surplus. The Joint Economic Committee regularly supported him. On only one occasion, in 1955, was a serious revolt initiated, when the House voted almost along party lines to approve a reduction in individual income taxes. But the Senate refused to go along.

With the onset of the third postwar recession, in the late summer of 1957, however, the policies of the two branches began to diverge. As the Congress convened in January 1958, President Eisenhower was still talking as though

33. Eisenhower himself acknowledged in his 1955 Economic Report that the reduction in military spending was a major factor in the 1953–54 recession. This reflects the consensus among economists. See James L. Sundquist, *Politics and Policy: The Eisenhower, Kennedy, and Johnson Years* (Brookings Institution, 1968), p. 16, note 8.

34. Wilfred Lewis, Jr., considered this to have been the administration's "major error" in economic stabilization policy during the 1953–54 recession. *Federal Fiscal Policy*, p. 183.

the prime economic peril continued to be inflation. This was in part a calculated position, based on the assumption that to "panic" would only make the recession worse by destroying confidence. Beyond that, the president and his advisers recalled that the 1954 recession—when they did not "get hysterical"—had turned out to be short-lived, while inflation appeared to be the more serious long-range problem.[35] The response of the Democrats who controlled the Congress was to chastise the Republican president for lack of leadership. Senator John J. Sparkman of Alabama, a member of the Joint Economic Committee, complained that the president's economic report contained no "overall, antirecession program." "Just what are the administration's plans?" demanded Senator Hubert H. Humphrey of Minnesota. "We have a right to know, and if there are no real plans we should know that too. . . . the American people will not accept excuses if this recession continues." House Majority Leader John W. McCormack, of Massachusetts, called for "drastic, affirmative action" by the administration.[36] Meanwhile, the Democratic Advisory Council, the national party's official policy organ, compared President Eisenhower to President Hoover for failing to present a program.[37]

Eventually, as the Democrats in the Congress continued to demand leadership from the Republican president, someone was bound to suggest, as Majority Leader McCormack did in March, that "the leadership in the Congress must fill the vacuum."[38] Yet there is no evidence that he or any other member of the House leadership ever took the first step to try to produce the program it claimed the administration lacked. Indeed, Speaker Sam Rayburn joined his fellow Texan, Senate Democratic Leader Lyndon B. Johnson, in agreeing to oppose any congressional effort for an antirecessionary tax reduction in the absence of a presidential initiative. But under great pressure from organized labor and Democratic senators from industrial states, Senator Johnson stepped forward as an alternative source of leadership. First he sponsored a resolution, which passed both houses almost without dissent, urging the president to accelerate civil and military public works to the limits of funds appropriated—which the president replied he was already doing.[39] Then he canvassed the committee and subcommittee chairmen to determine

35. Sundquist, *Politics and Policy*, p. 22; Lewis, *Federal Fiscal Policy*, pp. 204–07.
36. *Congressional Record*, January 31, 1958, p. 1434; March 6, 1958, pp. 3586–88; March 11, 1958, p. 4039.
37. "Economic Policy in 1958," a statement adopted by the Democratic Advisory Council, February 2, 1958.
38. *Congressional Record*, March 11, 1958, p. 4039.
39. The president announced a series of administrative steps to expedite spending and asked for supplemental funds in small amounts for some programs, which were promptly approved.

what additional programs might be legislated. Seven bills were ready for prompt action, and several others were developed later.[40] Not all of them could be classed as special antirecession measures. Some had been in process before the recession and would have been enacted in any event, although the committees took advantage of the favorable atmosphere to liberalize them. And some authorized new public works projects that could not be let to contract for a year or two, or even longer—when, if the economy righted itself, spending might need to be curtailed rather than expedited. In any case, the Senate pushed the program to passage in a piecemeal fashion, without benefit of any quantitative goal. The Joint Economic Committee, while calling for an acceleration of spending, offered no target figures. In cutting loose from the president's budget as a guide, the Senate was no doubt going in the right direction but it had no guide at all.

Of the measures that reached President Eisenhower, some he signed while expressing general misgivings and specific objections to particular provisions. Among these were an emergency housing bill and an increase in highway assistance to the states. But some he vetoed—a freeze of farm price supports, a liberalized grant program for airport construction, and a bill for loans and grants for depressed areas. None of the vetoes could be overridden.

Some of the measures initiated in the Senate died in the House, which was more easily intimidated by the president's attacks on what he called, in some of his milder language, "the wholesale distribution of the people's money in dubious activities under Federal direction."[41] A $1 billion loan program for community facilities approved by the Senate was killed on the House floor, after it had been raised to $2 billion by a House committee. An omnibus housing measure died there. And the House refused to accept a Senate amendment that would have granted an extension of unemployment compensation payments beyond what the president had recommended.

In every fundamental, then, it was the president's approach to the 1957–58 recession that prevailed. The Democratic majorities in the Congress had no mechanism for framing and adopting an alternative comprehensive policy; the Joint Economic Committee, bipartisan in composition and only advisory in its function, did not serve as a planning body for the leaders, and the leaders of the separate houses had no joint strategy—except the agreement *not* to propose the quickest-acting and most powerful antirecession measure

40. For a list of the bills making up the initial program, see *Congressional Quarterly Almanac, 1958,* p. 64.

41. "Letter to the Minority Leaders of the Senate and the House of Representatives Concerning Measure to Aid Economic Growth, March 8, 1958," *Public Papers of the Presidents: Dwight D. Eisenhower, 1958* (GPO, 1959), p. 208.

of them all, a substantial tax cut. Congress was able to add a bit of economic stimulus here and there—in housing and highway programs, mainly—and perhaps its partisan prodding caused the president to take administrative actions sooner than he would have otherwise. Though its contribution was, on balance, positive, it was no more than marginal.

President Kennedy and Congressional Deliberateness

Arthur Burns's first principle—that economic countermeasures must be taken promptly—was not heeded in 1957 nor when the economy turned down again in 1960—both occasions when a conservative Republican president was in the White House. But neither was it heeded in 1961, when the White House was occupied by a Democratic president.

John F. Kennedy was, as Herbert Stein observes, the first president who was not a pre-Keynesian, but he did not become the first Keynesian president until some time after his inauguration.[42] He had campaigned hard on the issue of unemployment and the need for economic growth, but he had also taken pains to reassure the business community that Democrats, too, were fiscal conservatives who believed in balanced budgets except in times of "a grave national emergency or a serious recession."[43] He made the symbolic appointment of a Republican banker, Douglas Dillon, as his secretary of the treasury, although he balanced Dillon with a Council of Economic Advisers composed of thoroughly committed Keynesians headed by Walter W. Heller. With the economy lagging well below its potential, Heller and his colleagues began bombarding the president with memorandums presenting arguments for more expansionary fiscal policy, and Kennedy showed early signs of being receptive.[44]

42. *Fiscal Revolution in America*, p. 375.

43. First debate with Richard Nixon, in *Freedom of Communications*, pt. 3: *The Joint Appearances of Senator John F. Kennedy and Vice President Richard M. Nixon, Presidential Campaign of 1960*, S. Rept. 994, 87 Cong. 1 sess. (GPO, 1961), p. 83. Other similarly stringent language can be found in his campaign speeches; ibid., pt. 1: *The Speeches of Senator John F. Kennedy, Presidential Campaign of 1960*.

44. Even before the inauguration, Kennedy had assigned Heller the responsibility of educating the public about the desirability of deficits in times of recession. Heller, *New Dimensions of Political Economy* (Harvard University Press, 1966), preface. In the summer of 1961 Kennedy suggested that a tax cut would have been the correct policy in the recession of 1957–58; "The President's News Conference of June 28, 1961," "The President's News Conference of July 19, 1961," "The President's News Conference of October 11, 1961," *Public Papers of the Presidents: John F. Kennedy, 1961* (GPO, 1962), pp. 482, 516, 663. Yet the boost in military spending occasioned by the Berlin crisis in mid-1961 led him to tentatively approve an offsetting tax increase, a decision averted only by the strenuous efforts of Heller and other economists. The evolution of Kennedy's thinking and his public positions during 1961 and 1962 are reviewed in Sundquist, *Politics and Policy*, pp. 34–40; Edward S. Flash, Jr., *Economic Advice and Presidential Leadership: The Council of Economic Advisers* (Columbia University Press, 1965), chaps. 6–7; and Stein, *Fiscal Revolution in America*, chaps. 15–16.

Yet throughout 1961 he resisted every effort in Congress to launch an emergency acceleration of public works spending; when he finally approved a $600 million program in March 1962, he insisted that it be limited to areas of exceptionally high unemployment. In his annual messages in January, he asked the Congress only to enact "standby" authority for tax reduction and public works acceleration, the authority to be triggered by a worsening of economic conditions.

But on June 7, 1962, the president reversed himself. An abrupt decline in the stock market ten days earlier—termed the Kennedy crash—had aroused fears of a new and deep recession, and demands that the government do something. The kind of drastic economic measures that had been politically impossible earlier now became feasible, and the president announced his intention to propose a substantial "across-the-board" tax reduction.

The crash may have been responsible for Kennedy's economic conversion, but perhaps he was already a convert only waiting for a politically opportune moment to change his public posture. According to Theodore C. Sorensen, his most intimate policy adviser, the president did not become truly "enthusiastic" about the tax cut until December 1962, six months after the June commitment.[45] Yet in the intervening months he had been presenting lucidly the Keynesian arguments for compensatory fiscal policy, a change in position that suggests he had already broken loose intellectually from his initial conservatism. Political considerations ruled out any reversal of his public position until the economy itself was shaken by some new event, for the Congress was unlikely to take seriously any proposal, in the absence of a new recession, to reduce taxes since to do so would—according to orthodox fiscal theory—increase the budgetary deficit.

Whatever the causes of the sixteen-month delay in Kennedy's endorsement of an expansionary policy, the twenty-month gap between that decision and President Johnson's signature on the tax reduction act in February 1964 is attributable to a single cause: the divsion of responsibility between the president and Congress. Those twenty months were spent in presidential wheedling, lecturing, pressuring, and maneuvering to win congressional support— and in going over the heads of the legislators to appeal to their constituents. In 1962, Kennedy's congressional relations staff advised him, the Congress simply would not approve a "quickie" tax cut. The key figure on Capitol Hill was Wilbur D. Mills, Arkansas Democrat who chaired the Ways and Means Committee, and Mills was on record as opposed to adjusting tax rates to stimulate or otherwise "manipulate" the economy, and doubly opposed to

45. *Kennedy* (Harper and Row, 1965), p. 429.

the notion of reducing taxes in a time of budgetary deficit. The House Appropriations Committee chairman, Clarence Cannon of Missouri, was contending that "any government—like individuals and families—cannot spend more than they take in without courting disaster."[46] So Kennedy used his news conferences and his speaking rostrums to educate the public on the modern economics of the time, and he made speeches more carefully focused on audiences of one, such as a speech dedicating a dam in Mills's Arkansas district. The president mobilized every department of the government in an intensive lobbying campaign and gave his sponsorship to a citizens' committee and a businessmen's committee supporting a tax cut. With these preparatory efforts under way, Kennedy made his specific proposals in January 1963. But the hearings and consideration in the Ways and Means Committee required seven months, because of a commitment to Mills to couple tax reduction with some complex and highly controversial tax reform measures that the president also favored as a matter of principle, and the bill did not pass until September. Then came the Senate. Hearings began in October. There was talk that some southern Democrats might try to stall the bill to win concessions on civil rights from the president, but when Kennedy was assassinated and Lyndon Johnson sworn in, that talk ceased and under Johnson's prodding the measure moved to passage quickly.[47] It cut corporate and individual income taxes by $11 billion, and economic revival followed.

Kennedy observed with chagrin in 1963, says Sorensen, that "the British prepared, proposed, passed and put into effect a proportionately larger tax cut than ours, and are getting the benefits from it, while we are still holding hearings."[48] Relations between the president and a Congress controlled even by his own party were such that, as of 1961–63 at least, the kind of prompt and decisive action called for by compensatory fiscal theory was institutionally impossible.

President Johnson and Congressional "Blackmail"

But after President Johnson's landslide election of 1964, which also brought into office an overwhelmingly Democratic Congress, quick action on fiscal policy was possible—for a time.

46. *Congressional Record*, September 26, 1961, p. 21541.
47. Kennedy's campaign for passage of his bill is described in Sundquist, *Politics and Policy*, pp. 40–53.
48. *Kennedy*, p. 433.

In May 1965 the president requested a $4 billion cut in excise taxes, for the same reasons of economic stimulus that justified the income tax cut of 1964, and he was able to sign the bill five weeks later, only slightly altered by the Congress. This apparent speed is somewhat misleading, because the subject had been thoroughly covered in the 1963 hearings, and Presidents Kennedy and Johnson had had to promise excise cuts later to stave off reductions then. Nevertheless, three other actions during the next couple of years indicated that, after the success of the 1964 tax cut, the Congress lost at least some of its resistance to manipulating tax rates on short notice as the needs of fiscal policy might dictate. In early 1966, when Vietnam expenditures had begun to rise, the president asked for repeal of some of the excise tax cuts passed the year before which had just taken effect, and the Congress complied in less than two months. In the fall, he asked for suspension of the investment tax credit as a measure of economic restraint, and both houses concurred within six weeks. Four months later, when investment appeared to have slowed too much, the president asked that the credit be restored, and the Congress again complied.

But to engage the ponderous weight of the legislative process in this kind of fine tuning left a strain on executive-congressional relations. Chairman Mills, who had had to explain to the House in 1966 why the investment credit should be suspended and a few months later why it should not, "felt this back and forth performance made him look foolish."[49] And it reinforced his skepticism about the accuracy of economic forecasts and the wisdom of the president's economic counselors.

At the beginning of 1966, when Johnson shifted from a policy of economic stimulus to one of restraint, his economic advisers urged him to ask for tax increases beyond the reinstatement of some of the excise tax rates that had just been cut. But they were overruled.[50] After consultation with labor and business and the congressional leadership, "it was evident that it would be impossible to get a tax increase" that year, the president said later.[51] So a year passed before he recommended that corporate and individual income taxes be raised through the imposition of a surtax, with another six months before it would take effect. As in President Kennedy's case, it is interesting to speculate how much faster President Johnson might have moved if he had

49. Lawrence C. Pierce, *The Politics of Fiscal Policy Formation* (Santa Monica, Calif.: Goodyear Publishing, 1971), p. 152.
50. Joseph A. Pechman, "Making Economic Policy: The Role of the Economist," in Fred I. Greenstein and Nelson W. Polsby, eds., *Handbook of Political Science* (Addison-Wesley, 1975), vol. 6, p. 56.
51. "The President's News Conference of March 30, 1968," *Public Papers of the Presidents: Lyndon B. Johnson, 1968–69* (GPO, 1970), vol. 1, p. 468.

not had to contend with a division of power between the executive and the legislative branches. Clearly, public opinion was not ready for a tax increase in early 1966, as his consultations indicated, and that might have been decisive in any case. The president was on the political defensive for having super-imposed the new spending for the Vietnam War on the added expenditures for his "war on poverty" and other Great Society innovations, and he had pronounced himself "unwilling to declare a moratorium on our progress toward the Great Society."[52] Perhaps he wanted to avoid stirring up a debate on Vietnam, or encouraging the military to believe he supported a rapid escalation of American participation in the war.[53] Hence he temporized on a demand for higher taxes that could only raise questions about Vietnam and heighten the demand for a moratorium on the Great Society, while he undertook to prepare public and congressional opinion.

When he finally took the plunge, in January 1967, his fears were realized. Republicans and conservative Democrats at once demanded that instead of a surtax—or at least accompanying such a tax increase—domestic spending be cut back. And among those seizing the opportunity to put the financial squeeze on Johnson's Great Society was Wilbur Mills. For nine months, the Ways and Means Committee calendar was too crowded to permit consider-ation of the surtax question. Finally, after a special message on August 3 in which the president declared that the prospective deficit of $24 billion to $28 billion, or even more, would be "fiscally and financially irresponsible," the committee held hearings. But then it "temporarily" deferred action "until such time as the President and the Congress reach an understanding on a means of implementing more effective expenditure reduction and controls as an essential corollary to further consideration of a tax increase."[54] The president protested that no such understanding was necessary: the Congress "can revise, repeal, or abolish any program they want abolished or cut, if the Congress sees fit."[55] But Mills insisted that the House would not consider

52. "Annual Message to the Congress: The Economic Report of the President, January 27, 1966," *Public Papers: Johnson, 1966* (GPO, 1967), p. 102. Later that year, however, he ordered a general slowdown in nonwar spending, which particularly affected highway and other construction projects.

53. James L. Cochrane, "The Johnson Administration: Moral Suasion Goes to War," in Craufurd D. Goodwin, ed., *Exhortation and Controls: The Search for a Wage-Price Policy, 1945–1971* (Brookings Institution, 1975), pp. 263–64.

54. *President's 1967 Surtax Proposal: Continuation of Hearing to Receive Further Administration Proposal Concerning Expenditure Cuts—November 1967,* Hearings before the House Ways and Means Committee, 90 Cong. 1 sess. (GPO, 1967), p. 1. The efforts by leading congressmen to force spending cuts by holding tax measures hostage are recounted in Allen Schick, *Congress and Money: Budgeting, Spending and Taxing* (Washington: Urban Institute, 1980), chap. 2.

55. "The President's News Conference of November 1, 1967," *Public Papers: Johnson, 1967* (GPO, 1970), vol. 2, p. 974.

increasing taxes unless agreement was reached concurrently to reduce expenditures.

He had ample reason to so interpret the mood of the House. On three separate occasions that autumn that body had overruled its own Appropriations Committee to vote for slashes in expenditures well below that conservative committee's recommended levels. In each instance it had adopted a Republican motion sponsored by Representative Frank T. Bow of Ohio that would have set a ceiling on expenditures $5 billion below the projected rate for the 1967–68 fiscal year, with the president to determine where the cuts should be made. In other words, it would have directed the president to undertake the very kinds of impoundment action that, a few years later, became the most incendiary issue between President Nixon and the Congress. In vain did George H. Mahon, Democrat of Texas, chairman of the Appropriations Committee, contend—foreshadowing the arguments of 1972 and 1973—that such a delegation of discretion to the president would be an "unthinkable abdication" of the power of the purse, a "confession . . . of our incompetence," and a concentration of "terrific, unheard of, and unbelievable power" in the executive branch to "defeat the will of Congress."[56] The Republicans voted unanimously to make such a delegation to the Democratic president, and they were joined by thirty-four Democrats, among them Wilbur Mills. However, the Senate refused to concur, and the two houses were deadlocked as some agencies ran out of funds.

With the tax bill as the hostage, Mills and his committee forced the president and the Senate to surrender. On November 29, the administration presented a plan to cut $2.6 billion by going back to the president's original budget and making reductions of 2 percent in personnel costs and 10 percent in all other "controllable" expenditures, both excluding Vietnam costs and all subject to "contingency" modifications in the formula totaling not more than $300 million. Where the Congress had made deeper cuts, those would stand; otherwise, the year's work of the appropriations committees and the two houses would be nullified.[57] This compromise passed both houses in December. Yet when the administration returned to the Ways and Means Committee in January, the president's budget for the next fiscal year, ending June 30, 1969, was before the Congress, and Mills now had a new hostage.

56. *Congressional Record,* September 27, 1967, p. 26961.

57. Testimony of Budget Director Charles L. Schultze, in *President's 1967 Surtax Proposal,* Hearings before the House Ways and Means Committee, 90 Cong. 1 sess. (GPO, 1967), pp. 29–30. The total reductions amounted to $4.1 billion; with congressional reductions of $1.5 billion the administration's reductions equaled $2.6 billion, or half the $5.2 billion contemplated under the Bow resolution. *Congressional Record,* December 11, 1967, p. 35801.

After two days of hearings, he sent the administration witnesses back to "take another look" to determine what further cuts in the new budget could be made.[58] Again, he took the position that without still further cuts in 1969 it would be futile to present a tax bill for House approval.[59] But it was the Appropriations Committee, not Ways and Means, that had authority to make the necessary cuts, and that panel was proceeding with the 1969 budget in its usual program-by-program fashion. Its aggregate recommendations would not be known until the last of its fourteen major appropriations bills was reported, in late summer at the earliest.

The impasse was broken in the Senate, where the more flexible rules permitted the surcharge and expenditure reduction measures to be joined. A measure dealing with excise taxes was amended on the Senate floor by incorporating the 10 percent income tax surcharge and a spending ceiling for the coming year $6 billion below the president's projections. This time there was little concern expressed about abdication of the power of the purse. Senator Jacob K. Javits, New York Republican, expressed concern about transferring "power and control" to the executive branch by directing the president to impound appropriated funds, but Senator John J. Williams, Republican of Delaware, the amendment's sponsor, argued that the Congress could enforce its own ceiling, since the 1969 appropriations bills were yet to be enacted.[60] Satisfied, Javits joined a unanimous Republican bloc in favor of the expenditure ceilings, which were approved 56 to 33. The surtax was also approved by a comparable margin.

This was acceptable to Mills, but agreement of the president and the Appropriations Committee had still to be won, and members of the latter body were aggrieved at the invasion of their jurisdiction by Ways and Means. A tense series of negotiations ensued, climaxed at an April 30 White House meeting at which Johnson claimed to have won approval of both Mills and Mahon for a cut of only $4 billion. While the Appropriations Committee had this figure under formal consideration, however, the president vented his pent-up resentment at a news conference:

> I think we are courting danger by this continued procrastination, this continued delay. . . . If they don't like that budget, then stand up like men and answer the roll call and cut what they think ought to be cut. . . . I think the time has come for all the Members of Congress to be responsible and, even in an election year, to bite the bullet and stand up and do what ought to be done for their country. . . . If they

58. *President's Surtax Proposal: Continuation of Hearing—January 1968*, Hearings before the House Ways and Means Committee, 90 Cong. 2 sess. (GPO, 1968), p. 162.

59. Pierce, *Politics of Fiscal Policy Formation*, p. 161.

60. *Congressional Record*, March 26, 1968, p. 7716.

want to effect reductions, then as each appropriation bill comes up, they can offer
their amendments like men out on the floor, and call the roll. But don't hold up
a tax bill until you can blackmail someone into getting your own personal viewpoint
over on reductions.[61]

Whether or not Mills was influenced by this personal attack, when the
Republicans insisted on a $6 billion reduction he joined them. So the House
conferees yielded to the Senate and accepted the larger reduction. By that
time price inflation had risen to a 5 percent annual rate, the highest since the
Korean War.

On signing the bill on June 28, seventeen months after he had first
proposed it, Johnson observed that "the decision should have come sooner
and should never have been in doubt." He called it "most unwise" for the
Congress to "shift to the President the responsibility for making reductions
in programs which the Congress itself is unwilling to do." And he suggested
two subjects for study:

How can we avoid in the future the costly inaction and the threat of the fiscal
stalemate we have just experienced?

How can we develop procedures to assure the timely adjustment of fiscal policy
and the closest cooperation between the executive and legislative branches in this
area?[62]

President Nixon and Congressional "Abdication"

By the time Johnson signed the surtax bill, consumer prices were rising
still faster, at an annual rate of 6 percent. And the surtax did not bring a halt
to inflation. Prices rose a bit more slowly in the fall but faster again in the
winter. During the first year of President Nixon's administration, the cost of
living rose by slightly more than 6 percent.

The Republican president placed the blame on the Democratic deficits of
the years preceding his inauguration, but the Democrats who controlled
Congress blamed the president. The inflation "demonstrates in dramatic
terms the utter failure of the Nixon administration's economic policies,"
House Majority Leader Carl Albert charged. "The vast and influential powers
of the Office of the President must be brought to bear against these sharply

61. "The President's News Conference of May 3, 1968," *Public Papers: Johnson, 1968–69* (GPO,
1970), vol. 1, p. 561.

62. "Statement of the President Upon Signing the Tax Bill," ibid., vol. 1, p. 756. The surcharge
was retroactive to April 1 for individuals and January 1 for corporations. Between them, President
Johnson and his successor, President Nixon, impounded a total of $8.2 billion, which was offset
by increases of $6.9 billion in "uncontrollable" items, such as interest on the public debt, and
exempted or excepted programs. Louis Fisher, "The Politics of Impounded Funds," *Administrative
Sciences Quarterly*, vol. 15 (September 1970), p. 372.

rising price increases of the concentrated industries."[63] Senator William Proxmire of Wisconsin, vice chairman of the Joint Economic Committee, likewise called for "leadership from the White House." Specifically, he demanded a return to the "guidelines" and "jawboning" of the Kennedy and Johnson administrations, which Nixon had explicitly abandoned on taking office, citing both practical and theoretical objections.[64]

Other Democrats called on the president to use the selective credit control authority that Congress had given him, unsolicited, at the end of 1969, and some suggested stronger antitrust action. But, said Albert, "it seems to be the continuing effort of the Republicans to reject the responsibility that goes with the control of the executive branch."[65]

Then how could the congressional majority impose its own economic policies on an unwilling president? By May, Representative Wright Patman, Democrat of Texas and chairman of the Joint Economic Committee, was declaring: "It is time for the Ninety-first Congress to assert its constitutional powers. . . . We must act on our own . . . if the administration continues to refuse to take the necessary steps." But, pointed out Proxmire, only the president could jawbone. "The leaders of Congress cannot effectively stop or roll back price increases." Said Senate Majority Leader Mike Mansfield: "Congress cannot itself draw up and administer a set of guidelines for reasonable wage and price behavior on the part of industry and labor."[66] All it could do, he said, was support the president if he chose to take those actions.

But the Democratic Congress could do one thing more. It could make absolutely clear that the Republican executive, not the Congress, was responsible for the state of the economy, by delegating even more power to the president. Out of Patman's Banking and Currency Committee, in July, came a measure to give the president blanket authority to impose direct controls on prices and wages. It was the "duty" of the Congress, said Patman, to give the executive branch "the widest latitude and flexibility," to give the president "all the power he needs when he needs it to protect the people against inflation." Nonsense, cried the Republicans. The delegation of power was "unneeded, unwanted, and unrealistic." It was "passing the buck,"

63. *Congressional Record*, January 20, 1970, p. 278.
64. Under the Democrats the guidelines (or guideposts) defined the limits of noninflationary wage increases, to which management and labor were asked to adhere voluntarily. The guidelines were pronounced without authority of law, but they encountered no significant objection at the time on Capitol Hill, and the technique was specifically endorsed by the Joint Economic Committee. Jawboning "did work," said Proxmire. Ibid. January 26, 1970, p. 1153.
65. Ibid., February 26, 1970, p. 5119.
66. Ibid., May 18, 1970, pp. 15832–33; June 17, 1970, p. 20155; June 24, 1970, p. 21232.

"dodging the issue," "sidestepping," "abdication," a "patently political gambit to embarrass the President." "If Members of Congress are convinced that such controls are necessary, let us have a new bill making them mandatory," argued William Widnall of New Jersey, ranking committee Republican. "In each case, it is the President's duty and responsibility not to make the policy decision, but to implement and carry out—to execute—the Congressional decision," agreed Garry Brown, Michigan Republican.[67] But an amendment to make the controls mandatory and another to create a joint committee of the Congress to decide when the discretionary powers would be used were defeated by overwhelming margins. The Congress might not be in session and its committee might not be able to assemble quickly enough in a crisis, the Democrats argued in rejecting the latter proposal. When the bill reached President Nixon, he accepted it grudgingly, because the legislation to which the price–wage control amendment was attached (extension of the Defense Production Act) was needed. He repeated the abdication charge: "If Congress believes that price and wage controls are needed in today's economy, despite all the evident disadvantages and against my strong recommendations, it should face up to its responsibilities and make such controls mandatory."[68] Almost exactly a year later, the president invoked the "unneeded" and "unwanted" authority and imposed controls. Twice, in 1971 and 1973, the legislators renewed his authority, adding some procedural safeguards. They permitted it to expire in 1974.

The Mismatch of Authority and Accountability

When the Employment Act of 1946 was passed, members of the Congress reassured one another that they were giving up none of their responsibility. The president would only propose; the Congress, as in the past, would make all the decisions that determine what the country's fiscal policy will be. Yet as the 1970 debate made vividly clear, the balance of responsibility has indeed been shifted. The president, probably more than the Congress, is held publicly and politically responsible for the stability of the economy. When things go wrong—whether recession or inflation, or both simultaneously—it is "the administration's policies," as well as those of the Congress, that are blamed. And the two branches, especially when controlled by opposing parties, then

67. Ibid., July 31, 1970, p. 26795, 26800, 26813, 26795, 26525, 26800, 26813.
68. "Statement Upon Signing Bill Extending the Defense Production Act, August 17, 1970," *Public Papers of the Presidents: Richard Nixon, 1970* (GPO, 1971), p. 675.

struggle to pass the censure to each other. Congressional Democrats in the Nixon period eagerly took the lead in heaping criticism on the president. And when the Republicans defended their president, they shifted the onus not only to the Democrats in the Congress but also—and mainly—to the former Democratic presidents, Kennedy and Johnson.

If the president was going to be held responsible for the state of the economy, Wright Patman could argue in the controls debate, it was the "duty" of the Congress to give him "all the power he needs when he needs it" to combat inflation. But while that principle may have guided the Congress in that decision, it has been by no means a universal principle. The legislators have been highly selective in delegating power, the criterion governing their decision usually being whether the power to be exercised is popular or unpopular, whether the actions to be taken will bring political reward or injury to those who take them. Controls were in the latter category, and the authority was thrust on the president, against his will. In budget decisions, the Congress developed the habit of passing politically popular appropriation measures one by one and then, if the aggregate turned out to be too high, placing on the president the burden of making the politically unpopular cuts—until 1972, when it refused to do that any longer. But most of the time, the manipulation of expenditures proved to be too clumsy and slow a process for compensatory fiscal policy; it was the revenue side that was subject to quick and massive adjustment. And when circumstances called for quick action on the revenue side of the budget, the Congress delegated no authority at all.

To make prompt action possible, many advocates of aggressive economic policies have urged a continuous, limited delegation of authority to the president to adjust tax rates. Alvin H. Hansen, the leading American disciple of Keynes, was arguing in the 1940s that to make possible a compensatory fiscal policy the president should have the power to adjust tax rates up or down, within limits, subject to a legislative veto.[69] President Kennedy asked for such a power on a standby basis in 1962—a request that was not even considered by the Ways and Means Committee—and the idea has been endorsed by such conspicuous Republican figures as Arthur F. Burns and Senate Majority Leader Howard H. Baker, Jr., of Tennessee.[70]

69. *Congressional Record*, August 8, 1944, p. 6759.
70. Baker, "What Presidential Powers Should Be Cut?" in Charles Roberts, ed., *Has the President Too Much Power?* (Harper's Magazine Press, 1974), pp. 42–43. Kennedy's proposal followed a recommendation in 1961 of the Commission on Money and Credit, a private group set up by the Committee for Economic Development. No member even introduced the president's bill, which was denounced on Capitol Hill as an attempt to usurp congressional prerogatives. Louis Fisher, *President and Congress: Power and Policy* (Free Press, 1972), pp. 165–73.

In the absence of such authority, the record on tax policy over the quarter century to 1973 was one of repeated vitiation by Congress of the fiscal policy of the president—in Truman's time, in Eisenhower's, in Kennedy's, and in Johnson's. Some of the time, in the 1940s and again in 1954, the Congress turned out to be more nearly right than did the president—though only by inadvertence. Sometimes the president failed to recommend the necessary measures, as in 1958, 1961–62, and 1965–66, and at such times the Congress could not overcome its dependence on his leadership and assert its own. But in the long deadlocks over tax reduction in 1962–64 and over the tax surcharge in 1967–68, after the president finally did make the appropriate proposals, the Congress inflicted severe damage by delaying the actions that it ultimately concluded it should take.

As the Congress worried in the 1970s about the broad problem of the power balance between the legislative and executive branches, the questions posed by President Johnson were still valid: How could costly inaction and the threat of fiscal stalemate be avoided in the future? What procedures could be devised to assure timeliness of action and effectiveness of executive-legislative collaboration? As long as the Congress insisted on a right to contradict, delay, or obstruct the fiscal policy of the president, without equipping itself to develop and enact a consistent and rational fiscal policy of its own, the country could not be sure of having any sensible policy at all. An "invisible hand" would truly guide the economy—the invisible hand of the political marketplace, of whatever power balance happened to be struck at any given time between the president and a torn, divided Congress.[71]

The Congress could have acquiesced to a further shift of power to the president, to make his authority commensurate with his public and political accountability. In its resurgent mood, however, it chose instead to reassert the legislature's authority and try to develop a commensurate capacity. It enacted as its instrument the Congressional Budget and Impoundment Control Act of 1974, which for the first time in modern history gave it the organizational strength to make the nation's fiscal policy.

71. The Federal Reserve Board is also part of the power balance that determines economic policy. But since it is independent of both the president and the Congress and may choose voluntarily to coordinate its monetary policies with the fiscal policy and other economic policies of the executive and legislative branches, it has not been involved in the struggle for power between those two branches and hence has not been discussed in this chapter.

CHAPTER V

The President as Foreign Policy Leader

IF THE president's executive power in domestic affairs is to carry out congressional policy as expressed in statutory law, his authority in international relations is not so limited. Since the beginning, presidents have taken it on themselves not only to execute the nation's foreign policy but to pronounce what the policy shall be, and even to use their authority as commander in chief to dispatch military forces to carry out their policies.

Whether the president is policymaker as well as policy executor in foreign relations became an issue as early as 1793, when President Washington proclaimed the country's neutrality in the war that had broken out between France and Britain. Then two who had been at the Constitutional Convention, and had collaborated in explaining the new charter in *The Federalist,* disagreed on whether it gave Washington the authority for his action. James Madison, in the Congress in 1793, said no. Since the Congress had the power to declare war, he argued, it also had the power, in effect, to declare peace—to adopt policies necessary to avoid war. Therefore, the president's role was to be the executive instrument of the Congress in foreign as in domestic matters, and his proclamation was improper. But Alexander Hamilton, a member of the first cabinet, saw things from the executive point of view: the president derives the authority to establish foreign policy from certain specific constitutional powers relating to foreign affairs, such as recognition of new governments, and from further powers implied in the general grant of "executive power."[1]

1. Edward S. Corwin, *The President: Office and Powers, 1787–1957,* 4th rev. ed. (New York University Press, 1957), pp. 177–82; Arthur M. Schlesinger, Jr., *The Imperial Presidency* (Houghton Mifflin, 1973), pp. 18–20; Abraham D. Sofaer, *War, Foreign Affairs and Constitutional Power: The*

President Washington backed off in this dispute and referred the matter to the Congress. But over the next century and a half, other presidents accumulated a wealth of precedents in support of Hamilton's position. James Monroe announced the doctrine that bears his name without asking the Congress for approval or consent, and it became accepted policy although it was not formally confirmed by the legislative branch until eight decades later.[2] Presidential initiative expressed in secret negotiations led to the annexation of Texas, and further executive initiative in dispatching troops into disputed territory brought on the Mexican War—a war promptly condemned by the House of Representatives as "unnecessarily and unconstitutionally begun by the President of the United States"[3] even though the legislators saw no choice but to support it with appropriations. "I took the Canal Zone and let Congress debate," boasted Theodore Roosevelt about a similar feat half a century later.[4] He sent the battle fleet around the world, prying the funds from grumbling congressmen by threatening to send the ships just halfway on funds already available and leave it to the Congress to bring them back.[5] President McKinley sent troops to China; Presidents Theodore Roosevelt, Taft, Wilson, and Coolidge sent them to various Latin American republics; and Wilson sent forces to Siberia, all without seeking prior congressional approval. Wilson announced his Fourteen Points without consulting Congress.[6]

When criticized, presidents were likely to reply along these lines: that American lives, property, and interests were at stake and quick decision was imperative; that the Congress was not in session to be consulted, or in any case the decision could not be subjected to the delays of congressional deliberation; that moves had to be made, or negotiations conducted, in secret, and only the executive branch could maintain confidentiality; that only the president has the essential information; that effective intercourse with other nations requires the United States to speak with a single voice, which can only be the president's; that policy has to be made not in the abstract but in the course of conducting day-to-day relations, which are the president's domain.

But, in the main, the Congress did not protest or resist the accretion of

Origins (Ballinger, 1976), pp. 111–16. Thomas Jefferson, also in the cabinet, had privately appealed to Madison to refute Hamilton, so the disagreement did not strictly follow executive-legislative branch lines.

2. Schlesinger, *Imperial Presidency*, p. 27.

3. *Congressional Globe*, January 3 and February 11, 1848, pp. 95, 343–44.

4. Joseph Bucklin Bishop, *Theodore Roosevelt and His Time Shown in His Own Letters* (Scribner's Sons, 1919), vol. 1, p. 308.

5. Theodore Roosevelt, *An Autobiography* (1913; Scribner's, 1925), pp. 552–53.

6. Schlesinger, *Imperial Presidency*, pp. 88–93.

presidential power. The issue was presented usually in substantive, not constitutional, terms. If the president's party in the Congress supported his policy, as usually it did, then it defended not only what he did but how he did it. When the opposition questioned his right to act, that was seen by his followers as a partisan attack grounded in the substantive dispute, and in defending the president's policy objective his followers in the Congress necessarily found themselves affirming as well the executive's right to seize the policymaking initiative. "In time," writes Louis Henkin, "the issue became not whether the President had authority to act . . . but whether he could act even contrary to the expressed wishes of Congress—whether Congress could direct, control, or supersede his decisions, whether Congress was constitutionally free *not* to implement his policies."[7]

The Supreme Court, in 1936, took a step toward affirming the Hamiltonian position. The president does indeed possess, in addition to powers delegated to him by statute, a "very delicate, plenary and exclusive power . . . as the sole organ of the federal government in the field of international relations," said the Court. "In this vast external realm . . . the President alone has the power to speak or listen as a representative of the nation. He . . . alone negotiates. Into the field of negotiation the Senate cannot intrude; and Congress itself is powerless to invade it."[8] But the scope and limits of the "plenary and exclusive" power were not defined, because the case did not require such a definition,[9] and the Court has not had occasion since to affirm, refine, or reconsider its broad language.

Nevertheless, the Congress has had its powers, too, and even the strongest presidents have found themselves unable to formulate and execute foreign policy over an extended period without enlisting congressional support.

Legislation and appropriations might eventually be needed and could always be denied. If the power of the president to negotiate treaties was exclusive, so was the authority of the Senate to reject them; of 786 treaties submitted to the Senate between 1778 and 1928, 15 were rejected—including the Treaty of Versailles—46 not acted on, and 51 nullified through unacceptable amendments. In a hundred cases during that period, Senate amendments to treaties were accepted by the signatory parties.[10] Only the Congress could declare war, even though the president could present the legislature

7. " 'A More Effective System' for Foreign Relations; The Constitutional Framework," in *Appendices: U.S. Commission on the Organization of the Government for the Conduct of Foreign Policy, June, 1975* (U.S. Government Printing Office, 1976), vol. 5, p. 12.

8. *United States* v. *Curtiss-Wright Export Corp. et al.*, 299 U.S. 304 at 319 (1936).

9. Indeed, in recognizing such a power, the Court went beyond the requirements of the case; its declarations about presidential power were obiter dicta. Louis Fisher, *President and Congress: Power and Policy* (Free Press, 1972), pp. 64–65; Schlesinger, *Imperial Presidency*, p. 103.

10. Royden J. Dangerfield, *In Defense of the Senate: A Study in Treaty Making* (University of Oklahoma Press, 1933), pp. 91–92, 150.

with faits accomplis that left it without choice. (But two wars of the nineteenth century—the War of 1812 and the Spanish-American War—were hastened, if not brought on, by agitation from the legislative branch that, reflecting public opinion, compelled a reluctant president to acquiesce.) And commercial relations were for the most part in the hands of the Congress, for tariff-writing was a legislative matter. So was immigration. In a very real sense, therefore, it has always been for the Congress itself, through its assertiveness or its passivity, to determine the actual limits of the president's "exclusive" power.

The height of congressional assertiveness in foreign affairs, in this century at least, was reached during the twenty-year period between the two world wars, when the legislature sought to control foreign policy through neutrality legislation. But with the outbreak of World War II, the Congress concluded that course had been a failure and that it must return discretion to the president. During the next three decades, although the Congress did assert a marginal influence through occasional minor budget reductions and restrictive amendments, its leaders came to acknowledge explicitly the president's primacy in the fundamental decisions of foreign policy. A long series of concessions by the Congress mark a perhaps unmatched period of congressional submissiveness in setting the country's world course.

The Failure of Congressional Foreign Policy: Neutrality

Reacting against involvement in World War I, the country slipped into the mood that came to be called isolationism and the Congress, reflecting the popular reprehension, sought to fix policies of nonintervention so firmly on the nation that no international-minded Woodrow Wilson of the future could upset them. The isolationists reasoned that if America's entry into the war had been compelled by the defense of neutral rights, the way to stay out of a new war was to give up those rights. Renounce freedom of the seas for shipping and for travel, and there would be no *Lusitania*s to inflame opinion, no freighters to defend against submarine attack. Moreover, if trade in armaments could be abolished, the possibility of war itself would be reduced. Take the profit out of war, and wars would be fewer and briefer.

The internationalists, however, had learned quite a different lesson from World War I. Forces other than a zeal for war profits, in their view, had dragged the United States into that conflict and would again if another world war broke out. So security lay not in isolation but in multilateral action to prevent new world wars. The internationalists had lost their struggle for U.S. entry into the League of Nations (in the first victory of nascent isolationism, though a majority of the Senate—short of the necessary two-thirds—had voted to approve it), but they envisioned a national policy that would permit the United States to work in concert with the League in deterring aggressors and imposing sanctions on them. They sought measures that would enable the government to control the arms trade in such a way that it could support some belligerents and penalize others. Resolutions along these lines were introduced in the Congress as early as 1927, and President Herbert Hoover late in his term was persuaded to endorse such a discretionary measure.[11] Franklin Roosevelt concurred, and a resolution conferring the power passed the House, 254 to 109, in 1933. The United States ambassador in Geneva, Norman H. Davis, assured the League powers that this country was prepared to join in collective action against aggressors.

But then the isolationists gained the upper hand, and the Congress achieved the first of a series of successes in support of the Madisonian principle that the Congress should fix the nation's international course, with the president as its instrument. Senator Hiram Johnson, Republican of California, led the forces seeking to enact a mandatory embargo applying equally to all participants in foreign wars, aggressors and defenders alike.

When the issue was joined in 1935, most of the president's supporters in the overwhelmingly Democratic Congress were willing to give discretion to the party's leader in the White House. "The President of the United States has a greater responsibility to prevent war and to sustain peace than any of you, and I am always willing to leave it to that office," Foreign Affairs Committee Chairman Sam D. McReynolds, of Tennessee, told the House.[12] Senator Tom Connally, Democrat of Texas, agreed that responsibility "must be vested in the Executive until the Congress steps in and makes a declaration of war."

> We cannot now put the United States into an international strait-jacket . . . a concrete cast internationally which will fit all future occasions and solve all future problems. . . . It is the President's function to conduct our international affairs. The history of the world demonstrates that never, in all the long years of strife and struggle, has a parliamentary conduct of international affairs been successful.[13]

Even some Republican internationalists were willing to place discretion in the president. Remarking that "no two wars are alike in their impact,"

---

11. Robert A. Divine, *The Illusion of Neutrality* (University of Chicago Press, 1962), pp. 26–37. This section relies heavily on Divine's research.
12. *Congressional Record*, August 23, 1935, p. 14370.
13. Ibid., August 24, 1935, p. 14432.

Representative James W. Wadsworth of New York wondered "if it is wise for America . . . to freeze its policy of neutrality in a statute."[14]

The neutralist bloc expressed the opposite view: With a "permissive neutrality" law, argued Louis Ludlow, Indiana Democrat, "the President would be supreme in his power to wage war." But "the judgment of no man is infallible, even though that man be the President of the United States. 'In multiplicity of counsel, there is wisdom,' says an old proverb, and it is not best to centralize authority in one man." The Congress should never "surrender . . . to the Chief Executive" the power to declare war, contended Maury Maverick, Democrat of Texas; "I want Congress to enact definite legislation. . . . Let us do our own duty." A New York Democrat, Fred J. Sisson, drew applause when he warned against permitting the president "to become a dictator in reference to our foreign policy."[15]

But the issue was settled before the debate began. With the Congress nearing adjournment, and with an Italian invasion of Ethiopia imminent, leaders of the Senate neutralist bloc threatened a filibuster. Nevada's Key Pittman, Democrat and chairman of the Foreign Relations Committee, advised President Roosevelt he would be beaten if he held out for discretionary authority to impose an arms embargo only against aggressors. Anxious to save some domestic measures that would be stacked up behind the filibuster, the president agreed to accept the resolution embodying the isolationists' mandatory and impartial arms embargo, provided it were effective only for the next six months—the embargo would be unneutral in its effect on an African war anyway, since only Italy had the resources to buy American arms. Three hours after the filibuster began, on August 19, Pittman made known Roosevelt's capitulation and the talk ended—"undoubtedly the shortest, and possibly the most successful, filibuster the Senate ever witnessed."[16] The resolution with its mandatory provisions then passed both houses easily, and the Congress's hand, not the president's, continued to steer the ship of state.

On signing the resolution, the president praised its purpose of keeping the country out of "any entanglements which would lead us into conflict" but expressed misgivings about its mandatory features. "No Congress and no Executive can foresee all possible situations. History is filled with unforeseeable situations that call for some flexibility of action. It is conceivable that situations may arise in which the wholly inflexible provisions of [the man-

14. Ibid., August 23, 1935, p. 14358.
15. Ibid., pp. 14359–60, 14357, 14358.
16. Divine, *Illusion of Neutrality*, p. 112.

datory embargo] might have exactly the opposite effect from that which was intended."[17]

When Italy invaded Ethiopia, in October, the president invoked the arms embargo against the belligerents. But arms were not Italy's crucial need. Oil was. The League of Nations voted economic sanctions against the aggressor, including an oil embargo, but exporting countries waited for parallel U.S. action before complying. Accordingly, as the Congress prepared to consider renewal of the temporary resolution, due to expire in February 1936, President Roosevelt asked for a new provision that would authorize him to prohibit shipments of strategic raw materials to belligerents in excess of peacetime trade levels. A new debate over placing discretionary power in the president was touched off, and the isolationists were joined in force this time by shipping interests, oil and cotton producers, and, above all, Italian-Americans. By all accepted principles of international law, the new provision "would amount to an unfriendly and hostile act toward a traditionally friendly nation," contended Representative Arthur D. Healey, a Democrat whose Massachusetts district contained many voters of Italian descent. "Thousands of our citizens of Italian extraction . . . are looking anxiously toward us," he told the House.[18] So many congressmen with similar constituencies appealed to Chairman McReynolds that he advised the administration the new discretionary provision—which his committee had loyally approved—could not pass the House. Meanwhile, Hiram Johnson was threatening another filibuster in the Senate. President Roosevelt again conceded defeat, and the resolution extending the neutrality policy—for fourteen months—passed without the new authority. In the 1936 campaign, the president talked again of the need for flexibility, but his position was not popular. The Gallup poll in January 1937 found that 69 percent of the people thought that the Congress, not the president, should make neutrality policy.[19]

When the legislation was made permanent in 1937, the Congress resolved the problem of strategic materials with a cash-and-carry provision: belligerents could purchase such goods, provided they were not bought on credit or carried in American ships. But the president was given the responsibility of deciding when the provision would be invoked and what items would be covered. Republican Senator Arthur H. Vandenberg of Michigan warned that the new provision would transfer a "substantial portion" of the war-making power to the executive because "the real war decision . . . is actually made

17. "Presidential Statement on Approval of Neutrality Legislation, August 31, 1935," *Public Papers and Addresses of Franklin D. Roosevelt, 1935* (Random House, 1938), pp. 345–46.

18. *Congressional Record*, February 17, 1936, p. 2247.

19. Divine, *Illusion of Neutrality*, pp. 164–65, 181.

when we choose our neutrality formula." It would, he said, permit a declaration of war "by Executive decree."[20] But his misgivings were overwhelmed by the Democrats' huge majority.

As the Japanese advanced in China and Hitler became more bellicose in Europe, President Roosevelt moved more openly to challenge the country's isolationist position. In October 1937 came his "quarantine the aggressors" speech, and by 1939 he was resolved to fight for repeal of the arms embargo. Hitler, after all, was armed, and in any conflict with him, Britain and France would need American munitions. After the Nazi seizure of Czechoslovakia, Democrats on the House Foreign Affairs Committee came to Roosevelt's support. On a party-line vote the committee reported a bill to place armaments under the same cash-and-carry rules that applied to other war materials. Again the cry arose: the Congress was surrendering its war-making prerogative. "The people of the United States do not want one-man government," pleaded Representative Robert F. Jones, Ohio Republican. "They do not want the discretion of life and death of their children lodged in the ambitious hands of one man."[21] Speaker William B. Bankhead of Alabama took the House floor to state the case for presidential power:

> We made a supreme and colossal mistake in policy . . . when we departed a few years ago from the time-honored and time-tested constitutional principle of leaving the management of our foreign and diplomatic affairs in the hands of the President of the United States and of the State Department of this country. It had been lodged there securely and definitely for 145 years. . . . Every incursion . . . in the last three years does but serve to teach us that it is absolutely impossible for the genius even of the Congress of the United States to enact a statute that contains real neutrality.
>
> I feel that the safest and surest way for us to proceed is to remove the shackles and impediments now resting on the President of the United States and the Secretary of State and give them absolute freedom of action, as the founders of our Constitution conceived they should have, to govern from day to day and from hour to hour the incidents that may occur in this storm-tossed and tempestuous world.
>
> The Congress of the United States is losing nothing by the passage of this bill. There is still reserved to us the constitutional power to declare war. Nothing can take that away from us. . . . I appeal to you . . . to return to the safe moorings of the Constitution and leave to him who is charged with that responsibility . . . always the President of the United States of America, the right in the first instance to control and manage our diplomatic and foreign affairs.[22]

But sixty-one House Democrats deserted their speaker and their president

---

20. The importance of the discretionary power to recognize the existence of belligerency had already been proved in the case of Japanese aggression in the Far East, for at the behest of the Chinese, President Roosevelt had declined since the beginning of that conflict to impose even the arms embargo. *Congressional Record*, April 29, 1937, p. 3943.

21. Ibid., June 29, 1939, p. 8265.

22. Ibid., June 30, 1939, p. 8510.

to support a Republican amendment restoring the mandatory arms embargo that had been in effect since 1935.

That, however, was the high water mark of isolationism, and of congressional control of foreign policy. Within a few days of the German march on Poland and the outbreak of the European war that autumn, the House reversed itself. The Senate concurred in the lifting of the embargo. The United States became "the great arsenal of democracy." An act of 1940 authorized export controls on defense items, which enabled the president to ban the sale of scrap iron to Japan. The president, on dubious constitutional authority, exchanged fifty overaged American destroyers for the lease of eight naval bases on British territory. In March 1941 the Congress abandoned neutrality altogether with passage of the Lend-Lease Act, a measure drafted by the administration.[23] Executing this congressional policy, Roosevelt authorized the Navy to convoy American shipping and approved the arming of merchant ships and their entry into combat zones. By executive agreement with Denmark, he assumed the protection of Greenland, and he ordered marines to Iceland. These initiatives were protested vigorously by the dwindling isolationist minority in the Congress as beyond the president's authority. But the majority, backed by public opinion, supported the chief executive, arguing questions of substantive policy and national interest rather than constitutional law. Agreeing with the end, the Congress chose not to examine carefully the means.[24] So the experiment in congressional management of foreign affairs ended. Control returned to the president, to remain there virtually unchallenged for three decades.

The Delegation of Tariff-Making Power

Even while it tried to restrict the president's power to embroil the country in war, the Congress had, in the 1930s, yielded its authority over an area that, more than any other single topic, had engrossed its energies for more than a hundred years—the tariff.

When the Democratic party reassumed control of the national government, it was committed to reversing the worldwide trend toward prohibitive tariff

23. James A. Robinson, *Congress and Foreign Policy-Making: A Study in Legislative Influence and Initiative* (Dorsey, 1962), p. 27. The Congress made only minor amendments to the administration draft.

24. Francis O. Wilcox, *Congress, the Executive, and Foreign Policy* (Harper and Row, 1971), pp. 7–9. Senator Jacob K. Javits, New York Republican, suggests that the majority of the Congress supported the president only because he concealed his "private" commitment to enter the war. Javits with Don Kellerman, *Who Makes War: The President versus Congress* (Morrow, 1973), pp. 217–22.

rates—reflected, in the United States, in the Republican-sponsored Smoot-Hawley Act of 1929—but it was ready to concede that tariff questions could no longer be handled in the accustomed way. The Congress was overwhelmed with the problems of the Great Depression; for it to undertake to adjust thousands of individual tariff schedules, as it had done on countless occasions for a century and a half, would engross it for an entire session to the exclusion of other crucial matters. Moreover, it now seemed clear that tariffs had to become a matter for international bargaining, rather than unilateral action, and the Congress could not negotiate. These considerations permitted but one outcome: the Congress must give up the power it had cherished for so long and assign the task to President Roosevelt and Secretary of State Cordell Hull.

The congressional debate that led to passage of the Reciprocal Trade Agreements Act of 1934 was extraordinarily revealing of the plight of the modern legislature in attempting to cope with complex subjects. The Republican opposition raised the accustomed plaint. "A supine, spineless, sycophantic Congress" was being "commanded to surrender absolutely to one man . . . the sole power, arbitrarily to make tariff rates," in the words of Representative Bertrand H. Snell of New York, the House minority leader. That, he said, was "unconstitutional to the core."[25]

Democrats responded to the constitutional question by arguing that the president would receive his power only by delegation, if the bill passed, and hence would be only the agent of the Congress. The Congress would be "instructing" the president to execute its will "promptly and thoroughly," said the bill's manager in the Senate, Democrat Pat Harrison of Mississippi.[26] Moreover, the bill established limits. The president could cut the Smoot-Hawley rates only by a maximum of 50 percent, and the delegation would expire in three years. But the main arguments were practical. "This is not a matter which can be satisfactorily disposed of in Congress," argued Representative Charles I. Faddis, Democrat of Pennsylvania.

> No Congressman has the time to make a detailed study of this matter in order to acquaint himself with the facts. Congress as a body does not have time to take up the consideration of such an intricate question and do it justice. It is a matter for slow and careful consideration. It must be gone into cautiously, step by step, with the idea of a general plan. Congress cannot do this, for in this country the tariff is to each Member of Congress a local issue. The tariff has always been a logrolling issue. . . . We must have a national tariff policy. At the present time we can have it in no way except by giving the authority to formulate it to the President.[27]

25. *Congressional Record*, March 26, 1934, pp. 5438, 5433.
26. Ibid., May 17, 1934, p. 8987.
27. Ibid., March 24, 1934, p. 5356.

Representative John A. Martin, Colorado Democrat, reminded the Republicans that even the Smoot-Hawley Act contained a provision allowing the president to revise its rates on the basis of investigations by the Federal Tariff Commission (a provision the Democrats, including then Senator Cordell Hull, had opposed as unconstitutional, and one that President Hoover never used). This, Martin said, was "a recognition of the fact that Congress, overwhelmed as it is . . . could no longer deal with the vast intricacies and complexities of tariff legislation."

> And what is true of the tariff is true of transportation, communication, of the banking and monetary systems, of internal revenue, of internal improvements, of the entire recovery program, and of every major national policy. The utmost that the Congress can do, and do intelligently, is to lay down policies and define limits, and it is difficult even to find time to do this.
>
> In the old days the problems of government were few and political, now they are many and are economic and sociological. . . .
>
> I am only able to apprehend this situation, not to meet it. Parliaments and constitutions are in the crucible.[28]

And there were memories of past fiascos. The Smoot-Hawley bill, observed Senator M. M. Logan, Kentucky Democrat, "was perhaps the most horrific monstrosity the world has ever seen."[29] While the president might make mistakes, agreed Senator David I. Walsh, Democrat of Massachusetts, "they will be no more numerous nor more injurious" than the mistakes the Congress might make in any tariff bill. And so the act passed, and tariff-making power shifted from the politicians of Capitol Hill, not to the president personally, of course, but to the diplomats and economists who occupied the executive buildings of "downtown" Washington.

When the act came up for renewal, in 1937—after fifteen agreements had been negotiated—the Republicans made no serious effort to take back the legislative initiative in tariff-making. They concentrated their efforts, instead, on an amendment to require Senate ratification of the trade agreements on the ground that they were properly treaties, which was defeated.[30]

In 1940, an amendment to require Senate ratification lost by a much narrower margin in that body—only three votes—and another amendment to require congressional approval of the agreements lost by just six votes. Again the practical arguments prevailed. "There are manifestly some powers given to Congress which it cannot appropriately exercise, or which it can

28. Ibid., March 26, 1934, p. 5456.
29. Ibid., May 29, 1934, p. 9814.
30. Democrats noted that fourteen trade treaties had been submitted to the Senate a generation earlier by President McKinley, but all had been rejected by the Senate (a fifteenth, after those rejections, was not even submitted); they argued that the same procedure now would be equally "impractical." Ibid., February 4, 1937, pp. 834-35.

exercise only with the utmost difficulty, if at all. . . . we have to look at it practically," said the veteran Senator Walter F. George, Democrat of Georgia. George W. Norris, the Nebraska Independent, was emphatic: "The idea that 435 Members of the House and 96 Members of the Senate can sit down and agree to a fair, efficient, scientific tariff act containing 5,000 separate items is simply absurd. . . . instead of being an admission of inefficiency, or lack of ability, it is a confession that we are, after all, only human beings." And Senator Bennett Champ Clark, Missouri Democrat, pleaded against a return to "the old, vicious, venal, disgraceful logrolling days of general tariff bills."[31]

The legislation was renewed that year, and ten more times between then and 1962, when a five-year delegation was approved on President Kennedy's request. The Congress occasionally altered the guidelines the president must follow. It steadily lowered the levels to which tariffs might be reduced. In 1951 it introduced escape-clause procedures that authorized the United States Tariff Commission to make investigations of injury to domestic industries and recommend tariff adjustments to the president. It also wrote provisions governing which nations would benefit from most-favored-nation treatment, and it specified organization and procedures for tariff bargaining. But only in one respect did the Congress reassert its decisionmaking power over individual items, when in 1958 it provided that the Congress by a two-thirds vote of both houses (reduced in 1962 to a simple majority) could override the president, if he disapproved a Tariff Commission recommendation for granting relief under the escape clause. The authority has not proved to be consequential, though its existence may have prompted the president to approve escape-clause recommendations he might otherwise have rejected.

Between 1967 and 1974 the delegation of authority to the president lapsed, and U.S. tariffs remained frozen. Presidents Johnson and Nixon both recommended renewal of their negotiating power, but the Congress denied the requests. With industrial tariffs already reduced so low that they no longer were a significant barrier to trade in most items, committees in both houses converted President Nixon's tariff negotiation bill into a protectionist measure that would have imposed import quotas on certain classes of industrial goods, and the liberals defeated that measure by a Senate filibuster. In 1974, negotiating authority was reinstated for five years without the offending quota provisions (although other restrictions, including a provision requiring congressional approval of agreements, were added). In 1979, agreements negotiated under the 1974 act were approved by the Congress, and authority

31. Ibid., March 27, 1940, p. 3514; March 29, 1940, p. 3674; April 3, 1940, p. 3918.

to negotiate reductions in nontariff barriers was extended for another eight years, still subject to congressional approval.

Even when it has had an apparent protectionist majority, the Congress has shown no disposition to take back its historic tariff-writing power, which it surrendered in 1934. The most comprehensive study of the subject, published in 1963, offered this explanation: "Responsibility brings with it intolerable pressures. . . . The power to dole out favors to industry is not worth the price of having to beat off and placate the insistent pleas of petitioners. . . . every favor which can be conferred is also a danger, because it must sometimes be refused. Responsibility involves blame. And, if the demands exceed what the congressman can effectively handle, then he may happily yield up a significant portion of his power." Now the congressman can gain credit with his constituents by inserting material in the *Congressional Record* or appearing as a witness before the Tariff Commission, "free to indulge the irresponsibility afforded those who do not participate in the final decision."[32] While containing a large element of truth, this language seems excessively cynical. One has to credit the explanations given by the members themselves over the years. The least irresponsible congressmen have been the ones most deterred from seeking for the Congress a duty too time-consuming and too intricate to be performed well and fairly by a large legislative body, and by its nature all but impossible for a legislator to approach from the standpoint of national, rather than constituency, interest.

Collaboration in the Postwar World

As World War II approached its close, the country looked to the future with a rare solidarity of purpose. The isolationism that had dominated the country's mood between the wars had been crushed by the Nazi panzers, then shattered by Pearl Harbor. This time the mistake of 1919 would not be repeated. The United States would join in creating a world order.

The change of purpose altered the relationship between the Congress and the president. The Congress could legislate isolation and neutrality in the 1930s, but only the president had the capacity to negotiate new international mechanisms in the 1940s. The Congress could support and encourage, but it could not act. When the United States became a full collaborator with other

32. Raymond A. Bauer, Ithiel de Sola Pool, and Lewis Anthony Dexter, *American Business and Public Policy: The Politics of Foreign Trade*, 2nd ed. (Aldine-Atherton, 1972), p. 38.

nations, the president perforce became the nation's leader and, given the nation's power, a world leader as well—*the* leader of the free world, as he was often hailed. And for those members of the Congress who shared the internationalist outlook—most of the Democratic party and a majority of Republicans as well—there was little to do beyond making peripheral suggestions and beating back any latter-day isolationist attempts to deny the president the legislative authority and the resources for the job.

For their part, however, presidents were vividly aware of the destructive potential of the Congress. If it could not create, it could assuredly negate. All who had lived through the battle for Woodrow Wilson's League of Nations, as had both Franklin Roosevelt and Cordell Hull, knew that. So, while the war went on, Roosevelt and Hull took pains to bring the Congress into collaboration in framing the institutions that would keep the peace once the fighting ended. With the Congress prepared to accept the necessity of presidential initiative and leadership, and the president equally ready to acknowledge the imperative of congressional participation and even partnership, a relationship of rare intimacy and mutual trust could be established.

The relationship almost got off to a bad start, however. As an early venture into multilateral institution-building, the administration in 1943 joined representatives of other nations in drafting a charter for a United Nations Relief and Rehabilitation Administration. But, as Senator Vandenberg said later, it "was to be launched exclusively by Executive agreement" with "never a purpose to consult either the Senate in respect to treaty obligations or the Congress in respect to appropriation responsibility."[33] The congressional leadership of both parties was consulted and raised no objections to the president's intended procedure but when Vandenberg, who was emerging as the Republican foreign policy spokesman, heard about it, he introduced a resolution calling for an investigation to determine whether the plan should be sent to the Senate in the form of a treaty. "I think this is clearly a preview of the method by which the President and the State Department intend to by-pass Congress in general, and the Senate in particular, in settling every possible international war and postwar issue by the use of mere 'executive agreements,' " he wrote in his diary.[34] Chairman Tom Connally of the Foreign Relations Committee, Vandenberg noted, was even more vehement; the resolution was immediately approved, and Hull was summoned to explain.

33. *Congressional Record*, February 16, 1944, p. 1739.

34. Arthur H. Vandenberg, Jr., ed., *The Private Papers of Senator Vandenberg* (Houghton Mifflin, 1952), p. 67. Writing at the time, Kenneth W. Colegrove asserted that this was indeed the State Department's plan. "The Role of Congress and Public Opinion in Formulating Foreign Policy," *American Political Science Review*, vol. 38 (October 1944), p. 961.

Connally chastised the secretary so severely that he walked out of the meeting, but what followed was the "closest and most sympathetic cooperation" in "rewriting the entire agreement."[35]

In the rewriting, neither side had to concede much. The administration accepted language stipulating that no funds could be committed without congressional approval, which was merely the recognition of the normal constitutional relationship. And the senators—citing the Trade Agreements Act as precedent—accepted the executive agreement. That, for the internationalist majority, was in fact not a loss but a gain, for it avoided the need for enabling legislation which an isolationist minority in the Senate—if it amounted to only one-third plus one—could kill with a filibuster.

Perhaps this episode impressed on the administration that it must arrange for full congressional collaboration when it moved to plan the permanent United Nations organization. More likely it would have invited such participation anyway, for the view had been widely held for a generation that if President Wilson had taken senators on his delegation to Versailles, the Senate would have accepted the League of Nations. As early as 1942, Secretary Hull had invited Senators Connally and Warren R. Austin, Vermont Republican, to serve on his Advisory Committee on Post-War Foreign Policy, and in 1944 when the department's plans for what was to become the United Nations were ready, he asked Connally to appoint a bipartisan committee to review them.[36] Two senators and two representatives were appointed to the seven-member American delegation to the San Francisco conference, and the two senators—Connally and Vandenberg—were among the most active and influential members.

The only issue of potential gravity in the Senate's consideration of the UN charter was the location of the power to commit U.S. forces to combat in support of Security Council peacekeeping resolutions. Speaking for the remnant of the prewar isolationist bloc, Senator Burton K. Wheeler, Montana Democrat, charged that the treaty would "turn over to one man"—the U.S. delegate to the Security Council—"the war-making power." But Connally, supported by administration testimony, cited the charter provision that before troops could be committed, each country providing such forces would have to enter into a formal arrangement with the council governing their use, and that such arrangement would be ratified by the country through its "constitutional processes." Asked repeatedly whether those processes required a

35. Vandenberg, in *Congressional Record*, February 16, 1944, p. 1739; Vandenberg, *Private Papers*, p. 68; Robert A. Divine, *Second Chance: The Triumph of Internationalism in America During World War II* (Atheneum, 1971), pp. 117–18.

36. Divine, *Second Chance*, pp. 5, 194–95.

treaty or merely an agreement that could be approved by joint resolution of the Congress, Connally successfully evaded the question, proposing that it be left for consideration when the time came.[37] In the end, only three senators opposed American entry into the United Nations.

The broad national consensus on foreign policy objectives—and even, most of the time, on tactics—continued for the next half dozen years, as the country assumed international responsibilities on a scale wholly without precedent, and as it moved with hardly a pause from a shooting war to the Cold War. Harmony within the country made possible, perhaps even compelled, harmony between the president and Congress on foreign policy, even when in 1947–48 the Republican-controlled Eightieth Congress bitterly fought, and often defeated, President Truman in domestic legislative battles. A whole series of radical postwar initiatives proposed by President Truman was approved, often without modification and rarely with any substantial change at all—the British loan, the Greek-Turkish aid program, the Marshall Plan, aid to China and Korea, the North Atlantic alliance, the Mutual Defense Assistance Program, Point Four. Liaison was so close between the branches that members of the Congress, particularly ranking senators on the Foreign Relations Committee, had opportunity to advise before policies were announced, as well as consent to them afterward, and potential breaches in harmony could be averted. And Vandenberg paved the way for the North Atlantic Treaty negotiations by sponsoring a resolution, approved by a large Senate majority, encouraging regional peace-keeping arrangements as authorized under the United Nations charter.[38] Once the measures, with whatever degree of advance consultation may have been involved, were sent to Capitol Hill, the members grumbled about the "blank checks" they were handing the president, but with the menace of Soviet expansion hanging over both Europe and Asia, they signed them. Truman's control of cold war and reconstruction was scarcely less solid than had been Roosevelt's control of wartime operations. Writing of the Marshall Plan, James A. Robinson described Congress's role as "plainly that of the modifier and the legitimator" of executive initiatives, and he reached the same conclusion about its role in the Greek-Turkish aid program and the North Atlantic Treaty—while not belittling the importance of legitimation and the careful planning, tactical skill, and hard work on the part of leaders like Vandenberg that were necessary

37. *Congressional Record*, July 24, 1945, p. 7987; July 25, 1945, pp. 8028–29; July 26, 1945, p. 8078.

38. This followed the precedent set by resolutions sponsored by Representative J. William Fulbright, Democrat of Arkansas, and Senator Connally adopted in 1943 that committed the Congress to join a world peacekeeping organization after the war and thus prepared the way for negotiations to form the United Nations.

to achieve it.[39] The majorities in the Congress beat back weakening amendments to the president's proposals, and the Congress confined its own initiative mainly to the distribution of the domestic benefits of the aid programs—such as the stipulation that half the aid cargoes must be carried on U.S. flagships. The legislature did initiate an additional blank-check appropriation in 1949 for assistance in "the general area of China," and in three successive years it forced on the president unsought funds for assistance to Spain.

The primacy of the president in the determination of foreign policy was formally, if tacitly, acknowledged in the 1947 legislation creating the National Security Council. The NSC was designed, explained one of its Senate advocates, Democrat Lister Hill of Alabama, as the place "wherein the complex and now uncoordinated problems of bringing foreign policy into harmony with the military means to enforce that policy may be brought to light and resolved."[40] Yet the council would be wholly in the executive branch, chaired by the president himself and advisory only to him. No corresponding steps were taken to bring into coordination in the Congress the separate committees handling foreign and military affairs. The picture was clear: the president would prepare the unified and coordinated policy; if legislation or appropriations were required, the Congress would review and respond.[41]

Presidential War-Making in Korea

President Truman continued to receive bipartisan support when, in June of 1950, he presented the Congress with a fait accompli by ordering American forces into combat in Korea. There was "no pretense of consulting the Congress," Senator Robert A. Taft, Ohio Republican, protested later.[42] The president merely called the leaders of both parties in the Congress to the White House, after he had issued the order, and informed them—only a few moments before issuing a statement to the press. In reaching his decision—

39. *Congress and Foreign Policy-Making*, pp. 40, 43, 46.
40. *Congressional Record*, July 9, 1947, p. 8506.
41. President Truman had seen no need for a statute instructing him which of his subordinates to consult. The council had been proposed originally by opponents of consolidation of the War and Navy departments as an alternative means of coordination, but proponents of the new department accepted it as an additional coordinating device. President Truman withdrew any objection once it was clear it would be entirely under the president's control.
42. *Congressional Record*, June 28, 1950, p. 9320. Dean Acheson, then secretary of state, offers a day-by-day chronology of the decisionmaking process in *Present at the Creation: My Years in the State Department* (Norton, 1969), pp. 402–13.

"the most important in my time as President of the United States"—the president reported:

> I turned the problem over in my mind in many ways, but my thoughts kept coming back to the 1930's—to Manchuria, to Ethiopia, the Rhineland, Austria, and finally to Munich.
>
> Here was history repeating itself. Here was another probing action, another testing action. If we let the Republic of Korea go under, some other country would be next, and then another. . . . And the United Nations would go the way of the League of Nations.
>
> . . . I met . . . with the Secretary of State, the Secretary of Defense, and General Bradley, and the other civilian and military officials who had information and advice to help me decide on what to do. We talked about the problems long and hard.[43]

The key words were "help me decide." He obtained advice from his subordinates, and discussed the issue "long and hard" in two evening meetings, on June 25 and 26, but it was a one-man decision. As Truman said, "the most heartening fact was that the American people clearly agreed with the decision."[44] That being the case, few questioned the propriety of the procedure. In the Congress the Democratic majority, to a person, defended the president's unilateral action as both wise and proper, and so did most Republicans. Hardly a word of protest was spoken in the House, and in the Senate only a few Republicans demurred. Most important among them was Senator Taft,who warned: "The President is usurping his powers as Commander in Chief. . . . there is no legal authority for what he has done. . . . if the President can intervene in Korea without congressional approval, he can go to war in Malaya or Indonesia or Iran or South America."[45]

Taft recalled the assurances given to the Congress, when the United States entered the United Nations, that the Congress would be consulted before military forces were committed in support of Security Council resolutions. The consultation was to have taken place on the specific terms of agreements negotiated between the council and the United States. But no agreement had ever been negotiated. Moreover, as was pointed out during the Senate debate, the Security Council resolution calling on UN members to support Korea with military forces was not adopted until the evening of June 27—*after* American forces had already been ordered into battle. Majority Leader Scott W. Lucas, Democrat of Illinois, with a reference to "communism creeping into every nook and corner where it can possibly go," defended the president's right as commander in chief to dispatch military forces if he believed "that the safety, the security, and the honor of this country are involved." He argued

43. "The President's Farewell Address to the American People. January 15, 1953," *Public Papers of the Presidents: Harry S. Truman, 1952–53* (GPO, 1966), p. 1200.

44. Ibid.

45. *Congressional Record*, June 28, 1950, pp. 9320, 9322–23.

that more than a hundred precedents existed for such action. Senator Taft replied that these instances all stopped short of "open warfare." But Senator Ralph E. Flanders, Vermont Republican, contended that the Korean action did not amount to war either—the position the administration took throughout the hostilities, insisting they were a "police action" rather than a "war."[46]

Senator William F. Knowland, Republican of California, urged "overwhelming" bipartisan support of the president's action, and internationalist Republicans such as Leverett Saltonstall and Henry Cabot Lodge, Jr., of Massachusetts, H. Alexander Smith of New Jersey, and Wayne Morse of Oregon backed him. Lodge added to his support of the president "the hope that he will not shrink from using the Army, if the best military judgment indicates that is the effective course to take." Morse noted that the president's powers in times of national crisis are "very broad." Democrats called on their colleagues and the people to "close ranks" behind the president. The most careful statement of the president's powers in the Senate debate was a brief entered by Paul H. Douglas of Illinois. "The speed of modern war requires quick executive action," argued Douglas; "even the slightest delay may prove fatal." But, he went on, congressional procedures were prone to delay; as few as one or two senators could filibuster the Senate to a halt under that body's rule of unlimited debate. And what would prevent abuse by the president of his right of "executive action"? First, "the sobering and terrible responsibilities of the office." Second, the "deterring influence" of the possibility of impeachment.[47]

But the essence of the situation is found in an exchange about the commitment of troops between Senator Arthur V. Watkins, Republican of Utah, and Majority Leader Lucas. Watkins: "A question that has never been finally determined is whether that can be done without the consent of the Congress." Lucas: "Well, it has been done."[48]

And the president stuck to his position. Senator Smith of New Jersey suggested informally to the president that he seek approval through a joint resolution, and on July 10 Senator Alexander Wiley of Wisconsin, the topranking active Republican on the Foreign Relations Committee, formally took the Senate floor to advise the president that it was still not too late to legitimate his action. The people were concerned, said Wiley, at the surrender by the legislative branch of "more and more of its authority and prerogatives" to

46. Ibid., pp. 9328, 9315. "We are not at war," President Truman told his news conference; "The President's News Conference of June 29, 1950," *Public Papers: Truman, 1950* (GPO, 1965), p. 503. (Curiously, the editors of Truman's papers disdained the euphemism; the only index entry under "Korea, Police Action in," is a cross-reference: *"See* Korean War.")

47. *Congressional Record*, June 27, 1950, pp. 9320, 9321; July 5, 1950, pp. 9648–49.

48. Ibid., June 27, 1950, p. 9233.

the executive. "If we are to sit by silently while the President takes action which might lead us into a third world war," he continued, "the people will wonder whether the legislative branch has continued strength and validity."[49] Truman showed himself not unreceptive to the idea initially but was apparently persuaded by Senator Lucas, among others, that such a resolution was unneeded and might touch off a damaging, divisive debate. The president was also, Dean Acheson has suggested, moved by his determination to pass to his successors a presidency "unimpaired by the slightest loss of power or prestige."[50]

The Congress displayed no equivalent determination to defend its prerogatives, and it in effect ratified the president's action by not responding to Wiley's suggestion—which the senator did not press—and then by approving the president's requests for military appropriations and for extension of selective service.

Delegation of the War-Making Power

For a dozen years after President Truman's declaration of "police action" in Korea, the question of the limits—if any—of the presidential war-making power arose repeatedly in the Congress. Truman tested those limits again in 1951 and precipitated a "great debate" in the Senate that ended in a stalemate. President Eisenhower, convinced that Truman's constitutional challenge to the Congress had been bad tactics, devised a new approach. In the two cold war crises of his administration—Formosa and the Middle East— he asked the Congress to delegate to him the power to decide whether to take the country into war. In each instance the Congress readily complied. These were the first two blank-check resolutions, and Presidents Kennedy and Johnson added two more in two later crises. Thus, in a series of steps, the Congress took itself out of the decisionmaking process altogether. The power of decision over war and peace—held in such tight and rigid control by the Congress in its period of self-assertion in the decade before World War II—slipped virtually wholly from its grasp.

The Great Debate. The exhaustive examination of the presidential-congressional balance of power that won recognition as one of the Senate's historic debates was touched off in 1951 by President Truman's decision to send four divisions of troops to Europe to serve in the international army to be set up

49. Ibid., July 10, 1950, p. 9737.
50. *Present at the Creation,* pp. 413–15.

under the North Atlantic Treaty Organization and placed under the command of General Dwight D. Eisenhower. As in the case of Korea six months earlier, the president chose not to share this decision with the Congress. Of course, the appropriate committees had been informed and their views obtained, the president told a news conference; that was regular practice, but it was strictly a courtesy. "I do not have to unless I want to. But of course I am polite, and I usually always consult them," he explained, and added: "I don't ask their permission, I just consult them."[51]

That was not good enough for the Republican leaders of the Senate. Senator Taft opened the debate with a denunciation of "secret executive agreements" that had brought the country "to danger and disaster." The Korean adventure, he reiterated, was "without authority of law," and so would be "the commitment of a land army to Europe" if that were done without congressional approval.[52] Senator Kenneth S. Wherry of Nebraska, the Republican floor leader, introduced a resolution expressing the sense of the Senate that no troops should be dispatched until the Congress had approved the policy.

The Democrats, likewise, repeated their constitutional arguments of the previous year. "If our forefathers had wanted Congress to be the Commander in Chief, they would have said so," argued Senator Connally, the Foreign Relations Committee chairman. They remembered too vividly, however, the "mistakes and troubles" of the Continental Congress in trying to conduct military affairs, so they made the president commander in chief. "It follows, furthermore, that with such power the President of the United States has the authority to send the Armed Forces to any part of the world if the security and safety of the United States are involved."[53]

The president held his disputed power in abeyance, however, while the combined foreign relations and armed forces committees held hearings on the Wherry resolution. In the end, the Congress sidestepped the constitutional question. The Senate did not attempt to set the country's European defense policy by law but only expressed its views by resolution, and the House declined the Senate's invitation to join in that expression. The resolution approved the sending of the contemplated four divisions but expressed the sense of the body that "in the interests of sound constitutional processes and of national unity and understanding," congressional approval should be obtained for any future expansion of the American commitment. The sena-

51. "The President's News Conference of January 11, 1951," *Public Papers: Truman, 1951* (GPO, 1965), p. 20.
52. *Congressional Record*, January 5, 1951, pp. 55, 61.
53. Ibid., January 11, 1951, p. 142.

torial suggestion would not have the force of law, however, and the president could still be guided by his own interpretation of his powers.[54]

Although the compromise was adopted unanimously by the committee members, it met some objection on the floor. "Instead of this resolution, we should take occasion to hammer out a foreign policy and establish it ourselves," argued Senator Knowland. And Senator William E. Jenner, Indiana Republican, was even more emphatic: "The whole responsibility for an honest, realistic American foreign policy . . . rests on the Congress. . . . Congress lays down policy, by law; and the President is supposed to carry it out. If the President can make whatever policy he likes, we are governed, not by law, but by the arbitrary whims of one man and the sycophants and the betrayers who make up his entourage."[55]

At the other end of the spectrum were those who thought the resolution invaded the executive prerogative by calling for congressional approval of future troop movements. Such a procedure, said Lister Hill, would subject decisions to "the hazards of parliamentary guerilla fighting." Brien McMahon, Democrat of Connecticut, warned of "pitched battles in this body upon every single deployment of troops which might be proposed." Senator Connally observed that the president as commander in chief must be able to "react with the speed of a totalitarian state" in "a day when atomic attack is possible," and therefore the Congress should not "whittle away" at his powers. Senator Herbert H. Lehman, New York Democrat, called it "bad government" for the Congress to undertake to legislate "on matters involving the central prerogatives of the Executive, and on which, by logic and reason, the Executive must exercise his discretion, based on information which can be available only to him, and to meet the exigencies of the moment. The country can pass its judgment upon his acts at the polls. The Congress has its opportunity to review in the course of its appropriations." Russell B. Long, Louisiana Democrat, said the best argument against congressional review was "what we have had going on for the past three months, on the floor of the Senate. . . . Somewhere along the line decisions must be made . . . and they must be made without hearing every Senator in complete detail while he states his views, without waiting for a Gallup poll and thinking the thing over for five or six months." And Lehman added a reminder that as long as the Senate permitted filibusters, decisions sometimes could not be made at all.[56]

54. The question has not arisen, because expansion of the American commitment to Europe has not been considered since the resolution was adopted.

55. *Congressional Record*, March 19, 1951, pp. 2594–95.

56. Ibid., March 29, 1951, p. 2966; April 2, 1951, p. 3079; March 16, 1951, p. 2543; March 21, 1951, p. 2738; April 2, 1951, p. 3079.

But, whatever their views on the constitutional question, the majority supported the North Atlantic alliance, the concept of the international army, the appointment of General Eisenhower, and hence the president's policy. So the compromise that evaded the issue of presidential power was satisfactory. Those who contended the president had no power to send the troops without approval could claim the resolution granted such approval—on behalf of the Senate if not the Congress as a whole—even though it did not have the force of law. And those who claimed the president had the power of unilateral action could support the resolution as an expression of national unity, telling themselves that since the measure did not have the force of law, it could not impair in any legal or constitutional sense the presidential power. It passed, 69 to 21.

Vietnam in 1954: A Resolution Not Adopted. The turmoil born of Harry Truman's confrontations with the Congress carried a lesson for his successor. Dwight Eisenhower believed that Truman had made a tactical blunder in committing American forces to Korea on his own, that the lack of unity between president and Congress at the outset contributed to disunity later when the war became unpopular.[57] So, when his administration confronted its first test—in Indochina in 1954—he made formal congressional support a prerequisite of intervention. By March, communist rebels were clearly driving the colonial French army out of northern Vietnam, and the crucial battle was under way at Dien Bien Phu, where a French garrison was besieged. The Eisenhower administration was split into the "hawks" and "doves" that were to become so familiar in later years, and the leading hawk, Admiral Arthur W. Radford, chairman of the Joint Chiefs of Staff, had prepared a plan to enter the war with air and naval power to rescue Dien Bien Phu. The plan was presented to the National Security Council, but Eisenhower made his approval conditional on "favorable action by the Congress," as well as "a favorable climate of free world opinion."[58] So Secretary of State John Foster Dulles tested congressional opinion at a secret meeting April 3 with eight leaders of both parties in both houses. The leaders, notably Senate Democratic Leader Lyndon B. Johnson of Texas, raised many questions, particularly about support by America's European allies, and Dulles later told Eisenhower that congressional approval of a resolution supporting intervention would depend on participation by other nations and on firm assurance that if the United States entered the war, the French would not pull out.[59] The secretary consulted ambassadors in Washington and then flew off to London and Paris,

57. Robert J. Donovan, *Eisenhower: The Inside Story* (Harper, 1956), p. 305.
58. Dwight D. Eisenhower, *Mandate for Change* (Doubleday, 1963), p. 340.
59. Ibid., p. 347.

but he failed to obtain the support required and Eisenhower stood by while the French capitulated.[60] Then followed the Geneva conference, which partitioned Vietnam between a communist North and a noncommunist South.

The reservations expressed by the congressional leaders undoubtedly contributed to the president's decision to stay out of war in 1954, but the single meeting with five senators and three representatives cannot be construed as any significant shift in the balance of presidential and congressional decisionmaking in favor of the legislators. The congressional leaders, in effect, shifted their role in the decision to America's allies. But this course was acceptable to the administration; some accounts, indeed, suggest that Dulles and Eisenhower had always made their support of the Radford plan contingent on allied participation and that the April 3 meeting only reached a consensus on the administration's previously held position.[61] There is little reason to doubt that if the president had made the opposite decision—with or without allied participation—the Congress would have gone along. His party was in the majority in both houses, and among the Democratic minority were those who said, like Senator Mike Mansfield of Montana, the assistant Democratic leader, "the President and the Secretary of State . . . and they alone, must lay down our official policy," or, like Senator Henry M. Jackson of Washington, "Then let us get behind that policy and let the world know that the Congress supports the President."[62] Or like the influential Senator Richard B. Russell of Georgia, who on being told by Assistant Secretary of State Thruston B. Morton that President Eisenhower had decided to send two hundred advisers to the government of the newly independent South Vietnam, reportedly responded that the number would inevitably be multiplied and "I think this is the greatest mistake this country's ever made. I could not be more opposed to it . . . but if he does it I will never raise my voice."[63]

The Formosa Resolution. Next year the Congress lined up behind the President. When the Chinese communists began to menace the Nationalist-held islands of Quemoy and Matsu in 1955, President Eisenhower asked for a congressional resolution authorizing the president to employ American forces in any way necessary to defend Formosa and other territories under Nation-

---

60. For an account of the April 3 meeting, see Chalmers M. Roberts, "The Day We Didn't Go to War," *Reporter*, September 14, 1954, pp. 31–35.

61. See, for instance, John Robinson Beal, *John Foster Dulles: A Biography* (Harper and Bros., 1967), pp. 207–08; and Marvin Kalb and Elie Abel, *Roots of Involvement: The U.S. in Asia—1784–1971* (Norton, 1971), p. 77. Eisenhower's own memoirs refer not to participation in the war by any allies except the French, but only to "a favorable climate of free world opinion"; *Mandate for Change*, p. 340.

62. *Congressional Record*, April 14, 1954, p. 5112; April 6, 1954, p. 4681.

63. David Halberstam, *The Best and the Brightest* (Fawcett, 1969), p. 181.

alist control. Eisenhower retreated only a little way from the Truman view that such a resolution was unnecessary: "Authority for some of the actions which might be required would be inherent in the authority of the Commander-in-Chief. I would not hesitate, so far as my Constitutional powers extend, to take whatever emergency action might be forced upon us." Yet the word "some" and the qualifying clause suggested the existence of a limit to the presidential power. However, unlike Truman, Eisenhower thought congressional action would be desirable in any case. It would remove any doubt about his power and "any doubt regarding our readiness to fight, if necessary."[64] Eisenhower was convinced that the Korean War was due at least in part to the "mistaken Communist notion" that the United States would not defend Korea, since the country's intention to do so had not been proclaimed.[65]

"How wise it is," exulted Republican Representative Hugh Scott of Pennsylvania, "to come to the Congress, in accordance with the Constitution. . . . How different from the action of the Truman administration which sent us to war first and told the Congress about it some hours later." Senator George, chairman of the Foreign Relations Committee, expressed his "profound belief that the President was right in coming to the Congress."[66] Speaker Sam Rayburn was less gracious; he was quoted as saying the president had all the power he needed "but he wanted it done this way, so it will be done this way."[67] The resolution drew only three dissenting votes in each house and was signed into law five days after the president sent his request to the Congress. The Chinese backed down, and the crisis passed.

The Middle East Resolution. Two years later, citing Soviet expansionism in the Middle East and the instability of the region in the wake of the brief Suez War of 1956, President Eisenhower asked for a grant of authority to employ American forces as he might find necessary in the Middle East.[68] But this time, in the absence of an immediate crisis, he encountered unexpected misgivings among the majority Democrats in the Congress. In the House, Clement J. Zablocki of Wisconsin protested against a blank-check delegation to the president of the Congress's constitutional power to declare war. Sidney R. Yates of Illinois complained that the president was asking the Congress

64. "Special Message to the Congress Regarding United States Policy for the Defense of Formosa, January 24, 1955," *Public Papers of the Presidents: Dwight D. Eisenhower, 1955* (GPO, 1959), pp. 209–10.
65. *Mandate for Change*, p. 467.
66. *Congressional Record*, January 24, 1955, p. 627; January 27, 1955, p. 814.
67. Arthur Krock, column in *New York Times*, inserted in ibid., January 27, 1955, p. 814.
68. "Special Message to the Congress on the Situation in the Middle East, delivered to a joint session in person, January 5, 1957," *Public Papers: Eisenhower, 1957* (GPO, 1958), pp. 6–16.

to share responsibility without sharing "the facts and information which he possesses and which provoked his doctrine." Abraham J. Multer of New York took a position just the opposite of Zablocki's: "The buck has been passed to us by the President. Under the Constitution it is his duty and he has the power to make the foreign policy." And James Roosevelt of California warned that the precedent of the president's "virtually giving over to Congress power which properly does not belong to the Congress" could have "fatal results," if a weak president faced a crisis when the Congress was out of session. William M. Colmer of Mississippi probably spoke for the House majority when he said: "We cannot make foreign policy in the Congress of the United States; that would be impossible. You know where that would lead to. So we must rely on the Chief Executive and those who would advise him. In fact, . . . it is the constitutional duty of the President to make our foreign policy."[69]

In the Senate a way was found to avoid a constitutional debate. Instead of authorizing the president to use the armed forces, an amendment by Democrats Hubert H. Humphrey of Minnesota and Mike Mansfield stated that "if the President determines the necessity thereof, the United States is prepared to use armed force to assist" victims of communist aggression. A proposal by Wayne L. Morse, now a Democrat, to make such use subject to subsequent congressional approval or disapproval was opposed by the administration and defeated, 64 to 28. But the second of the blank-check resolutions drew more opposing votes than did the original one dealing with Formosa. On the final roll calls, 19 senators and 61 representatives voted no.

Sixteen months later, the president ordered a landing of marines in Lebanon, at the invitation of the government of that country. In doing so, however, he relied on his powers as commander in chief (presumably because Lebanon was not threatened by "international communism," which the Middle East resolution addressed). A few members, including Morse, insisted that the president had exceeded his powers, but even Morse conceded that the Congress, once the flag had been carried into Lebanon, could only "close ranks behind that flag."[70]

69. *Congressional Record*, January 29, 1957, pp. 1152, 1200, 1199, 1183, 1149.

70. Ibid., July 15, 1958, p. 13769. When President Kennedy authorized an invasion at Cuba's Bay of Pigs in 1961, Morse was not so ready to close ranks. He revived the old Madisonian argument that "foreign policy does not belong to the President . . . and to the Secretary of State. They are but the administrators of the people's foreign policy" as determined by the people's representatives. And those representatives had not been consulted or even advised. Ibid., April 24, 1961, p. 6575. But Morse's was the only voice raised on the floor of the Congress to contest the use of force in the abortive invasion of Cuba. Senator J. William Fulbright, Democrat of Arkansas, chairman of the Foreign Relations Committee, had at Kennedy's invitation participated in the meeting where the decision to proceed with the operation was made, but as an individual rather than as a representative of the legislative branch. He advised against the plan. "The Lessons of the Cuban Disaster," *Saturday Evening Post*, June 24, 1961, pp. 26–27, 68–70.

The Cuba Resolution. In 1962 the threat of Cuban communism as a subversive, or even an aggressive, force elsewhere in the western hemisphere brought forth another resolution pledging the use of American force, if necessary to contain communism. This one evaded the constitutional question altogether,[71] by simply declaring the determination of the United States to prevent the spread of communism in the hemisphere. How the decision would be made, in an emergency, was left to be determined. But the president had asserted that "as President and Commander in Chief" he had all the authority he needed to use military force in any way that might be necessary. The Congress did not reject that view, and the debate left no doubt that most members thought it entirely appropriate to leave the decision to the president. Senator Humphrey, for instance, said the merit of the resolution was that "the President retains his flexibility to deal with the situation as he sees fit." Senator John Sherman Cooper, Kentucky Republican, also backed the president's right to act in whatever way he deemed advisable: "Only the President of the United States—by virtue of his powers as Commander in Chief, to direct the foreign policy of this country—can make the decisions . . . which this resolution supports. . . . the chief effect of this resolution is to give our support to the President of the United States in the use of his powers. I think that is proper." And in the House, Peter Frelinghuysen, Jr., of New Jersey, a Republican member of the Foreign Affairs Committee, acknowledged that the president "must make the final determination" regarding any action to be taken and "his definition of this Nation's security, or its vital interests, will be binding on us all."[72]

No one in either House arose to contradict that view. In a series of questions Senator John A. Carroll, Colorado Democrat, came closest. He suggested that if the president could establish a blockade, which is defined in international law as an act of war, then the war-making power had indeed been delegated. But Carroll seemed satisfied when he was assured that President Kennedy had promised to consult the Congress before taking any so drastic a step.[73]

And from one wing of the opposition party in the Congress came criticism that the president was not using his powers vigorously enough. Represent-

71. The original State Department draft asserted presidential authority and so raised the constitutional question, but when some senators objected the language was modified. Thomas F. Eagleton, *War and Presidential Power: A Chronicle of Congressional Surrender* (Liveright, 1974), pp. 77–78; Schlesinger, *Imperial Presidency*, pp. 174–75. When the time came to act, during the missile crisis of October 1962, the president cited his constitutional authority, which he said had been "endorsed" by the congressional resolution. "Proclamation 3504: Interdiction of the Delivery of Offensive Weapons to Cuba," *Public Papers of the Presidents: John F. Kennedy, 1962* (GPO, 1963), pp. 809–10.

72. *Congressional Record*, September 20, 1962, pp. 20051, 20033; September 26, 1962, p. 20866.

73. Ibid., September 20, 1962, pp. 20046–47.

ative Melvin R. Laird of Wisconsin (later secretary of defense) wanted the president to establish a clear policy to use force "to rid the Cuban people of their Communist masters." Kennedy's "inaction and indecision are almost unbelievable," said Laird.[74] No suggestion here that the Congress might be to blame, that the clear policy he demanded should be originated by the Congress, that the Congress indeed should declare the war he wanted.

The Berlin Resolution. A few days later, the Congress passed a similar resolution to deal with a crisis that developed over Berlin, when Soviet Prime Minister Nikita Khrushchev challenged the rights of the United States, Britain, and France to maintain military forces in the western part of the city and threatened to cut off their access to it. President Kennedy had responded with a categorical declaration that the United States would remain in Berlin, and members of both parties in the Congress moved to put that body on record in full support of his position. Like the Cuba resolution, the Berlin statement made no reference to presidential power, simply declaring that "the United States is determined to prevent by whatever means may be necessary, including the use of arms, any violation of [its] rights by the Soviet Union directly or through others." Since the president was already on record, the Congress acted—without dissent and almost without discussion—through a concurrent resolution, which does not require the president's assent.

The president's constitutional position appeared clearer in this case than in the earlier ones, because U.S. forces were in Berlin in accordance with a formal agreement signed at the end of World War II by the three western Allies and the Soviet Union. Yet the ambivalence of the Congress was reflected in the debate when one of the resolution's backers, Representative Katharine St. George, Republican of New York, was able to say in the same speech that the resolution "gives the President . . . all of the power that he could possibly need or desire" but "he does not, of course, come to us for that power; it is not necessary."[75]

So by this time a wealth of precedent had been established, through a dozen years of successive crises, that in the worldwide confrontation with communism it was for the president to set the policy, the Congress to support. In its blank-check resolutions, the Congress agreed in advance to whatever he might do. The Formosa resolution explicitly delegated the war-making power. The Middle East resolution avoided making an outright delegation, yet it gave an advance commitment to support whatever the president might do to effectuate the objectives of the resolution, including making war—

74. Ibid., September 24, 1962, pp. 20508, 20512.
75. Ibid., October 5, 1962, pp. 22619–20.

which amounts to the equivalent of delegation. The Cuba resolution only declared a national policy, leaving implicit—but spread on the pages of the *Congressional Record*—that it would be for the president to determine how, and when, the terms of the resolution would be applied. The Berlin resolution did likewise.

"In the decade after Korea," wrote Arthur Schlesinger, Jr., "Congress receded not alone from the effort to control the war-making power but almost from the effort to participate in it, except on occasions when national-security zealots on the Hill condemned the executive branch for inadequate bellicosity."[76]

Indeed, one of the most thoughtful and experienced members of the Congress, Senator J. William Fulbright, Democrat of Arkansas, chairman of the Foreign Relations Committee, argued for recognizing and regularizing the flow of power over foreign policy to the president, in perhaps as forceful an acknowledgment of the weaknesses of the Congress as has ever come from a member of that body.

> I wonder whether the time has not arrived, or indeed already passed, when we must give the Executive a measure of power in the conduct of our foreign affairs that we have hitherto jealously withheld.
>
> The source of an effective foreign policy under our system is Presidential power. . . . It is not within our powers to confer wisdom or perception on the Presidential person. It *is* within our power to grant or deny him authority. It is my contention that for the existing requirements of American foreign policy we have hobbled the President by too niggardly a grant of power.

76. *Imperial Presidency*, p. 169. In other aspects of military policy as well, the decline of Congress was evident. "Military policy is made by the Department of Defense. Our committee is a real estate committee," an influential member of the House Armed Service Committee told Lewis A. Dexter in the 1950s, and the same words were used by a committee staff member. Dexter, "Congressmen and the Making of Military Policy," in Robert L. Peabody and Nelson W. Polsby, eds., *New Perspectives on the House of Representatives* (Rand McNally, 1963), pp. 311–12. Francis Wilcox noted that "a proposal to close a navy base in Brooklyn excited far more interest [in the armed services committees] than building one in Cam Ranh Bay [in Vietnam]." *Congress, the Executive*, p. 84. Samuel P. Huntington, *The Common Defense* (Columbia University Press, 1961), pp. 127–28, observed that the congressional power over the size and composition of the armed forces had "faded away" and "the executive determined the overall level of military effort and the strategy by which it was shaped. . . . The fundamental decisions to maintain a massive nuclear retaliatory force, to construct a continental defense system, and to develop or not to develop forces for conventional limited wars were all made in the executive branch." Huntington attributes the congressional abdication to the consensus on broad policy objectives that prevailed during the cold war period and to the fact that the "interest groups" contesting military policy issues are almost entirely agencies of the executive branch, making those issues peculiarly appropriate for settlement by the executive (pp. 131–32). He observes that congressional influence is exercised by lobbying the executive (pp. 135–46). Holbert N. Carroll a few years later found members of Congress were giving low priority to the broad issues of foreign and national security affairs. "The Congress and National Security Policy," in David B. Truman, ed., *The Congress and America's Future* (Prentice-Hall, 1965), p. 171. These attitudes changed when the congressional revolt against the Vietnam War gained momentum, and the Congress began to assert itself on military questions, too, beginning with the curtailment of the anti-ballistic-missile (ABM) program. For a discussion of the ABM struggle, see Alton Frye, *A Responsible Congress: The Politics of National Security* (McGraw-Hill, 1975), chap. 2.

. . . It is exceedingly difficult—if not impossible—to devise unified policies oriented to a clear and definitive conception of the national interest through a system in which power and responsibility for foreign policy are "shared and overlapping." Policies thus evolved are likely to be ill-coordinated, short-ranged, and often unsuccessful, while the responsibility for failure is placed squarely on the President, neither "shared" nor "overlapping." . . .

. . . While Congress has many powers under the Constitution, having to do with foreign affairs, these powers do not enable the Congress to initiate or shape foreign policy, but to implement, modify, or thwart the proposals of the President. . . .

Foreign policy is scarcely ever the crucial factor in the election of Congressmen. . . . At no point in his rise to powerful office does the typically successful politician find it imperative to school himself in the requirements and problems of foreign policy. Indeed his preoccupation with local matters and with political machinery is virtually *bound* to prevent him from acquiring any breadth or depth of knowledge in the field of foreign affairs. . . .

. . . It is distasteful and dangerous to vest the executive with powers unchecked and unbalanced. My question is whether we have any choice but to do so.

. . . The President alone can act to mobilize our power and resources toward the realization of clearly defined objectives and to wean the American people and their representatives from the luxuries of parochialism and self-indulgence that they can no longer afford.[77]

The Tonkin Gulf Resolution. On the basis of the whole postwar record, presidents had every reason to believe that the Congress expected them to act decisively to check communist expansion wherever it might be threatening, and that it would support them when they did. The gravest of all the threats, after Korea, was in Vietnam; presidents did act, and congressional support was unstinting—as long as things went well.

The partition of Vietnam in 1954 had brought an end to overt hostilities, but not to communist guerrilla activities in the south supported from North Vietnam. By 1961, much of the South Vietnamese countryside had fallen under communist control, and the government of South Vietnam pleaded for an increase in the military aid it had been receiving since the French withdrawal. President Kennedy sent instructors, helicopter pilots, and support personnel, then 10,000 troops to train the Vietnamese army, then 5,000 more. There was not even grumbling in the Senate. Mike Mansfield, the majority leader, praised Kennedy (and Eisenhower as well) for keeping the

77. "American Foreign Policy in the 20th Century under an 18th-Century Constitution," a lecture delivered at Cornell University, May 1961, *Cornell Law Quarterly*, vol. 47 (1961–62), pp. 1–13. Fulbright often made this argument in legislative hearings and debates, as, for instance, in opposing an amendment designed to bar assistance to the United Arab Republic in 1963; *Congressional Record*, November 7, 1963, p. 21366. The amendment was adopted, and a month later President Johnson was criticizing "the growing tendency to hamstring executive flexibility with rigid legislative provisions wholly inappropriate and potentially dangerous in a world of rapid change." "Statement by the President Upon Signing the Foreign Assistance Act, December 16, 1963," *Public Papers of the Presidents: Lyndon B. Johnson, 1963–64* (GPO, 1965), vol. 1, p. 58.

Congress informed. "We have had, if anything, a surfeit of information on the situation in Vietnam and on our policies with respect thereto," he told the Senate. But, he added, "it is the President's responsibility to decide and to act. It is ours to advise . . . and, to the extent it is constitutionally required, to consent." But in advising, the Congress should not "look over the President's shoulder 24 hours of a day and . . . tell him how to conduct the foreign policy of the United States. That is the President's responsibility. . . . It is in the Nation's interest that he be supported in exercising it. It will be a disservice to the Nation . . . to impede him, for whatever reason, in exercising it." When President Diem was assassinated, another dove-to-be, Senator Frank Church, Democrat of Idaho, expressed the hope that "we will share in helping the leaders of the new Vietnamese Government to successfully prosecute the war against the Communists." Mansfield thought that was an "appropriate time . . . for the executive branch to reassess policies."[78] Significantly, he did not suggest a congressional role in the reassessment, or in the policymaking.

In this mood, it was a short step for the Congress to take itself formally out of Vietnam policymaking, through another blank-check delegation of power, at the time of the Tonkin Gulf incident. On August 2, 1964, President Johnson told the Congress and the country, the U.S. destroyer *Maddox* had been attacked without provocation by North Vietnamese torpedo boats, and two days later the *Maddox* and another destroyer were attacked again. The United States retaliated against the torpedo boats and against supporting facilities on the coast of North Vietnam. Johnson then asked for an expression of congressional support, such as those given his predecessors when trouble rose over Formosa, the Middle East, and Cuba. Chairman Fulbright rammed the resolution through the Senate Foreign Relations Committee after brief testimony from the secretaries of state and defense, and with but one dissenting vote—that of Oregon's Wayne Morse. It passed the Senate the next day, August 7, with only Morse and Ernest Gruening, Democrat of Alaska, voting in the negative. In the House there were no dissenting votes at all.

The authors of the Vietnam resolution went back beyond the Cuba resolution of 1962 to choose as their model the stronger language of the Middle East resolution of 1957, which explicitly committed the Congress to follow presidential leadership. The new measure declared that "the United States is . . . prepared, as the President determines, to take all necessary steps, including the use of armed force, to assist any protocol or member state of

78. *Congressional Record*, February 15, 1962, p. 2326; November 5, 1962, pp. 21056, 21061.

the Southeast Asia Collective Defense Treaty requesting assistance in defense of its freedom."[79] There was no question about the scope of the power that would be lodged in the president. The only issue was the recurrent constitutional question—the extent to which the president already had the power and the extent to which additional authority was being delegated—an issue the measure was drafted carefully to skirt.

Senator Fulbright, the sponsor of the resolution, interpreted its language both ways. The resolution, he said in answer to a question, "would authorize whatever the Commander in Chief feels is necessary," including the landing of large armies in Vietnam or China. But later in the debate he expressed doubt that the resolution "would in any way be a deterrent, a prohibition, a limitation, or an expansion of the President's power to use the Armed Forces in a different way or more extensively then he is now using them." And later, in even sharper words: "I do not believe the joint resolution would substantially alter the President's power to use whatever means seemed appropriate under the circumstances." If the Congress considered the action inappropriate, it could terminate the resolution. But still later, when John Sherman Cooper asked whether, "if the President decided that it was necessary to use such force as could lead into war, we will give that authority by this resolution?" Senator Fulbright answered in the affirmative. But he assured the Senate the president had no intention to commit combat forces to Vietnam.[80]

Democrats Frank Lausche of Ohio and Jennings Randolph of West Virginia, in supporting the resolution, asserted flatly that the resolution delegated congressional authority to the president. But Senator John J. Sparkman, Democrat of Alabama, referring to the power conferred by this and earlier resolutions, said, "I have always felt that the President had such power." Two veteran members of the Foreign Relations Committee, Hubert Humphrey and George Aiken, Republican of Vermont, concurred. So did Senator Everett Dirksen of Illinois, the Republican leader: "He does not have to ask Congress about the deployment of troops, submarines, bombers, and fighter planes." Wayne Morse argued that the "predated declaration of war" violated the Constitution and denounced "government by executive supremacy," but only Senator Gruening agreed with him. Senator Fulbright had the last word for the proponents: "But fundamentally, under our system, it is the President, as our representative in these activities, who must necessarily have the dominant role, however jealous we may be of our own privileges. . . . But

79. Ibid., August 6, 1964, p. 18398.
80. Ibid., pp. 18403, 18407, 18409.

in dealing with the Nation's security or with threatened warfare, we must rely to a great extent on the decisions of the Executive. We always have a reserve power. . . . We can always later impeach him, if we like, if we believe . . . that he has betrayed the interests of the country."[81]

A decade later, this same Fulbright was to say of this period that the Congress had permitted the United States to join "the global mainstream, becoming, for purposes of foreign policy, a Presidential dictatorship."[82]

Congressional Acquiescence in Presidential War

The mood of 1964 continued into the following year, when the Congress twice confirmed the president's power when he ordered U.S. forces into combat.

The first test came in the Dominican Republic. A revolution broke out on the Caribbean island late in April 1965, the government was unseated, and chaos ruled as separate groups of revolutionaries contended for power. On April 28, U.S. Ambassador W. Tapley Bennett, Jr., cabled an urgent plea for a landing of marines to protect Americans and nationals of other countries. "I thought that we could not and we did not hesitate," President Johnson explained later. "I knew there was no time to talk, to consult, or to delay. . . . I do not think that the American people expect their President to hesitate or vacillate in the face of danger . . . when life is in peril." And he ordered four hundred marines to land on the island.[83]

Then he consulted the leaders of the Congress. "I reported the decisions that this Government considers necessary," he said. "The members of the leadership expressed their support of these decisions."[84] Majority Leader Carl Albert told the House that the president's action "was not only correct; it was absolutely necessary."[85] Senate Majority Leader Mansfield concurred.

But a few days later the intervention took on a second purpose. Ambassador Bennett had warned Washington that one of the revolutionary factions was under communist control, and President Johnson dispatched another two thousand marines to the Dominican Republic on May 2. After another

81. Ibid., August 6, 1964, pp. 18419, 18422; August 7, 1964, pp. 18456, 18462; August 6, 1964, p. 18427; August 7, 1964, pp. 18442–48, 18462.

82. J. William Fulbright, "Congress and Foreign Policy," in *Appendices: U.S. Commission on the Organization of the Government for the Conduct of Foreign Policy*, vol. 5, pp. 58–59.

83. "Radio and Television Report to the American people, on the Situation in the Dominican Republic, May 2, 1965," *Public Papers: Johnson, 1965* (GPO, 1966), vol. 1, pp. 470–71.

84. "Statement by the President Upon Ordering Troops into the Dominican Republic, April 28, 1965," ibid., p. 461.

85. *Congressional Record*, April 29, 1965, p. 8855.

meeting with the congressional leaders later that day, Johnson announced that forty-five hundred more marines would be on their way "to help prevent another Communist state in this hemisphere."[86] Again the congressional leaders echoed the president. "It is the hope of everybody in this country that a repetition of what happened in Cuba has been prevented by the dispatch with which the President acted," Majority Whip Hale Boggs of Louisiana told the House. For the Republicans, Representative Leslie Arends of Illinois, the minority whip, applauded the president's action, and Hugh Scott of Pennsylvania observed that "had we moved as rapidly and effectively in Cuba as we have done in Santo Domingo, Cuba today would not be a Communist country."[87] Senate Republican Leader Dirksen reportedly assured Johnson, "We're behind you one hundred percent."[88] No member was more fervent in praise of the president than Senator Church; he "strongly commended" the president for his "swift action" to foreclose the "calamity" of a "Communist seizure of power. . . . His initiative . . . deserves the strongest praise. . . . we have every reason to applaud the President."[89] Not a word was spoken in opposition in either House. No member rose like Senator Taft fifteen years before to question the president's right to pursue his course without formal congressional sanction of any kind.

At this same time in 1965, the president had reached the conclusion that a communist takeover in South Vietnam could be prevented only by the commitment of a large contingent of American forces to actual fighting. While he asserted full power to act under the Constitution, the Southeast Asia Treaty, and the Gulf of Tonkin resolution,[90] he nevertheless sought an indirect form of congressional approval, by asking for a special appropriation of $700 million for military operations in Vietnam. "Each member of Congress who supports this request is also voting to persist in our effort to halt communist aggression in South Vietnam," he said in a special message to the Congress on May 4. "Each is saying that the Congress and the President stand united before the world."[91] On the same day, he summoned the members of the

86. "Radio and Television report . . . May 2, 1965," *Public Papers: Johnson, 1965,* vol. 1, p. 473. Eventually, 30,000 troops were on the island. *Congressional Quarterly Almanac, 1965,* p. 514.

87. *Congressional Record,* May 3, 1965, p. 9117; May 5, 1965, p. 9456.

88. Rowland Evans and Robert Novak, *Lyndon B. Johnson: The Exercise of Power* (New American Library, 1966), p. 517.

89. *Congressional Record,* May 5, 1965, p. 9451.

90. See, for example, "The President's News Conference of June 17, 1965" and "The President's News Conference of February 26, 1966," *Public Papers: Johnson, 1965,* vol. 2, p. 680, and *1966* (GPO, 1967), vol. 1, pp. 221–22.

91. "Special Message to the Congress Requesting Additional Appropriations for Military Needs in Viet-Nam, May 4, 1965," ibid., *1966,* vol. 1, p. 494.

three committees of each House most directly concerned to the White House for a briefing.

Both houses responded with the resounding expression of national unity the president had sought. Clamping strict time limitations on those who might dissent, the House passed the bill the next day and the Senate the day after that. The president signed it on May 7, three days after the request was made.

For the most part, the debate consisted of anticommunist orations, punctuated with praise of presidential leadership. House Appropriations Chairman George Mahon, Democrat of Texas, observed that the appropriation was not necessary, since the president already had the authority and could transfer funds from other accounts to the Vietnam operation but, he said, "I am glad we have a President who takes the Congress into his confidence on important international matters." There were a few dissenters, but they were lonely. One was Representative Edith Green, Democrat of Oregon: "I think it also clearly means the relinquishment by Congress of its Constitutional authority to declare war, for if the President can direct bombing raids on North Vietnam by simple Executive fiat, why can he not direct similar action against any other nation at any other time? Why bother to ask? . . . I cannot in good conscience lend myself to that kind of usurpation of Congressional power." Another was Senator Gaylord Nelson, Democrat of Wisconsin: "At a time in history when the Senate should be vindicating its historic reputation as the greatest deliberative body in the world we are stumbling over each other to see who can say 'yea' the quickest and the loudest." Another was Wayne Morse: "They [the houses of the Congress] will be voting to turn the conduct of foreign policy over to the Pentagon and the Joint Chiefs of Staff. They will be voting to amend the Constitution by taking away from Congress the power to declare war."[92] The vote was 408 to 7 in the House and 88 to 3 in the Senate, although this understated somewhat the opposition. A few members made clear that they opposed, or at least questioned the president's policy but would not vote to deny supplies and support to the forces that had been committed to the Vietnam War.

As those forces rose from 23,000 at the end of 1964 to 181,000 a year later, 389,000 a year after that, and 500,000 by the end of 1967,[93] the Congress expressed its support by giving the president, year by year, the funds he

92. *Congressional Record*, May 5, 1965, pp. 9518, 9536; May 6, 1965, pp. 9759, 9504.
93. Department of Defense announcements, summarized in *Congressional Quarterly Almanac, 1966*, pp. 393–94, and *1967*, p. 925.

asked, and it left to him the policy decisions. In the spate of studies of Vietnam decisionmaking during the period of escalation, hardly a reference is made to the nation's legislative body. The rising challenge to presidential war was centered outside the Congress, not within it, and the crucial arenas of policy debate turned out to be not the nation's legislative body but its campuses and its media, and then the 1968 Democratic national convention at Chicago and that year's presidential campaign. President Johnson chose to renounce his chance for reelection, and both major party candidates responded to the peace movement with promises to find ways to wind down the war.

After that, the Congress began also to respond. In 1969 it gingerly took the first steps to assert control over any phase of Southeast Asia policy, when it adopted a Church amendment to prohibit the use of ground troops in Laos and Thailand. Then, as it moved toward collision with President Nixon on a long series of issues, and as popular disillusionment with the Vietnam War continually broadened and deepened, the Congress was finally roused to undertake a searching reexamination of attitudes and processes that over three decades had made the president the virtually exclusive master of foreign policy—free to wage war wherever, by whatever means, and on whatever scale he chose.

CHAPTER VI

The President
as Chief Legislator

SOMETIME over the course of fifty years the nineteenth century attitude of the Congress toward the president-as-legislator reversed itself.[1] If in the 1880s presidents "did not sway the councils and guide the policy" of their own party in the Congress, as Lord Bryce wrote, they assuredly did by the 1930s. The legislators no longer took private pressure from presidents on legislative matters as a "personal affront," as Senator Hoar attested they once did, nor looked on advice from any outside source as "gratuitous impertinence," as Woodrow Wilson in 1885 said they did; by the later period they had come to expect advice, intervention, and pressure from the president as normal and proper conduct.[2]

If one had to choose a single turning point—the time and events that had the greatest impact on congressional acceptance of the president as chief legislator—it would be the famed Hundred Days of Franklin Roosevelt. In the hectic opening years of the New Deal era the Congress itself acted to institutionalize the president as legislative leader, or acquiesced in his assertion of that role. It conditioned and organized itself as primarily a responding rather than an initiating body. So the institutional mechanisms that would have been necessary for it to develop as the dominant initiator and determiner of policy atrophied, or were not formed at all.

Yet even before the Hundred Days, there were signs of erosion in the

1. "The President as Chief Legislator" is the title of a section of James MacGregor Burns, *Congress on Trial: The Legislative Process and the Administrative State* (1949; Gordian, 1966), and the term *chief legislator* is in Pendleton Herring, *Presidential Leadership* (Farrar and Rinehart, 1940), p. 12.

2. James Bryce, *The American Commonwealth*, 2d ed. (Macmillan, 1889), vol. 1, p. 210; George F. Hoar, *Autobiography of Seventy Years* (Scribner's, 1903), vol. 2, p. 46; Woodrow Wilson, *Congressional Government: A Study in American Politics* (1885; World, 1956), p. 270.

traditional Capitol Hill view that the chief executive should stick to executing and stay out of legislating. With each strong president of the new century, and even with some of the weaker ones, new precedents supporting presidential intervention were established. And, in facing a succession of aggressive leaders in the White House, the Congress turned out to be a weak antagonist. However individual members might feel about their constitutional prerogatives, some basic aspects of the whole institutional system as it had evolved from its constitutional base stood in the way of a successful collective defense of their institution against assertive presidential leadership.

The Constitution did not anticipate political parties and their national nominating conventions. But from the time they came into being, any presidential nominee emerging from his party's convention could lay claim to recognition as the preeminent leader of his party, if he chose to fill that role. He was its chosen spokesman and its standard bearer. And once vigorous direct campaigning by presidential candidates became the mode, in William Jennings Bryan's day, it was the candidate who took the party's case to the electorate and asked its mandate and, if victorious, received it. If after inauguration, therefore, he saw fit to press the Congress to execute the mandate, the legislators were in a weak position to claim that legislation was not properly within the scope of presidential leadership.

Moreover, if they had constitutional qualms about an expansive presidential role, they confronted a tactical dilemma in expressing them. In most circumstances, it is not possible for a legislator to oppose presidential leadership on institutional grounds except by opposing the substance of the policy. So the assertion of the congressional "right" to take the initiative on legislation tended to come mainly from the partisan opposition, and that in turn was bound to provoke a partisan response by supporters of the president. Inevitably when the president's allies rallied to support his substantive position, they found themselves defending and justifying his assertion of presidential power also. Thus when party control of the White House shifted, those legislators who had been criticizing presidential leadership ostensibly on constitutional grounds would find themselves (like Cordell Hull on the issue of delegating power over tariff rates) defending it. In time, as party control moved back and forth, the constitutional argument was bound to sound to both sides as partisan and hypocritical.

To the public at large, it must have seemed so from the beginning of the era of strong presidents, for there is no sign that the public penalized such presidents for their assertion of legislative leadership. Quite the contrary, the two Roosevelts and Wilson all won reelection, the Roosevelts by thundering majorities. After a time, the Congress would see resistance to the concept of the president as chief legislator as not only hypocritical but also futile and politically unpopular, and the institutionalization of the president's position as legislative leader could proceed.

Before the Hundred Days

That the nineteenth century norm of congressional initiative, and resistance to presidential leadership, lasted until the end of the century is attested by David W. Brady's study of congressional behavior during the McKinley administration. Congressmen then "did not expect a legislative program from the President; rather the *leaders* of the two houses of Congress provided the legislative program with which the Congress would deal. . . . Congress in the 1890s was the institution in which legislation was hammered out, and from which decisions were issued. . . . the House of Representatives in the late 1890s . . . served the function of chief legislator." In the Fifty-fifth Congress of 1897–98, for example, the measure given highest priority by the House leadership—a tariff bill—was written by the Congress evidently without even drafting help from the executive, despite the complexity of the measure. The House apparently "resented attempts by the presidency to become involved in the business of passing legislation."[3]

Theodore Roosevelt's accession to the presidency found a strong president confronting a Congress still wedded to the nineteenth century prerogatives, and so the legislature's ways were not to change abruptly. Roosevelt had a program—he was the first president, says Robert Luce, to speak publicly of "my policies"[4]—and he sent the Congress forceful advice, but always in general terms. He stopped short of appending draft legislation to his messages, as later presidents were to do, and to a critic who chided him about the generality of his antitrust recommendations he wrote: "Are you aware . . . of the extreme unwisdom of my irritating Congress by fixing the details

3. *Congressional Voting in a Partisan Era: A Comparison of the McKinley Houses and the Modern House of Representatives* (University Press of Kansas, 1973), pp. 19–21, 167. Mary Parker Follett observed in *The Speaker of the House of Representatives* (Longmans, Green, 1896), p. 325, that even the pre-Civil War practice of referring to the president's party in the Congress as the administration party had disappeared by the 1890s "simply because the President has had so slight a share in initiating the legislative policy. His message to the Congress is really an address to the country and has no direct influence upon Congress."

4. *Legislative Problems* (Houghton Mifflin, 1935), p. 212.

of a bill, concerning which they are very sensitive, instead of laying down a general policy?"[5] The Congress "even resents suggestions from administrative officers as impertinent invasions of its independence," Woodrow Wilson could still write in 1908, in the seventh year of Rooseveltian leadership.[6]

President Taft had a program, too, and he was the first modern president to formally present draft legislation to the Congress—arousing the predictable resentment by doing so.[7] Yet in 1912, even though Taft's standing with the Congress had sunk by then to an irretrievable depth, the Senate took occasion formally, if indirectly, to acknowledge his right to invade the legislative province. During the contest over the seating of William Lorimer as a Republican senator from Illinois, Senator Joseph W. Bailey, Texas Democrat, charged that Taft had sought to line up votes against Lorimer. Bailey introduced a resolution condemning presidential interference in questions "involving the right to a seat in the Senate or any other matter relating solely to the duties of Senators." Senator Albert B. Cummins, insurgent Republican of Iowa, thereupon sought to broaden the resolution to cover the ordinary legislative process (matters not exclusively within the jurisdiction of the Senate). It was "a greater impropriety," contended Cummins, "for a president to use the power of his office to induce men in Congress to vote for or vote against a bill which will affect the welfare of ninety millions of people," and he cited admissions by both Roosevelt and Taft that they had tried to obtain votes for bills "through personal solicitation, and under such circumstances as indicated the withdrawal of favor if the representations were not accepted." But the regular Republicans defended such presidential conduct as useful to senators as well as presidents, and Cummins's amendment was defeated on a voice vote. The resolution was passed in its original form.[8]

When the Democrats took control of the Congress in 1913, they went all the way to acceptance of the president as legislative leader. Woodrow Wilson approached this aspect of his job with deep conviction, having written for years of the necessity for the president to act as a prime minister in enacting

5. Letter to the Reverend W. S. Rainsford, December 27, 1902, in Joseph Bucklin Bishop, *Theodore Roosevelt and His Time Shown in His Own Letters* (Scribner's Sons, 1919), vol. 1, p. 233. See Lawrence H. Chamberlain, *The President, Congress and Legislation* (Columbia University Press, 1946), pp. 15–16, for comment about the generality of Roosevelt's recommendations.

6. *Constitutional Government in the United States* (Columbia University Press, 1908), p. 85.

7. W. E. Binkley, "The President as Chief Legislator," *Annals of the American Academy of Political and Social Science*, vol. 307 (September 1956), p. 95. "We challenge any member of Congress to point to any instance in the past history of our Republic where a bill was submitted to a committee of the Congress, drawn at the instance and aid of the President of the United States and declared to be the President's bill, and should be made a law," said the minority report of the House Commerce Committee on a railroad bill in 1910 (H. Rept. 923, 61 Cong. 2 sess., 1910), quoted by Chamberlain, *The President, Congress and Legislation*, pp. 422–23.

8. *Congressional Record*, July 16, 1912, pp. 9125–32.

a party legislative program. The new Democratic majorities, swept into office in the Wilson victory, looked automatically to him for leadership in carrying out the mandate given to a party long out of power. There was no longer even a congressional rival to the president as leader since the powers of the speaker had been stripped in the Revolution of 1910, instigated by Democrats and Republican insurgents.

Wilson seized the opportunity by presenting his legislative recommendations in person before joint sessions of the Congress—the first president in over a hundred years to address the legislature. To achieve the legislative objectives, a wholly new pattern of intimate congressional-executive relations was developed. The details of the New Freedom—tariff legislation, the Federal Reserve Act, antitrust legislation, and other measures—were worked out in joint meetings, some held at the White House, others on Capitol Hill. The press began to write, for the first time, about "administration bills."[9] Wilson "bypassed Speaker Champ Clark and dealt directly with committee chairmen."[10] He intruded into scheduling decisions that were normally the responsibility of legislative leaders—but without objection from them.[11] He put into use the long-neglected president's room in the Capitol for conferences with legislators, in addition to inviting them to the White House. When war broke out, wartime legislation flowed from the executive branch. In Wilson's time, no one inside the Congress or outside doubted who was legislator-in-chief. Some in the Congress cried alarm at this new surge of presidential power, as Senator John D. Works, Republican of California, did in his valedictory address on retirement from the Senate in 1917: "Never in the entire history of the country has the President so completely and defiantly usurped the law-making powers of the government and dictated and forced the course of Congress, and never has the Congress been so submissive or so subservient to a power outside itself. . . . Members of Congress have, under the lash of executive and party domination, surrendered their conscientious convictions and voted against their own sentiments of right and justice."[12]

Congressional committees, noted the *New Republic*, had "become less the moulders of legislation than the recipients who may alter its details. Even on the committees themselves the administration now has its avowed spokesmen . . . very much as a British minister in charge of a measure in the House of

9. Henry Campbell Black, *The Relation of the Executive Power to Legislation* (Princeton University Press, 1919), p. 35.

10. Neil MacNeil, *Forge of Democracy: The House of Representatives* (McKay, 1963), p. 32.

11. Randall B. Ripley, *Party Leaders in the House of Representatives* (Brookings Institution, 1967), pp. 56–57.

12. *Congressional Record*, January 5, 1917, p. 865.

Commons. . . . This is not, it is clear, the government envisaged by the Constitution. . . . But outside of Washington, the old suspicion of executive power is dead."[13]

Nevertheless, the new relationships between president and Congress were not institutionalized. Frank J. Goodnow described the Wilsonian methods of exercising influence as "somewhat secret and indirect, if not underhand."[14] Henry Campbell Black called them "subterranean, underhand, and extra-constitutional" and wanted them brought into the open. Get rid of the "tissue of pretense and camouflage," he urged,[15] by setting up in each house a committee on presidential bills to receive and handle presidential measures.

Early in his term, President Harding tried a feat of legislative leadership as bold as any during the heyday of Wilson's domination of the Congress. On July 12, 1921, he addressed the Senate from the vice president's desk, urging it to defeat a pending soldiers' bonus measure,[16] and in so doing set off angry repercussions in that body. During later debate on the measure, proponents of the bonus attacked the president's appearance as "unconstitutional." The Founding Fathers "were careful," argued Robert M. La Follette, the insurgent Wisconsin Republican, to withhold from the president "any express or implied authority to oppose legislation in the making or to participate in the deliberations and debate of either House in a pending measure." Where would one draw the line? asked William E. Borah, Republican of Idaho. Could the president have stayed for the whole debate, summed up, and rebutted? "So dangerous and far-reaching in its menace to our form of government," intoned Augustus Stanley, Democrat of Kentucky. But the president's supporters defended the constitutionality of his appearance. It was not only the chief executive's right but his "duty," in the view of Frank B. Kellogg, Republican of Minnesota.[17] Harding carried the day; the bill was recommitted. But he set no lasting precedent. In 1932, President Hoover addressed the Senate during consideration of a revenue bill, again arousing partisan recrimination. But since then no president has taken the floor of either house to discuss a specific measure pending before the Congress.

When the nation slipped into the Great Depression following the stock market crash of 1929, President Hoover was slow to assert legislative leadership. This may have been due in part to his limited conception of the

13. "The Future of the Presidency," September 29, 1917, quoted by Black, *Relation of the Executive Power*, pp. 38–39.
14. *Principles of Constitutional Government* (Harper's, 1916), p. 121.
15. *Relation of the Executive Power*, p. 62.
16. *Congressional Record*, July 12, 1921, p. 3597.
17. Ibid., August 22, 1921, pp. 5415–21.

presidential role. The president, he wrote many years later, "must demonstrate constant leadership by proposing social and economic reforms" in his capacity as adviser to the Congress on the state of the union, but "I feel deeply that the independence of the legislative arm must be respected and strengthened. I had little taste for forcing Congressional action."[18] This attitude was compounded by his conception of the role of the government as a whole. "Economic depression cannot be cured by legislative action or executive pronouncement," he told the Congress late in 1930; it must be met by "self-reliance" and voluntary action, and the "best contribution of government" was to encourage individual and community cooperation.[19]

Yet when the regular session of the Congress convened in December 1931, Hoover did present a program. Compared to the New Deal measures that came later, the program—mainly Hoover's proposal to create a Reconstruction Finance Corporation (RFC) to make loans to industries and financial institutions—was limited and timid, although as Hoover contended, his proposals went further than any previous president had been willing to go in earlier economic crises. The Congress promptly created Hoover's RFC, then spent a year demonstrating the futility of the legislative branch as an alternative source of leadership in a government that is politically divided. Democrats controlled the House, Republicans the Senate, and both parties were split internally. Eventually, the Democratic leadership of the two houses got together on a flood relief bill that would give direct aid not just to bankrupt corporations but also to destitute families and individuals, and with the help of insurgent Republicans, it passed. But Hoover vetoed it, and only a stripped-down version finally became law. The issue was left to be settled by the 1932 election, which brought into office a new leader and a Congress committed to support him.

During the Hundred Days

"You are simply placing responsibility on a great man who is willing to assume it," Representative John McDuffie, Democrat of Alabama, told the House one week after Franklin Roosevelt's inauguration during consideration of the first major controversial measure of the new president's program. "Your President, the President you followed, and without whose leadership

18. *The Memoirs of Herbert Hoover: The Cabinet and the Presidency 1920–1933* (Macmillan, 1952), pp. 216–17.
19. William Starr Myers, ed., *The State Papers and Other Public Writings of Herbert Hoover* (Doubleday, Doran, 1934), vol. 1, pp. 429–30.

possibly some of us could not be here, has called you to arms, and . . . the time has come to give the command . . . 'Full speed ahead!' "[20]

That set the tone for the Hundred Days that left their ineradicable mark on presidential-congressional relationships. McDuffie's military allusion was apt, and it was repeated in other forms by other members. Democratic majorities had marched into office behind their leader, and now their duty was to stay in line behind him. Outside the chambers, the emergency was of virtual wartime proportions. The banks were shut throughout the land, closed by presidential order. Nearly a quarter of the working population was unemployed. No one expected the Congress to lead the country out of the morass, nor had the experience of the three preceding years given anyone any reason to think it could. The people looked instead to the man whom they had just voted into office to set things straight. And the Congress looked to him, too—not just the Democrats but many of those in the depleted Republican ranks as well.

After an emergency banking bill to govern reopening of the closed banks had been enacted, the next Roosevelt measure was an economy bill, to grant the president the power to cut government salaries and pension payments, including those of veterans. He had handed it to the Democratic leaders at a night meeting, and they had emerged "a mixture of dazed, determined, and angry men."[21] Thirty-six hours later, it was on the floor of the House, under a rule limiting debate to two hours. Member after member rose to pledge his fealty to presidential leadership in defiance of the veterans' lobby, and the declarations of loyalty, each more passionate than the last, were greeted with applause. Among the Democrats in the crescendo that followed McDuffie's statement were John Young Brown of Kentucky: "The question for us to decide is: Have we confidence in the President of the United States? I had as soon start a mutiny in the face of a foreign foe as start a mutiny today against the program of the President of the United States." [Applause] J. Buell Snyder of Pennsylvania: "My people sent me here because they had faith in the President of the United States; and I am here to support that faith." Martin Dies of Texas: "The Commander in Chief . . . has summoned us to action." Sam Rayburn of Texas: "In every great emergency . . . I have upheld, without stint, the recommendations, and have followed the leadership of the President of the United States." [Applause] Clifton Woodrum of Virginia: "This vote . . . will show whether or not we in Congress are willing to submerge our own individual opinions and follow a great leader

20. *Congressional Record*, March 11, 1933, p. 201.
21. Ernest K. Lindley, *The Roosevelt Revolution: First Phase* (Viking, 1933), p. 88.

whom the people of America have selected to lead them out of this crisis." [Applause] Thomas Blanton of Texas: "The people . . . expect this Congress to open up the way and make it possible for the President to put into execution his promises and his policies." And Joseph W. Byrns of Tennessee, the majority leader: "This . . . is a time to get behind our great leader and to follow him and be guided by his judgment, rather than our own, in this critical period. The people are looking to him as their hope for relief. . . . What will the country say if . . . this Congress has failed to give him the support that he has asked?"[22]

There were Republican voices of warning about congressional abdication and presidential dictatorship. "If you gentlemen are afraid to meet this problem on your own responsibility," said Gardner Withrow of Wisconsin, "then cast your votes to declare the President dictator, and close up the doors of Congress and go home." But their own minority leader, Bertrand H. Snell of New York, went along with the majority. "If you are going to accomplish this purpose," he said, "you must put it up to the President of the United States and hold him responsible."[23]

And so it went throughout the Hundred Days. The newly elected speaker, Henry T. Rainey of Illinois, had appointed a steering committee and set up a network of assistant whips with the express purpose of facilitating the passage of "Mr. Roosevelt's program."[24] Bills were drafted in the White House, or elsewhere in the executive branch, and sent to the Congress in sequence. Sometimes key members of the Congress participated in policy and drafting sessions, but as "members of the administration" rather than as representatives of the Congress.[25] Even the congressional schedule was determined by executive decision. The phrase rubber-stamp congressmen appeared in the lexicon. The Congress as a body was not excluded altogether; it did amend administration measures (though not on the House floor, where "gag rules" forbade amendments by individual members),[26] but none of Roosevelt's proposals was rejected, or modified in any fundamental way. When the special session approached its end, Democratic Senator Josiah W. Bailey of North Carolina, who was later to break with the New Deal, could boast that the legislators had responded "unfailingly" to the presidential

---

22. *Congressional Record*, March 11, 1933, pp. 210, 213–14, 217.

23. Ibid., pp. 203, 215.

24. Quoted in E. Pendleton Herring, "First Session of the Seventy-third Congress, March 9, 1933, to June 16, 1933," *American Political Science Review*, vol. 28 (February 1934), p. 69.

25. James MacGregor Burns, *Roosevelt: The Lion and the Fox* (Harcourt, Brace, 1956), p. 187. Burns's reference is to Roosevelt's legislative leadership through 1933–34.

26. Sylvia Snowiss, "Presidential Leadership of Congress: An Analysis of Roosevelt's First Hundred Days," *Publius*, vol. 1, no. 1 (1971), pp. 81–82.

recommendations—just as, he noted, they had done in Hoover's term. The Congress had passed seventeen or eighteen major measures, he said, "each of them . . . enacted according to his recommendations."

> I think that the record of the responsiveness to the recommendations and the leadership of the Nation ought . . . to be made known. We have not failed to do anything we were asked to do, and . . . the Congress . . . has with singular regularity subordinated its judgment. . . . we . . . can go home with the sense of satisfaction that the Congress has responded, not in any small measure but in the utmost measure, to the recommendations of the chosen leader of our people in the present crisis.[27]

E. Pendleton Herring counted eleven important proposals emanating from the White House, passed with less than forty hours of debate altogether in the House and all enacted within sixty days of their submission. Only one major bill (a banking bill) originated within the Congress itself. The president, said Herring, had become a "prime minister." He directed the deliberations of the Congress. He used his patronage effectively to maintain discipline among the members. "His authority to dictate policy was unquestioned."[28]

Institutionalizing the President as Legislative Leader

The elections of 1934 and 1936 served to affirm and reinforce the pattern of presidential leadership established in the Hundred Days. Given the chance to vote for or against the revolution that Roosevelt had led, the people overwhelmingly endorsed it, and in doing so endorsed his form of leadership as well. For it was Roosevelt's New Deal, not the Congress's or even the Democratic party's. Democrats, indeed, divided into New Dealers and anti-New Dealers; the party image was blurred. So, for that matter, was the image of the Republican party during this period of realignment; Roosevelt Republicans (who voted for FDR but remained Republicans at state and local levels) appeared in the staunch GOP areas of the North and did well at the polls. The test of a politician was not what party he belonged to but whether or not he supported the Rooseveltian programs, and in this period when the president's popularity was cresting, Democratic candidates—and some Republicans as well—outdid one another in promising to follow wherever the leader led. Democrats back home in the states and districts enforced the test of loyalty to Roosevelt, denying renomination to anti-New Dealers, and selecting New Dealers to replace retiring Roosevelt opponents.[29]

27. *Congressional Record*, June 10, 1933, p. 5599.
28. "First Session," pp. 75, 65, 70.
29. James L. Sundquist, *Dynamics of the Party System: Alignment and Realignment of Political Parties in the United States* (Brookings Institution, 1973), pp. 211–12.

So developed the congressional posture of subordination to presidential leadership that members of the Congress four decades later were decrying. As party leader, Roosevelt pronounced the party program, and members of the Congress who owed their election to the president and his program looked naturally to the White House for the cues they were to follow. Randall B. Ripley identified 1933–37 as one of two periods when the president was the effective leader of the House and that body's own leaders "did not make a consistently major strategic or tactical input in planning the course of legislation."[30] In the Senate, too, Democratic leaders saw themselves as Roosevelt lieutenants, even one as out of sympathy with many New Deal measures as Joseph T. Robinson of Arkansas, the majority leader of the first Roosevelt years. Robinson's successor, Alben W. Barkley of Kentucky, felt constrained to dramatically resign his leadership post in 1944—only for a few minutes, it turned out—when he found he could not follow the White House lead.[31] And the president intervened in the selection of party leaders in the Senate and the House, to assure choices compatible with him.

Part of what became the New Deal still had its origins within the legislative branch, of course. Senator Robert F. Wagner of New York initiated both the National Labor Relations Act and the public housing program, and Senator Arthur H. Vandenberg of Michigan, a Republican, was the father of bank deposit insurance. Even in the follow-the-leader spirit of the Hundred Days, the Congress amended the president's proposals, and once the turmoil of that period had passed it resumed its role as careful and independent critic, refining and modifying presidential measures and, on occasion, rejecting them outright. But from that time on, the Congress expected and accepted presidential leadership in setting its direction and defining its agenda, and so it developed neither the organizational structure nor the institutional attitudes and habits that would enable it to do those jobs itself. Congressmen might bridle at being handed presidential "must lists," but their own leaders compiled no lists at all. At a later time, when the Congress was to reject the president as leader, those deficiencies would haunt it.

But the president, in the mid-1930s, was not well organized for the role of legislative leader either. The vast expansion of governmental functions that was the New Deal revolution made clear that someone had to fulfill that role. Someone had to conceive a strategy, set priorities, and coordinate the separate elements of legislation, and both ends of Pennsylvania Avenue agreed that

30. *Party Leaders*, p. 86. The other period was 1915–19, when Wilson led the House.
31. MacNeil, *Forge of Democracy*, p. 34. The president had vetoed a tax bill with a harshly worded message. Barkley was immediately reelected, his standing in the Senate only enhanced by his show of independence.

that someone had to be the president. Even after the honeymoon between the president and Congress ended and relations were severely strained in Roosevelt's second term, the legislators accepted that necessity, and the institutionalization of the president as chief legislator proceeded.

As early as 1934, President Roosevelt moved to gain control over all legislative proposals emanating from the executive branch. He had been "quite horrified—not once but half a dozen times—by reading in the paper that some department or agency was after this, that, or the other" without his knowledge.[32] Thus all agencies were instructed to submit all proposed legislation to the National Emergency Council for clearance, except for appropriations measures, which were already being cleared through the Bureau of the Budget.[33] The next year the system was extended to cover comments made by agencies on bills referred to them by congressional committees. By the end of his first term, then, Roosevelt had succeeded in harnessing the legislative initiative of the executive branch as a whole. When the National Emergency Council expired in 1937, the clearance function was ensconced in the Bureau of the Budget (in 1970 renamed the Office of Management and Budget), where it has remained.[34]

In examining a piece of proposed legislation from an executive agency, the Bureau of the Budget made a determination whether the bill was, in the bureau's language, "in accord with the program of the President." If not, the measure was either officially dropped by the agency or revised so as to win approval. Similarly, the bureau reviewed reports by agencies on pending bills and advised the agency, or the congressional committee, whether the measure was or was not "in accord" or whether by specific amendment it could be brought into accord. A "not in accord" ruling normally blocked a bill, because it carried the message that if passed, the measure would be vetoed. Whereas previous administrations had identified "administration bills," in the plural, Roosevelt now had a "program," in the singular. All presidential measures were considered to be related, making up a unitary package.

32. National Emergency Council, "Proceedings of the Nineteenth Meeting" (December 11, 1934), p. 7, quoted by Richard E. Neustadt, "Presidency and Legislation: The Growth of Central Clearance," *American Political Science Review*, vol. 48 (September 1954), p. 649.

33. The process for clearance of financial proposals through the bureau had been instituted in 1921 but did not become fully effective until 1926. Neustadt, "Growth of Central Clearance," pp. 643–47.

34. Ibid., p. 652. In 1938 the president assigned to the clearance staff, by then organized as a separate division, responsibility also for obtaining agency views and advising him on whether to sign or veto enrolled bills. Ibid., p. 654. In recent years, White House staff have taken increasing responsibility for the substance of the clearance process on major legislation, with the Office of Management and Budget continuing to handle more routine measures and coordinate the communication process. See Allen Schick, "The Budget Bureau That Was," *Law and Contemporary Problems*, vol. 35 (Summer 1970), pp. 526–28.

The next step was to systematize the preparation and communication of the program. The Hundred Days had been a period of helter-skelter legislation from crisis to crisis, and the next few years had been hardly more orderly. The president's annual messages tended to be general, followed by individual messages proposing legislation on particular subjects (the Seventy-fifth Congress in 1937–38 received seventy special messages)[35] and some of these messages arrived on Capitol Hill with little advance consultation or even notice. Senate and House Democratic leaders complained that if they were to be the president's agents on the Hill, they needed to be apprised earlier and more fully of White House strategy and they needed to be given opportunity to contribute to the timing and the content of party measures. Responding to these complaints, Roosevelt in late 1937 initiated what was to become another standing institution of presidential legislative leadership— the president's regular meeting at the White House with his party's congressional leaders. Roosevelt's meetings—held on Monday mornings, though not every week, when the Congress was in session—were between the leader and his lieutenants, the latter reporting on the progress of the presidential program, advising him of problems, and receiving information as to the timing of forthcoming executive proposals. "Throughout his twelve years the Congressional leaders—the elected leadership—accepted Roosevelt's position as initiator and source of party policies."[36]

By 1943, Roosevelt had appointed the first full-time writer of speeches and messages, Judge Samuel I. Rosenman, to the White House staff. He also brought legislative lobbying out into the open. Whereas before FDR the "role of presidential lobbyists was unofficial and almost clandestine," his legislative agents were highly visible, drafting bills and amendments and advising the legislative leaders during committee and floor consideration of presidential measures.[37] By the end of Roosevelt's long tenure, congressmen could complain that "bills originating in the departments have had the green light before the committees, and bills originating with the Members have been an idle fantasy." Even on the House floor, said one influential member, a bill that did not originate in the executive branch was considered by the members to be "no good."[38]

35. Edward S. Corwin, *The President: Office and Powers, 1787–1957*, 4th rev. ed. (New York University Press, 1957), p. 274.

36. Robert Leon Lester, "Developments in Presidential-Congressional Relations: F.D.R.–J.F.K." (Ph.D. dissertation, University of Virginia, 1969), p. 55.

37. Ibid., p. 43.

38. Comment, the first in the form of a rhetorical question, by Representative A. S. Mike Monroney, in *Organization of Congress*, Hearings before the Joint Committee on the Organization of Congress, 79 Cong. 1 sess. (U.S. Government Printing Office, 1945), p. 31. Monroney, vice

The contribution of Harry Truman was to make legislative leadership ever more orderly and systematic. This was a matter partly of temperament and partly of circumstance: the policymaking process had been complicated by passage of the Employment Act of 1946, which added another January message—the Economic Report of the President—to the Budget and the traditional State of the Union Message, and the first year's experience with drafting three related documents in separate corners of the Executive Office of the President, with contributions for each sought from the executive agencies, suggested the need for a coordinated approach. Accordingly, in September 1947 the president combined all the requests for legislative proposals and message suggestions into a single call. Truman's letter "may be said to mark the start of annual agency programming in contemporary terms."[39]

Truman likewise systematized the weekly meetings with the majority leaders of the two houses (the meetings resumed in 1949 after a hiatus during Republican control of the Congress in 1947–48). The agenda, prepared in the White House, was built around a list of presidential bills. Senate Majority Leader Scott W. Lucas, of Illinois, followed the Monday White House meetings with Tuesday meetings of the Senate Majority Policy Committee, and relations were so close and cordial that Lucas had a White House telephone installed in his office and asked for regular Bureau of the Budget reports on the administration stand on each piece of legislation coming up for action on the Senate floor.[40] Truman also assigned the first full-time specialists to congressional liaison, one to each House, although they were of relatively low rank within the White House and engaged in doing "favors" for the members rather than in lobbying.[41]

Dwight Eisenhower accepted and built on the institutional machinery his predecessors had created, and so did his successors. The congressional liaison staff was brought out of the "closet" by Eisenhower[42] to become a fixture in the White House. It gradually grew in size and under President Kennedy assumed leadership over the corresponding staffs in the departments, sometimes organizing a concerted, governmentwide lobbying effort on behalf of

---

chairman of the committee, drew agreement from Representatives Jerry Voorhis, Democrat of California, Albert Gore, Democrat of Tennessee, E. E. Cox, Democrat of Georgia, and Earl C. Michener, Republican of Michigan. Ibid., pp. 31, 389–91.

39. Richard E. Neustadt "Presidency and Legislation: Planning the President's Program," *American Political Science Review*, vol. 49 (December 1955), p. 1003.

40. Lester, "Developments in Presidential-Congressional Relations," pp. 74–80.

41. Stephen Hess, *Organizing the Presidency* (Brookings Institution, 1976), p. 51.

42. Ibid., p. 70.

a major administration measure. Each president met on a regular weekly basis with the Senate and House leaders of his party (even when they were in the minority), and he controlled the agenda and the attendance.

The "program of the president" became an accepted institution.[43] It was assembled annually, and the size of the White House staff assigned to program development grew. An identifiable speech-and-message-writing staff maintained general control over the content of the program, with the legislative clearance division of the Bureau of the Budget handling the details. During the Kennedy administration, the president himself rather than department heads began to transmit the draft bills and "no one noticed" the difference.[44]

The first two years of Lyndon Johnson saw a burst of presidential leadership that can be compared only to the early Wilson years and the first term of Franklin Roosevelt. Like those predecessors, he was intensely activist, and he brought to the office, in addition, experience in legislative leadership surpassing that of any president, possibly excepting Madison. Like Wilson and FDR, he had a Congress disposed to follow—at first out of respect for the slain Kennedy whose program Johnson was advancing, later because of Johnson's own landslide victory of 1964 that brought overwhelming Democratic majorities to both houses. So, like the New Freedom and the New Deal of the earlier periods, the measures that made up the Great Society were enacted. But Johnson, unlike his predecessors, had an institutional structure for presidential leadership in place, and he could devote his extraordinary energy to making effective use of it. He did, like every president since Franklin Roosevelt, make some marginal contributions to the structure itself; his were to enlarge the White House policy-planning group and augment it with formal task forces made up wholly or partly of experts from outside the government, sometimes working publicly, sometimes confidentially.

Richard Nixon continued the formalization and expansion of the policy-making apparatus. He also appointed outside task forces, but as a president of orderly administrative habits and a deep interest in governmental management, he sought a firmer institutional structure for policy development. Three days after his inauguration, he created by executive order an Urban Affairs Council to take responsibility for "the formulation and implementation

43. In 1953, when President Eisenhower was inaugurated, enterprising staff of the Budget Bureau's Division of Legislative Reference had already compiled for use in defining "the program of the President" a thick book excerpting policy positions Eisenhower had taken during the campaign or earlier in his public career. The volume was known, inevitably, as the "Ikelopedia." Similar materials were assembled during later presidential transitions.

44. Richard E. Neustadt, "Politicians and Bureaucrats," in David B. Truman, ed., *The Congress and America's Future* (Prentice-Hall, 1965), p. 111.

of a national urban policy."[45] Chaired by the president, the council included also the vice president and the heads of seven domestic departments, and its staff was located in the White House. In 1970 a reorganization plan presented to, and accepted by, the Congress broadened and converted this body into a new Domestic Council to embrace the whole range of domestic policy as a parallel to the National Security Council in the foreign and military fields.

The Domestic Council was overtly presented to the Congress as a structure for legislative as well as executive leadership. The council, said the president, would be a "streamlined, consolidated domestic policy arm" of the presidency to "coordinate policy formulation in the domestic area." It would assess needs, collect information, and develop forecasts "for the purpose of defining national goals and objectives."[46] The national goals would be translated into specific policies that, where new legislation was required, would be presented to the Congress. "By providing a means of formulating integrated and systematic recommendations on major domestic policy issues, the plan serves not only the needs of the President, but also the interests of the Congress," the president told the legislators.[47]

A majority of the House Government Operations Committee recommended rejection of the reorganization plan (which also converted the Bureau of the Budget into the Office of Management and Budget), partly because of the relation of the Domestic Council staff to the Congress. The council's executive director, argued the committee majority, should be subject to Senate confirmation, should submit an annual report to the Congress, should testify before congressional committees, and should provide other information directly to the legislators on request. The Congress should have "equal access" to the council staff, it contended.[48] But the House overruled its committee's objections to the plan, 193 to 164, and in the Senate no question was even raised.

During the entire period from the Roosevelt through the early Nixon years, there is no record of congressional resistance to the institutional development

45. "Statement on Signing Executive Order Establishing the Council for Urban Affairs, January 23, 1969," *Public Papers of the Presidents: Richard Nixon, 1969* (GPO, 1970), pp. 11–12. In November a Rural Affairs Council was established with essentially the same membership.

46. "Message to the Congress Transmitting Reorganization Plan No. 2 of 1970, March 12, 1970," *Public Papers: Nixon, 1970* (GPO, 1971), pp. 257–63.

47. Ibid. Also, see testimony of Roy L. Ash, chairman of the President's Advisory Council on Executive Organization, April 28, 1970, in *Reorganization Plan No. 2 of 1970 (Office of Management and Budget: Domestic Council)*, Hearings before a subcommittee of the House Government Operations Committee, 91 Cong. 2 sess. (GPO, 1970), p. 8.

48. May 8, 1970, in *Disapproving Reorganization Plan No. 2 of 1970: Office of Management and Budget, Domestic Council*, H. Rept. 91-1066, 91 Cong. 2 sess. (GPO, 1970), pp. 11–13.

of the president as legislative leader. That the man who combined the roles of party leader, chief of government, and head of the executive branch that originated much important legislation should also act openly as chief policy spokesman and chief legislator came to seem right and natural to the Congresses of the mid-twentieth century. Randall Ripley, interviewing House members of the Eighty-eighth Congress (1963–64), found that "over 80 percent of all Democrats assumed the party position to be the position of the President."[49] Congressional committees cooperated willingly, even eagerly, with the Bureau of the Budget in developing the clearance process.[50]

The President as Legislative Policy Planner

The posture of the Congress during this long period of presidential aggrandizement was, however, much more than one of simple acquiescence to the presidential initiative, as represented in such innovations as Roosevelt's legislative clearance process or Nixon's Domestic Council. Perhaps even more significant in reflecting the congressional attitude was the long series of affirmative steps the legislature took, on its own initiative, to assign to the president specific tasks for the planning and initiating of legislative policy— tasks that in earlier times the Congress might have considered to be more appropriately handled within the legislative branch itself. The Employment Act of 1946 (discussed in chapter 4) was only the first of a series of congressionally initiated postwar statutes establishing the president as legislative policy planner. Senators and representatives who found themselves dissatisfied with the way the government was coping with any of the complex problems of the day came almost routinely to demand that the president— not their own leaders—develop the new policies and programs that the times required.[51]

49. *Party Leaders*, p. 181.
50. Neustadt, "Growth of Central Clearance," pp. 670–71.
51. The planning activities were prefigured by the work of the National Resources Planning Board (NRPB), which evolved from the National Resources Committee created by President Roosevelt in 1934. That committee was formed in response to a joint resolution instructing the president to prepare for congressional consideration a comprehensive plan for development of the nation's rivers. The planning body, reorganized and renamed several times and lodged in the Executive Office of the President when that office was created, concentrated initially on public works and natural resources but later broadened its concern to encompass social and economic programs as well. In 1943 the agency was killed when the House Appropriations Committee terminated its funding. One argument used in abolishing NRPB was that postwar economic planning should be centered in the Congress. See remarks of Republican Appropriations Committee members Frederick C. Smith of Ohio and Everett M. Dirksen of Illinois, *Congressional Record*, February 8 and March 15, 1943, pp. 721, 1977. Senate and House committees did prepare reports on the postwar economy,

The Council of Economic Advisers (CEA), in particular, became a model. For groups dissatisfied with the way in which government policies were being formulated, the solution seemed clear: create a council in the Executive Office of the President to concern itself with the issue, and require the president to sign his name to a periodic report prepared by the council corresponding to the Economic Report of the President. The new council, by virtue of its location in the Executive Office, would be on a par with the Bureau of the Budget, able to argue its case for (presumably) new government activities on equal terms. Among the many bills introduced before 1973 to replicate the CEA planning process in other fields, and usually the CEA structure as well, four were wholly or partially successful.[52]

The first of these fixed responsibility in the president for planning manpower policy. The impetus for manpower planning came from a special Senate Committee on Unemployment Problems created following the 1958 recession, which recommended in a 1960 report that the federal government "maintain a continuing concern for the Nation's overall manpower resources, requirements, and utilization, including the problem of underemployment" and develop the capacity to anticipate and deal with "manpower dislocations resulting from automation and technological change."[53] To this end, the committee proposed either the creation of a national manpower planning commission in the Executive Office of the President or assignment of the responsibility to an existing agency. It also proposed a Senate subcommittee on employment and manpower, which was promptly created.

Pennsylvania Democrat Joseph S. Clark, a member of the special committee, offered a bill calling for a three-member council of manpower advisers in the Executive Office and an annual presidential report that "would focus attention on manpower problems and lead to the development of recommendations for action that the Congress does not now receive."[54] President Kennedy, however, preferred to designate his secretary of labor as the government's manpower planner, and Clark went along. Accordingly, the

but their merits were not sufficient to persuade the Congress to institutionalize within its own structure a comprehensive planning function. When the legislature came to grapple seriously with the problem of planning for economic stabilization, it placed the Council of Economic Advisers in the president's office and gave him the responsibility to prepare policy recommendations for congressional review.

52. No doubt with some hyperbole, the story is told that of the fourteen task forces appointed by Lyndon Johnson in 1964 to come up with innovative ideas in major fields of legislative concern, thirteen recommended in their confidential reports that a council be established in the Executive Office to give appropriate status, at the president's right hand, to whatever functional interest the task force happened to be concerned with.

53. *Report of Special Committee on Unemployment Problems pursuant to S. Res. 196 together with minority and additional views*, S. Rept. 1206, 86 Cong. 2 sess. (GPO, 1960), p. 126.

54. *Congressional Record*, May 16, 1960, p. 10318.

Manpower Development and Training Act of 1962, sponsored by Clark, instructed the secretary to report to the president on "manpower requirements, resources, utilization, and training" and the president to report in turn to the Congress. An annual Manpower Report of the President thereupon took its place with the State of the Union Message, the Budget, and the Economic Report of the President among the policy documents presented to the Congress at the outset of each session.

Even earlier than Clark's manpower bill was a proposal by Senator James E. Murray, Montana Democrat, for a council of resources and conservation advisers to the president, an annual report by the president, and a joint committee of the Congress on resources and conservation.[55] Introduced in 1959, the idea languished for a decade but in 1969 the proposed agency, converted into a Council of Environmental Quality, was created by the National Environmental Policy Act. Democratic as well as Republican members of the Congress were explicit in demanding strong leadership from Republican President Nixon and his administration in environmental policy. Representative John Dingell, Michigan Democrat, and principal House sponsor of the council, said the measure "clearly expresses my conviction that we need the vigorous involvement of the Executive Office of the President of the United States in this problem." Said Representative Sidney R. Yates, Democrat of Illinois: The council "will give Mr. Nixon the opportunity to seize the initiative in restoring the quality of our environment. He must not fail this important responsibility."[56] The law specifically directed the council to recommend legislation.

The third directive to the president to provide legislative policy leadership came in the Housing and Urban Development Act of 1968, which called on him to prepare a ten-year plan "for the elimination of all substandard housing" in the United States in order to realize, by 1978, a goal set in 1949 of "a decent home and a suitable living environment for every American family." The plan was to advise the Congress of the number of housing units that would need to be constructed or rehabilitated annually and to recommend legislation that might be necessary to achieve the goal. The president was to report annually on progress and on action being taken to prevent or remedy shortfalls. These planning and reporting requirements were added on congressional initiative to the administration's original bill, but the administration no doubt supported them. In this case, an existing department—Housing and Urban Development—would provide staff assistance to the president.

55. Ibid., August 17, 1959, p. 15980.
56. Ibid., September 23, 1969, pp. 26571, 26579.

President Johnson promptly set a goal of 26.2 million new or rehabilitated housing units for the decade.

Finally, an assignment of legislative planning responsibility, in part explicit and in part ambiguous, came in 1970 in the field of urban growth policy. President Nixon himself initiated the discussion in his State of the Union Message when, after citing the problems of the "violent and decayed central cities" and the "vast areas of rural America emptying out of people and of promise," he called for the nation to develop a "national growth policy" that would guide both urban and rural development.[57] But he did not suggest how the policy should be formulated, nor did he follow the original declaration with any more specific communication to the Congress. That left it to the members, and they responded in what had become the customary fashion. Bills were introduced in both houses to establish a council on urban growth in the Executive Office of the President and to require the president to submit each two years a national urban growth report. The president, then in the process of establishing the Domestic Council as a central planning body for domestic policy, protested against still another council, and the sponsors yielded; the legislation directed the president, in preparing his report, to "utilize the capacity of his office, adequately organized and staffed for the purpose, through an identified unit of the Domestic Council, and of the departments and agencies within the executive branch."[58] The law declared that the federal government "must assume responsibility for the development of a national urban growth policy," laid down general criteria as to the content of the policy, then directed the president to present in his biennial report data that would be useful "to assist in the development" of the policy and to make recommendations for programs and policies to carry it out, including legislative recommendations.

There is an important omission, curiously, in these instructions to the president. They cover what he shall do before and after the policy is developed, but they say nothing about the most crucial stage, the development of the policy itself. The language can be read to mean that the Congress reserved this responsibility for itself and needed only background data from the executive. Some of the legislative history, however, points in the other direction. The House Banking and Currency Committee in its report on the proposed council on urban growth said it was created to "develop a national

---

57. "Annual Message to the Congress on the State of the Union, January 22, 1970," *Public Papers: Nixon, 1970*, p. 14.

58. Section 703(a), Housing and Urban Development Act of 1970, P.L. 91-609.

urban growth policy,"[59] and Chairman Wright Patman, Democrat of Texas, in the debate over creation of the council, contended that "the Congress should simply authorize the President to develop an urban growth policy" and permit him to decide where to obtain his advice.[60] But it was the Senate version of the language that was ultimately incorporated into the act, and neither in the Senate committee report nor in the floor debate were the words relating to the president's role interpreted or amplified. As it happened, Presidents Nixon and Ford both chose not to seize the opportunity provided by the biennial report to take the lead in policy formation.[61]

Nevertheless, the experience with growth policy confirmed the pattern that had been developing since passage of the Budget and Accounting Act in 1921 and that had gathered momentum since the end of World War II. Whenever the Congress felt the need for development of broad and coordinated policies, it assigned that responsibility to the president. If he provided the leadership, the Congress could be led. If he failed to do so, the Congress lacked its own mechanisms for developing comprehensive strategy and taking broad initiatives. In seven broad policy fields—the budget, the economy, national security, manpower, the environment, housing, and urban growth—it had by statute directed or invited the president to be chief legislator.[62] These came close to defining the entire range of governmental policy concerns. As other, neglected areas of policy development came to be identified (as energy would be in the mid-1970s), the Congress would expect the president to step out in front there too. If he failed to do so, its members would complain of lack of leadership, pointing their fingers not at their own leaders but at the White House.

59. *The Housing and Urban Development Act of 1970*, H. Rept. 91-1556, 91 Cong. 2 sess. (GPO, 1970), p. 2.

60. *Congressional Record*, December 2, 1970, p. 39454.

61. James L. Sundquist, *Dispersing Population: What America Can Learn from Europe* (Brookings Institution, 1975), pp. 8–12, 239–40. In 1977, the Congress amended the law to eliminate the word *growth*, calling only for an *urban policy*, and redefined the coverage to eliminate the previous focus on the geographical distribution of economic growth and population. President Carter responded with proposals for a comprehensive national urban policy.

62. In narrower areas the Congress sometimes gave similar directives to individual department or agency heads to assume policy leadership. The Rural Development Act of 1972, for example, directed the secretary of agriculture to "establish employment, income, population, housing, and quality of community services and facilities goals for rural development and report annually to Congress on progress in attaining such goals" (sec. 603, P.L. 92-419). This act, too, was ambiguous as to the exact content of the required report, but it can be inferred that if the secretary reported insufficient progress toward goals he himself had set, he would recommend any congressional corrective action needed. "There seems little doubt that Congress intended the Secretary to develop a *national* program for rural development," concluded Morton J. Schussheim, in "Rural Development Goals," a critique of the secretary's second annual report, prepared at the request of the Congressional Rural Caucus (Library of Congress, Congressional Research Service, 1975), p. 2.

The President as "a Sort of Prime Minister"

By the mid-1960s, the relationship seemed fixed. Most scholars conceded that legislative initiative had passed from the Congress to the president. Whether they deplored the trend or applauded it, they acknowledged it. The textbook image of congressional-executive relations was one wherein, to use the common phrase, "the President proposes, and the Congress disposes."

One of the more vivid—and more categorical—descriptions was that of Samuel P. Huntington:

> The congressional role in legislation has largely been reduced to delay and amendment. . . . Since 1933 . . . the initiative in formulating legislation, in assigning legislative priorities, in arousing support for legislation, and in determining the final content of the legislation has clearly shifted to the executive branch. . . .
>
> Eighty percent of the bills enacted into law, one congressman has estimated, originated in the executive branch. Indeed, in most instances congressmen do not admit a responsibility to take legislative action except in response to executive requests. . . . The President now determines the legislative agenda of Congress almost as thoroughly as the British Cabinet sets the legislative agenda of Parliament. . . .
>
> The loss of congressional control over the substance of policy is most marked, of course, in the area of national defense and foreign policy. . . . In domestic legislation Congress's influence is undoubtedly greater, but even here its primary impact is on the timing and details of legislation, not on the subjects and content.[63]

Others concurred: "The president . . . bears almost the entire burden of the formulation of national policy and the definition of the national purpose."[64] He "is the energizer, the innovator. . . . New policies, new legislation depend almost entirely on the President."[65] He "has assumed the dominant role in the legislative process."[66] He "has now become a sort of prime minister or 'third House of Congress.' . . . he is now expected to make detailed recommendations in the form of messages and proposed bills, to watch them closely in their tortuous progress on the floor and in committee in each house, and to use every honorable means within his power to persuade the gentlemen of Congress to give him what he wanted in the first place. . . . We judge our Presidents today largely by their success in leading Congress."[67] That judgment, from Clinton Rossiter, was written during the time of Dwight Eisen-

63. "Congressional Responses to the Twentieth Century," in Truman, *Congress and America's Future*, p. 23.

64. Rowland Egger and Joseph P. Harris, *The President and Congress* (McGraw-Hill, 1963), p. 2.

65. Robert A. Dahl, *Pluralist Democracy in the United States: Conflict and Consent* (Rand McNally, 1967), p. 103.

66. John S. Saloma III, *Congress and the New Politics* (Little, Brown, 1969), p. 93.

67. Clinton Rossiter, *The American Presidency* (Harcourt, Brace, 1956), p. 83.

hower, who has appeared on no lists of "strongest" presidents and who contended with a party controlled by the opposition party.

And, added Rossiter, "what the country expects, Congress also expects."[68] The chairman of a major House committee in 1953 admonished an administration witness: "Don't expect us to start from scratch on what you people want. That's not the way we do things here—*you* draft the bills and *we* work them over."[69] Even when the two branches of government were politically divided, the Congress still looked to the president to set its agenda. During the Nixon administration, a Democratic House committee chairman complained: "The president hasn't given us anything to do. The president hasn't given us the bills to act on. . . . What can we do?"[70]

Lyndon Johnson, as Senate majority leader, "regarded the presidency as the one office in the American system which can give national leadership."[71] And Speaker Sam Rayburn, reporting on House achievements at the end of the 1955 congressional session, used as his benchmark President Eisenhower's program; his theme was that the Democrats had given the president more support than had his own party—around sixty of the president's proposals has been passed, which amounted to "cooperation . . . beyond expectations."[72] There was no mention of any other agenda than the one handed to the Congress by the president.

Majority Leader Mike Mansfield regularly measured the Senate's achievements in terms of action on the president's program, no matter whether a Democratic or Republican president sent it up.[73] Mansfield's more partisan House counterpart, Democratic Speaker John W. McCormack, was graphic in confessing to the congressional reliance on presidential leadership. At the close of what he called the Congress of Fulfillment—the 1965 session that climaxed Lyndon Johnson's Great Society—he asked what factors accounted for the spectacular record of the House of Representatives and found the answer "not only within the walls of this Chamber, but beyond it. . . . For, first, there was the dynamic, insistent, unrelenting, tireless . . . leadership of President Lyndon Baines Johnson . . . leadership on the highest standards

68. Ibid., p. 86.

69. Neustadt, "Planning the President's Program," p. 1015.

70. Chairman Wayne N. Aspinall (Colorado) of the House Interior and Insular Affairs Committee, quoted by Representative Bob Eckhardt, Democrat of Texas, *The Tides of Power, Conversations on the American Constitution between Bob Eckhardt and Charles L. Black, Jr.* (Yale University Press, 1976), p. 35.

71. Ralph K. Huitt, "Democratic Party Leadership in the Senate," *American Political Science Review*, vol. 55 (June 1961), p. 337.

72. *Congressional Record*, August 2, 1955, pp. 13147–49.

73. See, for instance, a press interview reported in ibid., November 13, 1963, pp. 22863–65, and end-of-session report, in ibid., December 23, 1969, pp. 41148–52.

of Presidential relationship between the executive and the legislative branches of our government."[74] Four years later, in his appraisal of Richard Nixon's leadership, he made clear that even an opposition Congress looked to the president to lead: "In every major field the committee chairmen moved promptly to fill the vacuum created by the lack of Presidential recommendations. In all too many cases, unfortunately, their efforts were severely handicapped by lack of recommendations and cooperation from the executive branch."[75]

What was true of the leaders was equally true of the rank and file. From his extensive interviews with senators and their staffs during the Eisenhower administration, Donald R. Matthews concluded that the expectation that modern presidents will lead the Congress "is as widespread on Capitol Hill as anywhere else." "Few, if any, senators expressed opposition to presidential leadership as such; rather, if they objected at all, it was to the direction, ineffectiveness, or lack of legislative 'leadership' from the White House."[76] And when another political scientist asked a sample of Democratic congressmen in 1965–66 whether they considered "the President's program to be the program of the Democratic party in Congress," 64 percent answered in the affirmative; several observed that the Democratic party in the Congress had no other program.[77]

If the president was chief legislator, then what had the congressional role become? In the prevailing textbook model, it was to exercise a simple choice: to follow or to obstruct. "The President is now the motor in the system; the Congress applies the brakes. . . . The President gives what forward movement there is to the system. . . . The Congress is the force of inertia."[78] But "Congress follows the Presidential lead with consistency only in crisis"; it

74. Ibid., October 22, 1965, p. 28699.
75. Ibid., December 23, 1969, p. 41168.
76. *U.S. Senators and Their World* (University of North Carolina Press, 1960), pp. 140–42. There were exceptions, of course. Senator Abraham A. Ribicoff, Democrat of Connecticut, in the *Saturday Evening Post*, March 21, 1964, expressed frustration that the Congress had "surrendered its rightful leadership in the lawmaking process to the White House" and resigned itself to "filtering" presidential proposals. But typical was Senator Jacob K. Javits, Republican of New York, who complained vigorously of President Johnson's failure to deliver a draft of legislation to deal with emergency strikes. "It is somewhat our fault, too," said Javits, "but I think more the responsibility is on the President. . . . It is uniquely this kind of situation where we are entitled to a recommendation from the executive department." *Congressional Record*, March 9, 1967, pp. 6095–96. In this case neither branch was able to reconcile conflicting political interests and take effective initiative, and each passed the buck to the other. See John R. Johannes, "Where Does the Buck Stop?—Congress, President, and the Responsibility for Legislative Initiative," *Western Political Quarterly*, vol. 25 (September 1972), pp. 396–415.
77. Vernon M. Goetcheus, "Presidential Party Leadership: Relations between President Johnson and House Democrats in the 89th Congress" (Ph.D. dissertation, University of Wisconsin, 1967), pp. 196–98.
78. Dahl, *Pluralist Democracy*, p. 136.

"is a highly negative body whose policy often is to have no policy."[79] In Huntington's view, "congressional assertion" had come to coincide with "congressional obstruction." "If Congress legislates, it subordinates itself to the President. Congress can assert its power or it can pass laws; but it cannot do both." He followed this reasoning to its logical conclusion: the Congress should give up legislating altogether, confining itself to either vetoing or legitimizing presidential policies. "Legislation has become much too complex politically to be effectively handled by a representative assembly."[80]

Yet even while these generalizations were being drawn, another school of political scientists was reaching quite another conclusion. Tracing the origin and development of specific laws, through case studies, they found the contribution of the Congress to go far beyond delay, amendment, and obstruction. After reviewing three decades of case studies of policy formulation, Ronald C. Moe and Steven C. Teel challenged "the conventional wisdom that the president has come to enjoy an increasingly preponderant role in national policy-making. . . . Quite the contrary, the evidence suggests that Congress continues to be an active innovator and very much in the legislative business."[81] One editor summarized seven studies of legislation affecting cities as casting "considerable doubt on the stereotype of a passive legislature simply responding to presidential initiatives." In some instances, Congress "may prove to be the dominant force."[82] Similarly, David E. Price, after tracing the history of thirteen bills enacted by the Eighty-ninth Congress (1965–66), rejected the "stereotype" that relegates the Congress to "delay and amendment." The processes and relationships are far more complex than that. Even in that period of exceptionally strong presidential leadership, the congressional role was not only one of checking the president and refining his proposals but also of "filling certain policy gaps on its own and stimulating, cajoling, and assisting the executive to fill others."[83] John F. Manley's study of the House Ways and Means Committee found that body, particularly in the area of taxation, to be "an independent force in policy-making . . . that is well-equipped to compete on equal terms with the expertise of the executive, and that stands as a formidable challenge to presidents and their programs."

79. Louis W. Koenig, *The Chief Executive* (Harcourt, Brace, and World, 1964), p. 127, and *Congress and the President* (Scott, Foresman, 1965), p. 141.

80. "Congressional Responses," p. 29.

81. "Congress as Policy-Maker: A Necessary Reappraisal," *Political Science Quarterly*, vol. 85 (September 1970), pp. 443–70.

82. Frederic N. Cleaveland and associates, *Congress and Urban Problems: A Casebook on the Legislative Process* (Brookings Institution, 1969), p. 356.

83. *Who Makes the Laws? Creativity and Power in Senate Committees* (Cambridge, Mass.: Schenkman, 1972), pp. 289, 332.

One member referred to that committee as "a bastion of congressional dominance."[84]

The Congress obviously can, and does, pass laws without subordinating itself to the president. Such major measures as the Taft-Hartley labor relations act and the McCarran-Walter immigration act have been passed over presidential vetoes. Among many measures initiated and pushed to passage within the legislative branch without presidential interest or support were the original National Labor Relations Act of 1935, the original minimum wage law of 1938, and federal grants for sewage treatment plants in 1956. Still more have been initiated and promoted by individual legislators, then added to the presidential program after a large measure of public support had been obtained. Thus Senator Norris fathered the Tennessee Valley Authority, long before Franklin Roosevelt made it part of his New Deal. Much of the Great Society legislation of the 1960s, such as aid to education, assistance for depressed areas, medicare, manpower training, and aid to mass transportation, was developed in the Congress during the Eisenhower period, and initiative remained there until a Democrat entered the White House and embraced the measures in his presidential program.[85] In some instances the executive branch forces the Congress to take the lead by deliberately withholding recommendations of its own, as in the case of the Agricultural Act of 1970.[86]

Nevertheless, if presidential dominance of the legislative process was never as stark as the textbook stereotype would have it, the president had certainly been established as the most important single participant in that process—the chief legislator in every sense. And it had all happened with the active assent of the Congress. A legislative program for the country had to be assembled, coordinated, made internally consistent, fitted within available resources, and coherently presented, and within it priorities had to be assigned. As the size and scope of government grew in the twentieth century,

84. John F. Manley, *The Politics of Finance: The House Committee on Ways and Means* (Little, Brown, 1970), pp. 379, 325.

85. James L. Sundquist, *Politics and Policy: The Eisenhower, Kennedy, and Johnson Years* (Brookings Institution, 1968), chap. 9; M. Kent Jennings, "Legislative Politics and Water Pollution Control, 1956–61," Royce Hanson, "Congress Copes with Mass Transit, 1960–64," and Frederic N. Cleaveland, "Legislating for Urban Areas: An Overview," in Cleaveland and associates, *Congress and Urban Problems*.

86. Remarks of Representative Delbert L. Latta, Republican of Ohio, *Congressional Record*, August 4, 1970, p. 27127. John R. Johannes has analyzed the many forms that congressional initiative and presidential response can take in "Policy Innovation in Congress" (Morristown, N.J.: General Learning Corporation, 1972), pp. 1–29; condensed in "Congress and the Initiation of Legislation," *Public Policy*, vol. 20 (Spring 1972), pp. 281–309; revised and updated in "The President Proposes and the Congress Disposes, but Not Always: Legislative Initiative on Capitol Hill," *Review of Politics*, vol. 36 (July 1974), pp. 356–70.

the capacity of the Congress to perform those tasks itself did not keep pace, and the Congress turned outside itself for the leadership it needed—to the president.

In time a kind of specialization developed: the president, as chief legislator, worried about the whole, the Congress about the parts. The president expressed the national interest, the Congress the state, local, or group interests. And the organs of the two branches evolved accordingly. The executive branch developed the integrative mechanisms in the Executive Office of the President and prepared the comprehensive policy documents. The legislature developed capacity to deal with the particular, through dispersed centers of specialized competence in committees and subcommittees. The structure tended to determine the scope of legislative initiative. The presidency, staffed to look at policy problems broadly, prepared the comprehensive programs. The Congress, organized to look intensively at narrower segments of the policy universe, filled the policy gaps, in Price's phrase, or acted as reserve initiator, in Johannes's.[87] While the president lobbied the Congress for enactment of his program, individual congressmen lobbied the president for inclusion of their pet measures in his program, as the surest means to speed their passage.

During periods when the president and the Congress lived together with a reasonable degree of harmony, this division of labor worked well enough. The president accepted his role as leader, and the Congress followed, amending and delaying and initiating as much or as little as it wished. But one of the prerequisites for a creative and constructive relationship (a necessary condition, not a guarantee, to be sure) was that the president and the majority of the Congress be of the same party, for opposing parties are—and in the nature of things have to be—bent on defeating and discrediting each other. For fourteen years—six of President Eisenhower's years and all eight of Nixon's and Ford's—this indispensable base for comity did not exist. Relations were increasingly strained during the Eisenhower period but stopped short of irreconcilable hostility; in the last two Nixon years, however, they reached that point, and the Congress found itself dependent for leadership on a presidency it had created for that purpose but could no longer follow. How to rid itself of that dependence? How to develop, overnight, a capacity to formulate and integrate a program of its own—not bits and pieces of a program, filling gaps, but a comprehensive program that it could enact under its own power and thrust on the president?

So, in confronting Richard Nixon, the Congress had also to look inward

87. Johannes, "The President Proposes," p. 369.

and confront its own traditions of structure and behavior. If the legislators were to recoup the long decades of decline they deplored in the introspective oratory of 1973, what were the implications for the organization, the processes, the habits, and the folkways of the Congress itself? It had had good and compelling reasons, or so it had thought, at least, at each stage in the process of making the president chief legislator. Could those reasons now be cast aside? And what would be the consequences, for the legislature's own behavior?

CHAPTER VII

Endemic Weaknesses of the Congress

THE POWERS of the modern presidency clearly were not wrested by self-seeking chief executives from a struggling but ultimately yielding Congress in a series of constitutional coups d'etat. On the contrary, every transaction embodying a shift of power and influence was one of mutual consent, for the shifts were made pursuant to law, and the Congress wrote and passed the laws.

Indeed, one of the striking facts of the modern presidency is the extent to which it was built through congressional initiative. It was the Congress that pressed for the crucial measure establishing the president as general manager—the Budget and Accounting Act of 1921. Similarly, the key measure fixing the president's role as chief economic stabilizer—the Employment Act of 1946—was the product of congressional initiative. In each instance the possibility of assigning the newly created staff agency—the Bureau of the Budget, the Council of Economic Advisers—to the legislative branch was considered, if only briefly. Had it so chosen, the Congress could have retained all of its power to assemble as well as review the government's budget, and it could have recaptured the initiative in formulating as well the country's economic policies—with results of profound significance for the nation's constitutional structure. Instead, it established the president as the responsible leader in those fields, just as it recognized his primacy in foreign policy and encouraged and accepted his role as agenda-setter and proposal-initiator in the legislative process as a whole.

Why did the Congress choose to shrink the range of the responsibilities it had claimed—and, to a degree at least, exercised—in a day when government was simpler? In the cases presented in the preceding chapters, two

155

themes recur, amounting to a self-appraisal by the Congress of its own limitations as seen during its long era of decline. First, the Congress could not act quickly. Second, it could not develop and coordinate comprehensive policies—in a word, could not plan. These are attributes (they may be called weaknesses only if seen as the obverse of some of the Congress's greatest strengths) that grew out of the fundamental structure of the U.S. Congress, as it was conceived in the Constitution and as it had evolved in the decades since.[1]

The Incapacity to Act Quickly

In the legislative process, speed is always at war with deliberation. In parliamentary governments where the legislature has fallen under executive domination—Great Britain's, for example—speedy action by the legislature can be attained whenever the leadership so wills, but only at the expense of deliberation. Issues are pondered mainly within the cabinet, which is the government's executive branch as well as a parliamentary committee; the legislature as a whole scarcely deliberates at all. The American Constitution, on the other hand, sets the legislature free to develop its capacity for deliberation by locating the capability for speedy action elsewhere—in a powerful executive outside the legislative branch. "Decision, activity, secrecy, and dispatch will characterize the proceedings of one man in a much more eminent degree than the proceedings of any greater number," wrote Alexander Hamilton in *The Federalist*, Number 70; "and in proportion as the number is increased, these qualities will be diminished." But a numerous legislature, he went on, is "best adapted to deliberation and wisdom, and best calculated to conciliate the confidence of the people." Indeed, "in the legislature, promptitude of decision is oftener an evil than a benefit. The differences of opinion . . . though they may sometimes obstruct salutary plans, yet often promote deliberation and circumspection, and serve to check excesses in the majority."

So with the president at hand to act when speed was required, the Congress developed the alternative virtue of deliberation. It became a forum for blending and reconciling the sharp and dangerous differences among the country's diverse and distant regions. From the beginning, the Congress has

---

1. Other factors, of course, may be influential. A large part of the motivation behind delegation of the tariff-making power, for instance, was the desire of congressmen to free themselves of a massive and difficult work load.

shown that its most deep-seated fear is not of obstruction but of quick majoritarian decisions, and its structures and procedures have evolved accordingly. Committees, and later subcommittees, were created for the thorough consideration of legislation, each with the right to proceed with virtual autonomy at its own unhurried pace, to act or not to act, as it might choose. The Senate adopted a rule of unlimited debate, a principle so cherished that even after the circumstances of the twentieth century forced members to reconsider and modify it, the votes of three-fifths of the body's membership are still required to terminate debate. And, of course, the constitutional division of the American legislature into two independent houses compounds its difficulties in attaining "decision" and "dispatch." When each house has acted, the two still must be brought into agreement with each other, which may be time-consuming or, on occasion, impossible.[2]

The inability to act quickly, then, virtually compels the Congress to delegate its powers—as the Founding Fathers presumably intended—on matters where the government must be prepared to respond speedily to events beyond its control. Either it authorizes the president to act, subject to review after the action, or it renders the government incapable of acting with speed and decisiveness at all.

Foreign affairs is, of course, the preeminent area in which the government must be capable of instant and resolute response. In wartime, this necessity has consistently been recognized, and the Congress has delegated to the president broad authority to prosecute the conflict, including the making of commitments to allied countries. Between the two world wars, the Congress experimented—in the Neutrality Acts—with the notion that it could prescribe in advance the course of action to be pursued by the government in any crisis that might arise; the experiment had to fail, and did. After World War II, the Congress found that the old distinction between war and peace was blurred, that peace itself had been renamed cold war. The Formosa, Middle East, Cuba, and Gulf of Tonkin resolutions were all concessions that in the modern era the Congress cannot debate how to respond to ultimatums, or when to issue them. Senator Douglas's declaration in the debate over Korea that "the speed of modern war requires quick executive action; even the slightest delay may prove fatal" reappeared in similar words in each of the subsequent debates on delegation of broad presidential power to act in various quarters of the globe.

2. In earlier decades, the fact that the Congress was in session for only a few months of the year was an additional, and powerful, argument for delegating authority for action to the president. But since virtual year-round sessions have become the rule, this argument, at least, has lost most of its force.

The Congress has been much slower to acknowledge that economic crises, which may also boil up with suddenness and intensity, call for an equivalent capacity for quick and forceful action in domestic affairs. When World War II imposed sudden strains on the economy, the Congress granted the president broad authority to impose direct controls on wages and on prices, as it did when the Korean hostilities began. During the Vietnam involvement, neither President Johnson nor President Nixon sought such authority, but the Congress ultimately thrust on Nixon the price and wage control powers that he exercised in 1971. A strong case can be made for a continuing delegation of authority to the president to impose controls and alter fiscal policy to counter inflationary or recessionary economic trends, on the ground that the Congress can rarely act with the speed and decisiveness that match the force of sudden and unexpected economic events. Presidents can procrastinate, too, but they are not compelled to do so by any institutional structure. In any case, the Congress has admitted the endemic weakness in its own capacity. Whenever it has recognized the necessity for speed of action, it has responded by building up the presidency.

The Incapacity to Plan

The many congressionally initiated directives to the president to propose comprehensive policies—the annual budget, the fiscal plan, the economic program, the national urban policy, and so on—reflect the Congress's second self-acknowledged weakness, as planner. So does its tendency to wait, in almost every other field as well, for the president's proposals before engaging in serious legislative activity. It is this attribute that has led the Congress to elevate the president to the position of chief legislator, the agenda-setter for the legislative bodies.

Again, it is the decentralization and fragmentation of power within the legislative body that impair the ability of the Congress. The incapacity to plan is the result of bicameralism and, particularly, the committee system. But a committee structure is an inescapable mechanism for a legislative body that truly legislates. It must assign some of its members to specialize in a given subject matter, inform themselves through hearings and discussion, avail themselves of expert staff, and then provide the information and advice on which the other members can rely. Committees can also serve as legislatures-in-miniature, undertaking the bargaining and compromising necessary to attain for their measures a sufficiently broad basis of consent within the parent body. From the standpoint of the legislature as a whole, specialization is the only way to get the work done; from the standpoint of the individual member, it is a way to escape the anonymity of the parliamentary back-bencher and attain a measure of influence and power, if only in a limited domain.

But just as the deliberativeness of a legislative body is at war with speed, so the specialization of standing committees is at war with comprehensive planning. The specialized committees, by their very nature, are instructed to think narrowly. And the problem has been compounded by the committees' division of their concerns, for the same reasons, into the still narrower confines of subcommittees.

This fragmented structure has enabled the legislative branch to develop a considerable measure of expertise, both in the members and in their staffs, that has proved indispensable for many purposes—for reviewing the specific proposals of the executive branch, for acting as a prod to the executive to produce such proposals and serving as an alternative source of initiative when it does not, for hammering out legislative compromises, and for over-seeing the executive in the administration of the laws. But specialized bodies, by their very nature, cannot be the source of the grand strategy that may be needed to inform and coordinate their individual products.

The Congress has not usually found that to be a disadvantage, for when the legislature has seen the need for planning—just as when it has seen the need for quick action—the executive has been available. The executive branch is appropriately designed for that purpose too, especially as the Executive Office of the President has been developed; and it is well staffed and usually willing, sometimes eager, to undertake the planning role. So, during the period of congressional decline, as individual legislators or committees looked beyond their piecemeal legislative labors for a broader framework within which to fit their measures—for a budget, an economic plan, a security policy, an urban policy—they turned to the president and assigned the task to him. Then the executive, when it took the initiative to formulate a plan, was in the best position to guide it through the legislative process afterward; and the Congress, not having staffed itself to prepare the plan, often was not well equipped to review and modify it.

As long as the president and the congressional majorities were of the same party—which until the mid-1950s was the normal state of affairs—this rela-tionship was acceptable enough. When the branches were under control of opposing parties, however, the Congress necessarily rejected the president as its leader and legislative planner, and then the weakness of the Congress in trying to set its own course became glaringly apparent. Then the legislators came to comprehend the importance to them of the function of agenda-setting that they had given up, and the consequences of their failure to develop the institutional capacity for planning.

The Void in Centralizing Institutions

In theory at least, the Congress could have achieved a better balance between its conflicting objectives. It could have developed a greater capacity for decision and dispatch, at the cost of some deliberation. And it could have developed its capacity for planning, synthesizing and coordinating, even as it was developing its specialized expertise through standing committees. It could have built centralizing institutions to offset the decentralizing ones, unifying influences to balance the fragmentation. The only constitutional limits would have been those of bicameralism.

(These limits, of course, are not to be lightly disregarded. There can be no unqualified assurance against deadlock in a bicameral legislature; if speed of action must be assured absolutely, the only recourse is to define the responsibility as executive. Yet not all matters require the same absolute assurance of the capacity for instant response. Economic crises break quickly, but still usually with less speed than military and diplomatic ones. If each house individually had the capacity to act quickly, both would bring greater decisiveness to the resolution of interhouse disputes, and the Congress would be in a far stronger position to make the kinds of decisions—such as the imposition of controls—that it has at times felt compelled to relinquish to the president.

(In the realm of planning, the consequences of bicameralism are not severe. If each house developed its separate capacity to plan, that would serve the purpose well enough. Unity between the houses in broad legislative strategy would be advantageous, but it would not have to be guaranteed. Moreover, because planning does not have to be accomplished with dispatch, time would be available for the reconciliation of differences in the programs of the two houses. Joint planning bodies, with joint staffs, are readily conceivable. Indeed, the general plans of the two chambers might be easier to reconcile than are disputes over concrete legislative measures, and the existence of jointly agreed plans might facilitate the harmonization of legislative differences.)

The role of chief legislator has in some periods of history resided in the legislative branch. Indeed, the president-as-chief-legislator is essentially a twentieth century conception. If the Congress is to reestablish its capacity to formulate and to set the legislative agenda, the requirements are easily identified. It must find means to subordinate its dispersed centers of power to an effective coordinating and synthesizing force. It must develop organs of some kind strong enough to make procedural decisions on behalf of the membership as a whole, to discipline the committees to conform their work to the policies laid down from the center, and to take matters out of the hands of committees when they are sluggish. This is the kind of control the president can exercise over the executive branch to enable him to act decisively and to plan—not that he always must or does, but he *can*. He stands at the top of a hierarchy, in a position to settle matters, to call in quarrelsome department heads, hammer out an administration position, and cement it in a statement or document that is binding on the whole executive branch, enforceable if necessary by the power to dismiss.

For the Congress to reclaim and exercise any significant share of its lost prerogatives, its two houses would have to organize as something like hierarchies too. They would have to pull back authority from the innumerable committee and subcommittee chairmen, and from the individual members, and subject them to an unaccustomed kind of discipline.

But members of Congress are independent-minded; fundamentally, they like the system the way it is. It has evolved in response to their needs, to the motivations that led the individual members to run for office and that keep them there. The rewards they seek are most easily and surely attained through a decentralized system, the punishments feared—first of all, defeat at the polls—most easily avoided. The greater the freedom of the individual members from leadership pressure and coercion, the greater their leeway to behave in whatever manner is best calculated to enhance the probability of reelection. Any change, then, is a threat to individual well-being.

There are other obstacles to be overcome as well. One is the mechanical problem of grafting a hierarchical authority onto the legislative structure without sacrificing the real values of pluralism and diversity. Another is the need to reconcile the principle of hierarchy with the democratic principle of equality among legislators, to assure that every member's constituents have the right to as great a share of influence on the legislative outcome as any other's.

Clearly, centralization of power in each house would have to be achieved through the auspices of the majority party, which assumes responsibility for organizing the body—and, indeed, exists for that purpose. From that flows another proposition: Power drawn back from the committees and the subcommittees would be retained somewhere within the majority party apparatus, because to share leadership and coordinating responsibility on any broad scale with the minority would be to relinquish power voluntarily—and to create one or another form of coalition government, inevitably an unwieldy arrangement—in the absence of any compelling reason for doing so. True, elements of the central planning and coordination function were lodged in the bipartisan joint committees of the Civil War and Reconstruction periods discussed in chapter 2 (although they were for practical purposes unipartisan) and the budget committees established in 1974,[3] but they operated within limited spheres. The exercise of a general coordinating and disciplinary role by a bipartisan body finally proved intolerable in the case of the House Rules Committee in the 1950s and 1960s.

Within the majority party apparatus, centralized power can be exercised by (a) the party leadership, (b) a policy committee, or (c) the caucus of all party members, or by various combinations of these. All three of these alternatives have been tested.

Power in the Leadership: The Era of the Czars

The apogee of leadership power came during a twenty-year period at the turn of the century. The leaders' rise in the post-Civil War decades had coincided with the solidification of tightly organized and well-disciplined party machines at state and local levels, held together by patronage, and the politicians who made their way to the Congress were accustomed to follow leaders—or obey bosses, as critics of the system put it. Ultimately, new currents of progressive thought triumphed over old-fashioned party discipline and the era of leadership power in the Congress came to an end.

In the House in particular the power of the speaker had been increasing since the Civil War.[4] The wartime speaker, Republican Schuyler Colfax of Indiana, was the first occupant of that office to assume the responsibility of "dictating to his followers [in the majority party] the policy to be carried out," according to Mary Parker Follett's study of the speakership. Before the opening of the Thirty-ninth Congress in 1865, Colfax laid down a program at odds with President Lincoln's policies on reconstruction, and it was his

3. The Joint Economic Committee has had a planning responsibility, but unlike the Civil War and Reconstruction bodies and the budget committees, it has had no legislative jurisdiction and hence no means to bring its plans before the two houses for adoption, or even for consideration.

4. In the first half of the nineteenth century Henry Clay had demonstrated the potentially great power of the speakership, but after he left the House in 1824 the office "went into eclipse." Roger H. Davidson and Walter J. Oleszek, *Congress Against Itself* (Indiana University Press, 1977), p. 21.

views that prevailed in the next two years.[5] James G. Blaine, the Maine Republican who succeeded Colfax in 1869, initiated party discipline "boldly as a first principle of political morality" and "carried to new extremes the manipulation of committee assignments to guarantee favorable action on desired legislation."[6] Samuel J. Randall of Pennsylvania (1876–81), a Democratic speaker, is credited with making absolute the speaker's control of the flow of House business by use of the power of recognition to decide who would be permitted to speak and in what order, no longer subject to appeal to the membership.[7]

Speaker John G. Carlisle, Kentucky Democrat (1883–89), like Colfax, had a program and used the power of recognition, the power over committee assignments, and "every other means which his office afforded . . . to impose his will on the House and to be the real source of the legislation of the United States." He converted the Rules Committee, which had been made a standing committee in Randall's time, into a "steering committee" that he and two of his appointees could dominate to schedule the business of the House.[8] All of these practices were solidified by his Republican successor, Thomas B. Reed of Maine, one of the ablest and strongest speakers to hold that office and the first accorded the sobriquet of *czar*. His famed Reed Rules also brought an end to dilatory tactics by which the minority had been able to frustrate the majority in the preceding decades.

By the time of Reed the office of speaker was being described as "the central feature of our actual system of government"[9] and its occupant as "next to the President, the most powerful man in the nation."[10] And with the arrival of a second Republican czar, Joseph G. Cannon of Illinois (1903–11), the speaker was adjudged even "more powerful than the President" because the president merely recommended legislation while the speaker "dictated" it.[11] "The House of Representatives," wrote Mary Follett, "is no longer the legislative power, but it is not even the maker of the legislative power; it is

5. *The Speaker of the House of Representatives* (Longmans, Green, 1896), pp. 98–99.

6. Neil MacNeil, *Forge of Democracy: The House of Representatives* (McKay, 1963), p. 30.

7. Albert V. House, Jr., "The Contributions of Samuel J. Randall to the Rules of the National House of Representatives," *American Political Science Review*, vol. 29 (October 1935), pp. 838–39.

8. Follett, *The Speaker*, pp. 115, 117.

9. Ibid., p. vii.

10. Albert Bushnell Hart, introduction to ibid., p. xi.

11. Hubert Bruce Fuller, *The Speakers of the House* (Little, Brown, 1909), p. 269. Such terms as *dictated* are, of course, overstatements. Both Reed and Cannon sometimes lost legislative battles. Reed personally opposed the Spanish-American War but was unable to "dictate" House policy. He also broke with President McKinley and the majority of his House colleagues on policies toward Cuba, Hawaii, and the Philippines after the war, and in 1899 resigned his House seat because of his disappointment with the party's policies. The first reclamation act was passed over Cannon's opposition.

but the maker of the real maker, the Speaker of the House of Representatives."
Ascendant on Capitol Hill, the speaker was bound to extend his influence
over the executive branch as well.[12]

An aspirant for the speakership might have to make commitments to other
important party figures to win his post, of course, and he had to maintain
their support to keep it; so his power was always less than absolute. Yet,
once elected, a skillful speaker had the resources to consolidate his position.
He had coveted rewards to bestow, and the means for inflicting heavy
punishment. Through his domination of the Rules Committee, and through
his power of recognition, he could block the pet legislation of an unfriendly
member and even deny the member the opportunity to make a speech. "The
power of recognition sent to the Speaker's anteroom, before the House
convened each day, humbly, and with hat in hand, every Member who
desired recognition of the floor for consideration of a bill or resolution."[13] But
most important were committee assignments, to be apportioned, at the
speaker's discretion, among his supporters. "I soon learned," wrote George
W. Norris, the insurgent Nebraska Republican, "that if I was to get any favors
in the way of appointments it would be necessary that I be ever faithful to
the leadership."[14] His loyalty being suspect, he got no favors. Although
speakers customarily deferred to seniority in reappointing chairmen and
members of existing committees, their power to discipline party members
was always in reserve, and in the Sixtieth and Sixty-first Congresses (which
convened in 1907 and 1909, respectively), Cannon visited wholesale punishment on Republican insurgents who had opposed him on legislative matters
and who were beginning to organize against him. Henry Cooper of Wisconsin
and Charles Fowler of New Jersey were relieved as chairmen of committees;
E. S. Henry of Connecticut and Gilbert Haugen of Iowa were passed over for
a chairmanship; Victor Murdock of Kansas was demoted on his committee;
and Norris, C. R. Davis of Minnesota, Elmer Morse of Wisconsin, and William
Lovering of Massachusetts were removed from committees.[15] Cannon explained that these members had either failed to participate in, or had refused
to abide by the decisions of, the party caucus—which, of course, Cannon
controlled. In the same reshuffling, Cannon even juggled Democratic com-

---

12. *The Speaker*, pp. 247, 326
13. George Rothwell Brown, *The Leadership of Congress* (Bobbs-Merrill, 1922), p. 86.
14. *Fighting Liberal: The Autobiography of George W. Norris* (Macmillan, 1945), p 97.
15. Charles O. Jones, "Joseph G. Cannon and Howard W. Smith: An Essay on the Limits of
Leadership in the House of Representatives," *Journal of Politics*, vol. 30 (August 1968), p. 623;
Kenneth W. Hechler, *Insurgency: Personalities and Politics of the Taft Era* (Columbia University Press,
1940), p. 215; Chang-Wei Chiu, *The Speaker of the House of Representatives Since 1896* (Columbia
University Press, 1928), pp. 66–67.

mittee assignments. Ignoring the Democratic leadership, he promoted out of order some Democrats who had supported him.[16]

Norris recalled several incidents that reflected the speaker's power. Assigned to a public buildings subcommittee on his arrival in the Congress in 1903, he heard the committee at its first meeting, on motion of the ranking Democrat, instruct the chairman to meet with the speaker to find out "whether or not we should be allowed to have a public building bill at that session." As a newcomer, adds Norris, he "could not understand why the Speaker should have anything more to say about it than anyone else, and especially the members of the committee."[17] On a later occasion, when a tariff subcommittee put petroleum on the free list, the speaker asked the chairman to call a meeting for reconsideration, in order to "abide by the promise which party leaders had made to the oil interests to place a tariff on petroleum and petroleum products." Obediently, the subcommittee reversed itself, although it was later reversed in turn on the House floor.[18]

The House in those days usually eclipsed the Senate, and senators, too, waited in the speaker's anteroom to solicit his support for measures their constituents desired. But the Senate was no less tightly controlled than the House. The Senate had no office equivalent to that of speaker, but Nelson W. Aldrich of Rhode Island—"probably the single most powerful senator in the history of the body"[19]—was at the center of a group of like-minded conservative Republicans who collectively dominated their chamber. Grouped around him were William B. Allison of Iowa, John Spooner of Wisconsin, and Orville Platt of Connecticut, and as a cohesive leadership they influenced committee assignments, managed the caucus, controlled the flow of business on the floor, and personally or through allies dominated the major standing committees.[20]

But the rise to power of Reed and Aldrich virtually coincided with the birth of the Progressive movement. The new century found Theodore Roosevelt in the White House, the muckrakers filling the popular magazines with their exposés, and political bossism and concentrated economic power—TR's "malefactors of great wealth"—under attack. Centralized power in the Congress was vulnerable on both counts. The congressional bosses offended the

16. Champ Clark, *My Quarter Century in American Politics* (Harper and Bros., 1920), vol. 2, pp. 272–73.

17. Norris, *Fighting Liberal*, pp. 95–96.

18. Ibid., pp. 101–02.

19. Randall B. Ripley, *Power in the Senate* (St. Martin's, 1969), p. 27.

20. Ibid. Also David J. Rothman, *Politics and Power: The United States Senate, 1869–1901* (Atheneum, 1969), pp. 44–61. Ripley points out that even at the peak of their power the Aldrich group suffered occasional defeats; *Power in the Senate*, pp. 27–29.

rising spirit of the new age not only by the coercive methods they employed to achieve their goals but also by the goals themselves. The dominant congressional oligarchy was closely linked to the trusts. The Senate, derided in the muckraking press as a Millionaire's Club, was soon to be remade by popular demand, through a constitutional amendment providing for its members to be elected by the people rather than by state legislatures. The Republican oligarchy in both houses was protariff, prorailroad, proemployer, antiprogressive, lacking in sympathy for any of the burgeoning protest and reform movements of the day—agrarian or urban, political or economic.

And, obviously, quite out of step with Roosevelt. Knowing their power, he dealt with them circumspectly. He met regularly with Cannon, and occasionally won concessions. Occasionally, also, he was able to defeat him, as on the reclamation act, when Cannon led the opposition but lost to a coalition of Democrats and western Republicans. But by the end of his presidency, the break with the congressional leaders was complete.

By then, too, Cannonism had become a national issue. Proclaimed the Democratic platform of 1908: "We demand that the House of Representatives shall again become a deliberative body, controlled by a majority of the people's Representatives and not by the Speaker; and we pledge ourselves to adopt such rules and regulations . . . as will enable a majority of its Members to conduct its deliberations and control its legislation."

And indignation was welling up on the House floor. John M. Nelson, insurgent Republican of Wisconsin, commented on the coming election: "What is it all for? . . . it will be in the power of a few, in the power of one . . . to defy, to ignore, and to defeat [the President's] recommendations. . . . It is the consensus of opinion that practically all the power of this body has been merged in the Speakership. . . . that the individual members have surrendered their constitutional rights, powers, and privileges."[21] William P. Hepburn, insurgent Republican of Iowa, complained:

> No member ought to be compelled to go to another man, his equal and no more, a representative of a constituency no whit superior to his own, and ask for the poor privilege of calling his measure to the attention of the House. [Applause.] And I do not hesitate to assert that if our constituents knew what we had done with their power, how we have betrayed our trust, how we have turned over their rights to another man, how we have imposed this wonderful difference between one constituency and another, not one of us would get back again. [Applause.][22]

During the campaign, Republican candidate William Howard Taft "complained that the greatest burden he had to carry was Cannonism, which was

21. *Congressional Record*, February 8, 1908, pp. 1652, 1649.
22. Ibid., February 18, 1909, p. 2654.

synonymous with 'reactionaryism'."[23] After his victory, Taft gave some encouragement to Cannon's opponents who planned a fight on his reelection to the speakership, but he gave up when he concluded the effort could not win.

The Republican progressives, unable to contest Cannon's election, set out to attack his powers. They reached an agreement with the Democratic leadership (who had an additional interest in scoring a partisan victory) on a joint proposal to strip from the speaker the power to appoint committees (except Ways and Means) and create an independent Rules Committee of fifteen members, excluding the speaker and reflecting the chamber's Democratic–insurgent Republican majority. The coalition held in rejecting adoption of the rules of the 1907–09 Congress, but enough regular Democrats bolted to prevent the adoption of the radical proposal. All that survived was a modification of the speaker's recognition power, which Cannon accepted "with good grace."[24]

Eventually, in March 1910, the Progressives found a new parliamentary opening, and, in the famous Revolution of 1910, the czar was dethroned.[25] An independent Rules Committee was established, elected by the House at large and excluding the speaker.

On its face, this was not much of a victory. The new ten-man Rules Committee included six Republicans chosen by the party caucus, which meant they were Cannon lieutenants. But in the next Congress the Democrats were in the majority and the new speaker was Champ Clark of Missouri, one of the conspirators and floor managers of the Revolution of 1910,[26] and with his full cooperation and consent, the Democrats now moved to take the last of the speaker's three great powers: his discretion in committee appointments. Assignments would henceforth be made through election by the House. And the Democratic caucus determined that nomination of the Democratic members would be made by a committee on committees, composed of the Democratic members of the Ways and Means Committee.

The day of the czars had ended. When the Republicans regained control of the House in 1919, "a return to the old order . . . was not seriously considered by anybody."[27] They deliberately passed over their minority leader of the preceding eight years, James Mann of Illinois, in favor of Frederick H.

23. George E. Mowry, *The Era of Theodore Roosevelt, 1900–1912* (Harper and Bros., 1958), p. 239.

24. Paul DeWitt Hasbrouck, *Party Government in the House of Representatives* (Macmillan, 1927), p. 5.

25. For a recent account of the revolution, see Jones, "Cannon and Smith," pp. 626–30.

26. Clark announced he would preside as an impartial moderator, a "Dean of Faculty." *Congressional Record*, August 24, 1912, p. 11840.

27. Brown, *Leadership of Congress*, p. 190.

Gillett of Massachusetts, in part because Mann was a protégé of Cannon and the members feared a recentralization of power.[28] And the public would not stand for it. When Nicholas Longworth, Republican of Ohio, who succeeded Gillett in 1925, declared his intention to use the powers of the speaker to enact the party's platform, he was greeted with cartoons of "Czar Nicholas" and editorial warnings against a return to Cannonism.[29]

But the powers of the speaker were by then too limited to permit any such development. No one had tried since the Revolution of 1910 to restore any of the speaker's old powers. And within the Republican party, the right to name committee members had—as in the case of the Democratic party—been transferred from the leadership to a committee on committees, which on the Republican side consisted of a member from each state that had sent one or more Republicans to the Congress. So the speaker who had been described in 1916 as "disarmed," as "simply a moderator, who keeps order and decides points of order"[30] remained in that relatively lowly status.

During the same period that saw the emasculation of the speakership, the power of the conservative oligarchy in the Senate was shattered too. Its ranks were thinned by retirement and death, and the Republican insurgents made their open break with the conservatives that foreshadowed the party split of 1912. Aldrich's ascendancy had rested on a personal rather than an institutional base, and with his departure no other leader, or small group, in either party could ever gain the same degree of dominance. Moreover, after adoption of the Seventeenth Amendment in 1913, direct election of senators further encouraged them to cultivate constituencies independently of party bosses.

Power in the Majority Caucus: The Sixty-third Congress

In the House the power wrested from the speaker had to repose somewhere, and when the Democrats took control of that body in 1911 the formal center of authority became the majority party caucus. As Speaker Clark, by both necessity and choice, stood aside, the leader of the House, for the first time in decades, "was not at the rostrum but . . . on the floor."[31] The majority leader, Oscar W. Underwood of Alabama, was also chairman of the Ways

28. Randall B. Ripley, *Party Leaders in the House of Representatives* (Brookings Institution, 1967), pp. 98–99; Brown, *Leadership of Congress*, pp. 191–92; Booth Mooney, *Mr. Speaker: Four Men Who Shaped the United States House of Representatives* (Follett, 1964), pp. 13–14.

29. Hasbrouck, *Party Government*, pp. 23–25.

30. DeAlva Stanwood Alexander, *History and Procedure of the House of Representatives* (Houghton Mifflin, 1916), pp. xii–xiii. Alexander had served as a Republican congressman from New York from 1897 to 1911.

31. Brown, *Leadership of Congress*, p. 176.

and Means Committee, whose Democratic members were the party's committee on committees which nominated the chairmen and majority members of the standing committees.

Underwood thus became the commanding figure in the House, but he elected to use the caucus as the formal instrument of control. It assumed the responsibility for making party policy. At a meeting on April 1, 1911, it approved a six-point program offered by Underwood and then "directed" the Democratic members of the various committees not to report any other legislation to the House during that session "unless hereafter directed by this caucus."[32]

Two years earlier, during the period of plotting that preceded the overthrow of Speaker Cannon, the Democratic caucus had adopted a set of rules, among them one that permitted a two-thirds majority to bind all members of the caucus.[33] The caucus could therefore not only set party policy but enforce it. Invariably it went along with the position established by the Democratic members of the appropriate committees, but in doing so it stifled dissent.[34] To violate the caucus directive would be to be "read out of the party," with accompanying loss of perquisites, including choice committee assignments.

In 1913, after President Wilson's landslide election, Underwood made the caucus the instrument of the Wilsonian attempt at party government, and the measures that became Wilson's New Freedom were passed through that mechanism. Caucus discipline was especially important in enactment of the Underwood tariff reduction act and the Federal Reserve Act in 1913, and it was helpful in staving off amendments to the president's antitrust legislation in 1914. These measures were first considered by Democratic committee members in meetings from which the Republicans were excluded, then presented to the Democratic caucus for binding votes, and only then presented to the full membership of the appropriate committees and to the full House

32. Wilder H. Haines, "The Congressional Caucus of Today," *American Political Science Review*, vol. 9 (November 1915), p. 697n.

33. A member could announce his intention not to be bound if the question involved constitutional construction or a matter on which he had "made contrary pledges to his constituents prior to his election or received contrary instructions by resolutions or platform from his nominating authority," but he had to advise the caucus (or, if absent, the majority leader) of this decision not to be bound. These qualifications were evidently not invoked often enough to seriously limit the impact of caucus decisions. The two-thirds majority had also to be a majority of House Democrats. The caucus rules of 1909 are reprinted in George B. Galloway, *History of the House of Representatives*, ed. Sidney Wise, 2d rev. ed. (Crowell, 1976), pp. 171–72.

34. On April 11, 1911, for instance, it endorsed several bills presented by the Democratic members of the Ways and Means Committee and pledged the caucus members to vote for the bills and against all amendments, except formal committee amendments, that changed "their text from the language agreed upon in this caucus." Wilder H. Haines, "Congressional Caucus," p. 698n.

for ratification without amendment. The House Rules Committee, which controlled the flow of business on the floor, was "completely subject to the direction of the caucus."[35]

Almost the same procedure was followed in the Senate, under the direction of its new majority leader, John W. Kern of Indiana. While the Senate Democratic caucus had had since 1903 a rule to permit the binding of its members by a two-thirds vote,[36] it adopted a less authoritarian procedure in 1913 that had about the same effect. Each member was called on to state publicly his position, and then a resolution was adopted that, while not binding, was "strongly worded" and put "great moral pressure" on members who disagreed with majority sentiment.[37] Thus procedures in both houses made it possible to exclude the Republicans from effective participation in the legislative process. The exclusion could even extend to House-Senate conference committees; on the tariff bill, the conference committee did not meet until its Democratic members from the two houses had reconciled all their differences and were able to present a solid front to the Republicans.[38]

Wilson, as a believer in party government, was determined to present a party program, and as the party leader he expected to take responsibility for the formulation of the program. But he recognized that the Democrats in the Congress represented the party also, and he frequently looked to them as his lieutenants for policy development. The Underwood tariff was essentially a congressional product, based on the Democratic bills of the previous Congress that President Taft had vetoed,[39] but Wilson intervened to change some of the decisions of the Ways and Means Democrats. In the case of the Federal Reserve Act, the president had no deep views of his own and looked to Representative Carter Glass of Virginia. His detachment turned out to be an advantage, because when conflict developed in the caucus the president could serve as a disinterested mediator.[40] The caucuses, not the floors of the

35. Ibid., p. 600. House Democrats spent a total of thirty days in caucus in 1913–14. Stephen Howard Balch, "Party Government in the United States House of Representatives, 1911–1919" (Ph.D. dissertation, University of California, Berkeley, 1972), p. 192.

36. Its exceptions were like those in the House rules; see note 33, above.

37. Randall B. Ripley, *Majority Party Leadership in Congress* (Little, Brown, 1969), pp. 65–66, 69. The use of the caucus by Senate Democrats for purposes of party discipline had a long history on both sides of the Senate aisle. Charges of "dictation" by the Democratic caucus were heard in the tariff debate of 1894, for instance, and three years later the Democrats were decrying the sacrifice of individual Republican consciences to the "omnipotent" party caucus.

38. Ibid., p. 59.

39. The bill was drafted even before Wilson was inaugurated. Ibid., pp. 67–68; Oscar W. Underwood, *Drifting Sands of Party Politics* (Century, 1928), p. 171.

40. Arthur S. Link, *Woodrow Wilson and the Progressive Era, 1910–1917* (Harper and Bros., 1954), pp. 49–52; Ripley, *Majority Party Leadership,* p. 59; George A. Curran, "Woodrow Wilson's Theory and Practice Regarding Relations of President and Congress" (Ph.D. dissertation, Fordham University, 1949).

two houses, were the legislative battleground. The House caucus considered the Federal Reserve bill for nearly three weeks of what Glass called "a lively time." Amendments that would have drastically altered the Glass plan were offered there but defeated with the help of Wilson and Secretary of State William Jennings Bryan, the leader of the party's agrarian wing. "Always excitement was at a high pitch and frequently the hall resounded with cheers," Glass recalled. "Once or twice the enthusiasm became a riot, men standing in their chairs and tossing hats to the skylights."[41] The Senate caucuses were more decorous, but as in the House the majority party meetings were where the legislative struggle was joined and the decisions taken.

But government-by-caucus provoked a tumultuous opposition too, both from the excluded Republicans and from Progressive reformers. Thus, the National Voters' League, organized in 1913 by prominent Progressives to agitate for congressional reform, found King Caucus no less objectionable than the czarism they had decried earlier. The league's secretary charged the Democrats with not abolishing Cannonism but only disguising it, by transferring power to the floor leader; thus "they adapted and blended together the worst elements of two bad systems, both Republican in origin." He particularly condemned the secrecy of the caucuses, terming them a device "employed repeatedly to shield and mantle with vague, shifting irresponsibility the obstructive tactics of so-called leaders. . . . The caucus has become the last refuge of the dodgers. Those actually responsible for not bringing politically dangerous questions before the House for an open vote seek shelter in the failure of the caucus to command them to do so." Moreover, it allowed a minority of the House, by dominating the majority caucus, to bind enough members from outside its ranks to enable it to prevail.[42] The caucus was pictured as "a shelter behind which members may prostitute their convictions in the dark," persuaded by the corrupting influences of "patronage, perquisites, and 'pork'."[43]

The Republicans wove the themes together, sensing the opportunity to win on the issue of King Caucus the same support the Democrats had gleaned from their attacks on Cannonism. Throughout 1913 and 1914, they attacked the procedures by which the Democratic program was formulated and enacted, and their charges were echoed in editorials in the press. They brought the issue to a climax in September 1913 after the House majority caucus had

---

41. Carter Glass, *An Adventure in Constructive Finance* (Doubleday, Page, 1927), pp. 133, 143.

42. Lynn Haines, *Your Congress* (National Voters' League, 1915), pp. 67, 76–77. Other critics were more pointed in identifying the southern Democrats as the minority whose advantage the caucus served.

43. Wilder H. Haines, "Congressional Caucus," pp. 704–05.

voted to bind its members on the Federal Reserve bill. The vulnerability of the caucus form of congressional leadership is clear from a reading of the Federal Reserve debate. Sydney Anderson of Minnesota decried the "rules of the House, written and unwritten," and the "system of legislation, visible and invisible," which "strips me of my prerogative as a representative of the people. . . . It is true that I am still permitted to cast my vote, but I do so with the foreknowledge that it will not count. . . . My membership [on the Ways and Means Committee] is at once a fraud and a farce."[44] And he dramatized his protest by resigning from the committee.

John Jacob Rogers of Massachusetts noted that minority members had "until a few days ago been kept from the committee room. . . . Is legislation by caucus to be substituted for legislation by the great House of Representatives? . . . Not in the palmiest days of Czar Reed and of Speaker Cannon was the monarchy a tithe as absolute as now. Never did the lash of the presidential and caucus whip cut so deep as today." Victor Murdock of Kansas denounced the secret caucus: "No man can serve two masters. No man can serve his people and the caucus. He will serve either the one or the other. He cannot serve both. . . . The unit of representation in this House is not the political party. It . . . is the individual Member representing a district."[45]

"The caucus destroys individuality," charged Charles H. Dillon of South Dakota; "it establishes tyranny; it sacrifices the best legislative instrumentality, the conscience; it makes weaklings of its members." In the Senate also, Republicans helped to make the case. Francis E. Warren of Wyoming deplored a system whereby "great statesmen, leaders of their party—heretofore independent beings . . . yield . . . to . . . domination. . . . great men prohibited . . . from offering amendments even of the most trivial character; great statesmen, heads of great committees of this body, men of long and brilliant service, proscribed and muzzled."[46]

Speaker Clark took the floor to defend the caucus:

> Responsibility rests upon the majority, and we shrink not from acknowledging our responsibility to the country and of acting accordingly. Being responsible and having an ample majority we intend to place our ideas upon the statute books on the great questions now pressing for solution. While we invite help from Republicans and Progressives we cannot, without shirking our duty to the country, permit them to spoil our bills.
>
> We must have organization in order to enact the will of the people into law, and we have got it, and we have had it for the last three years. . . . The people of the

44. *Congressional Record*, September 11, 1913, pp. 4759–60.
45. Ibid., pp. 4764–65; September 10, 1913, p. 4668.
46. Ibid., September 13, 1913, p. 4904; September 8, 1913, p. 4441.

United States . . . are much more interested in results than in the methods by which those results are worked out. They want results. They are going to get them, and we are responsible for them.[47]

Some Democratic representatives acknowledged they were voting for bills they opposed because of the caucus binding votes. Thomas W. Hardwick of Georgia, for instance, announced that he supported the Federal Reserve bill

not because I like it, not because it is my judgment that it ought to be enacted into law, but because I conceive it is my duty to do so because of the caucus action of my party. . . . The maintenance of party solidarity and discipline is essential, and party discipline can not be maintained unless on each question that is the subject matter of party action the majority of the party shall control its attitude. Otherwise, we would have chaos and anarchy. . . . When I vote for this bill it will be a sacrifice that I shall make for the Democratic party.[48]

But other Democrats expressed misgivings. Thus Senator Gilbert Hitchcock of Nebraska left the Democratic caucus when, in endorsing income tax legislation, the caucus ruled against permitting a floor amendment regarding the taxation of trusts. He protested that senators should have been allowed to vote their consciences on such a great and new issue as the income tax. "After all," he said, "Senators here were elected to the Senate and not to a caucus, and . . . great questions of this sort [should be] debated in public and decided in public."

It has been an unpleasant sight to me, as it has been to many Democrats during the last few days. . . . when Senators on the Republican side . . . have proposed amendments to the income-tax provision that appeal to the sense of justice, and appeal to the judgment of Senators on this side, but who, because of caucus rule, were compelled to vote against such amendments. I do not think that is a worthy sight in the Senate of the United States. . . .

Like all caucuses, I believe the fact to be that our Democratic caucus degenerated into a political machine.[49]

Newspapers echoed the criticism, among them the *Washington Times*, which called the caucus "the instrument by which a garrote is fastened on the throat of all individuality and independence. . . . Caucus rule, through which a few bosses imposed their will on the party and through it on the country, was the real thing that wrecked Republicanism. It will wreck Democracy, too, in time, and in a good deal shorter time than it required in the other case, for the country understands better now and is less willing to be patient with such methods."[50]

The caucus did not wreck Democracy, but perhaps only for the reason that the Democrats abandoned it. After passage of the Clayton Anti-Trust

47. Ibid., September 24, 1913, pp. 5157–59.
48. Ibid., September 12, 1913, p. 4801.
49. Ibid., August 29, 1913, pp. 3858–59.
50. Ibid., September 13, 1913, p. 4765.

Act of 1914 and two companion measures under binding votes in June 1914, caucus discipline appears not to have been imposed again during the Sixty-third Congress, and with that Congress the short career of government-by-caucus ended.

It would undoubtedly be going too far to attribute the abandonment of the caucus wholly to the drumfire of criticism from the Republicans and the supportive press, Progressive intellectuals, and restive Democrats like Senator Hitchcock. There were other factors. In 1914, Underwood was elected to the Senate, removing the pivot from the caucus system in the House. Even more important, with the outbreak of the war in Europe in that year, the Democratic party in both houses split over the issue of preparedness. Underwood's successor as majority leader, Claude Kitchin of North Carolina, was on the opposite side from President Wilson, and far from acting as a lieutenant to the president, he devoted much of his time and effort to marshalling the antipreparedness forces in the House.[51] It is probably a safe conclusion that binding caucuses in the American Congress are conceivable only in periods when the governing party has a high degree of internal unity, and in the Wilson period that lasted a scant two years.

But the caucus was never restored to its 1913–14 status by either party, even in times of extraordinary unity, and after the 1930s it lapsed into disuse as a means of setting—or even discussing—legislative policy.[52] Too many people, in and out of Congress, found the coercion of individual conscience to be, in Senator Hitchcock's words, an unworthy sight. Both parties were split on many questions, and insurgent factions sought freedom to form their coalitions with like-minded members across party lines. Beginning in the Progressive Era, America's political ethos became antiboss, antimachine, individualistic, even antiparty. If the representative could serve but one master, as Victor Murdock argued, the voters preferred that they, not the caucus or the boss who stood behind it, be that master—and so did the representatives themselves. As for senators, by constitutional amendment in 1913 they won the right to establish their direct link with the people through

51. The beginnings of the split were apparent in early 1914, when Clark and Underwood opposed Wilson on a bill relating to Panama Canal tolls and were beaten when Wilson lined up other Democratic leaders on his side. James Miller Leake, "Four Years of Congress," *American Political Science Review*, vol. 11 (May 1917), pp. 261–62. See Stephen H. Balch, "Do Strong Presidents Really Want Strong Legislative Parties? The Case of Woodrow Wilson and House Democrats," *Presidential Studies Quarterly*, vol. 7 (Fall 1977), pp. 23–38, for a discussion of the sometimes strained relations between President Wilson and the House leadership.

52. It was still used for organizational purposes, of course. In 1949 a binding vote was taken in the House Democratic caucus in support of the 21-day rule to curtail the power of the Rules Committee. James A. Robinson, *The House Rules Committee* (Bobbs-Merrill, 1963), p. 64, citing *New York Times*.

popular vote. The direct primary, an invention of the Progressive Era, went far toward taking bosses and party organizations out of the nominating process. Tightly controlled machines remained for a long time in some states and counties—and remnants can still be found—but when Cannonism became a national issue and was overthrown, bossism on a national scale was no longer possible. The Wilson-Underwood-Kern system of binding caucuses was too patently another form of Cannonism. As the years went by, such a device could only appear more and more anachronistic when it was occasionally used.

The Republicans, having made a virtue of opposing the "gag rule" of the Democratic Sixty-third Congress, went so far as to drop the word *caucus* from their lexicon for a decade or more. Their party meetings in both houses since then have been termed *conferences*, except for a brief period in the 1920s.[53] The Democrats changed neither the name nor the rules. Yet the House caucus invoked the provision for binding votes only once in the second Wilson administration, in 1920, against a Republican military training bill and also against the president's wishes. With the Democrats in the minority, there were three binding votes in 1921, all in opposition to Republican tariff legislation; one in 1922 in opposition to a ship subsidy bill; and one in 1923 against an income tax reduction bill.

The next attempt to use the House Democratic caucus was in 1933, when Franklin Roosevelt took office as the first Democratic president since Wilson, and one equally unchallenged in the party leadership. He and his House leaders failed in an effort to line up the party behind the president's first major bill—the economy bill, which among other things proposed to reduce veterans' pensions. Only 173 of 282 Democrats—less than the two-thirds majority necessary for binding—voted to support the president. During the remainder of the first Roosevelt term, the caucus met only nine times to discuss legislation, and only two binding votes were passed—one on veterans' benefits in June 1933 and one on public works in 1936.

That was the last time House Democrats imposed control on their members' votes on legislative issues. The caucus fell into disuse even as a discussion forum. During the Eighty-first Congress (1949–50) it met three times to consider legislative measures (once for only ninety minutes), but for the next couple of decades convened only at the opening of each Congress to deal with organizational matters—to nominate its candidates for speaker and other party offices and to ratify the committee slates presented by its committee

53. The caucus then was used for the discussion of legislation, but there is no record of any binding votes. Hasbrouck, *Party Government*, p. 32; Ripley, *Party Leaders*, pp. 45–46.

on committees.[54] Speaker Sam Rayburn, the party's House leader from 1940 to 1961, considered caucuses "a waste of time" and feared that they "could do more harm than good" by deepening the party's North-South split.[55] The Senate Democratic caucus evidently followed a parallel decline. When the party returned to power in 1933, the Democratic senators did adopt a rule permitting a binding caucus but there is no evidence that the rule was ever invoked.[56] The caucus occasionally discussed legislation, but less and less frequently as the split over civil rights and other issues deepened. Given the intensity of party factionalism, the notion that the caucus might be reborn as an instrument of party discipline on legislative matters was never seriously proposed by anyone.

So the majority party caucus, like the strong speakership, was tried, used successfully for a time as a means of centralizing power in the Congress, but then discarded. From the early New Deal period until the 1970s, restoration of the caucus as a means of setting the Congress's legislative course was not even seriously discussed. Discontent with the distribution of power within the Congress expressed itself in proposals for reform on other lines, but a return to either of the extreme forms of centralization discredited in the Progressive Era was clearly beyond the range of possibility.

Decentralized Power: The Era of the Barons

The power that had resided in the majority leadership in the era of the czars and in the majority caucus in the 1913–14 interlude devolved largely to the standing committees after the Wilson period. Particularly, it went to the chairmen, who controlled the scheduling and the agenda of committee meetings, the establishment of subcommittees and referral of bills, and the appointment of committee staff. And those worthies, elected by the members of the two houses presumably to act as their agents, slipped more and more

54. This summary is taken from the Journal of the Democratic Caucus of the House of Representatives, 1916–1964, deposited in the manuscript room of the Library of Congress after the Eighty-eighth Congress (1963–64) by Representative Clarence Cannon of Missouri, then the caucus parliamentarian. There are no entries for the 70th, 71st, 72d, 86th, and 87th Congresses (1927–33 and 1959–62), but these followed Congresses where the caucus had met only for organizational purposes and it appears safe to conclude that the gap in the journal reflects a continuance of the use of the body only for routine matters. I have found no reference to caucus meetings for legislative discussion during these periods, either in historical accounts of legislative action or in analyses of congressional organization.

55. Mooney, *Mr. Speaker*, p. 168; MacNeil, *Forge of Democracy*, p. 109; Richard Bolling, *House Out of Order* (Dutton, 1965), p. 66.

56. Ripley, *Majority Party Leadership*, pp. 80–81. The records of the Senate Democratic caucus have not been made public.

out of the effective control of the membership or its elected leaders, by virtue of another institution unique to the American legislature—the seniority system.

Seniority had long been a criterion in the selection of committee chairmen and in the reappointment of committee members. It was the easy way to avoid recrimination and divisiveness. Moreover, it made the most of the benefits of experience. If the purpose of a committee is to specialize, then continuity of tenure is the means to that end. And, logically, the most experienced and knowledgeable member of the specialized group—that is, its senior member—should be its leader. But during the periods of centralized power in the House and the Senate, seniority had not been the only criterion of selection. On many occasions the principle had been breached: Speaker Cannon had punished his enemies by departing from it, and in 1913 Senate Majority Leader Kern had freely sacrificed tradition in order to constitute committees that would support President Wilson's program. As long as the possibility of departing from seniority existed, that in itself meant discipline. The fact that chairmen could be stripped of their prerogatives prevented them from too egregiously opposing the leadership's desires.

Those who sought to prevent a return to the era of the czars, then, found it necessary to take from the leaders their discretionary power to discipline committee chairmen and members, by removal, demotion, or reassignment. Whatever committee assignments and rank a senator or representative had attained had to be guaranteed as a matter of right. So a rigid seniority principle came to be seen as essential to the realization of the progressive ideal. Members protected by seniority would no longer "serve two masters"; they would be free to represent faithfully, without interference, the people who sent them to Washington. "Subservience," "dictation," "fear," "intimidation," "subjection," "tyranny"—those colorful words with which the older leader-member relationship had been condemned—would disappear from the House and Senate vocabulary. In their place would rise the new ideals of "individuality," "freedom of conscience," "equality," "representation," "independence," "integrity."

By the mid-1920s the principle of seniority was firmly in place in both houses[57] and for the next four decades remained as an unwritten yet rigid,

57. In 1925 Republican leaders in both houses penalized party members who had supported the independent presidential candidacy of Robert M. La Follette, Sr., the year before, but this was not, strictly speaking, a departure from seniority since the bolters were considered to have left the party. In 1932, however, GOP party bolters retained their committee posts. The evolution of the seniority system is traced in George Goodwin, Jr., "The Seniority System in Congress," and Nelson W. Polsby, Miriam Gallagher, and Barry Spencer Rundquist, "The Growth of the Seniority System in the U.S. House of Representatives," *American Political Science Review*, vol. 53 (June 1959), pp. 412–36, and vol. 62 (September 1968), pp. 787–807; and Michael Abram and Joseph Cooper, "The Rise of Seniority in the House of Representatives," *Polity*, vol. 1 (Fall 1968–69), pp. 52–85.

all but unyielding, rule. Once assigned to a committee, a senator or representative would remain on that panel as long as he desired (unless the
committee were abolished or the number of seats assigned to a party were
reduced) and the member would advance up its ladder of seniority rung by
rung, ultimately—on the majority side—to the chairmanship. And the chairman could be removed only by voluntary retirement, defeat for reelection,
or death.

Under these circumstances, committee chairmen could develop a fearsome
degree of independence. They became a new class of congressional barons;
the party leaders could appeal to them, but without sanctions with which to
threaten. Indeed, it was the other way around; the leaders were far more
dependent on the goodwill of the committee chairmen than the chairmen
were dependent on the leaders. A president might be able to bargain with
the committee chieftains; he could offer patronage and threaten vetoes. But,
like the legislative leaders, he was often more dependent on the chairmen
for the success of his program than they on him for patronage. "The President
will find it difficult to lead the House if there is no authoritative agent with
whom he may deal," was Lindsay Rogers's prescient prediction in 1924.
"Speaker Cannon could promise Roosevelt that the House would do certain
things and the things would be done. There is no one in the House now to
make such promises."[58] In any case, the legislative leader became a go-
between, adding little to whatever influence the president could exercise.
Once seniority became entrenched, any party program became a wish list.
It might influence, might persuade, but could not command. The very concept
of a congressional program, whether initiated by the president or assembled
by the leaders, was out of the question.

The most important single committee, from this standpoint, was the House
Rules Committee, that funnel through which all legislation normally had to
pass to reach the House floor. When the speaker was removed from the
committee in 1910, the chairman of Rules became an independent power,
and once his position was assured by seniority, his authority came to rival
that of the speaker and the majority leader. The first Rules Committee
chairman to assert his authority aggressively was apparently Philip P. Campbell, Kansas Republican, who blocked several bills in 1921–22, including the
Muscle Shoals power bill and the bill that became the national prohibition
act. The latter had to be considered under suspension of the rules (which
requires a two-thirds vote). Regarding a measure proposing an investigation

58. "The Second, Third, and Fourth Sessions of the 67th Congress," *American Political Science
Review*, vol. 18 (February 1924), pp. 92–93.

of the Department of Justice, Campbell was quoted as saying to the other members of his committee: "It makes no difference what a majority of you decide; if it meets with my disapproval, it shall not be done; I am the Committee; in me reposes absolute obstructionist powers." And he similarly defied the entire House: "Even though every Member wants this resolution, what will that avail you? I have the resolution in my pocket and shall keep it there." The House upheld, 149–114, his right to exercise a "pocket veto" when a point of order was raised against his action.[59] By 1931, the chairman's powers were described by a colleague as "so far-reaching that he can choke to death any piece of legislation."[60]

Even if the chairman of the Rules Committee saw his own role as being "an arm of the leadership," as some chairmen did, he could not necessarily carry his committee with him. During the 1930s the committee consisted of ten Democrats and four Republicans, which meant that as few as three conservative Democrats, by siding with the Republicans, could block any New Deal measure they disapproved. And no fewer than five of the committee Democrats were southern conservatives, which was representative enough of the House Democrats in the pre-New Deal period but was quite out of proportion after the New Deal landslides of 1932, 1934, and 1936. Two of the five, according to George B. Galloway, had appointed themselves to "stand guard at the legislative gates and test all applications for admission by their own political and sectional predilections."[61] And under the seniority system, they could act with impunity. Even the northern chairman, John J. O'Connor of New York, turned out to be hostile to parts of President Roosevelt's program and became the only victim of FDR's celebrated attempt to purge anti-New Deal Democrats in the party primaries of 1938.[62]

The Demand for Responsible Party Government

To the pro-Roosevelt liberals who represented the preponderance of the Democratic voting strength in the country, the baronial structure within the Congress appeared increasingly anachronistic. The rule of seniority played

59. *The Searchlight*, vol. 6 (1922), pp. 5–6, quoted by Chiu, *Speaker of the House*, pp. 147–59.

60. Floyd M. Riddick, *The United States Congress: Organization and Procedure* (National Capitol Publishers, 1949), p. 123.

61. *Congress at the Crossroads* (Crowell, 1946), p. 114. One of these was presumably Howard W. Smith of Virginia, the celebrated chairman from 1955 to 1966.

62. The most dramatic instance of obstructionism during the New Deal was blockage in 1938 of the bill that became the original Wage and Hour Act. It had passed the Senate by a two-to-one majority and been approved by the House Labor Committee, but was forced out of the Rules

into the hands of the New Deal's enemies—a coalition of Republicans and conservative Democrats, the latter mostly from safe one-party states and districts in the South. To the liberals it made little sense to entrust the party's program—the party's mandate from the people in the elections of the 1930s— to Democrats who would only devote their energies to blocking it. The issue was expressed, however, as one of principle. The object should be "responsible party government." Whichever party won the election, that party should so organize itself in the Congress that it could carry out the program it had presented to the voters. Clearly responsible, it could be held accountable at the next election.

Two authoritative studies, each carried out over a period of several years and issued in 1945, expressed this theme. Both disapproved the seniority system, though neither was prepared to flatly recommend a substitute method of selection. One, a report by Robert Heller for the National Planning Association, concluded that on this emotional issue the solution "should be worked out within the Congressional family." But the seniority rule was "to be deplored." It enabled chairmen "to be arbitrary with impunity" and it impeded "efforts to achieve the degree of party responsibility and accountability needed."[63] The other, by a ten-member committee of the American Political Science Association (APSA) chaired by George B. Galloway, found the seniority custom "archaic" and offered a choice of solutions.[64] One was to rotate chairmanships by putting a time limit, possibly of six years, on any member's service as head of a standing committee. This reform would preserve the automatic feature of the existing system, in which the committee saw "great merit"; it was a "harmonious" way of averting "logrolling, factional fights, and political trading on a grand scale." The other solution, which the committee implied would risk those dangers, would assign the power of selection to the majority party's committee on committees. The committee observed, however, that "the attacks on the seniority rule would lose most of their force if the chairmen were to be deprived of their almost dictatorial

---

Committee only by the arduous instrument of a discharge petition (which requires 218 signatures, a majority of the House). Thus pried loose, it was passed by the House, 314 to 97. The bill had been released from Rules by discharge petition in 1937 also, but subsequently recommitted to the Labor Committee. James MacGregor Burns, *Congress on Trial: The Legislative Process and the Administrative State* (1949; Gordian, 1966), pp. 68–82. The bill was until 1960 the only one enacted after being released through a discharge petition; in many instances, however, committees reported bills only when it appeared they were about to be discharged. Committees sometimes helped the administration and the leadership, of course, by bottling up undesired bills that were strongly backed by pressure groups.

63. *Strengthening the Congress* (Washington: National Planning Association, 1945), pp. 30–31.
64. *The Reorganization of Congress: A Report of the Committee on Congress of the American Political Science Association* (Public Affairs Press, 1945), pp. 34, 37, 80.

power to control the committees' action." To this end, it recommended that a majority of members of a committee be empowered to force the calling of meetings, that committee chairmen be required to report bills the committee had approved, and that a complete public record of committee meetings be kept.[65]

The forum for discussing these and other proposals for congressional reform was the Joint Committee on the Organization of Congress, created in late 1944 to undertake the first comprehensive review of the structure of the legislative branch since the Congress was established. Headed by Senator Robert M. La Follette, Jr., Wisconsin Progressive, and Representative A. S. Mike Monroney, Oklahoma Democrat, the committee's assignment was to produce a plan for modernizing the Congress—"to protect our rightful place in the constitutional scheme of things," to bring an end to "legislative retreat and executive mastery."[66] George Galloway, principal author of the 1945 APSA report, was engaged as staff director.

Modification of the seniority system found no champion even among the reformers on the joint committee. Many witnesses suggested that something be done about it, but they did not agree as to what. Some would have put the choice of committee chairmen in the majority party—either in the leadership or in a committee on committees—some proposed election of chairmen by the committee members, some spoke favorably of the APSA committee suggestion for rotation of chairmanships. But committee members expressed misgivings about all of these. None seemed eager to return to the era of the czars. Monroney worried about the "friction between members on the committees" that would follow abandonment of the seniority rule.[67] If seniority were violated, it probably would mean "the ruination of the man who was passed over," observed Representative Earl C. Michener of Michigan, a Republican member.[68] Chairman La Follette said afterward that he had "never seen a solution better than the disease."[69] In the end, the committee "was unable to agree on workable changes" in the system.[70] Nor could it agree on any of the suggestions advanced by various witnesses that the powers of the

65. Ibid., pp. 37, 80.
66. Representative Everett McKinley Dirksen, Illinois Republican and member of the committee, *Congressional Record*, December 15, 1944, p. 9539, and Representative Monroney, ibid., January 18, 1945, p. 439.
67. *Organization of Congress*, Hearings before the Joint Committee on the Organization of Congress, 79 Cong. 1 sess. (U.S. Government Printing Office, 1945), p. 813.
68. Ibid., p. 998.
69. Testimony, in *Legislative Reorganization Act of 1946*, Hearings before the Senate Committee on Expenditures in the Executive Departments, 80 Cong. 2 sess. (GPO, 1948), p. 72.
70. Galloway, *Congress at the Crossroads*, p. 343. Also La Follette testimony, in *Legislative Reorganization Act of 1946*, Hearings, p. 61.

House Rules Committee to bottle up bills approved by standing committees be eliminated or curtailed.[71]

It did, however, adopt some of the APSA committee's recommendations to reduce the arbitrary power of committee chairmen. Each committee (except appropriations) would have regularly scheduled meetings, at which the members—not the chairmen alone—would determine the agenda. Chairmen would be required to report the bills the committee had approved and seek their consideration on the floor. And complete records of committee proceedings would be kept. These provisions were incorporated in the Legislative Reorganization Act of 1946, which was the result of the La Follette-Monroney committee's work.[72]

They turned out, however, to be less than self-executing. Some chairmen moved promptly to set up regular meeting schedules and establish majority control of committee activities, but these were principally the ones who would not have been arbitrary in any case. Those who had been accustomed to "one-man rule" still had ample means for avoiding both the letter and the spirit of the law. If a chairman simply took no initiative to put new procedures into effect, it was exceedingly difficult—given the traditions of the committees—for junior members to seize control, write the procedures themselves, and force their adoption. The 1953 *Congressional Directory* still listed seven of eighteen House standing committees without regularly scheduled meeting dates, assembling only "on call of the chairman."[73] A decade later, four House committees were still so listed. Even when committees scheduled regular sessions, it was still up to the chairman, and the staff controlled by him, to notify the members that the meeting would in fact take place—which was not much different from empowering him to schedule the meeting in the first place. Without his and the staff's facilitation and cooperation, it was little short of impossible for the members to organize in advance to show up at

71. In 1949 the Rules Committee was chastened by adoption of the 21-day rule, which permitted substantive committee chairmen to bring to the floor measures that the Rules Committee had not acted on in that length of time. In the 1949–50 Congress, eight bills were dislodged from Rules in that manner, of which seven were passed. But in the next Congress, after the conservative coalition had been strengthened in the 1950 election, the rule was scrapped. James A. Robinson, *The House Rules Committee* (Bobbs-Merrill, 1963), pp. 34, 63–71.

72. On the other hand, that act abetted the concentration of power in a small group of chairmen by drastically reducing the number of committees in each house and giving them more clearly defined jurisdictions.

73. This excludes the Appropriations Committee, which was exempted by the act. Senate committees were all in compliance with the law. Representative Stewart L. Udall, Democrat of Arizona, estimated in 1957 that about two-thirds of the standing committees of the two houses were by then "free of one-man control," the other third "still chairman-dominated." "A Defense of the Seniority System," *New York Times Magazine*, January 13, 1957, p. 17.

the appointed time, convene their own meeting, designate their own presiding officer, adopt an agenda, and transact business.

If the threat of such a coup forced the chairman to meet at the appointed time against his will—and if a quorum arrived on time—he still had many ways of stalling action. He could schedule business other than that which the rebels wished to talk about, he could refuse to recognize a member who wanted to amend the agenda or he could rule such a motion out of order, and he could find ways of dragging out the proceedings so as to block action to which he was opposed. And the Reorganization Act did not deal with some key elements of the chairman's power, notably his control over the constitution of subcommittees, referral of bills to them, and assignment of staff to facilitate their work.

Indeed, the instances of arbitrary conduct appeared to grow more frequent, rather than less so, after the 1946 act was passed. This was the period when the civil rights issue began to widen the schism between northern and southern Democrats, and southern chairmen were under constant pressure from their constituencies and their regional colleagues to use whatever powers they possessed to block legislation that in any way appeared to threaten the region's segregated institutions. And that pressure would usually outweigh the moral suasion of the 1946 act and the normal human desire for harmonious relations within any group that is compelled by circumstance to work together. The arbitrary exercise of power could be turned to advantage, of course, in political campaigns. Thus Senator James O. Eastland could tell his political audiences in Mississippi that his position as chairman of the Judiciary Committee, and only that, stood between them and the enactment of civil rights legislation—and if he were reelected, seniority would guarantee that the chairmanship remained in friendly hands.

Moreover, in the case of such a chairman, even his thwarted colleagues might be quite understanding, and forgiving. For a senator or representative to use, even ruthlessly, the power earned by many years of service was widely accepted within the Congress as normal enough practice for a politician who was under pressure from back home, and other senior members were loath to criticize because they looked forward to the day when they would inherit the right to act that way. Even junior members, who might normally be inclined to be restive, began to cherish the protection as they gradually acquired seniority.

Nevertheless, as the widening North-South split in the Democratic party brought with it a growing defiance of national party sentiment by the southern chairmen, each new instance of obstruction increased the demand from both within and without the Congress for fresh efforts at reform. The principal problem remained the House Rules Committee, its composition and powers essentially unchanged since the 1930s. It consisted of twelve members, of whom half (all four Republicans and two of the eight Democrats) were actively identified with the conservative Republican–southern Democratic coalition. Indeed, its chairman from 1955 through 1966, Howard W. Smith of Virginia, was the principal tactician for the coalition on the Democratic side, working in partnership with Charles A. Halleck of Indiana, who became House Republican leader in 1959. Smith pushed to the limit the powers of the committee to influence the substance of legislation, as distinct from simply managing the flow of business on the House floor. "My people," he liked to say, "did not elect me to Congress to be a traffic cop."[74] And he also pushed to the limit his prerogatives as chairman to dominate the decisions of the committee. During all his twelve years as chairman, his committee set no regular meeting date. Thus it was his decision whether a hearing was even held on a legislative committee's request for floor action on a bill it had approved.

In the 1950s, Smith denied hearings to about twenty bills each two years. Some of these were minor, and some were passed under suspension of the rules with two-thirds votes.[75] But others were significant and had strong Democratic party support. At the end of the 1958 session, for instance, Smith killed half a dozen bills, including an important housing measure, by simply disappearing to his Virginia farm and refusing to call a meeting of the committee.[76]

In 1959, he refused to convene his committee to consider a civil rights bill, resulting in a year's delay.[77] The next year, he released the bill only after a discharge petition had come within ten signatures of the necessary majority of the House membership.[78] To dislodge an area redevelopment bill in 1960, proponents had to resort to an equally difficult parliamentary maneuver— the "calendar Wednesday" procedure—and it was only the threat of that

---

74. Robert L. Peabody, "The Enlarged Rules Committee," in Robert L. Peabody and Nelson W. Polsby, eds., *New Perspectives on the House of Representatives* (Rand McNally, 1963), p. 137n. For a profile of Judge Smith, as he was called, and an account of how he used the chairman's prerogatives, see Robinson, *House Rules Committee*, pp. 81–88. Charles Jones paired Smith with Cannon as "the two spectacular cases of 'excessive leadership' in the House in this century," in "Cannon and Smith," p. 619.

75. Robinson, *House Rules Committee*, pp. 24–25.

76. MacNeil, *Forge of Democracy*, pp. 103–04.

77. Daniel M. Berman, *A Bill Becomes a Law: The Civil Rights Act of 1960* (Macmillan, 1962), p. 22.

78. Ibid., pp. 72–78; Galloway, *History of the House*, p. 105.

course that forced Smith to call a meeting to approve a school construction bill in that same year.[79] Both bills passed the House by comfortable margins once that body was permitted to vote. A dozen or so bills were killed in each Congress during the 1950s by the committee after hearings, including measures with strong party support, such as major housing legislation.[80] In many other instances, sponsors were forced by the committee to amend their bills to meet objections of the conservative coalition. And occasionally the committee used its power to kill a bill passed by both houses by refusing a rule permitting it to go to conference; that was the fate of the federal aid to education bill of 1960.[81]

Other chairmen rivaled Smith in their reputations as obstructionists. Graham A. Barden of North Carolina, as head of the House Education and Labor Committee, managed to block federal aid to education for years—in 1951–52 by refusing to call a session of the committee to discuss the subject, no matter what his responsibilities under the 1946 statute that required committees to establish regular meeting schedules;[82] in 1955–56 by dragging out the hearings for nearly three months and then consuming another two months in a line-by-line review of the measure.[83] Barden also blocked a juvenile delinquency bill after his committee had approved it, simply by declining to ask Chairman Smith to call a meeting of the Rules Committee to consider it—another clear violation of the 1946 law.[84] Another Democratic chairman, Wayne Aspinall of the Interior Committee, killed a wilderness bill in 1962 by going home to Colorado and remaining there until the Congress adjourned. The committee could not bring itself to act against his will in his absence.[85] On the Senate side, Judiciary Committee Chairman Eastland used still another tactic to block civil rights legislation; he simply declined to recognize the chairman of the subcommittee that had approved a bill to move its approval by the full

79. James L. Sundquist, *Politics and Policy: The Eisenhower, Kennedy, and Johnson Years* (Brookings Institution, 1968), pp. 71, 185–86. Under the calendar Wednesday rule, committees are called in alphabetical order to move for the consideration of legislation that may not have cleared the Rules Committee, but the procedure permits almost unlimited parliamentary obstruction and hence is rarely used.

80. Robinson, *House Rules Committee*, pp. 25–28; MacNeil, *Forge of Democracy*, pp. 106–07.

81. Sundquist, *Politics and Policy*, p. 186.

82. Frank J. Munger and Richard F. Fenno, Jr., *National Politics and Federal Aid to Education* (Syracuse University Press, 1962), p. 128.

83. Ibid.; Robert Bendiner, *Obstacle Course on Capitol Hill* (McGraw-Hill, 1964), p. 122; Sundquist, *Politics and Policy*, pp. 163–64.

84. Sundquist, *Politics and Policy*, p. 117. The Democratic majority of the House Education and Labor Committee finally forced Chairman Barden to accept a body of rules to govern the committee's operations, including regularly scheduled meetings and a guarantee of independence for subcommittees. MacNeil, *Forge of Democracy*, p. 173. However, MacNeil notes that the rules were not fully effective, as does Richard F. Fenno, Jr., "The House of Representatives and Federal Aid to Education," in Peabody and Polsby, *New Perspectives*, pp. 210–11.

85. Sundquist, *Politics and Policy*, p. 360; Bendiner, *Obstacle Course*, pp. 62–63.

committee.[86] To pass civil rights bills in the 1950s and 1960s, the Senate leadership had to resort to a series of extraordinary measures to circumvent Eastland, including the interception of House-passed bills on the floor before they could be referred to committee and initiation of legislation on the Senate floor in the form of an amendment to a pending measure.

Neither the Democratic party's leadership nor its rank-and-file membership had the means to bend the will of committee chairmen protected by seniority. During the 1950s the Congress was led by the two men generally considered to be the strongest leaders in modern times—Senate Majority Leader Lyndon B. Johnson and Speaker Sam Rayburn—yet even their effectiveness was severely limited by their lack of sanctions to bring to bear on the congressional barons. "On many occasions Rayburn virtually had to beg [Rules Chairman] Smith to release important bills," wrote the speaker's confidant and a committee member, Representative Richard Bolling of Missouri.[87] "Sometimes, Rayburn could persuade; many more times he couldn't."[88] "There is no patronage; no power to discipline; no authority to fire Senators," only "the power of persuasion," Johnson said in 1960.[89] Johnson's capacity to persuade—to wheedle, bluster, cajole, and browbeat—was legendary, and Rayburn could exploit his extraordinary personal prestige and long-standing friendships. But both leaders were necessarily limited in the number of issues to which they could devote their full energies, and if the committee chairman felt strongly enough, even Johnson and Rayburn could not prevail.

The men who succeeded the two Texas leaders in 1961, Mike Mansfield of Montana as Senate majority leader and John W. McCormack of Massachusetts as speaker, lacked their predecessors' powers of persuasion and, at least in the case of Mansfield, the disposition to try to impose their wills on their colleagues. "I'm not their leader, really," Mansfield said shortly after succeeding Johnson. "They don't do what I tell them. I do what they tell me."[90] In 1963, responding to criticism in the press and in the cloakrooms that had compared him unfavorably with Johnson, Mansfield took the Senate floor to protest that he was not "a circus ringmaster . . . a tamer of Senate

86. Howard E. Shuman, "Senate Rules and the Civil Rights Bill," *American Political Science Review*, vol. 51 (December 1957), pp. 961–62.

87. *House Out of Order*, p. 71.

88. Richard Bolling, *Power in the House: A History of the Leadership of the House of Representatives* (Dutton, 1968), p. 194. According to Douglass Cater, a Washington journalist, Rayburn lacked the means "to get Rules Committee action even when he asked for it" and "was always extremely chary about challenging the oligarchs." *Power in Washington: A Critical Look at Today's Struggle to Govern in the Nation's Capital* (Random House, 1964), pp. 168, 167.

89. Interview in *U.S. News and World Report*, June 27, 1960, quoted by Ralph K. Huitt, "Democratic Party Leadership in the Senate," *American Political Science Review*, vol. 55 (June 1961), p. 337.

90. *Washington Post* editorial, March 12, 1976.

lions, or a wheeler and dealer." The "whips," he said, were "nonexistent." "After all, what power do the leaders have to force these committees, to twist their arms, to wheel and deal . . . to get them to rush things up or to speed their procedure? The leaders in the Senate, at least, have no power delegated to them except on a basis of courtesy, accommodation, and a sense of responsibility." Indeed, the sanctions operated in the opposite direction. Senators had threatened him that if he did not accommodate them, "they would see that there was a lot of talk and no action would be taken on the floor."[91]

Power in Policy Committees: A Senate Experiment

To provide a central planning capacity for the Congress, both the Heller and APSA committee reports of 1945 proposed the creation of central policy-making machinery in each house under the auspices of the majority party. In Heller's scheme a majority policy committee in each house, composed of the majority leader and the chairmen of the major standing committees, would "coordinate all work of the several standing committees in each house," achieve "synthesis of the divergent interests," engage in "over-all planning," establish fiscal and monetary policy, and provide a "focus for party responsibility and accountability." When the president was of the majority party, he would meet with the two majority policy committees as a means of institutionalizing communication with the Congress. The minority party in each house would have a corresponding policy committee.[92] The APSA committee proposed a joint body—a legislative council—also made up of the majority leaders and standing committee members but including the vice president and the speaker. It would "prepare and initiate" a "coherent and coordinated program of legislation," seeking "an organic, overall approach to public problems instead of the piecemeal, splinter approach now prevalent," and "promote more effective liaison and cooperation with the Executive," both "in the development of balanced legislative programs and in the determination of legislative priorities."[93]

91. *Congressional Record*, November 27, 1963, pp. 22862–64. See John G. Stewart, "Two Strategies of Leadership: Johnson and Mansfield," in Nelson W. Polsby, ed., *Congressional Behavior* (Random House, 1971), pp. 61–92; Ripley, *Power in the Senate*, chap. 4. Johnson's leadership style is discussed in Huitt, "Democratic Party Leadership," and Rowland Evans and Robert Novak, *Lyndon B. Johnson: The Exercise of Power* (New American Library, 1966), chap. 6.
92. Heller, *Strengthening the Congress*, pp. 13–17.
93. APSA Committee, *Reorganization of Congress*, pp. 53–54, 79.

These proposals had some recent historical antecedents, but they were not impressive. Congressional Democrats had established a joint policy committee of ten members from each house in 1931, over the opposition of Speaker John Nance Garner.[94] It evidently faded quickly, because Henry T. Rainey of Illinois, running to succeed Garner in 1933, promised to create a steering committee, blaming failures in the preceding Congress on "the determination of policies . . . entirely from the Speaker's chair." Rainey was elected and carried out his pledge, and the Senate Democratic majority in that same year announced that it was making its policy committee "permanent."[95] Little was heard, however, from the Senate policy committee, as Democratic leaders looked to Franklin D. Roosevelt to set the party's policies. The House steering committee "occasionally played an influential role in the early days of the New Deal," but it too "lapsed into disuse and virtually disappeared."[96] Neither made enough of an imprint to be cited as precedent in the 1945 reports or in the report of the La Follette-Monroney committee in 1946.

Nevertheless, that committee went all the way in embracing the idea of party policy committees. It recommended a majority and a minority policy committee in each house, each to consist of seven members chosen at the beginning of each Congress, "for the determination and expression" of party policy. "We feel that if party accountability for policies and pledges is to be achieved, stronger and more formal mechanisms are necessary." No member would be bound to vote in accordance with the party policy, but the policy would be formally announced so that the party as a whole and its individual members could be held accountable. Moreover, the majority policy committees would meet regularly with the president and members of his cabinet as a joint legislative-executive council to "facilitate the formulation and carrying out of national policy."[97] The council, said La Follette, would "go far in helping to mitigate the deadlocks which occur between the President and the Congress, and which have caused dangerous crises in the conduct of the Federal Government."[98]

The Senate adopted these recommendations of the joint committee. But in the House, Speaker Rayburn exercised one of his office's remaining arbitrary

94. W. H. Humbert, "The Democratic Joint Policy Committee," *American Political Science Review*, vol. 26 (June 1932), pp. 552–54.

95. E. Pendleton Herring, "First Session of the Seventy-third Congress, March 9, 1933, to June 16, 1933," *American Political Science Review*, vol. 28 (February 1934), pp. 67–70.

96. Galloway, *History of the House*, p. 178.

97. *Organization of the Congress*, Report 1011 of the Special Committee on the Organization of Congress, 79 Cong. 2 sess. (GPO, 1946), pp. 12–14.

98. *Congressional Record*, June 5, 1946, p. 6345.

powers to block creation of the proposed majority policy committee in the House and, with it, the joint legislative-executive council. Deletion of these provisions was among the concessions he demanded before he would refer the Senate-passed bill for committee consideration. George Galloway surmised that the speaker saw in a House majority policy committee a diminution of his own power, and that he felt no need for a legislative-executive council since the leadership of the Congress was already meeting weekly with President Truman whenever the Congress was in session. "Political piracy" and "a travesty on the Constitution," Galloway termed the speaker's action.[99]

But the Senate proceeded independently to establish its own majority and minority policy committees— "for the formulation of over-all legislative policy of the respective parties," as the statutory language put it. The majority policy committee never functioned, however, in that capacity. It never laid down a party policy, or program, or strategy, to which the committee chairmen were expected to adhere. Occasionally it made a policy statement on some high-visibility, partisan issue, but for the most part its function was restricted to scheduling the flow of business on the Senate floor and planning floor strategy after the committees had acted. Up to that point, the barons were still in charge. Most senators, wrote Hugh A. Bone, preferred it that way; he found "no great desire" among the members to make the policy committees "effective instruments of party responsibility and discipline." The "habits of individualism and independence" were "too well entrenched." Public law

99. *Congress at the Crossroads*, pp. 345–46. Also *Congressional Quarterly*, vol. 2 (1946), p. 531. House Republicans converted their existing "lifeless" steering committee into a policy committee in 1949, but it remained lifeless too until it was revived in 1959. In 1961–62, it took positions on 28 bills, mostly in opposition to Democratic measures, but it has never had responsibility for initiating a program for the House majority. Charles O. Jones, *Party and Policy-making: The House Republican Policy Committee* (Rutgers University Press, 1964), especially pp. 21–27, 89–90, 139–43. The Reorganization Act of 1946 did attempt, although unsuccessfully, to bring order to the appropriations process. It set up a Joint Committee on the Budget, consisting of all the members of the two appropriations committees and the two revenue committees (House Ways and Means and Senate Finance), to agree by February 15 each year on an expenditure ceiling for the year, to be adopted through concurrent resolution of the two houses. In 1947 the two houses could not agree on a ceiling; the next year they did, but when the individual appropriations acts were totaled, the ceiling had been breached. Jesse Burkhead, *Government Budgeting* (Wiley, 1956), pp. 328–29. In 1949 the effort was abandoned. James P. Pfiffner suggests that the scheme broke down because of the early deadline, the rigidity of the ceiling, the unwieldiness of a committee of 102 members and its lack of permanent staff. *The President, the Budget, and Congress: Impoundment and the 1974 Budget Act* (Westview, 1979), pp. 111–13. In 1950 the Congress tried a different tack, consolidating all appropriations in a single omnibus bill. But that mammoth measure was not passed until September, more than two months after the new fiscal year had begun, and next year that approach was abandoned also, after a revolt by House appropriations subcommittee chairmen who felt the omnibus approach concentrated too much power in the chairman of the full committee. Ibid., pp. 113–14; Robert Ash Wallace, *Congressional Control of Federal Spending* (Wayne State University Press, 1960), p. 136; Burkhead, *Government Budgeting*, pp. 330–31. So the Congress reverted to its pre-1947 practice, which remained in effect until the Congressional Budget and Impoundment Control Act of 1974.

could create a Senate party policy committee but it could not create a "senatorial party" where none existed.[100]

The Congress saw little need for a program of its own because it had, by 1958, spent a quarter of a century building up the president as chief legislator. It had organized itself not to initiate but to respond. And, most of the time, that worked well enough to satisfy most senators and representatives. True, relations between Presidents Roosevelt and Truman and the congressional majorities were strained at times, and on occasion downright hostile. But the president was still acknowledged as the party leader, and his party colleagues in the Senate and the House were willing enough to let him propose as long as they were free to dispose. The last word would be theirs, so the president could have the first. And even in periods when the president's standing at the Capitol was at its lowest, his weakness did not necessarily extend to the cabinet members and other officials who actually presented the administration programs to the Congress.

But in the 1950s, something new developed. Before 1955 the presidency and the Congress had rarely been controlled by opposing parties, and not since 1889 had either house been organized by the out-party for longer than the span of a single Congress.[101] But beginning in 1955, they were more often than not—for fourteen of the next twenty-six years—in the hands of opponents, with Democratic Congresses confronting Republican presidents. That put a wholly new burden on the congressional majorities. Political dynamics compelled them to find matters on which to oppose the president, conspicuously and effectively. Otherwise they would be accepting his leadership and his programs—which would mean building him, and his party, for the next election. But it was awkward, and politically disadvantageous, to appear to be opposing blindly, without offering a coherent alternative program of their own. The need for independent capacity in the Congress to develop and present a program to its membership became a serious matter. Yet no such capacity existed, and the Johnson-Rayburn leadership had no disposition to create any. "With all his wisdom," wrote Representative Bolling, Rayburn "liked to operate on a hand-to-mouth basis legislatively. . . . he failed to plan beyond the session's short-range problems."[102]

100. *Party Committees and National Politics* (University of Washington Press, 1958), pp. 189, 195–96. He concluded the committees were "misnamed"; p. 186. Ralph Huitt observed that the committees did not "perform the functions hopefully suggested for them." "Democratic Party Leadership," p. 334. Malcolm E. Jewell, however, credited the Republican policy committee with an important mediating role on the Bricker amendment (relating to the treaty-making power) in 1953–54; the version of the amendment that came to a vote in the Senate was drafted under its auspices. *Senatorial Politics and Foreign Policy* (University of Kentucky Press, 1962), p. 94.

101. Jones, *Party and Policy-making*, p. 80.

102. *Power in the House*, pp. 194–95.

That left the activists within the party to grumble and to fill the gap as best they could. In 1957, eighty House Democrats agreed on a "liberal" legislative program that they offered as an alternative to President Eisenhower's. One of their number, the veteran Emanuel Celler of New York, chairman of the Judiciary Committee, complained publicly of "no leadership in the House. . . . no caucuses, no program."[103] But the House Young Turks, as they were inevitably called, were careful not to provoke any direct quarrel with Speaker Rayburn.

The provocation came, instead, in the Senate two years later, when the party's activists were in a far stronger position. The election of 1958 had given the Democratic party nearly two-to-one majorities in both houses—margins unprecedented since the halcyon years of the New Deal. The newcomers were overwhelmingly from the North and West—committed, progressive, activist. At last, argued Democratic liberals both inside and outside the Congress, their party was in a position to define a program, advance it in the Congress, confront President Eisenhower with whatever measures it could pass, and in so doing either enact them or provoke issues for the 1960 campaign. The outlines of the program were clear enough; they were found in the proposals of the House liberals and their Senate counterparts in 1957 and the earlier Eisenhower years, in the party platforms of 1952 and 1956, and in the pronouncements of a prestigious Democratic Advisory Council that National Chairman Paul M. Butler had appointed after the party's 1956 defeat.[104]

Even as the more senior liberal senators were meeting quietly to ponder how to raise the issue, it was carried to the Senate floor by one of that body's newest members—William Proxmire of Wisconsin, who had been in office only eighteen months. An "attack" on Lyndon Johnson's leadership, as it was portrayed—or an impersonal discussion of Senate organization and practice, as Proxmire described it—so premature and ill-organized could hardly succeed in its purpose of effecting change. Most Democrats, including liberals, were bound to rally around their leader. All the Proxmire effort could do was dramatize the impotence of the Democratic majorities to define and

103. *Congressional Quarterly Weekly Report*, vol. 15 (February 22, 1957), p. 224.

104. The council's policy declarations could be bold and unflinchingly liberal because the men who would have the responsibility for getting them written into law, Speaker Rayburn and Majority Leader Johnson, had declined the invitation to join the council. Speaker Rayburn's reaction was so forcefully negative that Johnson, as well as all the other House invitees, went along with his boycott. Senators Hubert Humphrey of Minnesota and Estes Kefauver of Tennessee were the only representatives of the Congress on the council, and both were identified with the liberal wing of the party. See Sundquist, *Politics and Policy*, pp. 405–15, for a discussion of the council and its impact.

discharge any mandate that Democratic voters may have thought the 1958 election gave their party. But that much it accomplished exceedingly well.

Democratic majority policy in the Congress, said Proxmire, did not exist. The party caucus—or conference, as it was then called—was "dead" as "an instrument of decision or even information." Indeed, it met only once at the beginning of each year to elect the party leaders and hear a speech from Johnson. The policy committee set up in 1946 "makes and purports to make no overall party policy." The majority leader, then, had "a blank check to exercise any kind of off-the-cuff, improvising direction for our party he chooses. . . . only the majority leader knows where our party is going, and even he does not have to make up his mind in advance." In fact, policy was "made entirely on an ad lib, off-the-cuff basis." Thus was the Democratic party in the Senate "evading our obligations to be responsible." It was "flying blind."[105]

Harking back to the days of Woodrow Wilson and Majority Leader Kern, Proxmire called for reinstituting the caucus as the basic policymaking body. The caucuses would not be binding, as Kern's were; Proxmire exalted the "individual conscience" that should guide each senator. But every Democratic senator's voice would be heard, and each would have "full opportunity to participate in making the important decisions now vested in the majority leader." The policy committee would amplify and apply the caucus policy decisions. Specifically, the caucus should produce "an overall budget and fiscal policy" that would set priorities for the committees and provide guidance as to the scale of the programs they would authorize. Eisenhower had presented a budget. Senate Democrats had in effect rejected it. "It is now up to us to set a standard of our own." A bipartisan committee such as the Joint Economic Committee could not do that.[106]

> Congressional policy, as it is formulated through the uncoordinated action of diverse and uncoordinated committees, necessarily lacks the unified, comprehensive direction which is dictated by the needs of a nation that is locked in a deadly struggle for survival. . . . the decentralized committee system cannot, without the influence of overall policy direction, produce a comprehensive policy which is consistent with a central purpose related to the Nation's central needs. . . . The majority party in the Congress is being backed into a fiscal corner by the plausible pleas of the President to balance the budget. We may think the President's budget proposals are wrong or even untrue; but we cannot escape the fact that it is the only budget that has been proposed by the responsible head of either party.[107]

The leadership and its supporters did not challenge Proxmire's description of how Senate policy was made, but they did find his remedies unworkable.

105. *Congressional Record*, February 23 and March 9, 1959, pp. 2814–15, 3560, 3567, 3572.
106. Ibid., pp. 3815–17, 3565, 3568.
107. Ibid., pp. 3567, 3570.

How, asked Assistant Leader Mike Mansfield, could a caucus prepare a budget that, in the executive branch, required a five-hundred-person bureau to produce? With the rule of "individual conscience" guiding every senator and without binding votes, how would a caucus discussion influence anybody anyway? Of course the policy committee did not make policy, said Mansfield, because that was the job of the legislative committees. The role of the policy committee was to schedule for Senate action the bills written by the legislative committees, and this it did; "very, very few" bills reported by the legislative committees were kept off the floor.[108]

To the argument that the legislative committees and individual senators would still be free to disregard party policy as it might be declared by the caucus or by the policy committee, Proxmire could only respond that they might be influenced. At any rate, under existing practice they had no way of even knowing what the party program was.[109]

Johnson did not respond until a few weeks later. Then, when Senator Albert Gore, Tennessee Democrat, and Proxmire were pleading for action on legislation to reduce interest rates, the majority leader told them to take their appeal to the appropriate committee.

> I hope the committee will face up to the problem. I hope it will hold hearings. I hope the committee will file a . . . report . . . so that the Senate can act. That is the only party policy I can offer.
> . . . the business of just waving a wand or pushing a button and saying, "Presto, you can get a policy" on this or that or the other thing does not hold true for the Senate.
> If they [Gore and his allies] cannot get their committees to go along with them, how do they expect a fairy godmother or a wet-nurse to get a majority to deliver it into their hands.
> I will say to any standing committee of this body . . . that if it makes recommendations to the Senate the policy committee will act promptly and will bring the recommendations to the floor of the Senate. . . . I do not know of anything else I can do.[110]

The frustration of the activists was not limited to the problem of getting a bill reported. If a reported measure fell short of the Democratic party program—assuming there was one—the leaders would not try to overturn the committee judgment.[111] And if the activists, without leadership support,

108. Ibid., pp. 3570, 3563.
109. Ibid., p. 3563.
110. Ibid., May 28, 1959, pp. 9259–62.
111. Senator Patrick V. McNamara, Democrat of Michigan, for instance, in a letter to Johnson complaining of the latter's refusal to intervene on an unemployment compensation bill, wrote, "It seemed very strange to me that you would say you could do nothing *until* the Committee acted and then say you could do nothing *because* it had acted." Sundquist, *Politics and Policy*, pp. 78–79. The civil rights bills were rare exceptions to the Johnson view that his job was to support and follow, not lead, the committees. Speaker Rayburn and other members of the House leadership had a similar relationship to the committees. Congressmen participating in Brookings discussions

were able to amend the committee's bill on the Senate floor, then seniority operated once again to stymie them; the Senate members of the House-Senate conference committee would be the very committee leaders who had lost the battle on the floor. Rarely did Senate conferees argue effectively for, and win acceptance of, the position they had fought against in their own body.

In any case, when Senator Gore at a party conference in 1960 moved to remake the policy committee into "an organization for evolving a coherent party policy on legislation," with the members to be elected by the conference, he was defeated, 51 to 12.[112]

But later that year the Democrats elected a president, and the question of congressional policy and program was once again moot. President Kennedy announced his program, and congressional committees accepted it as their agenda. After Kennedy's death, executive dominance of the legislative process reached a zenith in 1964 and 1965 under the frenetic leadership of Lyndon Johnson in the White House. Not since the Hundred Days of Franklin Roosevelt had bills written in the executive branch been passed by the Congress with such dispatch. So the problem of the congressional capacity to initiate and coordinate a legislative program would not arise again until a Republican was once again installed at the head of the executive branch, in 1969.

Then it would become vividly apparent again, as in Eisenhower's time, that neither house had established a capacity to plan. In the absence of any central apparatus for the purpose, there could be no comprehensive, internally consistent congressional program as such. When the Democratic majorities rejected the president's program that expressed the Republican conception of the nation's goals and priorities, as they were bound to do under the compulsion of party competition, they could offer in its place no alternative program that expressed coherently their own party's differing philosophy. And without the authority at some central point to make decisions and enforce them, there could be no capacity to act quickly.

As means to these ends, power in the leader and power in the caucus had been tried and had been discarded. Power in a majority policy committee had been essayed in a Senate rule but not in fact. They were all defeated by the overriding desire of most members, which had been growing ever since the Progressive Era, for independence of control and discipline by any form of central authority. When the Congress resolved, in 1973, to regain its

---

in 1959 agreed "that the intervention of House leadership in the committee process tends to be minimal." It "occurs less frequently than might be expected when major bills are being considered." Charles L. Clapp, *The Congressman: His Work as He Sees It* (Brookings Institution, 1963), p. 270.

112. *Congressional Quarterly Weekly Report*, vol. 18 (January 15, 1960), p. 91.

"rightful place" in the constitutional scheme of things, it had to confront the dilemma of its internal distribution of power—how to achieve a capacity for coordination and decision while respecting the desire for individual autonomy, how to organize itself to think and to act while still yielding to the demand for wide dispersal of power within the houses. To stem the decline of the Congress would require not just the resolve to do so but the artful creation of new forms and practices, an objective toward which so ponderous a body as the Congress would have to grope its way.

PART II

Resurgence

CHAPTER VIII

To Regain the Power of the Purse

THE dramatic confrontation of October 1972 between President Nixon and the Congress made one thing clear no matter which side won: the Congress had no mechanism for making fiscal policy.

Up to that time, the country's fiscal policy—its levels of taxing and spending, and of deficit or surplus, with all their importance to the economy—was whatever emerged from a piecemeal and haphazard legislative process. The president was directed, by the Budget and Accounting Act of 1921, to present each year a comprehensive and coherent program. But there was no compulsion on the Congress to act on that program in a similarly consistent and orderly way. The president's program was pulled apart. Its taxing and spending halves were assigned to different committees in the two houses and acted on quite separately The spending half was handled in a host of different measures: more than a dozen bills were produced by the appropriations committees but handled by separate subcommittees and considered independently of one another throughout the legislative process. And nearly half the outlays were beyond control of the appropriations committees, being authorized in diverse backdoor-spending provisions contained in laws written by various substantive committees.[1] Whatever the source of the spending authority, moreover, the actual expenditure might take place long afterward—as many as ten years later—so that at any time hundreds of billions of dollars

---

1. *Backdoor spending*, a Capitol Hill term used loosely to denote expenditures that are beyond review and control by the appropriations committees, includes, for example, farm price support payments, social security payments, general revenue sharing, public assistance, and certain other grants, and payments to retired military and civilian government employees. John W. Ellwood and James A. Thurber, "The Politics of the Congressional Budget Process Re-examined," in Lawrence C. Dodd and Bruce I. Oppenheimer, eds., *Congress Reconsidered*, 2d. ed. (Congressional Quarterly Press, 1981), p. 249, place backdoor spending at 44 percent of the 1974 fiscal year budget.

were in the spending pipeline. It was the total sum spent or obligated in a given year—not the total amount authorized—that measured the federal budget's impact on the economy. Yet the Congress did not have any way of controlling, and did not even examine, the spending totals. "The United States, it can be said, does not have a fiscal policy but a fiscal result," was one observer's apt summation.[2]

The Congress had been uneasy about these processes for a long time and had attempted to reform them in the Reorganization Act of 1946. Yet its methods were not quite so irresponsible as might appear. Whenever the president was of the same party as the congressional majority, the Congress normally accepted presidential leadership on fiscal policy as on other matters, and it did not usually depart from his spending recommendations far enough to upset his basic policy (although the legislature tended to be less responsive to tax recommendations). If the Congress proposed to spend too freely, the president could threaten—or use—his veto. When the executive and the legislature came under control of opposing parties, during the last six of Dwight Eisenhower's eight years, they became locked in a running battle over spending, and Eisenhower used the veto repeatedly and forcefully. As the result, even an opposition Congress was not able to break freely from the bounds the president set for it and put into effect its own independent fiscal policy.

Nevertheless, the absence of any system in the Congress for arriving at a considered and rational fiscal policy was bound to cause trouble again whenever the issue of spending became politically important. That time arose in Richard Nixon's first administration, in an even sharper partisan struggle, again between a Republican president and a Democratic Congress. And it was a period of inflation, which brought fiscal policy to the center of the political debate. Nixon could contend, quite validly, that the circumstances required a stringent control of government spending. And he could rightly condemn the "hoary and traditional procedure of the Congress" that "arrives at total Federal spending in an accidental, haphazard manner."[3] He repeatedly challenged the Congress on spending policy, through the veto and otherwise, with a rising force that culminated in the critical ultimatum of 1972 demanding that the legislators either put into effect a sensible fiscal policy of their own, or authorize him to do so. And, when they did neither, he felt justified in going ahead alone to override the Congress and impose his own fiscal policy on the country, by impounding appropriated funds.

2. Edwin L. Dale, Jr., *New York Times*, June 15, 1975.
3. "Special Message to the Congress on Federal Government Spending, July 26, 1972," *Public Papers of the Presidents: Richard Nixon, 1972* (U.S. Government Printing Office, 1974), p. 742.

When, on that occasion, many House Democrats voted to give the Republican president the power to fit total spending within a ceiling, some were saying, "All right, but just this once." After 1972, they announced, they intended to get the congressional house in order so that the legislators could impose fiscal discipline themselves. The climate was propitious for fundamental reform, for putting into place an institutional structure that would—in the single field of fiscal policy—overcome the legislature's endemic incapacity to plan. The result was the Congressional Budget and Impoundment Control Act of 1974, a landmark enactment that, with the War Powers Resolution of 1973, became an early symbol of the congressional resurgence.

In defining a new relationship in an ancient area of constitutional ambiguity, the Budget Act not only created the mechanism necessary for the Congress to recapture control of fiscal policy but also stripped from the president the power to impose his spending policies unilaterally through the device of impoundment. Thus, the shift of fiscal power to the president that had rapidly accelerated during both the Johnson and the Nixon administrations was reversed and, in this field, the Congress's goal of regaining its lost powers was achieved.

Nixon and the Impoundment Issue

President Nixon was not the first chief executive to impound appropriated funds. But others had exercised that power sparingly, usually in extraordinary circumstances where it was clear no constitutional conflict would be precipitated—where impoundment would carry out the will of the Congress rather than subvert it. If a president withheld money because a change in circumstances made its expenditure unnecessary to carry out the congressional purpose, that was one thing. But if he used it as a form of veto to prevent the achievement of that purpose, that was quite another. That was bound to destroy comity between the branches, because it smacked of a seizure of the legislative power, an assumption of an item veto over appropriations that many presidents had sought but that Congress had never seen fit to grant. In fact, recognition of the power of impoundment would amount to a grant of authority even stronger than the item veto, because under a formal veto procedure the Congress could override the president whereas the impoundment process permitted no such check.

The practice of impoundment grew out of a routine function of expenditure control, the apportionment of funds by time periods to prevent agencies from overspending early in a fiscal year: in 1905 the Congress, annoyed by the repeated requests for deficiency appropriations by agencies that had run out of money before the end of the year, ordered all agencies to apportion their funds. When the Bureau of the Budget was created, the director instituted a system of quarterly apportionments for all agencies. In this process, the director would also occasionally discover funds that turned out to be excessive for the statutory purpose and would place those in reserve also. The Congress accepted this practice as obviously desirable to prevent waste and encouraged it by law in 1950. There are times, of course, when what is waste becomes a matter of judgment, particularly under the rather loose language of the antideficiency act of 1950, which authorized impoundments when expenditures became unnecessary due to "changes in requirements" or "other developments subsequent to" the passage of the appropriation. Yet before Nixon, presidents were careful to use this power only when they could anticipate the support, or acquiescence, of the majority of the legislators and to steer clear of any circumstance where they could be accused of seizing an item veto power in defiance of the will of the Congress.

In this century, impoundment cases that went beyond the simple purpose of waste prevention were predominantly of two kinds.[4] First was the exercise of executive discretion to stretch out and defer nonmilitary expenditures in times of war. Franklin Roosevelt annually deferred several hundred million dollars of such spending (primarily construction projects) just before and during World War II. The Congress considered mandating certain of these expenditures but finally let the deferrals stand, thus in effect confirming discretion in the president.[5] President Truman took similar action during the Korean War under specific mandate of the Congress, and President Johnson followed Roosevelt's example and acted on his own as Vietnam expenditures mounted in 1966. The second large category of impoundment actions arose from disputes over weapons projects, and here the president could point not only to his general management responsibilities to prevent waste but to the

4. Louis Fisher has developed a useful classification of the types of impoundment, which this section follows. "Impoundment of Funds: Uses and Abuses," *Buffalo Law Review*, vol. 23 (1973), pp. 142–91. Two controversial cases of this type arose in the nineteenth century. In 1803 President Jefferson temporarily impounded funds for gunboats to patrol the Mississippi River. James D. Richardson, comp., *A Compilation of the Messages and Papers of the Presidents* (New York: Bureau of National Literature, 1897), vol. 1, p. 348 (hereafter *Messages and Papers*); Arthur M. Schlesinger, Jr., *The Imperial Presidency* (Houghton Mifflin, 1973), p. 235; Louis Fisher, *Presidential Spending Power* (Princeton University Press, 1975), pp. 150–51. And President Grant, in signing a public works bill in 1876, told the House that he would withhold expenditures on works that were "not clearly national," as distinct from private or local, in their benefits. Richardson, *Messages and Papers*, vol. 10, p. 4331.

5. Robert Ash Wallace, *Congressional Control of Federal Spending* (Wayne State University Press, 1960), pp. 145–46.

special duties imposed on the commander in chief by the Constitution, and on him and the secretary of defense by the National Security Act of 1947, to determine the roles and missions of the various elements of the armed forces. Presidents usually had the support of the majority of the Congress in their cancellations or deferrals of authorized procurement, and when it turned out their support was insufficient they yielded.

Only one president before Nixon—Harry Truman—appears to have expressly claimed a broad constitutional power of impoundment, and he did not specify either the source or the scope of the power. When the Congress, anticipating his opposition, not only authorized but "directed" him to make a loan to Spain in 1950, Truman issued a statement declaring that a directive would be "unconstitutional," without explanation. He said he would therefore treat the appropriation simply as authorized—that is, as permissive— and make his own decision as to whether the loan would be made.[6] Yet later, when the Congress directed him to cut back nonmilitary expenditures after the outbreak of the Korean War, Truman took the other side of the constitutional question, protesting that this was properly a job for the Congress itself to do. Perhaps—although there is nothing in the public record to indicate it—Truman claimed the constitutional power in the case of the Spanish loan only because it was in the field of foreign affairs, where presidents have, in the Supreme Court's words, their "very delicate, plenary, and exclusive power."[7]

President Nixon brought the impoundment issue to a climax by asserting that his power to withhold appropriated funds, derived from whatever constitutional and statutory sources, was without limit—and by acting accordingly. He carried both the volume and the scope of impoundment far beyond the actions of any previous president, and in so doing he breached the rule usually followed by his predecessors of avoiding a direct and open flouting of the will of Congress. Quite the contrary: he used the issue aggressively to provoke his political opponents who controlled the Congress. Government spending had been for forty years at the center of the quarrel between the parties, and now the chronic and rising inflation brought on by the Vietnam War made the issue more salient than ever. It was inevitable that a Republican president would try to exploit it—as Eisenhower had before Nixon—and in doing so attempt to discredit the Democratic foe. So Nixon could send up a tight budget. When the Congress loosened it—as it was

6. "Statement by the President Upon Signing the General Appropriation Act, September 6, 1950," *Public Papers of the Presidents: Harry S. Truman, 1950* (GPO, 1965), p. 616. After indicating for several weeks that he intended to defy the Congress, Truman finally did approve the loan.

7. *United States* v. *Curtiss-Wright Export Corp. et al.*, 299 U.S. 304 (1936).

bound to do, if only by reestimating expenditures under existing entitlement legislation and meeting new needs that might arise—he could demand that it set a spending ceiling. If it declined, he could set his own. If it did set a ceiling, he could set a lower one. In either case, he could enforce his own ceiling through the device of impoundment.

This was the pattern President Nixon followed throughout his first term. He took the stance of the economizer, the inflation-fighter. As for the congressional Democrats, some were eager to join wholeheartedly in the president's austerity crusade—or, if possible, get out in front of him—while others chose to exploit the opposite side of the issue, extending their sympathies to the state and local governments, the highway builders, the educators, the health researchers, the rural developers, and any other groups whose funds had been impounded. Both groups were handicapped, however, by the incapacity of the Congress to establish its own fiscal policy and stick with it.

As it happened, when Nixon took office in 1969 he found himself under a congressional directive to impound. The Congress had passed on to President Johnson in the tax bill of 1968 the unwanted mandate, referred to in chapter 4, to trim $6 billion from the spending it had approved for the 1968–69 fiscal year. After his inauguration, Nixon took up where Johnson had left off and brought the total impoundments, by the close of the fiscal year, to $8.2 billion.[8] By then the Congress had projected the spending results of its appropriations actions for the next fiscal year, 1969–70, and given the new president another grant of discretionary authority—but this time only to the extent of $1 billion. Only a few Democrats worried about endangering their party's Great Society programs by handing to Republican Richard Nixon the same kind of mandate they had given Democrat Lyndon Johnson; most of them were more anxious to be on the politically right side of the issue of spending and inflation. The appropriations bill that set a spending ceiling for 1969–70—$191.9 billion, or $1 billion less than projected under authorities

8. The term *impoundment* always presents a problem of definition. At any given time, the total of funds placed on reserve will include some that turn out to be unnecessary for the statutory purpose, some that the Congress intended for use in a future fiscal year, and some that the recipient agencies or state and local governments are not yet organized to use efficiently, as well as those which may represent a policy disagreement between the president and the Congress. By 1972 the Office of Management and Budget was distinguishing between funds reserved for reasons of "routine financial administration" (more than 80 percent of the total) and those reserved for "other"—that is, policy—reasons. When members of the Congress sought to maximize the impoundment issue, they cited the aggregate of the two categories; when the president or his supporters sought to minimize it, they referred to the latter, and they sought also to distinguish between expenditures that were merely deferred for one or another reason and those that were canceled. By the same token, Republicans commonly contended that every president since George Washington had impounded funds, failing to distinguish between those presidents who impounded only for reasons of routine administration and those, like Nixon, who impounded for policy reasons. Fisher, *Presidential Spending Power*, pp. 171–74; he claims the Nixon administration understated its impoundments by more than 50 percent.

separately enacted—passed the House by 348 to 49, and in the Senate the roll was not even called. But Nixon, it was clear, was even more determined to seize the spending issue. He announced that he would reduce spending by $3.5 billion and directed his department and agency heads to proceed accordingly. He cited no specific authority for going beyond the law, only his general "obligation under the Constitution and the laws."[9] Democrats seemed to agree that the president possessed the authority. As it became clear that the model cities and urban renewal programs would be among those bearing the brunt of the spending reductions, they complained (the president's policy "signals the end of our commitment to . . . urban areas," declared Senator Edward M. Kennedy, Democrat of Massachusetts),[10] but they did not challenge his right to make the reductions.

The peril to Democratic programs was becoming clear, however, and in 1970 the Congress set a looser ceiling on spending for 1970–71 than the ones it had imposed in 1968 and 1969. This time it set the limit at $200.8 billion— the amount projected in President Nixon's own budget—and provided that the ceiling would be modified if the Congress altered the president's proposed appropriations or if "uncontrollable" spending rose or fell. In other words, it did not mandate any reductions to be made at presidential discretion as in the previous years (except for a directive to cut spending by the Departments of Labor and Health, Education, and Welfare by $347 million, with a proviso that no program could be cut more than 15 percent).[11] Nixon denounced the congressional scheme as a "rubber ceiling" and demanded a firm one "within which the President can determine priorities."[12] When the Congress did not respond, he took the power into his own hands. He deferred spending on sixty-five new public works projects approved by the Congress beyond what he had recommended and made minor cuts in construction, land purchases, and several other programs.[13] As of February 1971, total funds withheld stood at $12.7 billion.[14]

By then, the constitutional issue could no longer be avoided. It was one

9. Louis Fisher, "The Politics of Impounded Funds," *Administrative Sciences Quarterly*, vol. 15 (September 1970), p. 372.

10. *Congressional Record*, October 2, 1969, p. 28213.

11. Fisher, "Politics of Impounded Funds," p. 372.

12. "Statement About Congressional Actions Affecting the Federal Budget, July 18, 1970," *Public Papers: Nixon, 1970* (GPO, 1971), p. 601.

13. Ibid., pp. 668–69, 824–25. Fisher, "Impoundment of Funds," pp. 168–69.

14. Office of Management and Budget statement, March 23–25, 1971, in *Executive Impoundment of Appropriated Funds*, Hearings before the Subcommittee on Separation of Powers of the Senate Judiciary Committee, 92 Cong. 1 sess. (GPO, 1971), pp. 164–65. This was the first tabulation ever provided the Congress. A subcommittee staff member was quoted as saying the subcommittee had been trying for three and a half years to get the data. Meanwhile, members of the Congress often learned of impoundments first through constituent complaints. Timothy H. Ingram, "The Billions in the White House Basement," *Washington Monthly*, vol. 3 (January 1972), pp. 44–45.

thing for a president to impound appropriated funds when complying with a specific statutory directive to do so, quite another to act on his own in the absence of a statute. The one was an orderly procedure carried out under strict congressional control, the other—in the legislative view—usurpation. Senator Sam J. Ervin, Jr., North Carolina Democrat and chairman of the Judiciary Subcommittee on Separation of Powers, opened three days of hearings in March with a declaration that the Founding Fathers intended that the president "execute all laws passed by the Congress, irrespective of any personal, political, or philosophical views he might have. He has no authority under the Constitution to decide which laws will be executed or to what extent they will be enforced. Yet, by using the impounding technique, the President is able to do just that."[15] Assistant Attorney General William H. Rehnquist, appearing for the Justice Department, was in essential agreement; the president, he said, had no general constitutional authority to decline to spend appropriated funds (with the possible exceptions of national security and foreign affairs appropriations).[16] But Caspar W. Weinberger, deputy director of the Office of Management and Budget, took a somewhat different view. The president's constitutional responsibility to "take care that the laws be faithfully executed" authorizes and sometimes requires impoundment, he argued, because the president must look beyond the language of particular appropriations acts to the whole body of statutes he is charged with executing. As of 1971, these included the expenditure ceiling enacted in the previous year and the statutory ceiling on the national debt—which establish that appropriations cannot be conceived as mandatory—as well as the Employment Act of 1946, which requires an anti-inflationary policy. Where the intentions of various statutes conflict, he argued, impoundment is one means by which the president can "insure that overall the will of Congress is maintained."[17] Only the president "has the overall responsibility and the overall knowledge of what the total expenditure picture of the Federal Government is at any one time."[18]

Yet, if the will of Congress was justification for an expenditure cut, the president followed his own will in deciding which particular programs must give way. Among those selected by President Nixon in 1970–71 were certain grant programs, such as urban renewal and model cities, that the president was recommending be eliminated in favor of revenue sharing. In selecting

15. *Executive Impoundment*, Hearings, pp. 2–3.
16. Ibid., p. 235. Rehnquist cited a 1969 memorandum from his office (in ibid., pp. 279–84) arguing this position.
17. Ibid., pp. 95–96, 101.
18. Ibid., p. 135.

those programs for impoundment, the president was not mediating among conflicting statutes already on the books so much as he was pressuring the Congress to pass new statutes more to his liking. He was impounding money "as a bargaining chip" for his legislative program, Democrats charged.[19] Weinberger himself virtually admitted as much in a letter to Representative Clement J. Zablocki, Democrat of Wisconsin, when he justified impoundment of funds for water and sewer grants on the ground that the president believed that revenue sharing—not yet enacted—was a better way of assisting cities.[20] Why were funds for urban renewal and model cities chosen for impoundment, a reporter asked a high OMB official. Because "Nixon doesn't believe in them," was the reply.[21]

But the bargaining worked both ways, for the Congress was not without means of striking back. The decisive votes that rejected the Nixon-supported supersonic transport in March 1971 were cast by members of Congress whose own projects had been frozen by the president, according to Republican House Leader Gerald R. Ford.[22] Chairman Allen J. Ellender (Democrat of Louisiana) of the Senate Appropriations Committee suggested that in the long run saying no to proposals dear to the president might be the most effective congressional tactic in the impoundment struggle and predicted "more and more of this thinking in the Congress."[23] In the foreign assistance appropriations bill in December, his committee formalized that approach. It prohibited spending any of the funds in that bill after December 31 unless the president first released all impounded funds, with the General Accounting Office as the arbiter. The House-Senate conference extended the deadline to April 30, 1972, and limited its application to three departments—Agriculture, Housing and Urban Development, and Health, Education, and Welfare— which by OMB figures would receive $2.268 billion. The president had no choice but to accept the bill, and the funds were released. But in the new fiscal year that began in July, the administration promptly impounded the same amounts all over again.[24]

Meanwhile, lawsuits were being filed in various federal courts, and bills were being introduced to curb the president's impoundment power. Following his hearings, Ervin introduced a measure to require the president to

19. Andrew J. Glass, "White House Report," *National Journal*, vol. 3 (May 15, 1971), p. 1027.

20. *Executive Impoundment*, Hearings, p. 310.

21. Glass, "White House Report," May 15, 1971, p. 1037.

22. Ibid., p. 1029. The House reversed its position in May, but this project was killed in the Senate.

23. Speech at Shreveport, La., April 13, 1971, inserted in *Congressional Record*, April 22, 1971, pp. 11465–66.

24. Andrew J. Glass, "White House Report," *National Journal*, vol. 5 (February 17, 1973), p. 236.

report all impoundments, with the reasons for his actions, and to provide that the Congress might override the president within sixty days. Subsequently, he changed the procedure to provide that the impounded funds would be released unless the Congress acted affirmatively in each case to approve the president's action. A version of this measure, which attracted twenty-eight Senate cosponsors, was approved by the Senate, 42 to 40, in the course of fixing a spending ceiling for the 1972–73 fiscal year, but the House preferred not to have a spending ceiling at all, and the legislation died.

When the Congress proved unable in October 1972 to enact a spending ceiling, Nixon once again took the power on himself and for the first time asserted an unconditional constitutional right to impound funds. The "constitutional right . . . to impound funds—and that is not to spend money, when the spending of money would mean either increasing prices or increasing taxes for all the people—that right is absolutely clear," he told a news conference.[25] With William Rehnquist now on the Supreme Court, the Justice Department reversed his position of 1971 and developed the legal case for the president's position along the lines of the Weinberger testimony of that year. Presenting the department's case in congressional hearings, Deputy Attorney General Joseph T. Sneed grounded the president's power on a combination of constitutional and statutory language but left little doubt that in the department's view the former was sufficient. To legislate against impoundment even in the domestic area would deprive the president "of a substantial portion of the 'executive power' vested in him by the Constitution," argued Sneed. "I question whether Congress has the power to convert the Chief Executive into 'Chief Clerk,' a position which he has never held under our Constitution."[26]

And the chief executive acted accordingly. Fresh from his massive reelection victory—after a campaign that had portrayed the Democratic Congress as profligate—the president made clear that such concessions to congressional opinion as might have marked his first term would have no place in his second. This time, instead of deferring particular projects as previous presidents had done, Nixon canceled entire programs. He eliminated a whole series of Department of Agriculture programs—a Rural Environment Assistance Program that dated back to 1936, the Water Bank Program to conserve wetlands for waterfowl, the 2 percent loan program of the Rural Electrification

25. "The President's News Conference of January 31, 1973," *Public Papers: Nixon, 1973* (GPO, 1975), p. 62.
26. Testimony, January 30–February 7, 1973, in *Impoundment of Appropriated Funds by the President*, Joint Hearings before subcommittees of the Senate Government Operations and Judiciary Committees, 93 Cong. 1 sess. (GPO, 1973), pp. 363, 369. The reversal of Rehnquist appears on p. 381.

Administration, the disaster loan program, and rural water and sewer grants. He cut in half the $18 billion made available to the Environmental Protection Agency for sewage treatment plants, despite language in the law that the Supreme Court later unanimously held to make allotment of the funds mandatory.[27] As in 1971, he withheld funds from urban community development programs that he had recommended be consolidated into a block grant. And his director of the Office of Economic Opportunity, Howard Phillips, refused to release funds for certain of that agency's programs after the president in his 1974 budget recommended that the agency be terminated. In both cases a presidential recommendation, as Louis Fisher remarks, was given higher status than a law on the statute books. The president also declared an eighteen-month moratorium on four housing programs on the ground that they were wasteful and ineffective.[28]

The beneficiaries of the programs that Nixon was eliminating or curtailing were prompt to take the administration into court, and during 1973 and 1974 the decisions accumulated. Despite the Nixon-Sneed argument, fewer than half a dozen of more than fifty cases decided in the lower courts by 1974 "upheld the President in any way," according to the Congressional Research Service of the Library of Congress.[29] And in 1973 and 1974, the Congress dealt with the entire problem in a fundamental way, in the Congressional Budget and Impoundment Control Act.

The Congressional Budget and Impoundment Control Act of 1974

In the 1972 imbroglio over Nixon's demand for a $250 billion spending ceiling, the House acceptance of the president's demand was based on the recommendation of its Ways and Means Committee. But in taking that position—in defiance of the House Democratic leadership—the committee took the first step toward making sure the Congress would not face similar

27. *Train* v. *City of New York*, 420 U.S. 35 (1975).

28. Fisher, *Presidential Spending Power*, pp. 177–97; James P. Pfiffner, *The President, the Budget, and Congress: Impoundment and the 1974 Budget Act* (Westview, 1979), especially chap. 5 and pp. 116–17.

29. *Presidential Impoundment of Congressionally Appropriated Funds: An Analysis of Recent Federal Court Decisions*, report to the House Government Operations Committee, 93 Cong. 2 sess. (GPO, 1974), p. 3. Most of the impoundment decisions were at the U.S. district court level. Two cases, involving sewage treatment plant grants, were appealed to the Supreme Court; the Justice Department chose to base its case on statutory interpretation rather than on constitutional grounds, losing one case (*Train* v. *City of New York*), while the other was remanded to the district court, so the constitutional issue was left unsettled. Pfiffner, *The President, the Budget*, pp. 100–04; Fisher, *Presidential Spending Power*, pp. 191–92.

dilemmas in the future. It wrote into the legislation a proposal by Representative Al Ullman of Oregon, the ranking majority member, to establish a special committee of both houses to examine how the Congress could regain control of the budget and of fiscal policy. When the Senate killed the extraordinary grant of power to the president, all that survived were the Joint Study Committee on Budget Control and a requirement that the president promptly report all impoundments to the Congress.

In presenting his proposal for the joint committee, Ullman chastised the Congress for long ago "abdicating" its own responsibilities:

> The only place where a budget is put together is in the Office of Management and Budget downtown. When they send their recommendations to us we go through a few motions of raising or lowering the spending requests, but we have lost the capacity to decide our own priorities in this Nation of ours. That is where the responsibility really is. . . .
>
> Somewhere we have to devise the vehicle to put it all together. Do not tell me the Appropriations Committee puts it all together. . . . the only thing that counts is the total expenditure level, whether it comes from within or outside the appropriations process. Until we can devise a vehicle for putting those nonappropriated funds into the same basket and coming up with an overall limitation we have not faced up to the issue at all.[30]

George H. Mahon of Texas, the Appropriations Committee chairman, agreed the backdoor spending had to be brought within the appropriations process, and that aggregate spending, as well as the total of new obligational authority, had to be considered annually.

When the Joint Study Committee on Budget Control met in January 1973, under the cochairmanship of Ullman and Representative Jamie L. Whitten (Democrat of Mississippi) of the Appropriations Committee, it received from Charles L. Schultze, a former director of the Bureau of the Budget, an outline of a budget process for the legislative branch. A budget committee would be established in each body, with competent analytical staff. Each year, after receiving the president's budget, it would recommend revenue and expenditure targets for the year; the two houses would act on the recommendations, and the Congress would thus by concurrent resolution officially adopt the targets. The legislative and appropriations committees would then go through their usual piecemeal process, but as each spending measure went through the two houses the budget committees would advise on whether the ceiling was being breached. Near the end of the session, the Congress in a second resolution would reconcile the sum of its individual actions with its original

---

30. *Congressional Record*, October 10, 1972, pp. 34600–02. The work of the Joint Study Committee and the subsequent development of the Congressional Budget and Impoundment Control Act are recounted in Allen Schick's definitive study of the congressional budget process, *Congress and Money: Budgeting, Spending and Taxing* (Washington: Urban Institute, 1980), chap. 3.

targets, by revising either the actions or the targets, or both. The Congress would thus, like the president, set its priorities for individual items "consistent with an explicitly chosen total."[31] This was essentially the scheme recommended by the joint committee in April, and bills were introduced to carry it into effect. To give authority to the budget process, the committee proposed that a two-thirds majority of each house be required to pass measures that would exceed the limits set by the budget resolutions.

So drastic a redistribution of power *within* the Congress is not accomplished quickly, however. House liberals raised a chorus of objections to the prospective domination of the new budget committees by members of the traditionally conservative appropriations and revenue (Senate Finance and House Ways and Means) committees. The joint committee, itself made up almost entirely of senior members of those four committees, had recommended that two-thirds of the members of the budget committees come from those committees, and that the chairmanships alternate between appropriations and revenue committee representatives. It also proposed that the members from the four designated committees be chosen by those committees. These provisions, said the Democratic Study Group, which claimed more than half the Democratic members of the House, "would lock the congressional budget process into a conservative mold for generations to come."[32] With the House Rules Committee acting as mediator, Ullman acceded to the liberal demands: only ten of the twenty-three members of the House budget committee would come from Appropriations and Ways and Means; and all of the members would be chosen by the party caucuses, and the chairman by the majority caucus. A four-year limit was put on the service of any member.

In addition to these questions of power, severe procedural problems had to be worked out. How could the budget committees' work be fitted into the annual appropriations timetable without resulting in further delays? As matters already stood, it was normal for several of each year's appropriation measures to be delayed well beyond the beginning of the fiscal year on July 1 while agencies operated under makeshift interim resolutions. The Rules Committee resolved this by shifting the fiscal year to an October 1 beginning date, and the two-thirds vote requirement for exceeding ceilings was dropped. Across the Capitol, the Senate Rules and Administration Committee recast that body's sixteen-member budget committee to provide that all members would be selected by the caucuses, in the manner of all other committees,

31. Schultze testimony, January 18, 1973, in *Improving Congressional Budget Control,* Hearings before the Joint Study Committee on Budget Control, 93 Cong. 1 sess. (GPO, 1973), pp. 11–12.
32. *Congressional Quarterly Almanac, 1973,* p. 248.

with no required Appropriations and Finance representation. Membership would be indefinite rather than rotated.

While all these problems were being tackled, Democratic members were straining to get back at President Nixon for the unilateral actions he had taken late in 1972 to terminate Democratic programs through the impoundment process. Senator Ervin reintroduced his impoundment control bill on January 16, 1973, and two weeks later his Separation of Powers subcommittee joined with a subcommittee of Government Operations to begin hearings at which appeared a parade of witnesses representing agricultural, rural development, housing, education, environmental, highway, and other interests whose programs had been eliminated or drastically curtailed by the president's impoundments—which the OMB then tabulated as totaling $8.7 billion but congressional staff, using a broader definition, estimated at a much higher figure. "The executive branch has been able to seize power so brazenly," said Ervin in opening the hearings, "only because the Congress has lacked the courage and foresight to maintain its constitutional position. . . . More-over, as individuals, too many of us have found it more comfortable to have someone else—the President—make the hard decisions and relieve us of responsibility. . . . The time has come when something must be done to restore the Congress to its rightful role, or our representative system of government cannot survive." It was "paradoxical and belittling," remarked Ervin, for the Congress to have "to lobby the Executive to carry out the laws it has passed." Other senators concurred. "Congressional power . . . has been not so much usurped by the Presidency as given up to the Presidency by Congress," declared Lawton Chiles, Democrat of Florida, and his Repub-lican colleague from that state, Edward J. Gurney, used similar language: the problem "was not created by the executive branch; it was created and can be solved only by the legislative branch." "We are engaged in a historic struggle," proclaimed Jacob K. Javits, Republican of New York, referring both to the impoundment hearings and to the battle over the War Powers Reso-lution taking place concurrently.[33]

In March, Ervin and his allies cut short the normal legislative procedure by attaching their measure as an amendment on the Senate floor to a dollar devaluation bill, but the House refused to accept so precipitate an action. So the Senate passed its bill in the regular fashion in May, without even a roll call, and the House followed in July by a vote that adhered closely to party lines, Republicans denouncing the action as a partisan political maneuver to embarrass the president. But then the bill bogged down in conference, for the Senate and House versions differed as to the basic procedure to be

33. *Impoundment of Appropriated Funds*, Hearings, pp. 1–3, 21, 27, 26.

established. The Senate would allow an impoundment only if both houses voted to sustain the president; the House, seeking to avert procedural burdens in the many instances where the Congress would agree with the president, provided for the president's action to stand unless either house voted to overrule him. In the end, the House approach was adopted for simple deferrals. But for cases where the president sought to terminate a statutory program, or impounded funds for reasons of fiscal policy, the Senate approach was adopted; unless a bill rescinding the original appropriation was passed within forty-five days, the impoundment was canceled.

The conference bill, which combined the impoundment control and budget provisions, set May 15 as the deadline for passage of the first budget resolution setting guidelines for the appropriations process. It required all authorizing legislation to be passed before that date. To allow the Congress time to consider such legislation, it added a less-than-enforceable provision directing the administration to submit its proposals for new programs more than a year in advance—that is, by May 15 of the year before the beginning of the fiscal year in which they would take effect. The second budget resolution reconciling the year's legislative actions with the original budget resolution would be adopted by September 15, to be followed by any necessary legislation. In addition to creating two budget committees, each with its own staff, the bill established an independent Congressional Budget Office, to serve not just the budget committees but the entire Congress.

The bill was passed with no dissenters in the Senate and only six in the House. "It is not going to be easy to implement," was Ullman's comment. "Unless we are determined to make it work, this will all turn out to be empty rhetoric" like the budget reform contained in the Reorganization Act of 1946, warned Richard Bolling, Missouri Democrat, the bill's floor manager.[34]

Just four weeks before leaving office, President Nixon signed the bill. He commended the Congress for finally imposing on itself the "disciplines" he had been urging. He grumbled a bit about the impoundment control provisions, saying they "may well limit the ability of the Federal Government to respond promptly and effectively to rapid changes in economic conditions."[35] But the administration had already announced it was abandoning impoundment as a tactic, as a result of the series of adverse court decisions,[36] and most of the withheld money had been released.

34. *Congressional Record*, June 18, 1974, pp. 19680, 19675. In 1975 the membership of the House Budget Committee was increased from twenty-three to twenty-five. Two seats are reserved for representatives of the majority and minority leadership.

35. "Statement About the Congressional Budget and Impoundment Control Act of 1974, July 12, 1974," *Public Papers: Nixon, 1974* (GPO, 1975), pp. 587–88.

36. *Washington Post*, June 30, 1974, reporting a speech by OMB Director Roy Ash to a regional meeting of the Council on International and Public Affairs on June 28.

Resolution of the Impoundment Issue

After passage of the 1974 act, the impoundment issue seemed to have disappeared. Presidents thenceforward could legally only propose to cancel or defer authorized spending; the Congress made the ultimate decision. Whenever the Congress reversed the president, the money was spent. Even the borderline impoundment cases that depended on the wording of the legislation and the purpose of the expenditure (foreign policy and national security expenditures having a special status) were brought within the procedural limits of the act. So, instead of a tug-of-war between the branches arising from the ambiguity of the Constitution, the act substituted a collaborative process in which each branch had a defined role. As both branches accepted their respective roles, the hostility and tension of the Nixon years over the impoundment question dissolved.

There remained considerable antagonism for a time, when President Ford adopted the practice of routinely impounding all funds appropriated by the Congress above his recommendations. This led to an equally routine reversal of his decisions by the Congress, with no result except delay, useless paperwork, and a prolongation of conflict between the branches. Eventually, the Ford administration wearied of the charade, and since then both the number of deferral and rescission actions and the proportion rejected by the Congress have been drastically reduced (from ninety-one rescissions involving $3.3 billion in expenditures, with Congress approving only $400 million or 12 percent, in fiscal 1975, to only eight rescissions totaling $644 million, with $55 million or 9 percent accepted three years later). In fiscal 1978, only six presidential deferrals of spending, totaling $70,000, were disapproved, compared to sixteen, involving $9.3 billion (almost entirely highway funds), rejected two years earlier.[37]

Disputes over spending policy did not end, of course. But they were fought out in the traditional way, through the use or threat of the veto power. By that means President Carter managed to kill off half of the water projects he objected to in 1977, as well as a $2 billion nuclear-powered aircraft carrier. But the Carter administration declared its unqualified support of the principle "that the Congress should be able to overturn Executive acts to withhold

37. Schick, *Congress and Money*, p. 404; the first nine months of 1979 fiscal year show an 80 percent approval rate on rescissions ($724 million of $909 million) and only 2 of 58 deferrals overridden.

funds."[38] The attitude of the Reagan administration seemed clear, too. Drastic expenditure cuts were announced in the early months of 1981 followed by proposed deferrals and rescissions under the terms of the impoundment control act. The proposals were generally approved routinely by the members of Congress, which accepted the president's broad objectives. Yet in April a group of congressmen filed a court action challenging the president's refusal to fill certain vacant positions in the Veterans Administration—a suit reminiscent of those provoked by the Nixon impoundments a decade earlier.

If the impoundment issue turns out to have been resolved by the 1974 act, the executive branch will be in one sense the gainer. The import of the earlier court decisions was that the president had no general constitutional power to impound funds for the purpose, or with the effect, of undoing the will of Congress. Under the 1974 act, however, he is conceded the right to temporarily withhold funds for any purpose while he asks the Congress to reconsider. And the temporary period can drag out. In instances where he recommends rescission of appropriations, the Congress has forty-five days in which to confirm his judgment; otherwise, he must spend the money. But the forty-five days must be a period of continuous session, and they begin when the president notifies the Congress. If the administration is slow in drafting the notification, and if the Congress is in adjournment or if it adjourns shortly afterward, the forty-five days may be stretched to a span of several months, which in itself may subvert the congressional intent. In 1975, for example, President Ford managed to defer expenditures for a summer jobs program until the summer was almost over and it was too late to spend most of the money.[39] Members of Congress have grumbled about this loophole in the act, and bills have been introduced to close it, but so far the responsible committees have not been eager to reopen a painful issue that has been reasonably well settled.

Establishment of the Budget Process

When presidential impoundment came under control, the power of the purse reverted to where it had traditionally resided, in the legislative branch. Whether the Congress could keep it would depend on how well the new

38. Testimony of Dale R. McOmber, assistant director of Office of Management and Budget, ibid., p. 24.
39. Joel Havemann, "The Immortal Impoundment," *National Journal*, vol. 9 (March 19, 1977), p. 433.

congressional budget process worked—or whether it in fact brought order to the legislative spending processes whose disarray, acknowledged by the Congress, had given Nixon a political, if not legal, basis for seizing the impounding power. If it failed, the question of a delegation of power to the president to control spending, such as had been granted to both Nixon and Lyndon Johnson, would again arise. But if the new process succeeded, it would solidify congressional control of fiscal policy. So it is one measure of the success of the new congressional budget system since 1974 that no suggestion has been made at any time by anyone in either branch that any new delegation of impoundment authority to the president might be necessary. Nor at any time, even during the critical period when power was being redistributed within the Congress, did any significant support develop for abandoning the new system. Because the sense of the Congress has been that the process had to be made to work, it has.

In many respects the congressional budget process replicates that of the executive branch. In formulating each year's fiscal plan, the budget committees and the Congressional Budget Office collectively employ macroeconomists of a number and stature that parallel those available to help the president formulate his fiscal policy recommendations, and the budget committees obtain the testimony of outside economists through public hearings. On the basis of their analysis of the economic outlook, the committees prepare their recommendations for basic fiscal policy—that is, determine the degree of stimulus or restraint that the economy requires and hence the optimum size of the budget deficit (or surplus) and the aggregate levels of revenue and spending outlays that will produce that difference. They also examine prospects beyond the immediate fiscal year and set ceilings on new spending authority (which may have its spending impact in future years) as well as on outlays. They allocate the budget authority and outlay totals by functions on the basis of recommendations from the substantive committees of the two houses, much as the OMB makes its allocations based on estimates from the executive agencies. The aggregate and functional figures are then reviewed by the two houses and embodied, each May, in the first annual budget resolution.

In all of these steps the Congress is now equipped to proceed quite independently of the president. And in the initial years, with a Republican in the White House, the two budget committees were bent on demonstrating their capacity and determination to do just that. In the House committee, the basis for committee consideration of the first budget resolution was not the president's budget but the "chairman's mark," a set of recommended numbers presented by the chairman.[40] The Senate Budget Committee worked from a set of option papers prepared by the committee staff. During the Ford years the budget that emerged from the Democratic-controlled committees reflected a fiscal policy quite different from what the president had proposed. When Democrat Carter succeeded Ford, the committees and the executive branch started with the same policy predilections and smoothed out their differences in consultation, so that the first congressional budget resolution each year was in harmony with the presidential views. But the Congress retained the capacity to develop and adopt its own fiscal policy whenever it might again be fundamentally at odds with the executive.

The congressional competence was clearly demonstrated in the crucial first year, 1975.[41] When the Congress met that year, the country was near the bottom of the worst recession since the Great Depression, with unemployment at 8 percent. President Ford responded with a fiscal policy that he termed one of "decisive action to restore economic growth," but one based on the belief "that tax relief, not government spending, is the key to turning the economy around to renewed growth."[42] It featured an immediate temporary tax reduction of $16 billion, accompanied by cuts of $17 billion in existing spending programs in the 1976 fiscal year, which would hold total expenditures that year to the 1975 level in real terms. The stimulus of the tax cut would be lessened not only by the spending cuts but by a permanent net tax increase of several billion dollars annually included in the president's comprehensive energy program.

The Democratic Congress found the president's recommendations far from a decisive response to a deep recession. The House Budget Committee termed his budget "in reality a very restrictive one that cannot meet the Nation's urgent economic needs," that would "provide virtually no new stimulus to the economy."[43] Senator Edmund S. Muskie of Maine, Democratic chairman of the Senate Budget Committee, declared that it was the responsibility of the Congress to "shape a recovery program that will help pull the United States out of the worst recession in a generation." "If we did not have an instrument for making overall fiscal policy and monetary policy judgments," he observed, "then we would be searching for one."[44]

40. This section relies on Schick's *Congress and Money*.

41. The process was not required to take effect until 1976, but the budget committees decided to establish the procedures in a dry run in 1975; it turned out to be a faithful application of the procedures that amounted to advancing the effective date of the act.

42. "Annual Budget Message to the Congress, Fiscal Year 1976, February 3, 1975," *Public Papers of the Presidents: Gerald R. Ford, 1975* (GPO, 1977), p. 147.

43. *First Concurrent Resolution on the Budget,* H. Rept. 94-145, 94 Cong. 1 sess. (GPO, 1975), p. 7.

44. *Congressional Record,* April 29, 1975, p. 12319.

In the end, the Congress did shape its own recovery program. It cut taxes deeper than the president proposed, by some $7 billion,[45] and directed a higher proportion of the benefits to lower-income taxpayers. It rejected the president's energy tax increases, while pondering at its own pace the rest of his energy proposals. And through the new budget process, it drastically reshaped the expenditure program. In the first budget resolution for the 1976 fiscal year, it discarded almost all of the proposed reductions, added about $7.5 billion in new spending, primarily for public works and public employment programs, and found part of the funds by reducing national defense and military aid outlays by $4.6 billion.[46] All of these actions raised to $69 billion the deficit that President Ford had projected at $52 billion, but the difference included updating and revisions of the president's estimates of both revenues and expenditures that accounted for almost $6 billion. Congressional action thus added about $11 billion to the stimulatory effect of the 1976 budget.

The congressionally shaped fiscal program cleared the Senate easily. In that chamber, Muskie as Budget Committee chairman and Henry Bellmon of Oklahoma as ranking Republican member had formed a bipartisan team committed to defending on the Senate floor whatever decisions the committee reached—an alliance that continued throughout their joint tenure on the committee (both left the Senate in 1980). Bipartisan solidarity, they reasoned, was essential to establishing the budget process—and their committees— solidly in the institutional structure of the Senate. In their first test, Muskie and Bellmon without great difficulty beat off attempts from both liberals and conservatives to alter their handiwork. In doing so, Bellmon joined in the committee's blunt rejection of the president's position.

In the House, there was no such bipartisanship and no such easy course. The House Budget Committee split at the beginning into partisan blocs (and remained divided on party lines for several years). The Democrats fashioned their resolution without Republican participation but they could not unify their own party either. At one wing was a conservative bloc that objected both to the size of the deficit and the reductions in military spending. At the other was a liberal faction that sought more economic stimulus and protested those of the president's cuts that the committee proposed to accept, particularly its modified acceptance of a proposal to place a limit on cost-of-living increases in federal workers' pay, social security payments, and other benefits

45. Estimate of the Joint Committee on Internal Revenue Taxation, *Congressional Quarterly Almanac, 1975,* p. 95.
46. Barry M. Blechman, Edward M. Gramlich, and Robert W. Hartman, *Setting National Priorities: The 1976 Budget* (Brookings Institution, 1975), pp. 233–35.

which by law were to be adjusted for inflation (Ford had proposed a 5 percent cap; the committee approved 7 percent). Eventually, two committee Republicans switched their votes in order to permit a resolution to be reported—and thus saved the heralded new system from being stillborn.

But that only transferred the impasse to the House floor. The resolution was saved there only by vigorous intervention by the Democratic leadership. Majority Leader Thomas P. O'Neill, Jr., first won over the liberals with a floor amendment eliminating the cap on cost-of-living increases. Then O'Neill, Speaker Carl Albert, and other leaders pleaded with Democratic conservatives to rally behind the budget process itself as a reassertion of congressional responsibility. "This is a historic moment," was Albert's appeal. "Only by supporting a budget resolution can we reestablish . . . the principle that the Congress will be a responsible partner, exercising its own judgment . . . in carrying forward the economic affairs of the nation. . . . Our national budget, and the budget resolution . . . are expressions of our mandate to carry out our constitutionally granted power of the purse."[47] Enough conservative Democrats responded to carry the resolution, 200 to 196—with the help of only three Republicans—and other Democrats were probably available to give the leadership their votes had they been needed.[48]

But passing a budget resolution did not, of itself, constitute discipline. It was easy enough for the Congress to declare an intent to hold the deficit to $69 billion—and some of those who voted for the first resolution in 1975 probably did so on the supposition that it was only hortatory anyway, that nothing would prevent the Congress from departing from it in the normal course of authorizing expenditures and appropriating for them. The first budget resolution set targets. The final expression of congressional policy did not come until the fall—in a second budget resolution after the individual appropriations bills had been acted on—and even that could not prevent the Congress from working its will on fiscal matters as it chose at any time thereafter. Not only could the limits be breached at any time, by simple majorities, but the second resolution could be replaced by a new one at any

47. *Congressional Record*, May 1, 1975, p. 12767.

48. The greater loyalty of Senate Budget Committee Republicans to their committee and to the process, observers suggested, might be due to the fact that senators were assigned permanently to the budget panel and thus had a stake in its status and influence, whereas House members were rotated on the committee, with a four-year limit on any member's term. John W. Ellwood and James A. Thurber, "The Politics of the Congressional Budget Process Re-examined," pp. 262–63; Louis Fisher, "Congressional Budget Reform: The First Two Years," *Harvard Journal of Legislation*, vol. 14 (April 1977), pp. 436–38. Fisher also notes that strong partisans were deliberately named to the House Budget Committee by both parties because the budget resolutions "are regarded as political documents." The House limit was extended to six years in 1979, with the chairman eligible for two more years and with no limit at all on the representatives of the majority and minority leadership.

time during the course of the fiscal year. So the congressional budget process possessed no power of enforcement beyond its moral authority. If the authorizing and appropriating committees chose to ignore the resolutions produced by the budget committees and adopted by the two houses, and if the two bodies supported them in doing so, then the Congress could be as irresponsible under the new system as the old. It could act in the same piecemeal fashion. Whether what emerged was a coherent fiscal policy, instead of a "fiscal result," would depend on the extent to which the two houses, in the course of acting on individual bills, elected to support the considered policy they had incorporated in their budget resolutions.

This situation inevitably pitted the budget committees against other committees in contests for the allegiance of their houses. The former, as authors of the budget resolutions, became perforce the fiscal consciences of the two bodies, defending the approved fiscal policy against assault by those who would spend more (or tax less). The members of the budget committees, obviously, could easily be outnumbered even if they held solidly together, and if enough of the other committees formed a common front to disregard the budget strictures the process could lose its meaning altogether. When the act was passed, this ultimate outcome was freely predicted. Yet it has not worked that way. The budget committees have not been proven invincible, by any means, but they have turned out to be formidable antagonists, their strength derived from their role as guardians of a process that virtually every member of the Congress tacitly recognizes as crucial to the standing of the legislative branch itself.

The authority of both budget committees was established impressively in the initial year. Senator Muskie in his first floor fight, with the powerful Armed Services Committee, led a successful effort to return to conference a bill authorizing military procurement on the ground that it exceeded by $800 million the amount contemplated in the first budget resolution. The vote in this first test of strength was 48 to 42. The conferees then took $250 million out of five air and naval procurement projects, which Muskie and his allies accepted as a sufficient triumph.[49] In a deft demonstration of even-handedness, the budget defenders coupled their rejection of the military authorization with an attack on a conference report on child nutrition programs that exceeded the budget target by $362 million. This report, too, was sent back, and a reduction of $75 million was obtained.[50] The media hailed the "victories" as proving the effectiveness of the budget process, and in the Washington

49. *Congressional Quarterly Almanac, 1975,* pp. 378–79. In the $250 million was $60 million as the initial outlay for a $1.2 billion nuclear carrier.
50. Ibid., pp. 674–75.

setting where facts tend to reflect images, all this helped. Other committees, not willing to risk controversy and possible humiliation on the floor, took care to keep their actions within the budget limits. And the same was true in the House, where Budget Committee Chairman Brock Adams (Democrat of Washington) undertook no floor fights but was credited with exerting potent pressure behind the scenes whenever the authorizing and appropriating committees appeared to be coming forth with "budget busting" measures. The House Appropriations Committee made a $9 billion cut in the administration's military spending request—described by Secretary of Defense James R. Schlesinger as "deep, savage, arbitrary"—which some members attributed to the committee's desire to avoid a floor fight with Adams. The House Budget chairman also was given credit for blocking a $3.4 billion increase in retirement outlays for federal employees.[51] So the discipline exerted on the spending totals was undoubtedly far greater than the net measurable savings of $325 million that accrued from the two battles on the Senate floor.

When the time came to pass the second budget resolution, in the fall of 1975, the spending total of the first resolution had to undergo only minor adjustments, except for reestimation of the cost of entitlements and other "uncontrollable" expenditures under existing law.[52] And the Congress then lived within its resolution for the remainder of the fiscal year. When the year ended, Adams was able to exult that "for the first time in its history the Congress . . . had developed and operated a comprehensive national budget," had produced "an economic policy that is distinctly that of the Congress, not the President," had "recaptured from the executive its constitutional role in controlling the power of the purse."[53]

The budget process scored still another triumph late in 1975 when it became the basis on which the Congress outmaneuvered President Ford in a confrontation over spending ceilings reminiscent of the clash of 1972 between Nixon and the legislature but with quite a different outcome. In October, Ford proposed that the Congress establish forthwith a spending ceiling of $395 billion for the fiscal year 1977 which would begin October 1, 1976, and

51. John W. Finney, *New York Times*, September 12 and October 21, 1975; Mary Russell, *Washington Post*, inserted in *Congressional Record*, October 8, 1975, p. 32462.

52. The most important adjustment was a floor amendment by Majority Leader O'Neill to add $900 million for foreign assistance in connection with the Egyptian-Israeli agreement on Sinai and another $200 million for additional public service jobs and job training. Without the latter addition to win liberal votes, the resolution—like the May resolution—was in jeopardy on the House floor. With the amendment, it passed by 225 to 191 but the final conference report survived by only two votes. "Once again," wrote Ellwood and Thurber, "The New Congressional Budget Process: Hows and Whys," p. 175, referring to the first vote, "the resolution was supported because of loyalty to the new process (in this case, leadership loyalty) rather than agreement with the content."

53. Edwin L. Dale, Jr., *New York Times*, July 2, 1976; Joel Havemann, *Congress and the Budget* (Indiana University Press, 1978), p. 56.

that the savings below what would be spent under a simple projection of current programs—$28 billion—be returned to the taxpayers as a permanent tax reduction.[54] Moreover, he promised to veto any tax bill, including one which merely extended the temporary cuts of 1975, unless a spending limitation were adopted.[55]

In the House, Republicans lined up solidly behind the president, but his proposal was so flagrantly in violation of the new budget procedures—demanding that the Congress commit itself far in advance of its first budget resolution, when its fiscal policy is supposed to be fixed—that Democrats were adamant against acting at that time. And in the Senate, they were joined by the ranking minority member of the Budget Committee, Senator Bellmon. "I personally seriously doubt that President Ford understands the changes that have been made since he was a member of Congress," he told the Senate in opposing the ceiling proposal. "I believe it would be a mistake to abandon the budget process in the first year of its infancy."[56] Earlier, he had suggested that the president's suggestion, coming when it did, had a "political purpose."[57] When the Congress refused even to consider the president's idea and sent him instead a simple extension of the 1975 temporary cuts, he stuck by his guns, too, and vetoed it, and the House upheld the veto. The two branches then tried to stare each other down, the executive threatening more vetoes and the legislature insisting that unless Ford yielded there would be no tax bill at all. In the end the president had to settle for some face-saving language the Congress wrote into the bill extending the temporary tax cuts. It committed the Congress to balance any extension of the cuts into fiscal 1977 with spending reductions—but only "if economic conditions warrant doing so"—and the decision would be made "through the procedures in the budget act." That act, this episode made clear, had given the Congress a strength to confront the president, and prevail, that it had lacked three years before. And in 1976 the Congress for the second time devised under its new procedures a fiscal policy of its own quite different from the president's, rejecting both his deep tax cut and the corresponding cuts in spending, and providing somewhat more stimulus to the economy. This time, Democratic unity was more easily attained and the resolutions passed more smoothly.[58]

54. "Address to the Nation on Federal Tax and Spending Reductions, October 6, 1975," *Public Papers: Ford, 1975,* vol. 2, pp. 1604–08.

55. "Interview with Reporters in Knoxville, Tennessee, October 7, 1975," ibid., p. 1609.

56. *Congressional Record,* December 15, 1975, pp. 40563–64.

57. Hobart Rowen, *Washington Post,* October 30, 1976.

58. But Chairman Muskie lost an important fight when the Senate Finance Committee failed to provide for enough revenue to meet the targets contained in the first budget resolution.

A "Bad" Year—and a "Good" One

When Democrat Jimmy Carter entered the White House, the eight years of bitter confrontation between the Congress and the president over fiscal policy—which had its roots in partisan rivalry—could be expected to end. Even before the inauguration, the two branches were moving toward agreement. The Congressional Budget Office issued a report entitled "The Disappointing Recovery" almost at the same time that the president-elect was announcing from Plains, Georgia, his intention to offer new measures for economic stimulus, amounting to $30 billion in tax cuts and additional spending divided between the 1977 and 1978 fiscal years. President Ford, in his final messages to the Congress in January 1977, also urged action to encourage investment and provide jobs, although as in the past his recommendations were to provide stimulus solely through tax cuts while slowing as much as possible the growth of spending.

The budget committees opened hearings at once and had no difficulty putting through the Congress a third budget resolution for the 1977 fiscal year to supplant the one adopted the previous autumn. They showed their independence by doubling President Carter's recommendations for new spending to $3.7 billion, while adhering strictly to his recommendations for nearly $16 billion in tax cuts, the major portion accounted for by a $50 income tax rebate for each taxpayer and dependent and for nontaxpayers as well. Six weeks after the Congress adopted the resolution, however, the president changed his mind and withdrew the proposal for a rebate, infuriating the budget committee leaders who had carried the burden of defending it on the House and Senate floors. Nevertheless, since the measure had proved to lack political appeal, they had no choice but to reverse direction with the president and carry still another revised budget resolution through the Congress.

The House leadership and the administration clashed again in May when the first budget resolution for the 1978 fiscal year reached the House floor. The House Budget Committee accepted the general fiscal policy reflected in the Carter budget, but it made some adjustments within the aggregate spending limits, including a hotly contested reduction of $4.15 billion in new budget authority and $2.3 billion in outlays for national defense. When Representative Omar Burleson, Democrat of Texas and a member of the committee, appealed this decision to the House, the administration swung in line behind him. Defense Secretary Harold Brown called House members and even persisted in doing so, members said, after Speaker O'Neill had obtained an agreement from Carter that the administration would remain neutral.[59] The motion carried. Once the committee's resolution was breached by this amendment (and an earlier one, minor in dollar terms, that rolled back a congressional pay raise), the gates were open for others. The House proceeded to increase outlays for the Law Enforcement Assistance Administration by $75 million and for World War I veterans' pensions by $500 million. At that, almost everybody deserted the budget resolution—liberals because defense spending was increased while cuts in other programs remained, conservatives because of the aggregate rise of $4.3 billion in the deficit, and some members because of the loss of the pay increase—and the resolution was defeated, 84 to 320.

At this, recriminations flew. Connecticut Democrat Robert N. Giaimo, the new Budget Committee chairman, accused the administration of trying to "dictate" to the Congress and of "breaking the delicate balance between defense and domestic spending proposed by the committee."[60] Next day, when tempers had cooled, the Budget Committee fashioned a compromise that restored the congressional pay raise and retained 25 percent of the funds provided in the floor amendments affecting the defense, law enforcement, and veterans' categories. Majority Leader James C. Wright, Jr., a member of the Budget Committee, wrote to all Democratic members pleading for votes to "redeem the commitment of the House to make this budget process work."[61] He and the other leaders followed up with active "arm twisting," and forty-three Democratic (along with four Republican) votes were switched on the Burleson amendment when it was again offered, and it was beaten. So were all other amendments except an additional $175 million for veterans' pensions, and the revised resolution was passed, 213 to 179. Once more the "budget process" had been "saved."

In the Senate, too, the Budget Committee found its resolution significantly amended on the floor for the first time. The Budget Committee, taking a deficit of $63 billion as the maximum allowable for purposes of fiscal policy, was forced to trim $15 billion in outlays from the spending estimates it received from the other committees. It could not find that amount in "obviously frivolous programs," Senator Muskie explained; it had to reduce "obviously meritorious programs."[62] But two chairmen successfully appealed on the Senate floor for restoration of funds they had sought. William Proxmire,

59. Joel Havemann, "Budget Process Nearly Ambushed by Carter and by Congress," *National Journal*, vol. 9 (May 21, 1977), p. 786.
60. *Washington Star*, April 28, 1977.
61. *Congressional Quarterly Almanac, 1977*, p. 195.
62. *Congressional Record*, May 4, 1977, p. 13565.

Democrat of Wisconsin, won an additional $6.2 billion in budget authority (as distinct from outlays) for housing assistance for low-income families and $500 million for community development. And Alan Cranston, Democrat of California, succeeded in adding $500 million in budget authority and $400 million in outlays for veterans' programs.

But this was only the beginning of the budget committees' 1977 problems. The first budget resolution had been on the books only six days when the Senate Agriculture Committee brought to the floor a farm price-support bill that breached the ceiling on fiscal 1978 outlays by about $1 billion. Declaring that if the first concurrent resolution were considered only "an open invitation to every committee" to ignore its targets "we might as well junk the process," Muskie offered two floor amendments to reduce the support price for wheat, which accounted for $500 million of the excess spending in the 1978 fiscal year.[63] Supported by Bellmon (who, as a farm state representative, was risking his political future) and a slim majority of the Budget Committee members— and by the Carter administration—but opposed almost solidly by members of the Agriculture Committee, he narrowly lost both amendments, by four and eight votes, respectively. But Muskie made another gesture in September, when he had his committee incorporate in the second budget resolution an instruction to the Agriculture Committee to bring in legislation to reduce spending on farm programs by $700 million. This time, he was beaten decisively, 64 to 27.

Once the second, or binding, resolution was adopted, the budget committees had to wage a continuing—and often a losing—battle to maintain its binding force. The most serious breach was an increase to $1.4 billion in authority for Small Business Administration disaster loans to farmers, which the administration supported but which was twenty-five times greater than the budget allowance. Muskie opposed the measure as a "runaway program . . . one of the most startling cases of uncontrolled spending in recent years . . . a multi-billion dollar money pump," and reiterated the old complaint that "we simply cannot afford the luxury of looking at one national need at a time and then ratifying runaway program costs to meet that need."[64] But he could muster only thirteen votes for his position. The Senate also voted $1.1 billion for tuition tax credits for higher education, a sum not included in the budget. And the energy program, as it went through the Senate, also contained tax reductions that would have increased the deficit by several billion dollars. The tuition tax credit, however, was rejected in conference,

63. Ibid., May 24, 1977, p. 16298.
64. Ibid., October 4, 1977, pp. 32318–19.

and the budget-breaching energy tax provisions were deadlocked in another conference committee for the remainder of the fiscal year.

As 1978 opened, Senator Muskie was expressing a grave concern that the budget process might already be in decline, portending its eventual abandonment. He saw "two disturbing trends"—a "threatened resurgence of the free spending mentality" and a "growing resistance and, unfortunately, resentment" toward the budget process by certain committees and members of the Senate. Had the process, he asked, "become simply a burden which most Members of the Senate no longer take seriously and are willing to ignore when it interferes with the spending or tax impulses of the hour?" Even members of the Budget Committee itself, he noted, had publicly abandoned "the philosophy and discipline of the budget process" by offering tax credit amendments that would raise the cost of the "already-too-excessive" energy bill. Senators, he said, "vote for budget resolutions with mental reservations and a purpose of evasion for when the specific votes on their favorite programs emerge later in the session." Senator Bellmon expressed a similar concern "that the level of commitment to the budget process and the will to make it function effectively are eroding." And Representative Giaimo was equally troubled. The farm price-support and disaster-loan cases indicated to him that some committees were "saying, in effect, that they will compel the Budget Act to adjust to their decisions, rather than to fit their actions into an overall budget."[65]

Yet when the Congress adjourned that year, the guardians of the congressional budget process found themselves greatly encouraged. The year had begun with another losing fight by Muskie and Bellmon against a farm bill, but the bill was later killed in the House, with Giaimo playing an important role.[66] But after that—and especially after the voters of California "sent a message to Washington" on June 6 with their approval of Proposition 13, the tax-cutting initiative—came a string of victories. The Senate voted by 60 to 21 to eliminate housing assistance funding that ran $5 billion beyond the congressional budget resolution and the president's budget request. The Senate Budget Committee also forced a considerable scaling down of tuition tax credit legislation and was sustained when the Finance Committee tried to expand the benefits on the Senate floor (the measure later died in a pre-adjournment deadlock).[67] And Muskie was able to invoke the budget act,

65. Testimony on January 17, 1978, in *Can Congress Control the Power of the Purse?* Hearing before the Senate Budget Committee, 95 Cong. 2 sess. (GPO, 1978), pp. 1, 3–4, 13, 6, 13.

66. Joel Havemann, "A Good Year for the Budget Process," *National Journal*, vol. 10 (September 23, 1978), p. 1501.

67. Ibid., p. 1502.

through points of order, to block floor amendments to the tax bill in October that would have reduced revenues below the figure in the budget resolution. Muskie said he was "pleased and proud" to be able to tell the Senate that it had shown itself willing "to accept budget reform as more than political propaganda." His warning against a "resurgence of the free spending mentality" had been heeded. "After a very bad beginning, it has been a good year," said Muskie. "I am much more hopeful now—than I could be last Spring—that the budget process is really taking hold in the Congress."[68]

The "Balanced" Budget of 1980–81

Two years later, in the late summer of 1980 (when Edmund Muskie, as President Carter's new secretary of state, was concerned with conflicts of another type) the budget process "took hold" in a far more rigorous fashion than in any previous year and came much closer to fulfilling the aspirations of its sponsors.

As early as 1977, the fundamental weakness of the new process had become apparent. It was the problem of "uncontrollable" spending—or "entitlements"—obligations fixed by law in a variety of fashions that the budget and appropriations committees, in their annual labors, could not reduce. The budget committees, in their resolutions, had anticipated savings in expenditures, or increases in revenue, that were dependent on new legislation to be written by other committees, and whenever those committees did not act the resolutions were to that extent vitiated. In 1977 Senator Muskie had tried to prevail on the Senate to *instruct* the Agriculture Committee to report legislation to reduce spending on farm programs, but he lost his battle.

The Senate Budget Committee renewed this course in 1979, by writing into its second budget resolution for the 1980 fiscal year a series of instructions to the Appropriations Committee and six other committees to prepare within ten days "reconciliation" measures that would result in savings of about $4.2 billion. After arduous debate in the Democratic caucus, Budget Committee Democrats agreed to reduce that figure by $400 million and extend the ten days to thirty, and with those concessions they were able to defeat decisively the efforts of some standing committee chairmen to further weaken the resolution on the Senate floor. But the House Budget Committee was in too weak a position to challenge similarly the array of spending committees in that body, and the reconciliation orders were stricken there. The Senate had

68. *Congressional Record*, daily edition, September 6, 1978, pp. S14607–08.

to settle for a "sense of the Congress" section of the resolution that warned the spending committees that the Congress would stick with the totals and, if the committees did not come up with the savings on which the totals were based, other spending needs that might arise later in the year—for which an allowance of $10.7 billion was contained in the budget—would be "crowded out": only about $7 billion of the $10.7 billion would be available for the original purpose. But when these needs did arise later (the result of inflation, recession, and such unanticipated events as the flood of refugees from Cuba and the eruption of Mt. St. Helens), the Congress simply could not crowd them out. A new budget resolution was adopted, and a supplemental appropriations bill providing $16.9 billion—far more than the $7 billion allowed in the second budget resolution in the absence of the reconciliation measures—was passed in July 1980. The appropriations would have been adjudged necessary in any event, but they were not offset in any significant part by the savings that had been sought through the reconciliation process.[69] As Muskie had anticipated, the "sense of the Congress" language had proved unenforceable.

By the time this issue was before the Congress in the spring of 1980, however, all attention was focused on the much more symbolically important first budget resolution for fiscal 1981. That resolution achieved its importance because President Carter, whose January budget had proposed a deficit of $15.8 billion, reversed himself in March—under the pressure of a sharp increase in the inflation rate and the imminence of his reelection campaign—and called for the 1981 budget to be in balance. Democrats in the Congress had independently, for the same reasons, determined the budget should be balanced, and early in March an extraordinary exercise in party policymaking took place. "Consultation of this type I've never seen in all my years in Congress," said Speaker O'Neill as the leadership and the two budget committee chairmen, as well as other key committee chairmen brought in by O'Neill and Senate Majority Leader Robert C. Byrd, of West Virginia, worked for more than a week in continuous session to reach a meeting of minds on how to bring the budget into balance.[70] The group's consensus was not binding on anyone—although Office of Management and Budget Director James T. McIntyre, Jr., did refer to "decisions" taken at the meetings[71]—but Chairman Giaimo of the House Budget Committee proceeded to put his

69. Representative Leon E. Panetta of California, a Democratic member of the Budget Committee, said that only $200 million of the savings assumed in the budget resolution for 1980 had been reported by the committees with jurisdiction over the necessary legislation. Ibid., May 7, 1980, p. H3319.

70. Martin Tolchin, *New York Times*, March 12, 1980.

71. Steven Rattner, *New York Times*, March 19, 1980.

version of a balanced budget through that body without waiting for the administration's revised proposals. The Senate Budget Committee moved less briskly but nonetheless independently, departing freely from the tentative administration figures that were available to it, and by early April it too had prepared a budget resolution embodying a slight surplus.

But the experience of earlier years had taught that no "sense of the Congress" resolution would suffice to bring about the legislative changes that would be necessary for either the Senate or the House version of the balanced budget (the two differed substantially in their particulars but were close together in their aggregates). Chairman Giaimo conceded that the voluntary approach had failed to trim 1980 expenditures as intended, and his committee's resolution for 1981, like the Senate committee's, contained reconciliation orders to the standing committees to report new legislation. A motion supported by sixteen House committee chairmen to strike the reconciliation section was overwhelmed, 127 to 289, by the budget-balancing sentiment that controlled the rank-and-file membership, and the budget resolution as adopted by both houses contained instructions to ten Senate and eight House committees to report legislation that would make $6.4 billion in further cuts and raise $4.2 billion in new revenues. The result of this $10.6 billion in reconciliation actions would be, as then estimated, a surplus of $500 million, and 1981 would be the first fiscal year without a deficit since 1969 and only the second such year in two decades.

Mandated to comply, the committees with varying degrees of protest did produce within the space of a few weeks the required legislation—a "monumental achievement," Giaimo called it.[72] Difficult decisions were made that would scarcely have been conceivable without the discipline of the budget process. The committees proposed, for instance, to reduce the number of children eligible for free school lunches; to remove some of the more liberal features of unemployment compensation, disability insurance, college student loan, and veterans' education programs; to limit medicare and medicaid payments to hospitals; to reduce highway and hospital construction; and—most controversial of all—to provide retired military personnel and civilian employees with only one cost-of-living adjustment a year, instead of two, in their pensions. On the revenue side they recommended a long series of adjustments, the most important of which was to extend the requirement for payment of estimated taxes to many corporations previously exempted. The Senate passed its reconciliation bill without delay, amid self-congratulatory comment. "This is a very proud day for the Senate and the congressional

72. *Congressional Record*, daily edition, July 21, 1980, p. E3484.

budget process," said Senator Ernest F. Hollings, Democrat of South Carolina, the new chairman of the Budget Committee. "This is the first significant step Congress has ever taken in a coherent fashion to bring the uncontrollable elements of the budget under greater control."[73]

Fearing a revolt in the House, supporters of the budget process sought to bring the reconciliation bill to the floor under a rule that would drastically limit the opportunity for amendments, but the Republicans on the Rules Committee declined to cooperate and the Democrats could not prevent enough defections to defeat the rule. After ten weeks of negotiations, the measure's sponsors had to accept a rule permitting several amendments, the most important being one to restore twice-yearly cost-of-living adjustments to government retirees, at a cost of $700 million during the 1981 fiscal year. With those modifications, the bill was passed and the reconciliation process saved. "A significant and historic day," proclaimed Majority Leader Jim Wright; "an important achievement in the field of fiscal responsibility."[74] After a conference lasting two months and involving a hundred senators and representatives, the Congress enacted the precedent-setting measure. A few cost-increasing provisions had been slipped in, over the protests of budgetary purists, along with the spending cuts, and the final version yielded only $8.3 billion instead of the originally projected $10.6 billion. Giaimo still found it "almost unbelievable."[75]

The two houses had gone ahead with the reconciliation process despite the fact that to balance the budget for 1981, which had been the purpose of the whole exercise, had become impossible. The deepening economic recession of 1980 had rendered invalid the assumptions on which the balanced budget embodied in the first budget resolution had been based. Those who fought to save the tiny "surplus" projected in the spring knew by midsummer that it would be wiped out by a slump-induced decline in revenue and an increase in unemployment compensation payments and other recession-related expenditures. Yet they pushed ahead with the reconciliation exercise because to retreat would be to strip the budget process of the discipline that had at last painfully been built into it. Moreover, the reconciliation measures would continue to bring their savings and increased revenues in future years when the recession would be over and budgetary balance would again be a feasible objective.

73. Ibid., June 26, 1980, pp. S8227–28.
74. Martin Tolchin, *New York Times,* September 5, 1980.
75. *Congressional Record,* daily edition, December 11, 1980, p. H12347. Provisions of the act are summarized in *Congressional Quarterly Weekly Report,* vol. 38 (December 6, 1980), p. 3488.

The New Congressional Capacity

In the sixth year of the budget process, the great potential of that process was beginning to be realized. The Congress had demonstrated the capacity to adopt a considered fiscal policy responding to the political and economic circumstances of a particular period, and then to enforce that policy on reluctant and resistant standing committees. A potent centralizing and co-ordinating force had been established to counter the long-dominant centrifugal trends within the congressional power structure. In one area of legislative activity, the Congress had overcome its inability to plan.

This achievement was not without its costs. The congressional budget process created new tensions within each house and intensified divisions within the majority party, which loaded heavy new burdens on the majority leadership. Particularly in the House, where most budget resolutions since the beginning had been written in an atmosphere of raucous partisanship, the majority leadership of the House and of its Budget Committee underwent an annual ordeal to frame a resolution acceptable to enough Democrats to win House approval. Sometimes they failed at first in floor votes, only to succeed later, and sometimes the ultimate success was attained only at the expense of the May 15 and September 15 deadlines set by the budget act for the first and second resolutions. In the presidential election year of 1980, the second budget resolution was delayed until the postelection lame-duck session in late November, to spare members the embarrassment of having to vote for a deficit of $30 billion–$40 billion after having promised a balanced budget in their first resolution in the spring. Appropriation bills were with increasing frequency delayed beyond the beginning of the fiscal year on October 1, a reversion to the inconvenience that the budget act had sought to correct when it changed the opening date from July 1. When, in 1980, Senator Muskie resigned and Senator Bellmon retired from the Senate, it appeared possible that that body, too, might lose the benefits of the bipartisan collaboration that had marked its proceedings since the beginning. But as Republican partisanship forced the Democratic majority to treat the budget as a party responsibility, that appeared to be producing benefits of a different, and perhaps ultimately more important, kind—in the form of an enhanced capacity for policy coordination through the party organs of the majority (a subject treated in later chapters).

As the year 1980 ended, the Congress, having made the reconciliation process work in one season, seemed likely to attempt it, and perhaps at an earlier stage in the process, in most future years—excluding only those when substantial deficit spending was the agreed policy. The extent of savings that individual committees would be called on to make in particular years would vary as the fiscal outlook became more or less stringent. (In the early months of 1981 a far more drastic budget-cutting effort than that of 1980 was under way, through the reconciliation process. On recommendation of its Budget Committee—which adopted President Reagan's proposals virtually without change—the Senate instructed its legislative and appropriations committees to reduce President Carter's 1981–82 budget by nearly $40 billion, which required major revisions in authorizing legislation. The House Budget Committee proposed adjustments on a comparable scale.) And even if the reconciliation process were unsuccessful in any particular year—that is, if the committees did not fully comply or if their compliance measures were rejected on the floor (as in the case of the cost-of-living pension adjustments), or even if the conferees failed to agree on a bill—that would not in itself necessarily brand the whole congressional budget process a failure. Indeed, even before the reconciliation process was attempted for the first time in 1980, the new process could be judged a success.

Whether the process works, as Allen Schick emphasizes, cannot be measured by simply counting how many times the budget committees win or lose in their disputes with agriculture, or revenue, or energy and natural resources committees.[76] The budget committees cannot expect to win in every conflict. Nor should they. Fiscal policy objectives are just one set of objectives, which have to be weighed against other national purposes. They should not necessarily be overriding. The budget act could have been written to give fiscal objectives a superior status. But the proposal to make the budget resolutions more controlling by requiring a two-thirds vote to set them aside was discarded, and the budget committees were established on a par with other committees, leaving the Senate and the House to make the choices by simple majority vote when objectives came into conflict. Under these circumstances, what Senator Muskie in 1978 called the "spending or tax impulses of the hour" were bound to prevail in many of the showdowns.

That this is as it should be was argued, also in 1978, by Senator Henry M. Jackson, Democrat of Washington, chairman of the Energy and Natural Resources Committee:

> I have no doubt that situations to which legislators must be able to respond

76. *Congress and Money*, pp. 569–71.

swiftly and with flexibility will arise again and again in our political system. Under these circumstances an overly rigid interpretation and enforcement of the provisions of the Budget Act may lead to unwise policy decisions. We cannot be constrained by decisions made on preliminary information and inadequate analysis in March when we have better information in June or when unforeseen crises arise in September. . . . Although the Budget Committees may sometimes have to act as policemen as they attempt to constrain a freewheeling system, they were not intended to diminish the responsibilities or prerogatives of other committees.[77]

This balance between restraint and flexibility is not unlike the one maintained within the budget process of the executive branch. In putting together his annual budget, a president must balance fiscal policy objectives with other goals; the Office of Management and Budget, like the budget committees, seeks to protect the former, and the spending departments, like the spending committees, advocate the latter. The fiscal policy that emerges may appear to have been controlling from the start, even when it was not, because the conflicts between the spenders and the savers, with the president as umpire, take place outside the public spotlight, and when the decisions are made the president presents them in the language of considered fiscal policy. Yet even after the president's budget is submitted to the Congress, he is free to revise it whenever he finds it necessary to do so, and it is a rare year that goes by without his sending significant supplemental estimates to Capitol Hill—along with occasional rescissions. Neither presidents nor Congresses have ever felt obliged to stick to their initial budget decisions when circumstances, including political circumstances, change. The popular proposal to write a requirement for a balanced budget (except in times of emergency) into the Constitution has been advanced as the means of removing the fiscal flexibility of a sovereign government that the budget act deliberately sought to preserve. In the absence of such a stricture, the government can, quite properly, modify its fiscal policy through normal legislative processes whenever its majorities elect to do so.

To say that the budget act preserved congressional flexibility is not to say that the Congress can now in fact proceed with as much abandon as it did before the act was passed. Even if reconciliation were not to be tried again, and even if the budget committees were to lose all their floor fights—which they have not, even in the worst of years—those would not be the only

77. *Can Congress Control the Power of the Purse?* Hearing, p. 47. Not many of the budget-breaching actions, however, resulted from unforeseen situations or genuinely new information—other than information about the views of constituency groups. But the substantive committees had justification for their argument that the schedule forces them to negotiate with the budget committees too early in the year, before their analysis of their information is "adequate." Though they could begin their analyses earlier, they have been reluctant or unable to recast their habits and cycles of activity to fit the budget cycle.

criteria for measuring the effectiveness of the budget process. The consequences of the committees' day-by-day, month-by-month activities—indeed
the consequences of the mere existence of the budget process—are of great
importance. The fact that a budget committee has been introduced as a new
force within each house affects the balance of power, and hence the outcome
throughout the legislative season. At each stage of the spending process the
budget committees are involved as a new source of pressure and restraint.

At the beginning of each year, before the preparation of the budget
resolution, the spending committees must justify to the budget committees
their spending programs, which they did not have to do before. The budget
committees try to accommodate the spending committees, for they need
friends and allies too, and they are limited in the number of confrontations
they can provoke. Yet they still have to scale down at least some of the
estimates they receive to fit within the general limits set by the fiscal policy
they are formulating, and the spending committees face the choice of going
along with the budget committees' decisions or appealing them on the House
or Senate floor. The same choice later confronts the advocates of spending;
either they live within the confines of the budget resolutions as adopted, or
they accept the pain and effort of a floor fight with a prospect of defeat.[78]
Thus the numbers contained in the budget resolutions are a significant
influence in debates within committees. They are an argument to be used by
those who would resist spending increases or revenue reductions. They are
a shield to help beleaguered committee members fend off lobbies. In a close
situation, they can be decisive.[79]

Even before the added savings to be attained through reconciliation were
attempted, the total impact of the budget process was considerable. Senator
Muskie estimated that in 1976 the process headed off $15 billion in spending
that would otherwise have been approved for the 1977 fiscal year.[80] This may
be near or far from the mark, but no one doubts that the act had had results
of *some* importance. As Senator Proxmire put it in 1978: "Without the act I
believe that spending would have been higher than it has been, that the
budget deficit would have been larger, and that inflation might have been
worse. The temptation for an orgy of spending, especially for public works,

78. Senator Muskie, who made it a practice to advise the Senate whether each spending
measure it considered was within the terms of the budget resolution, made 130 floor appearances
in the first three years. Schick, *Congress and Money*. The House committee chairmen, Representative
Adams and later Representative Giaimo, made fewer appearances but similarly made sure the
House was informed on all major departures.
79. Joel Havemann cites additional examples of the budget committees' influence in *Congress
and the Budget*, p. 132.
80. Joel Havemann, "The Congressional Budget—On Time and a Long Time Coming," *National
Journal*, vol. 8 (September 18, 1976), p. 1306. Havemann, *Congress and the Budget*, p. 131.

highways, weapons systems, et cetera in the name of offsetting unemployment would have been almost irresistible."[81]

Senator Bellmon concurred in milder language: "There is no question the budget procedure has had a restraining effect on the authorizing and appropriating committees. Fewer efforts have been made to increase spending, and not all of them have been successful."[82]

And even when the Congress was using its new procedures to upset the conservative fiscal policy of the Ford administration, President Ford's deputy OMB director, Paul H. O'Neill, gave the process credit for moderating what the Congress would otherwise have done.[83] So did Alice Rivlin, director of the Congressional Budget Office.[84]

These testimonials are reinforced by the outcries of those affected by the budget resolution spending limits. The AFL-CIO, for example, told the two national political conventions in 1976 that "the new budget process adopted by Congress threatens to undermine the ability of Congress to lead the nation out of recession and provide for the needs of the American people."[85] "I don't think it's worth continuing," groused Representative James C. Corman, Democrat of California, when the budget process ruled out consideration of an unemployment compensation bill early in 1976.[86]

These criticisms are analogous to the complaints of those who have judged the merit of the process narrowly in terms of the size of the resultant deficit and who condemned it for its failure to produce a balanced budget in its early years. The proper standard of judgment is whether the fiscal policy of the Congress is considered and rational, not whether it conforms to anyone's predilections as to what the policy should be. And, with the exception of an occasional Corman, the members of the Congress itself are judging the process by its rationality rather than by its outcomes—and supporting it. When on

81. *Can Congress Control the Power of the Purse?* Hearing, p. 21.
82. Alan L. Otten, *Wall Street Journal*, July 13, 1978.
83. Havemann, *Congress and the Budget*, pp. 195–96. O'Neill interpreted the establishment of the congressional budget process as actually increasing the president's power vis-à-vis the Congress, because it brought the congressional action closer to the presidential recommendations. "If power is being able to influence the outcome, the executive branch has more power now," he told an interviewer. (It may be argued, of course, that the influence toward fiscal conservatism is generated within the Congress itself by the budget committees, which by virtue of their structure and responsibilities tend to develop the same perspective and policy viewpoint as the president and his OMB.) The O'Neill analysis helps to explain why President Nixon urged budget reform on the Congress and welcomed it when it was enacted—even though the reform shifted the locus of decisionmaking in favor of the legislative branch.
84. Ibid., p. 195.
85. "The AFL-CIO Platform Proposals, presented to the Democratic and Republican National Conventions, 1976," p. 55. Four years later, the AFL-CIO platform proposals presented to the 1980 conventions contained no reference to the congressional budget process.
86. Joel Havemann, "The Congressional Budget Committees—High Marks after the First Years," *National Journal*, vol. 8 (September 25, 1976), p. 1346.

occasion, in the turmoil of trying to reach agreement on the annual budget resolutions, the process itself has appeared to be in danger, enough members of both houses have been rallied to set aside their substantive interests to assure its preservation. In a milieu where procedures are normally designed and sustained as means to substantive ends, the defense of the budget process as an end in itself, by liberals and conservatives alike, has been notable. Underlying that support, of course, is the postulate, often made explicit in the debates, that retention of the power of the purse by the Congress vis-à-vis the president depends ultimately on the orderly exercise of that authority, and the budget process is the symbol and the fact of order.

That a new orderliness has been achieved is the important thing. The Congress has established its own decisionmaking capacity, in the budget committees and the budget resolutions, and its own source of analysis and information independent of the executive branch, in the Congressional Budget Office. When it opposes the fiscal policy of the president, as it did when Gerald Ford was in the White House, it is able to fashion a coherent and well-considered alternative. If it amends its initial policy, during consideration of a farm bill or an energy bill or a tax bill, it does so deliberately. When it agrees with the president, as in the case of the initially projected balanced budget for 1981, it has the means—through the reconciliation process—to make even a stringent policy effective. It still may not make all of the politically unpopular spending reductions—particularly in legal entitlement programs—that might be justified in an objective weighing of costs and benefits, but no procedure can force that outcome. The reconciliation process has at least brought some reductions that, under former procedures, would hardly have been conceivable. The budget committees make sure that when the legislators consider individual measures they do so with full knowledge of the entire budget picture—not just the immediate consequences but the longer-term fiscal impact as well. The old charge that the Congress habitually acted irresponsibly in piecemeal legislative actions without regard for their aggregate effect—a charge to which the Congress pleaded guilty—has lost most of its validity.

In a strict sense, the Congressional Budget and Impoundment Control Act of 1974 does not represent a recapture of the power of the purse from the president by the Congress, because the power never left (except temporarily, in the late 1960s and early 1970s, in what can be looked on as aberrations, including usurpations by the executive, rather than settled practice). But the immensely important contribution of the act is to lay to rest the question of whether the Congress would someday be compelled by its own inadequacies to let that crucial power go. In that sense the Congress has indeed succeeded in resolving in its own favor the constitutional crisis of the Nixon years. It has taken the most important single step in restoring itself to what it conceived, during the depths of its humiliation in those years, to be its rightful, coequal place in the constitutional scheme of things.

CHAPTER IX

To Recapture
the War Power

WHILE President Nixon's claim to an unlimited power of impoundment may have been foremost among the issues that provoked the
historic executive-legislative clash of 1972–73—and the subsequent resurgence
of the Congress—the president's conduct of the war in Southeast Asia ranked
not far behind. As discontent with the failing military effort mounted, it fed
a gathering distrust of presidential leadership, a distrust compounded by the
secrecy that shrouded U.S. operations in Vietnam, Cambodia, and Laos.
Gradually, the Congress was impelled to recapture control of decisions governing the war. At the same time, it began to face squarely the question of
constitutional interpretation that underlay its dispute with the president, the
question it had skirted in passing the Gulf of Tonkin and earlier blank-check
resolutions: just how much power does a president have to lead the country
into war without the participation of the Congress? And alongside the constitutional problem lay a practical one: what is the feasible extent of participation of a deliberative Congress in war-making, anyway, in a time when
U.S. military forces may be stationed in any strategic segment of the globe
and the decision to use, or not to use, them may have to be made on the
briefest notice?

In its era of resurgence, the Congress wrote an end to the blank-check
version of strategic policy that had marked its era of decline. It even repealed
the Gulf of Tonkin resolution itself. Then it went on to define—or so it
hoped—a firmer constitutional relationship between the Congress and the
president in the taking of decisions that may plunge the country into war.
Its instrument was the War Powers Resolution of 1973, the earliest conspicuous symbol of the congressional resurgence. Unlike the Congressional

238

Budget and Impoundment Control Act, that resolution does not restore to the Congress the whole of the decisionmaking power (save for the presidential veto) in the matters it covers. Nor does it rest on as solid a constitutional foundation, for neither President Nixon—who vetoed it on constitutional grounds—nor any of his successors has conceded that it is in accord with the nation's basic charter. It has, nevertheless, altered significantly relations between the branches, by pronouncing rules that no president can ignore to govern consultation with the Congress on the movement of military forces into danger zones and to require the assent of the Congress to any prolonged military operations. Clearly, the legislative branch has restored in some substantial measure the authority over war and peace it had let slip away in its era of decline.

It was not the Vietnam War but Lyndon Johnson's intervention in the Dominican Republic in April 1965 that touched off the ultimately successful challenge to the president's war-making authority. Once it became apparent that the president's purpose in occupying the island republic was to take sides in an internal power struggle and not merely to save American lives, fundamental misgivings arose within the Congress—notably among members of the Senate Foreign Relations Committee and particularly in the mind of its chairman, Democrat J. William Fulbright of Arkansas. These dissenters held the view that the United States should align itself with progressive, reform movements in Latin America and elsewhere and saw in the Dominican case an intervention on the wrong side. Fulbright scheduled hearings and assigned a committee staff member to examine the State Department's cable file on the incident. This review not only confirmed the judgment of the chairman and his colleagues that the policy was wrong but led them to a conclusion even more damaging to executive-legislative relations: President Johnson had misled the Congress about the threat to American lives in the Dominican Republic and the true purpose of the intervention.[1]

Fulbright wrestled with his conscience for more than a month before breaking publicly with his old friend and former colleague, according to Pat M. Holt, a long-time member of the committee staff.[2] But on September 15 he took the Senate floor to denounce the intervention as a "grievous mistake," as an "overreaction," as a violation of the terms of the inter-American treaty, as an affair characterized "throughout . . . by a lack of candor."[3] "The

---

1. The sequence of events is set forth in chapter 5.
2. "Residue From the '65 Dominican Intervention," *Washington Post*, May 1, 1977. Francis O. Wilcox likewise identified the Dominican Republic episode as sowing the "initial seeds of executive-legislative distrust." *Congress, the Executive, and Foreign Policy* (Harper and Row, 1971), p. 22.
3. *Congressional Record*, September 15, 1965, pp. 23855–59.

credibility gap was open," wrote Holt. And the "embittered attitudes of mutual distrust generated by the Dominican affair" made the break between the Senate dissenters and President Johnson over Vietnam come earlier and become "sharper and deeper" than it otherwise would have been. Doubts already existed about Vietnam policy, "but before the Dominican intervention there was a predisposition to give the President the benefit of those doubts. Afterwards, this predisposition was reversed," Holt recalls.[4]

The September debate also touched off the congressional reconsideration of executive-legislative relations in the broad field of strategic policy and military operations. Senators took sides on the constitutional issue that had remained unsettled ever since the Washington administration. Reflecting the principles stated then by Madison, Eugene J. McCarthy, Democrat of Minnesota, contended that "our function in the Senate is not merely to find out what the administration policy is and then say yes or no to it—and oftentimes too late. We have a definite responsibility to develop policy ourselves." Not so, said George Smathers, Democrat of Florida, as the modern Hamiltonian; the "primary responsibility for establishing foreign policy" lies in the president. The responsibility, countered McCarthy, is shared equally between the president and the Senate. To which Smathers replied: "While the Senate has every right to speak about and discuss foreign policy, nevertheless the President has the responsibility for conducting foreign policy." He later added an adjective; the president has "final responsibility." Fulbright provided a Madisonian summing-up: "The concept of the President being permitted to do anything he likes in the field of foreign relations is a concept that has grown up. It is a misguided concept, dating back to certain resolutions adopted by the Senate. . . . It is true that he has the power, but that does not mean he has the legitimate, constitutional right to use it."[5]

Lyndon Johnson was not one to take such an attack passively. The administration supplied material to its Senate supporters for a series of rebuttals, and at the other end of the Capitol the House Foreign Affairs Committee produced a formal resolution interpreting the inter-American treaty as well as the Monroe Doctrine to authorize what the president had done. The resolution, said the committee, would place the House on record as supporting the president in any action he deemed necessary "to prevent in a timely manner Communist subversion in this hemisphere."[6] "Customarily the field of foreign affairs is left to the President," observed Julia Butler Hansen,

4. *Washington Post*, May 1, 1977.
5. *Congressional Record*, September 30, 1965, pp. 25622–23.
6. *Congressional Quarterly Almanac, 1965*, p. 518.

Democrat of Washington, during the House debate.[7] The resolution to continue the custom was approved by the full House by 312 votes to 52, but the
Senate's Madisonians, led by Fulbright, were not to let it rest at that.

The Deepening Distrust of Presidential Power

Senator Fulbright's contention that the president was using his de facto
power illegitimately and unconstitutionally was the equivalent of a charge
of usurpation, and senators who shared that view could not take the president's conduct lightly. Even before the end of the Dominican adventure,
attention shifted to Southeast Asia. As the Vietnam casualty lists mounted,
public opposition grew. The campus "teach-ins" began, and in November
1965 some twenty thousand students marched on Washington. In May and
again in September 1966, Gallup polls showed more than one-third of the
country believing that it was a mistake for the United States to have become
involved.[8] Division in the country was bound to be reflected in the legislative
branch, but the opposition on Capitol Hill was intensified by a growing
conviction that President Johnson had misled the Congress once again. The
credibility gap was widening, and the mutual distrust deepening. Suspicion
of the president was fed by a spreading belief that the 1964 episode that led
to the Gulf of Tonkin resolution had been misrepresented to the legislators,
as a pretext for winning the resolution, and by a widely held view that the
president was misinterpreting the intent of the resolution itself and hence
misusing it.

The doubt about the Gulf of Tonkin incident was at first only an under-
current in the debate over Vietnam policy, but Senator Fulbright brought it
to the surface in a Foreign Relations Committee hearing in May 1966, with
Secretary of State Dean Rusk on the witness stand. Since the passage of the
resolution, said Senator Fulbright, "there has come to my attention suggestions that the whole affair was very questionable as to the character of the
attack upon our ships on the high seas." But at the time, any suggestion
"that this might have been a deliberate provocation on our part to incite the
incident or that we had been inside the territorial waters of North Vietnam
in connection with some boats or South Vietnam, and all of that, was brushed
aside in the emotions that naturally arose from an allegation by the administration that this was a deliberate and unprovoked attack upon our ships on

7. *Congressional Record*, September 20, 1965, p. 24360.
8. Walter Isard, ed., *Vietnam: Some Issues and Alternatives* (Cambridge, Mass.: Schenkman, 1969),
p. 69.

the high seas." He had already publicly apologized, he said, for his "negligence" in not holding more thorough hearings—for, in effect, taking the president at his word.[9] But it was still a suspicion on Fulbright's part; it would not develop into a conviction until the committee had made its own investigation of the incident, in 1967 and 1968.[10]

On the second aspect of executive misrepresentation—on the meaning of the resolution—the dissenting senators had a complete legislative record to turn to. It was not, however, unambiguous, and the president could refer to it also in defending his course. During the debate, Daniel B. Brewster, Democrat of Maryland, had questioned whether the resolution would authorize or approve "the landing of American armies" in Vietnam. Senator Fulbright as floor manager of the resolution had responded:

> There is nothing in the resolution, as I read it, that contemplates it. I agree with the Senator that is the last thing we would want to do. However, the language of the resolution would not prevent it. It would authorize whatever the Commander in Chief feels is necessary. It does not restrain the Executive from doing it. . . . Everyone I have heard has said that the last thing we want to do is to become involved in a land war in Asia; that our power is sea and air, and that this is what we hope will deter the Chinese Communists and the North Vietnamese from spreading the war. That is what is contemplated. The resolution does not prohibit that, or any other kind of activity.[11]

Again, in a colloquy with Senator John Sherman Cooper, Republican of Kentucky, Fulbright had said: "This provision is intended to give clearance to the President to use his discretion. We all hope and believe that the President will not use this discretion arbitrarily or irresponsibly."[12]

Next day, Senator Gaylord Nelson, Democrat of Wisconsin, noting that "every Senator who spoke had his own personal interpretation of what the joint resolution means," had proposed an amendment to clear up the confusion. It would have expressed the sense of the Congress that the country's Vietnam policy would continue to be limited to "the provision of aid, training assistance, and military advice" and "except when provoked to a greater response" would "continue to attempt to avoid a direct military involvement in the Southeast Asian conflict." Senator Fulbright had replied that the proposed amendment "states fairly accurately what the President has said

9. May 9, 1966, in *Foreign Assistance, 1966,* Hearings before the Senate Committee on Foreign Relations, 89 Cong. 2 sess. (U.S. Government Printing Office, 1966), p. 622.

10. After a staff investigation and a closed hearing, Fulbright concluded that the administration had indeed misrepresented the facts about the Gulf of Tonkin incident and that the resolution, "like any contract based on misrepresentation," should therefore be considered "null and void." *Congressional Record,* March 7, 1968, p. 5645. Some members of the committee were more explicit, saying flatly that the United States had "provoked" the incident. *Congressional Quarterly Almanac, 1968,* p. 714.

11. *Congressional Record,* August 6, 1964, pp. 18403–04.

12. Ibid., p. 18410.

would be our policy, and what I stated my understanding was as to our policy." However, he had objected that as a practical matter he could not accept the amendment because it would delay the legislation, and Nelson did not press it.[13] In so casual a way did the Congress exercise its war power, in the decade before the War Powers Resolution.

When President Johnson committed large land armies to Vietnam less than a year later, he chose to interpret the resolution broadly and literally. He cited it in his public statements and correspondence and, so the Washington story went, carried a copy around in his pocket to whip out whenever he was challenged. His supporters could cite one strain in Fulbright's explanation: "it would authorize . . . whatever is necessary"; "the resolution does not prohibit"; "it does not restrain"; it "is intended to give clearance to the President to use his discretion." And the dissenters, their numbers growing, could cite the opposing theme: the resolution does not "contemplate" land armies in Asia; the president had said he had no such intention; "everyone . . . has said that the last thing we want to do is to become involved in a land war"; the president "will not use this discretion arbitrarily or irresponsibly." On the basis of the president's public statements and his private assurances in 1964, they felt betrayed as the country became steadily more deeply involved in the ground warfare in Vietnam.

In his 1966 confrontation with Secretary Rusk, Fulbright embraced the narrow interpretation of the resolution. The "whole reason" for the measure, he contended, was the incident itself—an attack on American ships on the high seas—and the language was intended to be confined to repelling such attacks. It "was not a treaty calling for deliberate determination of a policy with regard to the vital interests of this country in southeast Asia. . . . I do think in all fairness it is a distortion of that one resolution to make it equivalent to a declaration of war." Retorted Rusk: "I think the record makes it clear that the resolution was considerably broader than simply a quick and narrow reaction to a particular conflict in the exchange in the Gulf of Tonkin. . . . I believe as you yourself put it in your discussion on the floor—you hoped that the broader authorization of the act would not be necessary or not be used or called upon, that nevertheless you felt that the act itself did have in it such authority." "But the unfortunate part was that this was presented as a matter of great urgency," Fulbright replied. "There was practically no consideration. . . . I think we had 1 day's hearings. . . . I do not think anyone had the idea that this was the kind of broad commitment which it is now interpreted to be."[14]

13. Ibid., p. 18459.
14. *Foreign Assistance, 1966*, Hearings, pp. 622, 634, 636, 637.

Other senators shared Fulbright's recollection. "Nobody thought it would be what it turned out to be," recalled Senator Quentin N. Burdick, Democrat of North Dakota in 1969. Senator McCarthy said he had considered it innocuous, and other senators expressed the same sentiment. Even senators not identified as doves, such as John C. Stennis of Mississippi, ranking Democratic member of the Armed Services Committee in 1964, and Allen Ellender of Louisiana, joined Fulbright in the narrow interpretation of the congressional intent.[15]

But in Secretary Rusk's view, presidential power to use military forces was already unlimited, even without a Gulf of Tonkin resolution or a Southeast Asia Treaty. "No would-be aggressor," Rusk said, before the Preparedness Subcommittee of Armed Services, "should suppose that the absence of a defense treaty, Congressional declaration or U.S. military presence grants immunity to aggression." Senator Fulbright used that statement as his takeoff point in a long discussion of executive-legislative relations in foreign policy before the Separation of Powers Subcommittee of the Senate Judiciary Committee in July 1967. Secretary Rusk conveyed a significant message to the Congress, said Fulbright—namely, that the Congress was "irrelevant to American military commitments abroad." It was not a conscious message; "it seems more likely that this was merely assumed, taken for granted as a truism of American foreign policy in the 1960's." The senator cited a long series of presidential actions that had given rise to the assumption, from President Roosevelt's destroyers-for-bases deal in 1940, through the wartime agreements at Yalta and Potsdam, through the Korean and Vietnam wars, to small-scale actions in the Middle East and the Congo. "I do not believe that the executive has willfully usurped the constitutional authority of the Congress," he went on; "the cause . . . is crisis." The Congress cannot act quickly. "When the security of the country is endangered, or thought to be endangered, there is a powerful premium on prompt action, and that means executive action." The Congress participates in only two ways. One is through briefings after the fact, which pass for consultations but lack the substance. The other is through actions like the Gulf of Tonkin resolution. "Arranged in haste, always under the spur of some real or putative emergency, these resolutions and White House briefings serve to hit the Congress when it is down, getting it to sign on the dotted line at exactly the moment when, for reasons of politics or patriotism, it feels it can hardly refuse." The result: "The Congress has lost the power to declare war as it was written into the

15. Interviews with Walter Arnold Zelman, reported in "Senate Dissent and the Vietnam War 1964–68" (Ph.D. dissertation, University of California at Los Angeles, 1971), pp. 82, 91, 101. He found "few if any" senators who thought they had issued a blank check.

Constitution. It has not been so much usurped as given away, and it is by no means certain that it will soon be recovered."[16]

The National Commitments Resolution of 1969

So what were the next steps? Fulbright explained that he had been making his committee available as a forum for free and wide-ranging discussion, to provide an orderly outlet for dissenting views that would serve not only to educate but to restrain. He was serving notice that, as far as his committee was concerned, there would be no more "blank checks," no more "hasty responses to contrived emergencies."[17] Beyond that, Fulbright proposed to put the Senate as a body on record that thereafter no commitment to a foreign power would be valid without, in some form, the consent of the Congress. He introduced a "sense of the Senate" resolution to that effect.

Hearings on the resolution dramatized the wide and deepening split between president and Senate. The administration, through Under Secretary of State Nicholas deB. Katzenbach, opposed the resolution and, under intensive questioning, Katzenbach took an extreme view of the presidential prerogatives. Even without the Gulf of Tonkin resolution, he contended, the president would have the power to wage a ground war in Vietnam, "because of a variety of expressions of view of the Congress, including the SEATO [Southeast Asia Treaty Organization] treaty, as well as his own constitutional powers." The limits of presidential power have never been defined, nor has any president ever exercised his power to its limits, said Katzenbach; moreover, the limits should not be defined; they should be left flexible, to be worked out by the Congress and the president through "practical interaction between the two branches." The resolution and the SEATO treaty, in combination, were the "functional equivalent" of a declaration of war. When Fulbright mentioned the constitutional prerogative of the Congress to declare war, Katzenbach replied that "the expression of declaring a war is one that has become outmoded in the international arena." In the particular case, a declaration of war was unsuitable because the U.S. objectives were "limited." In any event, the Gulf of Tonkin resolution was "as broad an authorization

16. Testimony inserted in *Congressional Record*, July 31, 1967, pp. 20702–06.

17. The Congress had only recently rejected a request by the president for an advance commitment to increase aid to Latin America over a five-year period. Also in 1967 it refused to grant the Defense Department authority for procurement of "fast deployment logistic ships" designed for use in emergencies, extended for only a single year the revolving fund used by the Department of Defense for arms sales, and cut the foreign aid authorization by nearly one-quarter. *Congressional Quarterly Almanac, 1967*, p. 945.

for the use of armed forces for a purpose as any declaration of war so-called could be in terms of our internal constitutional process."[18]

The committee rejected Katzenbach's position in its entirety. The Congress's war power was not "outmoded," it asserted in its report, and in any case the executive was not "free to alter on its own authority" a provision of the Constitution it might consider to be obsolete. Only in recent years had the war power passed to the president, "as the result of erosion, inadvertency, expediency, and—in a few instances—usurpation." Why had the Congress acquiesced in the transfer of power? Because, said the committee, it lacked "guidelines of experience" in meeting the demands of the country's new role as a world power. Because great decisions of the postwar era had been made "in an atmosphere of real or contrived urgency." Perhaps because the Congress had been "overawed by the cult of executive expertise." Perhaps because it was "doing a kind of penance for its prewar isolationism," for the Senate's rejection of the Treaty of Versailles. The Congress had tacitly acknowledged a "lack of confidence" in its ability to adapt its war power to the nuclear age, the report conceded, but the executive, "though less susceptible to self-doubt than the Congress, is no less susceptible to error." The Congress "has demonstrated on many occasions that it is capable of acting as speedily as the executive," but "a useful distinction can be made between speed and haste," and none of the four postwar resolutions was a mattter of such urgency that a few days of deliberation would have done any harm. In the case of Tonkin, Congress erred in making a judgment as to how a *particular* president would use the power, rather than a judgment as to what power *any* president should have—or whether the Congress even had the right under the Constitution "to grant or concede the authority in question." In any event, the resolution was not the "functional equivalent" of a declaration of war. In the future, the Congress should take enough time to make its intent clear. It should explicitly make grants of power, to remove any doubt as to where the power to initiate war lies. And the grants should be explicitly limited in scope of power, and in duration.[19]

The national commitments resolution was scheduled for action in April 1968, but President Johnson's dramatic withdrawal from the presidential race on March 31 and his cessation of the bombing of North Vietnam led the leadership to delay it. Other matters intervened, but it was adopted in June

18. August 21, 1967, in *U.S. Commitments to Foreign Powers*, Hearings before the Senate Foreign Relations Committee, 90 Cong. 1 sess. (GPO, 1967), pp. 140–43, 76, 82, 81, 89. President Johnson had told a press conference three days before Katzenbach's testimony that "we did not think the resolution was necessary to do what we did and what we are doing." Ibid., p. 126.

19. *National Commitments*, S. Rept. 797, 90 Cong. 1 sess. (GPO, 1967), pp. 22, 23, 14, 26, 25, 24, 21.

1969 by a vote of 70 to 16—over the opposition of the Nixon administration, which reiterated the arguments of its predecessor.

The Beginnings of Congressional Control

The national commitments resolution simply expressed the sense of the Senate that commitments made without the assent of Congress were invalid; the resolution had no legal force. To enforce its will on the president, the Senate had to find ways to legislate. It had to detect commitments that had been made, were in the process of being made, or were contemplated, and intervene to stop them.

It was a measure of the extent of congressional abdication that the legislators had never even insisted on being informed by the executive what it was doing. Now, the first step was to find out. So, at the same time that it pressed forward with its resolution relating to future commitments, the Senate Foreign Relations Committee early in 1969 created a subcommittee chaired by Stuart Symington, Democrat of Missouri, to conduct a two-year inquiry into the extent of the commitments that already publicly or secretly bound the country. It began with hearings on Spain, which resulted in an expression of concern by the Foreign Relations Committee that the U.S. commitment to that country was being "upgraded" in a new executive agreement relating to bases, and a response by the administration that no upgrading had occurred.[20] Then the subcommittee turned its attention to the Philippines, Laos, Thailand, and Nationalist China.[21]

By midsummer it was clear that the United States was deeply committed in Laos and Thailand. "In effect," Symington told the Senate in August, the United States had been "at war in Laos for years" and much of this involvement had never been "taken up with the Congress."[22] As for Thailand, the United States had six major bases and forty-five thousand troops there,[23]

20. *Congressional Quarterly Almanac, 1969,* pp. 177, 179, 999.
21. Its findings are discussed in Merlo J. Pusey, *The U.S.A. Astride the Globe* (Houghton Mifflin, 1971); R. A. Paul, *American Military Commitments Abroad* (Rutgers University Press, 1973); and Arthur M. Schlesinger, Jr., *The Imperial Presidency* (Houghton Mifflin, 1973), pp. 200–06.
22. *Congressional Record,* August 12, 1969, pp. 23512, 23514. In October, the nature of the involvement was revealed in a series of *New York Times* articles (presumably using information leaked from the Symington group) and by Senator Fulbright after a Foreign Relations Committee closed briefing from Central Intelligence Agency Director Richard Helms. The CIA, said Fulbright, had been training, supplying, and transporting a 40,000-man army, made up mostly of tribesmen, fighting against the communists in northern Laos. The operation had been authorized by the National Security Council but "without the members of the Senate knowing it—and without the public knowing," according to Fulbright. *New York Times,* October 26, 28, and 29, 1969. *Congressional Quarterly Almanac, 1969,* p. 863.
23. Senator Fulbright, *Congressional Record,* August 12, 1969, p. 23514.

being used in support of the clandestine war in Laos. Moreover, senators heard of a secret "contingency plan" for joint action to combat internal guerrilla activity in Thailand, which they were seeking to examine. The Defense Department stalled for four months before bringing it to an executive session of the Foreign Relations Committee.[24]

Meanwhile, Senator Cooper, a member of the committee, saw a chance to put a limit on U.S. commitments. Observing that "wars start from small beginnings," as in Vietnam, Cooper proposed an amendment making clear that aid to Laos and Thailand should not encompass the sending of combat troops.[25] Defenders of the Vietnam War, and of President Nixon's conduct of it during his first year in office, raised the familiar cry of "trust the President." "The best thing to do today would be to stand behind our President and show unity," proclaimed Senator Strom Thurmond, Republican of South Carolina. All the resolution could do would be "to complicate the problems of the President, as he seeks to pursue disengagement" in Southeast Asia, said Gale McGee, Democrat of Wyoming. All that was needed was an understanding with the president, and his "good faith and assurances" could be trusted, argued John McClellan, Democrat of Arkansas, the Appropriations Committee chairman.[26] But for the first time since before World War II these arguments did not carry the day. What prevailed was the spirit of the national commitments resolution. The Congress would have to be a party to any new commitment; the day of blank checks for presidents was over.

Senator after senator rose to support forcefully the congressional prerogative, and to reveal bitter resentment of the executive branch's treatment of the Congress throughout the Vietnam period. The object of the amendment was to prevent the United States from "backing into" another war without congressional approval, explained Senator Cooper. If that could be done in Laos, it could be done "in Burma, Malaysia, Singapore, or anywhere else," argued Fulbright. The Senate had been "taken in" by the Gulf of Tonkin resolution, protested Mike Mansfield of Montana, the majority leader; Fulbright said it had been "deceived" and the representation of the incident "was not true." The Senate now had its first opportunity to apply its national commitments resolution, "reassert" its "constitutional responsibility," and prevent "another Vietnam," chimed in Frank Church, Democrat of Idaho. "This is the first time we are trying to match the power of the Senate with the power of the executive," declared Jacob K. Javits, Republican of New

24. *Congressional Quarterly Almanac, 1969*, p. 999.
25. *Congressional Record*, August 12, 1969, p. 23514.
26. Ibid., December 15, 1969, pp. 39165, 39161, 39164.

York.[27] A motion by Senator McGee to table the amendment lost by a vote of 41 to 48, and when that failed the Cooper amendment (modified to limit the prohibition to the introduction of ground combat troops) passed by 80 to 9. When the House accepted the amendment, it marked the first time since before World War II that the Congress had asserted control over military operations on foreign soil. The action did not change the status quo, since the Senate understood no ground troops were fighting in Laos—only air units[28]—but it set a limit on what the president could do in two countries without the consent of the Congress.

The next logical step, for those who would restrain the presidential power, was the repeal of the Gulf of Tonkin resolution itself. A resolution to that end was introduced by Senator Charles McC. Mathias, Republican of Maryland, and hearings were held in February and March 1970. The Nixon administration, which initially had opposed repeal, suddenly withdrew its opposition, on the ground that it had plenty of other legal and constitutional authority on which to base its current activities and its "contingency plans."[29] Republican Senator Robert Dole of Kansas, an administration supporter, cited a memorandum from the State Department's legal adviser asserting that the president's constitutional powers included "the power to deploy American forces abroad and commit them to military operations when the President deems such action necessary to maintain the security and defense of the United States," and noting that the president also derived power from the SEATO treaty.[30] Lyndon Johnson, even while invoking the resolution, had of course also held it to be unnecessary. Now, with Republicans and Democrats on Capitol Hill striving to outdo one another in identifying with disengagement, the Foreign Relations Committee had no difficulty voting to repeal a resolution that the "doves" considered undesirable and the "hawks" unnecessary.

Before the committee could report the resolution, however, the harmony was shattered by another unilateral action of the president—and one that provoked the strongest public outcry of the entire Vietnam period. President Nixon announced on April 30, 1970, that U.S. troops and those of South Vietnam had moved into Cambodia to wipe out bases that the North Viet-

27. Ibid., pp. 39148, 39156, 39163, 39162.
28. Remarks of Senators Stennis, Church, and John G. Tower, Republican of Texas, ibid., pp. 39157, 39168.
29. Letter from the State Department to the Senate Foreign Relations Committee, March 12, 1970, quoted in *Congressional Quarterly Almanac, 1970*, p. 950.
30. Memorandum from Lowell C. Meeker to the Senate Foreign Relations Committee, March 8, 1970, in *Congressional Record*, June 22, 1970, p. 20974.

namese enemy had established there. The mission, he promised, would be completed within two months, and the American troops withdrawn.

But the promise did not forestall what Nixon himself later termed "an unprecedented barrage of criticism."[31] Protest, both nonviolent and violent, erupted on campuses across the country. National guardsmen were called out, and four protesters were killed at Kent State University in Ohio and two a month later at Jackson State in Mississippi. An estimated 60,000 to 100,000 young people marched on Washington. The question was seriously asked at a presidential press conference whether the country was headed for a revolution.[32] And, on Capitol Hill, a Congress that had finally begun to look beyond the "good faith and assurances" of presidents was plunged into angry debate.

But debate was all. The Congress was, inevitably, as deeply divided as the public at large. It was split on the wisdom of the president's action, and on his constitutional right to have taken it. As on so many previous occasions, those who agreed with the president's objective found themselves constrained not to quibble about the source of his authority, while those who opposed the widening of the conflict were naturally quickest to charge that Nixon had usurped the congressional prerogative.

The Cambodian action was "one-man government," cried Senator Albert Gore, Democrat of Tennessee; it was "in direct contravention of the commitments resolution," and "a constitutional crisis impends." Senator Church agreed: "If the President . . . can make decisions of this character unilaterally with neither consultation with nor consent from the Senate, the Constitution has been scrapped and the Presidency has become a kind of Caesardom." And Senator Javits: "The President has apparently defined his authority as Commander in Chief in such a broad and comprehensive manner as to intrude upon, and even preempt, the powers reserved so explicitly to the Congress under the Constitution." But on the other side Majority Leader Mansfield, a cosponsor of the Cooper-Church amendment, argued that the president's conclusion "was his to reach under the Constitution." Assistant

31. "Address to the Nation on the Cambodian Sanctuary Operation, June 3, 1970," *Public Papers of the Presidents: Richard Nixon, 1970* (GPO, 1971), p. 479. The Congress learned much later that for more than a year before Nixon's announcement the Air Force had been bombing targets in Cambodia and that "at the express request of the President . . . an elaborate system of double reporting" had been devised to keep the information from foreign countries and from the Congress although a few friendly legislators were privately informed and leaks appeared in the press as early as May 1969. Leon V. Sigal, "Informal Communication Between the President and Congress," paper prepared for the 1974 annual meeting of the American Political Science Association, pp. 7–10. The full story was finally revealed in hearings before the Senate Armed Services Committee, *Bombing in Cambodia*, 93 Cong. 1 sess. (GPO, 1973).

32. "The President's News Conference of May 8, 1970," *Public Papers: Nixon, 1970*, p. 415.

Republican Leader Robert P. Griffin of Michigan contended that the Congress "cannot, and should not, attempt to make battlefield decisions." Senator Stennis, Armed Services chairman, took the familiar view that "when a man is Commander in Chief, as long as he is exercising a judgment that is within reason . . . he is the only one that we have to make decisions. We have no one else."[33]

While President Nixon carried out his Cambodian operation as planned, the Senate was unable to decide whether to interfere. Senators Cooper and Church offered another bipartisan amendment to forbid any support to Cambodian forces beyond the president's announced deadline of June 30, but defenders of the president dragged out the discussion until that very day. Then, when Nixon declared the troops had been withdrawn, they let the vote be taken. The amendment carried, 58 to 37.

But to get a majority even at that date on the policy question—to bar further operations in Cambodia—the amendment's backers had to finesse the constitutional issue altogether. Hawks such as Senator Sam J. Ervin, Jr., Democrat of North Carolina, had gone so far as to argue that, if it passed the new Cooper-Church amendment, the Congress rather than the president would be usurping power. The amendment was unconstitutional, said Ervin; "the Founding Fathers were not foolish enough to place the command of American troops engaged in combat operations in a Congress of the United States which is now composed of 100 Senators and 435 Representatives." A "war council" of that size would be "bedlam," he observed.[34] So the Senate adopted language declaring that nothing in Cooper-Church "shall be deemed to impugn the constitutional power of the President as Commander-in-Chief, including the exercise of that constitutional power which may be necessary to protect the lives of U.S. armed forces wherever deployed." It then unanimously approved a corresponding clause declaring the amendment should not "be deemed to impugn the constitutional powers of the Congress, including the power to declare war and to make rules for the government and regulation of the armed forces of the United States."

But the House rejected Cooper-Church by a decisive margin of 237 to 153,[35] and not until after a long deadlock that extended past the election did a lame-

33. *Congressional Record*, May 1, 14, and 15, 1970, pp. 13886, 13885, 13826, 15553, 15720.
34. Ibid., May 18, 1970, p. 15924.
35. Throughout the Vietnam period, the House tended to be more solidly supportive of the war, and of presidential conduct of it, than was the Senate, and particularly the Senate Foreign Relations Committee under Fulbright's leadership. It has been suggested this may be because of fundamental institutional characteristics: senators may be more willing to challenge presidents, for various reasons—their longer terms, which give them more freedom from constituency pressures; their greater public stature, which guarantees them media attention when they do mount a challenge

duck Congress finally reach agreement on its Cambodia policy. It adopted
a modified version of the amendment, prohibiting the reintroduction of
ground troops—but not air strikes—in that country. For the second time, and
in another country, the Congress drew a limit around presidential discretion.[36]
Finally, the Congress repealed the Gulf of Tonkin resolution, with the concurrence of the president who had said he did not need it anyway.

Still the constitutional issue remained unsettled. During the fighting in
Cambodia, Senator Fulbright had declared that it was "clear now beyond
doubt" that "the Congress shall have to resort to measures more binding
than a sense-of-the-Senate resolution."[37] And two such measures—the first
versions of what would become the War Powers Resolution—had been
introduced, one in the House by Dante B. Fascell, Democrat of Florida, the
other in the Senate by Javits of New York.

Deadlock on the Constitutional Issue

To recapture the war power through legislation, the activists on this issue
would have to find some way to satisfy the Ervins in both houses that
"bedlam" would not be the consequence of any redefinition of the congressional authority, and Javits recognized the problem at the outset. In introducing his bill in 1970, he acknowledged that in the nuclear age, the simple
constitutional stipulation that the Congress should declare war would at
times be out of date—so the president would have to act. But Javits sought
to define and limit those circumstances. He aimed to codify the rules of
behavior for both branches, in order to restore policymaking to the Congress
and to restrict the president to executing the legislature's policy—in short,

and hence encourages them to do so; their often lofty ambition, which causes them to look for
issues that might serve as launching pads for presidential campaigns; their traditionally greater
involvement in foreign affairs, because of their responsibility to ratify treaties, which has made the
Foreign Relations Committee attractive to energetic and ambitious senators; their stronger staff
support; and so on. Yet at other times in history the challenge to the president has come primarily
or equally from the House. Perhaps it is essentially accidental factors—the attitudes and capacities
of particular individuals who happened to make up a key committee—and leadership that are
decisive in determining the differing degrees of support for the presidency by Senate and House.

36. Again, it did not disturb the status quo, but the congressional attitude as expressed in
regard to Laos and Thailand, it could be surmised, played a part in inducing Nixon to set his
original 60-day limit on operations in Cambodia.

37. "The National Commitments Resolution One Year Later," statement by Senator Fulbright,
June 1970, in *Documents Relating to the War Power of Congress, the President's Authority as Commander-
in-Chief and the War in Indochina*, Committee Print, Senate Foreign Relations Committee, 91 Cong.
2 sess. (GPO, 1970), p. 42.

he said, to adapt the original constitutional principle to "evolving historical circumstances."[38] In the Javits bill, accordingly, the president could use the armed forces, without prior approval, only to repel an attack on the United States or on American forces on the high seas or lawfully stationed abroad, to protect the lives and property of Americans abroad, or to comply with national commitments to which both the executive and legislative branches were a party. The Fascell bill took the same approach but was even more restrictive; instead of "national commitments," its words were "specific treaty obligations." That, said its author, would have prevented both the major involvement in Vietnam and the Cambodian incursion, because the SEATO treaty was not specific regarding military operations.[39] Any such use of the armed forces must be reported—"promptly" in the Javits bill, within twenty-four hours in the Fascell version. And under the Javits bill, the president could not continue the operation beyond thirty days without affirmative congressional action.

The Nixon administration, of course, continued to oppose such restraints on the presidential power. If the whole idea was not to be killed by presidential veto, the bill would have to be toned down to meet the executive's objections. And the chairman of the House subcommittee examining the bill, Clement J. Zablocki, Democrat of Wisconsin, was emphatic in wanting a law, not another "sense of the Congress" resolution. So, after extensive hearings, he worked out in cooperation with the administration a wholly new resolution that imposed no restraint on the president. It specifically recognized "that the President in certain extraordinary circumstances has the authority to defend the United States and its citizens without specific authorization by the Congress," and it did not try to define or limit the circumstances. It urged "appropriate" consultation with the Congress whenever feasible before ordering military operations. It required the president to report "promptly" any such operations but put no time limit on them. Finally, instead of trying to resolve the constitutional issues by defining the president's authority, as Javits would do, it explicitly sidestepped that question, by asserting that nothing in the resolution "is intended to alter the constitutional authority of the Congress or of the President."[40] That language, said House Minority Leader Gerald R. Ford during the floor debate, was especially important, because "it means that this President can do as other Presidents have done,

38. *Congressional Record*, June 15, 1970, pp. 19657–58.
39. Ibid., May 13, 1970, p. 15332.
40. Comments of Zablocki and Fascell, June 1, 1971, *War Powers Legislation*, Hearings of the Subcommittee on National Security Policy and Scientific Developments of the House Foreign Affairs Committee, 92 Cong. 1 sess. (GPO, 1971), p. 5.

and as he has done, in those emergency situations."[41] No one contended the resolution changed very much, and it passed after a brief debate under suspension of the rules, 289 to 39, in November 1970. The Senate did not act on the subject that year.

In the next Congress the House repeated its performance, passing a slightly modified version of the Zablocki resolution by voice vote. But Javits and twenty-five cosponsors of his bill—including Chairman Stennis of the Armed Services Committee—were as insistent on a strong bill as Zablocki was on a "pragmatic" one. Javits dismissed the Zablocki resolution, offered as a substitute to his own bill on the Senate floor, as nothing more than an effort to give the president what he wanted, and termed it "inadequate to reclaim for Congress the powers under the Constitution in this area."[42] Senator William B. Spong, Jr., Democrat of Virginia, manager on the majority side of the Javits bill, found the reporting requirement of the Zablocki resolution desirable but otherwise agreed with Javits. The House approach was rejected, 56 to 22, and the Javits bill passed by an even larger margin, 68 to 16. The House then confirmed its own position, and the measure was still in conference when the Ninety-second Congress adjourned in October 1972.[43]

The War Powers Resolution of 1973

President Nixon broke the congressional deadlock.

In December 1972, he ordered what Senator Thomas F. Eagleton, Democrat of Missouri, called—with hyperbole reflecting the intense emotion of the time—"one of the most brutal bombardments in the history of aerial warfare" on the North Vietnamese capital of Hanoi and its port of Haiphong. As the Ninety-third Congress met in January 1973, the bombing had been halted, but, said Eagleton, "even now . . . the President has refused to come to the American people to explain why such action was necessary. If decisions of such moment . . . are made in secrecy . . . the democratic process will be undermined."[44]

41. *Congressional Record*, November 16, 1970, p. 37403.
42. Ibid., April 12, 1972, p. 12408.
43. Meanwhile, the Senate had mustered a two-vote margin for an amendment cutting off funds for the Vietnam War after four more months, but the House would not accept that measure either. The termination of the war, like its initiation and its conduct throughout, would be left to presidential decision. As an outgrowth of the Senate Foreign Relations Committee study of national commitments, however, the Congress approved without dissent a bill requiring the president to submit to the legislative branch the texts of all executive agreements with foreign countries. If necessary, they could be transmitted secretly.
44. *Congressional Record*, January 18, 1973, p. 1411.

Senator Javits reintroduced his war powers bill with fifty-seven cosponsors this time—a clear, bipartisan majority of the chamber. In the House, some thirty bills were introduced on the subject, embodying a dozen different approaches.[45] This was the moment of climax in the broad-ranging quarrel between Nixon and the Congress, with the war powers issue and control over budget and spending central to the struggle. The War Powers Act, Javits told the Senate, was "the fulcrum . . . of the broader attempt of the Congress to redress the dangerous constitutional imbalance . . . between the President and Congress. Unless Congress succeeds in reasserting its war powers I do not think it can succeed in reasserting its powers of the purse."[46]

Senator Edmund S. Muskie of Maine, a Democratic member of the Foreign Relations Committee and one of Javits's cosponsors, captured in purple language the mood of 1973. The bill would be "a first step," in ending the trend ever since World War II toward "more and more White House monopolization of our foreign affairs" that had reached "a real culmination" in "the ceremonial trappings, the trips, and the personalized rhetoric" of President Nixon—what Muskie called the "royal court." The characteristics of the royal court, he said, "are palpable. . . . Deliberations on anything of importance confined to a small circle . . . immunization of foreign affairs questions from congressional debate . . . increased anger that Congress cannot question the real makers of foreign policy—particularly the President's Assistant for National Security Affairs [Henry Kissinger]—because of Executive privilege claims . . . demoralization of the Department of State and the Foreign Service . . . increasing White House secrecy about foreign policy . . . a sense of moral certainty within the White House circle . . . this is the temper of Monarchs." The war powers bill would "fulfill" the Constitution, he said, not alter it.[47]

Everything Muskie had to say in the winter of 1973 about Nixon's sovereign disdain of the Congress seemed to be confirmed all over again in the spring. The war in Vietnam had ended in January, and U.S. forces were withdrawn by the end of March. But the country learned that, while the long Vietnam ordeal was over, the United States was still engaged in heavy bombing of Cambodia, in support of the Lon Nol government's effort to stave off a communist takeover of that country. The decision to bomb—again characterized by small-circle deliberations, immunization from congressional debate,

---

45. March 7, 1973, *War Powers*, Hearings of the Subcommittee on National Security Policy and Scientific Developments of the House Foreign Affairs Committee, 93 Cong. 1 sess. (GPO, 1973), p. iii.
46. *Congressional Record*, January 18, 1973, p. 1394.
47. Ibid., p. 1414.

secrecy and moral certainty—aroused another surge of angry outcries at the Capitol. "In my opinion," said Senate Majority Leader Mansfield, "there are no legal or constitutional grounds for our becoming involved in any way, shape, or form in the Cambodian civil war." Cambodia had explicitly refused to come under the protection of the SEATO treaty, Mansfield pointed out, and the Gulf of Tonkin resolution had been repealed.[48] Fulbright quoted Deputy Assistant Secretary of State William H. Sullivan as telling congressional staff at a briefing that the department's lawyers were trying to find a constitutional justification for the bombing of Cambodia, but that in the meantime he would "just say the justification is the reelection of President Nixon." Commented the senator: "For my own part, I retain total confidence in the ability of this administration to come up with some specious legal justification for doing exactly what it wishes to do. Like Humpty Dumpty, who would not be mastered by a mere word, the Nixon administration has shown that it will not be gotten the better of by anything so trivial as a law."[49]

The war-weary majorities in the Congress now asserted their opposition by invoking the power of the purse. Turning aside the plaint of Republican Leader Gerald R. Ford that the House, "that has a track record of strength and firmness, is now cringing and crumbling,"[50] the House on three consecutive votes—amid cheers—amended an appropriations bill to cut off funds for the Cambodian bombing. The Senate, by a 55 to 21 majority, supported an even stronger prohibition initiated by Senator Eagleton, which the House accepted. But the president vetoed the bill. A motion to override obtained a 68-vote majority in the House, but that was short of the necessary two-thirds. The Senate would repeat its action "again and again and again until the will of the people prevails," declared Mansfield.[51] He arranged for Eagleton to attach his amendment to a bill raising the limit on the public debt—a bill indispensable to the administration. Nixon found himself forced to negotiate a compromise. He agreed to a prohibition after August 15 not only of the Cambodian bombing but of all military operations in or over Vietnam and Laos as well.[52] The Congress had finally brought an end to the Vietnam adventure. True, the date chosen was one when hostilities would have been ended anyway, in all probability. But, however belated, the Congress had

48. Ibid., April 12, 1973, p. 12004.

49. April 11, 1973, *War Powers Legislation, 1973*, Hearings before the Senate Foreign Relations Committee, 93 Cong. 1 sess. (GPO, 1973), pp. 2–3.

50. *Congressional Record*, May 10, 1973, p. 15318.

51. *Congressional Quarterly Almanac, 1973*, p. 792.

52. See Thomas F. Eagleton, *War and Presidential Power: A Chronicle of Congressional Surrender* (Liveright, 1974), pp. 160–82, for an account of the maneuvering.

at least after more than a decade asserted its right to set the country's Vietnam war policy by law.

The undeclared presidential war in Cambodia provided a realistic backdrop for renewed consideration of the War Powers Resolution. No one could say that the Congress had acquiesced in the bombing of that small, remote country. By May, both houses had explicitly rejected it. Yet it went on. It was plain, as Senator Javits had said on introducing his bill in January, that for the Congress to rely solely on its powers to cut off funds was unsatisfactory, that the power of the purse was a "clumsy, blunt, and obsolescent tool."[53]

As soon as the Congress met at the beginning of 1973, it was clear that large majorities of the two houses were ready, and eager, to act on some kind of a war powers measure. But the practical problem remained of reconciling the divergent Senate and House approaches. Senator Javits opened the House hearings in March with a plea to Subcommittee Chairman Zablocki and his colleagues to abandon their objective—which Zablocki had just reiterated—of writing a bill that President Nixon would accept. "This is a struggle, between the Congress and the President. . . . a constitutional crisis . . . which we will not lose if we have character and resoluteness," Javits contended. "I do not believe that this legislation is of a character in which we can try to cut our cloth to suit a President. He is not going to be suited."[54] Some members of the subcommittee were already aligned with Javits. By May, Cambodia had converted almost all the others: by votes of nine to one in subcommittee and thirty-one to four in full committee, a measure was approved embodying provisions sure to make it unacceptable to Nixon.

The Senate passed the Javits bill in the same form as in 1972, and the House approved the Zablocki resolution essentially as it came from the committee, and a conference committee compromised the differences. In its final form, the resolution required a president "in every possible instance" to "consult with Congress" before introducing armed forces "into hostilities or into situations where imminent involvement in hostilities is clearly indicated by the circumstances," and regularly thereafter as long as hostilities continued. He would be required to report in writing within forty-eight hours to the speaker of the House and the president pro tem of the Senate any such movement of armed forces, stating the circumstances, the authority for the action, and the expected scope and duration of hostilities. If the Congress did not grant specific authorization for the operation through a declaration

53. *Congressional Record*, January 18, 1973, p. 1394.
54. *War Powers Legislation, 1973*, Hearings, pp. 11, 13.

of war or otherwise within sixty days, he would have to remove the troops (allowing an additional thirty days of action, if the president certified it as necessary, to cover the withdrawal), and the Congress could terminate the action at any time within the sixty days by concurrent resolution.

The most controversial issue in the conference was the Senate attempt to list the "only" circumstances under which the president might engage in hostilities, which was the heart of Javits's effort to "codify" the war power. The House accepted the word *only* but insisted that the list (which was condensed but retained the essential notion that use of force without authorization be limited to repelling attack) be placed in the Purpose and Policy section, rather than the substantive body, of the bill. The conferees then signed a statement explaining that the other sections of the resolution "are not dependent upon the language of this subsection, as was the case with a similar provision of the Senate bill."[55]

So again the crucial constitutional issue was evaded. The Senate had been ready to scrap the doctrine—reiterated so many times during the postwar period—that only the president had the capacity to act quickly in emergencies and take on itself the responsibility to make the instant decisions that might lie outside any list of enumerated presidential powers. But even in the mood of 1973 the House of Representatives was not ready.

The House victory on this point split the ranks of original sponsors of the War Powers Resolution. Senator Eagleton denounced the compromise version as "worse than no bill at all," and the language restricting the president's initial use of force as nothing more than a "sense of the Congress" resolution. The legislation was now "an open-ended, blank check for 90 days of warmaking." Javits made the best defense he could, contending that the Purpose and Policy section was as operative as any other section of the bill and that no president would dare ignore the clause, because it would cast a legal cloud on all his subsequent actions, including procurement and conscription. The statement of the conferees did not exclude other interpretations of the language, he continued, and anyway a clause at the end of the resolution expressly declared that the measure gave no power to the president beyond that which he already possessed under the Constitution. The New York senator, too, would have preferred his own original version, but the legislation would still "make history."[56]

55. Paragraph c, section 2 (Purpose and Policy) lists the circumstances as "(1) a declaration of war, (2) specific statutory authorization, or (3) a national emergency created by attack upon the United States, its territories or possessions, or its armed forces."

56. *Congressional Record*, October 10, 1973, pp. 33556–60. Once the legislation was enacted, Javits appeared to concede Eagleton's point about the significance of moving the language to the

The senators were more interested in doing that—in striking any kind of a blow at the now beleaguered president who had defied, ignored, and frustrated them in so many ways during the preceding couple of years—than in listening to a lawyers' wrangle over the significance of the location of words within a law. Only three senators who had voted for the original Senate bill joined Eagleton in opposing the conference report, and they were offset by four senators who switched the other way. Seventy-five senators, against twenty, voted to "make history"; Republicans voted almost two to one against their president. In the House, after a brief debate in which supporters of the president were joined in opposition by a few members who, like Eagleton, found the resolution too weak, the vote was 238 to 123.

If Eagleton was right in saying the president was getting an "open-ended, blank check," the current occupant of the White House did not see it that way. He flung the resolution back with a veto message reiterating the familiar position of the executive branch. Zablocki came back next day with a point-by-point rebuttal of the president's arguments, which was later refined and expanded in a joint statement by Zablocki and Chairman Thomas E. Morgan (Democrat of Pennsylvania) of the House Foreign Affairs Committee.

The Founding Fathers, argued the president, "acknowledged the need for flexibility." Not so, came the rebuttal; the war power was placed in the Congress, and "flexibility has become a euphemism for Presidential domination." The resolution "would seriously undermine this Nation's ability to act decisively and convincingly in times of international crisis," continued Nixon; does he really mean the whole nation, asked Zablocki, or just the incumbent in the White House? The world would find American behavior unpredictable, said the president; "recent events," responded the congressman, "have shown the President is not more predictable." The resolution might have prevented recent U.S. responses to crisis in Berlin, Cuba, Congo, and Jordan, claimed Nixon; each could have been conducted in exactly the

---

Purpose and Policy section. During a hearing in 1975 he acknowledged that the conference "did adopt the House approach," which "omitted" the definition of the president's emergency authority that the Senate bill contained. This contradicts his 1973 position that the definition was still "operative." *War Powers: A Test of Compliance,* Hearings before a subcommittee of the House International Relations Committee, 94 Cong. 1 sess. (GPO, 1975), p. 63. He made similar comments during an oversight hearing in 1977: "the House . . . completely omitted any effort to agree with the President upon the delineation of his emergency powers. In the conference, the House view had to be accepted. We couldn't have gotten any bill otherwise." *War Powers Resolution,* Hearings before the Senate Foreign Relations Committee, 95 Cong. 1 sess. (GPO, 1977), p. 197. Zablocki also confirmed Eagleton's interpretation. The language enumerating the president's powers, he said, "was intended as a statement of purpose and policy, a sort of sense of Congress." *War Powers: A Test of Compliance,* Hearings, p. 32. The State Department took the same view, in an opinion given to Senator Eagleton in December 1973. Eagleton, *War and Presidential Power,* p. 222.

same way within the terms of the resolution, was the reply. The resolution, said Nixon, would "strike from the President's hand . . . his ability to exercise quiet diplomacy backed by subtle shifts in our military deployments"; the president could still make the shifts, replied the legislators, subject only to consultation and reporting. And the president objected to the legislative veto of executive war-making by concurrent resolution (not requiring the presidential signature) rather than by law; to this congressmen responded that to check the president through legislation would require two-thirds of each house to override a presidential veto while a simple majority could reject a request from the president for a declaration of war. "It makes no sense," they observed, "to give the Congress less control over war powers simply because the President makes a commitment without first securing approval." The president suggested that a nonpartisan commission review the constitutional issues relating to the war powers as well as to executive agreements and executive privilege; Zablocki brushed this off as "a time-honored way of sidetracking an issue."[57]

The Congress overrode the veto, by votes of 284 to 135 in the House and 75 to 18 in the Senate, and the War Powers Resolution became law. Senator Eagleton still opposed it on the ground that the originally intended limitations on the president had been reduced to "pious chit-chat."[58] But the mood of the day was expressed by a senior senator who called him aside and said, "Tom, we wish you would keep quiet on this vote. We simply have to slap Nixon down and this is the vote to do it on." And another who expressed agreement with Eagleton but voted for the resolution explained to him: "I love the Constitution, but I hate Nixon more."[59] It was thus a symbolic issue— a timely triumph of Congress over president—and the personal antipathy to an aggressive president that had played a part in precipitating the whole resurgence contributed to its first tangible product. But in Senator Javits's view the victory was one of substance also. "At least something" had been done "about codifying the most awesome power in the possession of every sovereignty," he maintained. Wars in the future would have to have the consent and support of the people. There would be no more Vietnams—a "war that literally brought this country to its knees because . . . on the record it was essentially a Presidential war."[60]

57. "Veto of the War Powers Resolution, October 24, 1973," *Public Papers: Nixon, 1973* (GPO, 1975), pp. 893–95; Zablocki statement, *Congressional Record*, October 25, 1973, pp. 34992–93; Morgan-Zablocki statement, ibid., November 2, 1973, pp. 35868–69.
58. *Congressional Record*, November 17, 1973, p. 36189.
59. Eagleton, *War and Presidential Power*, pp. 215–16, 220.
60. *Congressional Record*, November 17, 1973, p. 36187.

The First Tests

In the first seven years of the War Powers Resolution, presidents made five reports to the Congress in accordance with provisions of the act. Four of these were made by President Ford in the spring of 1975, covering the use of military forces in Southeast Asia. The fifth was by President Carter five years later, reporting on the abortive mission to rescue the American hostages held prisoner in the U.S. embassy in Iran. Together, these incidents provided an inconclusive trial of the War Powers Resolution, for none of them involved prolonged military action. But they did test the reporting and consultation provisions of the law, with mixed and ambiguous results.

The Southeast Asia incidents of 1975 all occurred within a six-week span. In April 1975, U.S. naval forces reentered Vietnamese waters to assist in evacuating refugees from Danang and neighboring seaports to places farther south. A week later the marines evacuated U.S. citizens from Phnom Penh as the Cambodian capital fell. Two weeks after that, U.S. forces carried out a similar assignment at Saigon, where they removed many Vietnamese as well. And on May 12 they rescued the *Mayaguez*, a U.S. merchant vessel that had been seized by Cambodian naval patrol boats off that country's coast, and its thirty-nine-man crew. Retaliatory bombings of Cambodian targets were also carried out.[61]

In the first instance, the U.S. forces encountered no opposition. In the second, they were fired on but incurred no casualties. In the third, two helicopter crew members were lost at sea. The *Mayaguez* incident was more costly: forty-one U.S. servicemen killed.[62] In each of the three cases where weapons were employed, the operation was over by the time the president made his formal report to the Congress within his forty-eight-hour deadline; the fourth, the Danang rescue mission, lasted for about a week. So the Congress never had to face its own responsibilities under the resolution—to

61. In a 1977 lecture (at the University of Kentucky, inserted in *Congressional Record*, April 21, 1977, pp. 11700–03) former President Ford mentioned two other "military crises," involving the evacuation of Americans from Lebanon by naval vessels in 1976, when he said he did not feel bound by the resolution but "took note of its consultative and reporting provisions" and provided information (presumably orally) to members of the Congress. Pat M. Holt, *The War Powers Resolution: The Role of Congress in U.S. Armed Intervention* (Washington: American Enterprise Institute for Public Policy Research, 1978), pp. 11–20, summarizes all six incidents. Some members of the Congress felt that the rescue of Americans from Cyprus in 1974 should also have been reported. Senator Eagleton contended that the law had been violated (*Congressional Record*, July 31, 1974, p. 25916), but no committee took any action.

62. Of these, 23 lost their lives in Thailand when a helicopter engaged in the rescue mission crashed.

approve or disapprove the actions taken by the president pursuant, as he put it in his reports, to his "Constitutional executive power and his authority as Commander-in-Chief." He merely "took note" of the War Powers Resolution, careful not to acknowledge any responsibility to comply with its requirements.

The sponsors of the resolution concluded, after a House hearing, that it had weathered these initial tests reasonably well, although everybody concerned observed that procedural problems had to be worked out. The administration complained that in the *Mayaguez* case the forty-eight-hour deadline forced them to waken President Ford at 2 a.m. to sign the report so that it could be delivered to empty Capitol Hill offices by 2:30 a.m. Senator Javits found it unsatisfactory that the official reports to the Congress were treated as personal communications to the Speaker of the House and the president pro tem of the Senate; in the Danang case, the Congress was out of session and Speaker Albert received his report, on behalf of the House, in Peking. Javits also protested that the reports (which ranged from five to seven paragraphs in length) were "brief to the point of being in minimal compliance" and "almost worthless from an information point of view." "They do not suggest a readiness within the Executive Branch to provide the full and timely disclosure of relevant facts and judgments which the reporting provisions of the law were designed to elicit," he went on. "And, they do not provide an adequate informational base for informed Congressional action." Congressman Zablocki was more charitable. The reports, he said, did provide the Congress "with a grasp on the incidents to which they referred—a focal point around which to center informed debate."[63]

But the strongest criticism was leveled at the administration's compliance with the requirement to consult the Congress. In each case, the leaders of the two houses were "notified and informed" and their comments, if any, were relayed to the president.[64] But in at least two of the cases—the Saigon evacuation and *Mayaguez*—the notification actually took place several hours *after* the operation began. This was a far cry from what the congressional supporters of the resolution thought the word *consult*—which they had left undefined in the legislation[65]—really meant. "We were informed, not consulted," said Senate Majority Leader Mansfield, speaking of *Mayaguez*.[66] And

63. *War Powers: A Test of Compliance,* Hearings, pp. 77, 69, vi.

64. Testimony of Monroe Leigh, legal adviser, Department of State, in ibid., pp. 7, 78.

65. Thomas M. Franck and Edward Weisband, *Foreign Policy by Congress* (Oxford University Press, 1979), pp. 73–74.

66. *Washington Post,* May 25, 1975, in *War Powers: A Test of Compliance,* Hearings, p. 121. The House committee report on the legislation made clear that the consultation was to be more than notification, that it was to take place before the decisions were made, and that "in appropriate

in the House the speaker, majority leader, and the International Relations Committee chairman were quoted as making like statements.[67] It was the "old, discredited practice" of informing "selected members" after the decisions had already been made, said Javits of *Mayaguez*.[68] That was not the intent of the Congress, Zablocki agreed. The Congress meant to be "fully and accurately advised . . . in time to have meaningful input into the formulation" of the decisions themselves. The aim was "partnership and shared responsibility in foreign affairs." Measured against that clear intent, he said, "the executive branch proclivity is toward evasive and selective interpretation of the War Powers Resolution."[69]

There the matter was left. Various members of the Congress introduced measures to clarify and strengthen the resolution, but none was considered in committee. Javits, Zablocki, and the other principal backers of the 1973 measure were content for the time simply to put their complaints about the Ford administration's interpretation of the resolution on record, in the hope that his and later administrations would take heed.

But Ford, at least, left office convinced that consultation in the sense the Congress intended was impossible. In a lecture shortly after his retirement, he lampooned the whole consultation process as it had worked out in 1975 and 1976. The Danang evacuation, he recalled, had occurred during the Easter recess of Congress, when "not one of the key bipartisan leaders of Congress was in Washington."

> Without mentioning names, here is where we found the leaders of Congress: two were in Mexico, three in Greece, one was in the Middle East, one was in Europe, and two were in the People's Republic of China. The rest we found in twelve widely scattered States of the Union.
>
> This, one might say, is an unfair sample, since the Congress was in recess. But it must be remembered that critical world events, especially military operations, seldom wait for the Congress to meet. In fact, most of what goes on in the world happens in the middle of the night, Washington time.

And when Americans were evacuated from Lebanon, the Congress had adjourned for the day, again making it almost impossible to reach congressional leaders. "When a crisis breaks," Ford concluded, "it is impossible to draw the Congress into the decision-making process in an effective way."[70]

---

circumstances" the approval of the decision was to be sought. But language in a committee report is not, of course, legally binding.

67. Testimony of Representative John F. Seiberling, Democrat of Ohio, in ibid., p. 100.

68. Ibid., p. 67. While President Ford might have been expected to be more respectful of congressional sensitivities, he had been as House Republican leader a staunch defender of the presidential prerogative on this issue and had voted with the majority of his party colleagues against both the passage of the resolution and the override of Nixon's veto.

69. Ibid., p. vi.

70. University of Kentucky lecture, inserted in *Congressional Record*, April 21, 1977, p. 11702.

President Carter evidently reached the same conclusion, in the Iran operation of 1980. As rumors that a U.S. military operation of some kind in Southeast Asia was imminent spread through Washington in April—five months after the seizure of the Tehran embassy by Iranian militants and four months after the invasion of Afghanistan by the Soviet Union—leaders of the Congress itself had demanded that the consultation provisions of the resolution be invoked. On April 24, Senators Church and Javits, as chairman and ranking minority member of the Foreign Relations Committee, wrote to Secretary of State Cyrus R. Vance, reminding him of the language of the law and expressing the view that "the time has come" for consultaton on the crisis.[71] But on the morning of that very day, eight helicopters and six transport planes dispatched to rescue the hostages in Tehran had already entered Iranian airspace. A few hours later, they had withdrawn and the story of the failed mission was made public.

From the Congress, this time, came only a mild outcry against the absence of consultation; of members quoted by reporters, perhaps more approved the lack of consultation than protested it. At a closed Senate hearing, Acting Secretary of State Warren M. Christopher cited the resolution's qualifying clause that the Congress should be consulted "in every possible instance" and said the president had concluded that this was one instance where consultation was not possible, because the operation's success depended on "total surprise."[72] The suggestion that congressmen cannot keep a secret drew an indignant response from, among others, Senate Majority Leader Robert C. Byrd, Democrat of West Virginia, but some members agreed. "If they had been consulted," said Representative Robert E. Bauman, Republican of Maryland, "Tehran would have known about the whole thing within hours."[73] Asked what might have been accomplished through consultation, Byrd said the congressional leaders might have suggested the rescue mission be enlarged to include more helicopters.[74] Church expressed regret that the president did not consult, but Chairman Stennis of the Armed Services Committee said he had "no grievance."[75] Observing that "President Carter ignored the statute just as any other President will have to do," Senator Barry Goldwater, Republican of Arizona, urged that it be repealed.[76]

President Carter submittted a fourteen-paragraph report to the Congress dated two days after the incident and giving no more information than had

71. *New York Times*, April 25, 1980.
72. Ibid., May 9, 1980.
73. *Washington Star*, April 26, 1980.
74. Ibid., April 27, 1980.
75. Ibid., April 26, 1980.
76. *Congressional Record*, daily edition, May 6, 1980, p. S4726.

already been made public. Like Ford, he did not acknowledge that the report was obligatory under the resolution. He submittted it, the report said, "because of my desire that Congress be informed on this matter and consistent with the reporting provisions" of the resolution.[77] But once again, the Congress did not have to act on the report, for the operation was already over. What effect the resolution would have in a long engagement, like the one that precipitated its passage, remained untested.

Symbol or Substance?

"At least something," as Senator Javits predicted, has been accomplished by the resolution, but the constitutional issue that goes back to Madison and Hamilton is still unsettled. The presidential war powers have not been codified, as Javits had set out to do; neither the House nor the president would stand for that. There is no "compact" between the two branches, as he had sought; only the legislative branch's unilateral statement of the law. The resolution expressly recognized that the president's constitutional powers, whatever those may be, are not altered—a superfluous clause, since no simple act of the Congress, even if signed by the president, can change the Constitution. So whatever constitutional powers William McKinley used in sending troops to China, Woodrow Wilson to Mexico, Franklin Roosevelt to Iceland, Harry Truman to Korea, Dwight Eisenhower to Lebanon, Lyndon Johnson to Vietnam, and Richard Nixon to Cambodia remain, still fuzzy but intact. "A short, nonlegal summary of the issue," observes Pat M. Holt, Senate Foreign Relations Committee staff member for more than a quarter of a century, "is that, at any given moment, the relative powers of the President and Congress are what either feels it can get away with."[78] Constitutional powers left undefined are established in the practice, as the war powers have been since the beginning.

The resolution, says former Assistant Secretary of State Douglas J. Bennet, "has conditioned the executive branch's decision-making process in military crises," and other officials have concurred in that assessment. Bennet cites, for example, the episode in 1978 when the United States helped provide an airlift for French and Belgian forces that came to the aid of Zaire when guerrillas invaded that country from neighboring Angola. The U.S. commanders did not permit their planes and personnel within a hundred miles

77. *Weekly Compilation of Presidential Documents*, May 5, 1980, pp. 77–79.
78. *War Powers Resolution*, p. 1.

of the battle scene. "In the old days," said Bennet, "the planes would have landed in the heart of the action."[79]

Yet it is the practice of Congresses, more than that of presidents, that determines the tone of the relationship. It is the mood of the Congress, the degree of its assertiveness, that in normal circumstances set the tone. (It did not in Richard Nixon's later years, but that was the abnormal circumstance.) Presidents may prefer to ignore the Congress whenever they feel they "can get away with it," but whether they in fact do get away with it is strictly for the legislators to resolve. For quite apart from the War Powers Resolution, the legislative branch has enough uncontested constitutional powers—the power of the purse, for one—to make of an assertive legislature a formidable force that presidents normally must placate. Ralph K. Huitt's observation is apropos: "Congress cannot match the drama of the presidency, but any day it sits it can remind the executive that it must be taken into account."[80]

So in assessing the long-run effects of the resolution, the basic question is, will the Congress behave differently? Senator Eagleton has said yes. The Congress had lost its war powers, he observed during the 1973 discussion, "because, quite frankly, the individual members of this body have preferred to avoid more difficult questions facing our Nation." The resolution would oblige them "to fulfill their responsibilities."[81]

That may be true, but how would those responsibilities be seen? In the past, the members had invariably construed their duty as being to support the president, to rally behind the flag. Some members argued that still would be the case. They denied that the resolution would "prevent future Vietnams," as had been so often asserted during the debate. In fact, they contended, had the resolution been on the statute books, Vietnam policy itself would have been no different. The resolution would not "have given us the wisdom to know what course to take," argued Representative Peter H. B. Frelinghuysen, Republican of New Jersey; so the Congress would have approved the Gulf of Tonkin resolution just the same, or even declared war if the president requested it, and the Congress "would have been tied . . . more tightly to the massive involvement which followed." Representative Samuel

79. Quoted by Martin Tolchin, *New York Times*, December 24, 1979. On this occasion, Representative Paul Findley, Republican of Illinois, introduced a resolution to express the conviction of the Congress that President Carter should have consulted and reported under terms of the War Powers Resolution. *Congressional Record*, daily edition, August 10, 1978, pp. H8414–17. But the International Relations Committee accepted the administration view that the force did not go into places where "imminent involvement in hostilities" was indicated and took no action. For a view that it should have, see Franck and Weisband, *Foreign Policy by Congress*, p. 72.

80. "Congress: The Durable Partner," in Elke Frank, ed., *Lawmakers in a Changing World* (Prentice-Hall, 1966), p. 9.

81. *Congressional Record*, January 18, 1973, p. 1411.

S. Stratton, Democrat of New York, was more caustic. He called it "utter hogwash to say the President slipped this war over on us when we were not looking." The House "repeatedly supported the action that was taken," said Stratton, and the Congress "had plenty of opportunity to repeal the war if we had wanted to." As for the Gulf of Tonkin resolution, "this House could hardly restrain ourselves from rushing that measure through and sending it on the way to the Senate with a unanimous vote." He dismissed the War Powers Resolution as a vain attempt "to repeal the Vietnamese war . . . to square ourselves with the voters," and likened it to the Twenty-second Amendment, that "attempt to repeal the third and fourth terms of President Franklin Delano Roosevelt after he was in his grave."[82]

The Congress could have held up the Gulf of Tonkin resolution while it held hearings, questioned witnesses, examined cables, and demanded to know the president's full intentions in Southeast Asia. But that would have broadcast to the world a lack of unity and resolution in U.S. policy, and it would have told the American people that a Democratic Congress did not trust the leadership, or even the veracity, of a Democratic president—just three weeks before the party was scheduled to nominate that president by acclamation for a full four-year term. In 1964 the Congress was understandably loath to take that course; rather, as Stratton said, it rushed to display its solidarity behind the president. Would the members behave differently in, say, 1984?

Senator Church, soon to be chairman of the Foreign Relations Committee, did not think so. During the oversight hearings of 1977, he offered these views:

> I cannot imagine a situation where the President would take us into a foreign war of major proportions under circumstances that would not cause both the public and the Congress to rally around the flag, at least for 60 days. . . . It is only when a war is pursued for a period of time and the public begins to question whether it is a war in the national interest, or whether it is a winnable war, or a foolish one, that you will ever get a majority in the Congress to exercise the authority that we finally did exercise by pulling up the purse strings on the broadening theatre of war in Southeast Asia, and finally in forcing an end to the bombing in Cambodia.
>
> But, in both those cases it was done with Presidential acquiescence. It was not done by concurrent resolution. It was done by law, and the President joined and made it law by signing the legislation.[83]

Gerald Ford, who spent many more years in the Congress than he did in the executive branch, explained in his 1977 lecture why he felt the legislators would be barred from effective participation in the decisionmaking process.

82. Ibid., June 25, 1973, pp. 21216–17.
83. *War Powers Resolution,* 1977 Hearings, pp. 172–73.

"The institutional limitations on the Congress," he said, "cannot be legislated away." The members have a thousand things on their mind: "It is impractical to ask them to be as well versed in fast-breaking developments as the President, the National Security Council, the Joint Chiefs of Staff." A president cannot wait while a consensus among congressional leaders is being formed. And what if they disagree among themselves, or with the president, on an action he deems "essential"? Ford left that question unanswered, implying that the president must pursue the course he thinks essential in any case. Then there is the problem of disclosure of sensitive information, and the "question of how consultations with a handful of congressional leaders can bind the entire Congress." Foreign policy cannot be conducted nor military operations commanded by 535 members of the Congress, he concluded, "even if they all happen to be on Capitol Hill when they are needed."[84]

Nevertheless, the behavior of presidents did change, once the War Powers Resolution was on the books. Not immediately, of course; the initial reaction of the Nixon administration, in the combative spirit of 1973, was to embrace the Eagleton interpretation of the law that presidential power to act unilaterally had actually been expanded. Secretary of Defense James R. Schlesinger was quoted as saying late in 1973 that the legislation gave Nixon power to wage war for sixty days without congressional approval, and that the State Department was therefore examining the possibility of a resumption of the then-ended hostilities in Indochina.[85] (If the resolution were unconstitutional, as Nixon had contended in his veto message, how it could confer additional power was not explained.)

Any future president, either by interpreting the legislation as did Schlesinger or by ignoring it as unconstitutional, could flout the Congress and take his chances on public reaction and congressional retaliation. (The Supreme Court, it may be assumed, would stay clear of the issue as a "political" one.) Nixon's two immediate successors did not elect to take the chance. President Ford did not retreat from the Nixon position that the law was unconstitutional, yet he did "take note" of it in four reports to the Congress, all delivered within the time period specified in the law. He did take pains to consult, within his own definition of the word and his own judgment as to the appropriate time, even to the extent of tracking down congressmen in remote places.

The Carter administration at the outset was even more conciliatory. While equally careful in its official testimony not to yield the executive branch

84. *Congressional Record*, April 21, 1977, p. 11702.
85. Associated Press report on Schlesinger news conference, November 30, 1973, quoted in Eagleton, *War and Presidential Power*, pp. 220–21.

position on the constitutionality of the measure,[86] the administration took the stand that it would not challenge it. Secretary of State Vance, during his confirmation hearings, said he saw no problem with the good-faith observance of the law's provisions.[87] In an oversight hearing in 1977, Herbert J. Hansell, State Department legal adviser, urged that the constitutional debate be set aside while the executive and legislative branches together build "a body of practice . . . a consultation mechanism . . . a common law of operation in this arena."[88]

Hansell was bold enough to suggest that the Congress itself was negligent in not having established a "streamlined structure for carrying out consultations," and Assistant Secretary of State Bennet, speaking personally rather than as a representative of the executive branch, submitted the outline of such a structure. He proposed that each house designate a single individual to serve as a point of contact when a crisis developed and that that person be empowered to establish, under prearranged procedures, an ad hoc committee that would be the instrument for consultation under the War Powers Resolution.[89] Others have suggested a permanent consultative committee, always alert to meet on short notice with the president or the National Security Council and small enough to be fully trusted to protect secret information. But the Congress has taken no steps to act on these suggestions. The competing claims of the Senate and House majority and minority leadership, the foreign relations committees, and the armed services committees for the central role would make difficult the designation of a single individual or even a workably small committee as a standing consultative mechanism.

In the absence of some new "streamlined" structure, the choice of legislators, if any, to consult will continue to be left to the executive branch.

---

86. The president had called the resolution an "appropriate reduction" in the president's authority, which would appear to concede the question of constitutionality, but the remark was made in a television interview. "Ask President Carter, March 5, 1977," *Public Papers of the Presidents: Jimmy Carter, 1977* (GPO, 1978), p. 309. Herbert J. Hansell, State Department legal adviser, said he was not prepared to say the administration would concede the constitutionality of the resolution "in all respects." *War Powers Resolution, 1977* Hearings, p. 204.

87. January 11, 1977, *Vance Nomination,* Hearings before the Senate Foreign Relations Committee (GPO, 1977), p. 38. Asked by Senator Javits, "Do you challenge it [the War Powers Resolution] under the Constitution as to the President's power?" Vance answered simply, "No." In another confirmation hearing four years later, in January 1981, President Reagan's nominee for secretary of state, Alexander M. Haig, Jr., assured the Foreign Relations Committee "that I intend to live by the letter of the law and the spirit of the War Powers Act, and that I see no difficulty in doing so." *Nomination of Alexander M. Haig, Jr.,* Hearings before the Senate Foreign Relations Committee, 97 Cong. 1 sess. (GPO, 1981), p. 34.

88. July 15, 1977, *War Powers Resolution, 1977* Hearings, pp. 189, 211.

89. Ibid., pp. 199–203. Bennet was responding to a request from Senator Javits that the administration suggest a "methodology" for implementing the resolution. *Vance Nomination,* Hearings, p. 39.

Future presidents, like Carter, will doubtless use the "every possible instance" loophole. If consultation is attempted, the difficulties that President Ford encountered in locating the selected leaders will recur whenever the Congress is not in session. Any consultation is likely to take the form more of giving information rather than asking advice, and there will be no legitimated and reliable process for determining a quick congressional consensus. That a Congress that has demanded the right to participate as partner in crisis management has failed to grapple with the question of how to organize to do so is perhaps tantamount to admitting that it never seriously intended to take on the responsibility.

If the advance consultation called for in the resolution is liable to remain as unsatisfactory as in the past, the reporting requirement on the other hand has proved to be practicable. As long as presidents do not elect to challenge the constitutionality of the resolution frontally, there will be no more "secret wars." Congress will be informed, at least. But after the report, what then? In the mood of 1973, the Congress promised itself that it would ask harder questions of future presidents, that it would look behind the information presented to it in the midst of crisis. Yet no resolution was required for it to do that; even at the time of the Gulf of Tonkin incident, the Congress could have taken as much time as it needed to call as many witnesses as it liked. Whether the Congress will act deliberately before affirming the president's course in future crises will be a matter not of legislated procedures under the War Powers Resolution but a matter of how much trust the sitting president commands in any given set of circumstances. Representatives Frelinghuysen and Stratton were surely right in speculating that in 1964 the Congress would have backed the president's actions in Southeast Asia even if the War Powers Resolution had been in effect. What are the chances, then, that presidents will regain the trust that was lost in the Vietnam era and legislators will again turn their attention to the thousand other things that Gerald Ford referred to, leaving it to the commander in chief to decide when and how to deploy and utilize U.S. armed forces around the globe?

The first prerequisite for trust between the branches is a high degree of consensus on the country's basic foreign policy objectives and the strategy and tactics to attain them. From the end of the 1930s to the late 1960s the country was united to an extraordinary degree on its strategic goals—first on the defeat of Germany and Japan, after that on containing communist expansionism—and that unity was reflected in the Congress. During that long period the legislative majorities were willing to concede the war power to the president—even when they were his partisan opponents—because they had implicit confidence that those powers would be exercised on behalf of objectives, and by means and tactics, that they approved. Not until the national consensus on containing communism dissolved in Southeast Asia did that implicit confidence turn into doubt. Then the developing mistrust of the executive's purposes and methods was compounded by the loss of other requisites for confidence—by a lack of presidential candor in dealing with the Congress, by the executive's assertion of an unlimited right to withhold information, and in the end by the exceptionally bitter partisan and personal antipathy that developed, from many causes, between the Democratic majorities and the Republican who happened to occupy the White House.

With Richard Nixon's resignation in 1974, the level of trust turned upward. The personal animosity that had poisoned the relationship was gone. Gerald Ford proceeded to restore confidence by dealing more openly with the Congress. Executive privilege ceased to be a major issue. But the requisite of a new bipartisan, and hence interbranch, consensus on foreign policy was not attained.

When Jimmy Carter succeeded Ford, the prospects for heightened confidence in the presidency were bright. Harmony between the branches no longer depended on agreement between the two parties; if Democrats agreed among themselves, that was sufficient, and for the most part in the Carter years that seemed to be attained. Gradually, relations seemed to be returning to what in the postwar era had been normal. President Carter took congressional support for granted in responding to the Iranian and Afghan crises, including the movement of naval forces into the Arabian Sea, the pronouncement of a Persian Gulf doctrine, and the hostage rescue mission, and the Congress gave him that support.

Yet even if the Carter period presages a new period of congressional inattention, the war power cannot drift all the way back to the exclusivity of presidential control that prevailed in the years before the resolution was enacted. The resurgent Congress did win its point. Its right to be admitted to some degree of partnership in decisionmaking about war and peace has been conceded by the executive branch at long last, grudgingly by President Ford but openly and warmly by Jimmy Carter, if not as a constitutional matter then as a practical one, which is what counts.[90] The reporting procedures, if not yet the consultation procedures, protect an assertive Congress from

90. Graham T. Allison argues that the War Powers Resolution will make the advisory circle wider within the executive branch as well, because consultation with the Congress will require bringing political and legislative specialists into the process. The result will be to dilute the influence of national security advisors. "Making War: The President and Congress," *Law and Contemporary Problems,* vol. 40 (Summer 1976), pp. 103–04.

exclusion by the president and make it hard for a passive one to exclude itself. Future secretaries of state can be compelled by the Senate Foreign Relations Committee in confirmation hearings to swear allegiance to those procedures, as Cyrus Vance was. The legislators will be fully informed, which was not always the case before. And, when a report is received and military operations are continuing, the Congress cannot escape taking a stand. True, it may be caught up in patriotic fervor, as Senator Church expects. Perhaps it will never see fit to reverse a president. But the realization that it can will force presidents to make sure before they act that the Congress will support them. For the Congress cannot acquiesce just by doing nothing; it must affirmatively concur.

Thus, the War Powers Resolution compels joint decisionmaking on issues of war and peace. The Congress can still support automatically, without deliberation, the president's course of action, but it will be more difficult than before to evade the exercise of considered judgment and a full share of responsibility. The president is therefore restrained from rash, unilateral action; he will enter into commitments more cautiously. The War Powers Resolution is symbol of the congressional resurgence, and substance also.

CHAPTER X

To Take Command of Foreign Policy

WHEN the country lost its faith in the wisdom of the Vietnam War, the postwar national consensus on foreign policy disintegrated. For the consensus had been built on the broad strategic objective of containing communist expansion, and Vietnam had been only the logical and latest extension of that policy.

As the national mood changed, the legislative branch, always responsive to the shifting winds of public opinion, was quick to follow. But the executive branch resisted. It had accepted containment as an article of faith far too long—had nurtured it through the Truman Doctrine and the Marshall Plan, NATO and SEATO, the Berlin blockade and the Korean War, and now Vietnam—to give up easily. So a policy gap between the branches opened, and widened.

To the principal policymakers of the executive branch, the fundamental policies that had applied since World War II had by no means lost their validity. Intervention had failed in Vietnam not for lack of wisdom in the policy but for lack of national will. Communism still had to be contained— by détente if possible, by force otherwise. To that end, anticommunist regimes in any strategic area—the Far East, the Middle East, Latin America—had to be accepted as allies, and supported, however repressive their internal policies might be. The system of alliances that was the bulwark of containment, in both Europe and Asia, was still the heart of U.S. strategy, and the government even sought rapprochement with a mainland China that, though communist, was anti-Soviet. The relation between the United States and the economic and military giant of communism—the Soviet Union—was still central to every aspect of U.S. policy. Operational decisions of foreign policy therefore had still to be made on much the same ground as before.

But to a rapidly growing number of congressmen—who by 1973 had become the majority—Presidents Nixon and Ford, and especially Secretary of State Henry A. Kissinger, appeared to be clinging to policies that had been in some measure discredited, to alliances and commitments that ought now to be reviewed and in some cases discarded. The legislators did not know precisely what the new policies ought to be, but they had no doubt they would be different, would be less freely interventionist, and would be based less on realpolitik and more on morality and human rights.

So the policy gap grew broader and, as it did, so did the "credibility gap" that had been poisoning relations between the branches since the middle 1960s. With each new burst of combat activity in Indochina, each new resumption of fighting after each lull, each new revelation of information the executive branch had kept hidden from the public, the Congress—or its Democratic and antiwar majorities, at least—felt more deeply misled, deceived, and betrayed by presidential leadership. Then came Watergate, which could only intensify the distrust of the president and everybody near him. But even after Richard Nixon gave way to Gerald Ford, the credibility gap by no means closed, for Secretary Kissinger remained as a conspicuous link between the new administration and the old. In congressional eyes, Kissinger was still compromised in Indochina, as war continued despite the peace agreement that had won him the Nobel prize. He was compromised in the wiretapping of government officials and newsmen, and by reports of U.S. implication in the overthrow of President Allende of Chile in 1973. He was blamed for the secret billion-dollar grain sale to the Soviet Union, which raised prices in the United States, and he happened to be the secretary of state when the petroleum-producing countries imposed their embargo and launched their spectacular series of price hikes. And he appeared as the friend of corrupt military dictatorships.[1] Distrust reached the point where a House committee in 1975 took the unprecedented action of voting to cite the secretary of state for contempt for refusing it information on the Central Intelligence Agency's covert operations.[2]

As both policy agreement and mutual trust eroded, the inhibitions that for a generation had kept the Congress from taking control of foreign policy

1. These roots of the congressional antipathy toward Kissinger are well summarized in Laurence Stern, *The Wrong Horse: The Politics of Intervention and the Failure of American Diplomacy* (New York Times Books, 1977), pp. 137–39, 150–51.

2. The Select Committee on Intelligence dropped its recommendation after the information (withheld under the doctrine of executive privilege) was supplied orally to designated committee members. *Congressional Quarterly Almanac, 1975*, pp. 407–08.

washed away. The power to take command was always in the legislative branch; it had been used in the 1920s and 1930s to confine executive action within strict bounds. Now it would be used again.

But it would be used piecemeal. The Congress, when it substituted its own judgment for that of the executive branch in the 1970s, would have no grand design—no concept of the national interest as clear as the one that led the nation into Vietnam or, even, the one that governed the period of congressional ascendancy between the wars, when isolationism was the dominant philosophy and neutrality the operating legislative principle. This time, it was plain to the vast majority of legislators that nothing so simple as a return to isolationism could be the answer. Yet it was equally evident to a majority that the postwar policy of universal "containment" of communist expansion, which could involve the United States anywhere in the world and had led to the fiasco in Southeast Asia, must die with the defeat there. With such simple goals as involvement nowhere and involvement everywhere eliminated, that left only the in-between option—a policy of involvement on occasion, at some times, in some places. But there was no simple and reliable principle to decide the when and the where. That left the Congress free to act in individual cases as its mood might dictate, without the constraints imposed by broader policy considerations. It could let feelings and emotions, even impulse—and the constituent pressures behind them—be the guide.

The New Congressional Ascendancy

The Congress reaffirmed and reinforced its authority to take command of foreign policy in a series of actions: the War Powers Resolution of 1973 and the requirement that all executive agreements be submitted to the Congress, the establishment of congressional surveillance over the covert activities of the CIA, and the application of the legislative veto to arms sales and international atomic energy agreements. Then it used its new access to information and its strengthened authority to reverse the presidential policy in a series of operational decisions. Four of these in the 1973–76 period, in particular, represented the most aggressive reassertion of congressional control of foreign policy since the era of neutrality before World War II.

Ending the Vietnam War. Quite a few years of failure of U.S. policy in Vietnam were required before the majorities of the two houses wholly lost their trust in presidential handling of affairs there. But slowly, gingerly, and with great internal dissension the legislators did finally reach the point where they had more confidence in their own judgments than in the president's. By 1973, they were ready to take control of Southeast Asia policy. From then on, they retained control to the end of the country's involvement there, and they rejected presidential policies repeatedly, uninhibitedly, and almost as a matter of course.

The first assertion of congressional authority, in an area peripheral to Vietnam, was the Cooper-Church amendment in 1969 that prohibited the introduction of American combat troops into Laos and Thailand. But that was to forestall a presidential action, not to reverse one, and the Congress could achieve no such clean resolution of an issue when President Nixon the next year sent combat troops into another bordering country—Cambodia. All the opponents of the action could do was to vociferously denounce it. They could not force a termination earlier than the date the president had originally set.

Three years later, however, when the administration once again intervened in Cambodia—this time with air strikes against communist forces that were seeking to overrun the country—the antiwar forces in the Congress had become a clear majority, and a resolute one; they were at that very time pushing the War Powers Resolution of 1973 to passage over the presidential veto. The administration explained that its action in Cambodia responded to the request of the government of that country, then headed by Lon Nol, and was necessary to support the U.S. goal of self-determination for the peoples of Southeast Asia. But the Congress was unimpressed with the prerogatives of either chief executive or commander in chief, and, utterly weary of the divisive war in Asia, it adopted an appropriations rider commanding the president to halt the bombing. The president vetoed the bill, and the House could not muster the two-thirds majority to override him. Finally, as the fiscal year approached its end and the funding bill was imperative, Nixon and the legislators worked out a compromise—with Representative Gerald Ford among the intermediaries—setting a cutoff date of August 15.

But the congressional doves exacted an additional price; through a floor amendment in each house, they extended the prohibition of further combat activity to cover Vietnam, where hostilities had been ended by the cease-fire agreement signed in Paris in January of that year. What they did not learn until two years later was that that amendment—which President Nixon was forced to accept—contravened assurances he had given to President Nguyen Van Thieu of South Vietnam at the time of the signing of the cease-fire agreement. "You have my absolute assurance," Nixon had written Thieu on November 14, 1972, "that if Hanoi fails to abide by the terms of this agreement it is my intention to take swift and severe retaliatory action. . . . I repeat my personal assurances to you that the United States will react very strongly and rapidly to any violation of the agreement." And on January 5, 1973, he had written Thieu, "you have my assurance of continued assistance in the post-settlement period and that we will respond with full force should the settlement be violated by North Vietnam."[3]

With these promises, Thieu joined in the cease-fire agreement. But the assurances he had from Nixon were necessarily worth only the value that the Congress, in the absence of any commitment on its own part, was willing to assign at any given time to continuing to sustain South Vietnam; that turned out to be not much.[4]

The first test came on the postsettlement assistance. When hostilities were suspended with the signing of the agreement, the administration request of $2.1 billion for assistance to the South Vietnamese and Laotian forces in fiscal 1974 was scaled down to $1.6 billion, but the Congress cut almost another half billion out of that, setting a ceiling of $1.126 billion. Next year, as inflation pushed costs up, Nixon appealed for the restoration of the cut, but the Congress held firm. Turning aside protests that it was abandoning its ally, it also cut the authorization for 1975 from a requested $1.6 billion to $1 billion. But when appropriation time came around, even that was too high. The Congress allowed less than half the administration's original request—$700 million.

Late in 1974, the North Vietnamese and Viet Cong flagrantly betrayed the cease-fire agreement and began moving on Saigon, at the same time that communist guerrillas in Cambodia approached Phnom Penh. President Ford—prohibited from carrying out the "swift and severe retaliatory action"

3. *New York Times*, May 1, 1975. The agreements were made public on April 30, not by the Ford administration but by a minister of the fallen Saigon government. The U.S. government has never released the letters. When members of the Senate Foreign Relations Committee sought them after their appearance in the *Times*, Secretary Kissinger reportedly claimed executive privilege. *New York Times*, May 7, 1975.

4. "The argument was later advanced that it was not within the President's power to give such assurances without explicit authorization by the Congress," Henry Kissinger writes. "This idea not only did not occur to us; it would have struck us as inconceivable that the United States should fight for years and lose 45,000 men in an honorable cause, and then stand by while the peace treaty, the achievement of their sacrifice, was flagrantly violated. Diplomacy could not survive such casuistry." *White House Years* (Little, Brown, 1979), p. 1373. Apart from the question of power, it would be surprising if Kissinger meant that it did not occur to the administration that such an authorization would be *practically* necessary, or at least extremely useful, in order to compel the Congress to fulfill the promise in the event the United States was ever called on to do so. One of Kissinger's predecessors as special assistant to the president for national security affairs, McGeorge Bundy, suggests that the reason no authorization was sought, and the commitment was kept secret, was to avoid "an explosive reaction" from a country and a Congress that were not "the least bit eager to go back to war in Vietnam for any reason whatever." "Vietnam, Watergate and Presidential Powers," *Foreign Affairs*, vol. 58 (Winter 1979–80), p. 402.

pledged by Nixon—responded only by asking for the $300 million that had been cut from the Vietnam appropriation, to be used to replace equipment lost in combat, plus $222 million for Cambodia. But freshman Democrats chosen in the "Watergate" election of 1974, led by M. Robert Carr of Michigan, rounded up the fifty signatures needed to call an emergency caucus of House Democrats and succeeded in passing, by a 189 to 49 margin, a resolution opposing even that much help. Three days later the Senate Democratic caucus opposed Ford's request by an equally decisive margin, 34 to 6.

President Ford kept up the fight. Army Chief of Staff General Frederick C. Weyand returned from Vietnam in April 1975 with a report that South Vietnam still had "the spirit and the capability to defeat the North Vietnamese" if the United States would reequip several of its battalions, and the president went before a joint session of the Congress to request an immediate $722 million in new military aid, plus $250 million in economic and humanitarian assistance. The quick action was essential, he said, to permit the South Vietnamese "to stem the onrushing aggression," to make possible a negotiated settlement, and to make good on "our profound moral obligation" to our ally. Moreover, he argued, there were considerations of "our posture toward the rest of the world and, particularly, of our future relations with the free nations of Asia. These nations must not think for a minute that the United States is pulling out on them or intends to abandon them to aggression."[5]

But the Nixon-Thieu letters were still secret, and the Congress was not a party to the administration's "moral obligation." As Senator Henry M. Jackson, Democrat of Washington and a ranking member of the Armed Services Committee, had put it a few days earlier:

> The administration has intimated the Congress has reneged on "commitments" and "obligations" to the South Vietnamese government. The fact is that Congress is being accused of violating commitments and obligations it never heard of.
>
> I have been reliably informed that there exist between the governments of the United States and South Vietnam secret agreements which envision fateful American decisions, yet whose very existence has never been acknowledged.[6]

In any event, the Congress was not prepared to accede instantly to the president's request. As hostile forces closed in on Saigon and the two houses were still deliberating, the president laid the blame squarely on the legislature for the impending loss of South Vietnam to communism. He told a news conference on April 16:

> In the agreement that was signed in Paris in January of 1973, the United States,

5. "Address before Joint Session of the Congress Reporting on United States Foreign Policy, April 10, 1975," *Public Papers of the Presidents: Gerald R. Ford, 1975* (U.S. Government Printing Office, 1977), vol. 1, p. 463.

6. *Congressional Record*, April 8, 1975, p. 9281.

as part of its agreement with South Vietnam, agreed to supply replacement war material and to give economic aid. The Soviet Union and the People's Republic of China, I assume, made the same commitments to North Vietnam. It appears that they have maintained that commitment. Unfortunately, the United States did not carry out its commitment in the supplying of military hardware and economic aid to South Vietnam. . . .

I am absolutely convinced if Congress made available $722 million in military assistance by the time I made [sic]—or sometime shortly thereafter—the South Vietnamese could stabilize the military situation in South Vietnam today.[7]

A few days later, Ford chastised the Congress for refusing to countenance the use of American military forces. He told a group of correspondents that "unfortunately, the Congress in August of 1973 . . . took away from the President the power to move in a military way to enforce the agreements that were signed in Paris."[8]

In other words, President Ford would have resumed the war, or at least issued an ultimatum to do so, if he—rather than the Congress—had been making policy. President Nixon said much the same thing in his memoirs. "The effect" of the 1973 funds cutoff, he wrote, "was to deny me the means to enforce the Vietnamese peace agreement." Congress "reneged on our obligations under the agreements," and when it did so, "the war and the peace in Indochina that America had won over 12 years of sacrifice and fighting were lost within a matter of months."[9]

In this atmosphere of recrimination, before the Congress could complete its action on emergency aid, at the end of April Vietnam fell.

Linking Soviet Trade to Jewish Emigration. Among the most promising of the agreements stemming from President Nixon's 1972 trip to Moscow was the one covering trade between the two countries. The United States offered the Soviet Union the most-favored-nation (MFN) status granted most other U.S. trading partners and Export-Import Bank credits to help finance its imports from this country. The Soviets, for their part, promised to pay the balance of their World War II Lend-Lease debt of over $700 million when the MFN status and credits were received.

The agreement promised considerable benefits for the United States. The Soviet Union offered enormous potential as a market. As of 1972, the United States already enjoyed a trade surplus of $500 million with the Soviets—the largest with any single country—and the next year the surplus was $1 billion.[10]

7. "Remarks and a Question-and-Answer Session at the Annual Convention of the American Society of Newspaper Editors, April 16, 1975," *Public Papers: Ford, 1975*, vol. 1, p. 498.

8. "Interview with Walter Cronkite, Eric Sevareid, and Bob Schieffer of CBS News, April 21, 1975," ibid., p. 543.

9. *RN: The Memoirs of Richard Nixon* (Grosset and Dunlap, 1978), p. 889.

10. Statement of William D. Eberle, U.S. special representative for trade negotiations, *Trade Reform Act of 1974*, Hearings before the Senate Finance Committee (GPO, 1974), p. 317.

The Department of Commerce foresaw a rise in the surplus to $2 billion by 1980.[11] But beyond the economic benefits were the political gains. As a special study mission of the House Foreign Affairs Committee put it, "trade can serve as a catalyst toward the improvement of political relations by reducing animosities and providing a basis for working out mutually acceptable solutions to common problems."[12]

And Secretary of State Kissinger similarly linked the trade agreement to this country's broad foreign policy strategy: "We are trying to encourage the Soviet Union to maintain a moderate course in foreign policy, to move step by step to an attitude of real coexistence with the United States, and to create linkages between the Soviet Union and the United States such that whenever a potential crisis arises, there would be at least enough influence to put a brake on a conflicting course."[13]

But the strategy foundered on two amendments—one to the 1974 trade bill making both the credits and the MFN status conditional on liberalization of Soviet policies toward Jewish emigration, the other to an Export-Import Bank bill limiting the amount of credit the bank could extend to the Soviet Union.

The first of these was couched in general language, denying the trade and credit benefits to any non-market-economy country that refused its citizens the right to emigrate or charged more than a nominal fee to those exercising the right, but it was aimed at the plight of Soviet Jews desiring to emigrate to Israel. After the Soviet Union eased emigration restrictions late in 1968, the number of emigrants rose from a few hundred a year to 32,000 in 1972, but many more who were eager to leave were held back not only by an apparent quota system but by a tax of $5,000 to $25,000 per emigrant, levied ostensibly to compensate the Soviet Union for the cost of their education.[14] A few American Jewish activists, incensed at the treatment of their coreligionists in the USSR, conceived the idea of linking the expansion of American exports sought by the Kremlin to a further relaxation of its emigration policies. They were rebuffed by the Nixon administration—at least publicly[15]—as well

11. *Detente: Prospects for Increased Trade with Warsaw Pact Countries*, Committee Print, House Foreign Affairs Committee, 93 Cong. 2 sess. (1974), p. 1.

12. Ibid.

13. *Trade Reform Act of 1974*, Hearings, p. 466.

14. Paula Stern, *Water's Edge: Domestic Politics and the Making of American Foreign Policy* (Greenwood Press, 1979), pp. 4–5; Joseph Albright, "Pact of two Henrys," *New York Times Magazine*, January 5, 1975, p. 17. This section relies particularly on *Water's Edge*, a case study of the amendment.

15. President Nixon said later that the subject of emigration was discussed during the 1972 meeting in Moscow. Assurances were evidently received that the policies resulting in an outflow of 30,000–35,000 emigrants a year would be continued. Paula Stern, *Water's Edge*, pp. 10–15.

as by the major American Jewish organizations, but they found a champion in Senator Jackson and an aggressive organizer in his aide, Richard Perle. Jackson, although not a member of any of the committees concerned with foreign relations, trade, or credit policy, had been a candidate for president in 1972 and would be again in 1976. The initiative was his, but a large segment of the organized Jewish community at once—and virtually all of it eventually—lined up behind him. Representatives of Jewish organizations participated in the development of his amendment, lobbied for it on Capitol Hill, and organized a massive campaign to generate mail supporting it from senators' and representatives' constituencies. Organized labor also backed the measure, not only on its merits but also as a tactic to block passage of the general trade liberalization bill. Jackson obtained more than three-quarters of his colleagues as cosponsors of his amendment, and in the House, where Charles A. Vanik, Democrat of Ohio, was its principal sponsor, two-thirds of the membership joined him. It appealed alike to conservatives suspicious of the Soviet Union and détente and to liberals declaring their support of human rights, as well as Democrats who saw a chance to embarrass the Republican president, and to members from all sides who were susceptible to the intense pressure being exerted by Jewish constituents.

The Vanik amendment passed the House in December 1973 (a motion to strike from the committee bill a section containing the amendment was defeated, 106 to 298), after an administration effort to work out a compromise failed. Threatening a presidential veto, Secretary Kissinger denounced the House bill as one that "would do serious and perhaps irreparable damage to our relations with the Soviet Union."[16] At this point, both sides sought compromise—and so, to almost everyone's surprise, did the Soviet Union. Secretary Kissinger entered into a series of discussions with Soviet representatives, acting as a kind of mediator between the Soviet Union and Senator Jackson and his allies. Based on his conversations with the Soviets, Kissinger gave the senator "assurances" that the emigration tax, which had already been suspended, would continue in abeyance, that "punitive actions," "unreasonable impediments," and discrimination would not be permitted, and that the number of emigrants would rise.[17] In a letter of reply, Jackson insisted that the number of emigrants be specified, citing 60,000 a year—or 70 percent above the 1973 rate—as "a minimum standard of initial compliance."[18] At a

16. *The Trade Reform Act of 1973,* Hearings before the Senate Finance Committee, 93 Cong. 2 sess. (GPO, 1974), p. 457.
17. Letter from Henry Kissinger, in *Congressional Record,* December 13, 1974, p. 39785.
18. Ibid., pp. 39785–86.

televised news conference, Jackson boasted about having brought about "a complete turn around" in Russian policy.[19] The Soviet response was immediate. In a letter to Secretary Kissinger, Foreign Minister Andrei Gromyko denounced Kissinger's assurance that the number of emigrants would rise, as well as Jackson's use of a specific figure. Gromyko charged the secretary with knowingly distorting the Soviet position and insisted that emigration policy would remain "entirely within the internal competence of our state." The secretary in turn, without releasing the Gromyko letter, warned the Senate that the Soviet government could not be held accountable for any specific figure and that "any attempt now publicly to nail this thing down in the form of a legal obligation is likely to backfire."[20] Nevertheless, Jackson held to his position, as the Senate approved his amendment without dissent.

Meanwhile, the Senate Banking and Currency Committee had voted to restrict the authority of the Export-Import Bank to extend credits to the Soviet Union. Noting that $470 million had already been lent, it expressed concern "that pressure for detente may interfere with the analysis" such loans should have, including consideration of the effect of the credits on the Soviet military potential.[21] Particularly upsetting to the senators had been the bank's financing of a tractor factory and of oil and gas exploration.[22] Their proposed solution was a two-house legislative veto of any loan of $50 million or more to any country, recommended over the protest of a minority that "the Congress has neither the time nor the expertise" to "exercise programmatic decision-making authority on a day-to-day, case-by-case basis."[23] An amendment on the Senate floor by Adlai E. Stevenson, Democrat of Illinois, changed the veto to a prenotification procedure but placed a limit of $300 million on new commitments to the Soviet Union. The House accepted this provision, and the two houses also agreed to prohibit any aid for extraction of fossil fuels and to limit aid for research and exploration to $40 million.

All this was too much for the Soviet government to take. Shortly after the trade and banking bills were passed in December 1974, it announced its withdrawal from the 1972 trade agreement. The U.S. legislation, it said, violated both the principle of noninterference in domestic affairs and the terms of the 1972 agreement itself, which called for unconditional elimination

19. Paula Stern, *Water's Edge*, p. 163.

20. *Emigration Amendment*, Hearings before the Senate Finance Committee, 93 Cong. 2 sess. (GPO, 1974), pp. 53, 68. The letter, made public in Moscow, was printed in *New York Times*, December 19, 1974; see also Paula Stern, *Water's Edge*, pp. 168–69.

21. *Export-Import Bank Amendments of 1974*, S. Rept. 93-1097, 93 Cong. 2 sess. (GPO, 1974), pp. 11–12.

22. *Congressional Quarterly Almanac, 1974*, p. 215.

23. *Export-Import Bank Amendments*, S. Rept. 93-1097, p. 44.

of discriminatory trade restrictions.[24] Analysts of Soviet policy disagree as to what factors were decisive in the Kremlin's action—the Stevenson amendment, the controversy over Kissinger's interpretation of the agreement on Jewish emigration, the public boasting in the United States about the Russian "capitulation," or simply a wariness of overreliance on the United States as a trading partner.[25] Specifically citing the Soviet trade case, President Ford blamed the Congress for placing "rigid" restrictions on the ability of the president to conduct foreign relations.[26]

The immediate consequences were drastic. From its high of 35,000 in 1973, Jewish emigration from the Soviet Union fell to an annual average of fewer than 15,000 in 1975–77 (but later rose to 50,000 in 1979).[27] Trade between the two countries, which peaked at $2.3 billion in 1976, dropped to $1.6 billion in 1977 and $1.8 billion in 1978.[28] The effect on general U.S.-Soviet political relations is harder to assess, but 1974 did see the introduction of new tensions, and Soviet activities in Africa and elsewhere called into question the substance of détente. By 1977, the Carter administration, despite its outspoken commitment to human rights, was, like its predecessor, hoping for repeal of the Jackson-Vanik amendment.[29] In 1979 the administration was searching for a formula that would make the 50,000 annual emigration rate the Soviet Union had attained acceptable to the Congress as conforming to its Jackson-Vanik amendment. Vanik announced during a visit to Moscow that it was acceptable to him,[30] but Jackson was still holding out for a flat Soviet commitment to "free emigration."[31]

Penalizing Turkey for Its Cyprus Invasion. During the two and a half decades when executive leadership in foreign affairs was taken for granted, presidents were allowed wide latitude in determining how foreign assistance funds could best be distributed to further the national objectives. But in 1974, when harmony between the branches had given way to hostility, and a crisis broke

---

24. *New York Times*, January 15, 1975.

25. See, for instance, Daniel Yergin, "Politics and Soviet-American Trade: The Three Questions," *Foreign Affairs*, vol. 55 (Spring 1977), p. 532; Michael Kaser, "Soviet Trade Turns to Europe," *Foreign Policy*, no. 19 (Summer 1975), pp. 123–35; William Safire, *New York Times*, February 3, 1975; Joseph Kraft, *Washington Post*, January 21, 1975.

26. "Address Before a Joint Session of the Congress Reporting on the State of the Union, January 15, 1975," *Public Papers: Ford, 1975*, vol. 1, pp. 36–46.

27. *Congressional Quarterly Weekly Report*, vol. 37 (March 3, 1979), p. 360; Paula Stern, *Water's Edge*, p. 198; *Congressional Record*, daily edition, September 5, 1980, p. H8374 (figures compiled by the National Conference on Soviet Jewry).

28. Richard Burt, *New York Times*, July 24, 1978; Craig R. Whitney, ibid., December 30, 1978.

29. *Washington Post*, June 17, 1977.

30. Ibid., April 22, 1979.

31. Richard E. Cohen, "Carter Trying to Breach Trade-Emigration Barrier," *National Journal*, vol. 11 (May 26, 1979), p. 865.

in the eastern Mediterranean, the Congress overrode the president and made its own decision on military aid.

After a coup inspired from Athens had overthrown the government of Cyprus, Turkey invaded Cyprus to forestall, as it claimed, the union of the island with Greece. The Congress quickly responded with legislation to cut off further military aid to Turkey, on the ground that that country had used U.S. arms in an offensive military action in violation of both the law and the bilateral agreement with Turkey.[32] President Ford and Secretary Kissinger struggled, with their allies on Capitol Hill, to block precipitate action that might drive Turkey out of the NATO alliance and result in the closing of U.S. military bases used for electronic surveillance of the Soviet Union. When they failed, Ford twice vetoed the aid embargo. "Should this measure become law," he said in his first veto message, "it would be impossible for the U.S. to continue to play any meaningful role in assisting the parties to resolve the Cyprus dispute . . . because the Congress would have taken from us the tools we need to affect the outcome."[33] Contingency funds were available that the President could have used at his discretion, but he chose not to directly flout the forcefully expressed will of the Congress. With the second veto he won a postponement of the effective date of the embargo to February 5, 1975, but when the negotiations showed no substantial progress by that date, it took effect. In July 1975, after one more attempt at legislative compromise was blocked in the House, Turkey suspended operation of some of the U.S. bases.

That Turkey had acted illegally in using U.S. arms to overrun half of Cyprus was not controverted, and it provided a strong moral basis for the congressional action. But the passion for the enterprise did not come mainly from abstract morality (the moral issue was not even raised in another case that to many observers appeared analogous—Israel's use of U.S. weapons in military action outside its boundaries). It came, rather, from Americans of Greek descent who were enraged by the Turkish occupation of areas of Cyprus inhabited by ethnic Greeks. Among them were two House members in the forefront of the legislative effort, Chief Deputy Majority Whip John Brademas of Indiana and Paul A. Sarbanes, Democrat of Maryland. The easy

32. Agreements with Turkey and Greece under the Truman Doctrine in 1947 prohibited use of U.S. arms in offensive actions, and the policy was made applicable to military aid recipients in legislation of 1961 and later acts. See letter of October 7, 1974, from Elmer B. Staats, comptroller general, to Senator Thomas F. Eagleton, in *Congressional Record*, May 19, 1975, pp. 14975–79; Congressional Research Service, "Military Aid Cutoff to Aggressor Recipients," in *Congressional Record*, September 19, 1974, p. 31921.

33. "Veto of Continuing Appropriations Resolution, October 14, 1974," *Public Papers: Ford, 1974* (GPO, 1975), p. 299.

majorities for the embargo—both houses voted by three-to-one majorities for the original action, and the House came within two votes of overriding the second Ford veto—were due in considerable measure to the effective organization of what was called the Greek lobby. "The Greeks were not a big lobby, but fierce," one reporter quoted congressmen as explaining.[34] Greek–American organizations generated thousands of telegrams to members of Congress, a pressure that Representative Thomas E. Morgan of Pennsylvania, chairman of the House International Relations Committee, had not seen equaled in his thirty years in the House "by any company or union."[35] The leadership of the committee agreed with the administration that the issue should not be brought to a vote but "the foaming, boiling pot outside of the leadership . . . frightened" it "into going along," according to one committee member.[36] "There are more Greek restaurants in my district than there are Turkish baths," one congressman told a London journalist.[37] House Republican Leader John J. Rhodes some years later caustically noted that "in 1976, the entire Democratic leadership of the Congress supported the embargo. It should be borne in mind that that was an election year and the votes of the Greek community were very important. It is also well known that there are not a great number of Turks in this country."[38]

The intense distrust of Secretary Kissinger that was pervasive in the congressional majority at the time was heightened by his handling of the Cyprus affair. He appeared to disdain the humanitarian issues and legal arguments and to "tilt toward Turkey" for purely pragmatic reasons, and in doing so he was undercutting the new democratic government of Greece and carrying out a policy that, in the words of one senator, "rewards aggressors and oppressive regimes and punishes innocent people."[39] Moreover, he delayed obtaining a legal opinion on the validity of the Turkish action and,

34. Mary McGrory, *Washington Star*, July 25, 1975. See also Laurence Stern, *Wrong Horse*, pp. 139–41; Morton Kondracke, "The Greek Lobby," *New Republic*, April 29, 1978, pp. 14–15.

35. *Congress and Foreign Policy*, Hearings before the Special Subcommittee on Investigations of the House Committee on U.S. International Relations, 94 Cong. 2 sess. (GPO, 1976), p. 91.

36. Larry Winn, Jr., Republican of Kansas, ibid., p. 32.

37. Godfrey Hodgson, *Congress and American Foreign Policy* (London: Royal Institute of International Affairs, 1979), p. 11. Mary McGrory, *Washington Star*, July 25, 1975, similarly quoted unnamed congressmen. I heard one new member of the Congress explain at a meeting of American and European legislators: "I have a large Greek-American constituency, so I spoke on the floor of the House against aid to Turkey."

38. *Congressional Record*, daily edition, August 1, 1978, p. H7636. John J. Rhodes, *The Futile System* (McLean, Va.: EPM Publications, 1976), pp. 53–54, recounts how Rules Committee Chairman Ray J. Madden, Democrat of Indiana, who was instrumental in blocking House action to lift the embargo in July 1975, told the House he found constituents at Greek picnics in his district "almost unanimous" against aid to Turkey.

39. Adlai E. Stevenson, *Congressional Record*, September 19, 1974, p. 31914.

when pressed into getting the opinion—which, inevitably, was adverse—suppressed it, even after it had been "leaked" to interested members of the Congress.[40]

Once the embargo was in effect, however, it became clearer month by month that its purposes were not being served. The United States had lost the use of its Turkish bases, but Turkish troops were still in Cyprus. President Ford continued to appeal to the Congress to lift the embargo, saying in 1975 that the congressional action had undermined the North Atlantic Treaty Alliance in the eastern Mediterranean, "jeopardized vital common defense installations," "contributed to tensions which are not helpful to Greece," and reduced American influence in trying to assist negotiations for a peaceful settlement.[41] He did win some concessions, permitting cash sales and limited credits, but these were not enough to change the Turkish stand. No Turkish prime minister, it was clear, could yield to American pressure and keep his post. Not until 1978, when a Democratic president was in the White House, was the Congress willing to relent. Under intense pressure from the Carter administration, it implicitly acknowledged the failure of its policy and lifted the embargo, conditional on certification by the president that Turkey was acting in good faith to achieve a Cyprus settlement. Turkey thereupon permitted reopening of the U.S. bases.

Blocking Intervention in Angola. When the revolutionary government of Portugal decided to liquidate its African empire in 1975, there was in one of the colonies—Angola—no single liberation group with a clear claim on leadership of the new state. Three separate guerrilla forces had been contending against the colonial regime, and as the Portuguese prepared to withdraw, they turned their fire on one another. At least five powers from outside of black Africa—the Soviet Union, the United States, China, Cuba, and South Africa—intervened in support of one or another of the guerrilla groups, and neighboring African states served as the conduits for military supplies and equipment.

The most forceful intervention was by the Soviet Union and Cuba on behalf of the Popular Movement for the Liberation of Angola (MPLA), which had had Soviet backing for more than a decade. Soviet and Cuban personnel began to arrive in Angola in August 1975, and when independence was proclaimed in November the USSR immediately recognized the MPLA as the government of Angola and began massive airlifts of tanks, rockets, and other

40. Laurence Stern, *Wrong Horse*, pp. 142–44.
41. "Letter to the Speaker of the House Urging Resumption of United States Military Assistance to Turkey, July 9, 1975," *Public Papers: Ford, 1975*, vol. 1, pp. 946–48.

sophisticated equipment. By February, some 11,000 Cuban troops supplied with Soviet equipment were fighting beside the MPLA against the alliance of the other two groups, the National Front for the Liberation of Angola (FNLA) and the National Union for the Total Independence of Angola (UNITA), who were getting supplies—but no personnel—from the United States and China.[42]

South Africa invaded the country with an armored column in October 1975 in support of the FNLA-UNITA combination but did more harm than good. African states that had been neutral and had denounced foreign intervention were pushed into recognizing the MPLA and condemning their opponents as stooges of South African racism. The South Africans, recognizing the hopelessness of their involvement, pulled their forces back, leaving the MPLA in control of most of the country.

American covert involvement apparently began in 1974—or perhaps earlier—but was stepped up in January 1975 with a commitment of $300,000 to the FNLA.[43] In June or July, the Ford administration decided to send military supplies as well as cash, evidently on the scale of $30 million or so. The decision was based not on the importance of Angola to the United States, primarily, but on global considerations, as Secretary Kissinger testified later:

> If the United States is seen to emasculate itself in the face of massive, unprecedented Soviet and Cuban intervention, what will be the perception of leaders around the world as they make decisions concerning their future security? . . . The question is whether America still maintains the resolve to act responsibly as a great power—prepared to face a challenge when it arises, knowing that preventive action now may make unnecessary a more costly response later.[44]

The covert activity, Kissinger said, was reported to eight congressional committees in more than twenty briefings, in accordance with the requirements of the Foreign Assistance Act of 1974 that all such ventures be disclosed to those committees "in a timely fashion." When he learned about it, Senator Dick Clark, a freshman Democrat of Iowa, who although in his first year on the Foreign Relations Committee was chairman of its Subcommittee on African Affairs, introduced an amendment to a foreign aid authorization bill to prohibit further covert aid. Meanwhile, Senator John V. Tunney of California, a freshman Democrat not on any relevant committee but a candidate in search

---

42. Charles K. Ebinger, "External Intervention in Internal War: The Politics and Diplomacy of the Angolan Civil War," *Orbis*, vol. 19 (Fall 1976), pp. 690–91.

43. Seymour M. Hersh, *New York Times*, December 19, 1975; Neil C. Livingstone and Manfred von Nordheim, "The United States Congress and the Angola Crisis," *Strategic Review*, Spring 1977, p. 37.

44. *Angola*, Hearings before the African Affairs Subcommittee of the Senate Foreign Relations Committee, 94 Cong. 2 sess. (GPO, 1976), p. 130.

of an issue for his reelection campaign,[45] stepped out in front with an amendment to the defense appropriations bill to eliminate $33 million he estimated was in the measure for Angola. Rejecting a plea by Senator Robert P. Griffin of Michigan, the Republican whip, that the executive branch be granted "the flexibility necessary to carry out U.S. foreign policy in a dynamic and changing situation,"[46] the Senate adopted the Tunney amendment to cut off the funds by an overwhelming 54 to 22 margin.

The majority protested the covert operation on principle, contending that the United States should not secretly assist one faction in a civil war. They objected to the policy itself, holding that the United States would be backing the losing guerrilla faction and would isolate itself from black Africa by intervening on the same side as South Africa. They remembered Vietnam: "Although we are told that there is no intention of producing another Vietnam on the continent of Africa," warned Senator Edward M. Kennedy, Democrat of Massachusetts, "the dangers of step-by-step increments of U.S. money, manpower and prestige are clear."[47] And in Senator Clark's words, Angola was the wrong place for "an open-ended confrontation with the Soviet Union."[48] But President Ford saw the cutoff of funds as "a deep tragedy for all countries whose security depends on the United States" and as an "abdication of responsibility" with "the gravest consequences for the long-term position of the United States, and for international order in general."[49] By January it was even clearer that the MPLA, with an estimated sixteen thousand Cuban troops assisting it, was going to govern Angola in any case, and the House approved the aid cutoff by an even larger margin, 323 to 99. Senator Clark later added an amendment to a military aid bill making permanent the ban on U.S. support for military or paramilitary operations in Angola.

The Soviet Union had gained "a stronghold in Africa" because members of Congress "lost their guts," the president told reporters at the time.[50]

Two years afterward, Henry Kissinger was still blaming the Congress. "We had them defeated in Angola and then we defeated ourselves," he said.[51] But Nathaniel Davis, who as assistant secretary of state for African affairs in 1975 had advised against the covert operation, was defending his judgment too. The limited U.S. intervention had only produced "counter-

45. Livingstone and von Nordheim, "United States Congress," pp. 38–39.
46. *Congressional Record*, December 17, 1975, p. 41197.
47. Ibid., December 18, 1975, p. 41625.
48. *Washington Post*, December 18, 1975.
49. "Remarks on Senate Action to Prohibit United States Assistance to Angola, December 19, 1975," *Public Papers: Ford, 1975*, vol. 2, p. 1981.
50. *Washington Post*, February 11, 1976.
51. "Is There a Crisis of Spirit in the West," a conversation with Dr. Kissinger and Senator Daniel P. Moynihan, *Public Opinion*, May–June 1978, p. 8.

escalations"; only by intervening "quickly, massively and decisively" could the United States have turned the tide, and President Ford and Kissinger were not prepared to be that bold.[52]

"Impermissible Shackles" on the President

During 1974–76, when the four conflicts sketched above were boiling to a climax, the president and the Congress were at odds on a wide range of other, less spectacular issues. The Congress singled out certain countries for legislative penalty, by eliminating or sharply reducing military assistance allowances recommended by the president; thus, it cut off military assistance to Chile and Uruguay for violation of human rights, reduced assistance to South Korea for the same reason, and slashed assistance to India because that country persisted in developing nuclear weapons. After the Arab embargo on oil shipments to the United States, the Congress denied to all members of the Organization of Petroleum Exporting Countries the preferential tariff treatment being extended to other developing nations, and in doing so penalized friendly countries that had not participated in the embargo—including Ecuador, Venezuela, Indonesia, and Nigeria. It regained a substantial degree of control over trade policy when, in enacting a new trade agreement act in 1974, it subjected a wide range of executive actions to a one-house or two-house legislative veto or a requirement for affirmative congressional action.[53] It struck at international bodies, too; it withdrew the United States from the International Labor Organization because of that organization's political positions, withheld the U.S. contribution to the United Nations Educational, Scientific, and Cultural Organization in 1975 when that body excluded Israel from its activities, and cut the contribution to the United Nations itself after the world organization accorded the Palestine Liberation Organization observer status.

In the Middle East, the Congress—using the legislative veto procedure over arms sales established in 1974—forced the president to withdraw the proposed sale of an antiaircraft system to Jordan until President Ford imposed restrictions on its mobility and employment that King Hussein, in accepting them, denounced as "insulting."[54] Congressional opposition forced the administration to reduce from 3,500 to 1,500 the number of missiles sold to

52. "The Angola Decision of 1975: A Personal Memoir," *Foreign Affairs*, vol. 57 (Fall 1978), pp. 114, 123.
53. *Congressional Quarterly Almanac, 1974*, p. 554.
54. Ibid., *1975*, p. 358.

Saudi Arabia.[55] At a crucial point in Secretary Kissinger's peace-seeking maneuvers in the Middle East, when the secretary was reportedly pressing Israel for concessions, seventy-six senators intervened with a letter to the secretary backing the Israeli position. When Israel and Egypt reached agreement on Israeli withdrawal from the Sinai, the Congress accepted Kissinger's commitment of U.S. civilian monitors to help enforce it, but only—fearing the existence of secret commitments—after writing strict, explicit limitations on the U.S. role. The Congress delayed for several years the construction of a naval base on the island of Diego Garcia in the Indian Ocean. In African affairs, the Congress insisted on retaining a policy first imposed in 1972 over administration opposition (and finally repealed in 1977) forbidding the administration to support the UN-imposed boycott of Rhodesia by banning the importation of chrome. And the Congress intervened in internal organization of the State Department, by establishing the position of coordinator of human rights and humanitarian affairs, who would prepare for the Congress an annual report on observance of human rights by every country receiving security assistance.

There would have been many more restrictions—on aid to Zambia, Zaire, and Mozambique, to name a few—if the administration had not battled the congressional activists, week by week and clause by clause, as each of the annual foreign assistance bills went through the committees, the two houses, and then the conference committees. And in 1976, only by wielding his veto could President Ford win modifications in a bill that, he said, "would forge impermissible shackles on the President's abiliity to carry out the laws and conduct the foreign relations of the United States."[56] Having enough votes in both houses to sustain the veto, he forced the Congress to eliminate several of the more onerous restrictions—a ceiling on total private as well as government arms sales, an amendment forbidding limitations the president had imposed on trade with Vietnam, and a legislative veto on assistance to countries violating human rights. But he had to accept several other restrictions that he protested in his veto message.

In the message, Ford referred to the multiple "shackles" contained not only in that bill but in other legislation passed and pending during that contentious period and summarized the case for executive flexibility:

> The President cannot function effectively in domestic matters, and speak for the nation authoritatively in foreign affairs, if his decisions under authority previously conferred can be reversed by a bare majority of the Congress. Also, the attempt of

55. *New York Times*, September 2, 1976.
56. "Veto of the Foreign Assistance Bill, May 7, 1976," *Public Papers: Ford, 1976–77* (GPO, 1979), vol. 2, pp. 1481–85.

Congress to become a virtual co-administrator in operational decisions would seriously distract it from its legislative role. Inefficiency, delay and uncertainty . . . would eventually follow.

In world affairs today, America can have only one foreign policy. Moreover, that foreign policy must be certain, clear and consistent. Foreign governments must know that they can treat with the President on foreign policy matters, and that when he speaks within his authority, they can rely upon his words.[57]

From the standpoint of the Congress, however, America's foreign policy was anything but "certain, clear, and consistent." The legislators were as confused and uneasy as any foreign government as to where U.S. policy was leading. President Nixon early in his first term had announced a "new approach" to foreign policy, in which new commitments would be made only "in the light of a careful assessment of our own national interests."[58] But, as Seyom Brown points out, the reassessment never appeared in any concrete form that could be used by the executive and legislative branches as an agreed-upon basis for operational decisions. "Consequently, what was supposed to be a new conceptual basis for reforging the shattered foreign policy consensus turned out to be a plea to Congress and to the public to trust the executive's wisdom in understanding what the national interest required."[59] But that was precisely what the Congress was not prepared to do. Trust in the executive had been tried, with catastrophic results.

The mandate of Vietnam was to change existing policy in whatever way was necessary so that that kind of disaster, at least, could never happen again; "no more Vietnams" seemed likely to be as much the touchstone for the next generation of policymakers as "no more Munichs" had been for the generation that preceded it, and "neutrality"—or "no more World Wars"— for the one before that.[60] But in the conflicts over the Vietnam withdrawal and the Angolan intervention, and even to a degree in the very limited Sinai involvement, the Congress saw what seemed to be the old policies being pursued, and so it was impelled to take command.

Running through the series of clashes was the corollary theme of human rights. When, after Vietnam, the country moved to reduce its commitments around the globe, the latent revulsion against repressive regimes who had been accepted out of presumed necessity could rise to the surface and on

57. Ibid., pp. 1483, 1485.

58. "First Annual Report to the Congress on United States Foreign Policy for the 1970s, February 18, 1970," *Public Papers of the Presidents: Richard Nixon, 1970* (GPO, 1971), pp. 116, 119.

59. *The Crises of Power: An Interpretation of United States Foreign Policy during the Kissinger Years* (Columbia University Press, 1979), p. 7.

60. In Michael Roskin's terms, it would represent a shift from an interventionist to a noninterventionist generational paradigm, as Pearl Harbor marked a switch the other way. "From Pearl Harbor to Vietnam: Shifting Generational Paradigms of Foreign Policy," *Political Science Quarterly*, vol. 89 (Fall 1974), pp. 563–88.

occasion dictate policy—as it did in the actions of the Congress curtailing aid to South Korea and Chile. The human rights appeal to the Congress proved stronger, in the case of Soviet Jewry, than the attraction of détente. And in swaying the Congress to impose penalties on Turkey, the backers of Greece pleaded not only the rights of Greek Cypriots but another moral issue—the sanctity of law.

The new assertiveness of the Congress in foreign policy provoked a confrontation between the president and Congress that transcended the individual cases and continued as a general constitutional issue throughout Ford's brief term. The president's objection to legislative restrictions on his ability to negotiate and to act were perhaps predictable enough. But there was strong support for his view, also, on Capitol Hill. Some members went even further than did Ford in condemning congressional intervention. Thus Senator Barry M. Goldwater, Republican of Arizona:

> For the first time in the history of our country, we in Congress are forcing a President to come to this body for prior permission to do what he is charged to do under the Constitution—to manage foreign policy as he determines necessary for preserving the safety, the property, and the freedom of Americans. . . . in the context of attitudes toward foreign policy, we as Americans have never really become a nation of Americans. We are still a nation of hyphenated origins. . . . So, when the problem comes upon the floor of the Senate or House . . . involving any of the countries with whom substantial numbers of Americans have ancestral ties, you can lay a pretty good sized bet that these ethnic relationships are going to have a strong bearing on how that foreign policy is going to be formulated or implemented.
>
> This is why I believe that . . . Congress should not assert its distinct power, but should realize that a single elected official, who would not be disturbed by the politics of the moment, would use these powers far more wisely in the long run of history than a Congress which is constantly looking toward the political results.[61]

Similarly, Representative William S. Broomfield of Michigan, ranking minority member of the Committee on International Relations, worried about the role in international affairs of congressmen "elected to represent approximately 450,000 people, a sampling that is not necessarily an accurate reflection of national opinion. . . . I am disturbed when I sense that individual legislators might assess a foreign policy issue not by the standards of the national interest, but by what is right politically or will look good in the district."[62] Senator Griffin, the minority whip, put it more bluntly. He attributed both the Jackson-Vanik amendment and the congressional action on Cyprus largely to "domestic ethnic politics" and protested that "the foreign policy of a great power cannot be based on such considerations."[63]

61. *Congressional Record*, January 21, 1976, pp. 377–78.
62. *Congress and Foreign Policy*, Hearings, p. 85.
63. *Congressional Record*, February 5, 1976, p. 2465.

Senator Charles H. Percy of Illinois, a Republican member of the Foreign Relations Committee, questioned the competence of the Congress to take "control over Executive action." Referring specifically to the legislative veto on arms sales and the demand for prior approval of covert intelligence activities, Percy contended that "Congress simply does not have the expertise, the capability, or the authority for dealing with the daily operations of government." It was time, he said, to stop "overreacting to . . . the abuses of the recent past" and "accept that the Executive Branch also wishes to serve the common good."[64]

The criticism was not confined to Republicans, and even some of the leading activists among the Democrats had their misgivings, while defending their action in individual cases. Thus, Senator Stevenson, author of the Export-Import Bank amendment that helped to scuttle the U.S.-Soviet trade agreement, took the Senate floor for a blistering attack on Secretary Kissinger's style and, one by one, on his positions on the whole range of administration policies the Congress had reversed. He called for a foreign policy of "morality" rather than one of "bribes, false promises and gesticulations upon the stage of world opinion." Yet, in defending legislative intervention, he conceded that

> the Congress is poorly suited for a major role in the formulation and implementation of foreign policy. It is not a role which the Congress seeks. The strong inclination in the Congress is to give the President free rein so long as his power in foreign affairs is not abused and for so long as the judgments are sound. And there lies the rub. The power has been abused, and in the minds of many the judgments have been calamitous. That being so, the Congress is compelled to choose between licensing the continued misconduct of foreign relations or of exercising powers which it is not altogether equipped to exercise. It has no choice except to prevent further miscalculations in the world, as best it can, privately begging for the day when foreign policy is managed by men in whom it can confidently repose authority.[65]

The Senate Foreign Relations chairman-to-be, Frank Church, likewise conceded late in 1976 that the policy decisions imposed by the legislature through statute, as in the Turkey-Cyprus affair, were "awkward at best and often unworkable."[66] "The Congress cannot and should not run foreign policy," agreed Senator Hubert Humphrey of Minnesota, the former vice president.[67]

64. Address at the University of Alabama at Huntsville, May 20, 1976, in ibid., June 3, 1976, pp. 16407–08.

65. Ibid., February 21, 1976, pp. 3027–28.

66. Remarks at meeting of Foreign Relations Committee with President-elect Jimmy Carter, *Washington Post*, December 5, 1976.

67. *Congress and Foreign Policy*, Hearings, p. 175.

The Pendulum Swings Back—Partway

Gerald Ford's wish for his successor was "that this new congress will reexamine its constitutional role in international affairs." In his final State of
the Union Message, he reiterated, on behalf of Jimmy Carter, his oft-stated
plea for an end to "obstruction" and for presidential flexibility:

> There can be only one Commander-in-Chief. In these times crises cannot be
> managed and wars cannot be waged by committee. Nor can peace be pursued
> solely by parliamentary debate. To the ears of the world, the President speaks for
> the Nation. While he is, of course, ultimately accountable to the Congress, the
> courts and the people, he and his emissaries must not be handicapped in advance
> in their relations with foreign governments as has sometimes happened in the
> past.[68]

But as Carter was preparing to take office, the legislators did not seem to
fit Senator Stevenson's portrait of a body "begging for the day" when they
could once again "confidently repose authority" in a president. Key spokesmen for the Congress were putting him on notice that there would be no
return to the "normal" times of presidential supremacy and congressional
acquiescence in foreign relations. Indeed, argued the new chairman of the
House International Relations Committee, Clement J. Zablocki, Democrat of
Wisconsin, the so-called normal period of 1941–67 was in fact an aberration,
if one looks at the whole course of history, and the new period of congressional
assertiveness was in truth the norm. Congress, Zablocki went on, was not
going to forget the lesson it had learned well in the Vietnam era—"that
unbridled Presidential power in foreign affairs can be just as wrongheaded,
just as destructive, and just as harmful to the Nation as unbridled Congressional power"—and it did not matter that a Democrat was now in the White
House. "In other words, we are not going to roll over and play dead just
because Jimmy Carter is President."[69]

On the other side of the Capitol, Senator Humphrey was asserting that
a future Democratic president and a Democratic Congress should collaborate,
but collaboration did not mean acquiescence. To enable the Congress to
participate in major foreign policy decisions, "the progress made towards
the development of an independent congressional decision-making process
. . . must not be curtailed."[70] Most of a score of members of Congress

68. "Address Before a Joint Session of the Congress Reporting on the State of the Union,
January 12, 1977," *Public Papers: Ford, 1976–77*, vol. 3, pp. 2916–27.
69. Address to the Southern Council on International and Public Affairs, Charleston, S. C.,
December 4, 1976, in *Congressional Record*, January 4, 1977, pp. 246–47.
70. *Congress and Foreign Policy*, Hearings, p. 175.

interviewed in a *New York Times* survey in 1976 agreed that the "re-emergence" of the legislature in foreign affairs should and would continue, even with a Democratic president.[71]

Important institutional changes of the Nixon-Ford period were alone enough to prevent anything like a return to the old relationships. The War Powers Resolution would compel the Congress to become involved instantly in any crisis requiring the use of the armed forces, whether it might wish to be or not. The legislative vetoes it had reserved would necessitate its passing judgment on a wide range of foreign policy operations, the most important being arms sales to foreign countries. Information once made available to only a few members of the Congress or none at all—on covert intelligence operations, on agreements and commitments—would be available on a far wider scale. And vastly expanded staff resources now entrenched on Capitol Hill would enable the legislative branch to study the information and prepare to intervene. The greater number of subcommittees, and the developing norms of individualism and assertiveness, would make it possible for far more members—indeed, any member, as experience had shown—to initiate the intervention. No longer would the legislative branch be compelled to delegate authority because the executive had a monopoly of information or of expertise. Finally, well over half of the Democrats in each house had entered Congress in 1969 or later and had never known a collaborative relationship with a president of their own party.

Nevertheless, inauguration of the new Democratic president did make a difference. Before Carter took office, both foreign affairs committees met with him to press their demand for a collaborative role in making foreign policy. They insisted on full and timely information, and they demanded to be consulted in advance, before policies were formed and commitments made that would make congressional intervention awkward and embarrassing. And the president-elect agreed.[72] An era had passed. To avoid the conflict of the Ford years, he knew he would have to live with the Congress on its terms.

To a large extent, the Congress was satisfied with the flow of information from the Carter administration. The complaints so prevalent in the Nixon and Ford years that the Congress was kept uninformed and then confronted with faits accomplis were still heard,[73] but less frequently, and they were

71. Leslie H. Gelb, *New York Times*, April 19, 1976.
72. Zablocki address, in *Congressional Record*, p. 247.
73. See, for instance, the comments of Representative Lee H. Hamilton and Michael H. Van Dusen, "Making the Separation of Powers Work," *Foreign Affairs*, vol. 57 (Fall 1978), p. 25, that "far too little . . . consultation" preceded the Carter proposal to withdraw U.S. ground forces from

couched in less bitter language. Where Secretary Kissinger had been perceived by many as characteristically devious and secretive, Secretaries Cyrus Vance and Edmund S. Muskie were seen as open and direct. The administration promised to live by the spirit, as well as the letter, of the War Powers. Resolution and kept that pledge to the satisfaction of the legislators. One of the prerequisites for harmony between the branches on foreign policy was on its way to being restored, then, from the beginning of the Carter administration. The Congress had confidence that it at least knew what the executive was doing.

Progress toward a second prerequisite, however—consensus between the branches on the objectives of foreign policy—was not so evident. The Carter administration did make the policy shifts that the most vociferous Democratic critics of Kissinger had been demanding. Carter pledged during the campaign to build his foreign policy on the foundation of a concern for human rights, and he promised to reduce American arms sales abroad and cease supporting repressive military regimes. And, on taking office, he restated these objectives.

But it was easier to announce new policies and goals than to pursue them with consistency, for that would mean elevating them over other established objectives of foreign policy with which they might be at times in conflict. The country was caught in the later 1970s, as in the earlier years of the decade, in innumerable contradictions. It was torn between withdrawal and involvement in Asia and Africa—that is, between the "no more Vietnams" resolve and the long-standing containment policy that had by no means been wholly abrogated. The necessity for "standing up to the Russians" conflicted with détente. So did the emphasis on human rights, when applied to the Soviet Union; pressed on a global scale, human rights clashed with the need for stable allies. The national devotion to Israel confronted the national interest in Arab oil. Many of these contradictions, as Thomas L. Hughes has emphasized, are insoluble and must simply be accepted and managed.[74] Leslie Gelb and Richard Betts, looking back on the Vietnam experience, go further;

Korea and the initiation of discussions to normalize relations with Vietnam. In both cases the president was forced to postpone or modify his plans. Late in 1978 the president caught the Congress by surprise in recognizing the People's Republic of China and denouncing the U.S. defense treaty with Taiwan, resulting in a Senate vote rebuking the president. In 1979, Majority Leader Byrd and other senators expressed annoyance that the president did not consult with them on the handling of the Iranian crisis during the first couple of weeks after the seizure of the U.S. embassy, but Carter promised to correct the "inadvertancy" by holding daily sessions with the leaders of both parties. *Washington Post*, November 18, 1979.

74. "Carter and the Management of Contradictions," *Foreign Policy*, no. 31 (Summer 1978), pp. 34–55.

consensus on any "overarching" foreign policy doctrine, such as containment in the postwar period, is undesirable, they contend, for it leads to rigidity.[75] A doctrine tries to solve the insoluble, by selecting from among conflicting goals in advance, instead of balancing them and deciding case by case.

Yet the implications of all this uncertainty for executive-legislative relations are clear. Possible or not, desirable or not, agreement on the broad objectives and principles that will govern the conduct of foreign policy remains a precondition to the acceptance by the Congress of presidential leadership. If the legislators do not agree with the president on where he intends to drive the foreign policy vehicle, they are unlikely to grant him an unfettered control of the steering mechanism. Moreover, they must have confidence that he as driver knows how to get it there. They must trust not only his objectives but his competence.

In the early Carter years, as exponents within the administration of the various conflicting goals of foreign policy vied with one another, sometimes in public, the administration appeared to vacillate, and the administration's professional capability to produce and carry out a coherent foreign policy came into question.[76] Chairman Zablocki himself felt obliged to write Carter in mid-1978 protesting "confusion and doubt" and "apparently conflicting statements" from the administration on foreign policy matters.[77]

Relations between the branches during the Carter term were marked not, as in the Ford years, by a series of drastic reversals but by a mixture of successes, narrow escapes, minor setbacks, and issues deferred to forestall confrontation. The Congress yielded to the new president in lifting its ban on aid to Turkey and repealing its prohibition of an embargo on the importation of Rhodesian chrome. It approved the results of the multilateral trade negotiations conducted in Geneva in 1978–79. The Senate rebuked Carter in a "sense of the Senate" vote for acting unilaterally to recognize Communist China and terminate the mutual defense treaty with Taiwan—in spite of the Senate's earlier resolution specifically asking the president to consult before any such action—but the Congress accepted the result and passed the nec-

75. Leslie H. Gelb with Richard K. Betts, *The Irony of Vietnam: The System Worked* (Brookings Institution, 1979), pp. 365–69. The authors acknowledge the need for "some doctrine," but advocate "doctrine with escape hatches, doctrine that is susceptible to easy adaptation, that guides rather than restrains, and that does not take on a life of its own"; pp. 366–67.

76. I. M. Destler stresses the importance of congressional confidence in an administration's professional competence. In his view, the failure of the Carter administration to convince the Congress of its administrative capability weakened it especially in the 1979 debate over the Strategic Arms Limitation Treaty.

77. William J. Lanouette, "Who's Setting Foreign Policy—Carter or Congress?" *National Journal*, vol. 10 (July 15, 1978), p. 1122.

essary enabling legislation.[78] The Senate went against powerful constituency pressures to give Carter the benefit of the doubt on the Panama Canal treaties, but this was one of the narrowest of escapes. It was achieved only with enormous effort by the administration, Senate Majority Leader Robert Byrd, and administration supporters on the Foreign Relations Committee, and only after a reservation offered by a Democratic senator barely into his second year, Dennis DeConcini of Arizona, and accepted by President Carter, aroused passionate resentment in Panama and nearly scuttled the treaties. Byrd succeeded in working out a compromise that saved the enterprise, but it was an extraordinarily hard-won victory, and, perhaps, a "severely tarnished" one that did not fully serve the original purpose of strengthening relations with Panama and the rest of Latin America.[79] Heroic efforts were likewise needed to prevent the Congress from reversing the president on other actions. He was able to complete the sale of advanced radar aircraft to Iran in 1977 only after withdrawing the proposal and modifying it. With great effort, Byrd was able to prevent the Senate from repudiating Carter's proposal to withdraw U.S. troops from Korea over a five-year period, leaving the question in abeyance until the president later reversed himself. Carter narrowly escaped defeat on the sale of fighter planes to Saudi Arabia in 1978. His proposal for aid to the revolutionary government of Nicaragua was delayed for eight crucial months in 1979 and 1980. Only by the most intensive lobbying did the administration prevent, by a two-vote Senate margin, reversal of a Carter decision to sell nuclear fuel to India. And the Strategic Arms Limitation Treaty (SALT II) submitted for Senate ratification in 1979 was facing a likely defeat when consideration was suspended following the Soviet invasion of Afghanistan.

Like President Ford, Carter also soon came to complain of the restrictions on his freedom to conduct the country's foreign policy. While some of the constraints that had bedeviled Ford had been lifted, others—notably the

78. The Senate vote, taken June 6, 1979, was 59 to 35 on language expressing the sense of the Senate that approval of that body was required for terminating any mutual defense treaty, but the leadership was able to defer adoption of the resolution pending disposition of a legal challenge filed by Senator Goldwater and others to set aside the president's action. In a decision issued December 13, 1979, the Supreme Court sidestepped the broad constitutional question but allowed the treaty termination to go into effect. The resolution was never finally acted on.

79. I. M. Destler, "Treaty Troubles: Versailles in Reverse," *Foreign Policy*, no. 33 (Winter 1978–79), pp. 46, 52. A paper by I. M. Destler, "Learning from Panama: An Analysis of Executive-Congressional Relations," details the arduous struggle for ratification, involving "literally thousands of contacts with senators" by administration officials or others encouraged by them. Thomas M. Franck and Edward Weisband, *Foreign Policy by Congress* (Oxford University Press, 1979), p. 8, suggest that "on balance" the congressional language may have improved the text by "clarifying several unresolved issues which might have caused friction in the future."

Jackson-Vanik amendment on trade with the Soviet Union and the ban on involvement in Angola—remained. It was the last of these that caused the restriction issue to flare up in the spring of 1978, in the course of another African crisis. Cuban forces in Angola—then estimated at twenty thousand— were threatening an invasion of Zaire, and the CIA, according to news accounts, approached Senator Clark with a suggestion of U.S. aid to the UNITA guerrillas, who were still operating in the southern part of Angola, in order to "tie down" the Cuban troops there. Clark rejected the overture, and the White House, when confronted by reporters, professed no knowledge of it and no intention of intervening again in Angola.[80] But President Carter did tell a news conference that "the tragedy in Zaire as well as other recent developments has caused me to reflect on the ability of our government, without becoming involved in combat, to act promptly and decisively to help countries whose security is threatened by external forces." He said he had asked for a review of existing restrictions and, meanwhile, would resist further ones.[81] But Senate Majority Leader Byrd, among others, reacted testily to the complaint, and the White House soon let it be known that the president was not looking for a confrontation. That year, the Congress banned aid to Cuba, Uganda, Vietnam, and Cambodia. But those countries were not on the administration's assistance list anyway. Restrictions passed by the House to which the administration objected more strenuously were diluted or discarded in House-Senate conference. Again in the next Congress, major legislative struggles ensued on aid to Panama, Turkey, Zaire, Syria, and Somalia, as well as Nicaragua. In the end the president was granted somewhat less discretion and less money than he had sought, and appropriations—including those for contributions to international aid agencies—were seriously delayed.

At the end, Vice President Walter F. Mondale expressed the Carter administration's exasperation in words more than faintly reminiscent of Gerald Ford's. The president, he said, was "enfeebled" in offering aid to other nations.

> I could give you a hundred examples. It took us a year to get the little help we got in Nicaragua. Whatever you think of what's going on down there, certainly the president ought to be able to act decisively. With Pakistan we could only come up

80. Walter Pincus and Robert G. Kaiser, *Washington Post*, May 25, 1978, and Don Oberdorfer, ibid., June 25, 1978. An abortive invasion of Zaire by Zairian guerrilla bands based in Angola did occur, but without Cuban participation. The U.S. airlift of French and Belgian troops to Zaire—the operation that precipitated a War Powers Resolution controversy—contributed to the easy defeat of the guerrillas. In 1981 President Reagan asked the Congress to repeal the Clark amendment.

81. "The President's News Conference of May 25, 1978," *Public Papers of the Presidents: Jimmy Carter, 1978* (GPO, 1979), pp. 971–79.

with a small amount—they called it peanuts. You can say the same of the situation in Liberia, in El Salvador. . . . I wish we'd give a president a fund that he could use quickly, expeditiously, albeit requiring accounting, so that he could be effective and decisive in a crucial area where he cannot be today.[82]

Groping toward Collaboration

Even as the Congress continued to assert itself in foreign policy decision-making, some of its leading spokesmen continued to express the same misgivings about the congressional role that they had begun to articulate in the Ford years. "I recognize that the President is the chief architect of American foreign policy and that we ought not to occupy our time second-guessing the president on every decision he makes," Senator Church said just before assuming the Foreign Relations chairmanship.[83] "The President of the United States is, and must be, the ultimate spokesman of American policy," said House Majority Leader Jim Wright. "He must have sufficient flexibility, and sufficient tools."[84] And House Majority Whip Brademas, a leader in the fight against aid to Turkey, conceded, in the same words Senator Humphrey had used two years before: "Congress cannot—nor should it—run foreign policy on a day-to-day basis. This is a truism."[85]

Then what did they think the role of the Congress ought to be? "Participation" in major decisions, said Humphrey. "Consultation and accommodation of views," said Brademas, quoting Professor Edward S. Corwin. "Collaboration" and "cooperation" were other words running through the long debate. "A genuine dialogue" was Representative Lee Hamilton's goal.[86] Often quoted was the line attributed to Senator Vandenberg: "Let us in on the takeoffs if you want us in on the crash landings." But each of the catchwords begs a host of questions. Consult: with whom? Participate and collaborate and cooperate: on what decisions? in what manner? And if, after all the consultation, views are not accommodated, what then? Who has the last word?

Even the simplest of the principles—full and free and open consultation—turns out on examination to be less simple than it appears. Witness President Ford's claimed difficulty in finding leaders of the Congress when a crisis

82. Interview with Meg Greenfield, *Washington Post*, January 20, 1981.
83. *Washington Post*, December 31, 1978.
84. *Congressional Record*, daily edition, August 3, 1978, p. H7802.
85. "The Role of Congress in American Foreign Policy," address at the American embassy, London, July 6, 1978, in ibid., August 2, 1978, pp. H7762–66.
86. "Foreign Policy: Can Congress Play Effectively?" *Washington Post*, October 25, 1975.

occurred when the Congress was not in session. But consulting just the leaders is no longer enough. Brademas quoted a description, no doubt exaggerated, by a Truman administration official of the consultation process in his day: "We used to call 'Mr. Sam' and Tom Connally, and that was it."[87] In today's decentralized and individualistic Congress, Brademas added, "that's not 'it' any more!" Leadership now can come from anywhere—from obscure, junior members who are not even on the foreign affairs committees. Freshmen congressmen took a leading part in the congressional uprising against Vietnam policy. The key vote on the Panama treaty turned out to be held by a second-year senator with no record of foreign policy concern. The prime mover in the Soviet emigration–trade amendment was a veteran senator but not a member of a committee responsible for either foreign policy or trade. In the Cyprus case, the leadership of the House International Relations Committee was in accord with the administration, but it was outvoted. "Now we virtually have 535 Secretaries of State," complained Representative Broomfield, the committee's ranking Republican, in 1976, "and as Secretary Rusk pointed out, they are all minnows in one bucket." Even if a president and his secretary of state consulted widely, Broomfield protested, "more than ninety per cent of the members of Congress will remain unconsulted, unsatisfied, and unimpressed."[88]

For an administration to protect its measures against adverse floor amendments, therefore, the need for consultation is limitless. Learning from the recent record, the Carter administration extended the consultation process on some major matters far beyond the accustomed limited circle of party and committee leaders. Destler reports that in the months before the Panama treaties were signed, the treaty negotiators and other officials consulted with no fewer than seventy of the one hundred senators on the questions involved—forty-four on the financial arrangements alone.[89] But they learned what other executive branch officials had known before: it is difficult to get legislators to focus their attention on a treaty that has not been written yet. Senators are busy. For the most part, as former Secretary of State Dean Acheson observed, foreign policy questions bring trouble to senators and congressmen, rarely benefit,[90] and Panama was such a case; there was always a chance the treaty would never be negotiated, and if a member put off grappling with it, he might never have to struggle with it at all. There is an

87. "The Role of Congress," p. H7765. Sam Rayburn was speaker of the House and Connally chairman of the Senate Foreign Relations Committee.

88. *Congress and Foreign Policy,* Hearings, pp. 89, 87.

89. "Learning from Panama," p. 3.

90. *Present at the Creation: My Years in the State Department* (Norton, 1969), p. 99.

advantage in remaining uncommitted; it strikes a more judicious posture before one's constituents, and—in some senators' thinking, at least—it affords the opportunity to bargain with the administration for a quid pro quo.

Moreover, consulting members may be fruitless—except in creating good will—because the legislators may simply not know where they stand on matters that are not yet before the public. They are, after all, representatives— both in principle and of necessity. By long habit, they tend to reserve judgment until they have heard from their constituents. "The role of critic after the fact is often more politically rewarding than that of a constructive participant," writes Nicholas deB. Katzenbach, a former under secretary of state. "The temptation in both parties is to let the President assume responsibility, and to let future events determine the length of the coattails."[91] So the administration may consult, but a speaker of the House cannot tell for sure what the views of the body will be, and a committee chairman cannot always advise even as to what the committee will do, because their colleagues—even if they could be sounded out—do not themselves know, until the issue is in the headlines and they have heard from home.

This raises, of course, the question of secrecy. The need for concealment in foreign affairs has no doubt been exaggerated in recent years; yet in times of crisis—or even in the absence of crisis, as in the promotion of human rights—pressure may best be exerted, and threats issued, in private. When private pressure is converted into public threatening, concessions that another state may have been ready to promise the United States often must be repudiated, for domestic reasons and reasons of face—as appears to have been the case with the Soviet Union on the Jewish emigration issue. Similarly, if concessions that this country may be considering in a negotiation are made known prematurely, they may lose their bargaining value. The Congress has a good record on keeping secrets—contrary to the public impression—but only when the circle of consultation is kept relatively small. Yet if consultation is restricted, with those spoken to forbidden to seek counsel with others whose views they are presumed to represent, most of the value of the consultation process is lost. Katzenbach's view is that the advantages of wide congressional participation so outweigh the damage done by the occasional leak that openness in dealing with the Congress should be the general rule. But he acknowledges that there will be exceptions.[92] Openness, of course, would rule out altogether the possibility of again attempting covert operations anywhere.

91. "Foreign Policy, Public Opinion and Secrecy," *Foreign Affairs*, vol. 52 (Fall 1973), p. 14.
92. Ibid., p. 15.

Given these difficulties, consultation can be a time-consuming, frustrating, and sometimes fruitless endeavor. And it vastly complicates the lives of executive branch officials who may exhaust themselves in hammering out agreement among executive agencies and are hardly looking for additional variables to enter into the equation. Nevertheless, genuine consultation has to be pursued as the indispensable basis for any degree of harmony between executive and legislature. The exchange of views broadens the outlook of the participants from both branches.[93] It "often brings to the surface embarrassing facts and sloppy executive branch thinking and thus makes it more difficult to continue policies that make little sense."[94] Moreover, since the day has passed when the executive could simply withhold information from the Congress as the means to guarantee its right of unilateral action, it will usually have everything to gain and nothing to lose by a maximum of consultation, for then it is less likely to be reversed. In any case, almost everybody, at both ends of Pennsylvania Avenue, now endorses the general objective of consultation.

Out of the dialogue between the branches can come, at best, the "accommodation of views" that Brademas identified as the objective. When that is possible, again both branches have all to gain by trying to reach agreement. The more severe dilemma often is that of whom to agree with. When the country is divided on the basic issues of foreign policy, as it has been of late, the Congress will be divided, too. Consultation will discover that. But if the administration reaches an accommodation with one side in a congressional schism, it is bound to open or widen differences with the other side. Administrations, of course, try to bring about an accommodation within the Congress with the help of their party leadership in the two houses, and sometimes— as in the case of Panama—the leadership of both parties. But in the age of congressional individualism, unifying the Congress becomes increasingly difficult. Senator Byrd gets high marks in the Panama treaties' case, but as Destler's analysis shows, the process of communication and negotiation between Senator DeConcini and Panama, with the administration in the middle, was immensely complicated, and the efforts of the middlemen—the White House, the State Department, and the majority leader—carried out under intense time pressure, were not well articulated.[95]

93. The strengths, and weaknesses, of the Congress as a participant in foreign policymaking are summarized by Hamilton and Van Dusen, "Making the Separation of Powers Work," pp. 29–32, and by Douglas J. Bennet, Jr., "Congress in Foreign Policy: Who Needs It?" *Foreign Affairs*, vol. 57 (Fall 1978), pp. 43–45.
94. Gelb with Betts, *Irony of Vietnam*, p. 363.
95. "Learning from Panama," pp. 18–29; also, Destler, "Treaty Troubles," pp. 49–52, 60–61.

If, in the end, the views are accommodated, then all will be well. The country will have a policy that is fully legitimated because the two branches of government have united, and both will be satisfied, presumably, that the action taken is consistent with the nation's broad strategic objectives. But trouble arises when views cannot be accommodated, when after all the consultation and discussion and negotiation the majority of the Congress and the president are still not agreed. That was the problem in the quarrels over Vietnam, Soviet trade, Turkey, Angola, and Rhodesia. In each case, the Congress exercised its ever-present power to do exactly what both Senator Humphrey and Representative Brademas said the Congress cannot and should not do—"run foreign policy." So the right to participate or collaborate becomes the right to decide, whenever the Congress elects to use its power. And leading spokesmen for the legislature have made that point explicit too. "When we think we are right," said Senate Majority Leader Mike Mansfield in 1976, "we will do what we think is right in the matter of holding back appropriations or passing legislation."[96] And two years later John Brademas was saying, "A vigorous and, at times, feisty Congress can check and curb the missteps of the Executive in the life-or-death area of foreign policy." How? Not just by giving advice, as Brademas's own record in cutting off Turkish aid makes clear. He meant, by direct intervention—by "running" foreign policy. That was really the ultimate purpose of all the recent forceful measures enacted by the Congress to assure itself a full and timely flow of information on every aspect of foreign relations.

Here lies the dilemma. When the branches cannot arrive at a common policy to govern a particular set of actions, one or the other branch must prevail, and for either to make the decision unilaterally is less than satisfactory.

Those who argue that in such circumstances the Congress should give way contend that that is the only way the United States can have a foreign policy at all. President Ford made the standard argument: "America can have only one foreign policy," and that can only be the president's. If the Congress imposes its will on the executive, the United States winds up with two policies, one pursued by the administration within the sphere of its discretion, the other by the legislative branch. Or, more accurately, with no policy at all in the broad sense, for the Congress in frustrating a presidential initiative acts simply on the case at hand. It does not define new comprehensive policies or strategies to replace those—assuming they exist—whose application it is rejecting.

96. *Congressional Record,* February 5, 1976, p. 2464.

That would be all right, if broad strategies were unnecessary. But every president and secretary of state since World War II has taken for granted that each element of American foreign policy must be constantly weighed against other elements, on a regional scale at least and, in many cases, in the light of global conflict between freedom and communism. "The central fact," said President Nixon early in his administration, "is the inter-relationship of international events. . . . political issues relate to strategic questions, political events in one area of the world may have a far-reaching effect on political developments in other parts of the globe."[97] In a bipolar world the United States and the Soviet Union were seen as engaged in a gigantic chess game in which each side moved its pawns or pieces according to what would most weaken its opponent's position and protect its own. Pursuing the chess analogy, General George Brown, when chairman of the Joint Chiefs of Staff, put well the problem of congressional "participation" in foreign policy. In the U.S.-Soviet game, he said, one of the players has to contend with a kibitzer who "occasionally reaches in and moves a piece and thereby screws it all up."[98] Vice President Nelson A. Rockefeller's metaphor was the "image of 536 individuals' hands on the tiller of the Ship of State."[99] Or, in a military analogy, conducting foreign policy in the United States can be likened to waging war with competing command headquarters empowered to countermand one another's orders.

At most, moreover, the Congress can take responsibility for only a part of foreign and national security policy, not the whole. Many foreign policy decisions belong to the president under the Constitution, with no provision for congressional participation. The Congress might have found a way to reverse the president's decision to recognize communist China, but only the president could take the affirmative action.

The capture of a *Pueblo* or the seizure of an embassy in Tehran is a crisis for presidential management. The president negotiates with foreign powers, receives and delivers ultimatums, deploys the armed forces, asserts the power and influence of the United States in the domestic politics of other countries. For the Congress to control foreign policy in opposition to a president, its formal and only effective means is legislation—a tool as clumsy now as it

97. "First Annual Report to the Congress on United States Foreign Policy for the 1970's, February 18, 1970," *Public Papers: Nixon, 1970,* p. 179.

98. Speech at the National War College and Industrial College of the Armed Forces, Washington, D.C., May 21, 1976, quoted in *Washington Post*, March 27, 1977.

99. "Supplementary Remarks by Hon. Nelson A. Rockefeller, Vice President of the United States," *Report: Commission on the Organization of the Government for the Conduct of Foreign Policy* (GPO, 1975), p. 237. (Hereafter the Murphy Commission Report, for its chairman, Robert D. Murphy.)

was in the 1930s. General resolutions setting broad objectives (like the Ful-bright-Connally and Vandenberg resolutions of the 1940s) have proved useful, and it can be well argued that the Congress should spend more time debating and establishing these;[100] but when the Congress has tried to govern the conduct of foreign relations by law, as with the Neutrality Acts, the result has not been happy. Foreign policy by statute was no less "awkward" and "often unworkable" in the Ford years, as Senator Church acknowledged. Even in the War Powers Resolution, that symbol of congressional resolve to reduce the president's dominance in foreign and national security affairs, the Congress had to concede the necessity for presidential freedom to act—subject only to a requirement of advance consultation with the Congress and to the possibility of subsequent reversal. If the Congress does not command the whole of foreign and national security policy, then it follows that it cannot hope to integrate it. It can act negatively, to disrupt the policy the president pursues, but it cannot act affirmatively to carry out a comprehensive substitute policy of its own, even if through structural reform it could develop the capacity to create it.

America's best friends abroad have been complaining discreetly for at least a decade that the policies of the United States are inherently unpredictable, that the word of the president cannot be relied on because the Congress may at any time repudiate him, that the United States will not necessarily be able to act in unison in a crisis,[101] that those who negotiate a deal with the executive must be prepared to negotiate it all over again with the Congress—if they can find someone to speak for the Congress. (No fewer than forty senators went to Panama to subject Panamanian officials to questioning and, in some cases, to present demands.) When the president meets at the summit with other heads of state, he alone cannot bargain authoritatively and commit his government. Only if it is assumed that the president of the United States usually makes bad bargains, that flexibility to negotiate is therefore more of a danger than an opportunity, and that there would be more to be lost than gained if he were able to act as a world leader—in forging a common attack by the advanced nations on the world energy problems, for example—can this be considered an advantage.

To all of this, the advocates of congressional assertiveness reply: if the Congress cannot be brought into agreement, the country cannot have a foreign policy anyway. Policies established unilaterally by the executive,

---

100. Bennet so argues in "Congress in Foreign Policy," p. 46.

101. David M. Abshire, former assistant secretary of state, "Foreign Policy Makers: President vs. Congress," *The Washington Papers*, vol. 7, no. 66 (Sage, 1979), p. 5, reports illustrations of the foreign concern.

without congressional support, are not fully legitimated; they are at best tentative, subject to overturn at any time, and hence, from the standpoint of foreign countries, cannot be relied on.

There is no more justification for a unilateral executive policy to be imposed without congressional participation and consent than for the opposite to happen, the argument runs, for an executive policy is just as likely to be ill conceived as a policy initiated by the Congress and imposed on the executive. Anyone who lived through the 1973–76 period when the Congress was regularly countermanding executive decisions is likely to shy away from a blanket judgment that the Congress, however sporadic its attention and fragmented its authority, is necessarily always wrong and the president always right. He also is not likely to take for granted that the executive branch always has a sensible and consistent global strategy and the competence to apply it wisely to individual issues. Executive branch policies are not themselves fully coordinated, given rivalries between executive agencies and officials, and the executive is by no means immune from the domestic ethnic politics that influence the Congress. It was secret and unwise executive policies, not congressionally initiated ones, that dragged the country to its failure in Southeast Asia. Under these circumstances, goes the argument, if the branches are at odds on foreign policy, it would be just as irresponsible for the legislature to abdicate as to assert its own decision.

This is an argument not likely to be settled, because there is too much merit on both sides, and too much historical evidence supporting each. Most objective observers, surely, would agree that the Congress has "screwed things up" at times but has "curbed the missteps of the executive" at other times. One can appropriately counsel congressional self-restraint, recognizing the fundamental truth in the argument that if the country is to "speak with one voice" on the world scene, that voice can only be the president's. Most of the time, most congressmen themselves respect that counsel; they give the president the benefit of the doubt and accept his leadership. The early and middle 1970s were the exception, not the rule.

But there must be a limit to congressional self-restraint, to keep the country from reverting to the imperial presidency that the last two decades have discredited. The fact is that the Constitution did not give the country a single voice in world affairs. It established three separated power centers—a Senate and a House of Representatives as well as a president, and if it gave the executive some exclusive powers it gave the legislative bodies some as well, including the appropriation of funds and, most important, the ratification of treaties. When differences between the branches are profound, the cause will be deep divisions in the country. At such times it is hardly realistic to insist that members of Congress tell their constituencies that, while they disagree with the president, they will not, in the interest of keeping him free of shackles, use the constitutional powers they possess to set things right. They too speak for the country, and will not so easily be hushed.

Parliamentary governments are spared this kind of conflict, for the chief executive—the prime minister—is chosen by the legislature in the first place and, if he loses its support for his policies, he resigns or is removed from office by a vote of no confidence. No such safeguards exist in the American system. A president may come into office lacking any broad experience in foreign and national security affairs, and he can hardly expect to be followed blindly. Trust has to be earned before it will—or should—be given. A president may even be the leader of the party opposed to the majority of the Congress, and to suggest that the members of that majority should naturally and automatically follow as their leader the man who at the next election will be campaigning to turn them out of office is to defy human nature and political reality.

So, while congressional restraint is a reasonable expectation, it is also reasonable to expect that restraint will have its bounds. The key to harmony in foreign affairs is continuous and genuine consultation. If the two branches can reach common understanding of the goals and strategy of foreign policy and on the tactics to be employed to reach them, the president's leadership will be secure and he will be granted relative freedom to conduct foreign relations and handle individual issues as they arise. If differences cannot be resolved, the nation will inevitably speak with more than a single voice and, regrettably but also inevitably, its influence on the course of world affairs will be reduced.

Searching for a Structural Solution

Some of those who have confronted this dilemma—who have deplored the lack of coordination of United States foreign policy—have tried to devise a structural solution. From time to time, suggestions have been advanced that some type of formal link be forged between the branches, by adding congressional members to the National Security Council or creating a new form of executive-legislative council that would force joint discussion of foreign policy and national security if not joint decisionmaking.[102] But such proposals have been dismissed by most of the intended participants in both branches as creating an unwieldy apparatus, one not worth the trouble and the risk if it were only a discussion seminar, and one violating the constitutional principle of separation of powers and restricting the freedom of both branches if it were more than that. During the recent intense conflict between president and Congress, such ideas were not even revived.

Discussion has centered, instead, on improving the ability of the Congress to discharge the greater degree of responsibility it has assumed, by establishing central coordinating machinery within the legislative branch. Two high-ranking members of the foreign affairs committees, Senator Humphrey and Representative Zablocki, introduced legislation in the Ninety-third Congress (1973–74) to create a joint committee on national security matters of the various committees concerned with international and military affairs. The joint committee would consist of Senate and House leaders and the leaders of the standing committees concerned. Those committees would retain their legislative and investigative jurisdictions, but the joint body would oversee the work of the National Security Council, serve as a central repository of national security information, and provide a "more comprehensive framework" to guide the activities of the legislative committees.[103] Humphrey also suggested the joint committee might serve as a "crisis management team" for the Congress.[104]

The idea was given a further boost in 1975 when it was endorsed by the Commission on the Organization of the Government for the Conduct of Foreign Policy, a joint executive-legislative-citizen study group headed by Robert D. Murphy, a retired ambassador. The Murphy Commission envisioned a compact group of no more than twenty members, which would represent the majority and minority leadership of the two houses as well as "the leaders of the key foreign, military, and international economic policy committees from each House."[105] The joint committee would have oversight

102. One proposal, advanced in Francis O. Wilcox, *Congress, the Executive, and Foreign Policy* (Harper and Row, 1971), pp. 157–59, is for a joint executive-legislative committee on national security affairs, consisting of the president, the vice president, cabinet officers and other senior officials, and leading members of the Congress—about twenty in all—that would meet regularly for a "full exchange of views." It would make no decisions.

103. Senator Humphrey, introducing the measure, *Congressional Record*, January 15, 1975, p. 213.

104. Testimony, *Congress and Foreign Policy*, Hearings, p. 172.

105. Twenty members (say, six from the majority party and four from the minority in each house) would have difficulty representing the leadership and the multiplicity of committees involved in foreign and security affairs. Hamilton and Van Dusen counted seventeen House and sixteen Senate committees as having some involvement; "Making the Separation of Powers Work," p. 31.

jurisdiction in the intelligence field (a responsibility assigned to separate select committees on intelligence in the two houses) and would be the point of reception for intelligence information and for the reports required under the War Powers Resolution. Its only legislative responsibilities would be information classification and intelligence.[106]

To create such a central coordinating body, however, would run directly against the temper of a Congress that has been in the midst of diffusing power.[107] Senate Majority Leader Mike Mansfield, a member of the commission, filed a strong dissent to the report, blasting the scheme as inevitably impinging on the authority of existing committees, as squeezing out junior members of Congress, and as liable to "fall under executive dominance" and become "a favorite tool of the executive" for diminishing the scope of congressional oversight.[108] The junior members themselves saw little merit in it. A House International Relations subcommittee headed by Representative Lee Hamilton of Indiana, after general hearings on Congress and foreign policy in 1976, dismissed the proposed joint committee as a "palliative." The body would be cumbersome in size; it would be made up of senior members who would have "many competing interests and commitments"; and it would not deal with the basic problems of executive-legislative relationships, which were not structural but "attitudinal"—on the executive side, the attitude of disdain felt by officials toward congressional participation, and, on the part of the Congress, its members' parochialism, irresponsibility, and lack of sustained interest.[109]

106. Murphy Commission Report, pp. 207–10. Assistant Secretary of State Robert J. McCloskey of the Ford administration endorsed the idea in *Congress and Foreign Policy,* Hearings, p. 57. One advantage he saw was a reduction in "repetitive testimony" by administration witnesses before committees with overlapping jurisdictions. Graham Allison and Peter Szanton, staff members of the Murphy Commission, propose a committeee on interdependence in each house whose jurisdiction would extend beyond security and intelligence matters to encompass economic, political, and technological matters as well; *Remaking Foreign Policy: The Organizational Connection* (Basic Books, 1976), pp. 110–12. Bayless Manning, president of the Council on Foreign Relations, proposes a joint committee on international and domestic affairs, made up of the chairmen and ranking minority members of the committees of both houses concerned with aspects of international, or "intermestic," affairs, that would not have legislative jurisdiction but would review the actions of other committees and make reports to the two chambers; "The Congress, the Executive, and Intermestic Affairs: Three Proposals," *Foreign Affairs,* vol. 55 (Winter 1976–77), pp. 311–14.

107. The Murphy Commission found only 29 percent of House members and 28 percent of senators in a random sample in favor of a somewhat different proposal (to combine the armed services and foreign relations committee into a committee on national security in each house), although a majority approved the idea of a joint executive-legislative committee to exchange information and views. Appendices to the Murphy Commission Report, vol. 5, pp. 135, 170–71.

108. Murphy Commission Report, p. 231. The other congressional representatives on the commission—Senator James B. Pearson, Republican of Kansas, the commission vice chairman, and Representatives Zablocki and Broomfield—indicated no dissent from the recommendation.

109. *Congress and Foreign Policy,* Report of the Special Subcommittee on Investigations of the House Committee on U.S. International Relations, 94 Cong. 2 sess. (GPO, 1976), pp. 2, 21.

Instead of endorsing the joint committee, the subcommittee proposed that the Foreign Relations and International Relations committees be given the broad coordinating role in their respective houses, with the assumption of additional jurisdiction—specifically, over trade—and the right of concurrent or sequential referral of bills affecting foreign policy assigned to other committees. It recommended more joint hearings. It suggested the appointment of joint, bipartisan, ad hoc groups by the leadership to be responsible for consultation with the executive branch on particular crises or problems, which would transfer from the executive to the legislative branch the decision as to which legislators should be consulted. And it revived an old proposal for a question hour, like that in the British House of Commons, when the secretary of state and other cabinet officials would subject themselves to interrogation on the floors of the two houses. But nothing came of these proposals either.

So the Congress, which when it established the National Security Council acknowledged the necessity for integrating foreign and military policy in the executive branch, has created no comparable mechanism for itself. Significantly, even in passing the War Powers Resolution it evaded the question of how its own activities in response to that resolution would be coordinated, and it has ignored, subsequently, even the modest suggestion of the Carter administration that just for the purposes of the consultative provisions of that resolution a central point of contact needs to be established.

The analogy between organizing to integrate foreign policy and organizing to integrate fiscal policy is apparent. When the Congress in 1921 created the Budget Bureau and called for an all-encompassing executive budget, it did not unify to the same degree its own budget and fiscal policymaking processes. For the next half century the Congress acted piecemeal on the president's comprehensive fiscal plan. If it dismantled that plan, it lacked the capacity to substitute an equally well-considered policy of its own. By the 1970s, that was no longer tolerable. The process was reformed. Budget committees were finally established to produce an integrated fiscal program to control the whole range of individual taxing and spending decisions.

What Senator Humphrey, Representative Zablocki, and the Murphy Commission were saying is that piecemeal decisionmaking in the field of foreign policy is no longer tolerable either. In a world where the central fact, as Nixon put it, is "the interrelationship of international events," the Congress, like the executive branch, must have the capability to see the world whole and to interrelate the elements of its own policies when it chooses to reject those that the president has offered. Yet so seasoned a congressional leader as Mike Mansfield feared the creation of such a capability, for the very reason that an integrating committee would, in all likelihood, see the world much as did the president, with the result that it would become his tool—in other words, that the Congress would reject fewer of his proposals. No doubt Mansfield was right; a Congress acting on foreign policy piecemeal, in response to events, in the mood of the moment, without the discipline of broad strategy formulated centrally—yielding, as House Majority Leader Jim Wright put it, to the "many temptations to lash out in anger against past events of which we disapprove," in a "zeal to punish wrongdoing"[110]—is a more assertive Congress. It is likely to be one with a greater impact on the course of history, if that is the criterion. But it is also a less responsible Congress. In the case of the budget, the legislators gave up some of their individual power and their collective impact in the interest of responsibility.

In applying the pattern of the budget process to the national security field, however, practical difficulties immediately arise. First is the jurisdictional problem, the rivalry among the foreign relations committees, the armed services committees, and the many committees dealing with international economic matters. A merger of committees in each house would be hopelessly unwieldy. Internal redistributions of power do not come easily in the Congress; it took a constitutional crisis to bring about creation of the budget committees, and conflicts over foreign policy far more severe than any experienced lately would be required to force the legislators to come to grips with the coordination problem in this field.

A second difficulty in the area of foreign and national security policy is the lack of an integrating instrument like the annual budget. The country does not adopt an all-inclusive foreign policy at regular intervals, though some have proposed that it try to do so. Graham Allison and Peter Szanton suggest that the president prepare biennially "a comprehensive statement of U.S. purposes and commitments in the world, a document that would articulate basic foreign policy goals and specify their relation to proposed and continuing policy."[111] Committees on interdependence in each house would receive and debate the statement and prepare comprehensive congressional responses and propose means of coordinating congressional action accordingly.

The authors of this idea admit that attempts at such basic foreign policy statements by the Eisenhower, Kennedy, and Nixon administrations tended to retreat into meaningless generalities. Perhaps the prospect of intensive congressional review, debate, and response would force the administration

---

110. *Congressional Record*, daily edition, August 3, 1978, p. H7802.
111. *Remaking Foreign Policy*, p. 94.

to speak more concretely, but one may question whether it would be able to go far in that direction—or ought to. Foreign policy goals can be stated and probably agreed on readily enough, but only in general terms. It is in the application of the goals that controversy arises, because goals conflict. And the United States cannot always say in advance which goal will be preferred, in a given case. It can do so when it takes the initiative, as in negotiating treaties or extending assistance to friendly countries. Yet much of foreign policy is not initiative but response, and then policy must be made quickly, adaptively, defensively as well as offensively, and integration can be attained—if at all—only through continuity of decision by the same individuals. A joint committee on national security, or separate interdependence committees, would help to meet the need for continuity of attention, participation, and decision on Capitol Hill. But central leadership would be unacceptable to many; junior congressmen would resist being "squeezed out," as Senator Mansfield recognized. In an effort to get around such concentration of power, the Hamilton subcommittee proposed ad hoc committees, to be created on a crisis-by-crisis basis with varying membership; that, of course, is the very antithesis of policy integration through continuity of attention by the same individuals.

The theoretical case for an integrating mechanism is powerful. It would make genuine consultation with the executive more feasible. It would facilitate an accommodation of views, if not with the entire Congress, at least with its most influential elements. Perhaps Senator Mansfield was right in fearing that a joint committee would come to see the world much as the executive sees it. But the composition of such a committee would be so diverse that deferral to the executive would hardly be automatic and unanimous. In cases where accommodation was reached, the committee would be an instrument for mobilizing and sustaining congressional—and public—support for the common executive-legislative policy. And in instances where accommodation failed and the Congress chose to impose its own decisions, its policies would be conceived with a broader perspective than individual committees and subcommittees now possess.

But there remain crucial questions as to how the mechanism should be designed. The problem of policy integration in the Congress is a universal one, that transcends individual areas even as broad as fiscal or foreign policy. Even if foreign policy in all its aspects—security, economic, political—could be brought together, that would not be enough: international policy must be integrated with domestic policy; or, to slice the universe of interrelated policies along a different axis, the country needs a comprehensive energy policy with both domestic and international elements, and an economic policy with both components. Domestically, it needs a comprehensive urban policy and an environmental policy, and these have to be reconciled with economic policy and fiscal policy, and so on. The problem of policy integration is not, then, one that can be satisfactorily resolved by a series of sectoral actions to establish separate integrating mechanisms. We return to this fundamental structural and behavioral dilemma in chapter 14.

CHAPTER XI

To Tighten Control over Administration: Oversight

IN THE 1970s a new, harsh tone of suspicion and distrust suffused the relations of the Congress with the executive branch. The specific grievances that reached their climax in 1972–73—over impoundment, the conduct of the Vietnam War, executive privilege, reorganization—all sprang from a common attitude within the executive branch, one that to the legislators appeared as arrogance. More than that, members of the Congress and their staffs had been the victims of deception, or so they thought; they had heard half-truths and what appeared to them as outright falsehoods. In their Watergate investigations, they had uncovered crime and malfeasance at the highest as well as at lower levels. Small wonder that during this unhappy decade the long tradition of respect on Capitol Hill for at least the honesty and good intentions of political executives was shattered, and confidence in the expertise and judgment of the career officials of the government was undermined as well. These attitudes were sharpened by the ad hominem animosity of the large Democratic majorities toward a particular Republican president, Richard Nixon, but they continued after Nixon, even after the Republicans had left the White House and a Democrat, Jimmy Carter, came to live there.

In a climate of deep and pervasive distrust, it was not enough for the Congress to reclaim powers that had been allowed to drift away or had been usurped—the war power and the power of the purse, in particular. The Congress felt impelled, also, to move in whatever ways it could to assert tighter control over the executive branch in the exercise of the still vast authority that the executive of necessity retained.

In doing so, the members were responding as well to the pressures of constituency. In the 1970s, opinion polls were revealing an appalling loss of public confidence in all institutions, governmental and nongovernmental, and the Congress was consistently among those held in low esteem. Voters were unhappy about many things within the purview of their representatives—not just Vietnam and Watergate but inflation and, what was seen as one of its causes, the waste and inefficiency in federal spending. A particularly vocal segment of the electorate was inveighing loudly against governmental overregulation, of business, of education, and of local government. For what went wrong, the legislators could not shift the blame wholly to Richard Nixon, or after him to Ford or Carter. "You're in charge there, aren't you?" constituents asked, or implied, with at least a vague sense that the legislators had some kind of ultimate control over the executive.

As the decade progressed, more and more candidates for Congress were responding to popular discontent by promising, more or less explicitly, that they would indeed take charge. They would reduce the size of government, reduce its impact on the citizenry, curb the bureaucrats. "I ran for the Senate in part because I am dedicated to bringing the Federal Government under control," Max Baucus, the young Democratic senator from Montana elected in 1978, told his colleagues. "There is no greater challenge before this Congress than the challenge of bringing the Federal bureaucracy under control. Citizens in Montana, and throughout the country, are fed up with their Federal Government. They believe that it is too large, that it is insensitive to their regional and individual needs, and that it is not accountable to them or their representatives." Abolish outdated agencies, eliminate excessive regulation, reduce bureaucratic red tape, demanded Senator Baucus.[1]

Cutting down the size of government is one thing; Congress can do that, if it is willing to pay the political price. But making the bureaucracy "sensitive" and "accountable" is something else. How can a congressman discharge a mandate from the people to make the bureaucracy accountable to their "representatives"—by which he means, to him? The controls over the bureaucracy that the Congress exercises by constitutional right are put to use only through collective action, which can pose formidable problems to the individual member. And even when the Congress acts collectively, its controls are normally applied either before the fact or after the fact, not during— which is when, usually, they count the most.[2]

---

1. *Congressional Record*, daily edition, June 12, 1979, p. S7465.
2. Weaknesses in the instruments available to the Congress to control the executive are discussed

Before the fact, the Congress can prescribe the processes of administration and impose restraints on the administrators as specifically as it may wish. It can narrowly limit executive discretion, but only subject to grave practical difficulties. It can, at any time, modify any of its own decisions that contributed to making the president the general manager of the executive branch and attempt to exercise management responsibility by statute, assuming that it can find a way around the president's vetoes or muster the votes to override them.[3] Before the fact, also, the Senate has the power to confirm or reject appointees to top administrative posts. But when the laws are passed and the administrators confirmed, discretion passes to the executive branch. Except as the Congress may specify otherwise in the statutes themselves—and what may be specified is an unsettled constitutional issue—the Congress has no enforceable, constitutional right to participate in the exercise of that discretion, or even to be consulted. Through their oversight activities, committees can find out what an agency intends, and they can give advice and make demands, but they cannot impose these over an administrator's resistance, except by going through the whole legislative process to redefine the administrator's discretion. If a member of Congress finds a law maladministered, he can advise, coax, cajole, heckle, harass, and browbeat those who administer it—which is often sufficient, of course—but they are not required to obey his orders, and he cannot dismiss them. Legal directives come only from administrative superiors, through the echelons of the executive branch hierarchy, at whose apex sits the president. And even the president's control may be limited by law, especially in the case of independent regulatory agencies.

After the fact, the Congress has a virtually unlimited oversight authority, to review, examine, and investigate—the limitation being only the undefined boundaries of executive privilege. In its oversight capacity, exercised through committees and subcommittees, the legislators can call any official to account for any action, or lack of action. These bodies, and individual members, possess so many means of making life miserable—or pleasurable—for officials that they can often control administration simply by making suggestions. But if the administrators resist, the only recourse is new legislation, always a cumbrous process and one always subject to the presidential veto.

in James L. Sundquist, "What Happened to Our Checks and Balances," in Charles Roberts, ed., *Has the President Too Much Power?* (Harper's Magazine Press, 1974), pp. 96–108.

3. The one limit on congressional control over administration that had been enforced by the Supreme Court is the prohibition against the legislators' laying formal claim to the appointive and removal powers that inhere in the executive. In 1974 the Congress tried again to invade that sphere when it established the Federal Elections Commission. Of six members, two were to be appointed by the speaker of the House and two by the president pro tempore of the Senate. The Supreme Court ruled that provision unconstitutional in *Buckley* v. *Valeo*, 424 U.S. 1 (1976).

This, then, is the frustration of legislators with regard to the administration of the laws: they cannot ordinarily anticipate, and so take measures to forestall, administrative actions of which they disapprove; they lack information and authority to intervene while the action is going on; and while they can punish administrators afterward, and propose corrective legislation, by then the damage will have been done.

Difficulties of Before-the-Fact Control

As the Congress pushed and probed for ways to bring the execution of the laws under tighter supervision in the Nixon and post-Nixon years,[4] it learned again what earlier Congresses had known—that the traditional before-the-fact controls offered only limited opportunity for strengthening.

In the review of nominees for executive positions, Senate committees did introduce more systematic procedures and more rigorous examinations.[5] To guard against conflict of interest, most committees required full disclosure by appointees of their assets and income. With larger committee staffs, investigations were more thorough. Nominations were held long enough to permit interest groups to provide information and register their views. The Democratic majority of the Senate Commerce Committee, in particular, toughened its standards; in 1973, committee Democrats persuaded the Senate to reject a regulatory agency nominee for the first time since 1950, and within the next three years it could claim five more rejections.[6] A few other Nixon and Ford nominees to executive posts were rejected by other committees. The Congress in 1973 extended Senate confirmation to two important positions—the director and deputy director of the Office of Management and Budget—that had been exempt from approval because of the closeness of their relation to the president.

But this flurry of activity had a partisan tone, and when a Democratic president took office in 1977, his nominations did not appear to be subjected

4. Though the impulse toward tighter control was especially marked in the 1970s, it predated that decade. Richard E. Neustadt, "Politicians and Bureaucrats," in David B. Truman, ed., *The Congress and America's Future* (Prentice-Hall, 1965), pp. 105–06, discusses the congressional "reach for control" of the expanding bureaucracy, expressed in efforts to control appointments, annual authorization of agencies and programs, and multiplication of requirements for "committee clearance" of agency decisions. The object was "bread-and-butter for home districts."

5. G. Calvin Mackenzie, "Senate Confirmation Procedures," in *Committees and Senate Procedures*, papers prepared for the Commission on the Operation of the Senate, 94 Cong. 2 sess. (U.S. Government Printing Office, 1977), pp. 103–06.

6. Senator Warren G. Magnuson, Democrat of Washington and Commerce chairman, *Congressional Record*, March 22, 1976, p. 7310.

to any more searching scrutiny than had been given by earlier Democratic Congresses to appointees of Democratic presidents. Only one major nomination had to be withdrawn—Theodore C. Sorensen as director of the Central Intelligence Agency—and late in 1977 the reform organization Common Cause could chastise the Senate for becoming once more a rubberstamp machine.[7] Earlier that year, when President Carter's first budget director, Bert Lance, was forced to resign after information on his record as a Georgia banker came to light, members of the Senate Governmental Affairs Committee were embarrassed at how cursory had been their confirmation proceeding.

More rigorous examination might conceivably have blocked the Lance appointment, though under the circumstances of Lance's close personal friendship with Carter it would have been at an enormous cost in goodwill between the branches. Yet few nominees have backgrounds that, even under the most stringent investigation, would disqualify them. The problem facing senators is not how to detect past misbehavior but how to predict future conduct, by people whose records are unblemished. Looking back at the long roster of officials implicated in the crimes of Watergate—many of whom were confirmed in 1969—one can reasonably conclude that no matter how searching the Senate's examination process might have been and how exacting the standards applied, every one of them would still have been confirmed, because no one then could possibly have foreseen how they would behave in office. Senators cannot divine which executive officials are going to display bad judgment, fail to lead or control the agencies they head, or abuse their power.

So, beyond screening out the few cases where conflict of interest or impropriety is obvious, they can do little more than exact promises from nominees to respect the prerogatives of the Congress and to report to it fully and honestly, then approve them and take their chances. If senators were allowed to reverse their initial judgment—to unconfirm the nominees, so to speak, by the simple majority vote that confirmed them in the first place (as distinct from the extremely difficult impeachment process)—they would have a powerful control indeed, but that authority is quite wisely denied them by the Constitution. In its absence, the confirmation process can never be more than a weak instrument for controlling the executive branch.

7. *The Senate Rubberstamp Machine: A Common Cause Study of the U.S. Senate's Confirmation Process* (Washington, D.C.: Common Cause, 1977). The study concluded that none of the committees reviewing fifty major Carter nominations did a "thorough job." Summarized in Bruce Adams and Kathryn Kavanaugh-Baron, *Promise and Performance: Carter Builds a New Administration* (Lexington, 1979), pp. 162–69. In 1981, when the administration and the Senate were both controlled by the Republicans, the term seemed still appropriate. None of President Reagan's initial appointments was rejected or forced to be withdrawn.

As legislators cannot foretell how administrators will behave, neither can they foresee the problems the executives will confront, and that defines the obstacles to tightening control through the other before-the-fact instrument available—by restricting administrative discretion and constraining administrators by law. In the 1970s, they may have tried harder to do that. Some executives and former executives have seen in recent statutes a pronounced trend in the direction of greater restraint on the freedom of administrators. John Quarles, deputy administrator of the Environmental Protection Agency (EPA), for instance, discerned "recent ballooning in the length of statutes." Whereas earlier enactments had "set forth general principles of law, the modern style of legislation is to spell out all the details."[8] Assistant Attorney General Patricia Wald, like Quarles, associated the trend toward more specific legislation with the proliferation of congressional staff.[9] On the other hand, Hale Champion, on resigning as under secretary of health, education, and welfare in 1979, criticized the Congress for mandating a program to protect the rights of the handicapped with but "one line" of statutory language. "They're frequently very unhappy with what we do after they give us a mandate like that," said Champion. "But the trouble is, the mandate is broad, they deliberately are ambiguous where there is conflict on details and they leave it to us to try to resolve the ambiguities."[10]

Whether or not statutes are, on the whole, becoming more restrictive, the Congress would encounter severe practical obstacles if, as a matter of principle, it tried to make its delegations specific.[11] Clearly, it cannot always anticipate the circumstances that will arise in the administration of its laws and prescribe the solutions in advance. If wages and prices have to be controlled, for instance, the Congress can hardly decide which wages and prices should be controlled and which exempted, and when the controls

8. "Runaway Regulation? Blame Congress," *Washington Post*, May 20, 1979.

9. Juan Cameron, "The Shadow Congress the Public Doesn't Know," *Fortune*, January 15, 1979, p. 42.

10. Interview with Linda Demkovich, *National Journal*, vol. 11 (June 16, 1979), p. 998. Champion's reference to "one line" was only mild hyperbole; he referred to sec. 504, P.L. 93-112, 87 Stat. 394 (1973), which is a single sentence five lines long.

11. Theodore J. Lowi, in support of the ideal of a "rule of law," argues that presidents are "virtually obliged to veto a congressional enactment whenever Congress has not been clear enough about what should be executed, and how." Yet he concedes that the need for delegation of power to administrative agencies could never be eliminated. *The End of Liberalism: The Second Republic of the United States*, 2d ed. (Norton, 1979), pp. 301–02. Not since the 1930s has the Supreme Court invalidated a statute because of an excessive delegation of legislative power. For a view that broad delegations of administrative discretion are never justified and that the courts should once again insist that clear standards be established by the Congress to control administrators, see Joel L. Fleishman and Arthur H. Aufses, "Law and Orders: The Problems of Presidential Legislation," *Law and Contemporary Problems*, vol. 40 (Summer 1976), pp. 1–45, and Paul Gewirtz, "The Courts, Congress, and Executive Policy-Making: Notes on Three Doctrines," ibid., pp. 46–85. The constitutional history of the issue is reviewed in Sotirios A. Barber, *The Constitution and the Delegation of Congressional Power* (University of Chicago Press, 1975).

should be applied and when removed, and, having so decided, act in time. Even in less difficult instances, if committees and subcommittees deliberately choose ambiguity, the Congress is helpless to devise the restraints and standards on the House and Senate floors. Many reasons may lead committees to choose such a course. They may lack time, expertise, or dedication required to write a detailed law. Or members may simply foresee far more political trouble if they make the hard decisions themselves than if they "pass the buck" to the administrators. As Senator Bob Packwood, Republican of Oregon, put it: "We can delegate powers to the President, then sit back and carp or applaud, depending on whether what he does is popular or unpopular. If it's unpopular, we can say, 'What a terrible thing. We wouldn't have done that.'"[12]

Moreover, when the Congress does try to resolve the difficult questions itself, the law it produces is liable to be unworkable. Quarles described the EPA as a "regulatory juggernaut" operating "at excessive speeds and often out of control"—not by bureaucratic choice but because of rigid specifications in the law. Against its better judgment, in response to court orders interpreting precise statutory language, the EPA has had to write unrealistic regulations and impose unmeetable deadlines, Quarles contends, but the bureaucracy—not the Congress or the courts—gets the blame. "Detailed new requirements" in the law "applied with nationwide rigidity . . . predictably . . . make no sense in certain individual cases."[13] In an amendment to the Food and Drug Act, the Congress established a rigid standard for control of carcinogens: any substance found to cause cancer in laboratory animals should be outlawed. When the Food and Drug Administration found it had no choice but to ban saccharin, the resulting outcry forced the Congress to enact another law to defer the application of its standard to this one substance. Obviously, while an occasional case can be decided expeditiously by the full Congress, not many can. The only way to avoid such a necessity is to grant some degree of authority to administrators to exercise their judgment.

Limitations in After-the-Fact Control

Whatever the extent of discretion granted, there is always the chance that—in the eyes of some congressmen and the groups they represent—it will be abused. In giving authority to the Occupational Safety and Health

12. *Time*, January 15, 1973, p. 15.
13. *Washington Post*, May 20, 1979. The point is amplified in John Quarles, "Federal Regulation of New Industrial Plants" (1979), p. 4.

Administration, asks Representative Elliott H. Levitas, Democrat of Georgia, "did Congress intend that an employer would be fined because the fire extinguisher was too high off the ground?"[14] Congressional hearing records are full of horror stories of purported bureaucratic excess.[15] To challenge the administrators, if they do not yield to the congressional complaints, the aggrieved lawmakers may go to court just like any other citizens. But court processes are slow and costly, and the courts have traditionally given administrators the benefits of any doubt. Moreover, if the issue is not one of defiance of the law but only disagreement as to what is proper public policy within the boundaries of the law, not even the courts offer recourse. In the absence of a legislative veto, the aggrieved lawmakers are left to try somehow to correct matters by using their normal legislative powers—or threatening to use them—after the injury, if any, has been suffered.

And here they may be thwarted also, because the legislative devices available to the Congress have obvious difficulties and limitations. Sometimes, the Congress can penalize a transgressing agency by cutting its budget, or even by abolishing the agency. But if the agency's activity—such as tax collection—is essential, the question is how to change the behavior of its administrators. Sometimes, if the Congress does not like an agency's policy, it can amend the law to provide more explicit statutory direction for the future. But this risks the rigidity of detail that John Quarles complained of. Moreover, while the Constitution gives the Congress no share in executing the laws, it does give the president a part in their enactment—his veto. If the president insists on his policy preference and rejects the Congress's corrective legislation, he can usually muster the votes of one-third plus one of the membership of one house that is all he needs to sustain him. Even Nixon, facing an almost unprecedented level of hostility in a Congress dominated by the opposing party, was overridden only seven times in forty-three vetoes. The Congress can often, of course, circumvent the president's veto power by attaching an unwanted provision to an appropriations bill, an authorization bill, or some other measure that the president—particularly at the end of a session—is compelled to sign. But such a legislative vehicle is not always available.

So the Congress has to fall back on indirect instruments of control. It can expose and investigate, hoping that the media will pay attention and public opinion will be rallied to its side. And its offended members can exert many

14. Testimony, July 11, 1979, in *Regulatory Reform and Congressional Review of Agency Rules*, Hearings before a subcommittee of the House Rules Committee, 96 Cong. 1 sess. (GPO, 1980), p. 5.

15. See examples in John R. Bolton, *The Legislative Veto: Unseparating the Powers* (Washington: American Enterprise Institute for Public Policy Research, 1977), pp. 15–17.

kinds of informal pressure, backed up by threats to use their various formal powers—a kind of legislative blackmail. They can threaten to hold up the president's appointments, or legislation he most desires, or to cut budgets for his favorite programs. Often the threat suffices. The executive normally needs and wants the goodwill of the Congress, individually and collectively, and will pay some price to get it—especially when the president and the congressional majorities are of the same party, but even when they are not. So the executive branch will bargain, and sometimes its ways will be changed.

But if the executive is adamant—as Nixon was in 1972–73—the course of legislative blackmail is a hard one. The protesting legislators find threats of retaliation difficult to make credible, and to carry out. The members who are most distressed by the administration of a particular program will not be the ones necessarily in the best position to hold hostage some other program or appointment. The president may well turn out to have the stronger bargaining position—more favors to grant or withhold from the legislators, in projects and in patronage, than they have to withhold from him. In any case, the Congress is not organized to bargain effectively with the presidency. Decentralized into its multiplicity of committees and subcommittees, its members have no way of arriving at a common strategy to combat an executive branch that, while fragmented also, can be centrally led and directed in times of confrontation. And the members of the legislature have not delegated to their leaders the responsibility to strike deals in their behalf.

Moreover, much of what concerns the members of the Congress and their constituents about administration is not the subject of intense, high-level confrontation. The conduct of inspectors of the Occupational Safety and Health Administration, or the content of the regulations of the Consumer Product Safety Commission, is not the stuff of constitutional crises. Nor does it appear to the Congress to be even the stuff of presidential attention, and that is a large part of the problem. If the president had the means and the time to find out what was going on, they believe—if only he knew what they know—he would be bound to agree with them. Then, if he had the means and the time to make his will felt down the long echelons of the bureaucratic hierarchy, he would make the necessary changes—except as the statutory independence of some regulatory agencies would limit him.[16] But he has

16. There is also a legal question as to the president's authority to overrule subordinates in organizations not considered independent, such as the Environmental Protection Agency and the Department of the Interior, when the laws put the power to issue regulations in the heads of those agencies. His clear prerogative to remove offending officials, however, gives him extralegal means of making his will prevail. President Carter in 1978 established a mechanism for presidential review of regulations that have significant economic impact; no information on its implementation is available.

neither. To the legislators, as to their constituents, the bureaucracy often appears to be controlled by nobody, neither by the Congress nor by the president. And if that is the case, somebody needs to control it—not before the fact when the problems cannot be anticipated, not after the fact when the damage has been done, but during the fact.

It is a short step in reasoning from that point for congressmen to conclude that as elected representatives of the people, they should be the controllers. The president, too, is elected but he is remote and inaccessible and too easily becomes the captive of his bureaucracy. Members of Congress are "the human connection between the citizen and his Government," says Representative Levitas, a leading sponsor of measures to tighten congressional control of administration; "we are his Government. . . . It is making the public cynical [to] think their Government is being run by unelected officials." Concurs Senator Sam Nunn, Democrat of Georgia: "The reason people are losing confidence in Government is because they see their elected officials are unable to really get much done. . . . But they see that the bureaucracy is able to make profound decisions every day, whether they agree with them or not."[17]

To get something done, the Congress in the 1970s developed two broad approaches. One was to systematize and intensify its traditional function of oversight of governmental programs by the responsible congressional committees—predominantly an after-the-fact review but sometimes before the fact as well. The other was the expanded use of a relatively new device that by the end of the 1970s had become hotly controversial—the legislative veto.

The Intensification of Congressional Oversight

When the House Select Committee on Committees held its hearings on structural reform of the House of Representatives in 1973, no single weakness commanded more attention than "the failure . . . really to engage . . . in anything like the beginning of an adequate oversight function," according to its chairman, Richard Bolling of Missouri.[18] "Not sufficient oversight"; "the greatest shortcoming of Congress today"; "I felt very strongly our committee was not doing a good job on oversight"; "Congress has been derelict"; "Congress is just barely making a scratch on the oversight of the executive

17. *Regulatory Reform and Congressional Review,* Hearings, p. 16; *Regulatory Reform,* Hearings in June–July 1979 before a subcommittee of the Senate Judiciary Committee, 96 Cong. 1 sess. (GPO, 1980), pp. 116–17.
18. *Committee Organization in the House,* Hearings before the House Select Committee on Committees, 93 Cong. 1 sess. (GPO, 1973), vol. 3, p. 320, quoted by Roger H. Davidson and Walter J. Oleszek, *Congress Against Itself* (Indiana University Press, 1977), p. 99.

branch on any one year" were some of the comments of House members during the hearings.[19]

They spoke at a time when Senator Sam Ervin's Watergate investigating committee was every day uncovering new details of the secret, scandalous conduct of executive branch officials. One of its major responsibilities, the Bolling committee concluded, must be to improve oversight—to develop means to "systematically assess the quality" of governmental programs "in a responsible and effective way," as Representative John C. Culver, Democrat of Iowa, put it. "If there is any disenchantment in the country," said Culver, "it derives from the validity of the thought that in this respect Congress is pathetic."[20] The neglect of oversight was still as apparent as it had been in 1946, when the Legislative Reorganization Act first specifically mandated "continuous watchfulness" by standing committees of the administration of programs, or in 1965, when Senator A. S. Mike Monroney, Democrat of Oklahoma, one of the authors of the 1946 act, could assert that "regular committee oversight . . . is not carried out to any degree whatever."[21] And the need had grown, as more and more discretion was delegated to executive branch officials.

The solution the Bolling committee proposed was to assign clear responsibility to special oversight groups who would be separate from the legislative committees and subcommittees. The Government Operations Committee, given a governmentwide investigating authority by the Legislative Reorganization Act of 1946, would be made broadly responsible for coordinating oversight activities of all committees. At the opening of each Congress, Government Operations—in consultation with the majority and minority leadership and standing committee chairmen—would issue an oversight report, which would review the plans of each standing committee and make its own recommendations as to priorities. In addition, six committees would be given special oversight responsibilities for program areas that overlapped standing committees' jurisdictions. Finally, each standing committee (except Appropriations) would be required to create an oversight subcommittee separate from the legislative subcommittees. The findings of the Government Operations Committee and of the oversight subcommittees in their appraisal of individual programs would be required to be incorporated in committee reports on authorizing and appropriating legislation.[22] These proposals were

19. *Committee Reform Amendments of 1974*, H. Rept. 93-916, 93 Cong. 2 sess. (GPO, 1974), p. 63.

20. June 13, 1973, in *Committee Organization in the House*, Hearings, vol. 2, pp. 15–16.

21. Hearings of the Joint Committee on the Organization of Congress, 1965, quoted by Morris S. Ogul, *Congress Oversees the Bureaucracy: Studies in Legislative Supervision* (University of Pittsburgh Press, 1976), p. 13.

22. *Committee Reform Amendments of 1974*, H. Rept. 93-916, pp. 63–70.

adopted by the House in 1974, except that the standing committees were given the option of creating special oversight committees or assigning the responsibility to their regular subcommittees. As of 1979, the alternative methods were being used about equally.

Congressional oversight, as defined in the rules adopted in 1974, is an information-gathering function; "review and study" are the operative words. Oversight encompasses the efforts of the Congress to find out, after a law is passed, what happens as a consequence, and its purpose as stated in the rule is to enable the Congress to determine the need for modifying existing law or enacting new law. In practice, some review and study activities have only a remote legislative intent; they may be undertaken to influence the way in which officials administer the law, or their object may be to expose misconduct. But it is useful to limit the term *oversight* to information-gathering and use other terms to denote the wide range of actions that may be undertaken on the basis of the information; otherwise much of the legislative process itself is encompassed under the heading of oversight.[23]

Oversight activities may range from informal staff inquiries and casual or incidental information-gathering to formal oversight hearings, reauthorization and appropriations hearings, investigations, and evaluation studies. While oversight is largely after the fact, it is sometimes used to examine an agency's plans and intentions as well as past conduct, and through casework and inquiries about project applications, it may have an influence on individual decisions and transactions as they occur.[24] In either case, any action growing out of oversight, except legislation, is always, in a legal sense, advisory; even though administrators may heed suggestions made in oversight hearings and reports or in informal communications or even "sense of the Congress" resolutions growing out of oversight, they are not compelled by law to do so.

23. Rule X (b) (1), as written in 1974, assigns "general oversight" duties in these words: "Each standing committee . . . shall review and study, on a continuing basis, the application, administration, execution, and effectiveness of those laws . . . within the jurisdiction of that committee and the organization and operation of the Federal agencies having responsibilities in or for the administration and execution thereof, in order to determine whether such laws and the programs thereunder are being implemented and carried out in accordance with the intent of the Congress and whether such programs should be continued, curtailed, or eliminated." Common usage on Capitol Hill tends to include at least some types of action, in addition to information-gathering, under the heading of oversight. So does much of the scholarly writing on the subject. Ogul's definition of oversight—"behavior by legislators and their staffs, individually or collectively, which results in an impact, intended or not, on bureaucratic behavior" (*Congress Oversees*, p. 11)—seems both too narrow and too wide. It excludes information-gathering that does not happen to have an impact on bureaucratic behavior but encompasses all activity of legislators and their staffs that does have an impact, presumably including even the enactment of laws.

24. See John R. Johannes, "Casework as a Technique of U.S. Congressional Oversight of the Executive," *Legislative Studies Quarterly*, vol. 4 (August 1979), pp. 325–51.

Oversight was neglected, congressmen and political scientists had told the Bolling committee, because members found the function politically unrewarding in relation to the time and effort that were required. It was tedious work, often technical, requiring careful preparation to be done well. The government was too big, anyway, for "continuous watchfulness" of more than a small fraction of its activities. Except in instances where the prospect of gaining headlines through exposing misconduct existed, oversight therefore had little appeal to the typical senator or representative. And even in those cases, committees might be deterred by considerations of party loyalty, if the administration and the congressional majority were of the same political persuasion, or by fear of interest groups that might be offended. Or committee members might be deterred by the cozy relations that often exist between the overseer and the overseen. Thus the chairman of the House Agriculture Committee, W. R. Poage of Texas, expressed a deep reluctance to engage in intensive review of Department of Agriculture programs: "About all we would accomplish, as I see it, is to create hard feeling, a loss of confidence on the part of our farmers that the Department of Agriculture could render them a service, because we can be so critical of the Department . . . that there won't be any farmer in the nation that will have any confidence."[25]

Nevertheless both houses devoted more effort to oversight, spurred by the reforms of 1974, responsive to the rising popular clamor against government that marked the whole decade of the 1970s, and facilitated by the growth in the number and independence of subcommittees and the expansion of their staffs. The Congress also steadily broadened the operations of its general investigatory and oversight agency, the General Accounting Office, which made twice as many reports on executive branch activities in 1976–80 as in 1966–70, testified before committees five times as often, and attempted far more comprehensive program evaluations than before.[26]

In the first half of 1975, House committees and subcommittees spent two-thirds again as many days in oversight hearings and meetings as they did in the corresponding period in 1973 and more than three times as many as in the first half of 1971. The Senate, which had taken no formal action to

---

25. *Committee Organization in the House,* Hearings, vol. 1, p. 66, quoted in Davidson and Oleszek, *Congress Against Itself,* p. 98. The barriers to effective oversight are well summarized in Ogul, *Congress Oversees,* chap. 1; *Study on Federal Regulation,* S. Doc. 95-26, 95 Cong. 1 sess. (GPO, 1977), vol. 2, chap. 9; and in Walter J. Oleszek, "Toward a Stronger Legislative Branch," *The Bureaucrat,* vol. 3 (January 1975), pp. 456–58. See also Allen Schick, "Congress and the 'Details' of Administration," *Public Administration Review,* vol. 36 (September/October 1976), pp. 520–22. A new comprehensive analysis of congressional oversight of committee activities is in preparation by Joel D. Aberbach of the Brookings Institution.

26. U.S. General Accounting Office, *Annual Report, 1980,* pp. 1, 4.

emphasize oversight, showed a slightly smaller increase in oversight activity.[27] In both houses, committees and subcommittees were devoting more than one-sixth of their hearing and meeting days to oversight in 1975, compared to about one-ninth two years earlier. Because "most everyone is getting into the act in a bigger way than before," the specialized oversight units accounted for only part of the House increase.[28] By 1977, the proportion of all House hearings devoted to oversight had risen to 34 percent, and two years later the figure was 39 percent, according to a report released by Speaker O'Neill.[29]

Moreover, the Congress was more frequently requiring that administrative agencies notify the appropriate committees in advance of contemplated actions, so that the committees could call hearings, if they chose, and so bring their influence to bear informally in a timely fashion, or initiate preventive legislation. Usually the law specified a waiting period, typically of thirty or sixty days, between the time of the notification and the date when the action would take effect. In 1978 alone, the Congress enacted thirty-six such report-and-wait provisions, the most significant and controversial covering all regulations of the Department of Housing and Urban Development, and others such diverse matters as relocation of activities among military installations, the terms of contracts for energy production facilities on military property, extension of foreign aid to countries in violation of human rights, and revisions of the boundaries of national parks. Between 1973 and 1979 the Congress employed the notification device ninety-five times, more than twice as many as in the entire preceding four decades.[30]

Despite all this intensification of effort, the barriers to effective oversight that were noted in the 1973 hearings had by no means been swept away. A Senate committee concluded in 1977 that "Congress still lacks a continuous, systematic oversight process; Congress oversees in an episodic, erratic manner."[31] A House study in the same year found that very few of the members

27. The Temporary Select Committee to Study the Senate Committee System, chaired by Senators Adlai E. Stevenson, Democrat of Illinois, and William E. Brock, Republican of Tennessee, recommended in 1977 that Senate committees be assigned broad oversight responsibilities that might, on occasion, extend beyond their specific assigned legislative areas. This proposal was adopted, but a recommendation that each committee be required to publish annually an account of its oversight activities and plans for the coming year was not acted on. A recommendation by the Commission on the Operation of the Senate in 1976 that the Governmental Affairs Committee be given a general responsibility to monitor oversight activities of all committees was also shelved.

28. Joel D. Aberbach, "Changes in Congressional Oversight," *American Behavioral Scientist*, vol. 22 (May/June 1979), pp. 493–515.

29. "Congressional Oversight," *National Journal*, vol. 12 (January 12, 1980), p. 70. O'Neill's definition of an oversight hearing may not be identical with Aberbach's.

30. Clark F. Norton, "Congressional Review, Deferral and Disapproval of Executive Actions: A Summary and an Inventory of Statutory Authority," report 76-88 G (Congressional Research Service, April 30, 1976), as supplemented by his reports 78-117 Gov (CRS, May 25, 1978), 79-46 Gov (CRS, February 12, 1979), and 80-86 Gov (CRS, April 17, 1980).

31. *Study on Federal Regulation*, S. Doc. 95-26, vol. 2, p. 94.

thought the House did a "very effective" job of oversight and only one of six spent "a great deal of time" on it.[32] Chairman Bolling of the House Rules Committee observed in 1979 that members still had "no political incentive" for comprehensive and systematic oversight.[33] Representative Bill Frenzel, Republican of Minnesota, deploring the lack of public confidence in government in 1979, could still cite as one reason "the total failure of congressional oversight."[34] The job was still impossibly large, and of necessity could only be done spottily, and the subjects to be covered would still be chosen on the basis of public interest and attention. An obscure agency such as the General Services Administration, where mismanagement and corruption came to light in 1978, had not been the subject of congressional oversight for years, Representative John F. Seiberling, Democrat of Ohio, reported.[35] A large share of oversight activities still was designed to promote and protect, rather than critically review, particular programs; Representative John Brademas, the majority whip, announced hearings on programs to aid the handicapped with a frank acknowledgment that "I'm interested in expanding its appropriations." The House Government Operations Committee had not assumed the leadership role assigned it in 1974; its annual report simply compiled the reports of the various House committees, with no attempt to appraise them, and it did not advise or assist the other committees. Speaker O'Neill could declare that "America is crying for us to put oversight to work, and that is what we are going to do in this Congress," and the House Democratic caucus could formally resolve that its committees and subcommittees "shall vigorously pursue oversight," as both did early in 1979,[36] but providing the political incentive for the subcommittee members to devote a greater portion of their time and effort to so unglamorous, tedious, and unrewarding an aspect of their duties was another matter.

One widely supported scheme for forcing committees to attend to oversight was sunset legislation. Passed in 1978 by the Senate, but blocked in the House, sunset legislation would impose a time limit on the life of programs

32. Thomas E. Cavanagh, "The Two Arenas of Congress: Electoral and Institutional Incentives for Performance," paper prepared for the 1978 annual meeting of the American Political Science Association, pp. 24, 29; tables 4, 10. A poll of 153 House members undertaken by the House Commission on Administrative Review found that only 4 percent judged the House's oversight performance as "very effective," 18 percent "fairly effective," 33 percent "only somewhat effective," and 44 percent "not very effective." While 56 percent considered oversight activities "very important," only 16 percent spent "a great deal of time" on them. Cavanagh attributes the neglect of oversight to the absence of demand for it from the members' constituencies.

33. Richard E. Cohen, "Will the 96th Become the 'Oversight Congress'?" *National Journal*, vol. 11 (January 13, 1979), p. 45.

34. *Congressional Record*, daily edition, June 12, 1979, p. H4411.

35. Cohen, "Will the 96th?" p. 49. Oversight activities are not likely, however, to uncover misconduct not already exposed by law enforcement agencies or the media.

36. Ibid., pp. 44, 47.

and agencies, thus necessitating a periodic review. Skeptics observed that a sunset law would not solve the problem of motivation. It would not prevent a committee uninterested in oversight from making only a cursory, pro forma review, and the already overwhelming workload of the Congress would be increased with little advantage. Concern for the added burden was probably decisive in checking the measure again in the Ninety-sixth Congress of 1979–80. Meanwhile, however, the same end was being achieved piecemeal, as authorizing committees came routinely to fix time limits on all new agencies and programs, extend the limits to many established ones, and shorten the time periods, until the ultimate was being reached—annual authorizations for whole departments.[37]

Lifting the Shrouds of Secrecy

One feature of the post-Watergate oversight explosion was that committees began intensive reviews of agencies whose activities had hitherto been hidden in secrecy. An amendment to the 1974 foreign aid bill required that all covert actions of that most secret of all agencies—the Central Intelligence Agency (CIA)—be reported "in a timely fashion" to the "appropriate committees" of the Congress, and the agency accepted the claims of four committees in each house to fall within that definition.[38] The next year, both houses created select committees to examine the operations of the CIA and other intelligence organizations; the Senate committee termed its study "the only thorough investigation ever made of the United States intelligence," [39] and the House

37. The State Department was the first to be so covered, in 1971; the Justice Department and the Central Intelligence Agency and other intelligence agencies followed in 1976. By the end of the decade, 10–15 percent of federal expenditures were covered by annual authorization. Allen Schick, *Congress and Money: Budgeting, Spending and Taxing* (Washington: Urban Institute, 1980), pp. 171–72.

38. The amendment, sponsored by Senator Harold E. Hughes, Democrat of Iowa, and Representative Leo J. Ryan, Democrat of California, named only the two foreign affairs committees. The armed services and appropriations committees were added by agreement, as were the intelligence committees when they were created in 1975. The House Armed Services Committee later decided against receiving the reports. In most cases, information is presented to only the senior members and top staff of the committees, with others included only by special arrangement, at their request. Earlier attempts to establish oversight of the intelligence community are detailed in Cecil V. Crabb, Jr., and Pat M. Holt, *Invitation to Struggle: Congress, the President and Foreign Policy* (Congressional Quarterly Press, 1980), pp. 137–46. On oversight of the Central Intelligence Agency before 1975, see also Louis Fisher, *Presidential Spending Power* (Princeton University Press, 1975), pp. 217–19. By 1980 the congressional attitude toward covert operations had shifted, particularly as the result of Soviet expansionism in Afghanistan, and the Hughes-Ryan amendment was modified to require operations be reported only to the two intelligence committees, presumably to encourage the CIA to resume types of operations that had been suspended because of fear of exposure.

39. Senate Report 94-755 (April 26, 1976), quoted in *Congressional Quarterly Almanac, 1976*, p. 303.

committee noted in its report that the intelligence agencies had long been "beyond the scrutiny" of the Congress.[40] Both committees were subsequently made permanent and, according to their annual reports, they have conducted a wide range of special investigations in addition to exercising a continuous general surveillance over intelligence activities. The findings of the initial committees contributed to a reorganization of intelligence agencies by President Ford, including the issuance of "charters" containing new and more specific guidelines for their conduct.

As it probed into the secret areas of government, the Congress asserted something like an absolute right to information—as unlimited as the right that President Nixon had claimed, up to the eve of his resignation, to withhold it.[41] And, unlike Nixon, it came close to enforcing its position. While the Supreme Court's decision striking down Nixon's contention of unlimited "executive privilege" came in a case involving a demand for information by the Watergate special prosecutor,[42] the verdict could only undercut the president's position in dealing with the legislative branch as well. So, in two important test cases in 1975, congressional committees pressed their advantage; for the most part, they were successful. When the House Select Committee on Intelligence issued a demand to Secretary of State Henry A. Kissinger for documents on covert intelligence operations, the administration initially claimed executive privilege. But after the committee voted to cite Kissinger for contempt, the administration agreed to supply the information sought (although not all of the original documents). Chairman Otis G. Pike, Democrat of New York, found that this constituted "substantial compliance" and the charge against Kissinger was dropped.[43] Similarly, a House Government Operations subcommittee voted to charge Secretary of Commerce Rogers C. B. Morton with contempt when he refused for several months to give it the names of American companies that had been asked to participate in an

40. *New York Times*, January 26, 1976. For a review of both committees' work, see Crabb and Holt, *Invitation to Struggle*, pp. 149–52; and Thomas M. Franck and Edward Weisband, *Foreign Policy by Congress* (Oxford University Press, 1979), pp. 118–22.

41. The right of the president to withhold the contents of executive agreements with foreign countries—some of which, dealing with joint defense agreements or other national security matters, had been kept secret—was revoked by statute in 1972. The law, passed without opposition in either house, required that all such agreements be submitted to the full houses or, if the president believed secrecy to be required, to the two foreign affairs committees. The State Department had initially opposed the bill, but after the Senate passed it by 81 to 0 the department accepted it. *Congressional Quarterly Almanac, 1972*, p. 619.

42. *U.S. v. Nixon et al.*, 418 U.S. 688 (1974). In rejecting the claim that executive privilege was unlimited, however, the Court for the first time acknowledged the existence of the privilege—without, of course, going beyond suggesting the circumstances when it could be asserted.

43. *Congressional Quarterly Almanac, 1975*, pp. 406–07. Pike probably feared the House would not sustain him if he pressed the case; the committee had discredited itself through leaks, and when its report was submitted, the House voted not to publish it. Franck and Weisband, *Foreign Policy by Congress*, p. 119.

Arab boycott of Israel. In this case, the legislators' victory was complete; Morton backed down and surrendered the list.

The Carter years saw several similar flurries over executive privilege. One, in 1980, led to the initiation of a contempt citation against Secretary of Energy Charles W. Duncan, Jr., for refusing to release internal departmental memorandums relating to President Carter's imposition of an oil import fee, on the ground that such an action would inhibit free discussion among department officials. Duncan, like Secretary Morton, yielded. In two other confrontations in 1980—over the State Department's internal communications relating to a United Nations vote on Israel, and over the Justice Department's criminal investigation files—the administration held its ground and the committees gave way.

When the Congress in 1978 consolidated audit and investigation functions in twelve departments and agencies into new offices to be headed by presidentially appointed inspectors general, it specified that findings of the inspectors would be reported to the Congress as well as to the heads of the agencies and made public as well. No longer would those agencies be able to discover and correct their own deficiencies outside the glare of the congressional and public spotlight. In signing the bill, President Carter did not protest this additional limitation on executive privacy and concealment.

By the end of the decade, the Congress appeared to have won its point. There could be no more secret wars, no more secret covert operations, not even secret scandals. The release of internal documents to investigating committees would still be negotiated case by case, as it always had been, but the attitude of defiance toward the legislature's claims that characterized the later years of the Nixon administration was gone. During the Carter years, both branches sought accommodation. Whether this represented a durable change in relations would not be tested until the next time that the executive and legislative branches were controlled by opposing parties.

The Uses and Pathology of Oversight

To the extent that oversight has been intensified, so have certain questions of impropriety associated with the process. At its best, congressional oversight exposes and prevents misconduct, helps to maintain a salutary degree of constituency influence on administration, and in doing so protects the country from imperial presidencies and bureaucratic arrogance. But, at its worst, oversight becomes irresponsible meddling in administrative matters, producing undesirable strain and tension between the branches, imposing burdens of time and paperwork and harassment on the executive, blurring lines of responsibility, and inducing administrators to stretch or even violate the law to give preferential treatment to particular constituents at the expense of others, sometimes with added cost to the treasury.

The suggestion that the Congress is carrying oversight too far has been heard from both ends of Pennsylvania Avenue. As early as 1974, just when the Bolling committee was recommending more attention to oversight, Senator George Aiken, the thirty-four-year Republican veteran from Vermont, protested that the Congress was overreacting to its loss of status and its clash with Nixon. "Congress wants to tell the executive how to run things, down to small details," he said. "We just can't do it."[44] And executive branch officials were complaining about congressional "micromanagement" of programs, as exemplified by an 862-page report of the House Agriculture Committee advising the Department of Agriculture how to administer the food stamp program, or a 446-page House Appropriations report "littered with demands for information on scores of subjects" from the Department of Defense.[45] Congressional questioning, in both legislative and oversight hearings, was an endless drain on executive time. Secretary of Energy James R. Schlesinger made twelve appearances before congressional bodies in less than two months in early 1979, most of them being general briefings at which he gave "updated answers" to questions he had answered before.[46] Other Department of Energy officials appeared at nearly a hundred hearings in a little over a month, with as many as five scheduled in a single day. Said one of those officials, "The more we're on the hill, the more trouble we have attending to business at the department, and the more that happens, the more they demand to see us up there."[47]

To obtain an authoritative sampling of executive and legislative branch views on the nature and consequences of congressional oversight as it was developing in the era of congressional resurgence, the Brookings Institution convened a pair of conferences—one of present or former officials of the executive branch, the other of staff members of the legislative branch. There was surprising agreement between the two groups on the strengths and

44. What's Wrong with Congress," *U.S. News and World Report*, May 6, 1974, p. 24.

45. Cameron, "Shadow Congress," p. 42.

46. J. P. Smith, *Washington Post*, March 13, 1979. Part of the difficulty for Schlesinger was jurisdictional competition on Capitol Hill. Committees and subcommittees staking out claims to parts of the energy field required, as a matter of prestige, that the secretary rather than a subordinate official appear.

47. Walter S. Mossbert, *Wall Street Journal*, April 9, 1979. Some of these were legislative hearings essential in the consideration of specific bills; others were oversight hearings that "too often" were more of a public-relations exercise "than an information-gathering process"; ibid.

weaknesses, the health and pathology, of oversight.[48] The comments of the participants are excerpted here not only for what they reveal about the oversight function in the 1970s but also for the light they shed on the institutional problems of the Congress following the reforms of the 1970s.

Both groups agreed that the amount of oversight activity had increased markedly in the 1970s. A veteran executive branch official put it this way:

> It has been the proliferation, especially at the committee level, of an enormous staff, but on top of that there has been the insertion of new organs (Office of Technology Assessment, Congressional Budget Office) and augmentation of existing organs (Congressional Research Service, etc.) . . . which in effect are creating a depth of competence in institutional and staff backing which equips the Congress to intervene, second-guess, review, investigate, penetrate the undertakings of the executive branch to a degree that would not even have been dreamt of in, say, the beginning of the first Nixon term.

A former assistant secretary concurred that "on the whole, Congress is far more intrusive on a day-to-day basis than it was ten or fifteen years ago." And a staff member of a congressional support agency commented that "the oversight role of the legislative branch is enhanced by the proliferation of power to committees, subcommittees, to individual members."

The nearest thing to a dissent came from another support agency staff member:

> In some critical ways, there is much less oversight than there ever has been on Capitol Hill. There is more evaluation, there are more evaluators, there is more staff. . . . The growth in staff . . . would seem to give each member as a discrete unit an opportunity to be an overseer, whereas once you needed a committee, or at least a subcommittee to be the overseeing unit. In that sense, there perhaps is more oversight. . . .
>
> However . . . you have to look back at the incentives . . . of the staff. There are very few staff people who arrive on the Hill who seek career goals in Congress. . . . It's a stepping-stone, and except for those who are muckraking in instinct, which are very few, career advancement is in terms other than oversight. You don't make your mark that way. So to think that you're going to populate Congress with thousands and thousands of people and that they will be overseers thereby, I think is wrong. This particular year, if there is more talk about oversight, it's because there is less talk about legislation.

48. The quotations and generalizations in this section are taken from verbatim transcripts of the two conferences held at the Brookings Institution on June 5 and 7, 1979. The discussions were held on a not-for-attribution basis in order to encourage candor. The executive branch conferees consisted of one current and one recent assistant secretary for congressional relations, two recent assistant secretaries for administration, one commissioner of a regulatory agency, two top executives of regulatory agencies, a deputy assistant secretary, a special assistant to a secretary, a departmental inspector general, a bureau chief, a deputy bureau chief, and two recent deputy bureau chiefs. Some of these were veteran civil servants who had held more than one top post that involved dealing with the Congress and some were political appointees who had had earlier experience on Capitol Hill. The congressional conference participants included one person from the staff of a full committee, six from subcommittees (equally divided between oversight and substantive groups), one from a party leadership, two from senators' offices, and two each from the General Accounting Office and the Congressional Research Service. Both majority and minority staffs were represented.

But if there was a consensus that oversight activity had increased, the change related only to quantity. No one at either conference saw any notable improvement in quality. One House staffer of more than twenty years of service stated the consensus: "I don't think we're getting our money's worth." Another saw the increase as having been "for purposes of press more than purposes of major change." "If you talk to individual congressmen up on the Hill," observed a recently retired executive, "and ask them where legislative oversight stands on their priorities, it's still constituent service, number one; legislation, number two; and oversight is still running a poor third."

And what are the weaknesses? One executive official found the procedure "very ad hoc. It is very unsystematic and unplanned. Then, after whatever steps are taken, generally there is inadequate follow-through." And these were three views from the congressional perspective:

> You are not going to do reasonable, effective oversight by taking somebody who just got out of Harvard Business School . . . or somebody who . . . just graduated from Boston College Law School. They are just not ready to take on . . . the career bureaucracy that has seen them come and seen them go.
> The destructive things are the fragmentation of attention. . . . Oversight requires persistence. That's one thing a member doesn't have today, virtually no member.
> The basic incentive structure of Congress has not changed. . . . The authorizing committees . . . have virtually no incentives to be hard-nosed overseers of the agencies in their care. Things which have occurred in recent years [the new budget process, short-term authorizations] actually diminish their effectiveness. . . . They have got to lobby for the programs that they care about.

One of the congressional participants emphasized that the oversight function was just too complicated. "You hold oversight hearings, you do it right, you try to find out what they're doing, and if everything they are doing is wrong, there is almost nothing you can do about it, because there are 435 members of the House and 100 members in the Senate, and nobody concentrates on it." Several participants commented on the impossibility of covering all of the subjects within a committee's or subcommittee's jurisdiction, pointing out that the body could oversee effectively a single agency or a single area of policy only if it neglected the rest of its domain.

As might be expected, executive branch officials felt that their legislative overseers too often crossed the line that separated constructive oversight from irresponsible intervention in the details of administration. They referred to "dabbling," to "abuse" and "personal vendettas," to "individual members who have taken on missions that are irrational and perhaps politically motivated," to "incursion into administration in the name of oversight," to "a pretty serious problem in terms of accountability." Said a regulatory agency official: "The idea of their getting into whether or not something ought to be three pounds or five pounds or two inches or seven inches is just . . . put up for a political trade-off. [It] is really kind of ludicrous."

But what was less expected was the extent of agreement in the congressional group. "I think that what we've got now, instead of oversight, largely is intervention," said one long-time congressional assistant. "I think Congress on the whole is so suspicious of the executive as a result of the decade of the '60s that what they're really interested in is running the thing rather than oversight, and I think that is really a fundamental mistake." And another veteran legislative staffer noted that what the authorizing committees "have become interested in is not so much overseeing the executive branch. . . . They are massively interested in intervention."

Intervention in the details of administration, it was argued in both conferences, diverted committee and staff efforts from the larger matters that deserved oversight attention. One executive suggested that the Congress drifted into details because it is "easier to deal with individual specifics" than with "the basic policy issues." Said a former congressional relations officer:

> There is a lot more retailing than I have ever seen in recent years in the Congress. . . . This is routine [now]. You go in, you testify, you've got a bill, there are major issues, and you wind up having to talk about why somebody wasn't appointed the district director or assistant district director, or why a grant wasn't made to a particular city or county. [In] preparing a secretary or an assistant secretary for testimony . . . the bulk of the time is spent in preparing on the case matter and not on the bill.

Of course, "retailing" may serve the agency's purpose, too, if it does not want attention concentrated on the basic policy issues. But if an administrator genuinely wants policy guidance from his oversight committee—even if only to avoid the committee's ire later—the concentration of the members on details rather than broad policy questions can be vexing. Said a regulator:

> We are told to enforce the law . . . and I expect to go to oversight hearings and have a group of people argue with me about what is unreasonable. . . . What we wind up getting is who in the hell went to Hawaii last year, apparently to tell you about spending taxpayer's money. . . . I wind up going back and saying I haven't got any guidance, no guidance at all about the policy matters that we are supposed to enforce . . . and I have spent hours up there waiting for one more member to come so we can hold a damned hearing. . . . I am criticized, mind you, daily for doing the things inappropriately, yet they weren't there to say [what they considered inappropriate].

Congressional interest in particular details can distort the allocation of the agency's resources. One former administrator gave as an example a senator who

> took upon himself to be very, very concerned about [certain] delinquent accounts. Now these are a minuscule portion of the delinquent accounts owed to the federal

government, but [the] senator . . . for reasons, I suspect, that had something to do with publicity at home, took upon himself an annual listing in the *Congressional Record* of [these] accounts in congressional districts throughout the country. . . . It took [the bureau's] effort and turned it almost completely upside down, because the effort every year was to give a better report card to [the] senator on delinquent accounts. That was not what the [bureau] was supposed to be doing. That to me was a classic example of congressional oversight which, well intentioned as it may have been at the time, perverted, distorted, and biased the efforts of the executive branch. . . . I think we overresponded because we were weak, but we did it.

Another executive illustrated how oversight can force an undesirable centralization of administrative decisionmaking:

You have a field apparatus with people some distance from Washington who are called upon, in order to make a program work, to exercise discretion and to grant waivers. Then you get a lalapaloosa of a GAO investigation and an oversight hearing and everything freezes, and every decision which would leave a field operating bureaucrat to a degree exposed is not going to be made in the field. . . . It will go to Washington and it will take six to eight months to get an application approved.

Executives complained of conflict in the directions they received from the oversight committees and the Office of Management and Budget, respectively. They also told of conflicting guidance from different members of the same committee, and from different oversight committees:

I'll walk into a hearing in which the oversight committee says, "How come you spent so long getting [this action taken]?" and be dragged in front of [another] committee the next day and be asked, "How come you moved so fast?" So I'm getting a lot of conflicting legitimate pressures on the same issues, and yet I still read the legislation that says to act independent of political influence.

If two or more agencies were involved in a project, the conflict could be much worse. One former official in the Executive Office of the President charged with developing a governmentwide approach to a common procedural problem reported:

When you had . . . one project that would involve several different agencies, you could have as many as five or six subcommittees in the House and five or six subcommittees in the Senate going in ten different directions. There is no way . . . that you can coordinate the Congress, even if you are in a very strong agency . . . when there are strong emotional issues involved. When you are in a run-of-the-mill agency, of course, or a weak agency, it's laughable to think you can deal with that.

The congressional staff added illustrations of conflict among oversight committees, including an instance in which House and Senate committees were pulling in opposite directions. Under these circumstances, the executives testified, they had to assess the relative power of the conflicting committees; the appropriations committees, if they were among the contenders, usually won "because they make it count," as one participant put it.

To bring the oversight process under control, executive branch participants pleaded for more discipline on Capitol Hill. "Party discipline on the Hill should be . . . stronger than it is," said one former deputy agency head, "so that a [Senator Joseph R.] McCarthy . . . is not turned loose to turn any particular segment of the administrative branch upside down because of his particular political or ideological whim." An assistant secretary thought that in part the frustrations of the executive branch were

> a result of the breakdown in Congress of traditional structural leadership mechanisms by which . . . it was much more difficult for an individual or a junior member of Congress to move in as directly on an agency without running into difficulty with his subcommittee chairman. . . . You sort of had maybe a half a dozen members that were key people that were concerned with your agency and were predictable. . . . Now it can come from three hundred different [members] and each of them has an ability to move. . . .

A special purpose of discipline, the executive participants argued, should be to reduce the burden on the executive branch of redundant activity. One observed: "If you've got three or four or five different subcommittees looking at the same time, all pulling you, it creates an enormous distraction of resources to try to satisfy those needs. Often they are pulling in roughly the same direction, but in terms of the resources required to respond, it's enormous." Another participant complained:

> With the democracy within the committee system, one of the ways to get elected committee chairman is by . . . having a lot of subcommittees. . . . Everybody gets to chair one, and each one has its own staff and its own offices. Once you've got a subcommittee with a staff, they've got to do something, so of course they hold hearings and . . . summon administration witnesses. There was a period for about six months at the beginning of this administration, when everybody was always up on the Hill testifying, and you wondered who the hell was running the departments.

One of the executive participants wondered how "just the sheer numbers of individual members injecting themselves into your business . . . can be controlled in the absence of a return to the seniority system." His view found sympathy at the congressional round table. The staff director of an oversight subcommittee told of "chasing down" a regulatory commission chairman while "seven other committees were doing the same thing. . . . He was up there four days a week for six weeks in a row. You can't run an agency and have to do that. . . . I felt we truly were beleaguering an executive . . . to such an extent that he just couldn't get his job done."

To deal with an undisciplined Congress, one long-time executive branch official insisted that an agency simply needs "a little courage." In particular, oversight subcommittees—which are not in a position to deny either legislation or appropriations—can be ignored. Another participant contended that an executive agency was guilty of "complicity" if it yielded to a congressional request it opposed on principle. But others had found it more expedient to yield—resistance, even to oversight groups, "wasn't worth the effort." Oversight chairmen served on other committees where they might handle matters concerning the agency they were questioning, and in any event their influence extended beyond their own committees. But in the case of appropriations and authorizing groups, there was no question they had to be propitiated. Said a recent assistant secretary: "The appropriations subcommittee staff are the people who are going to kill you up there. When they get interested in your programs and start telling you how to run them, there is a natural response to try to accommodate them. . . . There was a pattern or a practice developing where you really had to jump through hoops, because if you didn't you were going to get scorched in the appropriations. . . . You can pay a high price if you say no." Another agreed: "Everybody knows that there are staff people on the Hill who virtually run agencies . . . and the public accountability is nonexistent. It's just nonexistent."

Congressional staff members acknowledged the difficulty of getting "neutral" oversight. The process is "co-opted," one said. A member of the staff of a substantive subcommittee was frank to say that its oversight hearings were "to seek business," to develop support against the current "general environment" of budget-cutting. He defined hearings as of three types, one of them "being objective and bringing out both sides of an issue. I think that would characterize a relatively small percentage of the oversight hearings. The other two are much more likely to be . . . saying, 'it stinks,' or . . . 'it's great,' because there's really not an awful lot to be gained in the political sense by having this really careful analytic and neutral presentation of a fairly close issue." "The neutral objective," an oversight subcommittee staffer agreed, "doesn't sell." Another broke in: "And the media won't pay much attention to that, either."

Despite their emphasis on the limitations and weaknesses of oversight, both groups found much to praise. The executive branch officials cited major improvements in management brought about by congressional investigations and persistent oversight—for instance, creation of the Defense Supply Agency as the culmination of a series of investigations of defense procurement practices. One executive probably expressed the consensus when he said:

> No federal bureaucracy will be completely on its toes if it does not expect that it's going to be subject to some kind of review, and I mean more than the classical review by the President and OMB. I always found . . . that three out of four GAO

reports were really worthwhile. They frequently made it possible to energize an agency to do something they just couldn't get the inertia of the agency to address until that report hit the public press.[49]

The executives, of course, found of particular value the hearings that were organized to build support for their programs. "We had a number of cases where the legislative committee, looking deeply at a problem, a policy issue we had, would take a position that we later could use very effectively in the appropriations process," one executive said. "Time and again this occurred in terms of a helpful approach." Participants acknowledged that often—some said usually—such committee hearings, studies, and investigations were suggested by the agency itself. When relations were good, some agencies initiated oversight by voluntarily submitting proposed regulations for review and advice, and they found this course both prudent and helpful in clarifying congressional intent.

From the standpoint of every participant in both groups, in sum, oversight has mixed results—a compound of benefit and harm. This can be said, of course, about every other check and balance in the American institutional system, but the problem of improving the mix is especially intractable in the case of oversight, because the process is so diffused. Institutional means can be found to increase the volume of oversight activity; special subcommittees can be created, more staff can be hired, sunset legislation can compel more hearings, and so on. But institutional means to improve the quality are not so easily found, and as the congressional staff members were the quickest to point out, it is in quality more than in quantity that the process is deficient.

Sunrise Legislation and Other Remedies

More than three hundred members of the Congress, by Senator Baucus's count, had introduced legislation in the first five months of the 1979 session to improve, in one way or another, the oversight process.[50] These included

49. These comments parallel those of a regulatory official who appeared at an oversight hearing on the Natural Gas Pipeline Safety Act in 1975: "Your oversight hearings have a salutary effect, perhaps more than you realize. The scheduling of an oversight hearing triggers a review of an organization's activities, with appropriate corrective action. The administrator of a program really finds out what is going on; he is probably never better acquainted with his organization than the day he appears before you. Perhaps more frequent oversight hearings would have prompted correction of some of the deficiencies we are discussing today. Your failure to hold hearings may have led OPS (Office of Pipeline Safety) to believe that its performance was satisfactory." Testimony of William C. Jennings, former director, Office of Pipeline Safety, in *Natural Gas Pipeline Safety Act Amendments of 1975*, Hearings before the Subcommittee on Surface Transportation of the Senate Commerce Committee, 94 Cong. 1 sess. (GPO, 1975), p.63.

50. *Congressional Record*, daily edition, June 12, 1979, p. S7465.

sunset and legislative veto bills and also "sunrise" legislation—a concept developed and advocated by the General Accounting Office, as the congressional support agency most specifically charged with assisting the legislators in their oversight function. As laid out in a manual of advice to congressional committees[51] and in other GAO documents, sunrise legislation emphasizes laying the groundwork for oversight in the authorizing legislation itself. Each authorizing bill (or its accompanying committee report) would include an "oversight requirements" section that would specify the goals of the legislation and pose oversight questions to the administering agency. The agency would periodically report accomplishments against the goals, respond to the oversight questions, and transmit the findings of formal evaluation studies. These reports would provide a basis for the committees' oversight activity, for which the authorizing legislation would establish a schedule.

Legislation has been introduced in both houses, with more than a hundred cosponsors, to apply the sunrise principle to every authorizing bill. But the effects of such legislation would appear to be mixed also. The oversight requirements would generate an enormous volume of reports—"the staff resources required to support the process may be substantial in the executive agencies, the committees, the GAO, and the other congressional support agencies," Comptroller General Elmer B. Staats acknowledges.[52] But the reports would have only as much utility as committees were motivated to give them, and sunrise legislation in itself would not affect motivation. If the agency performance fell below the standards, the reports would add marginally to the ammunition available to subcommittees that wanted to take hostile action; conversely, positive reports would help advocates to make the case for higher budget allocations. But whether they would cause a subcommittee to act in the absence of substantial other stimulus to do so is conjectural, given the enormous workload that each member of the Congress carries. The existence of the performance goals and standards and the prospect of review would, however, carry benefits—insofar as they were an additional spur to administrative performance by agencies already under constant prodding from their constituencies, their administrative superiors in the executive branch, and the Congress.

On the other hand, as opportunities for beneficial oversight were enhanced, so would be the dangers. "The process," says the GAO manual, "carries the potential for involving an oversight committee quite extensively

---

51. Comptroller General, *Finding Out How Programs Are Working: Suggestions for Congressional Oversight*, Report to the Congress (GPO, 1977).

52. Testimony, May 23, 1979, *Sunset, Sunrise, and Related Measures*, Hearings before a subcommittee of the House Rules Committee, 96 Cong. 1 sess. (GPO, 1980), p. 164.

in the administering agency's implementation of a program. . . . If carried too far, the involvement can represent an unwarranted intrusion into matters which should be primarily the responsibility of the executive branch and can be an impediment to timely and effective implementation of a program."[53] The paperwork burden would be great, on both ends. Sympathetic committees would, presumably, try to avoid specificity in setting goals in the first place; executive agencies in their reports would try to cover up shortfalls in performance, and the committees would not expend much effort to ferret them out. When Senator Baucus said, in introducing the general sunrise legislation, that "we in the Congress must hold ourselves accountable for the failure of our Government agencies to perform responsively and responsibly" and that the administration is only expected to provide "some leadership,"[54] he went far toward discarding the concept of the president as general manager that previous Congresses had spent half a century in building. Lines of accountability would be even more clouded than they are now.

Critics of the quality of oversight have suggested as another avenue of improvement the training of committee personnel. But the training would of necessity be voluntary, and given the autonomy of each oversight unit, the random manner of staff selection and assignment, the high rate of turnover, and the absence of a sense of professionalism among oversight personnel—and congressional staff in general—the reach of any formal instruction program would be limited. Moreover, the doctrine dispensed in a training program would presumably be the "neutral" ideal—taught by the "objective, bringing out both sides of an issue" school—but that is not the political objective of most oversight activity, as the congressional staff at the Brookings conference made clear.

Participants in the two conferences had no trouble identifying the characteristics of good and bad oversight. Given the facts of particular cases, they had no trouble agreeing within each group—and would undoubtedly have agreed as a single group, if they had met together—as to which cases were well or badly handled and which had mainly positive or mainly negative results. But the effort to generalize from case experience, to develop doctrine and principles to govern oversight, yields little beyond platitudes. Congressional committees should behave constructively and not destructively. They should put aside petty or political motives and act in the general interest of the whole government. They should avoid publicity seeking. They should prevent abuse and refrain from meddling. They should examine broad policy

53. Comptroller General, *Finding Out*, pp. vi–vii.
54. *Congressional Record*, daily edition, June 12, 1979, p. S7465.

issues and avoid details. They should expose incompetent or corrupt officials but not pillory able and dedicated ones. They should be a conduit for good ideas from the interested public but should not allow themselves to be used as tools by interest groups that carry on their own oversight activities for their own purposes. They should require enough reports to be informed but not so many as to be burdensome. And so on. No one would disagree. But what is "constructive" or "meddling" or "incompetence" or "burdensome" is now decided by every subcommittee and, to a degree, by every individual. The problem, as one veteran congressional aide put it, was the absence of accountability within the Congress, "our own lack of internal oversight."

Simply to intensify oversight, as the Congress has done and is still striving to do, without attention to quality control may, if anything, impair the mix. Officially encouraged to delve into administrative matters, more staff members without the background, experience, or training for the job will be engaged in it. Harried by relatively junior—often very junior—legislative employees, more senior executives will, in the words of one of them, "wonder why in the world they ever went to work for the government."

But, in the field of oversight as in every other area of legislative activity, decentralization is the order of the day. Any notion of central control, or discipline, within each house as a means of improving the quality of oversight is wholly foreign to the temper of the new, resurgent Congress.

CHAPTER XII

To Tighten Control over Administration: The Legislative Veto

FROM the standpoint of the Congress, the normal processes of congressional oversight of administration have two fundamental limitations. First, they do not prevent maladministration. Oversight occurs usually after the fact; by the time the oversight hearing takes place, the administrative action has been taken. Second, except as it may lead eventually to new legislation, oversight produces only advice, not mandatory direction, to administrators; during or after oversight hearings, committees and individual legislators have no authority to issue directives to administrators telling them how to do their jobs. It is these twin shortcomings of oversight—too late and too weak—that have impelled the Congress in its period of resurgence to develop a more timely and authoritative means of intervention in the administrative process. That means is the legislative veto—the device that was used, for instance, in the Wars Powers Resolution and the Congressional Budget and Impoundment Control Act. It goes back to the 1930s but until the 1970s was employed only occasionally, on a limited scale.

Through the veto, the Congress resolves its problem of trying to legislate detailed prescriptions to restrict and control administrative action; instead, by reserving the right to review and disapprove contemplated action, it can launch a program with broad discretionary powers but make mid-course corrections. In the veto, the Congress has found its long-sought means to exercise authoritative control of administration during the fact, when the regulations that govern its constituents have been developed and are ready to be promulgated, or other actions that affect them are about to be taken.

The legislative veto takes a variety of forms. The Congress can require that both houses concur in the veto or even a two-thirds vote of each house (as in a 1958 tariff law). It can permit either house alone to veto the action. It can delegate the authority to one or more committees, or even a subcommittee. In 1952, it even authorized the chairman of the House Appropriations Committee to veto proposals of the director of the budget to amend a budget circular. And in 1979, it gave one of its agencies, the Office of Technology Assessment, the power to veto the research design for a Veterans Administration study.

No set of figures measures so well the resurgence of the Congress in the 1970s as does the number of legislative veto provisions written into law. In the forty-eight years from 1932, when the instrument was introduced, through 1979, a total of 113 laws were enacted with legislative veto provisions.[1] However, 62 of these were passed in the last seven years of that span, the period of congressional reassertion. If the legislative veto continues to be applied as freely as it was in the 1970s, it will work profound change in the constitutional relation between the executive and legislative branches—assuming that the Supreme Court does not eventually find it impermissible.

A Half-Century Constitutional Tug-of-War

The legislative veto was born in innocence. Early in his term, President Herbert Hoover, noting Congress's failure to reorganize the executive branch, asked for authority to do it himself, subject to Congress's "power of revision."[2] The Congress did not respond until June 1932; by then the Democrats were in control of the House for the first time in a dozen years, and they were unwilling to grant their political opponent carte blanche to reshuffle and consolidate government agencies. Yet they also recognized that the Congress was in no position to take the initiative on reorganization and that not much

1. Clark F. Norton, "Congressional Review, Deferral and Disapproval of Executive Actions: A Summary and an Inventory of Statutory Authority," report 76-88 G (Congressional Research Service, April 30, 1976), as supplemented by his reports, 78-117 Gov (CRS, May 25, 1978), 79-46 Gov (CRS, February 12, 1979), and 80-86 Gov (CRS, April 17, 1980). The figures here differ from Norton's in several respects. They omit legislation that amended laws containing a legislative veto or that reenacted existing vetoes. They also exclude statutory provisions sometimes defined as legislative vetoes that authorize the Congress to act by concurrent resolution (which does not require presidential approval) to terminate the authority for programs, or in a few cases to initiate action under the authority (provisions introduced principally during World War II), or that authorize a program or a project to be planned but reserve authorization to undertake it, or appropriations, or both, for later legislation.

2. John D. Millett and Lindsay Rogers, "The Legislative Veto and the Reorganization Act of 1939," *Public Administration Review*, vol. 1 (Autumn 1940), p. 176.

could be accomplished through the normal legislative process. Out of this deadlock emerged an institutional invention: as the reverse of the usual legislative procedure, let the president write the equivalent of law but subject to a congressional veto—with no authority in the executive to override. Hoover was given power in June 1932 to reorganize the government by executive order, but each order was to be transmitted to the Congress and could be disapproved by either house within sixty days.[3]

The lawyers in the Justice Department evidently let this one slip by, for seven months later they found constitutional objection to the concept of the legislative veto as embodied in another bill.[4] Then Attorney General William D. Mitchell first presented the argument that has been used ever since by presidents and attorneys general—but not yet tested before the Supreme Court. The issue concerned a proposal by the Congress to allow one of its committees to override the Treasury Department on large refunds of taxes illegally or erroneously collected. If approving the refunds was a legislative function, Mitchell contended, it could not be delegated to a committee of the Congress. And if it were an administrative function, the veto constituted an improper invasion by the legislative branch of the executive's constitutional territory.[5] Hoover disapproved the bill, and the Congress withdrew the offending provision.

In the course of reviewing precedents for his position, Mitchell belatedly raised "a grave question as to the validity" of the government reorganization procedure established earlier, but that bridge had been crossed. The legislative veto, in one form or another, has become a standard provision of reorganization legislation, and presidents have preferred to set aside their constitutional objections rather than get no reorganization authority at all.

In 1944 the first legislative veto by committee was adopted, and the constitutional struggle during the next two decades centered on that form of the device. The 1944 measure required the secretary of the navy to "come into agreement" with the two naval affairs committees on the terms of any land acquisition or disposal. President Roosevelt, in the midst of a war, did not protest this incursion,[6] but when the Congress in 1951 extended the

3. The House rejected all of Hoover's proposals, which were submitted in December, after he had been defeated for reelection. Richard Polenberg, *Reorganizing Roosevelt's Government: The Controversy over Executive Reorganization, 1936–39* (Harvard University Press, 1966), pp. 5, 6.

4. Hoover, in signing the reorganization bill, protested that the procedure would delay reorganization but he did not object on principle. "Statement About Signing the 'Economy Act,' June 30, 1932," *Public Papers of the Presidents: Herbert Hoover, 1932–33* (U.S. Government Printing Office, 1977), p. 283.

5. "Veto of a Bill to Supply Deficiency and Supplement Appropriations," ibid., pp. 969–77.

6. But when signing another bill that required the Navy Department to consult with the naval affairs committees on "all . . . details" of contracts relating to the Navy's petroleum reserves, he

requirement to the entire Department of Defense, as well as to the Federal Civil Defense Administration, President Truman rejected the bill. In his veto message he contended that congressional review would result in "severe and unnecessary administrative burden . . . continuing delays . . . inability . . . to plan . . . uncertainties . . . centralization in Washington of real estate operations." And he expressed concern "over what appears to be a gradual trend on the part of the legislative branch to participate to an ever greater extent in the actual execution and administration of the laws," which were functions belonging to the executive branch.[7] But the Congress was not without resources to impose its will. The House overrode the president's veto, 312 to 68, but the Senate leadership chose not to bring the issue to a vote. Instead, both houses simply wrote the provision into the annual act authorizing military construction, which the president could not afford to veto.

President Truman did manage to kill with a pocket veto, after the Congress adjourned in 1952, a bill authorizing the Post Office Department to enter into lease-purchase agreements but requiring it to obtain the approval of each contract by two Senate and two House committees. The veto, however, only caused the Congress to invent a new, two-stage approval procedure that offered, if anything, tighter control of the executive branch. In the Public Buildings Purchase Contract Act of 1954, the General Services Administration and the Post Office were required to submit to the public works committees a prospectus for each proposed lease-purchase project, and no appropriation could be made for a project until the committees had approved it. This was presented as an internal congressional rule governing the manner in which appropriations would be made and President Eisenhower, presumably accepting it as such, approved it without protest. The same procedure was adopted a couple of weeks later when the Congress approved a program for small watershed projects to be carried out by the Department of Agriculture, and it was also incorporated in a small reclamation projects act in 1956 and in the Public Buildings Act of 1959, which superseded the 1954 law.

---

did object that legislative committees should stay out of the administration of the laws. Joseph P. Harris, *Congressional Control of Administration* (Brookings Institution, 1964), pp. 219–20.

7. "Statement by the President Upon Signing Bill to Facilitate the Financing of Defense Contracts, May 15, 1951," *Public Papers of the Presidents: Harry S. Truman, 1951* (GPO, 1965), pp. 281–82. The provision covered all transactions over $25,000 for either acquisition or disposal, as well as rental agreements exceeding $25,000 a year. Harris, *Congressional Control*, p. 220, quotes Representative Carl Vinson, Democrat of Georgia, author of the provision, and chairman of the Armed Services Committee when it was organized in 1949: "I want this committee to have something to do with running the departments instead of the departments just telling the committee what they are going to do. . . . when we are guiding the destinies of the Navy we feel that the committee should have a hand in a great many things."

While the two-stage procedure seemed to circumvent the constitutional issue,[8] Eisenhower like Truman staunchly defended the presidential prerogative whenever the committee veto was written in its original form. Eisenhower vetoed two bills containing a committee veto, announced he would disregard another such provision, and got another removed by threatening a veto. But the Congress in most instances had its way, either by withholding the authority and substituting a two-stage procedure or by some other means.

Having won this series of victories—if, in practical terms, they could be called that—President Eisenhower undertook a final challenge to the committee veto applying to Department of Defense real estate transactions. In his budget messages of 1958 and 1959 he called for its repeal but was ignored. In 1960 he went further, declaring that his attorney general had found the provision "violates fundamental constitutional principles," and that he had no alternative but to instruct the secretary of defense to disregard it if it were not repealed.[9] When the Senate Armed Services Committee went along with the president, accepting a thirty-day report-and-wait procedure in lieu of the veto, the House Armed Services Committee finally gave up—after sixteen years of reviewing contracts.[10] But the change was less than might appear. The House committee's chairman, Carl Vinson of Georgia, would be able to "establish a reasonable working agreement with the military departments so that no real difficulty will arise with respect to proposed real-estate actions,"[11] and the prediction was backed by his enormous power over matters of greatest concern to the Department of Defense.

Meanwhile the Congress had been gradually extending the one-house or two-house veto to additional types of administrative action, mainly property

8. The constitutionality of the two-stage procedure went unchallenged until 1967, when President Johnson announced that he would recommend no more projects under the four acts that made appropriations dependent on committee approval of project plans. The Johnson administration contended that the two-stage procedure did not in practice differ from the committee veto that presidents beginning with Truman had rejected, because appropriations were usually made first and project approval came later, putting the committees in the position of approving expenditure of funds duly appropriated and thus intervening in administration—although they rarely disapproved any project. Appropriation for the unapproved projects would be subject to a point of order during the appropriations process, but points of order were seldom if ever raised. Johnson's protest died with his administration, however, for President Nixon resumed the programs that had been suspended. Virginia A. McMurtry, "Legislative Vetoes Relating to Public Works and Buildings," in *Studies on the Legislative Veto*, prepared by the Congressional Research Service for a subcommittee of the House Rules Committee (GPO, 1980), pp. 462–77.

9. "Annual Budget Message to the Congress: Fiscal Year 1961, January 18, 1960," *Public Papers of the Presidents: Dwight D. Eisenhower, 1960–61* (GPO, 1961), pp. 49–50.

10. Harris, *Congressional Control*, pp. 222–23, reports that 1,510 cases were reviewed between 1951 and 1959, with very few rejected, but he concludes that the procedure undoubtedly had the effect of preventing closing of obsolete military installations.

11. *Congressional Record*, June 1, 1960, p. 11585.

transactions, and presidents—for the familiar reason that they wanted the legislation—could not fight them all. President Eisenhower did veto a bill conferring on the Department of Defense the authority to settle small claims with a proviso that the governing regulations be subject to a two-house veto, and President Johnson even found "repugnant to the Constitution" a report-and-wait procedure that applied to the closure of military installations or reduction in their missions.[12]

In 1967 the legislators adopted the veto as a way of avoiding the politically dangerous course of setting their own salaries; the president's recommendations for pay scales for congressmen, judges, and top officials in the executive branch, based on a report by an independent commission, would take effect unless turned down by either house.[13] Three years later, the same principle was applied to pay-setting throughout the executive branch. In 1972, the Congress began to extend the veto to the issuance of agency rules and regulations, beginning with the schedule of expected family contributions under the Basic Educational Opportunities Grants Program of the Office of Education. President Nixon accepted these, but he did protest committee vetoes written into two public buildings laws in 1972. In one case, he announced that he would not comply.[14]

The War Powers Resolution and the Congressional Budget and Impoundment Act well illustrate the utility of the veto as a device for breaking impasses in the allocation of responsibilities between legislative and executive. In the war powers case, it made the legislation possible. Some form of legislative veto was the only possible compromise between what, in the majority congressional view, would be unworkable—trying to codify the president's discretion to act—and what in the post-Vietnam political climate would have been unthinkable, conceding the virtually unlimited right to act that presidents had been claiming. In vetoing the War Powers Resolution, incidentally, Nixon used the familiar argument that the Congress would be trying to legislate, unconstitutionally, by concurrent resolution, that is, without giving the president the chance to approve or veto.[15] In the impoundment control features

---

12. "Veto of Military Authorization Bill, August 21, 1965," *Public Papers of the Presidents: Lyndon B. Johnson, 1965* (GPO, 1966), vol. 2, pp. 907–08. When, after he vetoed the bill, the Congress reduced the proposed 120-day waiting period to 30 days, Johnson accepted the revised version.

13. This proved to be even more dangerous politically. In 1977, after members of Congress received heavy criticism for managing under the procedure to get their own pay raised without even voting on it, they enacted a new law requiring affirmative action by both houses on the recommendations.

14. "Statement About Signing the Public Buildings Amendments of 1972, June 17, 1972," *Public Papers of the Presidents: Richard Nixon, 1972* (GPO, 1974), pp. 686–88.

15 "Veto of the War Powers Resolution, October 24, 1973," *Public Papers: Nixon, 1973* (GPO, 1975), p. 893.

of the budget act, the veto device was not the only way for the two branches to resolve the vexing question of how to make routine adjustments in spending authority, but it was certainly the simplest way. The alternative would have been to require each simple deferral to go through the full legislative process— as rescissions must (and as the House bill had proposed for deferrals)—with an added procedural burden on the two houses and the likelihood of unnecessary delay.

Just as these two acts symbolize the congressional resurgence, so did they set a precedent for the proliferation of veto provisions as convenient weapons to be seized by a Congress resolved to do battle against the president. After 1973, the device was proposed almost routinely whenever the Congress found itself forced to delegate some new, broad authority to the executive branch. It was not always accepted by both houses, the Senate being more resistant than the House. Sometimes the Senate converted a House-proposed legislative veto into something less than a veto, such as a report-and-wait provision. But in more than sixty pieces of legislation in the six years from 1973 through 1979 a veto was adopted, and sometimes in up to a dozen or more separate sections of a law. The one-house veto became the most common form, but the two-house veto—less onerous from the standpoint of the executive because it was more difficult for the Congress to impose—was also employed, and the committee veto, more onerous, was still occasionally used, particularly on the kinds of matters where it had been introduced in earlier decades.

The one-house legislative veto appears throughout the stream of energy legislation enacted in the years of oil supply crisis that followed the Arab embargo of 1973–74. It found its way into laws dealing with railroads, education, financial aid for New York City, election finance, the disposition of President Nixon's tapes and papers, the call-up of military reserve units or members, and advance payments or loans to military contractors.

Through a two-house veto, the Congress retained control of aid to Middle East countries, of military arms sales in the Middle East and elsewhere, of the export of nuclear materials and agricultural products, and of public land withdrawals. Through both kinds of vetoes, it retained authority over tariff policy. In 1980, after a three-year battle, the House forced the Senate and the president to accept a two-house veto provision covering all regulations of the Federal Trade Commission, in order that the agency would survive at all. In 1974 the Congress reserved a two-house veto over all rules, guidelines, interpretations, and orders issued by the Department of Health, Education, and Welfare to govern the conduct of local school districts, and in 1980 extended it to virtually all rules and regulations of the new Department of Education.[16]

The House of Representatives was eager to go much further. In 1976 it came within two votes of a two-thirds majority (necessary under a procedure suspending the rules) favoring a bill offered by Representative Walter Flowers, Democrat of Alabama, to make all rules and regulations by all agencies subject to a legislative veto.[17] Meanwhile, in the Ninety-fourth Congress (1975–76), it systematically attached veto provisions to individual pieces of legislation authorizing rule-making as they came before it. Some became law, and some died in the Senate or in conference, either because of the veto issue or for other reasons.[18]

In the next Congress, the Senate blocked a series of far-reaching veto proposals approved by the House. One, which covered all regulations of the Department of Housing and Urban Development, was converted into a report-and-wait procedure—the Senate having rejected the original proposal by a decisive 65 to 29 vote.[19] Another, applying to regulations issued under the president's emergency powers, was dropped in favor of a procedure permitting the Congress to terminate an emergency by concurrent resolution—which President Carter, on signing the bill, protested was equally unconstitutional. Veto proposals covering Department of Transportation and Department of Energy regulations were dropped in conference, and the bill to redefine and extend the Federal Trade Commission's powers was carried over to the succeeding Congress after the House twice rejected a conference

16. From 1960 through July 1978, 19 one-house and 13 two-house vetoes were exercised, and 49 impoundments were disapproved under the Congressional Budget and Impoundment Control Act. Clark F. Norton, "Data on Congressional Veto Legislation (1932–1978) and Extent of Its Usage" (Congressional Research Service, March 2, 1979). These figures understate the impact, however. Intended administrative actions may be modified to avoid vetoes (which is the equivalent of an actual veto), and a threat to veto is a legislative "bargaining chip" that can be used against the executive on related, or unrelated, matters.

17. The vote was 265 to 135. The House Rules Committee had declined to clear the bill, thus making suspension of the rules necessary.

18. In addition to the bills that became law, House measures applied the veto procedure to bills dealing with regulation of toxic substances, youth camp safety, water and air pollution, the outer continental shelf, mine safety, and various programs of the Consumer Product Safety Commission, the Federal Energy Administration, and the Environmental Protection Administration (all lost in the Senate or in conference), and bills relating to pesticides regulation, civil service, navigation, fire prevention, long-range resource planning, and foreign aid (vetoed by President Ford; in the last two cases for reasons beyond the veto provisions alone). Eleven of these measures are listed in *Congressional Quarterly Almanac, 1976*, p. 508. President Ford also vetoed a military construction authorization bill because of its long report-and-wait provision; "Veto of the Military Construction Bill, July 2, 1976," *Public Papers of the Presidents: Gerald R. Ford, 1976–77* (GPO, 1979), vol. 2, pp. 1953–54. But he signed the measure after the waiting period was reduced. Ford continued the practice of earlier presidents in formally protesting when forced to sign a bill containing a veto provision.

19. As of the end of 1980, no resolution of disapproval had been reported by a committee during the waiting period.

effort to excise the veto provision. Another House proposal, to subject all National Labor Relations Board regulations to a congressional veto, was killed by a Senate filibuster, and two House-passed postal service bills containing veto provisions also died in the Senate.

But the Senate sometimes accepted veto provisions or even, as in the New York City loan guarantee case, initiated them. And many bills containing what presidents considered to be encroachments on their power were too important to their objectives and to normal governmental operations for the president to veto because of the constitutional objection. President Carter rejected only two bills on this ground—a Department of Energy authorization bill, in which the legislative vetoes it contained were probably the least influential of his objections, and a bill requiring approval of a Health, Education, and Welfare study design by the Congress's Office of Technology Assessment. But he had to accept many veto provisions added to administration-backed legislation, and on occasion even to request them, as in a governmental reorganization act that recognized the decades-old tradition of a one-house veto.

Unable to use his own veto consistently to defend the presidency, Carter in 1978 sought recourse to the tactic of ignoring the vetoes as unconstitutional. In so doing, he meant to force the Supreme Court to settle the issue. In a special message to the Congress, the first ever delivered on the subject, he protested the "proliferation" of vetoes—forty-eight in four years, by his count, which was more than in the preceding two decades. Where he could, he would veto the bills containing them, and where he had to sign the bills, he would consider the provisions not legally binding.[20] The administration made clear it was not seeking a "major confrontation"—it would not flout a congressional veto of an arms sale, for instance—but only a Supreme Court resolution of the question, and for that purpose it would choose a minor issue.[21] Even that choice was delayed, and in 1979 Carter had to make a tactical retreat in at least one instance, when it became clear that he could not obtain standby gasoline rationing legislation without a provision for a legislative veto. Acknowledging the practical side of the constitutional issue, he told a news conference: "I don't object to the one-house veto if it's done

20. "Legislative Vetoes, June 21, 1978," *Public Papers of the Presidents: Jimmy Carter, 1978* (GPO, 1979), pp. 1146–49. The administration's constitutional arguments were presented by Attorney General Benjamin R. Civiletti, September 26, 1979, in *Regulatory Reform and Congressional Review of Agency Rules*, Hearings before a subcommittee of the House Rules Committee, 96 Cong. 1 sess. (GPO, 1979), pt. 1, pp. 364–449.

21. Transcript of news briefing at the White House by Attorney General Griffin B. Bell, presidential assistant Stuart E. Eizenstat, and John Harmon, Office of Legal Counsel, Department of Justice, June 21, 1978, pp. 8, 3–4.

expeditiously. . . . if either house wants to veto it they can do that."²² But a year later, Carter was still denouncing the legislative veto (this time as applied to Federal Trade Commission regulations) as unconstitutional and looking forward to a court challenge.²³

Meanwhile, congressional proponents of the legislative veto were giving no ground. Representative Elliott H. Levitas, Democrat of Georgia, who in his second term had made himself the leading sponsor of legislative veto bills and amendments pertaining to agency regulations, greeted the president's message with: "The gauntlet has now been thrown down. . . . The issue is who makes the laws in this country. Is it the unelected bureaucrats or is it the elected Congress which is responsible to the people? Regrettably, the President has come down on the side of the bureaucracy. The House will come down on the side of the people [who are] fed up with Washington bureaucrats running their lives."²⁴ House Majority Leader Jim Wright said he "respectfully disagreed" with the president; the veto was necessary to control the "voracious thirst . . . of nonelected bureaucrats to write regulations that have the force and effect of law, without the inconvenience of running for Congress."²⁵ By 1979, two hundred members of the House had joined Levitas in reintroducing the Flowers bill of 1976 to make all rules and regulations issued by all administrative agencies subject to a legislative veto, and a companion measure had been introduced in the Senate by Harrison H. Schmitt, Republican of New Mexico. Hearings were held on both bills, but both were buried by hostile, or at least skeptical, committees. Meanwhile, the Congress continued to write legislative vetoes into individual bills, sometimes applying the procedure to the regulations of entire agencies, such as the Federal Trade Commission and the Department of Education. Yet, sometimes, the opposition prevailed even in the House; in 1980, only a few days after it joined in subjecting all Federal Trade Commission regulations to a congressional veto by concurrent resolution, it declined by three votes, 189 to 192, to apply an identical requirement to regulation of the trucking industry by the Interstate Commerce Commission and the Department of Transportation.

A test case did not arise until mid-1980, when the House and Senate

22. "The President's News Conference of July 25, 1979," *Weekly Compilation of Presidential Documents*, vol. 15 (July 30, 1979), p. 1311. The law as enacted contains a complex series of legislative veto compromises. Under its provisions, a standby plan was presented to the Congress in 1980 and, not being disapproved, became official.

23. "Federal Trade Commission Improvements Act of 1980," ibid., vol. 16 (June 2, 1980), pp. 982–83. The act contains a provision intended to expedite such a challenge.

24. *Congressional Record*, daily edition, June 21, 1978, p. H5880.

25. *New York Times*, June 22, 1978.

vetoed four sets of education regulations in a dispute over interpretation of the law. Attorney General Benjamin R. Civiletti instructed the new secretary of education, Shirley M. Hufstedler, that she was free to enforce the regulations anyway. But the Congress had the last word; it simply inserted language in appropriation bills—not only the bill funding education programs but other appropriation measures as well—prohibiting expenditure of funds to enforce regulations that had been rejected under any legislative veto provisions, and Secretary Hufstedler announced she was reconsidering the disputed rules. The administration finally found another case, when the Ninth Circuit Court of Appeals in December struck down a legislative veto provision in the law establishing procedures for deporting aliens. In Carter's last week in office, the White House announced that the Justice Department would ask the Supreme Court to review the case and issue a definitive ruling.

A few days later, the first president to have expressed support of the legislative veto was inaugurated. In a campaign speech in October, Ronald Reagan endorsed "greater authority" for both the Congress and the president to veto regulations approved by executive agencies.[26] His position reflected that of the Republican platform of 1980. Nevertheless, he authorized the Justice Department to proceed with the test the Carter administration had initiated. The prospect for judicial determination was clouded, however, by the prospect that any Supreme Court decision might not apply to all of the widely varied veto provisions contained in scores of statutes.[27]

Never, or Always, or Sometimes?

As the 1970s drew to a close, the legislative veto was the most forceful continuing expression of the congressional resurgence. The House of Representatives and the presidency were polarized on the issue of how far the

26. Ibid., January 15 and March 19, 1981.
27. Attorney General Bell argued, for instance, that the legislative veto as contained in reorganization legislation applied to matters sufficiently different from those covered by other veto provisions to pass the constitutional test while the others failed. He contended that to call the reorganization act provision a legislative veto was a misnomer "because there the President decides which programs to submit. He doesn't lose any of the Executive's power under the Constitution." Transcript of news briefing, June 21, 1978, p. 2. Similar language was contained in the president's message of the same day. How the fact of presidential initiative distinguishes the reorganization act provision from any other—since all matters subject to legislative veto originate in the executive branch—is likely to escape the layman, but the argument does suggest that the substantial differences in circumstances surrounding particular veto provisions might make the reach and applicability of any initial Supreme Court decision unclear. The one-house veto and the committee veto raise constitutional questions additional to those raised by the two-house veto, in which the whole Congress participates.

legislative veto process should extend, with the Senate somewhere in between. The House in 1976 had said "always" in regard to regulations, with almost two-thirds of its members ready to alter profoundly the constitutional balance of power by making the legislative veto universal in its coverage of agency rule-making. Like every president since Hoover, Jimmy Carter, officially, was saying "never"; he would outlaw legislative vetoes altogether. The arguments are both constitutional and practical.

On the constitutional question, presidents and attorneys general have consistently reiterated the contentions of Herbert Hoover's attorney general. "Such intrusive devices," President Carter said, "infringe on the Executive's constitutional duty to faithfully execute the laws. They also authorize congressional action that has the effect of legislation while denying the President the opportunity to exercise his veto."[28] The opposing argument is summed up by Representative Levitas:

> Certainly, Congress delegates rulemaking authority to the executive branch agencies, but the separation of powers doctrine does not preclude that the delegation be absolute and cannot be conditioned by legislation enacted according to the constitutional design. In short, if Congress has the power to delegate rulemaking authority, it is axiomatic that it can delegate all that power, or it can condition or limit that delegated power by making it subject to a Congressional veto.[29]

These two central arguments have been refined and embellished by constitutional scholars[30] and rehearsed in lawsuits. When the Court of Claims upheld the one-house veto in the Federal Salary Act of 1967,[31] the Supreme Court passed up the opportunity to review that decision on appeal, but in another case Associate Justice Byron R. White offered a dictum affirming the constitutionality of the legislative veto "in light of history and modern reality

---

28. "Legislative Vetoes, June 21, 1978."

29. Testimony, July 11, 1969, *Regulatory Reform and Congressional Review of Agency Rules*, Hearings before a subcommittee of the House Rules Committee, 96 Cong. 1 sess. (GPO, 1980), p. 10. The argument, directed at rulemaking, applies equally to other grants of authority by the legislature to the executive—power to contract, expend funds, use military forces, etc.

30. Among recent analyses of the constitutional issue are the statements in *Regulatory Reform*, Hearings, of Attorney General Civiletti, Circuit Court Judge Harold Leventhal, and academicians Joseph Cooper, Robert G. Dixon, Jr., Eugene Gressman, and Antonin Scalia; John T. Melsheimer, "Discussion of the Congressional Veto Provisions Contained in the Federal Election Campaign Act of 1971, as Amended, in Light of the *Buckley* Decisions" (Congressional Research Service, February 20, 1976); Thomas J. Nicola, Clark F. Norton, and John T. Melsheimer, "Congressional Veto of Executive Actions," Issue Brief IB76006 (Congressional Research Service, February 3, 1976, updated May 4, 1979); H. Lee Watson, "Congress Steps Out: A Look at Congressional Control of the Executive," *California Law Review*, vol. 63 (July 1975), pp. 983–1094; Robert G. Dixon, Jr., "The Congressional Veto and Separation of Powers: The Executive on a Leash," *North Carolina Law Review*, vol. 56 (April 1978), pp. 423–94; John R. Bolton, *The Legislative Veto: Unseparating the Powers* (Washington: American Enterprise Institute for Public Policy Research, 1977); and Louis Fisher, "A Political Context for Legislative Vetoes," *Political Science Quarterly*, vol. 93 (Summer 1978), pp. 241–54. The last two and the Cooper testimony also discuss the practical issues.

31. *Atkins v. United States*, 556 F. 2d 1028 (Ct. Cl. 1977). The court divided four to three.

. . . at least where the President has agreed to legislation establishing the disapproval procedure or the legislation has been passed over his veto."[32]

Justice White's language does not offer much of a clue as to where the Court might eventually stand on this issue. His "at least" clause is particularly puzzling. Since all legislative veto provisions have been in bills either agreed to (signed) by the president, or passed over his veto, White must have meant to distinguish between those accepted willingly and those accepted under protest as evidenced by presidential statements. The distinction has perhaps been obliterated by President Carter's subsequent blanket protest against all such provisions. But, if not, for the Court to draw the line between the branches wherever the president says he wants it drawn would be a most unusual form of judicial compromise, and one that would set awkward precedents for future courts. Traditionally, the justices have been reluctant to concede that the president and the Congress, simply by agreeing to do so, can alter the Constitution. Even more dubious is Justice White's suggestion that the Congress can strip the president of a constitutional power simply by overriding his veto. Yet the reference to "history and modern reality" reflects the reluctance with which the Court would move toward prohibiting the use of a device that both the Congress and the executive have repeatedly found valuable in reaching their own compromises over the form and content of delegations of authority. And that is the key point: both branches have found the legislative veto a realistic way of resolving practical issues in their relations.

The Executive Would Regret "Never"

Were the executive branch to succeed in getting the legislative veto outlawed, it would in all likelihood come to regret it. In too many cases, the legislative veto has been the key to getting the very delegation of authority the executive wants. If the Congress were faced with a stark, no-compromise choice of giving the executive either an absolute delegation of power or none at all, its decisions would depend on its mood at the time and the extent of its trust in a president and his subordinates. Given the temper of the Congress in the 1970s, it very likely would have, at least in many important cases, written its delegation in the narrowest terms or withheld it altogether.

32. Separate opinion in *Buckley* v. *Valeo*, 424 U.S. 1, at 285 (1976). The case concerned the Federal Election Campaign Act. The court as a whole did not confront the legislative veto issue; its finding that certain provisions of the law were unconstitutional was based on other grounds. Ibid., at 140, note 176.

Rather than approving blanket reorganization authority, for instance, it would have said in effect, "Work out your plans, then send them up and we will consider passing them by statute." All of the advantages to the executive of the long-established system for reorganizing—the no-amendment, take-it-or-leave-it procedure; the victory for the president in the case of congressional inaction—would be lost. In the debate on the 1977 reorganization act, significantly, those who argued that the legislative veto was unconstitutional were proposing a no-delegation, not a blanket-delegation, law. In other cases the Congress would have adopted one or another two-stage procedure like those it devised in the 1950s to overcome presidential objections to legislative vetoes. In the impoundment control act, if the legislators had been prohibited from controlling deferrals of spending through a simple veto process, they surely would have insisted on either approving each one by statute or granting a delegation limited to small amounts. In setting up Amtrak, the national railway passenger service, they would have asked the administration to recommend criteria and standards for statutory enactment, instead of delegating authority for their adoption subject to veto; in effect, they would have felt compelled to draw the service map by law, as they ultimately did voluntarily anyway after failing to exercise their available veto. In the case of the various committee vetoes of individual contracts or projects, the alternative is well-established; the committees would return to line-item authorizations and appropriations, approving each undertaking when and as the proposal was firm. This is the alternative that would have been available, likewise, for the two-house vetoes adopted to control arms sales and the allocation of foreign aid.

The Congress could also accomplish much of what it seeks by falling back on report-and-wait procedures, whose constitutionality the Justice Department has usually conceded.[33] During the waiting period, the Congress could take the same types of action it now takes under legislative veto provisions. Disapproval could be expressed by a subcommittee or a committee, or by a single house, or by both houses concurring. Administrators do not normally ignore such expressions, though they are not binding (and though committees and subcommittees may not reflect the views of their houses). Beyond these types of formal action lies the whole range of informal ways of bringing

33. The only exception appears to have been President Johnson's 1965 veto on constitutional grounds of a military construction authorization bill containing an unusually long waiting period. President Ford's 1976 veto of another military construction bill for the same reason was based on policy rather than constitutional objections.

pressure on administrators through suggestions and requests backed up by explicit or implicit threats.[34]

If the agency persists in doing what was disapproved, the Congress can legislate in such a way as to escape the presidential veto—by inserting amendments into authorizing acts (and prohibition of the legislative veto would doubtless accelerate the trend from permanent or multiyear to annual authorizations) or as riders on appropriations bills. These equivalents of the legislative veto were used countless times before that instrument appeared in 1932 and have been used steadily—and with increasing frequency—since. Through these means, the Congress has reversed administrative policies and regulations on school busing, for instance, and on abortion. Among its interventions in administrative detail in 1978 were bills prohibiting the Fish and Wildlife Service from requiring (except where the states agreed) that waterfowl hunters use steel rather than lead shot; prohibiting the Bureau of Alcohol, Tobacco, and Firearms from carrying out a proposed rule requiring serial numbering of firearms and reporting of sales; prohibiting the Energy Regulatory Administration from paying for public participation in hearings; prohibiting Radio Free Europe from allowing communist nations to use its facilities unless those nations reciprocated; denying the Defense Department permission to reduce Marine Corps basic training from eleven to nine weeks; prohibiting the consolidation of the Navy's training program for helicopter pilots at Pensacola, Florida, with Army and Air Force programs; exempting twenty Colorado river projects from any requirement for a comprehensive environmental impact statement; preserving the Navy's air shuttle service for carrying reserve officers to their drill units; and rebuking the administration for allowing former Budget Director Bert Lance to continue to carry an official passport after he left office.[35] Appropriation riders, of course, have their own unique pathology. The normal processes of hearings and committee deliberation are circumvented, and appropriations bills are delayed, sometimes for months, in disputes over substantive issues. Indeed, in the 1980 fiscal year, the regular appropriations bill for the Departments of Labor and Health, Education, and Welfare could not be passed because of a deadlock on a rider

34. The House Commerce Committee succeeded in delaying the authorization of pay television by the Federal Communications Commission for ten years without ever reporting legislation for that purpose and without benefit of any formal veto procedure. It accomplished its end by "threats, letters, resolutions, and hearings." Harold H. Bruff and Ernest Gellhorn, "Congressional Control of Administrative Regulation: A Study of Legislative Vetoes," *Harvard Law Review*, vol. 90 (May 1977), p. 1421.

35. *Congressional Quarterly Almanac, 1978*, pp. 122, 99–100, 411, 144.

dealing with abortion, and the departments had to be funded for the entire year through makeshift interim legislation.[36]

President Carter's handling of the legislation on gasoline rationing in 1979 illustrates the dilemma any president would face if the legislative veto were outlawed. Struggling with the Congress over a pressing practical problem, the president took the position best calculated to get the bill through Congress. Acceptance of the legislative veto was one of his bargaining chips, and one he was willing to expend. He got the legislation, and when his standby rationing plan was presented, no veto was interposed and it became official, for use if necessary. Had the legislative veto been outlawed, the country in all probability would have gotten no gasoline rationing plan, for the Congress would not have been able to agree on one.

Facing the same reality, President Kennedy included a provision for legislative veto in the bill he presented to the Congress in 1962 asking for a standby authority in the president to make temporary reductions in tax rates when necessary to stimulate the economy.[37] This conformed to the recommendation made the previous year by a prestigious private group, the Commission on Money and Credit, except that body had proposed presidential authority—subject to veto—to adjust tax rates upward as well as downward.[38] Since then, the idea has received support from such experienced practical figures as Arthur F. Burns, long-time chairman of the Federal Reserve Board, and Senate Republican Leader Howard H. Baker, Jr.[39] To cope with a related economic problem where decisions, if they are made, must be made quickly,

36. See the denunciation of appropriations riders as an "insult to the legislative process," by Senator Harrison Williams, Jr., Democrat of New Jersey and chairman of the Labor and Public Welfare Committee, *Congressional Record*, daily edition, September 11, 1980, pp. S12402-04. The number of appropriations riders adopted on the House floor rose from no more than seven annually in the 1963–68 period to more than twenty each year in 1977–79 and fifty in the first nine months of 1980. *Congressional Quarterly Weekly Report*, vol. 38 (November 1, 1980), p. 3252. The increase prompted discussion of ways to restrain the practice, but no action was taken.

37. "Annual Message to the Congress on the State of the Union, January 11, 1962," and "Letter to the President of the Senate and to the Speaker of the House Concerning Standby Authority to Reduce Income Taxes, May 8, 1962," *Public Papers of the Presidents: John F. Kennedy, 1962* (GPO, 1963), pp. 6, 371–72.

38. *Money and Credit*, Report of the Commission on Money and Credit (Prentice-Hall, 1961), pp. 136–37. The commission, headed by Frazar B. Wilde, was established by the Committee for Economic Development. Even broader proposals had been made by other observers of the smooth working of the Reorganization Act. See Thomas I. Emerson, "Administration of Stabilization Policy," in Max F. Millikan, ed., *Income Stabilization for a Developing Democracy* (Yale University Press, 1953), p. 688 (covering tax measures, spending power, and direct controls); and Peter Schauffler, "The Legislative Veto Revisited," *Public Policy*, vol. 8 (1958), pp. 324–26 (covering tax and expenditure policy).

39. Baker, "What Presidential Powers Should Be Cut?" in Charles Roberts, ed., *Has the President Too Much Power?* (Harper's Magazine Press, 1974), pp. 42–43.

Arnold R. Weber, who had wage and price control responsibilities in the Nixon administration, has urged that the president be given permanent authority for selective controls subject to congressional approval of their use within fifteen to thirty days of his action.[40]

All this suggests that the constitutional issue is of secondary importance, and that its resolution wholly in favor of the executive branch, were that to happen, would bring the executive more loss than gain. The legislative veto has proved its value repeatedly as a practical way of resolving vexing questions of relations between the branches. In most areas of government, whenever the Congress desired to assert control, it would still find ways of doing so. Only the form of the veto would be changed and the alternative procedures would add to the burden on the Congress, would make relations between the branches more cumbersome, and would lead to a net reduction in the authority that the Congress would be willing to delegate.

The Congress Would Regret "Always"

But if the Congress were to go all the way in the other direction and apply the veto to all rules and regulations, as in the Levitas bill, it would surely come to regret that decision. In arguing against the Levitas and Schmitt bills, congressional opponents drew a gloomy picture of a Congress overwhelmed with the responsibility of passing on seven thousand rules a year. The Congress would be encouraged to "pass the buck" to the executive on hard questions, knowing that if it legislated loosely it would have a chance to reconsider after the executive branch had made up its mind. Then, if it exercised the veto, the administrators would know only what the policy should not be, not necessarily what it should be—leaving a void. Accountability and responsibility would be lost. They envision a Capitol Hill flooded with lobbyists seeking to overturn administrative decisions. Issues deliberately taken out of the political arena because of their technical complexity and turned over to experts in the executive branch would be brought back. The well-heeled interests who could afford expensive lobbying campaigns would have the advantage. The Congress would be swamped with minutiae, on the one hand, and questions inappropriate for political decision, on the other. The result would be a vast expansion of staff to review the regulations,

40. "The Continuing Courtship: Wage-Price Policy through Five Administrations," in Craufurd D. Goodwin, ed., *Exhortation and Controls: The Search for a Wage-Price Policy, 1945–1971* (Brookings Institution, 1975), pp. 382–83.

hear the pleas of the aggrieved citizens, and initiate the veto procedures. The staff would be just as "unelected" and "nameless" as are the maligned bureaucrats—"we turn them over on our own payroll so fast, we don't even know their names," remarked Senator John C. Culver, Democrat of Iowa, at a Senate hearing.[41] It would neither be as expert as its executive counterpart nor bound by the rules of fair play required for executive agencies by the Administrative Procedures Act. Decisions would necessarily not be made on the record of the regulatory hearings; in many cases, the record would be too long even to be read. The Senate and the House would have to make decisions on engineering and scientific issues that the membership could not possibly master. Anyone who heard, for instance, the Senate floor debate on the merits of a five-mile-per-hour as against a two-and-a-half-mile-per-hour standard for automobile bumper safety—actually a quarrel between the steel and aluminum industries—can only share such misgivings.[42]

President Carter, of course, did not base his opposition on the convenience or inherent inadequacies of the Congress but on the damage that he claimed would be done to the administrative process. In his 1978 message, he argued, first, that the legislative veto "greatly compounds" the problems of delay and "uncertainty which cripples planning by business, state, and local governments, and many others." It took three vetoes and three years, for instance, for the Senate, the House, and the administration to reach agreement on the disposition of President Nixon's papers, and such "lengthy, expensive procedures could easily become commonplace under legislative veto statutes." Second, a legislative veto "can seriously harm the regulatory process." Carter explained:

> Regulators operating under such laws would seek to avoid vetoes. They would therefore tend to give more weight to the perceived political power of affected groups and less to their substantive arguments. Meetings of regulatory commissions could degenerate into speculation about how to write rules so they would escape future disapproval of future Congressional reviewers who are not present nor represented when the rules are being drafted. Many regulations would be evolved in negotiations between agency officials and Congressional staff members, subverting requirements in present law for public notice and comment and for decisions based on the record. Parties to regulatory proceedings, never knowing when a decision might be vetoed, would have to reargue each issue in Congress.
>
> These problems would lead many regulators to reverse the constructive trend toward adopting uniform rules. They would revert to acting on a case-by-case basis,

41. *Regulatory Reform,* Hearings in June–July 1979 before a subcommittee of the Senate Judiciary Committee, 96 Cong. 1 sess. (GPO, 1980), p. 114.

42. *Congressional Record,* daily edition, July 11, 1979, pp. S9159–65. On the inadequacy of the congressional process, see the excellent case, pertaining to immigration, offered by Fisher, "A Political Context," pp. 251–53.

because the legislative veto cannot be applied to such decisions. This lack of uniformity would not reduce the scope of regulation, but it would reduce clarity and certainty.[43]

Instead of blaming the regulators, Carter went on, the Congress should reexamine the laws that authorize or mandate the undesired rules, and deregulate where appropriate.

Representative Levitas and his allies see the opponents' fears as highly exaggerated and envision no great change were his bill to be enacted. The lobbyists, they argue, come to the Hill now, seeking redress through the means the Congress always possesses—appropriations riders, special legislation, special legislation, oversight hearings, informal pressure, and so on. They have to be heard. Congressional staffs have already been expanded for purposes of oversight and review of regulatory activity. They and the members would select only cases appropriate for congressional intervention, and very few of those, because the mere existence of the veto procedure would cause regulation writers to be more careful of congressional intent and more sensitive to citizen opinion. That has been the experience, they say, in the states that have adopted legislative veto procedures.

Given these opposing sets of predictions, what can be induced from the experience thus far with the vetoes enacted piecemeal in individual laws? Harold H. Bruff and Ernest Gellhorn's penetrating study of five acts passed in the 1970s confirms most of the criticisms leveled at the legislative veto.[44] The authors found delay: in the case of the decontrol of petroleum prices by the Federal Energy Administration, the House vetoed two agency proposals in 1975 and finally established its own policy in legislation. This case, conclude the authors, "shows the veto's potential for interbranch deadlock. It demonstrates how, in cases of disagreement on basic policy between Congress and the agency, the veto power can cause the frustration of important agency programs or the failure to formulate any programs at all." Again, the case of the Nixon tapes and papers illustrates how "a legislative veto may only lead to deadlock and inaction where there are substantial policy differences between Congress and the rulemaking agency."[45]

The studies confirm President Carter's fear that regulations would be evolved not through public processes but through negotiations between agency and congressional staffs. "Significant negotiation occurred in all five

43. "Legislative Vetoes, June 21, 1978," p. 1148.
44. "Congressional Control of Administrative Regulation," pp. 1369–1440. The five case studies, made for the Administrative Conference of the United States, included two concerned with the Office of Education and one each the Federal Energy Administration, the General Services Administration (Nixon's tapes and papers), and the Federal Election Commission.
45. Ibid., pp. 1390, 1402.

programs despite their disparate natures, and it was often intense," the authors found, and agencies bent their rules in favor of interest groups that were known to be influential on Capitol Hill.[46] The negotiations were "of low visibility" or even secret, which "violates two of the fundamental standards for informal rulemaking: reasoned decisionmaking based on a record and an opportunity for public participants to contest opposing presentations." Indeed, they smacked of the kind of ex parte influences in administrative decisionmaking that has led the courts in some cases to invalidate decisions.[47] The processes favored groups "having greater resources or prior influence with congressional committees," which violates "the ideal of equal access to the rulemaking process." Indeed, once time and energy have been spent negotiating an agreement with the Congress, the proposed rule may become "substantially harder to change through subsequent public comment." The studies also documented the lack of quality and thoroughness of congressional review; the congressional members and their staffs lacked the time to master, or even examine, all the facts the agency possessed, and on technical questions they lacked expertise. And there was no assurance that the individual legislators or staff members who negotiated and settled policy issues with the administrators—without bringing the questions to the floor of either house through formal veto resolutions—interpreted the law, or effectively amended it, in the same way as would the full membership of the Congress if it had had the opportunity.[48]

On the question of delay, it may be argued in response that where delays occurred as in the presidential papers case, they were not due to the legislative veto as such but to the fact that the Congress was not ready to establish policy. In the absence of a veto procedure, the legislative body would in all likelihood have withheld delegation, instructing the administrative agency to return with proposed legislation rather than with proposed rules. The ultimate delay would have been greater, because once agreement was reached the rules would have had to go through the entire legislative process rather than just a designated waiting period.

Bruff and Gellhorn conclude, on the basis of their cases, that the legislative veto should be abandoned altogether as a device for the oversight of rulemaking. Certainly, their findings weigh heavily against making the veto universal, bringing before the Congress thousands of regulations annually

46. Ibid., pp. 1410, 1413.
47. Ibid., pp. 1413–14, 1433–37. While the decisions invalidated have usually been of a quasi-judicial rather than a quasi-legislative character, in at least one case, *Home Box Office, Inc.* v. *FCC,* no. 75-1280 (D.C. Cir., March 25, 1977), the court set aside a rule because of ex parte activity.
48. Bruff and Gellhorn, "Congressional Control of Administrative Regulation," pp. 1413–18.

on matters where the legislators have not felt impelled to reserve a review power heretofore. But as to whether the veto should be used selectively to control rulemaking, the question in each case is the one that was asked in regard to the use of the device in reorganization, or impoundment, or war powers legislation, or project authorization: what, in the given circumstances, would be the alternative? If the practical alternative is no delegation at all, then delegation with a veto may prove to be the most expeditious means of resolving the divergent points of view of the two branches. When the Congress is in doubt as to the exact nature of program and policies to be carried out, the quickest way to get the information necessary to decide those questions may be to create an administrative organization and let it proceed. But without the veto, it might be properly reluctant to give the administrators any such carte blanche. To say "never" to the veto, even if the negative applies only to rulemaking, may on some occasions mean longer delay and more cumbersome processes in initiating necessary governmental action.

If Sometimes, When and How?

Thus, neither of the extreme positions is satisfactory. For the executive branch—or the courts—to say "never" to the legislative veto would be, for the executive branch itself, self-defeating. And for the Congress to say "always," as in the Levitas bill, would weigh it down with an enormous burden that it does not need and is not equipped to handle and that would certainly lead, in many instances, to abuse and impropriety. The only remaining conclusion is "sometimes." That is the position taken by congressional opponents of the "always" approach—as, for instance, the Senate Government Operations Committee after its intensive year-long study of federal regulation.[49]

That leaves to be resolved the questions of when and how. The Government Operations Committee suggested the veto is useful in "limited situations" where the initiative has traditionally lain with the executive and flexibility is essential but "Congress' responsibilities require it to review executive action." That definition does not resolve very much, however. The committee identifies arms sales and government reorganization as among the limited situations, but others would find that "Congress' responsibilities" require review of a far wider—or even the whole—range of executive initiatives. Perhaps,

49. *Study on Federal Regulation,* S. Doc. 95-26, 95 Cong. 1 sess. (GPO, 1977), vol. 2, chap. 10. Fisher eloquently espouses the same "pragmatic approach" in "A Political Context," pp. 253–54.

in time, general guidelines can be evolved, but in the meantime the best course is to leave the questions to be resolved case by case, in the normal course of designing and enacting legislation. With each delegation of authority to the executive, the desirability of a veto and the form of any that is to be employed are among the issues to be debated within the Congress and between it and the executive branch. As in bargaining over other provisions of legislation, the executive branch begins from a position of not inconsiderable strength; its position can be backed by the threat of presidential veto and by actual vetoes, which have forced the Congress to back down so often in the nearly half a century of struggle on this issue. The executive can consider in each case what the alternative to a proposed veto is likely to be. Where the alternatives are likely to be worse, from its standpoint, it may accept some vetoes—as President Carter did in the standby legislation for gasoline rationing. In other cases, it may draw the line.

In this as in every other aspect of congressional control of the executive branch, the executive must depend largely, in the end, on congressional self-restraint. It is a constitutional fact of life that nothing can prevent the Congress from exercising a tight control over the execution of the laws if it elects to do so. So nothing can prevent it from finding some way to assert an effective veto over administrative action whenever its displeasure is deep enough. The problem, for the Congress, is to attain the degree of internal discipline that will enable it to distinguish constructive from destructive intervention and to avoid the latter. Skeptics will question whether such a prescription is realistic in the light of the evident congressional self-interest, but up to the Nixon years, self-restraint—encouraged by presidential protests and presidential vetoes—did characterize the slow evolution of the legislative veto. It also characterized the behavior of the Congress in general; throughout its long period of decline, it was not grasping for power, and it voluntarily divested itself of much of its control over the executive—from line-item budgeting to Senate confirmation of postmasters. Congressional self-restraint dissolved in the 1970s only as part of the general dissolution of trust between the branches. The present level of distrust, one may hope, is a transitory phenomenon, growing mainly out of the peculiar circumstances of the Nixon period. As trust is gradually restored, one happy consequence should prove to be greater restraint and selectivity on the part of the Congress in enacting legislative vetoes. In the meantime, when and as the Congress does find them necessary, they are a good place for application of the sunset doctrine. Legislative veto provisions contain so much potential for abuse that their number should be strictly minimized; each such enactment should be made subject to review and reenactment, if it is still found to be necessary, at periodic intervals. The sunset idea was adopted, incidentally, when the two-house veto was written into the 1980 Federal Trade Commission legislation and was scheduled to expire on September 30, 1982, unless renewed before that date.

CHAPTER XIII

To Strengthen Congressional Capacity

THE MOOD of unease and rebellion within the Congress induced by the clash with Richard Nixon was seized on by reformers of every stripe. "The fault lies not in the executive branch, but in ourselves, in the Congress," Mike Mansfield had said in 1973, and his view was echoed both within and outside the legislature. So at the same time that the Congress looked angrily down Pennsylvania Avenue to the White House, determined to cut an overweening presidency down to size, it looked anxiously inward too—at its own structures, practices, habits, folkways. The substantial element in the Congress that had been advocating reforms of various kinds for a long time—and had gained some momentum in effectuating change—became even more vocal, and they were joined by newcomers chosen by a reform-minded electorate. Clamorous voices outside the Congress were charging the legislature with nonfeasance for permitting executive misfeasance, and under these circumstances the reformers were heard.

The half dozen years surrounding the crisis of 1972–73 saw the greatest spurt of congressional reform since the Revolution of 1910 transformed the House. It is not too much to say that in the 1970s the Congress was transformed again. Its new form is not yet clearly defined, just as the import of the earlier changes was not fully delineated on the morrow of 1910. But that the mores and organization and procedures of the legislature are profoundly different at the beginning of the 1980s from what they were at the start of the preceding reformist decade is unmistakable.

Some of the reforms were deliberately designed to ameliorate the endemic weaknesses of the Congress that the members themselves recognized—its difficulty in formulating programs of its own, independent of presidential leadership, and in pulling itself together to act coherently and decisively. Preeminent among these changes was the new congressional budget process. The time-honored seniority system was at last shorn of its absolutism in both houses, breaking the power of committee chairmen to obstruct action; in the process, leadership institutions were strengthened, although power flowed outward in greater measure, to subcommittee chairmen and individual legislators. The House majority party caucus, long quiescent, was revived for a time. The Democratic Steering and Policy Committee of the House was brought under leadership control and reactivated. Both House and Senate set up committees to review and revamp their standing committee structures, although the House effort was not notably successful. The Congress dramatically expanded the staffs of committees and individual members, created a second new organization for independent policy research and analysis—in addition to the Congressional Budget Office—in the Office of Technology Assessment, and broadened the research and program evaluation functions of the General Accounting Office and the Congressional Research Service of the Library of Congress. By the end of the decade the resources at the call of the Congress for policy analysis and development had in many critical areas the capacity to compete effectively with, and serve as a check on, those of the executive branch itself.

Still other reforms were aimed primarily at improving the reputation of the Congress, by opening up hitherto hidden processes to public scrutiny. Subcommittee and committee "mark-up" sessions—where compromises are struck and bills rewritten—were brought into the full view of lobbyists and journalists. So, even, were conference committee meetings. Previously unrecorded teller votes in the Houses were placed on record, as that body introduced electronic voting. The House even introduced televised recording of its proceedings. Both House and Senate introduced new, tight rules limiting what members could earn outside the Congress and requiring disclosure of income and investments.[1]

When the surge of reform had spent itself at the end of the decade, however, the endemic weaknesses of the Congress—its inability to act quickly and its inability to integrate policy—were by no means fully remedied. Some

---

1. Reforms relating to openness of processes, ethical conduct, and introduction of technology are not discussed further, because while they affect the moral tone and public reputation of the Congress, they do not bear significantly on its capacity to do its work or on the balance of power between the branches.

changes, notably the budget process, did create a new integrative capacity. But centrifugal as well as centripetal forces were at work, and even as centralizing institutions were developed in the 1970s, the accelerating trend toward democratization and individualism was affecting the character of the Congress.

Underlying the transformation of the Congress in the 1970s was a change in the psychology of the individual members of the House and Senate. It is the difference between the members of today and those of a generation ago that made reform possible—indeed, probably made it inevitable, so that Nixon and Watergate served only to advance the timing. That difference determined also the direction and character of the reforms themselves. And it explains the difficulty the Congress encounters in mobilizing its resources to act coherently and decisively.

From Party Regularity to Political Individualism

Everyone who has participated in the affairs of the Congress, or observed them, since the 1940s or 1950s can testify to the differences in the goals and attitudes and temperament of the typical member of the 1970s. These are the consequences, surely, of the gradual transformation in this century of the political system from which the holders of elective office emerge. The dominant element of the new political order is individualism. Political individualism—the antithesis of party regularity and party cohesion—is at once a cause and a product of the decay of the strong political party organizations that once dominated American politics, a decay that dates from the Progressive Era and has been accelerating especially since World War II.

The old-style organizations declined and disappeared when reformers struck at the two pillars that sustained the "machines" and their "bosses." Civil service systems and other reforms drastically reduced the amount of patronage at the disposal of the party leaders. And the direct primary undermined and eventually took away their control of nominations. Today, in many places, party organizations scarcely exist, or where they do exist many have ceased even to try to exert influence in the party's choice of candidates.

The old-style organizations manned by professional politicians in the wards and precincts have in some places been superseded by new-style organizations led and dominated by amateurs—persons who are in politics, in James Q. Wilson's definition, not primarily for a livelihood or a pecuniary reward but because they find political activity "intrinsically rewarding because it expresses a commitment to a larger purpose."[2] They differ from professionals not in the degree of their dedication or skill—amateurs may devote as much time to politics and be as effective as professionals—but in their goals and motivation. Prototypically, the new amateur organizations are concerned with issues rather than patronage, manned by volunteer workers rather than by public jobholders and their relatives, motivated by programmatic goals (Wilson's "larger purpose") rather than by the prospect of material reward, led by men and women chosen through processes involving wide and open participation by the party rank and file. Compared to the old machines, even the strongest of the new-style groups are relatively undisciplined, essentially individualistic, with participants taking orders from no one and making individual voluntary choices as to what leadership they will accept and follow. In the nominating process, they tend to encourage rather than restrict competition; even when they hold preprimary endorsing conventions, they typically open those assemblies to wide participation, and the proceedings are individualistic and undisciplined.[3] Yet in many places no significant structure of any kind has appeared as the old ones withered away, and individualism is the whole of the political order. Or nearly the whole, for the vacuum is partly filled by the single-issue groups—antiabortionists, environmentalists, anti-gun-control groups, or whatever—who are a kind of organized individualism, their power magnified by the absence of broad and disciplined parties as political competition and as mediating influence.

The difference in the political milieus from which candidates spring could not help but produce a different type of candidate for Congress as well as other offices. So the new-style congressman differs from the old as radically as the new-style political organization—or none at all—differs from the old political machine. Individualism in the constituencies put individualists in office, and when enough of them were in the Congress, the nature of the place was bound to change.

2. James Q. Wilson, *Political Organizations* (Basic Books, 1973), p. 106. The new-style organizations have not yet been widely analyzed. James Q. Wilson, *The Amateur Democrat* (University of Chicago Press, 1962), is the basic work; Stephen A. Mitchell, *Elm Street Politics* (Oceana, 1959), presents the reflections of a Democratic national chairman; John W. Soule and James W. Clark, "Amateurs and Professionals: A Study of Delegates to the 1968 Democratic National Convention," *American Political Science Review*, vol. 64 (September 1970), pp. 888–98, applies the Wilson criteria to examine differences between amateur and professional convention delegates; Raymond E. Wolfinger, *The Politics of Progress* (Prentice-Hall, 1974), chap. 4, especially pp. 95–106, uses definitions similar to Wilson's in a study of local politics.

3. James L. Sundquist, *Dynamics of the Party System: Alignment and Realignment of Political Parties in the United States* (Brookings Institution, 1973), especially pp. 239–44, 265–69, sketches the rise of new-style party organizations in various states.

The typical member produced by an old-style pre-Progressive party organization—whether Republican or Democratic, liberal or conservative, urban or rural—had been trained to be deferential. Coming from a political apprenticeship in which leadership and hierarchy were normal and accepted, he accepted them in the Congress, too. His views on political issues were compatible with those of his organization. He was content to follow his party leadership, in the House or Senate, or in the White House, and his orthodoxy in voting was predictable. Since the nomination was, in some measure, a reward for past services, he might look on the job as largely honorary, and he might or might not work hard at it. Except for one aspect of his job: getting material returns for his constituents—judgeships, postmasterships, jobs in Washington, pork in its many forms for his state or district. His power to obtain these benefits increased with seniority, and as long as he performed acceptably in these respects, he could count on the organization that sent him to the Congress to keep him there. His career did not depend on any showing of brilliance in the conception or advocacy of legislative measures, and he was not likely to mount a challenge to the way the Congress was organized or run.

The new-style member contrasts with the old in political manners, political vocabulary, interests, and conception of the proper nature of the institution in which he serves. As a congressional candidate, he was self-chosen. Nobody handed him the nomination; he won it in open competition, usually by the vote of the party rank and file in a direct primary. He won it by identifying and articulating the issues better than his competitors. Hence he is usually well educated. His background is likely to be less in party service than in intellectual and advocacy organizations, of all kinds. His interest in patronage is minimal, though pork retains its value and he may be proficient in obtaining it. His absorbing interest is governmental policy. He came to the Congress with a sense of mission, even a mandate, to have an impact on the legislative process. He is impatient, for those who backed him expect legislative results. An upstart as a candidate—self-selected, self-organized, self-propelled, self-reliant—he will be an upstart in the House or Senate, too. He has no habit of being deferential to the established and the powerful, and he will not be so in the Congress, either in committee or on the floor.

At the moment the first of them arrived, the new-style members began demanding that bossism in the House and Senate give way to equality and democracy, and their first triumph—supported, of course, by many old-style members for purely partisan and factional reasons—was the overthrow of

Czar Cannon in 1910. But they were soon to learn that an oligarchy of seniority-protected committee chairmen could be as oppressive as the autocracy they had just brought down, and seniority—along with such other antidemocratic institutions as the Senate filibuster—became the new targets for reform. Bosses were being dethroned and disciplined party machines were disintegrating back home, but it would be some time before party organizations in the Congress fell apart as well. First, the new-style congressmen and senators had to attain a critical mass of numbers within the majority party in each house.

That day did not arrive for nearly half a century, but when it did come it came abruptly—in 1958. November of that year saw a Democratic landslide, which turned on issues of economic policy. The fifteen freshman Democratic senators and threescore representatives who made up the class of 1958 were preponderantly of the new type, more markedly in the Senate than in the House. A large majority of them supplanted Republicans; hence they came from states or districts where the Democratic party had been relatively weak, where it may have scarcely existed until the postwar period. Many came from areas where the Progressive tradition was strong early in the century and where the Democratic party was the inheritor of that tradition. Most of the newcomers, then, arrived as individualists or as the product of new-style Democratic organizations that took shape after the war in areas of traditional Republican predominance. The new-type congressman, who before 1958 had appeared as something of an aberration, became overnight almost the norm.

So the norms of the Congress as a body changed too. The new members expected a full share of responsibility from the beginning; those coming from Republican areas had to make their reputations quickly to survive. The tradition that a freshman member should be seen but not heard soon disappeared. Senators made their maiden speeches early, and kept on talking. In time, the formal organization and distribution of power were drastically affected. The Democratic Study Group (DSG) was formed in the House to mobilize liberal congressmen behind structural reform. The reforms got under way before the Nixon era, and as each new election brought more new-style senators and representatives to replace the old, it gathered speed, and the climate became more propitious for radical reform. By the 1970s the time was right. Then, in 1975, came the largest new class of House members since 1949, mostly Democrats elected by the Watergate scandal and the Nixon resignation, mostly young, and most of them wholly committed to finding new and better ways for the Congress to conduct the public's business.

Remolding the Power Structure in the House

The baronial structure of the House of Representatives, which centered decisionmaking authority in chairmen of standing committees protected by the tradition of seniority, seemed impregnable as late as the 1950s. But a generation later it appears as such an anachronism that one wonders how it survived as long as it did. The Democratic party was predominantly liberal. Its presidents in the 1960s, Kennedy and Johnson, were squarely in the liberal tradition. So was a clear majority of Democrats in both houses, ever since the 1958 landslide that gave their party a durable preponderance of the membership. Then how could the liberals tolerate a system that had permitted a small bloc of conservative Democrats, holding strategic chairmanships and allied with the Republicans, to block important legislative measures that the party, in the Congress as well as outside, overwhelmingly supported? And how could the Democrats' leadership in the House, even if it wished to, withstand the demands of the liberal majority to change the system? The answer to both questions is that, in the long run, they could not.[4]

First Stirrings of Reform. After the 1958 election, the leaders of the House Democratic activist wing who had prepared the 1957 liberal program (see chapter 7) turned their attention to the problem of how to make the House more responsive to its new majority (later, in 1959, they formed the Democratic Study Group). Clearly, their policy goals depended on institutional change— on finding ways to strip power from the barons—and their first target was identified easily enough: the Rules Committee. They pressed Speaker Rayburn to act, but he declined. Two years later, however, the speaker—frustrated by a series of obstructive actions by the committee,[5] and recognizing the unlimited damage that body could do to the Democratic party program the new president, John F. Kennedy, was about to put forward—finally resolved

4. The following discussion of changes in organization and procedures deals almost exclusively with Democratic policies and actions, since the Democrats were the majority party in both houses throughout the 1960s and 1970s. In general, the Republican party in the Congress has undergone a parallel evolution, so that the main features of reform—reduction of the powers of committee chairmen in favor of a diffusion of power to subcommittees and individual members—seem likely to be preserved under Republican majorities.

5. During the 86th Congress, 1959–60, the Rules Committee refused 31 requests for hearings and denied rules to 11 bills, its most controversial action being one that barred a federal aid to education bill from going to a House-Senate conference committee. Charles O. Jones, "Joseph G. Cannon and Howard W. Smith: An Essay on the Limits of Leadership in the House of Representatives," *Journal of Politics,* vol. 30 (August 1968), p. 638.

that a collision was unavoidable. Even then, rather than challenge the seniority tradition head on, as many of the activists had urged, he chose the less defiant course of enlarging the committee.[6] Three members would be added, two of them Democratic party loyalists. Even with the new president's open and active support and with Rayburn's drawing on all his accumulated store of goodwill, the victory was precariously narrow, 217 to 212. And the arch conservative Howard W. Smith of Virginia was still chairman. He could be outvoted, but it was still he who called committee meetings and fixed agendas. During the 1961–62 Congress, the Rules Committee bottled up no fewer than thirty-four measures, many of them fundamental to the Kennedy program.[7] The committee was not finally tamed until 1965, when the Democratic Study Group, taking advantage of the party's expanded and liberalized majorities following the 1964 election, won readoption of the 21-day rule of 1949–50 as well as a change that stripped from the committee the power to block bills from going to conference committee.[8] In 1966, Smith was defeated for re-nomination in his Virginia district and William Colmer, the senior Democrat, agreed to hold regular weekly meetings as a condition of assuming the chairmanship. The 21-day rule, as in its previous trial, was dropped after a single Congress, following Republican gains in the 1966 election,[9] but Smith's

6. Rayburn could have displaced William Colmer of Mississippi from the committee for bolting the Democratic party in 1960 to support Richard Nixon for president, as the Republicans had penalized party bolters in 1925. However, several other southerners on other committees would presumably have had to be disciplined for the same reason. And four years earlier the party had failed to discipline Adam Clayton Powell of New York for supporting President Eisenhower's candidacy for reelection; see James A. Robinson, *House Rules Committee* (Bobbs-Merrill, 1963), p. 77. In what appears to have been the only departure from the seniority tradition in either house from 1925 to 1961, Rayburn had in 1949 "arbitrarily removed" John E. Rankin of Mississippi and F. Edward Hébert of Louisiana from the House Un-American Activities Committee because of their "antics" on the committee (J. Hardin Peterson of Florida was also removed); Neil MacNeil, *Forge of Democracy: The House of Representatives* (McKay, 1963), p. 159. The Republicans in 1953 had removed Senator Wayne Morse of Oregon from his committee assignments, but he had left the party and declared himself an independent during the 1952 campaign. See MacNeil, *Forge of Democracy*, pp. 412–47, for a detailed account of the 1961 struggle to reform the Rules Committee; and Jones, "Cannon and Smith," pp. 638–44, for a review of the arguments used in the debate.

7. Walter Kravitz, "The Influence of the House Rules Committee on Legislation in the 87th Congress," in Joseph S. Clark, ed., *Congressional Reform: Problems and Prospects* (Crowell, 1965), pp. 127–37. See also Robert L. Peabody, "The Enlarged Rules Committee," in Robert L. Peabody and Nelson W. Polsby, eds., *New Perspectives on the House of Representatives* (Rand McNally, 1963), pp. 151–54; Robinson, *House Rules Committee*, p. 79; Jones, "Cannon and Smith," p. 643, note 52; and MacNeil, *Forge of Democracy*, pp. 447–48. The enlargement of the committee was made permanent in 1963, but *Congressional Quarterly Almanac, 1963*, p. 370, lists a series of measures blocked in that year.

8. Roger H. Davidson, David M. Kovenock, and Michael K. O'Leary, *Congress in Crisis: Politics and Congressional Reform* (Wadsworth, 1966), chap. 5, describes the successful DSG-led efforts to reform House rules in 1965.

9. The rule was employed eight times in 1965–66 to release bills from the Rules Committee. The threat of its use undoubtedly resulted in the release of other bills. *Congressional Quarterly Almanac, 1967*, p. 180. The rules reform of 1965 relating to conference committees was retained.

successors as chairman were generally responsive to the leadership and to the party majority in scheduling meetings, and the committee finally ceased to be a major source of frustration for the House majority.

In 1965 the House Democratic caucus, with Speaker John W. McCormack persuaded to remain neutral, also took the step that Rayburn had declined to attempt four years earlier and stripped seniority from two southerners who had supported the Republican candidate, Barry Goldwater, for president. One of those penalized, John Bell Williams of Mississippi, was thus denied the chairmanship of the Interstate and Foreign Commerce Committee that would have been his in the next Congress, and he retired from the House. The other member penalized, Albert Watson of South Carolina, resigned his seat, changed parties, and was returned to the House as a Republican.

The Joint Committee on the Organization of the Congress, set up in 1965 as a successor to the La Follette-Monroney committee of twenty years before, was specifically barred from examining the rules, practices, and parliamentary procedures of the legislature (except committee jurisdictions); but it did include in its recommendations what it called a committee bill of rights that would have been a significant advance toward carrying out the intent of the Legislative Reorganization Act of 1946 to limit the abuse of power by arbitrary chairmen. A majority of a committee would have been empowered to call a meeting if the chairman failed to act on their request, and to force a bill to be reported if the chairman refused to do so. A bill containing these provisions passed the Senate in 1967 but was buried by the Rules Committee in the House.

This decade of experience was instructive. House rules could be written in two ways—either by the whole House, or by the majority party in its capacity as organizer and manager of the house. And to write them through the Democratic caucus was clearly, from the standpoint of the liberals, the more efficacious method, for while they might be a minority or a tenuous majority in the House, they were a clear majority in the Democratic caucus. After 1958 the party's liberal majority and the Democratic leadership, whenever they agreed on a rules change, could easily put it through the caucus, where acceptance of party discipline on organizational matters prevails, and thus assure its adoption by the House. As the years went by, the liberals and the leadership found themselves as natural allies on the issue of seniority and oligarchical control, for power wrested from the barons would be, in effect, divided between the leadership and rank-and-file members.

Beyond that, as a matter of survival the leadership could not resist making common cause with the liberals once the latter became a clear majority of the party in the House. Speaker Rayburn had been a bit distant when the DSG was formed; he did not discourage the new group but neither did he give it any public recognition, and he communicated with it largely through an intermediary, Representative Richard Bolling of Missouri.[10] But those on the leadership ladder who aspired to succeed to Rayburn's post could not stand aloof, for it was clear where the future lay. Each successive election added a class of Democratic freshmen who were nearer in age and outlook to the DSG reformers than to the elders whom seniority had elevated to the seats of power. The newcomers, obviously, had no stake in the seniority system, and much to gain from diffusing power in the House. No ambitious member could ignore them. And besides, the leadership inevitably had a representation of northern liberals within its ranks, sympathetic to the substantive goals of the reformers—beginning with John W. McCormack of Massachusetts, the majority leader. Even when Rayburn was maintaining his distance from the DSG in its formative period, McCormack was privately urging likeminded colleagues to join the DSG, and when he succeeded Rayburn as speaker in 1962 his support became more open. By 1965, more than half the members of the Democratic caucus attended the DSG organizing session (and by 1979, 247 of the 276 House Democrats). McCormack collaborated actively in drafting the rules changes of 1965 and even turned up at a reception given by the DSG for new members.[11]

After the setbacks of 1967–68 to the reform movement came the Nixon election, which carried with it the prospect that some of the conservative Democratic chairmen would become de facto lieutenants of a Republican president. Democratic liberals in the House were aroused to a new awareness of the need both to mobilize their strength and to attack the institutional barriers that stood in the way of making their strength effective. Late in 1968 the DSG leaders held a series of meetings to revitalize their organization, still demoralized by the counter reforms of the preceding two years, and to plot a strategy of reform.[12] Recognizing that the instrument of reform would ultimately be the Democratic caucus and that that body was also the best available mechanism for spreading the reformers' message, the group agreed to propose regular monthly caucus meetings. Speaker McCormack accepted

10. Richard Bolling, *House Out of Order* (Dutton, 1965), pp. 55–56. Kenneth Kofmehl, "The Institutionalization of a Voting Bloc," *Western Political Quarterly*, vol. 17 (June 1964), pp. 256–72.

11. Davidson, Kovenock, and O'Leary, *Congress in Crisis*, pp. 135–37. Carl Albert continued the friendly relations and his majority leader, Thomas P. O'Neill, Jr., of Massachusetts, became the first person from DSG ranks to hold that post—and later the first to become speaker.

12. The following account of House reform efforts up to 1973, and of the role of the DSG, draws particularly on Arthur G. Stevens, Jr., "The Democratic Party in the House of Representatives, 1958–73," and on an interview with Richard P. Condon, DSG executive director, March 9, 1979.

the suggestion and the DSG established a committee to plan how the organization would make use of the caucus.

Thus the reformers set in motion a chain of events that led, over the next decade, to a radical redistribution of power in the House. Who lost power—the committee chairmen—is clear enough. But what the pattern of redistributed authority will be, when it finally stabilizes, is not yet fully apparent. Centrifugal and centripetal forces are still at work together; power is still being both centralized and decentralized.

Breaking the Power of the Barons. In the course of their negotiations with Speaker McCormack on rules reform in 1965, the DSG liberals had won his agreement that when the party's Committee on Committees designated the chairmen and the Democratic members of House standing committees at the opening of each new Congress, the list would no longer go directly to the House floor for perfunctory approval—the practice since 1951—but would be submitted to the caucus for confirmation. That gave the liberals the opportunity to challenge the seniority principle whenever the time was ripe. In 1967, they used the new procedure to relieve Representative Adam Clayton Powell of New York, who was accused of misusing House funds, of the chairmanship of the Education and Labor Committee, and two years later they stripped of his seniority John Rarick of Louisiana, who had supported George Wallace for president the previous autumn. (This was the same penalty inflicted on Representatives Williams and Watson for party disloyalty four years earlier, but in that instance the caucus had instructed the Committee on Committees in advance of its preparation of the committee rosters.) But they were not ready yet to challenge the credentials of Democratic committee chairmen who merely opposed the party's program as distinct from its presidential candidates. Soundings among their House colleagues had convinced the DSG activists that the House was not ready to respond favorably to any frontal attack on the seniority system as a whole. The system was taken for granted; some members assumed it was embedded in House rules, one even thought it was in the Constitution.[13] Before a chairman could be deposed on ideological grounds alone, more education and discussion among House Democrats would be necessary, and the tactics would have to be carefully planned. Progress could be made only "one inch at a time," in the words of Representative James G. O'Hara of Michigan, the DSG chairman.[14] So beyond its action against Rarick, the DSG's only move against seniority in 1969 was to conduct research and begin an educational campaign. Among

13. Mary Russell, *Washington Post*, February 4, 1975.
14. Ibid.

the research findings: one-third of the one hundred and fourteen Democratic committee and subcommittee chairmen voted more often with the Republicans than with the Democrats.[15]

Early in 1970, help came from an unexpected quarter; House Republican Leader Gerald R. Ford—"partly in an effort to upstage the Democrats on the seniority issue," according to one reporter[16]—responded to the urgings of young party members and appointed a committee of the GOP caucus to study the question. The Democrats could hardly do less, and on the petition of eighty-two members of the DSG, the House caucus chairman (Dan Rostenkowski of Illinois) appointed an eleven-member committee to make recommendations by the end of the year. The committee was representative of the body of House Democrats—mostly northern and western, mostly liberal and moderate. Chaired by a member of medium seniority, Julia Butler Hansen of Washington, it included DSG leaders O'Hara, Frank Thompson, Jr., of New Jersey, and Phillip Burton of California.[17]

When the Hansen committee reported at the beginning of the Ninety-second Congress in 1971, the seniority barrier to majority rule in the House, which had been steadily eroding, finally washed away. The committee, being representative, had to reflect the majority sentiment of House Democrats, and in the end all agreed that the seniority principle should no longer be rigidly adhered to. The committee proposed a party rule that the Committee on Committees "need not necessarily follow seniority" in nominating committee chairmen and members, and that the caucus should vote separately on any chairman or member on demand of ten or more members.

The proposals were approved, and the effect was immediate. Members noted the "new responsiveness" of committee chairmen. Even the eighty-year-old chairman of the Rules Committee, William Colmer of Mississippi, "was often seen . . . trying to strengthen his position with his colleagues . . . to fend off any challenge to his chairmanship in the new caucus."[18] No chairman was rejected that year, 1971, but John L. McMillan of South Carolina, head of the District of Columbia Committee, survived by only thirty votes, 126 to 96.[19]

But the process was still difficult. Ten members had to initiate a reversal of the Committee on Committees by what liberals called a "kamikaze" action—

15. Neal Gregory, "Congressional Report," *National Journal*, vol. 3 (January 2, 1971), p. 18. For a DSG report on the history of the seniority system, possible alternatives or modifications, and arguments pro and con, see *Congressional Record*, February 26, 1970, pp. 5169–72.

16. Gregory, "Congressional Report," p. 24.

17. Several others were probably affiliated with the liberal group, but were not so identified. The DSG has never released its membership list.

18. Gregory, "Congressional Report," p. 17.

19. *Congressional Quarterly Almanac, 1973*, p. 43.

a public accusation, "in the nature of an impeachment"[20]—which exposed those taking the action to reprisal if they lost. And not even the subsequent vote was required to be secret. An automatic vote, by secret ballot, had been the object of the reformers, but they had not been able to win over the Hansen committee to that view. "No rule we could pass would give guts to the gutless," remarked Mrs. Hansen in rejecting the idea.[21]

Once again the Republicans showed the way. The rule they adopted in 1971, as proposed by their special committee headed by Representative Barber B. Conable, Jr., of New York, likewise provided that seniority need not be followed in the nomination of ranking minority members of committees (or chairmen whenever the Republicans were in control) but also called for automatic votes and secret ballots. The Hansen committee reconsidered the subject and in a second report, in 1973, recommended going part way, accepting the automatic vote on chairmen but still resisting the secret ballot. But when the caucus considered the Hansen report, Majority Leader Thomas P. O'Neill, Jr., of Massachusetts, came up with a "compromise" that in fact conceded the whole issue: a secret ballot would be taken if 20 percent of the members of the caucus asked for it. It would be a simple matter for 20 percent to ask routinely for a secret ballot on every vote, but the O'Neill procedure was adopted by the caucus, 117 to 58.

Meanwhile, those who despaired of being able to scrap the seniority tradition, or who saw the replacement of one chairman with another as less than a cure-all, had been pressing a less divisive line of reform—stripping chairmen of their arbitrary powers through the kind of committee bill of rights recommended by the Joint Committee on the Organization of Congress in 1966 that was considered on the floor, rather than in the Democratic caucus, and defeated. If reforms of this character were carried far enough, it would scarcely matter who presided over the committee meetings. The advocates of this approach took their case to the Hansen committee, which agreed that it was appropriately a matter for the majority caucus to decide. Then the Hansen committee went much further than had the joint committee. Its plan, which was approved by the caucus in January 1973 and came to be known as the subcommittee bill of rights, directed the Democratic members of each committee to form a caucus to secure the adoption of committee rules that met certain criteria. In effect, subcommittees would be freed from the control of the committee chairmen; their jurisdiction, their right to meet, automatic referral of bills, and the right of their own chairmen to choose their staff

20. *Congressional Quarterly Weekly Report*, vol. 31 (January 20, 1973), p. 69. Comment of Richard P. Condon, quoted by Stevens, "The Democratic Party," p. 24.
21. Gregory, "Congressional Report," p. 17.

would be guaranteed. In addition, the committee chairmen would lose their power to appoint subcommittee chairmen and stack key subcommittees; Democrats would bid in order of seniority for vacant chairmanships, with approval by the full committee caucus, and follow a like procedure in filling vacancies in subcommittee memberships.[22]

Even with these safeguards against the abuse of power by committee chairmen, the caucus went ahead anyway to end the absolutism of seniority. Armed with the weapon of the secret ballot gained in 1973, the "Watergate Congress" of 1975—with its infusion of seventy-five new Democrats, all carrying a popular mandate to clean up the discredited Washington establishment—wrote the epitaph. It dramatically ousted three of the most senior committee chairmen—Wright Patman of Texas, chairman of Banking and Currency for fourteen years and dean of the House with forty-six years of service; W. R. Poage, also of Texas, chairman of Agriculture for eight years and third in seniority in the House; and F. Edward Hébert, a thirty-four-year Louisiana veteran who had headed the Armed Services Committee for four years. In the last two cases, the Democrat next in seniority was advanced to the chairmanship, but Patman was replaced by the fourth-ranking Democrat, Henry S. Reuss of Wisconsin, who was the most senior member willing to run against the chairman. All three of the new chairmen were northerners, from the liberal wing of the party, but ideology was less a factor than was the reputation of the incumbents as autocrats in dealing with the members.[23] Their replacements were seventeen years younger, on the average, and had thirteen fewer years of service. "From now on," said Reuss, "the sword of Damocles hangeth over every chairman."[24] At the end of the year, Representative Burton, the caucus chairman, could boast that "for the first time in memory there was not a single instance when a committee chairman blocked a major bill."[25]

The caucus also decided to reserve to itself the right to confirm chairmen of Appropriations subcommittees, and two years later deposed the chairman of the Military Construction Subcommittee, Robert L. F. Sikes of Florida, a thirty-seven-year veteran censured by the previous Congress on a conflict-of-interest charge.

22. The rules and their consequences are more fully discussed in David W. Rohde, "Committee Reform in the House of Representatives and the Subcommittee Bill of Rights," *Annals of the American Academy of Political and Social Science*, vol. 411 (January 1974), pp. 39–47.

23. Glenn R. Parker, "The Selection of Committee Leaders in the House of Representatives," *American Politics Quarterly*, vol. 7 (January 1972), p. 83. Patman was aligned with the northern liberals on most issues. That other equally conservative members were reelected in this and later years also suggested that ideology was not the decisive factor.

24. John Pierson, *Wall Street Journal*, February 3, 1975.

25. David E. Rosenbaum, *New York Times*, December 23, 1975.

The revolt against seniority spread immediately to committee caucuses. Freshmen of the Watergate class on the Interstate and Foreign Commerce Committee provided the necessary support in 1975 to enable John E. Moss of California to unseat the committee chairman, Harley O. Staggers of West Virginia, from the chairmanship of the Subcommittee on Oversight and Investigations. The subcommittee chairmen then drew up a set of committee rules guaranteeing subcommittee rights and even went so far as to hold a meeting that Staggers had sought to postpone and, in his absence, approve a budget for the committee and the subcommittees. Another veteran, Leonor K. Sullivan of Missouri, lost her chairmanship of the Consumer Affairs Subcommittee of Banking, Currency and Housing, defeated by Frank Annunzio of Illinois.[26] Four years later, the Commerce Committee caucus disregarded seniority twice in choosing subcommittee chairmen. Representative Henry A. Waxman, a California Democrat entering his third term, defeated a six-term veteran for chairmanship of the Subcommittee on Health and the Environment, in a vote of the Commerce Committee caucus that turned, according to members, on Waxman's more liberal position on health issues (although allegations were heard that campaign contributions the Californian had made to some of his committee colleagues may have been a factor).[27] The same caucus chose Bob Eckhardt of Texas over a more senior opponent to head the Oversight and Investigations Subcommittee, with ideology again a factor. And another third-termer, Toby Moffett of Connecticut, defeated three more-senior candidates in the Democratic caucus of the Government Operations Committee to win the chairmanship of its Environment, Energy and Natural Resources Subcommittee.

Spreading the Action. In its 1971 report that ended the sovereignty of the seniority system, the Hansen committee proposed a series of corollary measures to assure dispersal of the power concentrated in the House oligarchy. The recommendations, which were adopted by the caucus, provided that no committee chairman should chair more than one subcommittee of his full committee, and every member would be limited to chairing one legislative subcommittee in the House as a whole. These two recommendations opened at least sixteen subcommittee chairmanships for rank-and-file Democrats. Each subcommittee would be assured at least one professional staff member,

26. Mary Russell, *Washington Post*, March 7, 1975. Norman J. Ornstein and David W. Rohde, "Revolt from Within: Congressional Change, Legislative Policy, and the House Commerce Committee," in Susan Welch and John G. Peters, eds., *Legislative Reform and Public Policy* (Praeger, 1977), pp. 60–61. The fact that Sullivan was chairman of a standing committee (Merchant Marine and Fisheries) had a bearing on her ouster in the "spread the action" spirit of the time, although she was eligible for a subcommittee chairmanship on another committee under the rules.

27. *Congressional Quarterly Weekly Report*, vol. 37 (February 3, 1979), pp. 183–84.

to be chosen by the chairman but approved by the committee Democratic caucus.[28] The caucus also ended the seniors' monopoly of questioning of witnesses in some committees, by requiring that no member be allowed more than five minutes of questioning until all members had had that amount of time.

The Democratic caucus of the next Congress, meeting in January 1973, continued to "spread the action," as the process came to be known. All Democrats were to be assured at least one major committee assignment. Democratic members on the three most prestigious committees—Appropriations, Ways and Means, and Rules—were barred from serving on other standing committees. And, no member could fill two subcommittee vacancies before each member, bidding in order of seniority, had claimed one.

Two years later, with Wilbur Mills's retirement as chairman of the Ways and Means Committee, the caucus undertook to spread the action within that body, which had been under the chairman's tight personal control, by requiring it to establish subcommittees. The committee was enlarged from twenty-five to thirty-seven members, with ten of the new seats going to the Democrats (reflecting the 1974 Democratic landslide). In addition, the rule against any member's serving as chairman of two committees was extended to nonlegislative as well as legislative committees and to joint committees.

The caucus of December 1976 ruled that no member could chair more than one subcommittee, whether legislative or nonlegislative, and no chairman of a full committee could chair a subcommittee on another body. Two years later, the caucus made one more change: a reelected member could retain only one subcommittee post—instead of the previous two—before new members were allowed to bid. At that point the action appeared to have been spread as far as it could go—with 150 subcommittees (up from 119 in 1972), chaired by that many members, each guaranteed its jurisdiction, its own budget and staff, and its right to proceed independently. In the 1978 caucus, a move to carry the process one step further—by denying to a committee chairman the right to chair a subcommittee even of his own committee—was defeated by a four-to-one margin. That, the opponents argued, would take the former barons of the House out of the action altogether, reducing them to figureheads. The defeat of the proposal, said Thomas S. Foley of Washington, the caucus chairman, reflected the feeling of most members that the

28. Norman J. Ornstein, "Causes and Consequences of Congressional Change: Subcommittee Reforms in the House of Representatives, 1970–73," in Norman J. Ornstein, ed., *Congress in Change: Evolution and Reform* (Praeger, 1975), pp. 94–100, recounts the development of the subcommittee reforms by the Hansen committee and their adoption by the caucus. The calculation of a minimum of sixteen new chairmanships is Ornstein's, p. 102. Stevens, "The Democratic Party," p. 11, puts the figure at nineteen.

diffusion of power had gone "far enough."[29] In 1981 the pendulum swung back a degree or two, when the caucus put a ceiling of eight on the number of subcommittees for any committee, thus requiring the elimination of five existing panels.

Broadening the Use of the Caucus. The majority caucus had proved to be a worthy instrument of organizational reform. Beyond that, the mere existence of the caucus invited its use by the liberals for purposes of advancing their legislative objectives as well. In other words, it could become a means of bringing pressure on recalcitrant committee and subcommittee chairmen, and as such contribute to diffusing power to the rank-and-file members of the majority party. It could also, however, enhance the power of the party leaders, for they too could use the caucus for their purposes. The binding caucus of 1913–14 could hardly be restored, but short of that the caucus could be an instrument of moral suasion, backed by its ultimate sanction of removing committee chairmen from their posts.

In the first year of regular monthly caucuses, 1969, the meetings were devoted largely to discussing the all-engrossing issue of that day, the Vietnam War, but with no attempt to form an explicit party policy on the issue. But on another legislative matter, the caucus did take a stand. It "urged" the Ways and Means Committee to "consider" legislation repealing a ceiling on welfare payments to the states under the program of aid to families with dependent children. At the suggestion of Mills, the resolution had been toned down from a mandate to report the measure, but the committee did report it, and it was enacted.[30]

In April 1972, Majority Whip O'Neill put the caucus on record on the crucial question of ending the war in Vietnam, and in forceful, precedent-setting terms. His resolution, adopted by a vote of 144 to 58, *directed* the Democratic members of the Foreign Affairs Committee to prepare and report legislation within thirty days setting a date for the termination of military involvement in Indochina. O'Neill argued that the Democratic committee members, while not being bound to support or vote for the measure on the House floor, were obliged as "agents of the Caucus" to report a bill, and that individual members must accept the views of the committee's Democratic caucus as to the bill's content.[31] Thomas E. Morgan of Pennsylvania, the

29. B. Drummond Ayres, Jr., *New York Times*, December 8, 1978.

30. In September 1969, the caucus approved a resolution sponsored by DSG leaders supporting preparation of a party program in the House, based on the 1968 platform, as an alternative to the Nixon administration program. Ibid., September 16 and 18, 1969. But the resolution did not lead to adoption of a comprehensive Democratic plan.

31. Letter from O'Neill to Democratic House members, May 1, 1972, in Stevens, "The Democratic Party," p. 17.

committee chairman, managed to bring out a measure drafted by the committee's Democrats responding to the caucus resolution, despite his personal opposition to the policy, but it required a hundred days to do so. Morgan's initial effort failed when five Democrats defied the caucus mandate and supported President Nixon's policy instead. When the measure was finally approved by the committee, in the form of an amendment to a foreign aid bill, five Democrats again voted against it. No attempt was made to discipline them, because it was clear such an effort would lose and the wrong kind of precedent, from the standpoint of the resolution's sponsors, would then have been established. The amendment was defeated on the House floor, but at least the House members were given the first chance they had ever had to vote directly on ending the Vietnam War.[32] In the end, a somewhat mixed precedent had been established: the caucus had proved able to cause a committee chairman to act against his own policy position and a committee to report a bill that a majority of its members opposed. But committee Democrats could also oppose and obstruct the effort, without penalty.

In 1973 an appropriations bill amendment to cut off funding for the bombing of Cambodia, offered by Representative Joseph P. Addabbo of New York was adopted on the floor, 219 to 188, after the Democratic caucus had endorsed it, 144 to 22. The caucus discussion and the lopsided margin of approval were credited with important influence in swinging over to the majority side some important senior Democrats who had been unswerving in their support of the war.

In that same year the caucus devised still another means of limiting the powers of recalcitrant committees. It instructed the Democratic members of the Rules Committee to vote against a closed rule (that is, one prohibiting floor amendments) on any measure where a majority of the caucus or one-fourth of the Democratic members of the substantive committee desired to support an amendment on the floor. The procedure was inconclusively tested the next year when the caucus instructed the Rules Committee to permit two amendments to a tax bill; on one of them, which would end the oil depletion allowance immediately, the Ways and Means Committee (the principal user of the closed rule and the main target of the new caucus procedure) insisted on a closed rule. Caught between the caucus and Ways and Means, chaired by the redoubtable Wilbur Mills, the Rules Committee simply shelved the bill. Next year, however, the caucus again instructed the Rules Committee— over the opposition of both Ways and Means and the Democratic leader-

32. Ibid., p. 18.

ship[33]—and the Rules Committee complied (Mills was no longer a factor to contend with, having relinquished his chairmanship). The floor amendment eliminating the depletion allowance was permitted, approved, and, with minor modifications imposed by the Senate, became law. A short time later, the caucus went on record 189 to 49 against President Ford's request for additional military aid to South Vietnam and Cambodia. While the vote was only an expression of sentiment, not binding on anyone, the International Relations (formerly Foreign Affairs) Committee thereupon postponed action, and the matter was still pending when the two governments fell to the communists.

This bold use of the caucus to bypass the committee system produced a reaction. "Some people were steamed," Chairman Burton commented. "We have to lay off using the caucus for a while." One of those "steamed" was Chairman Morgan of International Relations, who pointed out that the committee had not even had a chance to hold hearings. "If this is the way we're going to operate, let's abolish the committee system, open up the caucus and call witnesses," he reportedly told the caucus. Burton joined in complaining of members who, "whenever they had a problem they couldn't solve in subcommittee, would bring it to the caucus." A former DSG chairman, Donald M. Fraser of Minnesota, agreed that "the caucus shouldn't be overused to take positions on substantive issues." Many feared that if attempts were made regularly to put the party on record on divisive issues, members would stop attending and a quorum could not be mustered, as had been the case in 1971 during the height of the Vietnam War controversy.[34]

The Republicans, of course, were bound to raise an outcry at any sign of a shift in influence from the bipartisan legislative committees to the Democratic caucus, and they kept up a running attack on the institution from the time of its revival. Representative John B. Anderson of Illinois, chairman of the House Republican conference, exhumed the arguments used by his GOP predecessors against King Caucus in 1913 and leveled them against the latter-day heir apparent. King Caucus, he said, appeared to be "making a comeback, and in all the worst possible senses of that term, including secrecy, strict party unity and discipline, disregard for minority rights, restraints on the free operation of the legislative process in committees and on the floor, and resistance to meaningful reforms."[35] Other Republicans picked up the theme,

33. *Congressional Quarterly Almanac, 1975*, p. 101.
34. *Congressional Quarterly Weekly Report*, vol. 33 (May 3, 1975), pp. 911–12; Michael J. Malbin, "House Reforms," *National Journal*, vol. 8 (December 4, 1976), p. 1735.
35. *Congressional Record*, June 19, 1974, p. 19857.

as did some Democrats. As the result, the Democratic caucus in September 1975 repealed its long-established rule permitting the caucus to bind its members,[36] and also voted to open its meetings to the public when legislation, as distinct from organizational matters, was discussed.

In April 1978, the caucus urged the Democrats on the Ways and Means Committee to bring forth a bill that would avert a scheduled increase in social security payroll taxes. The Carter administration, the House leadership, the Ways and Means Committee and its chairman, Al Ullman of Oregon, were all opposed to reopening a subject that had aroused bitter controversy only a few months before. The caucus vote was a decisive 150 to 57, but the resolution stopped short of "directing" the committee members; and Ullman, after initiating some discussions to see if he could find a way to comply with the caucus action, finally gave up. He and his colleagues suffered no penalty for their inaction.

Before that episode, Speaker O'Neill had made clear his dislike of the caucus mechanism. Since 1972, when as majority whip he had played an active part in putting the end-the-war resolution through the caucus, he had come—like Sam Rayburn and other predecessors in the speakership—to see the caucus as more likely to be a source of embarrassment to the leaders than of help. After he reached the highest office in the House, Capitol Hill journalists described him as "quite candid in admitting that he doesn't want to be told what to do by the caucus."[37] "I don't like any of these matters coming from the caucus on a direct vote," he told a press conference before joining the losing side in the 1978 social security vote.[38] With the leadership against them, rank-and-file Democrats have rarely sought to put the caucus on record on legislative issues, and even when they have tried they have encountered difficulty because the regular monthly caucuses frequently fail to muster a quorum. Moreover, when they have been successful the effort has not paid off in legislative results, for committee Democrats have felt free to ignore resolutions that merely urge them to act, while sponsors of resolutions have not pushed their luck to the point of proposing directive lan-

36. The rule had been invoked only once since the revival of the caucus, on a matter of House organization where decisions had traditionally been made by the majority party in caucus. That was in 1971, when the caucus bound its members to vote to repeal a rule guaranteeing the minority one-third of committee staff positions.

37. Richard L. Lyons and Mary Russell, *Washington Post*, March 18, 1978. David W. Brady, Joseph Cooper, and Patricia A. Hurley, "The Decline of Party in the U.S. House of Representatives, 1887–1968," *Legislative Studies Quarterly*, vol. 4 (August 1979), pp. 404–05, explain the reemergence of the caucus since 1969 as the result of efforts by northern liberals to limit the power of southern chairmen and junior members to gain influence. Hence it has become an "arena for conflict and not an instrument for integration, thus threatening leadership power more than reinforcing it."

38. Ann Cooper, "Democrats Still Arguing Over Party Caucus Role on Legislative Issues," *Congressional Quarterly Weekly Report*, vol. 36 (April 15, 1978), p. 876.

guage. Thus in 1979, after the caucus endorsed public financing of congressional election campaigns (in a pro forma action without debate or a roll call vote), eight of sixteen Democrats voted to kill the bill in committee—even though Speaker O'Neill appealed to them to act and cited "the wishes of the caucus" in his plea.[39] In May 1979 the caucus voted by 138 to 69 against President Carter's plan to decontrol oil prices, but this had no evident influence either on the president or on the House.

Nevertheless, the latent authority of the caucus to direct committee Democrats to act—like its latent authority to depose committee chairmen—contributes to making the leadership and the committee structure responsive to the majority of the majority party. The 1975 caucus chairman, Thomas Foley, likened the ultimate power of the caucus to "a gun behind the door," which if kept in reserve for extraordinary matters would be a potent weapon then.[40]

Strengthening the Leadership. Sixty years after the downfall of Speaker Cannon, liberal reformers had come, if not full circle, surely no little distance back toward finding merit in the centralized system they had cast aside. Those who led the fight that began in the 1950s against the House's oligarchical structure needed all the help they could get from Speaker Rayburn and his successors, and so came to regret that a leadership deliberately rendered weak in the earlier struggle was now a necessarily less than powerful ally. Moreover, even as the norm of individualism was supplanting that of party solidarity in the House, many sensed that the House could drift too far in that direction. Parties did still exist. Members of the majority party could not dissociate themselves entirely from the party record when they ran for reelection. The better that record, the better off they were. So they had a common interest in making a legislative record—which requires organization, presumably through the party structure, which in turn requires leadership. Moreover, even from the standpoint of achieving individual rather than party goals, the argument for group action held. No matter how little an individualistic congressman might like to be coerced by the leadership to favor someone else's bill, when his own bill came up for action he always appre-

---

39. *New York Times*, May 25, 1979.

40. Cooper, "Democrats Still Arguing," pp. 875–76. Sidney Waldman, "Majority Leadership in the House of Representatives," *Political Science Quarterly*, vol. 95 (Fall 1980), pp. 380–81, describes how the latent sanctions influenced a reluctant Chairman George H. Mahon (Democrat of Texas) of the House Appropriations Committee to report out of committee, and give his personal support to, a public employment appropriation bill in 1975. In April 1981 the House Democratic caucus adopted a statement of Democratic economic principles intended to provide the basis for development by the party's majorities on standing committees of alternatives to President Reagan's program. While cast largely in generalities, it did take issue with some specific administration recommendations. While the caucus suggested no sanctions to compel committee Democrats to adhere to the principles, the action presumably would turn out to have some influence in promoting party cohesion.

ciated a bit of coercion of other members on his behalf. So he was ambivalent. On the one hand, he prized his freedom; on the other, he accepted a fundamental fact of political life: winning coalitions are not built without organized logrolling, and discipline. And those require leadership.

"There is no reason," wrote the most articulate member of the reform bloc, Richard Bolling, in 1968, "why a distillation, impervious to gross abuses, of the best in the historical caucus and the best in the historical speakership cannot be made. . . . It does not seem dangerous to me now . . . to restore a modified grant of power to the Speaker." Restore his powers to nominate committee chairmen, and the majority members of Rules and Ways and Means (who were then also the Democrats' Committee on Committees), Bolling argued, and "an element of accountability" would be reintroduced. "No longer could a Speaker blame the District of Columbia Committee for not passing out a local suffrage bill or Ways and Means for not reporting out a tax or Medicare bill. The Speaker would be obliged to answer as to why he did not change the membership of the Committee on Committees or change committee chairmen, or both, so as to achieve party objectives." This return part way to the structure of Cannonism would have "a built-in hedge against abuse," because a majority of the caucus could reject the speaker's nominations.[41]

The developing alliance between the leadership and the reformers moved only slowly in the direction that Bolling sketched out. The first step was taken in 1973, when the caucus approved a resolution adding the speaker, the majority leader, and the chairman of the Democratic caucus to the Committee on Committees, theretofore made up of only the fifteen Democratic members of the Ways and Means Committee. The leadership exercised its new power to make sure that the nominees to three vacancies on the Rules Committee were party loyalists.[42] With Ray J. Madden of Indiana succeeding the retired Colmer of Mississippi as chairman, that committee—with its vast powers over the flow of House business—came close for the first time in nearly three decades to being what it was in Cannon's day, an "arm of the leadership."[43]

41. Richard Bolling, *Power in the House: A History of the Leadership of the House of Representatives* (Dutton, 1968), pp. 266–68.

42. Robert L. Peabody, "Committees from the Leadership Perspective," *Annals of the American Academy of Political and Social Science*, vol. 411 (January 1974), p. 137.

43. After the House had reversed the Rules Committee eleven times during 1973, Madden abandoned his resolve to "go along with the leadership" as a matter of duty. "When bills come along that look like they are going to be upset on the floor, we hold them up until some more work can be done on them." The committee was criticized for blocking some bills in 1974, but it eventually released them. Spark M. Matsunaga and Ping Chen, *Rulemakers of the House* (University of Illinois Press, 1976), pp. 7, 115–18, 151–52. Bolling, who became chairman in 1979, had long taken the view that the committee should be an "arm of the leadership" and even went so far as to advocate making the speaker again the chairman of the body. Ibid., p. 7. See Bruce I. Oppenheimer, "The Rules Committee: New Arm of Leadership in a Decentralized House," in Lawrence C. Dodd and Bruce I. Oppenheimer, eds., *Congress Reconsidered* (Praeger, 1977), chap. 5.

The next year the caucus confirmed the relationship by empowering the speaker to nominate all Democratic members of the Rules Committee at the opening of each Congress, subject to ratification by the caucus. This was done even though Speaker Carl Albert, of Oklahoma, spoke against the proposal.[44]

The leadership also responded favorably in 1973 to the growing pressure to revive the Steering and Policy Committee as an executive committee of the caucus and, in doing so, moved to take control by enlarging it from fifteen to twenty-four members, nine of them appointed by the speaker (the others were the speaker, the majority leader, the caucus chairman, and twelve members elected by caucus members from regions). The next logical step was to make that body—instead of the Democratic members of Ways and Means, a group less representative of the caucus membership—the party's Committee on Committees, and that step was taken in December 1974.[45] Thus was one of the keys to Speaker Cannon's arbitrary power—domination of the committee assignment process—restored to the leadership, but with no likelihood, for the reasons that had been advanced by Bolling, that it would be used in the same ruthless manner.

The most significant attempt to use the party machinery for policymaking purposes came during the Ninety-fourth Congress, in the final two years of the Ford administration. Speaker Albert created a ten-member Task Force on the Economy and Energy, headed by Representative James C. Wright, Jr., of Texas, one of his lieutenants on the Steering and Policy Committee. The task force recommended a series of spending measures to stimulate the slack economy, and when those popular bills were produced by the appropriate committees, they were easily passed. But those involving large expenditures were vetoed by President Ford, and the Democrats were unable to mobilize their huge majority (then almost exactly two-thirds of the House) to override. On the far more controversial side of its job—energy—the Wright task force recommended consideration of some unpopular steps to reduce gasoline consumption, including a tax increase, rationing, and other types of sales restrictions, and corresponding measures affecting other forms of energy. On none of these matters did the committees respond, and the Wright committee and the majority leadership proved helpless to do anything about it.[46]

The speaker was also given power, on recommendation of the House

44. John Pierson, *Wall Street Journal*, December 12, 1974.
45. The action was taken as Wilbur Mills was stepping down from his long-time chairmanship of Ways and Means. Earlier, however, the caucus had assigned to the Steering and Policy Committee the responsibility for nominating Democratic members to the new Budget Committee, to prevent the old Committee on Committees from skewing the membership in favor of the conservatives.
46. Bruce I. Oppenheimer, "Policy Effects of U.S. House Reform: Decentralization and the Capacity to Resolve Energy Issues," *Legislative Studies Quarterly*, vol. 5 (February 1980), pp. 10–19.

Select Committee on Committees in 1974, to make joint, split, or sequential referral of bills and, with the approval of the House, to create ad hoc select committees. The last of these powers was used effectively in the next Congress by Albert's successor as speaker, Thomas (Tip) O'Neill, to coordinate the handling of energy and welfare legislation (discussed in chapter 15).

Redistributing Power in the Senate

The forces and events that remade the power structure of the House in the 1970s had their counterparts in the Senate, with results that closely correspond. There was the same dissatisfaction among liberal Democrats, as well as liberal Republicans, with the conservative oligarchy that held its power by virtue of seniority. There were the same centrifugal and centripetal impulses within the majority Democratic party—the demand by junior senators for full participation and a wider sharing of influence and authority, at the same time that they yearned for greater cohesion around a definable party program. But the changes in the Senate tended to be less tangible than in the House, often a matter of practice rather than rule, as befits a smaller and more intimate body where the power structure is often defined more by the interplay of personalities than by formal institutional arrangements.

Thus, where House Democratic liberals had a formally organized Democratic Study Group, complete with offices, staff, and publications, as a means of massing their strength and plotting strategy, their counterparts in the Senate relied on an informal communication network among like-thinking senators and their staffs. And the impetus for reform came from individual rather than concerted group initiative. In the late 1950s and early 1960s, a junior Democratic senator, Joseph S. Clark of Pennsylvania, through direct pressure on the leadership and, ultimately, in 1963, a series of speeches attacking the "Senate establishment," spurred Majority Leaders Johnson and Mansfield to broaden the Senate Democratic Steering and Policy committees to make them more representative of the party membership.[47] And when the

47. Following Clark's demand for enlargement of the Senate Democratic Policy Committee after the 1958 election that added 15 Democratic senators, most of them liberals (Democratic strength rose from 49 of 96 to 64 of 98), Johnson invited 3 freshman liberals to attend Policy Committee meetings. Whether they were full voting participants was not made clear, but the question was moot because the committee operated by consensus. For Clark's Senate speeches detailing the conservative bias in the makeup of the Steering Committee and alleging a consequent bias in the assignments of Democrats by that committee to the Senate standing committees, and debate on the issue, see Joseph S. Clark and other senators, *The Senate Establishment* (Hill and Wang, 1963). Two years later, a move to enlarge the committee from 15 to 17 to make it more representative, which had failed in 1963, was approved by the Democratic conference; as vacancies occurred, Mansfield filled them with liberals who, by 1967, constituted a majority. By the early 1970s the committee appeared to be reasonably representative of the Democratic membership.

election of President Nixon brought pressure on Senate as on House Democrats to mobilize their strength for partisan combat with the White House, it was another junior senator, Fred R. Harris of Oklahoma, who opened the campaign for Senate reform.

Citing the alienation and loss of confidence in government that he had encountered while moving about the country as chairman of the Democratic National Committee in 1969 and 1970, Harris in December of the latter year addressed a plea for "modernization and reform" of the Senate to his colleagues, particularly those on the Democratic side. The House, he said, had begun to move. Now was the time for the Senate to do likewise. Among other things, he asked for the abolition of the seniority system, regular meetings of the Democratic caucus, and modification of the two-thirds requirement for halting filibusters.[48] He then teamed with Senator Charles McC. Mathias, Republican of Maryland, to hold informal hearings, out of which grew a Harris-Mathias proposal to amend the rules to require a Senate vote on each committee chairman and ranking minority member and to provide that neither of the party conferences that made the nominations "shall be bound by any tradition, custom, or principle of seniority."[49] The resolution was soundly defeated on the Senate floor, 48 to 26. Harris and Mathias talked of the "principle of accountability" of committee leaders, but Senator Robert C. Byrd, Democrat of West Virginia, chairman of the Subcommittee on Standing Rules of the Senate, carried the day with profuse and colorful warnings of what would happen if the Senate balloted on each nomination and the tradition of seniority were scrapped: "the confusion, the chaos, and the exorbitant waste of time . . . to say nothing of the friction, the divisiveness, the bitterness, and ill-feeling that would result . . . politicking, logrolling, buttonholing, backslapping, and trading in . . . caucuses . . . blood-letting and scar-leaving battles . . . pork-barreling. . . . we can expect the pressure groups and the special interest groups to get into the act . . . and in all too many instances they will dictate the selection of the chairmen."[50]

Nevertheless, Majority Leader Mansfield gave ground, as he had done earlier on the issue of the Steering Committee composition, quietly, almost imperceptibly in his way. Instead of simply announcing the committee assignments in 1971 as he had done before, he presented them to the caucus for approval. Nobody challenged anyone, but the precedent had been set. The next step was to eliminate the handicap that House reformers had faced,

48. *Congressional Record*, December 3, 1970, pp. 39706–08. A floor amendment to the Legislative Reorganization Act offered by Senator Bob Packwood, Oregon Republican, that would have ended the seniority system by providing for election of chairmen by committee members of the majority party had been defeated earlier, 46 to 22. Ibid., October 6, 1970, pp. 35016–271.

49. Ibid., January 28, 1971, p. 870.

50. Ibid., March 16, 1971, p. 6701.

of having to bring their challenges in the open. In 1975, Senate Democrats agreed to vote separately on any committee chairman on request of 20 percent of the caucus members, and the request itself would be by secret ballot. The senators have done nothing so dramatic as their House colleagues' unseating of three committee chairmen in 1975, but it has not been necessary. Senate chairmen, like their House counterparts, began taking pains to run their committees democratically. Chairman Russell B. Long (Democrat of Louisiana) of the Finance Committee, who was a target of a Common Cause campaign before the 1977 Democratic caucus, bent the reformers' attack by yielding to one of their demands—that the committee create subcommittees with legislative jurisdiction for the first time. Long was "buttering up the liberals in a totally uncharacteristic way," according to one reporter.[51] As the result, only six votes were cast against him, and no other chairman received even that many negative ballots.[52] "We seek a change of attitude," Senator Mathias had said in 1971; the object was "to make clear that every steward has a day of reckoning."[53] The new Democratic caucus rule made it clear enough, and the change of attitude has since been evident.

Meanwhile, two other rule changes furthered the democratization of the Senate. One, in 1970, authorized Senate committee majorities to call meetings on occasions when their chairmen refused to do so. The other, in 1972, provided that in the appointment of Senate members of House-Senate conference committees the tradition of seniority should be set aside where necessary to make sure that the members reflected the majority view of the Senate on the principal issues in dispute.

When Nixon's inauguration in 1969 introduced a new period of partisan division of the government, Senate Democrats—like their predecessors in the Eisenhower years, and like their House contemporaries—became concerned about the absence of mechanisms for forming and expressing party positions to counter the Republicans' use of the White House rostrum. After a series of discussions, the Democratic Policy Committee agreed "reluctantly," according to Majority Leader Mansfield, to assume responsibility for delineating party positions. But Mansfield was careful to emphasize the limitations of the committee:

> For eight years, Democrats in the Senate looked to Democratic Presidents—to Presidents Kennedy and Johnson—for political as well as national leadership. . . . Democrats in the Senate could let the lead, so to speak, come from the White House. That is, obviously, no longer the case. . . . Democratic Senators were asking from time to time for a statement of the position of the leadership on national issues

51. Jack W. Germond, "Congress and Carter: Who's in Charge?" *New York Times Magazine*, January 30, 1977, p. 26.
52. *Washington Star*, February 11, 1977.
53. *Congressional Record*, March 16, 1971, p. 6705.

before the Senate. Heretofore, Democratic Presidents had largely supplied that yardstick.

. . . it was agreed that an effort should be made to delineate Democratic positions in the Senate on certain issues of significance in which there existed a substantial degree of unity among members of the Party. The responsibility is assumed reluctantly by the Policy Committtee.

I want to make it very plain that the Committee will not intrude, in any way, upon the functions of any of the legislative committees. . . . the Committee has not the slightest intention of presuming to replace a Senator's individual judgment with a party judgment.

In sum, the new procedures are designed simply to reintroduce among the Democratic members of the Senate some of the unifying cement which was formerly supplied by the Democratic President in the White House.[54]

During the Nixon-Ford years, the Policy Committee did take stands on a dozen issues or so, but never on matters that were deeply controversial. "Where an issue might divide us, we just don't touch it," Mansfield told an interviewer in 1971.[55] The nearest thing to an exception, perhaps, was a divided vote of six to one that put the Policy Committee on record, in February 1971, in favor of legislation to end the Vietnam War "at a time certain."[56] The Democratic conference followed suit with a 38-13 endorsement of the same objective. But that no senator's individual judgment had been replaced with a party judgment was confirmed a few months later when, on the McGovern-Hatfield amendment to set December 31, 1971, as the termination date for the war, Democrats were recorded only 34 to 19 in favor and the amendment lost. Next year, a similar conference vote was followed a few months later by legislation ending the war, but there is no indication that the conference action had any influence on the outcome. When the Policy Committee or the conference endorsed a legislative goal, the action was in the form of a recommendation to one or more standing committees, and their autonomy was in no way reduced. Such was the case with the recommendations of a five-member committee on energy, headed by Senator John Pastore of Rhode Island, appointed in 1975 as a counterpart to the Wright task force in the House.[57]

After the Democrats recaptured the White House in the 1976 election, the relationship reverted to that of the Kennedy-Johnson period that Mansfield

54. Ibid., May 20, 1969, p. 13101.

55. Andrew J. Glass, "Congressional Report," *National Journal*, vol. 3 (March 6, 1971), p. 504.

56. Ibid., p. 499.

57. In 1979, Majority Leader Robert C. Byrd effectively used a Democratic party committee to prepare a crucial amendment on budget policy. When a Republican amendment appeared likely to be adopted requiring two-thirds approval of both houses in the future for any budget not in balance, Byrd appointed a nine-member group, headed by Senator Edmund S. Muskie of Maine, Budget Committee chairman, to devise a Democratic alternative. The committee's proposal, which called for any unbalanced budget proposed by the Budget Committee to be accompanied by a balanced budget for the Congress to consider as an alternative, was approved, 57-42, after the Republican proposal was defeated by two votes. Richard E. Cohen, "Trying to Kick the Spending Habit," *National Journal*, vol. 11 (April 21, 1979), p. 633.

had described. Insofar as Senate Democrats sought policy leadership from any party source at all, they looked to President Carter and his administration. Senator Byrd of West Virginia, successor to Mansfield as majority leader, was credited with extraordinary skill in "making the Senate trains run on time" but he made no claim to policy leadership nor did he attempt to use the Policy Committee or the conference for that purpose.

With fewer members than the House to do its legislative work, the Senate had customarily spread power more widely than had the larger body. But it, too, saw further diffusion in the 1970s. As in the House, subcommittees multiplied, and as they did so, junior senators saw to it that chairmanships were widely distributed. The Legislative Reorganization Act of 1970 provided that no senator could serve as chairman of more than one subcommittee of the same committee. It also prohibited senators from being assigned to more than one of the four most prestigious committees—Appropriations, Armed Services, Finance, and Foreign Relations. And in 1977, junior members forced through a floor amendment to a committee reorganization act that as of 1979 limited committee chairmen to two subcommittee chairmanships, as against three for other Democrats. The result was to transfer a dozen subcommittee chairmanships to junior members. The 1977 act also expressed the view of the Senate that committees should assure each senator membership on one subcommittee of his choice before any member received two assignments. And whereas once the selection of committee staff was one of the important prerogatives that shored up the power of committee chairmen, by the late 1970s authority over most appointments had passed to the subcommittee chairmen.[58]

Finally, Senate reformers accomplished a minor change in rule 22, which governs filibusters. After struggling at the opening of nearly every Congress for two decades to modify the rule in order to make it easier to close debate, the liberals won acceptance of a compromise in 1975. It lowered the number required to end debate (except on rules changes) from two-thirds of senators voting—which would be sixty-seven if all members were present—to three-fifths of the Senate membership, or sixty. In the first five years after the rule was modified, the change would appear to have made only a little difference, since the majorities that succeeded in invoking cloture seventeen times would have been large enough under the old rule in all but two cases. However, one of the sponsors of the change, Senator Walter F. Mondale, Democrat of Minnesota, argued that this kind of statistic is misleading, because "the entire atmosphere . . . has changed." Cloture was being voted more frequently as

58. Norman J. Ornstein, Robert J. Peabody, and David W. Rohde, "The Changing Senate: From the 1950s to the 1970s," in Dodd and Oppenheimer, *Congress Reconsidered*, p. 16.

the result of the rule, he contended (nine times in 1975 alone); it was being invoked earlier, making filibusters shorter, and the existence of the simpler cloture procedure had in some instances deterred the organization of talkathons in the first place.[59]

Leadership in the Age of Individualism

The headlong trend toward democracy, and dispersal of power, in the Senate and the House has changed the task of leadership. Whereas the problem of Lyndon Johnson and Sam Rayburn, in the 1950s, was to wheedle and plead with committee chairmen who held the keys to legislative action, the problem of Robert Byrd and Tip O'Neill, in the 1970s, was to organize the new individualism—or new fragmentation—into some kind of working whole. And the leaders must do that without seeming to grasp for power, because the resistance of the rank and file of the new-style congressman to any hint of bossism would be instant. In their ambivalence, junior members will accept leadership only on their own terms, and subject to their continuous control. They insist on the right to decide day by day and case by case, without coercion, when they will be followers and when they will assert their right of independence.

"Nobody is telling anybody what to do," remarked Senate Majority Leader Mansfield in 1976. "There's no 'inner club' in the Senate any more. . . . Younger members are more assertive, as they should be. We don't have wallflowers any more unless a member deliberately sets out to be one."[60] Adlai E. Stevenson, a fifth-year Illinois Democrat, agreed, "The juniors are no longer on their knees. We're not asking, we're demanding. We're organizing and using power."[61]

59. *Congressional Record*, May 4, 1976, p. 12409. Cloture votes are in *Congressional Quarterly Almanac, 1975*, p. 37; *1976*, p. 27; *1978*, p. 5; and *1979*, p. 13. If the amended rule had been in effect between 1919 and 1975, cloture would have been invoked 25 times instead of 21, in the 100 attempts made under the old rule. Mondale challenged the validity of this comparison on the same ground. The change in the atmosphere, however, may be attributable in large part to the disappearance of civil rights as a legislative issue after passage of the civil rights laws of the 1960s, which freed anti-civil rights senators—who as a bloc had felt compelled to oppose any cloture motion as a matter of principle—to vote on each cloture motion on its merits. After the rules change, Senator James B. Allen, Democrat of Alabama, and others discovered that if they took advantage of every loophole in the rules, they could force the Senate to permit debate virtually without limit even after cloture had been voted. But at the beginning of the 1979 session, Byrd won a further amendment designed to put an effective limit on postcloture debate and thus made it impossible for a few senators, in his words, to "make the Senate a spectacle before the nation." Ibid., daily edition, January 15, 1979, p. S9. Senator Daniel Patrick Moynihan, Democrat of New York, said that 62 days of Senate time in 1978 were consumed by filibusters. Ibid., February 9, 1979, p. S1416.

60. *U.S. News and World Report*, August 16, 1976.

61. *Congressional Quarterly Weekly Report*, vol. 33 (December 13, 1975), p. 2717.

The changes of style and culture that characterize the "new Senate" of the 1970s are most fully documented in the book of that title by Michael Foley,[62] based on extensive interviewing in 1974 and 1975. The inner club of which William S. White spoke has disappeared, he found.[63] So has the tradition of apprenticeship, the notion that in their early years new senators "should be seen but not heard." That principle had to yield as subcommittees proliferated and responsibility was distributed more nearly equally among all the members, but Mansfield from the beginning of his leadership had encouraged younger members to assert themselves. "I believe that every member ought to be equal in fact, no less than in theory," was Mansfield's philosophy.[64] Equality meant decentralization, and that in turn meant individualism. "Distinctions between juniors and seniors became blurred," wrote Foley, "as the atmosphere within the institution became one of individual assertion."[65] The Senate became more informal, less clearly structured, less closely integrated. The norm of specialization also lost influence; more senators than before were policy generalists, spreading themselves over a wide range of issues and no longer looked on as "charlatans" for doing so. After John Kennedy's success in 1960, almost every quadrennial year has found a half dozen or so of these generalists in the top rank of presidential possibilities.

On the other side of the Capitol, new members were similarly seen as being different from their elders and bringing new modes of conduct to the House. "Sam Rayburn used to be able to glare people down," said Majority Leader O'Neill in 1974. "These new members are brighter, better educated, more talented. . . . You just don't glare these people down." The House, said O'Neill, was "extremely difficult to coordinate." Machine politics "is dead" in the country, he went on, and hence in the House as well.[66]

62. *The New Senate: Liberal Influence on a Conservative Institution, 1959–1972* (Yale University Press, 1980).

63. William S. White, *Citadel: The Story of the U.S. Senate* (Harper and Bros., 1956), especially chap. 7, drew the picture of an "Inner Club" made up of "Senate types" who dominated the "inner life" of the Senate. Foley uses as his starting point for describing institutional change in the 1960s and 1970s a composite of the descriptions of Senate norms of White and political scientist Donald R. Matthews, *U.S. Senators and Their World* (University of North Carolina Press, 1960). Many of Foley's observations correspond to those of Nelson W. Polsby, "Goodbye to the Senate's Inner Club," *Washington Monthly*, August 1969, pp. 30–34, reprinted in Nelson W. Polsby, ed., *Congressional Behavior* (Random House, 1971), pp. 105–10; Robert L. Peabody, *Leadership in Congress: Stability, Succession, and Change* (Little, Brown, 1976), pp. 8–9, 48–49; Ornstein, Peabody, and Rohde, "The Changing Senate," p. 8. In 1965 Randall B. Ripley, *Power in the Senate* (St. Martin's, 1969), p. 185, found senators "not sure" of the existence of the "club" but, in any case, not oppressed by it. At that time, Senator Clark, the original critic of the Senate "establishment," acknowledged it was "gone." "Democracy is now pretty much the rule in the Senate," he said. *Congressional Record*, September 13, 1965, p. 23495.

64. *Congressional Record*, November 27, 1963, p. 22862.

65. Foley, *The New Senate*, p. 253.

66. Mary Russell, *Washington Post*, March 31, 1974.

And that was even before the Watergate class of 1974—the largest class of newcomers since 1948 and surely the most assertive in many years. Observers of the Congress agreed as to the impact of that class on the style of the House—if not the patterns of its voting. House members responding to a *Washington Post* survey in June 1975 believed by a large majority—64 percent to 25 percent—that the new freshmen were indeed different from their elders. They were described as "wild, uninhibited . . . feeling their oats," "downright rude, intemperate," "less willing to go along to get along," "in a hurry to make a record," "younger, brighter, more active, involved and vocal," "more questioning of our institutions."[67] The younger members "resist the idea of elders calling the tune," was a news magazine's summary.[68] But the elders did not really try—not in the old manner, at any rate. "The 'go along' idea never has been pressed by the leadership," testified Jerome A. Ambro of New York, chairman of the freshman Democrats' organization in 1976. And a member of the leadership, Chief Deputy Whip John Brademas of Indiana, put it this way: "1976 is not 1966 and it's not 1956. I don't think, given the changes in American society, that intelligent and highly motivated young men and women will sit back and wait for a few years before speaking out."[69] The Republican leader, John J. Rhodes of Arizona, noted in that same year that the Congress had changed "atmospherically." Civility had declined. Whereas "the average Congressman of yesteryear was congenial, polite and willing to work with his colleagues whenever possible," a large number of the new members were "cynical, abrasive, frequently uncommunicative and ambitious to an inordinate degree."[70] But they were reformist: House Democrat newcomers thought reform had not gone far enough, by 60 percent to 38 percent, while veteran Democrats thought it had (64 percent to 34 percent).[71]

"No one can lead men and women who refuse to be led," complained journalist David S. Broder in 1975 in diagnosing the ills of a "floundering" Congress. "The House juniors have overthrown the old power centers. Yet they consistently refuse to heed even those they installed in power."[72] Of the 289 Democrats in the House, 120—including more than one-third of the freshmen and many liberals—voted against the leadership in at least one of the first three attempts to override vetoes by President Ford that year. All

---

67. William Greider and Barry Sussman, *Washington Post*, June 30, 1975. Sixty percent of the House members returned their questionnaires.
68. "Behind the Upheaval in Congress," *U.S. News and World Report*, April 14, 1975, p. 22.
69. Michael J. Malbin, "Congress Report," *National Journal*, vol. 8 (February 14, 1976), p. 194.
70. *The Futile System: How to Unchain Congress and Make the System Work Again* (McLean, Va.: EPM Publications, 1976), p. 7.
71. William Greider and Barry Sussman, *Washington Post*, June 30, 1975.
72. *Washington Post*, August 13, 1975.

three attempts failed. The Democratic Study Group found the lowest party unity scores in twenty years.[73] But at no time has the ambivalence of House Democrats toward leadership and discipline been better illustrated. Even while the individual members were exercising their full freedom to vote as they pleased, the press was filled with their complaints against the leadership for allowing this to happen. The *Washington Post* 1975 survey found 52 percent of all Democrats dissatisfied with the party leadership, with new and veteran Democrats about equal in their discontent.[74] Complaining of weak leadership, a group of freshmen organized what the press called a "confrontation" with Speaker Albert to protest his lack of "arm-twisting" on the votes to override vetoes and to demand stronger action to attain party discipline in the future. Yet Albert could point out that at that very time 35 freshmen were among the Democrats who provided the votes to kill the three-cent increase in the gasoline tax that the Ways and Means Committee had proposed as a key element in its energy conservation program. Some of them were his loudest critics, and some had directly refused his plea for help on the tax measure.

Albert retired at the end of that Congress, and his successor, O'Neill, has been generally credited with being the strongest speaker since Rayburn. Yet the attitude of the membership toward party discipline appears essentially unchanged. "It is . . . an atomized House, increasingly resistant to leadership," wrote a Capitol journalist.[75] The members themselves confirmed the judgment. "It's not enough any more to say to people that the leadership is for something, so they should be for it," remarked Representative Richard Gephardt of Missouri, a junior Democrat of rising influence; "people vote for things if they want to vote for them."[76]

In this atomized and egalitarian milieu, what can a leader do to mobilize the House or the Senate—assuming he sets out to try? He has few rewards to offer and few punishments to inflict. "When we say, 'vote with the party or else,' " Majority Whip John Brademas acknowleged, "we don't have much on the 'or else' side of the equation."[77] "You have a hunting license to persuade—that's about all," agreed Majority Leader Jim Wright.[78] And as to

73. *Congressional Quarterly Weekly Report*, vol. 33 (June 28, 1975), p. 1332.
74. William Greider and Barry Sussman, *Washington Post*, June 29, 1975.
75. Dennis Farney, *Wall Street Journal*, April 5, 1979.
76. Alan Ehrenhalt, *Washington Star*, February 27, 1979. In 1980, Speaker O'Neill formally chastised 44 House Democrats who had voted affirmatively on a Republican motion to overturn a procedural ruling of the chair relating to legislation on an appropriations bill. There had not been an appeal from a ruling of the House presiding officer for thirty years before 1968, O'Neill wrote the defectors, but since then there had been seven, three of them in 1980. He said the Democratic Steering Committee had discussed the problem of party discipline on procedural matters. "On Capitol Hill," *Washington Post*, September 4, 1980.
77. Speech to the National Democratic Club, Washington, D.C., March 6, 1979.
78. Steven V. Roberts, *Washington Post*, June 4, 1979.

the rewards, Representative Gephardt remarked, "You know, there is nothing the leadership can offer me, really nothing."[79]

"Nothing to offer" is hyperbole, of course. Most important among its powers, the House leadership can assert a controlling influence at times, through the Steering Committee (which it can normally dominate through the speaker's power of appointment), on committee assignments. Although this loses most of its meaning once a member gets on the committee he wants—Gephardt received the seat he coveted, on Ways and Means, as a freshman—it always retains some importance, for additional and special assignments are possible from time to time. In the case of new special and select committees, the speaker names the majority-party appointees. He also makes appointments to the majority party's Steering and Policy Committee. The leadership has a part in determining who sits on the Democratic Congressional Campaign Committee, which allocates campaign funds. It chooses delegations for interparliamentary meetings in pleasant overseas locations. The House Administration Committee, which may be (and now is) closely linked with the leadership, approves committee and subcommittee spending and controls the relatively small amount of House patronage. The Rules Committee, which acts now as an "arm of the leadership," controls the flow of business. All of these powers in the House leadership are paralleled in the Senate, but they may be enhanced in some respects. The Senate majority leader appoints all the members of the majority Policy and Steering committees (in the House, some are elected by regional caucuses), and the power of the Steering Committee to make assignments to the legislative committees is more important in the lives of senators because they serve usually on three such panels each, instead of only one or two.

Yet if the sum of these powers appears considerable, the more significant point is that the egalitarian ethic has pervaded the exercise by the leadership of all of its authority. A more accurate statement than "there is nothing the leadership can offer" would be "there is nothing the leadership would dare withhold." Mike Mansfield's benign philosophy—every senator is equal and deserves equal treatment—may simply have reflected the leader's temperament, yet if only by coincidence it was a sensitive response to the changing mood of his colleagues. The leader is, after all, an elected official, and the leaders who have followed Lyndon Johnson and Sam Rayburn in both houses have sensed that to be arbitrary or punitive in the exercise of leadership power—even to the degree that those two Texans on occasion were—would no longer be acceptable. Thus, most rewards have become a matter of right,

79. Thomas B. Edsall, "Congress Turns Rightward," *Dissent*, vol. 26 (Winter 1978), pp. 12–18.

and the leader's job is to see that they are passed out equitably. Campaign funds become a matter of formula. So does patronage. Majority committee assignments are in fact made through a collective process that the leader no longer dominates to the extent that, in the Senate, Lyndon Johnson once did.[80] On committee assignments, observed a Capitol Hill journalist, Speaker "O'Neill can get something done when he has to because he uses his influence very sparingly."[81] The House Rules Committee and the Senate Majority Policy Committee, in scheduling bills, look at them on their merits without regard to whether the sponsor has pleased the leadership. The spirit of egalitarianism even crosses party lines; where in the old days a bill or an amendment sponsored by a member of the minority would be rejected by the majority on principle, Republican initiatives by the late 1970s were accepted by the Democratic majorities in committee and on the floor on their merits, and bipartisan collaboration appeared to be increasing.

In this democratic milieu, the advice so often attributed to Sam Rayburn, "to get along, go along," has taken on a new meaning. The major rewards and punishments are now in the hands of committee and caucus majorities; they make the key decisions on committee and subcommittee chairmanships, and the ambitious member would find it more advantageous, if on occasion the leadership appeared to be out of step with the rank and file, to go along with the latter. It is noteworthy that in the famed rejection of the three House committee chairmen in 1975, the Democratic caucus overturned the recommendations of its own Steering and Policy Committee, which the speaker chairs, on two of those cases.[82] In 1979 the caucus rejected a Steering and Policy Committee nominee for a vacancy on Ways and Means who was sponsored by Majority Leader Jim Wright and turned down also a committee nominee for the Budget Committee. The intervention of House leaders on behalf of Richardson Preyer of North Carolina in his losing fight for chairmanship of the health subcommittee of the House Commerce Committee actually contributed to his defeat by Henry Waxman of California, according to one committee member.[83]

With such unruly followers, the tendency of the leadership in both houses

80. Peabody, *Leadership in Congress*, pp. 349–50.

81. Steven V. Roberts, *New York Times*, January 24, 1979. Interviews by Sidney Woldman confirmed that the leadership has used its power over committee assignments sparingly; "Majority Leadership in the House," *Political Science Quarterly*, vol. 95 (Fall 1980), p. 375.

82. The committee had approved the chairmanships for Poage and Hébert and had recommended removal of Patman, while Majority Leader O'Neill had recommended renomination of all three. The caucus also approved Wayne L. Hays of Ohio as chairman of the House Administration Committee, reversing the Steering Committee, which had in turn reversed O'Neill. Michael J. Malbin, "Congress Report," *National Journal*, vol. 7 (January 25, 1975), pp. 130–31.

83. Ann Cooper, "New Setbacks for House Seniority System," *Congressional Quarterly Weekly Report*, vol. 37 (February 3, 1979), p. 184.

has been to avoid trying to impose its will, or at least to choose its fights very carefully, so as not to risk defeat and expose its weakness. "I don't twist arms. I shake hands," was Speaker Albert's way of putting it.[84] Senate Leader Mansfield used the same words: "There has been no arm-twisting and there could be no arm-twisting any more."[85] "The Senate never wanted a leader," observed Senator Edmund S. Muskie, Democrat of Maine, "and it has seldom had one, at least not one in the sense of somebody who could mobilize a majority."[86] "I don't feel pressure to go along with the party position," said Senator Gary Hart, a first-term Democrat from Colorado, in 1979.[87] "You never know what they want," said Representative Peter H. Kostmayer, Pennsylvania Democrat, of the House leadership. "I'd like to vote with them more."[88]

Some reforms of the post-Watergate age that were designed not to redistribute power but simply to bring into the open the processes of government have had unintended and unexpected effects in making it harder for followers to follow and leaders to lead. Recording of previously unrecorded teller voters in the House now makes it possible for everyone back home to find out how a member voted; to the new ideal of openness is sacrificed the honored tradition of logrolling, the secret pledging and delivery of votes that may not be in the interest of one's constituency to serve the cause of party solidarity. Opening of committee meetings, including House-Senate conferences, to public view has had the same effect.

On organizational matters, the leadership cannot avoid risks; when decisions are necessary, it is compelled to make proposals. But on policy the leadership finds it easy to defer—to a president when he is of the same party, and to substantive committees of the two houses at all times. This has been the case for decades. During the Carter years, neither Speaker O'Neill nor Senate Majority Leader Byrd—any more than Carl Albert and Mike Mansfield before them—assumed the role of policy leader. O'Neill, as much as any speaker in the past, regarded himself as a loyal presidential lieutenant for the purpose of enacting the party—that is, the administration—program. Byrd, though saying, "I'm the President's friend, I'm not the President's man," steadily supported the Carter program[89] and, in any case, did not presume to put forward any alternative program of his own. Neither O'Neill nor Byrd

84. Richard L. Lyons, *Washington Post*, June 23, 1975.
85. "Face the Nation," CBS television program, March 28, 1976.
86. Germond, "Congress and Carter," p. 38.
87. Richard E. Cohen, "Freshmen in the Senate Being Seen—and Heard," *National Journal*, vol. 11 (March 17, 1979), p. 440.
88. Martin Tolchin, *New York Times*, October 24, 1979.
89. Richard E. Cohen, "Byrd of West Virginia—A New Job, A New Image," *National Journal*, vol. 9 (August 20, 1977), pp. 1295, 1299.

made policy pronouncements, and neither assembled a staff that in size or backgrounds would enable him to compete with the president or the standing committees as a source of policy initiation and leadership. The first Republican majority leader of the Senate in a quarter of a century, Howard H. Baker, Jr., of Tennessee, began his duties in the tradition of his Democratic predecessors, looking on the Reagan administration as the appropriate source of policy initiative. "I intend to try to help Ronald Reagan [carry out] the commitments he made during the campaign," said Baker.[90]

If the leadership of the House and Senate cannot impose their own notions of order on the proceedings of their respective bodies, even less, it should be added, can the president, or leaders of party organizations outside the Congress. The Congress still faces the problem of developing a capacity to formulate and adopt its own independent and comprehensive legislative programs.

Expanding Staff Resources

Just as the 1937 report of the President's Committee on Administrative Management—that landmark document in the history of the aggrandizement of the presidency—declared "the President needs help,"[91] so every study that has concerned itself with restoring the power and prestige of a declining Congress has declared, in one or another set of phrases, that the Congress needs help.

"The lack of skilled staffs for the committee work-shops of Congress was more complained of than perhaps any other matter before your committee," reported the Joint Committee on the Organization of Congress in 1946.[92] "The shocking lack of adequate congressional fact-finding services and skilled staffs sometimes reaches such ridiculous proportions as to make Congress dependent upon 'hand-outs' from Government departments and private groups or newspaper stories for its basic fund of information on which to base legislative decisions." The committee's proposed remedy for "the sad state of committee staffing" was assuredly, by today's standards, modest enough.

90. *Washington Post*, December 3, 1980. In March 1981 Baker obtained concurrence at the Senate Republican caucus to postpone consideration until 1982 of certain divisive social issues, including constitutional amendments on abortion and prayer in the public schools, in order to concentrate on Reagan's economic program. The action was in accord with the administration's desire.

91. President's Committee on Administrative Management, *Report of the Committee with Studies of Administrative Management in the Federal Government* (U.S. Government Printing Office, 1937), p. 5.

92. *Organization of the Congress*, S. Rept. 1011, 79 Cong. 2 sess. (GPO, 1946), p. 9.

It proposed that each Appropriations subcommittee, and each other standing committee, be authorized four professional staff members. It also recommended that the Legislative Reference Service (LRS) of the Library of Congress, created in 1919 and then staffed with about twenty-five professionals, be quadrupled in size to provide a "pool of experts" to assist the committees in policy analysis, and that the Office of Legislative Counsel of each house— the Congress's own bill-drafting service—be similarly enlarged, even though "comparatively little legislation originates in Congress today."[93] These recommendations were adopted in the Legislative Reorganization Act of 1946.[94]

With this impetus, the staff resources available to the Congress were gradually expanded over the next couple of decades. Professional staffs of committees multiplied, from 93 persons in 1948 to 588 in 1967.[95] The LRS, after an initial spurt, grew more slowly than contemplated, but by 1967 its staff was four times the 1946 level. The personal staffs of the members also grew in size, as did the staff of the General Accounting Office (GAO, a part of the legislative branch) engaged in investigation and evaluation work on behalf of the Congress. Yet studies of the Congress repeatedly demanded still further expansion. A committee of the Committee for Economic Development, for example, recommended in 1970 "that Congress strengthen its staff resources by recruitment of highly qualified specialists—physical scientists, engineers, environmentalists, physicians, economists and other social scientists, nutritionists, mathematicians, management experts, and others as occasion may require."[96] And members still complained. In a 1963 survey, House members placed the need for information and analysis at the top of their list of problems.[97]

The Legislative Reorganization Act of 1970 set in motion a second vigorous expansion of the LRS to meet the need of the Congress for "massive aid in policy analysis," as the House Rules Committee put it.[98] The LRS was renamed

93. Ibid., pp. 15, 11.
94. Except that the Appropriations subcommittees were given an unlimited authorization for professional staff. The act authorized the LRS appropriation to be tripled in three years, after which time it would not be limited, and converted the LRS into a broad-gauged policy analysis organization, with the duty of assisting congressional committees "in the analysis, appraisal, and evaluation of legislative proposals before it, or of recommendations submitted to Congress by the President or any executive agency." It was authorized to employ "senior specialists" who would be paid as much as the highest-salaried personnel in comparable jobs in the executive branch.
95. Samuel C. Patterson, "The Professional Staffs of Congressional Committees," *Administrative Science Quarterly*, vol. 15 (March 1970), p. 23.
96. *Making Congress More Effective* (New York: Committee for Economic Development, 1970), p. 51. Some of the resources, it suggested, should be located in the LRS or GAO.
97. Survey by the Dartmouth College Public Affairs Center, cited by Kenneth Janda, "Information Systems for Congress," in American Enterprise Institute for Public Policy Research, *Congress: The First Branch of Government* (Washington: AEI, 1966), p. 421.
98. *Legislative Reorganization Act of 1970*, H. Rept. 91-1215, 91 Cong. 2 sess. (GPO, 1970), p. 18.

the Congressional Research Service (CRS) to reflect the evolution of the organization since 1946. The Rules Committee suggested that the CRS should be tripled in size by 1975, and in fact it more than doubled in that time (to 644 employees in fiscal 1975) and continued to grow at a slower pace thereafter.

The act of 1970 also recognized the gradual transformation of the General Accounting Office from an auditing and accounting agency into a versatile organization with broader purposes. Specifically, it instructed the GAO not only to review agency programs from the standpoint of efficiency, economy, and fidelity of administration but also to "analyze the results of" governmental programs (changed in 1974 to "evaluate"). Elmer B. Staats, who became comptroller general in 1966 after a career in the Bureau of the Budget, had been applying executive-branch doctrine to remold the tradition-bound GAO, adding to its core of accountants and auditors persons with backgrounds in economics, systems analysis, operations research, engineering, the physical sciences, and other nonaccounting fields.[99]

In 1972 a third auxiliary research agency for the Congress was created—an Office of Technology Assessment (OTA), "to provide the Congress with new ways to evaluate the effects of technology, pro and con."[100] Finally, the Congressional Budget and Impoundment Control Act of 1974 created yet another analytical resource in the Congressional Budget Office (CBO), staffed by economists and budget analysts to serve not only the House and Senate Budget committees but other committees as well.

By 1975, then, the legislators had, in addition to their personal and committee staffs, no fewer than four organizations—CRS, GAO, OTA, and CBO—organized, or organizing, to assist them in evaluating governmental programs and developing and analyzing legislative proposals. While each had special strengths, all but OTA were authorized to concern themselves with the entire range of governmental programs and problems. Most observers, including members of the Congress, were not disturbed by the overlapping missions and, indeed, judged the resulting friendly competition to be useful. Collectively, they provided the substantive talent needed to supplement the political and manipulative skills of the committee and personal staffs.

And in many areas of legislative policy analysis, they could match the

99. Frederick C. Mosher, *The GAO: The Quest for Accountability in American Government* (Westview, 1979), pp. 191–95; Norman Beckman, "Congressional Information Processes for National Policy," in *Annals of the American Academy of Political and Social Science: Social Science and the Federal Government*, vol. 394 (March 1971), pp. 94–95; John M. Pearce, "Congress Report," *National Journal*, vol. 3 (February 6, 1971), p. 273.

100. *Establishing the Office of Technology Assessment (OTA) and Amending the National Science Foundation Act of 1950*, H. Rept. 92-469, 92 Cong. 1 sess. (GPO, 1971), p. 3.

resources of the executive branch in competence, if not in depth of numbers. In 1972, before two of these four agencies were organized, and before the great expansion of committee and personal staffs, Nelson W. Polsby could argue that the Congress was no longer "necessarily outgunned by executive agencies in the policy-making process. . . . When committee chairmen are able and intelligent, when they favor legislative activity, when they want to pursue an independent congressional course of action, the means are generally readily at hand for Congress to do the intelligence gathering job it needs to do."[101]

But this statement acknowledged some limitations. Some committee chairmen lacked the ability or desire to assemble a competent staff, or interest in using it (and, through it, the CRS and the GAO as well) to obtain policy analysis and advice independent of the executive branch. Under these circumstances, the traditional centralized control of the staff resources available to each committee was not acceptable in the 1970s to subcommittee chairmen, to whom legislative power was being rapidly devolved. Nor did it satisfy junior members, who in the individualistic congressional culture of that decade felt the responsibility to make up their own minds on each issue, and who might doubt the reliability of the information and advice provided either by the executive branch or by staff members beholden to committee seniors— assuming they could get access to the committee staff experts whose chairmen had first call on their time. Nor was it satisfactory to minority members, who could hardly turn to the majority staff for policy advice. (By this time, the concept in the Legislative Reorganization Act of 1946 that professional staff members should be politically neutral, able to serve Democrats and Republicans with equal dedication and detachment, had long since been discarded by most committees as unworkable.)

These cumulative dissatisfactions produced in the mid-1970s an explosion of legislative analysis staffs in both houses. The added staff was widely dispersed to subcommittees and individual members, paralleling the diffusion of legislative responsibility. In 1975, junior senators waged a successful fight on the Senate floor to win authority for every senator—not just committee and subcommittee chairmen and ranking minority members—to hire one senior staff member for each of the three committees to which he was assigned (or more than three persons, if he preferred to use his allotment for lower-paid, junior staff). And in that same year the House increased the permanent

101. "Does Congress Know Enough to Legislate for the Nation?" paper prepared for a conference sponsored by *Time* magazine, Los Angeles, December 7, 1972, printed in *Congressional Record*, March 7, 1973, pp. 6756–57. Mosher, *The GAO*, pp. 270–77, compares the four support agencies.

staff of each committee from twelve to forty-two, partly to make possible the assignment of two professional staff members (one majority, one minority) to each subcommittee. That year the House gave ten of its committees an aggregate increase of 79 percent in funds for staff hiring.[102] The Rules and Appropriations committees were providing one professional staff member for each member, on the Senate pattern.[103]

After years of incessant complaint from the Republicans, the Democratic majorities in both houses also finally made concessions on minority staffing—a decision for which Senate Democrats had occasion in 1981 to be grateful. In increasing committee staffs in 1975, the House guaranteed the minority sixteen of the forty-two permanent positions on each panel.[104] The additional temporary staff authorized each two years was not similarly divided, complained the Republicans, with the result that only about one-fifth rather than one-third of total positions were assigned the minority; the Democrats responded that many of the four-fifths were not in partisan positions and served majority and minority alike. Senate Democrats finally yielded in 1977, amending the rules to stipulate that the minority on each committee should be granted its proportional share—and must be granted at least one-third—of the total funds available for hiring nonadministrative committee staff if it so requested. The resolution allowed the committees four years in which to comply; by 1979, when the Republicans held 41 percent of the Senate seats, only two committees were still significantly below the minimum one-third in the allocation of committee funds to the minority.[105]

What had been a gradual expansion of legislative staff became an explosion in the mid-1970s. The influx of new members gave fresh force to the "spread the action" drive, and the clash with President Nixon heightened the demand for legislative self-sufficiency in information gathering and analysis to enable the Congress to counter and combat the executive branch on something approaching equal terms. Many members, said Representative Frank E. Evans, a sixth-term Democrat from Colorado in 1975, felt that the only way "to get Congress back on what we hoped would be a more coequal footing with the executive branch" was "to equip ourselves with people, people with skills and who answer to our requests. . . . We have done this."[106] Arguing

102. *New York Times*, March 12, 1975.

103. Richard L. Lyons, *Washington Post*, June 1, 1975.

104. House Democrats had been forced to accept a two-to-one division of committee staff funds in order to pass the Legislative Reorganization Act of 1970, but they reversed themselves through caucus action—or "reneged," as the Republicans preferred to say—when they organized the House in 1971.

105. Statement of Senator Mark O. Hatfield, Republican of Oregon, and table inserted in *Congressional Record*, daily edition, May 8, 1979, p. S5514.

106. *Congressional Record*, May 21, 1975, p. 15685.

for the establishment of the OTA, Senator Edward M. Kennedy, Democrat of Massachusetts, contended that without its own facility for "independent congressional evaluation," the legislative branch would be "more and more dependent on administration facts and figures" and hence its role would become "more and more perfunctory."[107] Senator Mike Gravel, Democrat of Alaska, who was the principal sponsor of the amendment authorizing additional legislative aides for rank-and-file senators, related the decline of Congress directly to its weaknesses in supporting staff:

> We have just passed through one of the most difficult periods in American history. One in which the Executive tried to run rampant over the American people, the Constitution, the Congress, the courts, and the press. . . . the Senate [was] a major contributor to creating the situation that led directly to this blatant, illegal, and unconstitutional abuse of power. For while we appropriated moneys year after year to expand the agencies, departments, and the White House staff, we have neglected to staff ourselves adequately to meet our legislative over-sight responsibilities. . . .
>
> Far too often we see the following scenario. The White House formulates a legislative idea; a department immediately breaks off 10, 20, or 30 staff to research and draft the proposal; it is introduced in the Senate and in the final analysis is referred to a subcommittee which may have no staff or simply a counsel and a secretary. Thus the stage is set for another steamroller job from the Executive. The Congress must stop performing its crucial functions in this passive fashion. We must enhance our factfinding, investigative, and technical capacity.[108]

The figures in table 1 are a rough indicator of the expansion in the 1970s of the staff resources available to the Congress for policy research and analysis.[109] The trend in every category has been upward, and in some cases sharply so, suggesting a tripling of analytical staff in the listed categories—from fewer than three persons per member to about nine, including both professional and clerical personnel.

By now, the Congress appears to have successfully established its independence of the executive branch for information, policy analysis, program

107. *Office of Technology Assessment for the Congress,* Hearings before the Subcommittee on Computer Services of the Senate Rules and Administration Committee, 92 Cong. 2 sess. (GPO, 1972), p. 37.

108. *Congressional Record,* February 5, 1975, pp. 2479–80.

109. The figures reflect the rapidity and magnitude of staff growth, but understate the total resources available. The GAO, whose staff grew from an annual average of 4,136 in fiscal 1966 to 4,713 in 1972 and 5,144 in 1978, is omitted because the allocation of staff time between policy review and analysis and other responsibilities is not known. The personal staffs of House members are omitted because no data are available as to the number of employees assigned to legislative research and analysis (it is relatively small, because House members rely on committee staffs for legislative assistance). The number of legislative and research aides to senators is limited to designated legislative assistants, omitting many with other titles whose duties may include a substantial proportion of legislative work. The figure for the OTA does not include the research and analytical services obtained through contract (nor do figures for Senate and House committees and the CRS, which do a minor amount of contracting). On the other hand, committee staff figures include employees who engage in casework and in investigative and oversight activities that may not be related closely to legislative matters.

Table 1. *Policy Analysis and Research Staffs Available to the Congress (Partial Listing), 1966, 1972, and 1978*

	Number of employees[a]		
Category	1966	1972	1978
House committee staffs[b]	566	851	2,073
Senate committee staffs[c]	624	899	1,275
Senators' offices (legislative and research aides)[d]	126	287	654
Congressional Research Service (policy and research units)[e]	175	275	520
Congressional Budget Office[f]	...	...	193
Office of Technology Assessment[f]	...	...	89
Total	1,491	2,312	4,804

a. Figures include both professional staff members and clerical personnel assigned to assist them, and are for actual employment rather than number of positions authorized.

b. Figures for 1966 from Kenneth Kofmehl, *Professional Staffs of Congress*, 3rd ed. (Purdue University Press, 1977), p. xxvi; for 1972, *Legislative Appropriations for 1974*, Hearings before a subcommittee of the House Appropriations Committee (GPO, 1973), p. 1018 (employment as of December 31); for 1978, *Legislative Branch Appropriations for 1980*, Hearings before a subcommittee of the House Appropriations Committee (GPO, 1979), pp. 1291–92 (employment as of October 30).

c. Figures for 1966 from Report of the Secretary of the Senate, July 7, 1966 to December 31, 1966 (employment as of September 30); for 1972, Report of the Secretary of the Senate, July 1–December 31, 1972 (employment as of September 30); for 1978, Report of the Secretary of the Senate, October 1, 1977 to March 31, 1978 (employment as of March 31).

d. Reports cited in note c. Figures include all employees whose job titles include the words *legislative* or *research* or otherwise indicate that the employee is assigned to policy analysis or research; exclude student interns.

e. Derived from *Budget of the United States*, Fiscal Years 1968, 1974, and 1980, by multiplying the proportion of the total budget of the Congressional Research Service (in 1966, the Legislative Reference Service) devoted to "research and analysis" or "policy analysis and research" by the average annual CRS employment for the fiscal years ending in 1966, 1972, and 1978.

f. *Budget of the United States*, Fiscal Year 1980.

evaluation, and legislative advice. Where it does not have the necessary specialists in its own burgeoned staff, it has the means to consult with experts outside the government. The Congressional Budget Office regularly produces independent estimates of the economic outlook, and these usually carry more credence with the Congress than do the estimates of the executive, which are always suspected of having been manipulated to support the policy objectives of the president. In May 1979, the CBO took issue with the White House on the costs and consequences of the decontrol of oil prices, in a study that was widely cited by those in the Congress who opposed President Carter's decontrol proposal.[110] The General Accounting Office likewise freely contradicts the administration in its evaluations of federal programs, regularly disputing, for instance, the Pentagon's official estimates on weapons costs and performance. In 1979, all four of the congressional support agencies separately advised the Congress that President Carter's goals for synthetic fuels production were out of reach.[111] The very existence of the congressional capacity

110. *Washington Post*, May 24, 1979. In March 1981 the CBO drew a denunciation from President Reagan when it claimed the administration had underestimated spending in its 1982 budget by $20 billion–$25 billion. *New York Times*, March 18, 1981.

111. Richard E. Cohen, "Congress Report," *National Journal*, vol. 11 (September 8, 1979), p. 1486.

to critically examine official reports serves to keep the departments and agencies honest. Even when the legislature has to rely on the executive for basic information, it has the capacity to verify what it receives. The executive's former monopoly of information and analytical capacity is broken, even in the national security areas, now that the responsible committees have gained a satisfactory degree of access to hitherto secret documents.

From the viewpoint of the executive branch, and some Capitol Hill critics as well, the myriad staff members are often laxly managed, allowed to "free wheel" in overseeing the executive branch and intervening in executive decisions.[112] The warning of Senator Herman E. Talmadge, Democrat of Georgia, when he led the unsuccessful opposition to the Gravel amendment in 1975, that the once tightly controlled committee staffs would be splintered into "a whole new army of employees, each going their own way, without any responsibility to their respective committees" seems in some measure to have been borne out.[113]

A common complaint of members is that the expansion of staff, while it may help a senator or representative cope with his workload, also adds to it. As Talmadge remarked in 1975: "We have got a lot of bright-eyed, idealistic young people right out of law school, seeking new worlds to conquer. They spend virtually all of their time writing speeches for Senators, preparing amendments for Senators, and developing broad new spending programs for Senators to introduce . . . and if you double the staff, you double the amendments and double the costly new programs."[114]

And Senator Pete V. Domenici, Republican of New Mexico, noted in 1979:

> Every Member of this body, and every person who works here, knows the frustrations imposed by too many hearings, competing with too many markups, producing too many bills, attracting too many extraneous amendments, requiring too many record votes. . . .
>
> What happens with all this staff? To justify its existence, staff generates new bills and new amendments and new hearings. More legislation . . . is not better legislation. More staff is not better staff. . . . We are simply inflicting complexities upon ourselves with more people winding up more and more ideas that produce more votes and more debates and more hearings and more markups.[115]

Even if the conservative bias of these two senators is taken into account,

---

112. The expansion of congressional staff available to assist in media relations, communication, meeting with constituents, answering mail, casework, and so on is not discussed here because it does not relate directly to the balance of power between the legislative and executive branches. But it does contribute to the magnitude of the management problems that individual senators and representatives now face.

113. *Committee-Related Senate Employees*, Hearing before the Senate Committee on Rules and Administration, 94 Cong. 1 sess. (GPO, 1975), p. 42.

114. Ibid., pp. 41–42.

115. *Congressional Record*, daily edition, April 4, 1979, p. S3922. Harrison W. Fox, Jr., and Susan Webb Hammond, *Congressional Staffs: The Invisible Force in American Lawmaking* (Free Press, 1977), quote other senatorial expressions of uneasiness, pp. 4–5, and sketch the growth of staff, chap. 2.

the question of the congressional workload has become a serious one. Once a seasonal institution, assembling for a few months each winter, the Congress now meets all year. Sometimes, it fails even to finish its work by the date of the election that passes judgment on its members; in 1980 it adjourned in October for the presidential campaign, but had to return in November to pass its second budget resolution (more than two months late), to enact most of the appropriations for a fiscal year already almost two months old (which in some cases it handled only through improvised interim resolutions), and to complete work on a series of other major bills. In the 1950s, the House met in session for an average of 1,064 hours for the two years of each Congress; by the 1970s, the figure was 1,650. Over the same interval, the Senate's hours in session rose from 1,809 per Congress to 2,260. The average number of recorded votes per Congress rose from 170 to 1,135 in the House (in part reflecting rules changes that recorded previously unrecorded teller votes) and from 312 to 1,140 in the Senate. The number of public laws enacted each two years did not increase, but the total number of pages did—from an average of 1,908 in the 1950s to 2,551 in the 1970s. The average number of committee meetings each two years rose from 2,542 to 3,813 in the Senate and from 3,340 to 4,628 in the House (excluding Appropriations).[116] The number of pages of the *Congressional Record*, as a rough reflection of time spent in debate as well as other activities of the members, rose from 20,814 in 1951 to 25,696 in 1963 and 42,450 in 1975.

That there is at least some association between the expansion of staff and the increase in workload seems clear enough. While the number of amendments offered to bills has not been counted, most Capitol Hill observers would surely agree with Senator Domenici that the number has increased, in part because of the availability of staff to initiate and develop them. More words are uttered on the floor, and more unspoken words are inserted in the *Record*, because staff is available to write them. As for oversight hearings—which are not necessarily reflected in floor activity—the number of days Senate committees spent in such hearings in the 1969–75 period varied almost exactly with the size of the staff.[117]

116. Figures from Arthur G. Stevens, "Indicators of Congressional Workload and Activity," report 79-159 GOV (Congressional Research Service, Library of Congress, May 30, 1979). For the 1950s, the averages are for all five Congresses except committee meetings, which are for the last three (1955–60). For the 1970s, the figures are for the first four Congresses (1971–78) for the number of votes and hours in session, for the first three Congresses for public law pages, and for the first two Congresses for committee meetings. Figures for the House Appropriations Committee are not included because they were not available for the earlier period.

117. Joel D. Aberbach, "Changes in Congressional Oversight," revision of papers prepared for the Commission on the Operation of the Senate and the 1977 annual meeting of the American Political Science Association; he cautions against drawing firm conclusions from data for so short a period.

That the increase in staff has also been working slow changes in the character of the legislative bodies—particularly the Senate, which has a higher ratio of staff to members—seems evident. Time spent by the members in recruiting, directing, and supervising staff is time not spent in face-to-face relations with other members. As members become managers of professional staffs, the chambers disintegrate as "deliberative bodies" in the traditional sense of legislators engaged in direct interchange of views leading to a group decision. With more and more votes taken on the floor, a smaller and smaller proportion of each member's votes can be cast on the basis of his personal grasp of the issue involved; votes, too, are cast on the basis of staff advice— cast, in effect, by the staff. With each passing year, the House and Senate appear less as collective institutions and more as *collections of* institutions— individual member-staff groups organized as offices and subcommittees. Each legislator is the head of an organization, who delegates to subordinates and reviews their product, much like an official in the executive branch or, in Malbin's simile, "a chief executive officer in charge of a medium-sized business."[118] And what is delegated moves always closer to the heart of the legislative process. A phenomenon of the 1970s in the Senate was the "staff markup"; once senior specialists were assigned to assist senators in the work of each committee, it was only a matter of time until they began to assemble to negotiate and compromise on behalf of their principals, producing an agreement for ratification—much as a committee of assistant secretaries in the executive branch might draft an interdepartmental agreement for approval by the cabinet officers, or foreign ministers might negotiate a treaty to be signed by heads of state at a summit conference.[119]

By the end of the 1970s, for all these reasons, signs of a reaction were appearing. The House Commission on Administrative Review in 1977 expressed concern "that Members are becoming too dependent on a permanent bureaucracy of staff aides, who by virtue of their tenure and expertise 'control' policy decisions."[120] The Senate Budget Committee in 1979 expressed a concern about the "cost effectiveness" of the legislative branch and agreed to consider whether the size of the staff was impairing congressional efficiency.[121] Senator Daniel P. Moynihan, Democrat of New York, who proposed the committee's

118. Michael J Malbin, *Unelected Representatives: Congressional Staff and the Future of Representative Government* (Basic Books, 1979), p. 6.

119. Malbin tells of a "phantom conference" between House and Senate in 1977, in which conferees were never appointed and staff members resolved the differences between House and Senate bills dealing with veterans' benefits. Ibid., chap. 5.

120. *Administrative Reorganization and Legislative Management*, H. Doc. 95-232, 95 Cong. 1 sess. (GPO, 1977), vol. 2, p. 59.

121. *First Concurrent Resolution on the Budget FY 1980*, S. Doc. 96-98, 96 Cong. 1 sess. (GPO, 1979), pp. 233, 312.

action, expressed the belief that staff expansion had become "self-defeating
or worse!"

> After a point—reached sooner, perhaps, than generally realized—increased as-
> sistance begins to defeat its purposes by consuming the very time and energy it
> was supposed to free up. The small group takes on a life of its own: it becomes an
> organization in its own right, and commences to behave like organizations behave.
> . . .
> We become administrators, looking to the activities and the logistical needs of
> our separate organizations, engaging in ever more complex patterns of cooperation
> and conflict with other such organizations, much in the manner that bureaucracies
> cooperate and compete in the executive branch. . . .
> Bureaucratization . . . now . . . appears in the Senate and the House, forced on
> us in some ways by the need to maintain a balance of forces with the increasingly
> bureaucratized Presidency.[122]

Nothing came of the Senate Budget Committee's agreement to consider
the matter, but when the Republicans took control of the Senate in 1981,
they imposed a 10 percent cut in the size of committee staffs—though not
in the personal staffs of senators. The committee staff cuts would work no
immediate hardship on the new majority, since several hundred new Republican staff members would be added in any case to fill the two-thirds
share of nonadministrative staff positions that the majority party could claim.

To the average Republican as well as Democratic member, the advantages
of bureaucratization appear still to outweigh the drawbacks. The expanded
staff enables a senator or representative to expand his reach, keep informed
on more subjects, exert influence on more matters, overcome the handicap
of amateurism in competing with the executive branch and with more experienced and specialized colleagues. A legislator's staff reflects and represents his views as faithfully, presumably, as a president's cabinet represents
the president's position, or a subcabinet member that of his cabinet member.
If staff members legislate, in effect, by negotiating the agreements that are
later ratified, the product is essentially the one that would have resulted if
the elected members themselves had been at the bargaining table.[123] If the
legislators reduce the number of matters on which they may act, that in itself
will not reduce the size and scope of government itself, as the conservatives
hope. It will simply unilaterally disarm the Congress in its struggle with the

---

122. Ibid., pp. 330–33.
123. Malbin questions this, on the ground that staff members tend to be "technocrats whose
self-interest is not the same as their bosses' and whose knowledge of the world is limited to what
they learned in school or from other participants in the specialized Washington issue networks."
He contrasts this with the knowledge an elected member gains from direct contact with constituents
in his representative capacity, and he expresses concern at the loss of the values that come from
direct conversations among members and the decline in "Congress' ability to act as a deliberative
body." *Unelected Representatives*, pp. 247, 240–44.

executive, for a vast bureaucracy in the executive branch cannot be overseen and controlled except by a Capitol Hill bureaucracy of corresponding competence and breadth. A strong argument can be made that the legislative branch is intervening excessively in administration, but withdrawal from oversight and control is not cited as an explicit objective by those on Capitol Hill who criticize the staff explosion, nor would it reflect the current mood of the Congress.

In sum, to blame the work overload of the Congress on the augmentation of staff resources, or to attempt to control the behavior of the Congress by limiting or reducing staff is to grasp the problem at the wrong end, to reverse the cause-and-effect relationship. Senate and House members made the decisions *first* to increase their individual workloads; then they increased their staffs to enable them to cope. Collectively, they resolved that the legislature must be far more assertive in the legislative process vis-à-vis the executive branch. That inevitably meant more bills originating on Capitol Hill and a more careful review of those sent up by the executive branch, with more amendments to limit and confine executive discretion. The legislators resolved to engage in more intensive oversight, which compelled more hearings and more staff to organize and manage them. Junior members demanded a greater share of resources, and so did the minority in both houses, and the demands could be met only by augmenting total resources. The spreading culture of individualism and equality led to diffusion of initiative and responsibility, with more bills, more amendments, and more participation, all of which required staff support. For those who are concerned about the overload of the Congress, and the difficulty of managing its large bureaucracy, it is not the staff as such but the role the Congress has chosen for itself that must be reexamined.

Staff is the currency with which members of Congress buy independence, Allen Schick has said—independence of the legislature from the executive branch, independence of rank-and-file members from the committee chairmen who once monopolized the available staff resources.[124] It follows, then, that staff can be reduced only if, and to the extent that, the Congress is willing to return to the attitudes and practices that prevailed when staff was small— if it returns, in a phrase, to the norm of deference, of individual members to committees, of juniors to seniors, of the legislative branch to the executive. In European parliaments, where deference of legislators to the executive is

124. "The Staff of Independence: Why Congress Employs More But Legislates Less," paper prepared for the White Burkett Miller Center for Public Affairs, University of Virginia, October 1980, p. 13.

the rule, there is little legislative staff and little expressed need for it. In this country, too, congressional staff grew slowly during the long period when Congress permitted each accretion of governmental power to be lodged primarily in an expanding executive. That the legislature has been, in the 1970s, by far the fastest growing branch of government is a direct reflection of its reassertion of authority vis-à-vis the president.

This is not lost on the Congress. The reaction that began in the late 1970s against the growth of the legislative bureaucracy is not wholly due to the practical problems of office space and management, reinforced by the conservative suspicion of staff activism. It reflects also an underlying feeling among many former champions of legislative reassertion that that course has been pursued far enough—perhaps too far. The conspicuously expanded staff is a convenient target for those who are not quite ready to admit, at least openly, that they think the Congress has reached the point of too much oversight, too much intervention in executive affairs, too much detail in legislation, too little reliance on the executive. In short, that they want an end to the period of congressional resurgence, and perhaps to have the pendulum begin a slow swing back.

PART III

Prospect

CHAPTER XIV

Missing Capabilities: Political Leadership and Policy Integration

"THE THING that is missing in the Senate today is that we get caught up so often in these day-to-day debates without a national or a broad perspective, without an overview, or foresight capacity." So complained Senator Bill Brock, Republican of Tennessee, cochairman of a committee established to reform the Senate's committee system, in 1976.[1] And the Democratic cochairman, Adlai E. Stevenson of Illinois, agreed:

> We are compartmentalists; we have sliced our daily routines into superficial fragments, and we have divided and subdivided large problems into a host of committee cubbyholes. It is no wonder that there is little consistency or coherence to what we do here. Do we have anything that could fairly be called a "policy" in such fields as energy conservation, environmental protection, or health care? If we do, it would be hard to find evidence of it in our fragmented committee system.[2]

That was in the fourth year of the congressional resurgence, but these were time-worn criticisms, by members of both houses. And they had led to the time-tested remedy: where "a broad perspective" and "consistency" and "coherence" were needed, the Congress had become accustomed to turn to an executive branch that at the top, in the person of a single individual and in the staff agencies that with him make up the presidency, has the capacity to blend and unify disparate views. So the Congress prescribed an annual executive budget as long ago as 1921, and subsequently, as it recognized the need for broad and integrated policies in other areas—economic

---

1. *First Report, with Recommendations of the Temporary Select Committee to Study the Senate Committee System,* S. Rept. 94-1395, 94 Cong. 2 sess. (U.S. Government Printing Office, 1976), p. 5.
2. *Congressional Record,* September 30, 1976, p. 34018.

growth and stability, national security, urban growth, and so on—it directed the president in successive acts to assemble and present those policies.

But these specific acts reflected, as well as abetted, the rise of the presidency to the preeminent position in American government and society that in the twentieth century it has come to occupy. The president has become the prime center of legislative initiation not merely because he heads the vast apparatus of the executive branch but, perhaps primarily, because he is given a mandate by the people as the political leader of the country. After his inauguration, he is expected by his opponents and supporters alike to restate authoritatively the philosophy and the programs that he presented in his victorious campaign—to pronounce the goals that he will seek, to define the programs and propose the allocation of resources to attain those goals, and to use his unmatched, and unmatchable, access to the media to mobilize public support. The short word for all this is to *lead*. By mid-century, what may be called the presidential leadership model was firmly in place. The president was accepted even as the legislature's own leader, expected to set the goals for its legislative sessions, to assemble the agenda, to plan the strategy for the passage of individual bills, to negotiate the necessary compromises, and then even to round up the votes for their enactment.

Within the presidential leadership model, the Congress had developed for itself a complementary role, which was more than one of simple followership. If the president in his program provided the broad perspective, the Congress contributed the narrow one; it examined the presidential program from the viewpoint of nearly half a thousand separate constituencies. The American congressman, deeply rooted in his state and district, constantly in touch with his constituents, individualistic, and not tightly bound to support any party line, specialized as *representative*, in the literal meaning of the word. The president proposed, from the national perspective, and the Congress disposed, from the perspectives of an aggregate of separate constituencies.

That was the implicit principle of executive-legislative relations that evolved in the age of congressional decline. The president would be the nation's policy planner and initiator. He would also be the decisive doer; when quick decision and action were required, he would be empowered to decide and to act. The Congress would not seek to alter the structural characteristics— cure the endemic weaknesses—that prevented it from fulfilling those roles. It would, instead, concentrate on doing what it does best, assigning to the executive branch those functions the latter could perform better.

When the system worked, the president set the general direction of national policy, and the Congress modified the specific policies and programs, to soften or enhance their impact on particular constituencies. The system did not always work, of course, for the president might not always lay out clear goals and programs, or the Congress might choose not to accept them if he did. At such times, the country entered one of the periods of "deadlock and drift" that James MacGregor Burns has characterized as the normal state of American democracy.[3] For there could be no alternative to presidential leadership, as long as the Congress had not organized within itself the capacity to proclaim an alternative set of national objectives and devise comprehensive and consistent programs to achieve them.

Turning Away from Presidential Leadership

The significance of the congressional resurgence of the 1970s is that it has challenged the fundamental concepts of the presidential leadership model. A resurgent Congress, by definition, is one that has turned away from its old dependence on the executive. But what, in the American system, is to take the place of presidential leadership? In its day of introspection and resolve, in 1973, the Congress did not confront that question in any abstract form. As always, its members were responding to a condition, not a theory. They knew the relationship they wished to overturn, concretely, but they were less clear as to the relationship they sought. While they denounced unilateral presidential government, only in their more extreme bursts of rhetoric did they talk of substituting anything like congressional government. When Senate Majority Leader Mike Mansfield declared, "The people have not chosen to be governed by one branch of government alone," he referred, presumably, to the legislative as well as the executive. The most common expression of a goal was "coequal" status for the Congress. What the advocates of change seemed to be groping for was a relationship of equality within which the two branches, harnessed somehow in tandem, would lead the government together. "The essential point," said one of the leaders of the debate, Representative Lee Hamilton, Democrat of Indiana, "is that the decisions of government, both domestic and foreign, be shared decisions."[4]

But when it came to defining that relationship in specific bills, over the ensuing years, the Congress had to confront the inherent fallacy in the conception. For the two branches can lead the government in tandem only when they agree on the direction it should go. When they agree, however,

3. *The Deadlock of Democracy* (Prentice-Hall, 1963), p. 2.
4. *Congressional Record*, June 24, 1974, p. 4176.

there is no problem with the old presidential leadership model. It is when they disagree that institutional relationships become crucial, because they determine the means by which deadlocks are broken, compromises forced, and when compromise is impossible which branch prevails. Who prevails on what matters defines the balance of power between the branches.

That balance of power was what the constitutional crisis of the Nixon years was all about. The policy differences between the president and the Congress were real, and they were sharpened by the struggle for partisan advantage. On some matters where the branches disagreed—welfare reform, for example—the usual deadlock ensued and could be accepted, for there was no compulsion for immediate action. But other issues simply had to be resolved. At any given time, the government had to have a budget and a fiscal policy. In its international affairs, it had to act, one way or another. When compromise could not be achieved, Nixon felt impelled to act to assure that the executive branch prevailed and, in so doing, shifted the balance of power decisively in favor of the executive. The Congress cried "usurpation" and moved to set the balance right, by its standards. That meant undoing not merely the specific shifts that Nixon had wrought but, to the degree it could, the whole of what it saw as forty years of continuous decline.

The congressional actions did not result in any tandem arrangements. As they grappled with specific problem areas, the advocates of change could set up institutional arrangements that encouraged consultation and a free flow of information, but in the end they had to assign responsibility clearly to one branch or the other in order to avert deadlock and permit the government to function. In fiscal policy, they claimed the last word for the Congress, by ending the practice of impoundment. In war powers, they conceded the first word to the president but instituted a procedure to require the Congress to affirm or reverse his course. Wherever the legislative veto was applied, they reserved the final decision for the Congress.

To assert its right to make the ultimate decisions, the Congress did not need to alter the role of the president as policy initiator. While Republican presidents were in office, the Democratic congressional leaders did encourage initiatives independent of the White House, but for reasons more of partisan than of institutional rivalry. "The Constitution does not require us to await proposals from the Executive Branch," Majority Leader Mansfield reminded the Senate at the opening of the heady Ninety-third Congress, in 1973, as he recited a list of pending issues, including measures vetoed by President Nixon the preceding year.[5] To an extent, in the next four years, the Congress did

5. Ibid., January 4, 1973, p. 325.

strike out on its own, most notably in developing and enacting its series of economic stimulus measures in 1973. But once the Democrats recaptured the White House, the democratic majorities lapsed back to their old habits. In a not untypical instance, when Senator Daniel P. Moynihan of New York learned in April 1977 that the new Carter administration would not be sending its welfare reform proposals to the Congress until autumn, he reportedly declared angrily that someone "with a first-rate mind and three months experience could draft legislation in a morning."[6] Moynihan had the experience and surely the mind—he was one of the principal authors of the Nixon family assistance plan of 1969—and presumably he could spare a morning. Yet neither he nor anyone else suggested that in a resurgent Congress the subcommittee on public assistance that he headed should draft its own bill. Moynihan himself would only promise to begin action immediately when the president's program arrived.[7]

The idea for a "summit" conference of business, labor, and other groups on the state of the economy early in President Ford's term originated on Capitol Hill, but the legislators prevailed on the chief executive to call it and preside over it. In this same period, Majority Leader Mansfield, appearing on national television, described graphically the congressional dependence on the executive on economic matters—even when that executive is the political opponent of the congressional majority. "We tried to do something about the inflation and the recession through advocating wage, price, rent and profit controls . . . and other matters, but we just can't seem to get the votes. That's why it is necessary, in my opinion, for one man, the President, to take the lead, and for the Congress to cooperate as much as it can." The lead has to come from the "chief of state," said Mansfield, because "535 men and women in the Congress cannot do so."[8]

None of the legislation that over the years had imposed on the president responsibilities to plan and to initiate was changed during the congressional resurgence. Even in setting up the congressional budget process, the Congress left intact the executive budget process it had established in 1921. The president still presents the budget as he always has, in the same form, and the new budget committees, like the appropriations committees, use it as a starting point. Moreover, the stream of directives to the president to prepare comprehensive plans, and the authorization of new units in the Executive Office of the President for the purpose, flowed unstemmed. In 1976 the legislators established in the Executive Office an Office of Science and Tech-

6. United Press International dispatch, April 26, 1977.
7. *Congressional Record*, April 25, 1977, p. 11965.
8. "Face the Nation," CBS television program, October 27, 1974.

nology Policy, to assist the president in, among other things, preparing an annual report to the Congress and a legislative program dealing with "critical and emerging national problems."[9] Senators who sought a national policy on "balanced growth" initiated legislation for a White House conference on the subject, to be convened by the president (and held in early 1978). In establishing the Department of Energy, the Congress directed the president to prepare and submit, by April 1 of each odd-numbered year, a National Energy Policy Plan. The Full Employment and Balanced Growth Act of 1978[10] specified that the president, in his annual Economic Report, should include numerical goals for levels of employment, unemployment, production, real income, productivity, and prices, and a program for achieving those goals. And the requirement for an annual report by the president on housing production objectives and a program of legislative and administrative action to achieve them, established in 1968 for a ten-year period, was made permanent.

Only in the Congressional Budget and Impoundment Control Act, among all these measures, did the Congress impose on itself the same requirement for comprehensive thinking and action. The case of the National Energy Policy Plan is particularly instructive, because sponsors of the idea—Senators Jacob K. Javits, Republican of New York, and John Glenn, Democrat of Ohio—originally proposed that the Congress do just that. As passed by the Senate, the president's plan would be referred to the "appropriate committees" in each house, which would modify the plan as they found necessary and desirable and report a joint resolution embodying the plan as modified. The Congress would then, by October 1 of the odd-numbered year, adopt a final plan, which would assure, said Javits, that the Congress would not revert to the "random and short-term energy policies that have been so characteristic of our actions in the past."[11] The weakness in the bill, however, was that, unlike the budget act, it did not create a centralized congressional machinery. Indeed, it did not even specify which of the existing committees would have responsibility for writing the joint resolution. So the Congress went on responding to crises, on a "random and short-term" basis.[12]

9. Public Law 94-282. This revived an office that President Kennedy had established by reorganization plan but President Nixon had abolished in a subsequent plan.

10. Better known as the Humphrey-Hawkins Act, for its principal sponsors, Senators Hubert H. Humphrey and, after his death, Muriel Humphrey, both Democrats of Minnesota, and Representative Augustus F. Hawkins, Democrat of California.

11. *Congressional Record*, May 18, 1977, pp. 15280–81.

12. Anticipating the statutory requirement, President Carter had already come forward, in April 1977, with a document bravely—and misleadingly—entitled "The National Energy Plan." It was not a *national plan*, at all, let alone *the* plan; it was only a proposal for a plan. And, in the absence of a congressional mechanism and process analogous to those created in the budget act, it never became a plan.

But while the Congress still looks to the president for comprehensive planning and for legislative initiative, it is in the response to that initiative that the relationship has changed. On decisions where the Congress once normally deferred to the president, in the 1970s it asserted its own views more aggressively and felt less compunction in substituting its judgment for the president's. A habit of deference, in other words, had given way to a habit of self-assertion.

Yet when the Congress deliberately turned away from the presidential leadership model that it had in large measure itself designed, it raised grave questions as to what might take its place. If the president was diminished as a leader, could the Congress fill the resulting vacuum? Could a legislative branch so long conditioned and organized to follow now step out in front and point the way? Two elements of the president's leadership responsibility are crucial: first, his position as the political leader of the nation; second, his function as integrator of the government's policies and programs. Neither of these roles, at the end of the resurgent 1970s, was the Congress prepared to play.

The Congress as Political Leader

"One of the most universal cravings of our time is a hunger for compelling and creative leadership," are the opening words of James MacGregor Burns's treatise on that subject. Leadership, he goes on, "is exercised when persons with certain motives and purposes mobilize, in competition or conflict with others, institutional, political, psychological, and other resources so as to arouse, engage, and satisfy the motives of followers."[13] In the presidential leadership model, it is the president who mobilizes the resources. Leadership in the presidency, Burns tells us, means identifying and enunciating the national values of liberty and equality, confronting "the overriding moral and social issues facing the country"—making that high office, in Franklin Roosevelt's oft-cited words, "preeminently a place of moral leadership."[14] As Burns acknowledges, some disagree that presidents ought to talk in moral terms about the national purpose and national values. But presidential leadership surely does consist, at a less exalted level, of defining national objectives, goals, and policies that "arouse, engage, and satisfy" the majority of the country. The Monroe Doctrine and the Truman Doctrine, the Emancipation

13. *Leadership* (Harper and Row, 1978), pp. 1, 18.
14. Ibid., pp. 389–90, xi.

Proclamation and the Atlantic Charter, the Fourteen Points and the Four Freedoms, the economic bill of rights and the war on poverty were all presidentially proclaimed goals that aroused, engaged, and satisfied the preponderance of national opinion—for a time, at least.

On a whole range of more prosaic matters, the country wants to be satisfied that it is heading, if not toward clearly defined goals, at least in the right general direction. It wants to be assured, at any time, that fiscal policy is sound, that the government is steering the economy wisely, that the United States is meeting its international challenges successfully, that tax and welfare policies are equitable, that the environment is protected, that the urban condition is being improved, that opportunities for human development are being extended. At this particular time, the country would like to think that its interminable energy problem is on its way to being resolved. All these are quite apart from leadership in crises like Iran or Afghanistan or Watts, when the people instinctively turn to the single individual in the White House as the only person who can unify the country and point the way.

In the presidential leadership model, it is the president who sets the direction of the country, who proclaims the policies and programs he contends will move the nation toward its goals. He does not do this arbitrarily, of course. He gets advice from a huge executive establishment and from a circle of close associates. He is sensitive to public opinion, he has the benefit of sophisticated polling data, and he tries to give the public what it wants. He listens to members of the Congress and to his own particular constituency. Sometimes he is more follower than leader. But, in any case, it is the president who in the end must announce where he means to take the country, and how he means to get it there. If he does not, the cry goes up, sooner or later, for "leadership," for "vision." Lack of leadership becomes a campaign issue and a president's challengers seek to displace or succeed him by promising a greater measure of the leadership the people want.

In the great quadrennial political competition, presidential leadership is legitimized—at times unmistakably mandated. In every presidential campaign, the candidates present their philosophies and their programs, and the people, in choosing one from among those candidates, decide the general direction of governmental policy. Sometimes they register their views incontestably, in favor of change or in favor of continuity, in a landslide election— as in 1932, 1936, 1952, and 1964—that endorses both the candidate for president and the congressional candidates of his party who share his policy commitments. After such elections, the presidential leadership model has every chance to work. The mandate is to a party as well as to a person, but the mandate to lead is clearly fixed—in the president. He was chosen for that purpose by the party itself, at its convention. He was the chief and only authoritative spokesman for the party, in the campaign. And he and his vice president were the only persons for whom the entire nation had the opportunity to vote.

In every less decisive election, however, the model is put on trial. In a split decision—and four of the seven elections from 1956 through 1980 chose the president and the majorities of one or both houses of Congress from opposing parties—who has the people's mandate? Even when the presidency and the Congress are of the same party, the presidential leadership model may be vitiated, if the president's victory is a narrow one. President Kennedy, in his brief term, found himself thwarted repeatedly by the conservative coalition. And President Carter, who ran weaker than the Democratic congressional candidates in virtually every state and district—and who, moreover, ran as an outsider to the party establishment—never won full acceptance as leader of his party in the resurgent and individualistic Congress of that time.

At all such times, when the presidential leadership model has been rejected—whether on principle during periods of divided government or as the consequence of defections from party discipline when majorities are small—there has been no alternative model of congressional leadership. The institutional structure of the Congress and its patterns of behavior have evolved to enable it to follow and to respond, but not to lead.

And that creates profound consequences for the democratic system. Even when the voters give the president an uncooperative Congress, he remains the only source of effective leadership, and the people understand that as a fact of life and expect him to be the leader. He is still the one person who presented a philosophy and a program to all the voters, asked for a mandate to lead the country in a more or less defined direction, and received it. The people sent him to Washington to take charge, and one of his jobs is to lead the legislature, to stop the incessant bickering and get things done. Even when they elect a president of one philosophy and congressmen of another, it is surely doubtful that the people are mandating deadlock and inaction. They may be expressing ambivalence and uncertainty, but they are more likely to be simply paying respect to incumbency or personal acquaintanceship in voting for Congress—particularly for members of the House. The superior mandate is still the president's.

If elections are to have meaning, then—which is to say, if democracy is to have meaning—the country must be able to make some progress in the direction the president told the people he would lead it, at least for the first two years until the voters can again express themselves. If it does not so move, the whole democratic electoral system has failed in its fundamental purpose: the people have not been able, by their votes, to set the course of government. The election, it turns out, did not make the difference that was promised; the voters might as well have stayed at home. Confidence is shattered, disillusionment sets in. One of the common complaints against Jimmy Carter throughout his term was that of "broken promises"—which in most cases reflected not a reversal of his own position but the rejection of his leadership by the Congress. So the normal rise of optimism that marks each quadrennial election and inauguration season was reversed more quickly than usual as President Carter failed to deliver on his pledges. And when Carter came down from Camp David in July 1979 and made his extraordinary televised speech deploring the national "malaise," his political opponents, at least, were quick to make the connection between the country's mood and the weakness of presidential leadership. As Senator Edward Kennedy opened his campaign against Carter, he made "leadership" the issue and found the "malaise" to reside "not in our people but in our leadership."[15]

Unless the presidential leadership model can somehow be restored, simply changing the occupant of the White House will not satisfy the "universal craving . . . for compelling and creative leadership." The Congress cannot make up the loss, short of radical changes in the constitutional and party systems. Alternative congressional structures tried out in the past are likely to be as faulty for the future as they proved to be when they were in effect. Stronger congressional leadership is not the answer: even if the trend of seven decades could somehow be reversed and the centralized power stripped from Czar Cannon and from Nelson Aldrich and his allies be restored to their successors, the new leaders still could not speak for all the people. The link that binds followers to leader was never forged through the process of a national election. So it was that when Cannon tried to govern the country from his post as speaker, Cannonism became an issue and Cannon inevitably lost. A modern speaker or Senate leader who sought to arrive at his policies through a truly democratic process—acting as spokesman for the party caucus and a representative party policy committee—would have a stronger claim to speak for the nation. Conceivably, leaders who renewed their mandates continuously through those instruments could compete with the president for public respect, particularly in a period of divided government. But for them to be effective in announcing, and then executing, a set of policies and programs would require radical change back to institutions and practices long

15. David S. Broder, *Washington Post,* November 19, 1979.

since discarded in most of the United States: binding caucuses and party discipline. In other words, a new political party system would have to take form on Capitol Hill, and it could not emerge unless a new party system evolved in the states and districts that send their representatives to Washington.

In the meantime, the present party system moves toward an ever more rampant individualism. No one can speak with authority for the Congress as a whole, or even for either house. Probably more than ever before in its history, unless the Congress follows the president it emits a cacophony of sounds. In crisis, it does not act with sureness, with decision, unless the president sets its course. Between crises, it does not have a program, or goals, or a sense of direction, of its own, for it deliberately has looked to the president for those. In sum, to the extent that presidential leadership is rejected, there is no substitute.

The Congress as Policy Integrator

To give the country a sense of progress toward any of its accepted goals, leadership must mobilize institutional, political, and psychological resources, as Burns points out. The activities of the government must be concerted in support of the objectives, and where objectives conflict—energy development and environmental protection, for example—the opposing considerations must be balanced through open processes and with apparent equity. The government's programs must support its goals, functional or sectoral policies must be brought into consistency with broad objectives, decisions that affect one another must be related so that the totality makes sense. All this calls for policy integration, or planning. The lack of capacity of a fragmented Congress to perform this function is one of the endemic weaknesses of the legislative branch that led it to erect the edifice of the modern presidency, brick by brick.

In the presidential leadership model of American government, then, policy integration was made the responsibility of the presidency. Whether or not it has always performed that function well, the executive branch is at least well designed for the purpose. With its hierarchical structure, it can represent diverse views in the many departments and agencies but reconcile them in the Executive Office of the President, with a point of decision in the chief executive himself.

In its policymaking processes, of course, the executive branch may appear more rational and orderly than it really is. And in its rivalry with the Congress, every public relations advantage is with the executive. Its strengths are exaggerated in the communications process, its weaknesses can be largely hidden. If on a given policy situation it flounders in indecision for months on end, if it is stalemated by internal policy conflicts, if it finally yields to the demands of narrow special interests, if its ultimate product is badly compromised and sloppy, all those weaknesses are likely to remain partially or wholly concealed. Dissenters within the executive branch do not take their case to the public, unless they resign. Investigative reporters can report and columnists can gossip, but their findings rarely make the seven o'clock news. The first the public at large hears of a policy decision is normally when the president announces it. Then he speaks with decision and authority, and his presentation is so well organized and well documented that his policies appear to flow from a systematic, balanced, and orderly consideration of the public interest—and only that.

The Congress, in contrast, does its floundering in public. Every conflict, delay, stalemate, and hastily-arrived-at compromise is in the open. So is every concession to the lobbyists. And the Congress, unlike the executive branch, is bipartisan, which means that on the inside of its deliberations at every stage is a minority whose political mission is to discredit the majority—to expose its weaknesses, disputes, and indecision. And the president, who may have temporized a year or more before making up his own mind, always presses the Congress for instant action, once he announces his program, and appeals for help to the people directly and through the media. The contrast in the public view is between a president who knows what he wants and where he is going and a Congress that cannot seem to come to grips with the agenda he has given it. The Congress is bound to look worse, and the executive branch better, than each really is.

But after that is said, the fact remains that the executive branch does have the capability of being more decisive than the legislative branch when it has to be, and of bringing its policies into a more consistent whole, simply because it is a hierarchy. At the top is an authoritative Executive Office of the President where policies can be looked at in relation to one another and their conflicts reconciled. In charge of it all is a single individual—the president—with the power to say "This is it" and command his subordinates to fall in line with his decision.

Each autumn the executive branch goes through an elaborate process of policy integration, out of which emerges "the program of the president."[16]

16. In a year of presidential transition, the program is that of the outgoing president, but it is

That program—and it is significant that it is viewed as a single program—is embodied at the beginning of each year in a series of state papers that are supposed to be, and in fact are in their major aspects, mutually reinforcing, with any serious contradictions usually discovered and ironed out. Beginning with the State of the Union Message, they include the Economic Report of the President and the Budget, followed by supplementary special messages spelling out specific legislative proposals. If the Congress rejects the program of the president, the question is whether it can substitute a corresponding, equally well-integrated, program of its own. Can it establish the necessary centralized institutions that it has lacked, and endow them with authority? If it cannot, if its own decisions lack national perspective and consistency and coherence, the resurgence of Congress must lead to an inferior policy product.

The problem of policy integration in the Congress appears at three levels: first, in each committee; second, in each house as a whole; third, between the houses.

The last of these is a territory almost wholly unexplored. To find a bicameral policymaking mechanism with broad responsibility one must go back more than a century, to the Joint Committee of Fifteen on Reconstruction. Recent years have seen only an occasional experiment, such as the Joint Committee on Atomic Energy, now abolished, and the Joint Economic Committee, which has never had legislative jurisdiction. In an era of fragmentation and individualism, the trend has been away from centralization of power even within individual houses, let alone in the Congress as a whole. Anyway, acceptance of presidential leadership of the legislative process by both houses made joint devices appear dispensable. Coordination of legislative policies and program was to be attained in meetings of the leaders of the two bodies at the White House with the president. Coordination of the details was to be left to committee chairmen and their staffs, with cabinet members and other administration officials acting as intermediaries if necessary.[17]

During the six Eisenhower and eight Nixon-Ford years of divided government, presidential meetings with the congressional majority leaders—when they were held—were limited in scope and inevitably took on the

---

presented to the Congress with the same formality as though the incumbent president were continuing in office. And much of it survives the change of incumbents, for the presidency—as distinct from the president—has its own continuity.

17. The *Washington Post*, April 22, 1978, relates an incident of shuttle diplomacy that is not atypical: "The separation of powers doctrine was fairly blurred Thursday night as congressional conferees on natural gas pricing . . . invited in the administration, in the person of Energy Secretary James Schlesinger, to help solve their differences. For much of the session, which lasted until 3 a.m., House and Senate members caucused in separate rooms . . . and Schlesinger in his shirtsleeves padded from one closed meeting to another trying to mediate differences and persuade one side or the other not to break off talks and go home."

character of negotiating and communicating, rather than policy planning, sessions. Presidents discussed legislative strategy on controversial questions at separate meetings with the minority Republican leadership, and the Democratic majorities were left to their own devices to coordinate House and Senate legislative policies and programs. Nevertheless, even in these periods the Congress did not develop any new joint mechanisms for integrating policy. In designing its new congressional budget process, it did create a central research and advisory organization—the Congressional Budget Office—but the legislative responsibilities were assigned to separate committees in the two houses in the usual fashion. So in this as in all other fields of legislation (except atomic energy, when the joint committee was still in existence), policy differences between the two houses were negotiated piecemeal, by conference committees appointed separately for every piece of legislation. From 1977 through 1980, the executive branch resumed its former coordinating role.

At the committee levels and in the separate houses the Congress has periodically grappled with the problem of policy integration, through internal redistribution of power. The degree to which these experiments succeeded is an indicator of the potential of structural reform.

The Limits of Committee Restructuring. At the committee level, improvement of the capacity for policy integration has been sought through reduction in the number of committees and elimination of jurisdictional overlap. The reform temper of the 1970s invited new attempts to simplify committee structure on the pattern of the highly successful effort of 1946 and the less productive undertaking in the mid-1960s. The Bolling committee was established by the House in 1973 and the Stevenson-Brock committee by the Senate in 1976. The former presented a plan to rationalize committee jurisdictions that was, for the most part, rejected by the Democratic caucus,[18] but the Senate group was more successful. It managed to eliminate three standing committees, reducing the number from eighteen to fifteen. And through its recommendation to limit the number of subcommittee chairmanships each senator could hold—a proposal made more stringent through amendment on the Senate floor—the number of subcommittees was cut from 135 in 1976 to 100 in 1978 (compared to 121 in 1972). This helped.[19] But reducing the number of committees and subcommittees cannot begin to solve the problem

18. The work of the House Select Committee on Committees, chaired by Representative Richard Bolling, Democrat of Missouri, is analyzed by two former members of its staff, Roger H. Davidson and Walter J. Oleszek, in *Congress Against Itself* (Indiana University Press, 1977).

19. The number remained at the new level in 1979–80. Meanwhile, as noted in chapter 13, the number of House subcommittees continued to rise, from 119 in 1972 to 144 in 1976 and 148 in 1979.

of policy integration. Policy still has to be sliced into segments—if not 150, then at least 100 or so—and even if that number could conceivably be cut in half, virtually every major problem would still be bound to overlap the defined jurisdictions. Yet, except in the field of budget policy, there is no continuing institutional machinery for reassembling the segments of an issue for consideration whole.

One of the aims of the Stevenson-Brock enterprise, for example, was to bring into a single committee responsibility for as many aspects as possible of the newly emergent problem of energy. The old Interior Committee was therefore converted into a Committee on Energy and Natural Resources; the Joint Committee on Atomic Energy was abolished, and its nonmilitary jurisdiction, along with some of the functions of half a dozen other committees, were transferred to the new committee. Yet when President Carter sent his National Energy Plan to the Congress in 1977, a large element of the legislative action concerned taxation, which remained the responsibility of Finance, and the conflict between two blocs of senators led by two aggressive chairmen— Henry M. Jackson (Democrat of Washington) of Energy and Natural Resources and Russell B. Long (Democrat of Louisiana) of Finance—deadlocked the Senate members of the House-Senate conference committee for over a year. The result, in the end, was anything but a comprehensive and coherent program. To transfer jurisdiction over energy taxation to the Energy and Natural Resources Committee would not solve the overlap problem, of course, for then consideration of revenue policy would be divided.

The Bolling committee in the House, struggling with the same problem, had earlier proposed a similar solution—a new committee on energy and environment, to be built on the existing Interior and Insular Affairs Committee, with areas of jurisdiction transferred from several other committees, including Commerce. But environmental and consumer groups, fearing capture of the new committee by producer interests, rallied to defeat it.[20] A new House Select Committee on Committees, appointed in 1979 as a successor to the Bolling group and headed by Jerry M. Patterson, Democrat of California, conceived a more limited approach, proposing to promote Commerce's Subcommittee on Energy and Power to full committee status with only minor disturbance to the jurisdictions of other committees. Rejecting this approach, the House renamed the Interstate and Foreign Commerce Committee the Energy and Commerce Committee but left important aspects of energy legislation outside its scope. The locus of policy integration therefore remained largely as before, in the whole House as the mediator among committees.

20. Davidson and Oleszek, *Congress Against Itself*, pp. 176–78, 196–97, 212–13, 250.

Even where jurisdiction over particular problems can be nicely concentrated in single major committees, moreover, the committees have lost much of their power as integrating forces. The autocratic chairmen of the past, however one may view their other attributes, could coordinate and direct the work of their committees and control the product if they chose to do so and possessed the necessary skill and determination. But in the new democracy, most of the jurisdiction, and the accompanying staff resources, have been assigned to the subcommittees, and full committee chairmen have been reduced in many cases to a first-among-equals—some say to a figurehead—status. What comes to the floors of the House and Senate now is usually less a committee than a subcommittee product. It may be routinely approved by the full committee, through a logrolling process among subcommittee leaders. It is managed by the subcommittee, rather than the full committee, chairman on the floor. Committee members are less inclined to support the committee product as a matter of principle. Floor amendments are more freely offered, and more freely accepted. In sum, what begins as piecemeal consideration of problems in subcommittees of limited jurisdiction continues as piecemeal action all the way through the legislative process.

An occasional committee chairman with the right combination of knowledge, skill, charm, and untiring effort can still dominate his committee. Russell Long of Senate Finance was perhaps the chairman most often cited as a surviving embodiment of the baronial tradition, but even he was not always able to carry his control of events from the committee to the Senate floor. No matter what his personal qualities, Al Ullman could never have become the force as chairman of House Ways and Means that his predecessor, Wilbur Mills, was for so many years; too much of the institutional power of the Ways and Means chairman was deliberately stripped away when the committee was enlarged and directed to establish subcommittees, and when it ceased to function also as the Democratic committee on committees. To some degree, the power of every chairman has been similarly diffused.

The Use of Ad Hoc Committees. At the level of the whole house, the most promising innovation in policy-integration machinery—apart from the budget process—has been the use by the House of Representatives of ad hoc committees which cut across the jurisdictional lines of the standing committees to deal with broad problems. Both the Bolling and Stevenson-Brock committees were aware that the problem of overlap, and the need for policy integration, could not be met by a reshuffling of committee jurisdictions, no matter how designed. The solution devised by the Bolling committee, which was adopted by the House, gave the speaker additional control over the flow of legislation by authorizing him to refer bills to more than one committee simultaneously or sequentially, to create ad hoc select committees with the approval of the House, and to make "such other provisions as may be considered appropriate" to expedite the consideration of important bills.[21]

Ad hoc committees showed some early promise of evolving as a mechanism for policy integration. Such committees had been created on occasion in both houses in the past to make studies and prepare reports, but until the Bolling committee recommendation was adopted in 1975 they had not, in modern times, had *legislative* jurisdiction;[22] the combined power of the standing committee chairmen was sufficient to forestall any invasion of their domain. But, with the barons gone from the scene, Speaker Albert used the new authority once in 1975, and Speaker O'Neill twice two years later. All three proposals, carefully negotiated by the leadership with the leaders of the affected committees, were approved by the House without opposition. All are worth attention as promising designs for the development of a capacity for policy integration in both houses.

In the first action, Speaker Albert had the House create a Select Committee on the Outer Continental Shelf, with members drawn from three standing committees, to review and bring up to date the 1953 law that governed the development of oil and gas in the seabed. Headed by Representative John M. Murphy, New York Democrat, it produced a bill that set new rules for oil and gas leasing, which was rejected by the House late in 1976 but enacted in modified form in 1978. The committee's life was then extended into 1980 for purposes of oversight.

Speaker O'Neill's first experimental body, the Ad Hoc Committee on Energy, was not, in contrast, assigned original jurisdiction over energy legislation but instead sat in a review capacity over the bills reported by the regular committees. Most of the measures called for in President Carter's 1977 National Energy Plan were referred to two committees—Commerce and Ways and Means—but minor elements went to three others. All five, as well as two more that had some interest in the broad subject, were represented on the forty-member ad hoc body, which was chaired by Thomas L. Ashley of Ohio, a twenty-three-year veteran who was not identified with either the producer or the consumer side of the highly controversial energy issue and

---

21. "Committee Reform Amendments of 1974," H. Res. 988, p. 35.

22. The only exception in the preceding thirty years, apart from groups (such as the Bolling committee itself) set up to deal with internal House matters, was a select committee on survivor benefits for deceased members or former members of the armed services. David J. Vogler, "The Rise of Ad Hoc Committees in the House of Representatives," paper prepared for the 1978 annual meeting of the American Political Science Association.

who could be counted on to work closely with the leadership. The other twenty-six Democratic members were "hand-picked" so as to make sure the committee would be "friendly" to the Carter program; "packed" was the Republican term for it.[23] In referring the measure's elements to the regular committees, O'Neill gave them a ten-week deadline—which all of them met. The president's program survived that stage almost intact, the main casualty being his proposal for an increase of five cents in the gasoline tax in any year during which consumption rose. The principal contributions of the ad hoc committee—which made its decisions through a caucus of its Democratic members—were to restore the proposed increase in the gasoline tax and to somewhat liberalize price controls on natural gas to stave off a move for deregulation on the floor. The strategy was half successful; the compromise on control of gas prices was accepted, while the gasoline tax lost. But all the other major elements of the Carter program survived the House. O'Neill, who had master-minded the entire exercise, was credited with an extraordinary feat of generalship in steering the whole complex package through the chamber in a bare three months. "A lot of people have been crying for leadership," commented Representative Toby Moffett, a second-term Connecticut Democrat. "And now they've got it."[24]

In the third experiment, O'Neill negotiated an arrangement with three committees for a combined "super-subcommittee" (as distinct from an ad hoc select committee) to consider the president's welfare reform program, transmitted to the Congress in August 1977. Headed by James C. Corman, Democrat of California, a Ways and Means committee member and supporter of the president's approach, the ad hoc subcommittee consisted of fifteen members of Ways and Means and seven each from Agriculture and from Education and Labor. In this case, however, the speaker set no deadlines. While the subcommittee served its purpose in holding a single set of hearings on the entire plan and in approving it nearly as submitted, the legislation subsequently bogged down in the three committees to which the Corman panel reported—particularly in Ways and Means, whose chairman, Al Ullman, had an alternate proposal.

The ad hoc structure served to facilitate negotiations with the White House, however, and in June 1978 a compromise was reportedly agreed on. But that turned out to be too late; O'Neill concluded that even if the scaled-down compromise measure could be put through the House, the Senate would not have time to act on it in that election year. So he pronounced the issue dead

23. *Congressional Quarterly Almanac, 1977*, pp. 721–22. Richard Corrigan, "Carter's Energy Crusade Becomes Tip's Party Caucus," *National Journal*, vol. 9 (July 30, 1977), p. 1196.

24. Corrigan, "Carter's Energy Crusade," p. 1197.

for the Ninety-fifth Congress. Despite the ultimate collapse of the effort, however, the structural device that was employed establishes a third useful precedent for the handling of complex problems where a comprehensive approach is required. The device did permit all of the facets of the welfare problem and the administration's proposed solution to be considered in an integrated way, and at the initial stage an integrated policy did emerge from the subcommittee. That the policy lacked sufficient support to pass the Congress does not reflect on the procedure.

With the Bolling committee recommendation as its model, the Stevenson-Brock committee recommended in 1976 that the Senate place in the majority and minority leaders, acting jointly, the same authority that the House had given to its speaker. But some members of the Senate Rules Committee, to which the Stevenson-Brock report was referred, contended that the leaders already had the authority to propose ad hoc arrangements at any time, and Majority Leader Byrd did not press the issue. If the power exists, however, it has not been used, and issues that overlap committee jurisdictions continue to be handled in a piecemeal fashion.[25] As a case in point, the Carter energy program that was put through the House with only minor modifications under the auspices of the Ashley committee was parceled out among Senate committees and nothing that could be called a national energy plan was ever put together. No significant energy legislation at all emerged in 1977, and after a deadlock that lasted throughout most of the next year the Carter plan was decimated, with no substitute congressional plan in its place. Thus ended an essay at national energy planning in the manner that the Senate itself had called for in the Javits-Glenn amendment to the Department of Energy Act of 1977.[26] In the House, Speaker O'Neill did not continue in the Ninety-sixth Congress of 1979–80 his experiments with ad hoc committees.

25. The Senate had, of course, utilized devices for coordination directly between existing committees, as distinct from creating new committees. G. Calvin Mackenzie, "Committee Coordination and Policy Integration in the Senate," in *Committees and Senate Procedures,* papers prepared for the Commission on the Operation of the Senate, 94 Cong. 2 sess. (GPO, 1977), pp. 74–93, reports that 7 percent of all Senate public bills in 1975 were referred to more than one committee (but this device, he notes, does not ensure agreement, and if it is not reached, some other mode of coordination must be employed), that committees held 107 joint hearings, and that assignment of members of one committee to be ex officio members of another sometimes helped to bridge the gap between committees. He also reviews the use of temporary study committees, which he finds are usually "regarded as weak stepsisters in the legislative process" that rarely seek "to provide balanced and integrated responses to complex policy questions" (p. 87). Mackenzie recommends invigorating the majority Policy Committee as the arbiter of committee jurisdiction and the coordination of legislative action.

26. In a letter to Majority Leader Mansfield in 1975, Senator Frank E. Moss, Democrat of Utah, pointed out that "twenty-six subcommittees held hearings or mark-up sessions on energy legislation in the first session of the 93rd Congress (1973) alone. This dispersal of responsibility prevented the Senate from developing a national energy policy." *Congressional Record,* February 18, 1975, p. 3344.

In sum, the period of congressional resurgence has brought about no fundamental improvement in the integrative capacity of the Congress, with the single, though major, exception of the budget process. The House and Senate Budget committees provide the perspective and the overview capacity that is missing elsewhere, and their budget resolutions are expressions of integrated policy, of general fiscal goals with which all program decisions are to be made consistent. What, then, is the potential for creating similar integrating mechanisms in other fields?

The Congressional Budget Process as a Model. When the Congress and the executive branch agree on their general fiscal policy—as during the Carter years—relations in this field resemble a modified version of the presidential leadership model. As party leader and chief legislator, President Carter was actually in a stronger position than were his predecessors, for the congressional budget committees exist to mobilize support for the party's consensus program and safeguard it from piecemeal damage. They provide a channel for orderly communication between the branches. Antagonisms are reduced and party cohesion improved, yet with the full participation of the assertive Congress.

But when the president and the congressional majorities are of opposite parties, or the branches disagree for other reasons, the budget process approaches what may be termed a congressional leadership model. In those times, when the president's fiscal policy is going to be overturned in any case, the new budget process enables the Congress to supersede the administration's integrated program with one of its own that is coherent also, assembled through a process not markedly less rational and orderly than the one the president used. That is what happened in the first two years of the act's operation, when Gerald Ford was in the White House.

True, the budget committees have no power of decision; they are on a par with other committees advocating other policy positions, and contested issues are ultimately resolved in trials of strength on the floors of the two houses between the broad and the particularist perspectives. But budget-makers do not necessarily have the last word in the executive branch either. There it is the president who balances the goals of fiscal policy against other policy objectives and makes the choices. This is as it should be. Fiscal policy is an element of national policy that has to be reconciled with other elements; it is not always, as those who seek to write the country's fiscal policy into the Constitution would have it be, the overriding element.

When the Congress each year completes the reconciliation process, and thus brings the fiscal consequences of every action into harmony with a general fiscal policy, it solves much of the total problem of policy integration. Once the fiscal reconciliation is achieved, the formation of tax policy, social security policy, agricultural policy, welfare policy, resource development policy, and so on can perhaps proceed well enough on a piecemeal basis, as they always have. If this means philosophical contradictions—government regulation being extended in some areas while being contracted in others, for example, or some programs being devolved to state and local governments while others are being centralized—that may be untidy but probably harmless enough.[27] Nevertheless, there are areas in addition to fiscal policy where the need for policy integration seems to be generally acknowledged. These include economic policy, urban or urban growth policy, environmental policy, and energy policy. Most crucial of all, perhaps, is the need for coordination of foreign and military policies—a need conceded when the Congress created the National Security Council in 1946. Then, in some aspects at least, foreign policy has to be linked to domestic policy, and energy policy and growth policy and fiscal policy all tied together. It is difficult to escape the conclusion that additional mechanisms are needed to enable the Congress to at least *consider* whether critical linkages exist among the policy decisions that it takes and, where it finds that the policies are interrelated, to make the decisions consistent. All of the arguments that have been accepted by the Congress for integrating all of the elements of fiscal policy can be put forward with equal force on behalf of integration in other policy areas—indeed, on behalf of integration of all policy into a "program of the Congress" that corresponds to the "program of the president."

There are severe limits, however, to the extent to which a model of congressional leadership could be applied. That model appears to be working in the field of fiscal policy; and in theory it could work in some other areas of domestic policy—such as urban growth policy, or energy policy, or economic policy. But it is not suited to national security and foreign affairs, or for linking foreign and domestic policy, for the reasons set out in chapter 10. And in domestic areas each new integrating committee inserted into the policymaking process compounds the total problem of integration at the same time that it may solve a segment of it. It is one thing to require that all policies have to be harmonized with a fiscal policy, but quite another to demand that they be harmonized with an energy policy, an urban policy, an economic

27. The classic argument for achieving coordination of policy *without* benefit of an authoritative central mechanism—through "partisan mutual adjustment"—is Charles E. Lindblom's, *The Intelligence of Democracy* (Free Press, 1965). But Lindblom acknowledges that neither mechanism is a complete substitute for the other, and that coordination of policy through central decisionmaking is the superior process in some circumstances (pp. 293–94).

policy, and perhaps an environmental policy, as well, and then that all of these be reconciled with one another. With each new integrating device that might be conceived for any one segment of the total policymaking process, the complexity advances by geometrical progression.[28]

Then what of a supercommittee to integrate them all and produce the *single* congressional program that would correspond with—and supersede if necessary—the program of the president? That, in one form, was what the Legislative Reorganizaton Act of 1946 contemplated, with its provision for a majority and minority policy committee in each house. But the idea failed then, and it would be rash to believe it would work better now. To produce an integrated program, the supercommittee would have to do more than react to policy proposals or individual bills after they came from the regular committees, which is about all the committees created since 1946 have ever done. It would have to do its work in advance, much as the budget committees now do, laying out the general policy and program to which—after adoption by the bodies—the regular committees would be obliged to conform. But such an undertaking would be all but impossible to fit into the already bulging annual congressional schedule. Moreover, it would require an extraordinarily able staff, which would have to be granted a large measure of power and influence, and that would hardly be acceptable to elected members of Congress who found their views overruled by mere employees. Even if the staff could be kept submerged, to place an effective power of program integration in an elite group of members in each house would run counter to all the forces that have produced the new individualism of the Congress. The other members, singly or in committees, would not be likely for long to submit peacefully to a supercommittee, even if they could be lured into creating it in the first place. The idea of a central policymaking apparatus for the Senate or the House has an engineer's simplicity of form, but the last time either house was organized on hierarchical lines was in 1910, and it turned out then that neither the members nor the public would stand for it. Since then, the centrifugal forces of individualism have gained strength with every passing year.

The capacity to produce a comprehensive and integrated program, then, remains missing in Congress. "The effort of the Congress to assert itself should not be misunderstood to mean that the Congress can truly become

28. This is especially true if the integrating body is simply imposed on the existing structure without a rationalization of the whole—as was the case when the budget committees were established. If the Congress were being organized anew, it may be doubted that a three-tier structure would be designed, with budget, authorizing, and appropriations committees all involved in the major decisions on every program every year.

an equal branch of the government," Representative Hamilton said in 1974, in the early days of the resurgence. "It is simply too difficult for strong-minded, aggressive persons 'to get it all together' on all the issues on the nation's agenda. The Congress cannot control inflation, solve the energy shortage, or negotiate trade agreements. Congress may win some battles, restrain the President here and there, but it will remain essentially a body which confirms or rejects Presidential proposals, and reviews them after the fact."[29] That was an accurate forecast. Three Congresses later, Senator Gary Hart, Democrat of Colorado, was complaining: "In the Senate . . . we almost never debate what this country's long-term strategy is." "The United States has no trade strategy," declared Senator Stevenson shortly afterward. "It has no industrial policy. It has no food policy."[30] His criticism was directed at the government as a whole, not just at the Congress, but insofar as either branch felt a responsibility for developing long-term strategies on such matters, it was the executive. Except in the fiscal field, policy coordination remained, no less than before the congressional revolt against the Nixon leadership, a function delegated to the executive. The Congress remained compartmentalized, organized as the executive branch would be if the latter had only departments and no Executive Office of the President—indeed, no president. The independent work of individual committees and subcommittees cannot be integrated without instrumentalities for that purpose, and the conceptual and practical obstacles to creating such instrumentalities appear insuperable. Moreover, the motivation to take any decisive steps in that direction is lacking.

29. *Congressional Record*, June 24, 1974, p. 4174.
30. Ibid., daily edition, October 5, 1979, p. S14173; December 20, 1979, p. S19286.

CHAPTER XV

Representation
and the Will
to Govern

REPRESENTATIVE Barbara Jordan, in the introspective days of 1973, admonished a resurgent Congress to "regain the will to govern."[1] Theodore Sorensen, less elegantly, saw the issue as one of "guts."[2] Many others found the Congress similarly deficient. "There is a deeply unheroic streak in Congress that does not covet responsibility nor welcome tests of courage," wrote John W. Gardner, a former cabinet member.[3] Journalist Arlen J. Large similarly diagnosed the congressional ailment as a "failure of nerve," which led it to express opinions but leave final decisions to the president.[4] "Congress is really a body of followers, not leaders," Representative Donald W. Riegle, Jr., Republican (later senator and Democrat) of Michigan, confided to his diary. "Congress usually won't face up to a problem until it has to, before it is forced to."[5] "Unfortunately, it is in the nature of the Congressional animal," agreed Representative Bob Eckhardt, Democrat of Texas, "to be overly concerned with the backwaters of public policy and too little disposed to make hard decisions on mainstream national issues."[6] Congressmen prac-

1. *Congressional Record*, April 18, 1973, p. 13170.
2. Theodore C. Sorensen, "The Case for a Strong Presidency," in Charles Roberts, ed., *Has the President Too Much Power?* (Harper's Magazine Press, 1974), p. 27.
3. "The Role of the Presidency: What Must Be Done After Watergate," *Current*, no. 153 (July/August 1973), p. 20.
4. *Wall Street Journal*, August 13, 1974.
5. Donald W. Riegle, Jr., and Trevor Armbrister, "A Congressman's Diary" (excerpt from *O Congress* [Doubleday, 1972]), in Peter Collier, ed., *Dilemmas of Democracy: Readings in American Government* (Harcourt Brace Jovanovich, 1976), p. 80.
6. "Alternative Policymaking Structures and the Democratic Legislative Initiative in the 94th Congress," in National Capital Area Political Science Association, *Short Essays in Political Science*

tice "collective avoidance" of important questions, said Representative Michael J. Harrington, Democrat of Massachusetts, on his retirement in 1978. "I'm not sure we really want to participate."[7] And their colleague, Representative Les Aspin, Democrat of Wisconsin, explained the reason: "Since only the most politically secure congressman can afford to offend constituents—and since there are so many ways to offend them—natural survival instincts dictate that a congressman will duck any tough issues that he can. Politically, it is often much safer to let the Executive do the leading."[8]

In this composite view, the long decline of Congress was not just an accident of history. It flowed from the very nature of the congressional animal, a creature compelled to nurture its relationship with the state or district that determines, at two- or six-year intervals, whether it lives or dies. The demands of the constituency are so urgent and incessant as to lead the members of Congress—House members in particular but senators as well—to concentrate on the role of *representative* of their areas, to deal with local and peripheral matters, avoid broader responsibility, and leave basic decisions to the president. If that view is correct, the will to govern, the necessary guts, will not be regained—or acquired in the first place—without radical change in the nature or the behavior, or both, of the members themselves. To the extent that they are oriented toward state, district, and constituency, they would have to be reoriented toward the nation, induced somehow to set aside local demands and interests in order to concentrate on the broad concerns of the whole country. The question is whether legislators elected from narrow constituencies can ever, in the nature of things, alter fundamentally the modes of conduct that have evolved out of the peculiar relationships they bear to their constituencies in the United States.

This question has both quantitative and qualitative aspects. First, the volume and diversity of constituent demands impose an enormous burden on the members' time, distracting them from concentration on fundamental issues of national policy. Second, constituency pressures impel individual legislators to consider broad policy questions from a local rather than a national viewpoint, producing the oft-criticized "parochialism" and "irresponsibility" of the Congress.

From *The Spring 1975 Conference Of The National Capital Area Political Science Association.* Eckhardt expands on the reasons for this characteristic of congressmen and traces the decline of Congress to it in Bob Eckhardt and Charles L. Black, Jr., *The Tides of Power: Conversations on the American Constitution* (Yale University Press, 1976), pp. 19–20.

7. Dennis Farney, *Wall Street Journal*, September 21, 1978.
8. "Why Doesn't Congress Do Something?" *Foreign Policy*, no. 15 (Summer 1974), p. 73.

Distraction

A member of Congress is "a special pleader and a sort of super-lobbyist for his constituents and his area," Representative Joe L. Evins, Democrat of Tennessee, wrote some years ago.[9] John Brademas of Indiana, later to become the House Democratic whip, used the same term in writing of the members' role: "With the defense budget at $50 billion, today's congressman may often have to become a kind of lobbyist for bringing more defense business to his own district. . . . I never know with complete assurance, when the contract is finally awarded, whether my effort made the difference or not. In any event, to be very candid about it, the effort has to be made because the public expects it."[10]

Another member, speaking of "the service we have to perform for constituents," complained: "Too much of our time and energy is diverted in that direction with the result that the opportunity for creative thinking in a legislative way is greatly lessened. It is too bad we don't have two members of Congress for each district, with one having the responsibility for handling constituent requests."[11]

That statement was made in 1959. Two decades later, the complaints were, if anything, more emphatic. A 1977 survey found that half the members of the House felt constituent demands interfered with the proper exercise of their legislative duties. These are representative comments:

> There's a role conflict. The incredible demands of constituent service interfere with constructive legislation.
>
> I spend too much time on things like finding a high school band a place to stay. . . . That actually consumed half a day—that's nuts!
>
> I have an ombudsman-like role. I came down to Washington with great ideas but I don't have the time to deal with them.
>
> One reason we are not able to formulate better national policy is because we have become the ombudsman and the last hope of individuals who are despairing of dealing with the federal bureaucracy.
>
> I would like to be exclusively a legislator, but custom has made that impossible.
>
> Legislation takes a back seat. It can be neglected without any immediate adverse impact on a congressman. . . . But he cannot avoid, except at the risk of peril of constituent hostility, responding to constituent requests. So constituent requests

9. *Understanding Congress* (Potter, 1963), p. 37.

10. "Technology and Social Change: A Congressman's View," in Aaron W. Warner and others, eds., *The Impact of Science and Technology* (Columbia University Press, 1965), pp. 146–47.

11. Charles L. Clapp, *The Congressman: His Work as He Sees It* (Brookings Institution, 1963), p. 55. This was representative of the comments on the subject by the congressmen who participated in the discussions that were the basis for Clapp's book; many, however, made a point of the usefulness and necessity of constituent service.

take a priority over legislation. You have a turning upside down of what the priorities ought to be.[12]

This is particularly true of the newer members. "I haven't been a congressman yet," a member in his fourth year claimed. "The first two years, I spent all of my time getting myself reelected. That last two years, I spent getting myself a district so that I could get reelected. So I won't be a congressman until next year."[13] Representative Bob Bergland, Democrat of Minnesota, who later served as secretary of agriculture, also admitted that most of his first two years went to getting reelected. "I decided there was nothing in Washington as important as one constituent, and I dropped everything when one called."[14] Another first-term member described his job: "Taking care of home problems. Case work, not necessarily having anything to do with legislation at all. Taking care of constituents. In the legislative part of it, getting legislation through that affects your district."[15]

After their first term or two, members may be well enough advertised, and well enough entrenched, in their districts to devote more of their time to general policy questions. But most members appear not to lessen their attention to their districts; one study showed a substantial increase in the time members, senior as well as junior, spent in their districts in the 1970s. Some congressmen remain essentially locally oriented throughout their careers, not only because of fear of reprisal from their constituents but because that is where their interests lie, that is their conception of their proper role, and that is where they get the satisfaction of seeing tangible results from their labors. Not every candidate for Congress aspires to be a statesman coping grandly with large issues, and the electoral process itself—at least in some districts—may tend to give locally oriented candidates an advantage both for nomination and for election. The majority of a group of seventy-seven House members interviewed in 1971 derived greater satisfaction from their representational and service function than from any other aspect of their jobs, including legislation. Constituent service was also the aspect they emphasized most in discussing their activities. The local orientation of the congressmen contrasted with that of federal executives interviewed in the

12. Thomas E. Cavanagh, "The Two Arenas of Congress: Electoral and Institutional Incentives for Performance," paper prepared for the 1978 annual meeting of the American Political Science Association, pp. 21–22. The survey was conducted by the House Commission on Administrative Review, of which Cavanagh was assistant survey research director. In all, 153 members were interviewed.

13. Richard F. Fenno, Jr., *Home Style: House Members in Their Districts* (Little, Brown, 1978), p. 215.

14. *Washingtom Post*, November 21, 1974.

15. Roger H. Davidson, *The Role of the Congressman* (Pegasus, 1969), p. 80.

same study; the executives said that "the most appealing aspect of their roles is to wrestle with policy problems."[16]

Senators and representatives of this turn of mind seek membership on committees that handle legislation of particular interest to their states or districts, or that distribute the federal projects collectively known as the pork barrel—rivers and harbors projects, public buildings, military bases, and so on. That committee members do in fact obtain greater benefits for their states or districts by virtue of committee membership—either through legislation or influence on administrative decisions or both—has been documented by several statistical studies.[17] Many types of projects are authorized separately, one by one, and appropriated for individually, to maximize the credit-claiming. Where appropriations are made in lump sums, administrative agencies take care that congressmen are allowed to announce the projects, to enable them to take the credit even when they may have had no influence at all on the decision.

A survey in the mid-1960s of how House members actually spent their time produced a figure of 28 percent devoted to constituent service, defined broadly and somewhat arbitrarily.[18] Another, covering eighty-seven House members, found that only 16 percent listed the "errand boy" function as their primary activity, but 59 percent named it as secondary.[19] Even at the very top of the congressional power structure, the most eminent members remain representatives while becoming statesmen. Mike Mansfield, when Senate majority leader, would "readily see any constituent from Montana who comes to Washington or . . . talk with any long-distance caller from the state with

16. Joel D. Aberbach and Bert A. Rockman, "The Overlapping Worlds of American Federal Executives and Congressmen," *British Journal of Political Science*, vol. 7 (January 1977), p. 46. First-term members were excluded from the random sample.

17. See R. Douglas Arnold, *Congress and the Bureaucracy: A Theory of Influence* (Yale University Press, 1979), which analyzes Army and Air Force employment, water and sewer grants, and model cities grants, chaps. 6–8; John A. Ferejohn, *Pork Barrel Politics* (Stanford University Press, 1974), distribution of rivers and harbors projects; Carol F. Goss, "Military Committee Membership and Defense Related Benefits in the House of Representatives," *Western Political Quarterly*, vol. 25 (June 1972), pp. 215–33, military bases; Gerald S. Strom, "Congressional Policy-Making: A Test of Theory," *Journal of Politics*, vol. 37 (August 1975), pp. 711–35, waste treatment plants; and Charles R. Plott, "Some Organizational Influences on Urban Renewal Decisions," *American Economic Review*, vol. 58 (May 1969, *Papers and Proceedings, 1968*), pp. 306–21. "The map of the old Atomic Energy Commission's national laboratories . . . was a near geographic rendering of districts from the old Joint Committee on Atomic Energy," a reporter wrote in the *Washington Post*, February 21, 1978. The location of the Houston center of the National Aeronautics and Space Administration was commonly attributed to the influence of that city's Representative Albert Thomas, Democrat, chairman of the appropriations subcommittee with jurisdiction over the program.

18. John S. Saloma III, *Congress and the New Politics* (Little, Brown, 1969), pp. 184–86. The computation was based on 160 responses.

19. Davidson, *Role of the Congressman*, p. 99.

a legitimate reason for telephoning him,"[20] and he took time to communicate forcefully with administration officials whenever any federal installation in his state, such as a veterans' hospital or an agricultural research station, was threatened. The intense interest of his successor, Robert C. Byrd, in federal expenditures in West Virginia is legendary. Speaker O'Neill, amidst his leadership duties, maintains a close watch over the welfare of the Boston navy yard.

In short, whether a member finds constituent service the most or least satisfying element of the job, none can escape its demands. If they let themselves, members can become wholly absorbed in errand running, in lobbying and case work, in garnering federal projects for their states or districts, and in returning home at frequent intervals to speak, listen, and be seen. Yet if they pay too little attention to that aspect of their jobs, that can bring a quick end to their political careers. Neglect is an issue political opponents are quick to seize on, and one constituents can understand. It has figured, to greater or less extent, in the defeat of many prominent Senate figures; Ralph K. Huitt, who knows that body well, lists two majority leaders, Scott W. Lucas of Illinois and Ernest W. McFarland of Arizona, and Wayne L. Morse of Oregon, J. William Fulbright of Arkansas, and Fred R. Harris of Oklahoma, all Democrats, among those turned out of office by constituents who felt a loss of interest in them.[21] Every two years, news stories carry fresh reminders of the potency of that issue. In 1978, for instance, Representative John B. Breckenridge of Kentucky was beaten in the Democratic primary by a challenger who "campaigned on the theme that Mr. Breckenridge was more concerned with what was going on in Washington than the needs of Kentucky residents."[22] In 1980 the same line of attack was used by the Republicans who defeated some senior Democrats, such as House Majority Whip Brademas and Senators Frank Church of Idaho, George McGovern of South Dakota, and Gaylord Nelson of Wisconsin, and by Democrats who almost defeated Senator Barry Goldwater of Arizona. Even if an incumbent is reasonably sure of reelection, neglect of his constituency may mean the difference between having to fight a primary election or running unopposed, or the difference between drawing in the general election a strong or a weak opponent, or none at all. "So members of Congress concentrate on constituencies," ob-

20. Andrew J. Glass, "Mike Mansfield, Majority Leader," in Norman J. Ornstein, ed., *Congress in Change: Evolution and Reform* (Praeger, 1975), p. 153.
21. "Congress: Retrospect and Prospect," *Journal of Politics*, vol. 38 (February 1976), p. 211. Other factors, of course, entered into these races.
22. United Press International dispatch, *Washington Post*, May 25, 1978.

serves Huitt.[23] Constituent service undoubtedly helps account for the anomaly that the voters, while they hold the Congress as a whole in low repute, usually reelect their individual members. Fenno, in his travels with representatives in their districts, found each invariably described as "the best Congressman in the United States,"[24] and a 1978 poll found that respondents gave their own representatives an approval rating exactly twice as high as the one they gave the Congress—62 percent as against 31 percent.[25] The Congress is expected to solve national problems, and is perceived to be doing that badly. But the individual member, particularly the House member, is judged by other criteria—among them, how accessible he is, how much time he spends in the state or district, how he performs as "ombudsman," how many projects he brings home.[26] When Julia Butler Hansen, Democrat of Washington, retired after seven terms, the Seattle *Post-Intelligencer* editorial lauding her service made no mention at all of her voting record, her policy stands, or her leadership position in the Democratic caucus. "Any doubt as to how much she will be missed by her Third District constituents," said the newspaper, "can be estimated by the revenue she has directed into the state through her job as chairman of the House Appropriations Subcommittee on the Department of the Interior."[27] A student of the House Public Works Committee quotes a member of that body: "We are all national legislators in a sense and we have to be but the national issues don't mean a damn thing back home—oh sure, they read about it in the newspapers but it doesn't mean much to them. They've got to see something; it's the bread and butter

23. "Congress: Retrospect and Prospect," p. 212.

24. Richard F. Fenno, Jr., "If, as Ralph Nader Says, Congress Is 'The Broken Branch,' How Come We Love Our Congressmen So Much?" in Ornstein, *Congress in Change*, p. 277.

25. New York Times/CBS News poll, *New York Times*, April 14, 1978. Louis Harris survey found a negative rating of 39 to 43 for individual representatives and a 29 to 63 negative rating for Congress as a whole. *Washington Post*, February 6, 1978.

26. Bruce E. Cain, John A. Ferejohn, and Morris P. Fiorina, "What Makes Legislators in Great Britain and the United States So Popular?" paper prepared for the 1979 annual meeting of the American Political Science Association (APSA), concludes (p. 28) on the basis of statistical analysis of polling data that "in both countries, legislators can insulate themselves from hostile national forces by attending district functions, by regularly seeking publicity, by diligently doing casework, and by protecting the special interests of the constituency." Other studies reaching essentially the same conclusion include Arthur H. Miller, "The Institutional Focus of Political Distrust," paper prepared for the 1975 annual meeting of the APSA; Glenn R. Parker and Roger H. Davidson, "Why Do Americans Love Their Congressmen So Much More Than Their Congress?" *Legislative Studies Quarterly*, vol. 4 (February 1979); Cavanagh, "Two Arenas of Congress," pp. 26–27 and tables 5–9; Stephen P. Brown, Beth C. Fuchs, and John F. Hoadley, "Congressional Perquisites and Vanishing Marginals: The Case of the Class of '74," paper prepared for the 1979 annual meeting of the APSA. All of these studies support the theory of Morris P. Fiorina, *Congress: Keystone of the Washington Establishment* (Yale University Press, 1977) that the "incumbency advantage" that results in the overwhelming electoral success of congressmen seeking reelection is derived from "pork barreling and casework."

27. Reprinted in *Congressional Record*, October 2, 1974, p. 33455.

issue that counts—the dams, the post offices and the other public buildings, the highways."[28]

Missouri Democrat Richard Bolling, after nearly two decades in the House, wrote that a flood control dam in his district had contributed more to his political reputation than all of the stands he had taken on major issues during his tenure. He expected the same political gains from a federal office building under construction in Kansas City. "Casework is the reason I got reelected," testified Representative Andrew Young, Democrat of Georgia, a black congressman from a district 60 percent white.[29] "A near idiot who has competent casework can stay in Congress as long as he wants, while a genius who flubs it can be bounced very quickly," a member told an interviewer in 1977.[30] Congressmen and their staffs devote considerable effort to stimulating requests for casework from constituents.[31] The importance of constituent service is confirmed in a 1978 election-day poll that asked which of three factors influenced the respondents most in voting for congressmen; 47 percent chose "what you think he can do for this community," 36 percent "because of his stand on national issues," and 17 percent "because you respect him as a person."[32]

"Part-time policymakers," concludes journalist Arlen Large, cannot give their attention to initiating a "coherent legislative program." Traditionally, congressmen are "nay-sayers and errand runners." "Collectively, they're incapable of command."[33]

Parochialism

It is when the Congress does try to take command, as it has done more frequently in its new mood of reassertion vis-à-vis the president, that the parochialism produced by incessant constituency pressure has an important bearing on the quality of government decisions. Constituency views are only

28. James Murphy, "The House Public Works Committee: Determinants and Consequents" (Ph.D. dissertation, University of Rochester, 1970), cited in Strom, "Congressional Policy Making," p. 714.

29. *Washington Post*, November 21, 1974.

30. Cavanagh, "Two Arenas of Congress," p. 16. Cavanagh's analysis shows that even unsuccessful casework—as long as the member and his staff appeared to have tried—is a plus factor in the member's rating (p. 27).

31. John R. Johannes, "Causes and Consequences of Congressional Casework Operations: An Analysis of Congressmen's Attitudes Toward, Time Spent On, And Efforts To Stimulate Casework During the 95th Congress," paper prepared for the 1980 annual meeting of the APSA.

32. CBS/New York Times survey, summarized in *Public Opinion*, November–December 1978, p. 22.

33. "Will Congress Grab the Reins?" *Wall Street Journal*, August 13, 1974.

one of the factors, of course, that enter into the complex "personal calculus," as Cavanagh calls it, by which the individual member determines his policy position and course of action. National priorities are a factor, too, and so is the value structure that the individual member brings to the job.[34]

On difficult questions, consequently, a large proportion of the membership may be ambivalent, pulled one way by one set of influences, the other way by another. If the member's constituency is never out of mind, neither are the member's party colleagues in the legislative body and the party leadership both inside and outside the chamber, including the president. When torn between the national interest, as expressed by party leaders, and the district interest, the member can only lose by taking any stand. Hence the urge to evade; hence the "deeply unheroic streak" of which John Gardner spoke.

When the issue cannot be avoided, some members yield more rapidly to constituency pressure, while others are more mindful of their standing with their colleagues and, if their party controls the executive branch, with the president and his administration. Members frequently assert that they go along with the party position, as expressed by the leaders, "whenever I can" or "all other things being equal," meaning whenever the risk back home is not too great.[35] Those who are ambitious for influence and leadership within the House or Senate—or perhaps for higher political office with a larger and different constituency—are likely to take a greater risk of offending their constituents for the sake of party regularity. And as they gain influence, that can perhaps be exploited to advantage with their constituents, offsetting in part at least the losses that regularity may have cost them. Fenno summarizes it this way: "Most members will trade off some of their personal commitment to reelection in order to satisfy a personal desire for institutional or policy influence. . . . All want reelection in the abstract, but not all will pay any price to achieve it; nor will all pay the same price."[36]

Political scientists have attempted to measure the relative weight of national and local factors in the voting decisions of individual congressmen. Davidson, on the basis of interviews with 87 House members in 1963–64, classified them as trustees or delegates, depending on whether they considered themselves primarily as independent decisionmakers or as followers of instructions. They came out about equal in numbers, but larger than either category was

34. Thomas E. Cavanagh, "Role Orientations of House Members: The Process of Representation," paper prepared for the 1979 annual meeting of the APSA, p. 2.

35. See, for instance, John W. Kingdon, *Congressmen's Voting Decisions* (Harper and Row, 1973), pp. 116–17.

36. *Home Style*, p. 221.

the group that was a blend of the two.[37] In the interviews, a majority emphasized their role as representative—as "discoverer, reflector, or advocate of popular needs and wants." And in this representational capacity, it was predominantly the people of their districts—rather than those of the whole country—for whom they sought to speak. "A Representative is interested primarily with his own little piece of land," said one of those Davidson labeled the "locals," the largest single grouping in his sample. "Represent the people," said a senior member. "That's the first duty . . . do exactly what the name implies." Asked whether, "if a bill is important for his party's record, a member should vote with his party even if it costs him some support in his district," 37 percent of the sample disagreed outright. Another 15 percent "tended to disagree," to make a majority of 52 percent responding in the negative. Only 9 percent agreed, and an additional 26 percent tended to agree, for a total of 35 percent.[38]

Members who admit to putting district interests foremost defend it on philosophical grounds. Representative Evins considered the role of the congressman as "special pleader" for his district to be "fundamental to our form of government" because it corrected the regional favoritism exhibited by the executive branch.[39] "I'm here to represent my district," a congressman told an interviewer. "This is part of my actual belief as to the function of a Congressman. . . . What is good for the majority of districts is good for the country. What snarls up the system is these so-called statesmen—Congressmen who vote for what they think is the country's interest. . . . Let the Senators do that . . . . They're paid to be statesmen; we aren't."[40] Representative Samuel L. Devine, Republican of Ohio, responded in much the same terms ten years later when President Carter accused the Congress of being "parochial" in rejecting his proposed gasoline rationing plan. "It seems to me," said Devine, "each of us is elected from our own parochial local

37. *Role of the Congressman*, pp. 116–17. Of the sample, 28 percent were trustees, 23 percent delegates, and 46 percent a combination of the two, which Davidson labeled *politicos* (3 percent were undetermined).

38. Ibid., pp. 79–80, 122–23, 145. In response to the last question, 7 percent were undecided and 6 percent did not respond. Republicans showed higher party loyalty scores than Democrats, leaders than nonleaders, juniors than seniors, holders of marginal than safe seats, northerners than southerners, urban than suburban (pp. 149–60). Kingdon found substantial evidence of district influence on votes even where "constituents' interest is probably nil." Like Davidson, he found that "safe congressmen take as much account of their constituents as do insecure ones." *Congressmen's Voting Decisions*, p. 64.

39. *Understanding Congress*, p. 38.

40. Lewis Anthony Dexter, *The Sociology and Politics of Congress* (Rand McNally, 1969), p. 154. The interviews probed congressional policymaking on trade questions.

districts to come here and express the views and vote the convictions of a majority of our constituents."[41]

Cavanagh, analyzing the 1977 survey of House members, found more of them national-minded than district-minded; only 24 percent described themselves as "primarily concerned with looking after the needs and interests of [their] own district[s]," compared to 45 percent "primarily concerned with looking after the needs and interests of the nation as a whole" and 28 percent declaring the two equally important.[42] These figures suggest a shift away from the parochialism Davidson found in 1963–64, which could perhaps be expected as a reflection of the increasing proportion of the "new breed" congressmen who arose from a political milieu in which the strength of local party organizations has declined. Asked the direct question, "When there is a conflict between what you feel is best and what you think the people in your district want, do you think you should follow your own conscience or follow what the people in your district want?" 66 percent of the Cavanagh sample were for conscience and only 6 percent for the district, with 26 percent saying it depended on the issue, and 3 percent not sure. Yet the question is not unambiguous; making the issue one of "conscience" rather than one of conflict between national and district interests eliminates the problem for the member who is by conscience a representative or delegate. Cavanagh found, indeed, that about a tenth of the members considered the question moot because, as one put it, "my conscience and my district's interests are the same." Those members who acknowledged some degree of conflict tended to follow their own consciences, they said, on moral issues, constitutional questions, and other matters of great national importance; on matters where district opinion was evenly balanced, or indistinct, or even nonexistent; and on questions where the member had strong personal convictions. They tended to follow constituent opinion, on the other hand, when the district had a distinct economic stake in the issue; when constituent feeling was clear, one-sided, and intense; and when the member did not feel strongly on either side of the question.[43]

41. *Congressional Record*, daily edition, May 14, 1979, p. H3070.

42. "Role Orientations," p. 2.

43. Ibid., pp. 3, 22. It may be a sign of the times that Cavanagh does not list the party's position as one of the elements entering into the member's calculus, along with national priorities, district interests, and an individual belief system. Perhaps it is subsumed in national priorities. However, the word *party* does not appear in any of his many quotations or in the author's discussion of the factors that influence the policy positions of house members, and the determination of national priorities appears as a personal rather than a party matter. This is in marked contrast with earlier writings on the subject, which gave considerable emphasis to party and leadership influence; the disappearance of the word may be an inadvertent but accurate reflection of party disintegration in today's individualistic Congress.

But whether parochialism is a dominant or secondary characteristic of the Congress, it is nevertheless one of its inbred and ineradicable traits. As members with important district interests seek membership on the committees that are in a position to advance those interests, then whole committees become special pleaders for segmental interests. Agriculture committees are profarmer, interior committees pro-West, labor committees prolabor, veterans' committees proveteran, armed services committees promilitary, and so on. With a long tradition of logrolling among its committees, the Congress is likely to permit parochial interests to prevail. Departments of the executive branch can be parochial, too, of course, and logrolling is far from unknown there. The difference is that the executive branch is equipped with a powerful Executive Office of the President that can offset parochial pressures and try to arrive at a concept of the broader national interest. To a degree, the president is compelled to try, because he is judged by the *whole* country on the basis of *general* conditions, while a congressman is judged by the *local* condition. And while the president may not always succeed in rising above the pressure of local and narrow interests, his office has a structural capacity to do so that the Congress (except for its struggling budget process) lacks.

Thus it is that in conflicts between the branches, the executive appears, usually, to reflect the *national* interest, the legislature the *local* or *special* interest. It is the president who tries to reduce the number of local water projects, as in Carter's case, the legislature to expand them. It is a succession of presidents who have tried to reduce and limit aid to "impacted" school districts, the Congress that has defeated them. The executive branch tries to consolidate or eliminate small and inefficient hospitals, research stations, post offices, and Amtrak schedules, and the legislature resists. The executive proposes broad plans to reorganize the government, and the legislature rejects them in response to the pressure from individual departments and bureaus and their constituencies. The executive tries to limit the diffusion of benefits designed for depressed areas or to restrict the number of model cities, and the legislature finds it necessary to extend the benefits until most of the 435 congressional districts receive a share. Presidents of both parties since the 1930s have supported liberal foreign trade policies, and often have had to fight hard for them against the resistance of congressmen responding to local producer groups. And foreign policy has sometimes been skewed because the Congress responded to pressure from ethnic groups in their constituencies; the philosophy of the congressman-as-representative that "what is desired in the majority of districts is good for the country," applied literally, would base foreign policy wholly on the distribution of Americans of particular ancestries across the map of the United States. Presidents are not unaffected by such local pressures, of course. But the conversion of a John Kennedy or a Lyndon Johnson to new views when he leaves the Senate for the White House testifies to the broader presidential outlook.

Parochialism can color and distort the major decisions of the Congress, when representatives of particular districts attain positions of leadership and power. Many years ago, Henry L. Stimson, for example, quoted a chairman of the House Naval Affairs Committee who, when asked, "Is it not a fact that the navy yard in your district will not accommodate our latest battleships?" answered, "That is true, and that is the reason I have always been in favor of small ships."[44] More recently, Senate Leader Lyndon Johnson and Speaker Sam Rayburn, as representatives of Texas, used their powers quite overtly to protect the oil depletion allowance from the attacks of tax reformers—a tradition maintained today in the open representation of oil interests by southwestern members of both houses, notably Russell Long of the Senate Finance Committee.[45] And this producer representation is balanced by an equally candid advocacy of consumer interests by senators and representatives of non-oil-producing states.

The representation philosophy has unquestionable merit, up to a point. It ensures that local and narrow interests can get a hearing, that they are not ridden over arbitrarily, as they can be in the executive branch. Yet the theory that the national interest can be arrived at by adding or balancing the 535 parochial interests of the individual members does not stand up under either theoretical or practical analysis. The congressional budget committees were created because the Congress found that, when most members represented their local interests, budgets were pushed far above the levels that, in the national interest, should be sustained. If each member reflected only a local interest, that would automatically doom any measure bringing benefits to fewer than half the Senate, or House, constituencies, whether it were a New York City loan guarantee, a farm price-support bill, an Appalachian development program, or a depressed areas program. Actually, such measures do get enacted, through an elaborate and sometimes quite open logrolling process, with rural and urban, or southern and northern, members trading support for one another's programs and party leaders acting as brokers.[46] Yet

44. *National Budget System,* Hearings before the House Select Committee on the Budget, 66 Cong. 1 sess. (U.S. Government Printing Office, 1919), p. 641.
45. On Rayburn's activities, see Richard Bolling, *House Out of Order* (Dutton, 1965), p. 68.
46. For a case study of a typical trade—one that became all but explicit—see Randall B. Ripley, "Legislative Bargaining and the Food Stamp Act, 1964," in Frederic N. Cleaveland and associates, *Congress and Urban Problems: A Casebook on the Legislative Process* (Brookings Institution, 1969), pp. 279–310.

congressional parochialism, in making sure that as many districts as possible share the benefits, often comes close to destroying the purpose of a bill. Thus uneconomic projects are added to omnibus bills in order to spread the gains and add support; job-creating measures designed for areas with heavy unemployment are made national in scope and consequently less beneficial where the need is greatest; the Appalachian program is enacted only after promises are made to create similar commissions in other areas (they came to virtually blanket the country, including depressed and prosperous regions alike, although benefits were not uniform); and so on.[47] Anything like a national growth policy as intended in the Urban Growth and New Community Development Act of 1970—which would seek deliberately to influence the geographical distribution of economic growth to assist declining central cities and rural areas—becomes a near impossibility. The prospect that any such measure would founder in the geographic divisiveness of the Congress helps to account for the fact that, despite the mandate of the law, no policy was ever drafted in either branch.

That parochialism can immobilize the Congress on more urgent matters is illustrated by the energy deadlock of 1978. The deadlock occurred because the decision lay in the hands of conference committee members, particularly senators, who were evenly balanced between producer and consumer points of view, and who found no incentive for compromise. A president, when executive agencies disagree, finds himself compelled to mediate clashes, seek to discover the elusive "national interest," and take a stand, but a Congress may find itself immobilized, unable to arrive at any stand at all. Its members individually have to take positions, and in the energy case they did. But the stands they took reflected the starkly opposing viewpoints of producer and consumer states and interests, and put the evenly balanced group of conferees at loggerheads. A state either sells or buys, and the interests are opposite; there turned out to be no interest in the middle, and so no senator stood there. As the stalemate dragged on through the entire 1978 session—until the final day—the Congress as a whole was discredited but each member of

47. As an example of parochialism carried to the point of absurdity, consider this incident. The Public Works and Economic Development Act of 1965, as reported by committee, defined eligible "redevelopment areas" according to an objective statistical formula based on unemployment and other factors. But Representative Patsy T. Mink, Democrat of Hawaii, arose on the House floor to offer an amendment requiring the administrator to designate at least one area in every state as eligible—that is, economically depressed—whether it met the statistical criteria or not. With the support of representatives of other states excluded from benefits under the original formula, her amendment was adopted by a voice vote. Sec. 401(d), P.L. 89-136, enacted August 26, 1965. A similar provision, less clear in its wording, had been contained in the earlier Area Redevelopment Act of 1961. Some areas designated as depressed when they did not feel that way protested, but the provision remains in the law.

the conference committee could only enhance his position with his own state and his own political supporters the longer he stood fast. Far better for a senator to campaign for reelection on the slogan, "I fought for your interests to the last ditch" than "I worked out the compromise that settled the question." To the latter boast an opponent can simply add the words: "by sacrificing the position and the interests of the state he was sent to Washington to represent." On highly visible questions, a president is expected to find a compromise, and gains by doing so. But a congressman is expected to struggle to the end, and if necessary go down battling for his constituents. Out of this fact of legislative life comes the foot-dragging, the sluggishness, the evasion of hard questions that are indelible elements in the congressional image.

Irresponsibility

Political responsibility for the condition of the nation is borne unequally by the president and the Congress. When things go wrong, it is the executive who is held primarily accountable; and congressmen find it far easier to escape blame. When the voters are deeply disgruntled, of course, they are liable to visit retribution on the president's party colleagues in the Congress as well as on the president himself, producing a party landslide, as was the case in 1932 and 1952. And in mid-term elections, such as those of 1946 and 1974, an electorate unable to chastise the president personally may vent its dissatisfaction on the president's party in the Congress. But even when presidents are being rebuked for failures of governmental policy, senators and representatives are not punished with equal severity. That was well demonstrated in 1980, when public disapproval of the government's record was registered most decisively in the rejection of President Carter. The Democratic Senate shared the blame but to a lesser degree; twelve members of the majority were defeated, yet as a group they ran far ahead of Carter, and except for the massive margin of the Reagan victory many of them would have survived. And the Democratic House was even given another two-year lease of power, though with a smaller majority. Clearly, those who split their tickets perceived the president as carrying the burden of responsibility and found reason to absolve their congressmen. The concept that the representative, and to some degree the senator as well, should be judged more on his capacity as a constituent servant than as a policymaker must surely account in large part for the more favorable treatment the incumbent legislators were accorded. Moreover, as David Mayhew has emphasized, the individual member of Congress, to the extent he is judged on issues at all, tends to be judged not by whether specific pieces of national legislation are enacted, nor by the content of the legislation, or the effects, but rather by the position he has taken. Political credit at home comes from the speech and the press release and the recorded vote, not from the hours of internal maneuvering that produce the legislative outcome. So the temptation is to shirk the latter duties. "On matters where credit-claiming possibilities wear thin," writes Mayhew, "members display only a modest interest in what goes into bills or what their passage accomplishes."[48] This is an exaggeration if applied indiscriminately to all members, but the opportunity exists for individual congressmen to be irresponsible in terms of producing results, without penalty from the voters. If the Congress obstructs the president without offering an alternative program of its own, the institution may be criticized but the individual member may escape responsibility. He, after all, was only one member among many. Presidents have to live with the consequences of what the Congress does to a much greater extent, ironically, than do the congressmen themselves.

Francis O. Wilcox, who served both as chief of staff of the Senate Foreign Relations Committee and as assistant secretary of state, has cited both parochialism and irresponsibility as reasons for the inability of the Congress to order the nation's priorities. His observations on foreign policy are equally applicable to economic policy, or energy policy, or any other aspect of national affairs:

> The great bulk of congressmen are simply too busy, too distracted, too willing to take chances abroad for the sake of scoring points at home. Too many congressmen, in short, are irresponsible in the literal, not the pejorative, sense. If there is a failure of American policy, most likely it will be the President, not Congress, who is held responsible, though some congressional action or omission contributed to the failure. And even if Congress is held responsible, it is even rarer that the responsibility devolves on an individual member—especially if he has been serving the parochial interests of his state or district by his action.[49]

The more irresponsible, in Wilcox's literal sense, the members are permitted by institutional rules and practices to be, the safer they are individually. The ultimate in political safety for congressmen is to be free to behave exactly as they wish, to have no responsibility to follow the lead of anyone else in Washington—not the president, not the elected leaders of the Congress, not the party caucus, not a policy committee, not the chairman or the majority of a standing committee. Then they will be free to follow the lead of their constituents whenever a constituency view can be discerned, to cultivate

---

48. David R. Mayhew, *Congress: The Electoral Connection* (Yale University Press, 1974), p. 122. The argument is developed on pp. 115–25.

49. *Congress, the Executive, and Foreign Policy* (Harper and Row, 1971), p. 79.

them, to avoid giving them offense, and so to make their seats as safe as any seat can be, for as long as they desire. Even when the party's record is a disastrous one, they stand a chance to avoid identification with it. And, as many members have attested, an overt show of independence—an open defiance of those who seek to lead or constrain the individual member—can actually be turned into a political asset to exploit back home. The stalwart, unbossed legislator, heeding only his conscience and his constituency, uncompromising to the end, is still the American ideal.

But a body made up of individuals looking out for themselves cannot, as a collectivity, act responsibly. It cannot govern. Individuals do not conceive, adopt, and enact coherent programs. Only groups having a degree of discipline, a measure of individual subordination to the group, do that. Given the forces that militate against discipline, that make for irresponsibility in the Congress, it follows that the stronger will to govern will be found in the executive branch, which is held accountable and so cannot avoid responsibility. Senator Gale W. McGee, Democrat of Wyoming, made the argument directly and forcefully in a 1965 lecture:

> I advance the contention, as a member of the Senate, that the need for increasing executive power is very much the requirement of the day. . . . There is no other single repository of responsibility that could be held accountable for what happens. . . . No Senator really has that common responsibility to so many at all levels of the economy, in all segments of the social framework. . . .
>
> . . . in our political legislative bodies . . . the chances to pass the buck to someone else, to duck the responsibility for failure and, conversely, to seize the credit for success, is one of the dilemmas that face us. . . . You can duck responsibility within your committee (and we have all done it); you can blame somebody else's committee; you can disappear behind the facade of your party allegiance, or of the philosophical group within your party to which you belong; or you can blame it on the other House; and if none of those happens to . . . work, you can dump it on the shoulders of bureaucracy and red tape downtown.[50]

From Representation to Decline—and Resurgence

Through a chain of causation, then, the long decline of the Congress in relation to the president can be traced to its roots in the principle of representation, which is unchangeable—embodied in the Constitution, necessitated by the size and diversity of the United States, and hallowed by tradition. Representation produces individualism and parochialism. Individualism produces fragmentation and dispersion of authority within the Congress. Frag-

50. "The Role of Executive Leadership," in Nathaniel Stone Preston, ed., *The Senate Institution* (Van Nostrand Feinhold, 1969), pp. 21–22.

mentation and dispersion vitiate the capacity of the Congress to integrate policy, to lead, and to govern. Parochialism produces irresponsibility, and irresponsibility undermines the will to govern. Deficient in both capacity and will, the Congress lets authority over broad public questions—as distinct from local and peripheral matters—drift to the executive branch. Representative Aspin set out the linkage from representation to irresponsibility to decline in simple terms: it was to take the "safer" course in relation to their constituents that congressmen established the president in his role of leadership; "tough issues" could then be evaded. The purpose was not necessarily always acknowledged, or even understood, but at times it became explicit, as in the Budget and Accounting Act debate of 1919–20, when members openly sought to transfer to the president the political accountability for future budget deficits.

The decline of Congress appears, then, to have been a natural historic trend, flowing from the fundamentals of the political system. As soon as strong presidents willing to assume responsibility became the norm, the Congress was equally willing to let them have an increasing share of the totality of decisionmaking as the scale and range of governmental activity expanded. That responded to the needs of the members, and their wants.[51] It relieved them of responsibility to do things they did not wish to do, things that were politically dangerous to do. Indeed, it gave them the best of both worlds, the right and the opportunity to intervene in the affairs of government when there was political credit to be gained, but the freedom to leave matters to the president when that appeared to be the safer course.

If the decline was natural, even historically inevitable, what then of the resurgence? The constitutional crisis of the Nixon period wrenched the legislators out of their complacency and thrust reponsibility on them, whether they liked it or not, in spite of the burgeoning culture of individualism. It produced institutional changes. Some power—over fiscal policy and war, in particular—flowed back. The conflict also generated new attitudes in the Congress—the new assertiveness. But it did nothing to change the structure of incentives that control and motivate congressmen, for it did not alter in any way their relations with their constituencies, did not lessen their representational responsibilities. As time passes and the memory of Nixon and

51. For a discussion of the cyclical pattern of the internal distribution of power in the Congress, from centralization to decentralization and back again, and its relation to the balance of power between the Congress and the president, see Lawrence C. Dodd, "Congress and the Quest for Power," in Lawrence C. Dodd and Bruce I. Oppenheimer, eds., *Congress Reconsidered* (Praeger, 1977). Dodd's analysis leads to the same conclusion reached here: that the period of resurgence (which in his analysis parallels the centralization period of the internal cycle) will be followed by a new period of decline.

his "usurpations" fades, and congressmen live with presidents they respect and trust, the links in the old causal chain are likely to reappear. The will to govern will again wane. The capabilities that are missing will not be acquired, because the members will not be willing to sacrifice their individual freedom and, in the literal sense, their irresponsibility. Nor, even if they wished, would their inescapable role as representatives permit them to. "No matter how assertive [Congress] is, or how creative and qualified for leadership individual members are," said Senator Edmund Muskie of Maine in 1978, "maybe the institution is not really equipped to act as a strong leader."[52] This from the chairman of the Senate Budget Committee who, perhaps more than any other member of the Congress, was carrying the burden of asserting the restored authority of the legislative branch.

The institutional changes will work to inhibit a new decline, but they are not enough to stop it altogether. The War Powers Resolution does compel the Congress to arrive at a decision to affirm or overrule a presidential course of action that utilizes military force, but legislators who wish to evade responsibility can hide again behind the president's constitutional prerogatives as commander in chief and the superior information and expertise of his advisers—as they did in the long series of postwar crises from Korea to the Gulf of Tonkin. The Congressional Budget and Impoundment Control Act establishes a process, but it does not require the process to reject, or even significantly alter, the president's budget; and the process itself is never out of danger of collapse. Perhaps the most important force for maintaining congressional authority will be the expanded staff, not likely to decline much in numbers (despite the gestures in that direction by the new Republican majority in the Senate) and not likely, either, to abet a congressional relapse into passivity. To a member of Congress, irresponsibility may discourage action, but for the bright and transient young people who make up the bulk of the legislative staff it has the opposite effect. They can act, enjoy power, and perhaps affect history, without having to face either the political consequences in a constituency or administrative accountability in an executive department.

With the Ninety-seventh Congress, party control is divided in a way not known for nearly half a century, since Herbert Hoover's time. Interparty competition will not spill over into conflict between the executive and legislative branches, as in the Nixon-Ford years, but primarily into clashes between the House (when the Democratic majority is able to prevail) and the

52. "The Great Congressional Power Grab," *Business Week*, September 11, 1978, p. 91.

Senate, with the latter allied with the president, and with the conference committees the main battleground.

The record of the past five decades, however, suggests that the divided Congress of 1981–82 will prove transitory, and the two houses will shortly be restored to the similarity of composition and outlook that has been the normal pattern. When that time comes, the balance of power between the branches will not be static, as it has not been in the past. But in all probability it will fluctuate within a narrower range than in the 1970s. The Congress will not soon again reach as low a point as the nadir of 1972. Nor will it soon again be as assertive as in the crisis years of 1973 and 1974.

CHAPTER XVI

The Unending
Conflict

BY THE TIME the Congress was ready to claim its first victories in the drive to attain "coequal" status, as early as 1974, many of its more thoughtful members were already warning against carrying their struggle to excess. Representative Barbara Jordan of Texas, she who in 1973 had admonished the Congress to regain the will to govern, was the next year denouncing the extreme of "legislative dictatorship" as well as its opposite, "an imperial president with a subservient congress." The "revitalization of Congress need not result in a weak presidency," she declared. "The need for a strong President in the years ahead is beyond challenge."[1] Lee Hamilton, Democrat of Indiana, even denied the objective of coequality. "The effort of the Congress to reassert itself should not be misunderstood to mean that the Congress can truly become an equal branch of government," he told the House in mid-1974. "It is simply too difficult for 535 strong-minded aggressive persons 'to get it all together' on all the issues on the nations's agenda. . . . No one advocates a weakened Presidency . . . a shackled Presidency would not be wise. Our system requires a strong Presidency, but a strong President under the Constitution."[2] A few years later, Representative Morris K. Udall, Democrat of Arizona, reported, "I'm starting to hear talk in the cloakrooms now that wouldn't it be nice if we had a stronger President who could provide solid leadership." But he added, "The power of Congress is a new sort of idea. Members haven't tired of it yet."[3]

1. Speech to the Democratic mid-term conference in Kansas City, Mo., inserted in *Congressional Record*, December 11, 1974, p. 39244.
2. *Congressional Record*, June 24, 1974, p. 4174.
3. "The Great Congressional Power Grab," *Business Week*, September 11, 1978, pp. 91, 99.

Perhaps the wisest and most reflective view, as so often had been the case, came from J. William Fulbright of Arkansas. The former Senate Foreign Relations Committee chairman, observing events from the vantage of retirement, wrote in 1979:

> Our proper objective is neither a dominant presidency nor an aggressive Congress but, within the strict limits of what the Constitution mandates, a shifting of the emphasis according to the needs of the time and the requirements of public policy. In times of presidential excess, such as in the 1960s, an assertive Congress is a necessary corrective. In a time, such as the present, when Congress is asserting its prerogatives aggressively, but without a commensurate demonstration of public responsibility, there is much to be said for a revival of presidential leadership.[4]

Regardless of whether he or anyone else believed the emphasis should shift back and forth between the branches, it almost surely would. The balance between president and Congress had gone through nearly two centuries of ups and downs; in the third century the seesaw would continue. With each shift, the automatic stabilizer would be public opinion, as the politicians responded to what the people wanted—or lost their jobs to those who would. Thus, Gerald Ford and Jimmy Carter were quick to reverse the practices of Richard Nixon that had so deeply offended the Congress, and by 1977 the Congress in its turn was ready to pull back from the extremes of assertiveness—particularly in the field of foreign policy—to which its post-Nixon enthusiasm had carried it. When crises erupted in Southwest Asia in 1979, President Carter seemed to be as much in charge of the national security as his predecessors Johnson and Nixon had been when another corner of Asia was the center of attention. He unilaterally proclaimed the "Carter doctrine" for defense of the Persian Gulf, he moved naval forces to the Indian Ocean, he announced sanctions against Iran and later the Soviet Union, and organized the abortive mission to free the hostages held in Tehran—all without any visible interference or influence from the Congress. If Carter formally consulted with the leaders of that body, it was not considered important enough for public mention; and if he did not, nobody complained. The test would be in the results, as always; there had been little congressional objection to presidential domination of decisions regarding Vietnam, either, until things began to go sour there.

As the campaign of 1980 developed, the public seemed to be in about the same mood as Fulbright, ready for a revival of presidential leadership. Carter had gained support—for a time had seemed to salvage a failing presidency—by what was seen as resolute handling of the Iran and Afghanistan crises, and there was no evidence that the country was reacting adversely to any

4. "The Legislator as Educator," *Foreign Affairs*, vol. 57 (Spring 1979), pp. 726–27.

candidates when they promised, as all of them did, that they would be strong leaders.

In any case, those who may have feared "legislative dictatorship" could be reassured. The Congress had recognized that it lacked the capacity to lead, to integrate policy, and, preoccupied as ever with the demands of constituents, it lacked the will to dominate on any broad and continuing basis. Nevertheless, it lacked neither the will nor the capacity to intervene whenever it chose, to the degree and on whatever subject it wished, and to impose its own notion of coequality. The compulsion to do so is always present; as Harold J. Laski wrote, the Congress "is always looking for occasions to differ from" the president, "and it never feels so really comfortable as when it has found such an occasion for difference. In doing so, it has the sense that it is affirming its own essence."[5]

Even if the self-righting tendency—monitored by public opinion—can be relied on to check or correct excesses by either branch, the governmental system can be damaged and public confidence severely shaken, as in 1973–74, before the corrections take effect. Even more important, the national interest can be gravely disserved by the stalemates that occur while the branches are locked in contest. The issue, then, is both one of how power is divided—the balance between the branches—and one of how it is shared. It concerns who will have the last word on particular decisions, and also how decisions can be reached jointly—for on a host of matters there can be no effective governmental policy until the branches reach, if not an agreement, at least an accommodation. So the question becomes one of how the partners of the forced and sometimes loveless marriage of president and Congress can come to live together with a reasonable degree of harmony and with enough unity of purpose to make the government functional.

This has been the concern of statesmen and of scholars for decades. Almost a century ago Woodrow Wilson worried that "the federal government lacks strength because its powers are divided, lacks promptness because its authorities are multiplied, lacks wieldiness because its processes are roundabout, lacks efficiency because its responsibility is indistinct and its action without competent direction."[6] Walter Lippmann, reading the record of "unending conflict" between president and Congress forty years ago, fretted that the "lack of a working arrangement between them exposes our government to continual trouble. We have not found a way to give the President his necessary

5. *The American Presidency: An Interpretation* (Harper, 1940), p. 123.
6. *Congressional Government: A Study in American Politics* (1885; World, 1956), p. 318.

powers without impairing the control of Congress. And we have not found a way to give Congress control without depriving the President of essential power."[7] "The American system is so constituted that it produces a conflict between the Executive and Congress every time the Executive tries to be positive and strong," Thomas K. Finletter, later to be secretary of the air force, wrote at the end of World War II. "You cannot have a government capable of handling the most difficult problems that peacetime democracy has ever faced with the two main parts of it at each other's throats."[8] And the British scholar Herman Finer wrote in 1960: "The separate elections of the President, the Senate, and the House of Representatives fractures the nation's vision and will, destroys cogency of thought, and pits legislature and executive branch against each other."[9] And, among today's troubled observers, Douglas Dillon, former treasury secretary and under secretary of state, doubts that, in a world of military confrontations and economic threats, "we can long continue to afford the luxury of the division of power and responsibility between our executive and legislative branches of government."[10]

To overcome the built-in separatism of the governmental structure, the presidential leadership model was evolved. Yet, though the dominant model—accepted by presidents, congressional majorities, the media, and the public—it was less than universally approved. For it was largely a liberal creation, supported most fervently by those who, idealizing Franklin Roosevelt, wanted government to continue to strive for great and noble ends, both at home and abroad, in the New Deal manner. So it was the liberal bloc in the Congress who initiated the concerted attack on the institutional obstacles to presidential leadership of the legislative branch—the seniority system, the veto power of the House Rules Committee, the Senate filibuster—and conservatives of both parties who defended them.

The issue of strength and unity in government may by now, however, have lost some of its ideological content. The experience of Presidents Nixon and Ford demonstrated that governmental disunity could hamper conservative as well as liberal objectives; Nixon was frustrated by the Democratic Congress in many of his initiatives for retrenching the responsibilities of government and reducing its cost. And ever since the end of the cold war

7. Newspaper column of February 8, 1941, quoted in Arthur N. Holcombe, *Our More Perfect Union* (Harvard University Press, 1950), p. 270.

8. *Can Representative Government Do the Job?* (New York: Reynal and Hitchcock, 1945), p. 9.

9. *The Presidency: Crisis and Regeneration* (University of Chicago Press, 1960), p. 302.

10. James Reston, *New York Times*, December 23, 1979.

consensus, it has been the conservatives rather than the liberals who have been the leading advocates of a stronger military posture and forceful foreign policy that require national unity behind the president.

The Issue of Constitutional Reform

Many who have deplored the disunity of the U.S. government have despaired of finding a remedy within the constitutional structure and have looked longingly across the water to Great Britain or across the border to Canada. There, as in most Western European and British Commonwealth countries, the parliament is sovereign and the legislative and executive branches are joined at the top, in a cabinet that dominates the former and directs the latter. The nineteenth century produced a considerable volume of scholarly and journalistic writings advocating that the U.S. Constitution be revised in the direction of parliamentary government (the most trenchant and influential contribution to the discussion being that of the young Woodrow Wilson).[11] In this century, whenever internal dissension seemed to be robbing the government of strength to meet its basic responsibilities, the arguments were revived.

The conflicts over New Deal legislation provoked extended treatises on constitutional reform. Writers of that period, upset by the recalcitrance of the Congress toward the Rooseveltian leadership, urged adoption of the device used in parliamentary governments to attain party discipline and, when necessary, to break deadlocks—dissolution of the legislature, followed by elections. William Y. Elliott suggested that the terms of House members be extended to four years, concurrent with the president's, and that the executive then be given authority to dissolve the House of Representatives once during his term. The people could then choose, in effect, between president and representatives. They could elect candidates who promised to support the president or, by voting for the opposition candidates, give the president a mandate to resign. To avoid the cost and political jeopardy of a special election, Elliott reasoned, the House would become "a much more disciplined body." But when the president called an election, he would give up his veto power for the rest of his term, enabling the Congress to set policy.[12] Henry

11. See James MacGregor Burns, *Congress on Trial: The Legislative Process and the Administrative State* (1949; Gordian, 1966), pp. 146–48; Henry Hazlitt, *A New Constitution Now* (New York: Whittlesey House, 1942), pp. 15–45.

12. *The Need for Constitutional Reform* (New York: Whittlesey House, 1935), pp. 200–01, 234–35. Elliott suggested that the power of dissolution might extend to the Senate as well; to curtail the

Hazlitt advocated a full-fledged parliamentary system, with the executive chosen by the Congress. The legislature could at any time vote a lack of confidence in the executive—as in the House of Commons—and the executive (who might be designated premier rather than president) would have the option of dissolving the House and calling new elections or simply resigning. In the new election, the executive as well as all members of Congress would be obliged to run, and if the executive lost, the Congress would choose his successor.[13] Finletter, writing in 1945, proposed that the terms of senators, representatives, and the president all be six years, with simultaneous election; that dissolution power be vested in the president; and that upon dissolution a new election be held for the presidency and the entire membership of the Congress. Presumably, the same party would win control of both branches and the government would be unified under presidential leadership.[14] None of these proposals gathered any support, either inside or outside the government, and the discussion of constitutional reform lapsed.

President Lyndon B. Johnson revived one aspect of the earlier plans when he endorsed the idea of electing House members for four-year terms concurrent with that of the president. In a 1966 message to the Congress[15] he based his case on the desirability of reducing the burden and cost of campaigns every two years, and he justified putting the election in the presidential year on the democratic principle that more voters turn out then than in the off years. Congressional opinion on the president's proposal was splintered among those members who preferred no change at all and those who supported variants of the plan—election of all members during the presidential year, all members in the mid-term year, or half in each. Of these four positions, a Brookings Institution survey showed that the Johnson proposal had the least support, and presumably for the very reason that led its original advocates (and no doubt Johnson himself, no matter what he said in his message) to support it—it would tie the House members' fortunes too closely to the president's. Republicans, who had just seen many of their party colleagues swept away in the Johnson landslide of 1964, were unanimously opposed to a four-year term coincident with the president's. The survey found "very

Senate's powers, he would strip it of power over money bills and reduce the majority required for approval of treaties from two-thirds to a simple majority. He argued that the dissolution power would eliminate the need for presidents to use patronage as an instrument of discipline and hence would make possible the extension of civil service to top administrative jobs, again on the British model.

13. Hazlitt, *A New Constitution Now*, pp. 9–10, 102–06.

14. Finletter, *Can Representative Government Do the Job?* chap. 12.

15. "Special message to the Congress Proposing Constitutional Amendment Relating to Terms for House Members and the Electoral College System, January 20, 1966," *Public Papers of the Presidents: Lyndon B. Johnson, 1966* (U.S. Government Printing Office, 1967) pp. 36–41.

little enthusiasm" for any change at all and no prospect that two-thirds of the members could agree on the form a constitutional amendment should take.[16] In any case, Judiciary Committee Chairman Emanuel Celler, Democrat of New York, was among those opposed to any change, and after hearings the measure died in his committee.

The Watergate scandal aroused another flurry of interest in constitutional change, centered on the problem of removing presidents. Noting the limitations of the impeachment process—which in practice permits removal only for provable criminal misconduct[17]—several members of Congress introduced constitutional amendments either to broaden the impeachment power or to make the president removable by the Congress by a simple vote of no confidence. Their purpose was not to break policy deadlocks but to remove a president who through incompetence, mental or emotional instability, misfeasance, nonfeasance, or any other reason had lost the public confidence a nation's leader must possess. The principal measure on the subject, offered by Representative Henry S. Reuss, Democrat of Wisconsin, required that if the Congress deposed the president (with a 60 percent majority required in each House), all members of the Congress as well as the president would have to submit to a special election—a provision designed to ensure that the Congress not remove a president for trivial or partisan reasons.[18] After the resignation of President Nixon, however, the problem seemed to be solved, and interest in a simpler process for removing presidents melted away.[19] The problem remains unsolved, of course, insofar as presidents may lose leadership capacity for reasons other than crime.

However grave the structural weaknesses of the American government, those that are embedded in the Constitution are quite beyond the reach of reformers—barring some governmental breakdown more catastrophic than any so far experienced.[20] The amendment process is so formidable that any

16. Charles O. Jones, *Every Second Year: Congressional Behavior and the Two-Year Term* (Brookings Institution, 1967), pp. 104–12. Of the House members, 318, or 73 percent, returned their questionnaires.

17. Whether the Constitution intended broader grounds in its language ("Treason, Bribery, or other high Crimes and Misdemeanors") is a moot question because the requirement of a two-thirds vote for removal of a president means that the views of thirty-four of the one hundred senators determine what the grounds shall be, and the experience of the Nixon case makes clear that at least that many will always insist on the narrower interpretation.

18. H. J. Res. 1111 (introduced August 15, 1974).

19. *George Washington Law Review*, vol. 43 (January 1975), contains a thirteen-article symposium on the Reuss resolution, with some support—including an essay of mine—but many theoretical and practical criticisms.

20. Lloyd N. Cutler, "To Form a Government," *Foreign Affairs*, vol. 59 (Fall 1980), pp. 139–43, discusses a series of alternative amendments to mitigate the difficulties arising from the separation of powers; he proposes a bipartisan presidential commission to conduct a full-scale study. Charles M. Hardin, *Presidential Power and Accountability: Toward a New Constitution* (University of Chicago

basic structural change that arouses controversy and determined opposition is doomed at the start. A proposal can be blocked by one-third plus one of the membership of either House or, if it hurdles that obstacle, by as few as one-eighth of the nation's state legislative bodies—one house in each of thirteen states. Far more than that small number would surely resist any proposal to tamper with the country's fundamental institutions, given the aura of reverence that surrounds the Constitution and the specter that adverse, unintended consequences would attend a basic change. The overwhelming public demand necessary to overcome both inertia and well-founded opposition arguments would hardly form around an issue as abstract as the structural reform of institutions. Accordingly, any practical remedies to the problem of disunity among the elements of the governmental structure at this time must be sought within the bounds of an unamended Constitution.

Reform without Constitutional Amendment

The Constitution clinches the separation of powers by prohibiting a member of Congress from also holding executive office. Any step toward formal unification of the branches on the parliamentary model is forbidden, then, but over the years many proposals have been advanced to move toward that end through devices that would institutionalize consultation between the branches, joint consideration of policy issues, and even joint decisionmaking. One set of proposals would introduce officials of the executive branch into congressional proceedings; another would insert congressional leaders into executive decision processes. Or, in the shorter phrases of Stephen Horn, one would put the cabinet *in* Congress, the other construct a cabinet *from* Congress.[21]

Proposals to put the cabinet in Congress have been advanced by two sets of advocates, for opposing reasons. One group has sought to enhance executive influence over the legislature, by permitting the cabinet members to participate in debates on measures concerning their departments (but not to vote, for that would transgress the constitutional separation). The other has pursued the objective of greater legislative influence over administration, by bringing cabinet members to the floors of the House and the Senate at stated times for questioning. A bill authorizing both of these was approved by a

Press, 1974), is an earlier, comprehensive presentation of the case for constitutional reform, with proposals for amendments.

21. *The Cabinet and Congress* (Columbia University Press, 1960), p. 211; the summary of proposals to put the cabinet in the Congress is largely derived from his study.

special House committee and debated on the floor in 1865 but not passed. A measure providing only for a question period was pressed by Representative Estes Kefauver, Democrat of Tennessee, in the mid-1940s and received considerable support from outside the Congress.[22] But Speaker Sam Rayburn and other House elders were adamantly opposed, and the measure did not emerge from committee.

A survey by Horn in 1957 found that members of Congress who chose to comment were opposed, by about three to one, to admitting cabinet members to their respective floors even for a question period. The opponents feared an enhancement of executive power and, with a few exceptions, saw no benefit for the Congress. Information and advice from the executive branch, they held, were gained more efficiently through committee hearings and other existing communication processes, and many feared that the question period would degenerate into harassment and badgering of the executive officials.[23] As for the executive view, two earlier presidents, Taft and Harding, had endorsed the idea, with the support of some or all of their cabinets, presumably for the same reason that legislators have found for opposing it— enhancement of executive power (Secretary of War Henry L. Stimson, a strong advocate, contended that the proposed executive budget, which Taft was supporting, would "carry very little distance" unless cabinet members were present to explain and defend it in the floor debates).[24] But when Kefauver advanced his proposal in the 1940s, Franklin Roosevelt gave it no encouragement, and seventeen former cabinet members responding to Horn's 1957 survey were unanimous in seeing no potential gain in executive power from a legislative question period even if it were broadened to provide for participation of cabinet members in debate. Half of the former executives thought the Congress would gain in power, and they expressed an "intense" suspicion of potential legislative interference with administration.[25]

Perhaps the idea is bound to fail at any time because, quite apart from the normal human resistance to institutional change, too many in each branch will see the other as the gainer. When the executive is in the ascendancy and aggressive, as it was during most of this century, the Congress will resist the highly symbolic intrusion into its affairs that appearance of cabinet officers

22. See ibid, pp. 229–31; George B. Galloway, *Congress at the Crossroads* (Crowell, 1946), pp. 212–19.

23. Horn sent a questionnaire to all members of both houses; 182 representatives and 36 senators—42 percent and 38 percent, respectively—responded. Horn analyzed only the House returns (*Cabinet and Congress*, pp. 193–210).

24. Letter from Stimson to Taft, November 11, 1912, quoted in ibid., p. 117. After he left office, Taft withdrew his support for the idea.

25. Ibid., pp. 176, 185.

on the floors of the Congress would represent.[26] Conversely, when the legislature is resurgent, as in the 1970s—or even when it is relatively docile, as in 1957—the executive will be more aware of the potential harassment and interference than of the opportunity to educate the Congress. It may be significant that while, before their election, both President Carter and Vice President Mondale endorsed the proposal for a question period,[27] there is no record of their having reiterated that view after their inauguration.

The alternative approach, to put Congress in the cabinet, has likewise been advanced at intervals over the years, but it has attracted even less support and has never found favor with any president. Several academic proposals stimulated discussion in the 1940s, particularly a scheme advanced by Edward S. Corwin, the constitutional scholar, for a cabinet constructed from a joint legislative council created by the two houses and made up of its leading members. The members would not be officers of the executive branch with administrative responsibility, to avoid the constitutional prohibition, but as an advisory group they would both control the president by bringing "presidential whim under an independent scrutiny which today is lacking" and support him by getting his legislative program, as agreed to by them in cabinet, enacted.[28] In an amplification of the plan by Corwin and Louis W. Koenig some years later, the notion of a compact between the branches was introduced, whereby in exchange for seats in the cabinet the leaders would pledge themselves to guarantee action on all of the president's legislative proposals within a reasonable time.[29]

The nearest the Congress has come to considering any scheme for a legislative council was in 1946, when the La Follette-Monroney committee on congressional reorganization endorsed a less formal version of it. In recommending creation of a majority policy committee in each house, the committee also recommended that these meet regularly with the president and his

26. In earlier years, cabinet officers were occasionally admitted to the House or Senate floor, but now when members desire to assemble to hear an executive official (other than the president)—usually the secretary of state—they use an auditorium at the Library of Congress.

27. Jimmy Carter, *Why Not the Best?* (Nashville: Broadman Press, 1975), p. 147; Walter F. Mondale, *The Accountability of Power* (McKay, 1975), pp. 148–51, 216. Both urged that the question periods be televised. Mondale had sponsored legislation along the lines of the Kefauver bill.

28. *The President: Office and Powers, 1787–1957*, 4th rev. ed. (New York University Press, 1957), pp. 297–98. Finletter gave the idea strong support in *Can Representative Government Do the Job?* chap. 11.

29. *The Presidency Today* (New York University Press, 1956), p. 95. The arrangement would be effected without a constitutional amendment, simply by a "gentlemen's agreement." Senator Joseph S. Clark, Democrat of Pennsylvania, revived part of this proposal with a suggestion that the two houses bind themselves by concurrent resolution to bring to the floor any measure designated by the president as a priority matter within six months of the time he sent it to the Capitol; *Congress: The Sapless Branch* (Harper and Row, 1964), pp. 205–06. But his colleagues were not attracted to the idea.

cabinet as a joint legislative-executive council, in order to facilitate reaching a common policy and mitigate deadlocks. But when Speaker Rayburn rejected the idea of having a policy committee in the House, the joint council proposal died with it.[30] Since then, the notion has been revived in a limited form for application to the national security area alone, but without gaining significant support either from inside or outside the government. Francis O. Wilcox proposed a joint executive-legislative committee on national security affairs to be made up of the president, the vice president, and top executive officials and congressional leaders dealing with foreign and military policy,[31] and Senator Hubert H. Humphrey, Democrat of Minnesota, picked up the idea in a modified form in 1975, in a bill to create a congressional joint committee on national security that would not only coordinate policy and action in the legislative branch but also meet regularly with the president.[32] But presidents and other congressional leaders have been satisfied with the existing practice of informal meetings at the White House. This arrangement has the advantage, from their view, of providing opportunity for consultation while preserving the freedom of action of all parties to go their separate ways when the conversations end.

The weakness in all of the joint cabinet or council proposals is that when the president and congressional leaders are in harmony, new formal mechanisms would add little to the existing opportunities for consultation and communciation, and when they are not in harmony, the devices would fall into disuse. One can visualize, for instance, the treatment that President Nixon, or President Johnson before him, would have given a legislative-executive council or committee when Senators Fulbright, Mansfield, and others were leading the Senate rebellion against the Vietnam War. The president would have simply ceased to call meetings. If the structure provided that the congressional members could initiate meetings (it is hard to visualize presidential assent to any such provision in the design of such a structure), the president could find his schedule too crowded to permit him to attend. If adverse public reaction to such stalling finally forced him to meet with the group, he would be sure to find the legislative members of the committee divided, so that he could accept the advice of those who agreed with him and do as he wished anyhow. Britain's unwritten constitution makes the

30. See pages 187–89 above.

31. *Congress, the Executive, and Foreign Policy* (Harper and Row, 1971), pp. 157–59.

32. *Congressional Record*, January 15, 1975, p. 213. In 1943 Senator Alexander Wiley of Wisconsin, a senior Republican member of the Foreign Relations Committee, had introduced a resolution to create a joint foreign relations advisory council, but the measure never received a hearing. Horn, *Cabinet and Congress*, pp. 171–72. However, Secretary of State Cordell Hull created a temporary executive-legislative advisory committee on postwar foreign policy.

cabinet collectively responsible, which forces discussion and the attainment of a sufficient consensus to ward off resignations and party splintering. But the United States' written charter forbids collective responsibility through the formal merger of separated powers, and any gentlemen's agreement to unify the branches through informal practice would last only as long as the participants agreed on the substance of the policies discussed—in which case it might become a time-consuming nuisance bringing no particular benefit. A president who wants to consult with the Congress will do so and select his own consultees—as President Truman did with Senator Vandenberg. One who does not want to can hardly be compelled by statute to do so, and to avoid being under pressure that he might not welcome, no president, it is safe to say, would ever approve the statute in the first place.

The Responsible Party Model

If reformers could not ameliorate the unending conflict between the branches by constitutional amendment or by joining cabinet and Congress, another avenue appeared open. That was to remodel a political institution that is outside both the Constitution and the government itself—the political party.

Here again, the reformers looked to Europe, but they also looked to America's political past. At times in U.S. history the president and the Congress had managed to work together in constructive and creative harmony. What was the explanation? And could that explanation, whatever it was, be captured and institutionalized so that harmony would be not the rare exception but the rule? Political scientists thought the secret of successful collaboration in any period that might be chosen as the ideal—the administration of Jefferson, say, or the early Wilson, or the early Franklin Roosevelt—was not hard to identify. President and Congress were united, and impelled to work together, by the bonds of party. "For government to function," wrote V. O. Key, Jr., "the obstructions of the constitutional mechanism must be overcome, and it is the party that casts a web, at times weak, at times strong, over the dispersed organs of government and gives them a semblance of unity."[33]

Yet in the twentieth century the web of party has been, most of the time, weak and getting weaker, and there lies the root of the trouble. Even before this century, American political party organizations rarely attained the degree

33. *Politics, Parties, and Pressure Groups*, 5th ed. (Crowell, 1964), p. 656.

of cohesion and discipline characteristic of the parties of Britain and continental Europe. Here the national parties have always been federations of state parties, some of which in turn have been little more than federations of county and city organizations. And most of these organizations have been steadily losing strength, as observed in an earlier chapter; in states without effective two-party competition, they might barely exist. The national parties have had no control over nominations for the national legislature. Nor have they usually had organs to pronounce party policy, except for the quadrennial platform hastily put together by the presidential nominating convention. And even then there has been no means for, or tradition of, requiring anyone running as the party's nominee—even its presidential candidate—to adhere to the platform's policy positions. So presidents, senators, and representatives elected at the same time by the same party have been free to pursue their independent courses once they took their seats in Washington. Governmental cohesion in the capital has been undermined by the absence of cohesion in the apparatus that nominated and elected presidents and congressmen—the party structure.

The prevailing model of how the U.S. government could be made to work, the presidential leadership model, thus came to be seen by the more analytical of the reformers as simplistic. President and Congress had to be bound together by a principle more reliable than congressional acquiescence to the presidential will, for how could the Congress be made to acquiesce? And the principle had to be a safer one, too. For running through the liberal disparagement of the separation of powers structure over the years had not been one theme but two: the president had not only to be supported but also to be checked and controlled. So some who worried about the deadlocks of the U.S. government went beyond the presidential leadership model and evolved one that was more complex and more subtle, the responsible party model.[34]

The authoritative presentation of this concept is the 1950 report of the Committee on Political Parties of the American Political Science Association, headed by E. E. Schattschneider. Entitled *Toward a More Responsible Two-Party System*, the report proposed a new party institution to provide the missing elements of unity and cohesion. It would place at the top of the national party a party council of fifty members, including the president and vice

34. John S. Saloma III, *Congress and the New Politics* (Little, Brown, 1969), pp. 37–47, presents such a model as the "presidential responsible party model," with no reference to a distinct presidential leadership model. I believe that the concept of attaining governmental unity through presidential preeminence, without the development of the new party organs or party functions that the responsible party model incorporates, has gained such widespread acceptance and support that the distinction should be made.

president (or in the case of the opposition party, its nominees for those offices), senators, representatives, governors, and party officials chosen by the national convention. The council would have broad responsibility not only to link the executive and legislative branches of the national government but to unify all elements of the party, state and local as well as national. It would be responsible for party management and, most important, would pronounce party policy in between conventions. It would draft a platform for submission to the convention and interpret the platform afterward. It would also make recommendations "in respect to congressional candidates," discuss presidential candidacies, and even perhaps screen the candidates. Within the council might be a smaller group of advisers to the president—a party cabinet.[35]

In this unified system the president would occupy "a central place"—an understatement, surely, for a strong and popular president, with the executive patronage at his disposal, could easily dominate the party council. Yet the report in a prescient section warned of "overextending the presidency," of relying exclusively on one man's program and leadership, of turning the presidency into "personal government."[36] Accordingly, the concept was one of collective leadership, with the president subject to restraint by a group, many of whose members—the congressional representatives, the governors, officials of state party committees—would have independent bases of political support.

The nearest thing to an American precedent for the committee's concept of the "responsible" party would therefore not be Republican or Democratic party organizations at all, for the strongest of them were autocratic "machines" run by bosses; it would be the local nonpartisan reform organizations that had risen in various localities since the Progressive Era to smash the old-style machines. This was the kind of party organization the committee conceived on a national scale—issue-oriented, programmatic, dominated by no single person but led by a plural elite whose distinguishing characteristic was its ability to design and articulate the goals of governmental policy. Neither the president alone nor even the president and the Congress together would be responsible for the record of legislative and executive action; the party would be.

Six years after the report appeared, it was one of the influences that led the Democratic National Committee to organize a Democratic Advisory Coun-

35. *Toward a More Responsible Two-Party System* (Rinehart, 1950), pp. 39–44. The committee cited as precedent a party council created by the Republican National Committee in 1919, which "evidently ceased to function after a few years"; p. 42.

36. Ibid., pp. 93–95.

cil with an intended membership similar to that the political scientists projected. And nothing better illustrates the defects in the committee's model that render it unworkable in the American setting than the experience of the council. Its design failed in the first instance when the leaders of House and Senate declined to join; once more the desire of responsible elected officials for independence from the executive, or anybody else, was overriding. Organized with some legislative members but without the leaders, the council issued policy pronouncements, but while they gained publicity for the party, they did little more than that; no senator or representative felt any more bound by its decisions than by analogous declarations in the party platforms.[37] Finally, the council was disbanded by the Democratic party's own president after John F. Kennedy was elected in 1960; like the leaders of the Congress earlier, he too cherished his independence and felt quite capable of interpreting the party platform and enunciating party policy by himself, without the help of any formal party structure. The old presidential leadership model was good enough for him.

Thus, while the Committee on Political Parties made an excellent academic argument for its model, it made no practical case at all. It did not explain how presidents would be persuaded to share their power with a group outside their control and submit to its restraints, nor why congressional leaders would wish to do so either. It did not explain what sanctions the council would apply to enforce its policy positions. The sanctions, indeed, ran all the other way; the council would be at the mercy of the president and the other elected officials who would be its most powerful members, for they could wreck it with their individual or collective resignations the first time it sought to restrain them. If the council evaded tough issues, it would be innocuous. If it tried to grapple with them, it would dissolve.

Nevertheless, Key was right. The party remains the web that gives the dispersed organs of government their semblance of unity. When at times the web is strong, it is not because the party imposes discipline directly but simply because presidents, senators, and representatives who carry the same party label exhibit a stronger interest than they do at other times in their collective party record. Discipline is voluntary. Congressmen of the president's party recognize that they have an interest in making him look good, because either he or another nominee running on his record will head their

37. The experience of the Democratic party in its attempts to adopt policies at mid-term conferences in the 1970s confirms the lesson of the council. The party's mini-conventions in 1974 and 1978 had publicity value, but there is no record that President Carter or any member of Congress altered a policy position because of their resolutions. Moreover, the conferences were deliberately scheduled after the mid-term elections to avoid creating any policy conflicts for Democratic candidates.

common reelection ticket. Accordingly, they give him the benefit of the doubt on policy issues and follow his lead whenever constituency pressures are not too strong. And the president, for the same reasons, is respectful of the views of his congressional party. Thus the bonds of party generate centripetal forces to counter the centrifugal forces inherent in the relations between the branches; they engender impulses toward harmony to offset the natural tendencies toward dissension.

That is one of the reasons that the recent deterioration of parties in the United States must be a cause of grave concern. The trend toward party disintegration is measured by the increase in the proportion of voters who do not identify with any party, who call themselves independents, and who split their tickets with abandon. It is manifested in the decay and disappearance of old-style party organizations and the failure in many places of new-style structures to arise to fill the vacuum. It is reflected in the rise of individualism within the Congress. In this respect, too, the Committee on Political Parties was foresighted; it warned that unless parties became responsible, by adopting and carrying out party programs as a collective responsibility, public cynicism about parties would spread and the parties themselves would disintegrate.[38] That, it is clear, is happening. Millions of young people, in particular, do not identify with any party, do not understand the differences between the major parties, what they stand for, why they matter, even why they exist. Meanwhile, the power and significance of single-issue groups are enhanced by the lessening of competition from the multi-issue, more broadly based, parties.

In the days when parties were stronger, the president and the main body of his party in the Congress were usually bound in a close relationship long before the inauguration, because no candidate for president could be nominated without the assent of the congressional elders. That was before the hegemony of the presidential primary, when the party elite, including leaders of its congressional wing, performed a screening function in the nominating process. To be eligible for nomination, a candidate usually began with some established standing as a leader, and in any case he had to be acceptable to, and accepted by, the elite. During the campaign, then, the party organization was prepared to mobilize its adherents on the candidate's behalf, and after the election, it was prepared to follow his lead.

But both as a cause and a consequence of the disintegration of parties has come the explosion in the 1970s of the presidential primary. As the primary method of selecting convention delegates has spread to most of the states,

38. *Toward a More Responsible Two-Party System,* pp. 14, 95.

and as the others have adopted—under directives from the national parties—widely participatory caucus systems, the party's screening function has all but disappeared. Now a presidential candidate may be someone who is in no sense the natural leader of his party, who has no ready and established following among the party's senators and representatives. Indeed, he may be someone who has campaigned *against* the party establishment, including its congressional leadership, and who arrives in Washington in an atmosphere of suspicion and hostility. He may be someone without experience and skill in dealing with the members of the Congress he is supposed to lead, perhaps without even any extensive acquaintanceship with them. All of this was the case with Jimmy Carter, and it goes far toward explaining the difficulties in executive-legislative relations that developed at the outset of his administration and characterized—although with some improvement toward the end—his entire term.[39]

But, to lessen still further the prospect for united government, the president may not even be a member of the party that controls the Congress, much less its leader. With the disintegration of political parties in the United States has come a decline in straight-ticket voting. In choosing among candidates for president, Senate, and House, the voters are influenced by their party preference but also by their estimates of the candidates' personal competence and character, particularly in presidential voting, and by local and district considerations, especially in electing representatives. As the result, while the voters chose a Republican president in four of the last seven elections—from 1956 through 1980—they returned a Democratic House on all of those occasions and a Democratic Senate in all except the last. Thus, more than half the time, control of the government has been divided—something rarely known before the past quarter-century.

At such times, the normal tendency of the American system toward deadlock becomes irresistible. The president and the Congress always pledge themselves to seek harmonious collaboration, but ultimately they are compelled to quarrel. No presidential proposal can be accepted by the opposition in the legislature without raising the stature of its partisan adversary. Simi-

39. A *Washington Post* poll taken in July 1979 found that two-thirds of the people felt that President Carter and the Congress had not worked well together. Of those, 86 percent said that lack of cooperation was harmful to the country. They absolved neither side, although they considered the legislature somewhat more at fault. *Washington Post*, August 5, 1979. Early in the Watergate period, in February 1973, a Louis Harris poll found that a majority of respondents with opinions believed that it was good for the country to have a president of one party and a Congress controlled by the other, because it kept both president and Congress in line. Fifty percent thought divided government was better and 29 percent worse, with 16 percent saying it made no difference, and 5 percent with no opinion.

larly, no initiative of a Congress controlled by his opponents can be approved by the president without conceding wisdom to his political enemies. Sometimes, to be sure, the lack of cohesion within the Democratic party has enabled Republican presidents to lead effectively on some matters with the support of a bipartisan conservative coalition, especially when the Democratic majority has been a narrow one. But such coalitions tend to be loosely organized and unstable, for Democratic conservatives are subject to conflicting pressures; and, in any case, the resources of the leadership and most committees and subcommittees are in the hands of Democratic moderates and liberals anxious to distinguish their party position from the president's. So in times of divided government, the natural struggle between the parties for political advantage inevitably spills over—sooner or later, depending to a great extent on how well the president's public popularity holds up—into a struggle between executive and legislative branches. The bickering and tension that are rarely absent from relations between the branches are intensified, tending toward open conflict and recrimination of the kind that marked the last years of Eisenhower's term and virtually the whole of the Nixon-Ford period.

If the trend toward disintegration of political parties could be reversed, their revival would strengthen the ties between president and Congress without having to alter the Constitution, or establish joint executive-legislative mechanisms, or even create new party structures. Unfortunately, the outlook for party renewal is not much more favorable than the prospect for basic constitutional or institutional reform.

For the revitalization of political parties cannot be willed. If it could be, it already would have been; party leaders have not lacked the desire to preside over stronger organizations. But the people who are not now identified with either party—more than half the voters in the youngest age brackets consider themselves independents—will not commit themselves to parties, support them, and believe in them as an end in itself. They will join a party only when they see it as a useful means toward achieving some other desired end. Some attachments are formed in every election, while others are weakened or broken. But a massive reversal of the trend toward political independence must await the appearance of some great issue—like the slavery question in the 1850s, or the plight of the farmers in the 1980s, or relief of hunger and unemployment in the 1930s—which arouses the country and impels people to seek solutions through the political and governmental system. At such times the voting public is polarized, and new parties spring into being or old parties take on new meaning, because they become instruments for the achievement of goals about which the voters deeply care.[40] Yet powerful issues come and go, and when they have gone the parties may lack relevance to new issues that arise. The last period of polarization, when the current alignment of the two-party system was shaped, is almost half a century old and the Democratic and Republican symbols have lost much of the meaning and appeal they then possessed. But revival depends on something happening outside the parties themselves—some kind of sustained crisis that will arouse the people, polarize them, and impel them to organize politically, through parties, to attain their ends. In short, the party system is a dependent, not an independent, variable.

On the other hand, even as the parties have become weaker, the gradual realignment of the party system that is taking place—especially in the South, which after decades of lag is slowly conforming to the national liberal-conservative alignment of Democrats and Republicans established in the 1930s— makes both parties more homogeneous ideologically in the nation at large. This is reflected in the Congress and is a force for cohesion there in an era of individualism. Ideological kinship will also facilitate cooperation between presidents and their congressional party colleagues.

Comity within the System

All the broad avenues toward fundamental reform to ameliorate the unending conflict between the branches seem, therefore, to be closed. Grafting some features of the parliamentary system to the American constitutional structure might help, but the issue is academic; basic change in the Constitution is impossible. Formal merger of legislative and executive powers in a joint cabinet or council runs counter to the self-interest of the responsible politicians in each branch in maintaining their freedom of decision and independence of action within their respective spheres. The responsible party solution runs afoul of the same objection. Restoration of strong political parties as the tie that binds the branches is beyond anyone's control, dependent on the emergence of new forces and events that will arouse a mass public desire to form and utilize parties to attain political ends.

That leaves the question of how the system of relationships between the branches, as they now exist, can be made to work better. The four Cs

40. The processes of party realignment and renewal are analyzed in James L. Sundquist, *Dynamics of the Party System: Alignment and Realignment of Political Parties in the United States* (Brookings Institution, 1973) and in works cited there; chap. 13 is a theoretical summary.

enunciated by President Ford in his first address to the Congress—communication, conciliation, compromise, and cooperation[41]—define well the goal. But there are no panaceas to secure them. No systematic improvements in the tone and practices of interbranch relations can be adopted and fixed permanently in place, as by a constitution or a statute. The only recourse left for those who worry about the disunity of their government is exhortation, the offering of gratuitous advice to presidents and congresses and to voters who elect them. Exhortation will not satisfy the souls of systems designers, but it is the only option that is practically available.

Presidential Behavior. Some of the more obvious lessons for presidents, or those who would become presidents, can be drawn from well-publicized mishaps of the Carter administration. At the outset, a would-be president should not get off to a bad start by campaigning against the Congress and the rest of the Washington establishment—even if that appears to be the easiest road to the White House—because he is going to have to work with them when he gets there. On taking office, a president should staff his office of congressional relations with persons who know the Congress and can interpret it to him, as well as him to it, and who will do the little things—like returning congressional telephone calls—with care and dedication. Other White House aides should be reminded that they are congressional relations officers too and must behave accordingly (cabinet and subcabinet officers will not need to be reminded).

The president's legislative program and schedule should be planned through genuine collaboration with his party leaders in the Congress; the weekly meetings instituted by Franklin Roosevelt are still as good a technique as any. Unilateral commitments by the president as to what the Congress will or must do, and when, must be avoided. The timing of messages transmitting legislation should be worked out with the leaders, and the priorities should be scaled down to what the Congress can be reasonably expected to handle. The president should not let himself appear to be picking fights with the Congress, as Carter did when he chose to make an issue of local water projects at the very opening of his term.[42]

Yet it is not easy for a president to form a genuine partnership with the Congress, no matter how earnest his intention. The problems of policy formulation *within* the executive branch on any complex matter are so enor-

41. "Address to a Joint Session of the Congress, August 12, 1974." *Public Papers of the Presidents: Gerald R. Ford, 1974* (GPO, 1975), p. 7.
42. Thomas E. Cronin, "An Imperiled Presidency," *Society*, vol. 16 (November/December 1978), pp. 59–60.

mous—the data that must be analyzed, the departments and agencies and interests that must be reconciled, the outside views that must be taken into account—that the responsible policymakers often have all they can do to resolve their differences and arrive at an administration position without the added complication of trying to incorporate the views of the congressional majority, which to make matters worse is likely to be in serious disagreement within itself (and which may be led by the administration's partisan opponents). So once the executive branch has reached its own conclusion, the impulse is always strong to encase the policy in a presidential message so that all the settlements and compromises will not have to be reopened.

Having taken his position, the president is then obliged to fight for it, if he is to maintain the image every president seeks as a person of principle and courage. But this, of course, is what offends the Congress; its members don't like to be given their marching orders from downtown, handed their policies on a take-it-or-leave-it basis, with the implication that if they leave it they are doing so for narrow, parochial, benighted, or even corrupt reasons.

Yet the periods of fruitful executive-congressional collaboration, such as those of the early years of the Wilson, Franklin Roosevelt, and Johnson administrations, show that mutual goodwill and harmony can at times be attained, even though not necessarily sustained for long. The explanation probably lies less in the skill and tactics of a president in communicating with and handling the Congress—which are generally overrated as the determinant of presidential success with the legislature—than in a wholly external factor, his standing in the country. A president who wins by a landslide, carries both houses with him, and runs ahead of his congressional candidates, as Lyndon Johnson did in 1964, will get off to a good start with the Congress no matter how he deals with them—although Johnson's experience and skill did stand him in good stead until he overplayed his hand and drove the legislators too hard. Conversely, a president who slips into office narrowly, running behind his ticket, like Kennedy in 1960 or Carter in 1976, begins at a disadvantage, even if he handles his congressional relations with finesse. Later, however, if the president maintains a high rating in the public opinion polls and seems to be headed for reelection, his party in the Congress will be inclined to accept his leadership. To the extent he is in command of the country, in other words, he is likely to be in command of his party in the Congress, too. Among other things, a popular president can always go over the heads of the Congress and appeal to the people; senators and representatives know that and try to avoid giving him the excuse to do so. Conversely, when the president stands low in the polls and threatens to drag his party down with him in the next election, the legislators will dissociate themselves from his policy positions and find reasons to oppose him.[43]

Congressional Behavior. As a generalization, the Congress should strengthen its capacity to do the things that it does best, and that the executive branch cannot do, and should stop trying to do what it can do only poorly and the executive does better. The special strengths of the Congress, like its weaknesses, arise from its representational role; the other side of parochialism is responsiveness and sensitivity. Congress as representative provides the citizen access to the policymaking process, makes possible a personal relationship to government that can help to offset the impersonality of the administrative agencies. The Congress can set localism against centralism, the micro view of events against the macro view. It can improve national policy by bringing to bear on the executive branch's proposals a sensitive regard for the local and individual consequences of policies designed from the national perspective.

Collaboration is therefore not only a practical imperative but a theoretically desirable end. But Congress can make its own mistake if it permits parochially minded members who occupy strategic committee posts to impose their own policies on the country, or if it assumes that an amalgam of local interests arrived at through logrolling is the equivalent of the national interest. The party caucuses have recaptured the power to instruct and to discipline chairmen and committee members who do not respond to the sentiment of the caucus membership, and this power should not be allowed to lapse through disuse if circumstances again arise that demand its exercise.

The representational role of the Congress gives it a special competence for oversight of administration, but while the potential for constructive contribution in the review of administrative processes and actions is immense, so is the potential for abuse. The boundary between useful and damaging oversight cannot be drawn with precision, and the Congress can only be admonished to proceed vigorously with the former but abjure the latter, in the hope that common sense will somehow define the difference, case by case. With the multiplication of provisions for legislative veto, the potential for inappropriate and burdensome intrusion into administration becomes even greater, and the Congress should add new vetoes with great restraint,

43. Jon R. Bond and Richard Fleisher, "The Limits of Presidential Popularity as a Source of Influence in the U.S. House," *Legislative Studies Quarterly*, vol. 5 (February 1980), pp. 69–78, found that as a president's public popularity rises, he gains significantly in support from his own party but loses support from opposition members at a lesser rate. Doe C. Shinn, "Toward a Model for Presidential Influence in Congress," paper prepared for the 1980 annual meeting of the American Political Science Association, likewise found that the president's public popularity rating is an important factor bearing on his level of congressional support.

only in individual cases when the need is demonstrable beyond a reasonable doubt.

Individual members need to recognize that the trend toward individualism in the Congress can go too far. For the Congress to legislate efficiently and responsibly requires some reasonable degree of cohesion within the majority party, and that in turn requires a subordination of personal and local self-interest to the will of the party majority. The centralizing instruments of the controlling party—that is, its leadership, policy and steering committees, and caucus—need to be more assertive, and given stronger powers if necessary, to balance the forces making for dispersion and fragmentation of power. The need for cohesion within the majority party is especially great whenever the legislative body is controlled by the party opposing the president, or when it rejects his leadership for any other reason. Then the majority leadership should take the initiative to use the caucus to help define and build a consensus around party policy, based on preparatory work assigned to existing policy committees or ad hoc bodies reporting to the caucus. Steps in this direction go against the grain of the men and women who make up the Congress these days, but that is the direction in which the institutional structure should be moved. Special bipartisan committees to integrate policy in each house, like those created by Speakers Albert and O'Neill, also show promise for use on a more regular and expanded scale.

The Congress will never have the capacity to play its full potential role in government until that last, anachronistic institutional barrier that prevents the legislature from acting when a majority is ready to act—the Senate filibuster—is modified to permit the majority to rule after an issue is fully debated.

Voter Behavior. The individual citizen and voter should act to protect and strengthen the web that gives to the government its semblance of unity—the political party. If, as a corollary to that action, the voters curb their penchant for splitting tickets, they can save the country from divided government.

The New Equilibrium

The conflict is unending. But its tone, and its terms, and the balance between the combatants, change constantly. The 1970s were a period of upheaval, of change so rapid and so radical as to transform the pattern of relationships that had evolved and settled into place over the span of half a century or more. But by the end of the decade the spirit of resurgence, at least, had waned. The Congress seemed for the most part satisfied with what it had achieved in its quest for equality—except for the agitation for further legislative vetoes. Members no longer complained of an overweening and overreaching presidency, and presidents, since 1977 at least, seemed in general to accept the new balance of power that had been reached. So the 1980s should be a period of relative stability, with a new cycle of slow decline of the Congress in favor of the president probably beginning some time in the decade.

Meanwhile, there are grounds both for foreboding and for optimism in the institutional and behavioral changes that the period of congressional resurgence has brought about. On the negative side, the new assertiveness of the Congress has not been fully matched by new capability, by institutional forms that would assure responsibility in the more aggressive exercise of power. The weaknesses that arise from the fragmentation of the Congress have not been wholly overcome; that would require the development of strong centralizing institutions, and that runs counter to the temper of the times.

On the positive side, however, of immense significance in the long run will be the destruction during the 1970s of old barriers to effective and responsive government. The obstacles to harmonious legislative-executive relations and constructive legislative achievement so apparent in the 1930s, the 1950s, and even the 1960s have for the most part been overcome. The enemies of governmental competence then were the absolutism of the seniority system in both houses, the obstructionist power of the Rules Committee in the House, and the filibuster in the Senate. Of these, the first two have been destroyed and the third has been modified.

In a sense, no relationship between president and Congress is ever normal, for the country passes from one special pattern of association to another, each influenced by the unique personality of a president, a particular configuration of congressional leaders, and the political setting of the time. Yet the beginning years of the congressional resurgence were, by any standard, more abnormal than most, with executive-legislative relations reduced to a level of bitterness matched perhaps only during the time of President Andrew Johnson. In 1977, when one period of divided government came to a close, a tone at least of cordiality reappeared, and it continued into at least the early months of the new period of division that began in 1981. While the conflict between the branches is unending, it has not always been so acrimonious nor so destructive of the governmental process as it was during much of the decade of the 1970s. Nor, in all likelihood, will it be so soon again.

Index

Abel, Elie, 114n
Aberbach, Joel D., 327n, 328n, 410n, 444n
Abourezk, James, 7
Abram, Michael, 177n
Abshire, David M., 306n
Acheson, Dean, 107n, 110, 301
Activists: Congress, 191, 193–94; economic, 63; in fiscal policy, 68; presidents as, 20n; reform efforts by House, 373–74
Adams, Brock, 221, 234n
Adams, Bruce, 319n
Adams, John, 22, 24n
Addabo, Joseph P., 384
Administration, congressional control over, 17, 316–17; arguments for, 324; confirmation process, 318–19; indirect means, 322–23; legal limitations, 322; report-and-wait procedure, 357; restrictive statutes, 320–21; riders on appropriations bills, 358–59. See also Oversight, congressional; Veto, legislative
Administrative Procedures Act, 361
Afghanistan, 264, 271, 298, 461
AFL-CIO, 235
Agriculture Committee, House, 333
Agriculture Committee, Senate, 225
Agriculture, Department of, 333, 347
Aiken, George, 122, 333
Albert, Carl: ad hoc committees, 433; congressional budget process, 219; Dominican Republic, 123; inflation, 86–87; leadership, 398, 401; Nixon invasion of congressional power, 1, 2, 3
Albright, Joseph, 280n
Aldrich, Nelson W., 165
Alexander, DeAlva Stanwood, 168n
Allen, James B., 395n
Allison, Graham T., 271n, 310n, 312
Allison, William B., 165

Ambro, Jerome A., 397
American Political Science Association (APSA): Committee on Political Parties, 472, 474–75; congressional policymaking, 187–88; seniority system, 180–82
Anderson, John B., 6, 385
Anderson, Sydney, 172
Angola, 286–99
Annunzio, Frank, 381
Antideficiency Act, 46n, 57
Antitrust action, 28, 32n, 87
Appalachian program, 452, 453
Appleby, Paul, 34
Appointments, presidential, 38
Appropriations, 40, 41, 42–44, 46. See also Budget process, congressional; Impoundment of appropriated funds
Appropriations Committee, House, 41, 44, 45n, 85, 221
Appropriations Committee, Senate, 44, 45n, 394
APSA. See American Political Science Association
Arends, Leslie, 124
Armbrister, Trevor, 440n
Armed services, 55–56
Armed Services Committee, House, 57, 330n, 348
Armed Services Committee, Senate, 220, 348, 394
Arms trade, 95, 96–99
Arnold, Peir E., 58n
Arnold, R. Douglas, 444n
Ashley, J. M., 15n
Ashley, Thomas L., 433, 435
Ash, Roy L., 142n, 213n
Aspinall, Wayne N., 149n
Atomic Energy, Joint Committee on, 429, 431